Human Communication:
A Unified View

INTER-UNIVERSITY ELECTRONICS SERIES

Books in Series

Vol. 1: *Jamieson et al.* Infrared Physics and Engineering, 1964
Vol. 2: *Bennett and Davey.* Data Transmission, 1965
Vol. 3: *Sutton.* Direct Energy Conversion, 1966
Vol. 4: *Schwartz, Bennett, and Stein.* Communications Systems and Techniques, 1966
Vol. 5: *Luxenberg and Kuehn.* Display Systems Engineering, 1968
Vol. 6: *Balakrishnan.* Communication Theory, 1968
Vol. 7: *Collin and Zucker.* Antenna Theory, Part 1, 1969
Collin and Zucker. Antenna Theory, Part 2, 1969
Vol. 8: *Zadeh and Polak.* System Theory, 1969
Vol. 9: *Schwan.* Biological Engineering, 1969
Vol. 10: *Clynes and Milsum.* Biomedical Engineering Systems, 1969
Vol. 11: *Huelsman.* Active Filters: Lumped, Distributed, Integrated, Digital, and Parametric, 1970
Vol. 12: *Oliver and Cage.* Electronic Measurements and Instrumentation, 1971
Vol. 13: *Smit.* Magnetic Properties of Materials, 1971
Vol. 14: *Cruz.* Feedback Systems, 1972
Vol. 15: *David and Denes.* Human Communication: A Unified View, 1972

INTER-UNIVERSITY ELECTRONICS SERIES, VOL. 15

Human Communication: A Unified View

EDITED BY

Dr. Edward E. David, Jr.
Science Advisor to the President
The White House

Dr. Peter B. Denes
Head, Speech and Communication
Research Department, Bell Laboratories
Murray Hill, N.J.

McGRAW-HILL BOOK COMPANY
New York St. Louis San Francisco Düsseldorf Johannesburg
Kuala Lumpur London Mexico Montreal New Delhi
Panama Rio de Janeiro Singapore Sydney Toronto

David, Edward E.
Human communication: a unified view.
(Inter-university electronics series, no. 15)
Includes bibliographies.
1. Speech. 2. Speech perception. 3. Speech processing systems. I. Denes, Peter B., joint author. II. Title. [DNLM: 1. Communication—Collected works. 2. Computers, Digital—Collected works. 3. Speech—Collected works. P121 D249h 1972]
BF455.D275 001.54'2 72-5092
ISBN 0-07-015446-5

1234567890 KPKP 765432

The editors for this book were Tyler G. Hicks, Karen Kesti, and Lydia Maiorca, the designer was Naomi Auerbach, and its production was supervised by George E. Oechsner. It was set in Caledonia by The Maple Press Company.

It was printed and bound by The Kingsport Press.

Contents

Series Purpose

The explosive rate at which knowledge in electronics has expanded in recent years has produced the need for unified state-of-the-art presentations that give authoritative pictures of individual fields of electronics.

The Inter-University Electronics Series is designed to meet this need by providing volumes that deal with particular areas of electronics where up-to-date reference material is either inadequate or is not conveniently organized. Each volume covers an individual area, or a series of related areas. Emphasis is upon providing timely and comprehensive coverage that stresses general principles, and integrates the newer developments into the over-all picture. Each volume is edited by an authority in the field and is written by several coauthors, who are active participants in research or in educational programs dealing with the subject matter involved.

The volumes are written with a viewpoint and at a level that makes them suitable for reference use by research and development engineers and scientists in industry and by workers in governmental and university laboratories. They are also suitable for use as textbooks in specialized courses at graduate levels. The complete series of volumes will provide a reference library that should serve a wide spectrum of electronic engineers and scientists.

The organization and planning of the series is being carried out with the aid of a Steering Committee, which operates with the counsel of an Advisory Committee. The Steering Committee concerns itself with the scope of the individual volumes and aids in the selection of editors for the different volumes. Each editor is in turn responsible for selecting his coauthors and deciding upon the detailed scope and content of his particular volume. Overall management of the Series is in the hands of the Consulting Editor.

Frederick Emmons Terman

Contributors

BRUCE P. BOGERT
Head, Ocean Systems Research Department
Bell Laboratories, Whippany, New Jersey 07981

RICHARD H. BOLT
Chairman of the Board
Bolt Beranek and Newman Inc., Cambridge, Massachusetts 02138

FRANKLIN S. COOPER
President
Haskins Laboratories, New Haven, Connecticut 06510

EDWARD E. DAVID, JR.
Science Advisor to the President
Director
Office of Science and Technology
The White House, Washington, D.C.

PETER B. DENES
Head, Speech and Communication Research Department
Bell Laboratories, Murray Hill, New Jersey 07974

J. L. FLANAGAN
Head, Acoustics Research Department
Bell Laboratories, Murray Hill, New Jersey 07974

IRA J. HIRSH
Dean of the Faculty of Arts and Sciences
Washington University, St. Louis, Missouri 63130
Director of Research
Central Institute for the Deaf, St. Louis, Missouri 63110

S. R. HYDE
Joint Speech Research Unit, Ruislip, Middlesex, England

BELA JULESZ
Head, Sensory and Perceptual Processes Department
Bell Laboratories, Murray Hill, New Jersey 07974

K. C. KNOWLTON
Member of Technical Staff
Bell Laboratories, Murray Hill, New Jersey 07974

H. LEVITT
Associate Professor of Speech
The City University of New York, Doctoral Program in Speech
The Graduate School and University Center, New York, New York 10036

ALVIN M. LIBERMAN
Professor of Psychology
University of Connecticut, Storrs, Connecticut 06268
Research Associate
Haskins Laboratories, New Haven, Connecticut 06510
Adjunct Professor of Linguistics
Yale University, New Haven, Connecticut 06520

ANTHONY G. OETTINGER
Professor of Linguistics, and Gordon McKay, Professor of Applied Mathematics
Aiken Computation Laboratory
Harvard University, Cambridge, Massachusetts 02138

JAMES M. PICKETT
Professor of Speech Communication Research
Gallaudet College, Washington, D.C. 20002

DONALD P. SHANKWEILER
Professor of Psychology
University of Connecticut, Storrs, Connecticut 06268
Research Associate
Haskins Laboratories, New Haven, Connecticut 06510

ROGER N. SHEPARD
Professor of Psychology
Stanford University, Stanford, California 94305

KENNETH N. STEVENS
Professor of Electrical Engineering
Research Laboratory of Electronics
Massachusetts Institute of Technology, Cambridge, Massachusetts 02139

MICHAEL STUDDERT-KENNEDY
Professor of Communication Arts and Sciences
Queens College and The Graduate Center of City University, New York 11367
Research Associate
Haskins Laboratories, New Haven, Connecticut 06510

EDWARD E. ZAJAC
Head, Economic Analysis and Graphics Research Department
Bell Laboratories, Murray Hill, New Jersey 07974

Preface

Communication between people, whether face-to-face or at a distance via electrical connections, has long fascinated man. It is the fabric of human society as we know it. Clearly human communication involves the coding of meaning into language followed by generation, transmission, and perception of speech. The latter events correspond to psychological, physiological, and physical activity in man. As a result of these processes, the basic communication information changes form as it passes from level to level; from nerve signals to gestures of tongue, teeth, and lips, to acoustic form for example. These are not independent processes: each is influenced by and plays an essential part in one another. Human communication is, therefore, very much a matter of interrelated events on numerous levels of activity. In fact, the effect of one level on others is profound, not secondary as was once thought. This fact was not realized for many years and, as a result communication events at each of these levels were studied separately, and unjustified assumptions about a one-to-one correspondence of events on one level to adjacent levels were made. It has only been within the past decade or two that newly emerging knowledge has made us recognize the unity of the communication process across the many different levels involved. This knowledge also made us aware of the complex transformations from one level to the other, transformations that are explainable only against the unifying teleological background: semantics. This new viewpoint has come from physiology, anatomy, psychology, linguistics, physics, information theory, and communication engineering. It is the purpose of the book to present the essentials of this unified view rather than an exhaustive account of the contributing disciplines.

Interestingly and significantly, attempts to develop communication technologies of speech recognition ("voice typewriters") and speech generators ("talking machines") have often foundered on the lack of this unitary view. Even today we find that the quality of artificially produced speech and the scope of automatic speech recognition devices are constrained by limited knowledge or even an appreciation of the semantic and linguistic overlay. Another typical example is the recognition of individual speakers from their utterances. Anecdotally, we know that some listeners, at least, are adept at recognizing members of their cohort entirely by listening to their voices. However, experiments indicate that this ability is actually highly fallible *unless* the semantic context is taken into account; and this is a highly personal matter, not one on which an identification technology can depend. So as with all aspects of human communication, the identification process is tied tightly to the overall framework and refuses to be isolated usefully.

The integrated viewpoint taken in this volume concerns the vertical dimension: from semantics and linguistics to acoustics and physiology. No attempt has been made to encompass all forms of human communication which can be regarded as forming a horizontal dimension. Actually, the unifying principles discussed here generalize reasonably well across this dimension. It is important to remember, however, that human communication does take many different forms and utilizes one or more of our sensory modalities—vision, touch, smell, hearing—and also facial or manual gestures.

A special form of communication developed by human civilization is linguistic communication. Here man has learned to use symbols in a variety of sophisticated and flexible ways so as to enable him to communicate his thoughts, his feelings, and his accumulated wisdom on matters relating to his emotions and to his survival. The linguistic system of communication also offers the open-ended flexibility necessary for dealing with man's everchanging and expanding interests and knowledge.

The two forms of linguistic communication that modern man uses most extensively are writing and speech. There is little doubt that, of these two, speech is historically earlier and also more universal than writing. There is no known human society which does not use speech communication. Writing, on the other hand, probably came much later in our development and is used only by some civilizations.

Furthermore, speech is also a remarkably efficient form of communication. It resists an exceptionally wide range of deteriorations in any of its several stages. In production, it remains largely unaffected by dialectal differences, by speech defects, and by individual peculiarities of millions of different speakers. In transmission, it is highly resistant to the effects of noise, amplitude limitation, and bandwidth restrictions. In perception, it bypasses many hearing defects and resists interference from simultaneous competitive perceptual tasks. This remarkable efficiency of speech communication is partly due to numerous redundancies. Some of these arise from the semantics of the communication situation, some from the necessity of conforming to grammatical rules, and others from linguistic statistics, such as the frequency of sound occurrences. Redundancy arises also from the intricate acoustical constraints inherent in the shape of the vocal tract and the mobility limits of individual articulators. These factors are probably important in man's remarkable ability to distinguish between speech and nonspeech sounds even for foreign languages that he does not understand and even when the sounds have been subjected to severe distortions. The study of speech communication, therefore, is likely to provide rich rewards not only in the better understanding of human information processing, but also in what it teaches us about communication pathology and its correction, and about the design of man-computer and perhaps even computer-computer communication.

In this volume, therefore, we decided to concentrate on speech communication and use it as an example for presenting a unified view of how semantical, linguistical, physiological, and physical events interact to bring about human communication.

The importance of the semantic overlay seems the very essence of the human communication process and is discussed in Oettinger's chapter. He indicates that the earlier investigations of the speech process were hampered by concentration on the most obvious manifestation of speech, namely, the acoustic phenomenon. It has proved unrewarding to begin with acoustic analysis and then drive back toward a literal form, for in doing so the semantic aspects of the speech process has not been invoked.

Semantics then provides an overall framework. To understand the process as a whole, however, we must understand its nature at every level. The various levels and their interrelations are discussed in the chapters by Liberman, Cooper, et al., and by Stevens. They attempt to take a global view of the speech process by detailing the interplay between the acoustic, articulatory, linguistic, and semantic levels.

The significant finding is that the events at any level are not uniquely specified by the levels nearer the semantic framework. This is quite clear in comparing meaning with the linguistic level. Even in one language there are many different sentences which can convey the same meaning. Which one is used depends upon factors such as the events preceding and those to follow, the lexicon of the speaker, and so on. This same lack of uniqueness shows up in the transformation from each level to the next as we progress down the speech chain from semantics to acoustics and thence to hearing and comprehension in the overall process of human communication.

Quantitative knowledge about speech communication is essential for its proper explanation. Shepard's chapter presents one method for structuring and measuring the speech perception process. He applies this method to show that perception of speech is compatible with the phonetic-linguistic classification of sounds. By contrast, Levitt's chapter indicates that the perceptual process operates very differently when the task is not speech oriented but concerns detection and recognition of elementary signals which are far from speech. The two papers show the diversity of human perception. It adapts to the task at hand and so is profoundly dependent on the semantic context.

The properties of the auditory system are obviously an important ingredient of the total communication picture. Flanagan's chapter illustrates the application of modern signal processing techniques in relating auditory physiology to perception. Flanagan's chapter discusses the transformation of signals from the acoustic domain into the neurophysiological one. It examines this stage of auditory physiology by applying modern signal processing techniques. These tools become more important as the signals to be treated approach speech in complexity. Flanagan's signals are speech-like in the sense that their spectra contain multiple harmonic tones and yet their perceived pitch is not simply related to the presence of a fundamental tone.

Bogert's chapter presents a variety of modern signal analysis tools, most of which have proved so important for analyzing and synthesizing speech, and for modeling the human speech production and perception mechanism through the use of the digital computer.

Most of this volume concerns a particular aspect of human communication; namely, speech communication from a vertically integrated viewpoint beginning with semantic factors and terminating with perception and comprehension. Along the horizontal dimension are other facets of human communication. A particularly vital one today concerns the link between man and computer. This is important, for example, in data analysis, the study of functional relations, and dynamic processes. Knowlton and Zajac's chapter discusses how digital computers can be adapted to the requirements of human communication. This example shows many of the same features found in the speech chain but with less ambiguity and contextual effects. Man-computer communication does validate the importance of meaning and language in the process. Thus the Knowlton-Zajac chapter indicates that many aspects of speech communication are significant across the whole scope of human communication.

The unified view of human communication has its impact on engineering. Two examples, in which the multilevel view of speech communication is particularly relevant, are discussed in the chapters by Bolt, et al., and by Hyde. The former concerns identification of speakers from the acoustic characteristics of their voice, while the latter examines the automatic recognition of words. These chapters emphasize our earlier comments in this Preface on how machine identification and recognition have been constrained by lack of the unified view.

The familiar topics of speaking machines and speech processors for narrowband speech communication and reading machines for the blind have been omitted from this volume because they are documented extensively elsewhere. It is interesting to note though that recent research on speaking machine design has also profited greatly from the unified view. No longer do investigators concentrate their efforts solely on defining the spectral properties of the synthesized speech waves. Instead, they recognize the great importance that linguistic description has long assigned to the intonation and rhythm of spoken language. As a result, they now devote considerable attention to defining the pitch, intensity, and duration of the sounds in a way required by the stress pattern and semantic content of the speech to be produced.

We hope that this volume will illustrate both the difficulties and the fascination of basic research on a human process, which involves not only psychological, physiological and physical events, but also the uniquely human process of linguistic communication with its vital overlay of meaning.

Edward E. David, Jr.
Peter B. Denes

Human Communication:
A Unified View

CHAPTER ONE

The Semantic Wall

ANTHONY G. OETTINGER

Introduction

Two decades of linguistic research of unprecedented intensity have revealed only how miraculously the process of human communication performs its everyday wonders. So simple that nearly every child masters it almost unconsciously, this process is so complex that all our efforts at understanding it have yielded only fragmentary and superficial insights.

Elaborate and varied theories of physical, phonetic, phonemic, morphemic, syntactic, and semantic phenomena have pleased some, confused others, spawned schools, spurred controversies. "A grammar of a language," says Chomsky, "purports to be a description of the ideal speaker-hearer's intrinsic competence" [1]. Others seek understanding of those properties of language that affect or are affected by its transmission, transformation, and storage; some study the psychology of language, and still others the problems of communication between man and machine. Card-carrying linguists somewhat defensively tend to regard technical or psychological questions as "devoid of linguistic significance," i.e., as not interesting to themselves; fortunately this has not seriously deterred anyone from taking a broader look at language.

Chomsky admits that "the tentative character of any conclusions that can now be advanced concerning linguistic theory . . . should certainly be obvious . . . ," adding that to make this point "it is sufficient to consider the vast range of linguistic phenomena that have resisted insightful formulation in any terms."

Specifically, we are more than ever baffled by how language performs its primary function, to convey meaning. All our understanding of the mechanics of language, built up from real or fancied elementary building blocks, stops dead before the question of meaning. It is almost as if meaning were primary and everything else a consequence of understanding meaning. If this is true, linguistics must be built anew and we face a formidable challenge.

In what follows, I choose to concentrate on the physical vehicles of symbols, on syntax, and on semantics, ignoring other aspects of linguistics without denying their importance in contemporary theory or practice. It should quickly become clear that progress has been made only in the first two and only insofar as they could be divorced from semantics. Semantics remains shrouded in an obscurity significantly pierced only by occasional rays of classical philosophical inquiry.

In fact, the boundaries among these three aspects have grown indistinct. Serious difficulties now apparent on the frontiers of the study of physical vehicles and of syntax can be eliminated from these realms only by circumscribing them very narrowly and sweeping interesting but difficult problems under the rug of semantics, or else by admitting that problems one might have wished to characterize as purely physical or syntactic do, after all, have properties common not only to one another but also to semantics.

The Physical Vehicles of Symbols

The most splendid scientific and technological successes have been realized in the realm of the physical manipulation of symbols, where one deals with the physical embodiments of symbols ("tokens" in C. S. Peirce's terminology) without regard to their role as vehicles of meaning. Progress in electrical and electronic communications and the development of the modern computer speak for themselves.

Yet however remarkable it may be in other respects, the invention of the telephone and most of the subsequent improvements in telephony require no understanding of syntax or semantics beyond a vague concern for their preservation. This concern could long be safely limited to requiring that whatever is in the sound waves impinging on a microphone at one end be also in the sound waves recreated by the earphone at the other. Indeed, in terms of the parameters such as bandwidth which characterize the quality of transmission channels, music and other forms of information are far more demanding of their vehicle than speech.

The same applies to computer design to the extent that the meaning of the symbols acted on can be ignored. Where there is a concern for interpretation, as in advanced programming systems or "software," all of the general problems of linguistics reappear, together with the characteristic frustration they produce. Only the great freedom to define one's way around problems precludes stalemate in this area.

The mathematical theory of communication as sketched by Hartley, brought to a fine flowering by Shannon, and since elaborated by many successors is essentially a physical theory. This theory addresses itself to a fundamental and pervasive problem expressed both concisely and eloquently by Quine [2]:

> In logical and mathematical systems, either of two mutually antagonistic types of economy may be striven for, and each has its peculiar practical utility. On the one hand we may seek economy of practical expression—ease and brevity in the statement of multifarious relations. This sort of economy calls usually for distinctive concise notations for a wealth of concepts. Second, however, and oppositely, we may seek an economy in grammar and vocabulary; we may try to find a minimum of basic concepts such that, once a distinctive notation has been appropriated to each of them, it becomes possible to express any desired further concepts by mere combination and iteration of our basic notations.

In a limited but significant realm, Shannon's theory provides a clear-cut and quantitative description of the range of choices available in resolving the antagonism Quine describes. Given the need to transmit or to store a message worth b bits of information, we can calculate precisely how many characters of a large alphabet or how many more characters of a smaller alphabet would be needed to encode the same message. If the messages are selected from a population according to some probability distribution, an algorithm proposed by Huffman tells us how to encode each message in a given alphabet so as to minimize the cost of transmission.

Contemporary coding theory is an elaboration of these basic ideas to accommodate a variety of other conditions, including, for example, the desire to minimize the error rate, to delimit the maximum length of that portion of a message which a local error can garble, or to minimize the cost of this or that component of the transmission channel.

In any of these cases, whether the bits transmitted mean anything or not is of no concern to the theory, nor, in general, is any structural relation among the symbols beyond certain statistical dependencies.

When this same problem appears with a semantic component, as in such matters as word formation, paraphrase, ellipsis, definition, or anaphoric construction, Quine's principle applies, but little more can be said.

Superficially, the problem of speech recognition seems to fall in a class with the problems solved by Shannon. The problem innocuously presents itself as a question of code conversion much like that of transforming a string of characters of the conventional alphabet into a corresponding string of binary digits. So, at one time, did the problem of automatic language translation [3].

The analogy may seem flimsy since, after all, both the alphabetic string and its binary counterpart are denumerable sequences of discrete symbols chosen from very finite sets, while speech-as-sound-wave or speech-as-electrical-signal intercepted at a fixed point in space are continuously varying functions of time. However, linguistic theory not only rescues the analogy but in fact suggests it through the intervention of the phoneme.

The fact is widely accepted among linguists that all "linguistically significant" features of the sound systems of most languages may be accounted for by describing speech as a concatenation of discrete "phonemes," each chosen out of a set of 40 or so characteristic of the particular language.

A phoneme is defined as an abstract class of elemental sounds which, though varying from speaker to speaker, from context to context, and from time to time, are sufficiently like each other and distinct enough from any sounds in any other phoneme class to be clearly perceived, say as /b/ rather than as /p/, in spite of the multitude of idiosyncratic variations.

The status of the phoneme was further bolstered by the elaboration of a system of elementary "distinctive features" whose individual properties and combination rules are believed to be sufficient to account both for the total number of possible phonemes in a language and the apparently invariant characteristics distinguishing one from another [4].

The abstract nature of the phoneme was tempered by "the methodological demand that any distinctive feature and, consequently, any phoneme treated by the linguists, have its constant correlate at each stage of the speech event and thus be identifiable at any level accessible to observation," and further justified by the assertion that "our present knowledge of the physical and physiological aspects of speech sounds is sufficient to meet this demand" [5].

Indeed, to trained eyes, spectral analyses of speech showed, for example, that the energy of consonants is spread in characteristic ways over the whole spectrum, while in vowels it is concentrated in three distinct bands or "formants," whose relative pitch and intensity reflect the expectations of the distinctive-feature characterization. From this point of view, the continuity of the supporting speech wave is of no greater significance than the continuity of the electrical signal supporting a train of binary digits.

There was considerable initial success in building apparatus that would eke a sequence of discrete phonemes out of a continuous speech waveform. Although phonemic analysis has been prominent, numerous other approaches to this "decoding" problem were followed. Almost all shared the same degree of initial success. Yet all have proved incapable of significant extension beyond the recognition of (1) the speech of a very few distinct individuals, and (2) the recognition of a very few distinct sound patterns, be they phonemes, words, or whatever. Similar restricted initial successes followed by total failure to generalize have been evident in research on automatic language translation, game playing, problem solving, and pattern recognition. A penetrating critical analysis of these fields by Dreyfus [6] could equally well apply here.

The essentially discrete and invariant nature of the phoneme, so evident to the linguist concerned with phonemic analysis or even to people who have trained themselves to read speech from sound spectrograms, has turned out to be most unexpectedly elusive in the absence of a human agent. The invariance of perception is clear. A sound wave can be mauled by bandwidth compression, elimination of formants, and a great variety of other forms of torture. The resulting speech, perhaps degraded in aesthetic quality, nevertheless remains surprisingly intelligible. Yet the phoneme, or for that matter the boundaries between words or sentences, seem undetectable by any nonhuman device yet tried except under the most artificial and restrictive conditions.

One is therefore forced to raise once again the question, if not of the reality of the phoneme, then of its usefulness. Perhaps the phoneme plays a role in human speech perception, perhaps not. However, the value of the phoneme as a building block for automatic speech analysis is very dubious indeed.

Perhaps it is the case that, in perception as well as in conscious scholarly analysis, the phoneme comes after the fact, namely, that it is constructed, if at all, as a *consequence* of perception, not as a step in the process of perception itself. If so, the separation of phonology and phonemics from syntax and semantics must be regarded as fruitless and artificial when seeking something beyond explanation after the fact, which can be tolerated only when dealing with human beings with their marvelous but as yet unexplained faculties for speech generation and perception.

Syntax

Syntax has followed the same pattern of early success, then disillusionment accompanied by a deepening sense of wonder at the mystery of language, then new challenge to a more vigorous scholarly probe into the fascinating realm of linguistic structure. There is, by now, a rich and accessible literature of contemporary syntactic studies concerned with syntactic theory and with the problems of automatic processing of natural and formal languages [1, 7]. Linguists, logicians, and computer people have all been concerned with various aspects of the problem and have contributed to its study in an increasingly unified and coordinated fashion. Details of theory or technique need not concern us here.

Wisely taking into account the difficulties of speech analysis, those concerned with syntax have worked primarily with printed materials where the problems of symbol identification, segmentation, and machine input, while not negligible, are much simpler than for speech, especially if one is willing to invest in an appropriate number of keystrokes to make material available in machine-readable form.

The starting point for any of the superficially divergent but fundamentally similar techniques of analysis or synthesis is a lexicon where each word is accompanied by syntactic (part of speech) markers of various degrees of complexity and refinement. The lexical entry for "flies," for example, might include mention that the word may serve as a plural noun or as a verb form in the third person singular.

With each part of speech, and with each syntactic role the word may play when used as that part of speech, there is associated one or more senses which the word may assume. For example, "flies" as noun denotes an annoying domestic insect, while as a verb it denotes locomotion through the air by an agent represented by a subject in the third person singular. "Bank" as noun may denote a financial institution or the edge of a river, and it may serve attributively in either sense as, for example, in "the bank teller." As a verb, it may denote either the transacting of banking business as in "I bank at Farmers' Trust Company" or the act of relying on someone as in "I bank on you to do such and such."

Some languages have incorporated as purely formal syntactic features distinctions that have a semantic flavor. Gender in French and the animate/inanimate distinction in Russian are prime examples.

When generating a sentence, it seems possible in principle, although little is known about practice, to make a deliberate choice of a unique marker to accompany an instance of a word in a sentence and hence to produce a sentence whose structure is unambiguous and even one whose meaning is both unambiguous and free of anomalies.

The same freedom does not apply when trying to recover the structure of a sentence as presented in a text. The string "time flies like an arrow" carries no explicit indicators of its structure or of the history of its construction in terms of choices made for each word. Nevertheless, its meaning is obvious to any normal speaker of English. Why this should be so is not understood.

A typical machine program for analyzing this sentence would first look each word up in a dictionary. For example, the entry described above would be recovered for "flies." The problem of determining the structure of the sentence—typically, determining what part is the subject, what part is the predicate, and so on—is therefore complicated by the fact that "flies" out of context might be either verb or noun. Which role it serves in this particular context can be determined only by examining its relation to the other words in the sentence, each of which in turn is usually identified by the dictionary as capable of assuming more than one role.

A five-word sentence where each word form may represent either of two parts of speech thus represents 32 distinct sequences of syntactic markers. Each of these 32 must be examined to see whether it is a valid sequence according to the grammar postulated for the language. In general, if words have k syntactic markers on the average, a sentence n words long yields n^k distinct sequences for examination. This exponential growth was one of the major obstacles that had to be overcome in the development of practical syntactic-analysis systems.

While the exponential explosion has now been controlled, the resulting syntactic analysis of sentences yields many surprises. Of course, every combination of syntactic markers does not yield a viable structure for the sentence. For example, "bank" in "the bank" can quickly be ruled out as a verb form, although it is acceptable in that context as either an attributive ("the bank teller") or a noun. Nevertheless, almost every sentence subjected to purely syntactic analysis, however unambiguous it might appear to most people, turns out to have a high degree of syntactic ambiguity. In general, sentences are assigned many structures, some of which reflect genuine semantic ambiguities and are therefore desirable products of a grammar intended to describe "the speaker-hearer's intrinsic competence," as Chomsky [1] put it, while others are semantically anomalous.

"Time flies like an arrow" must, if a given grammar pretends to describe English with any degree of accuracy, be analyzed in the obvious way that yields "time" as the subject of the verb "flies," with "like an arrow" as an adverbial phrase modifying the verb. But "time" can also function attributively, as in "the time bomb," and "flies," of course, can serve as a noun. Together with "like" interpreted as a verb, this yields an analysis whose structure becomes obvious if one thinks of a species of flies called "time flies" who happen to like an arrow as a meal. Moreover, "time" as an imperative verb, with "flies" as a noun, yields a structure of the sentence appropriate to an order to someone to take out his stop watch and time flies with great dispatch or swiftly, like an arrow.

Too-hasty reflection would suggest that minor modifications of the grammar should be sufficient to eliminate the anomalous structures. Unfortunately, there is no such easy way out. First of all, one might argue that the structures are legitimate even if the sentences are meaningless. It is, after all, only an accident of nature, or for that matter merely of nomenclature, that there is no species of flies called "time flies." Second, the nature and scope of anomaly are highly debatable both in general and in many specific instances. Finally, any minor modification which would rule out the anomalous syntactic structure that refers to the nonexisting species of "time flies" must also rule out the identical and legitimate structure of the sentence "fruit flies like a banana."

To make matters worse, the latter sentence is itself given an anomalous structure, namely the one which is quite legitimate for "time flies . . ." but which is nonsensical here since we know quite well that fruit in general does not fly and that, when it does, it flies like a maple pug rather than like a banana.

What becomes painfully clear at this point is that only an appeal to semantics can resolve the choice among the three syntactically acceptable structures of "time flies like an arrow." Surely the reader is also aware that this sentence, harmless and clear enough when first introduced, now seems rather confusing and complex. Its meaning will never be quite the same again.

Semantics

Having demonstrated our inability to solve the problem of speech analysis and having brought the problem of syntactic analysis about as far as the formal study of linguistic structure will permit, the only path remaining open is to readmit to full consideration the relationship between the linguistic symbols or their physical vehicles and the real world or, at least, the speech community's view of this real world.

One of the few things that contending schools of linguists have agreed on in the past few decades is the banning of semantic considerations from linguistic theory. Semantics has been left to philosophers, poets, and assorted cultists. The current return of semantics to linguistic grace is marked by the appearance in 1963 of Katz and Fodor's "The Structure of a Semantic Theory" [8], although Katz and Fodor did not develop a semantic theory but merely tried to state what such a theory should look like if one had it.

Katz and Fodor proposed to extend the notion of syntactic marker (e.g., "noun") by adding to the lexical description of a word semantic markers which describe appropriate semantic features. Thus, for example, "bachelor" in "John remained a bachelor until he met and married Sara" would be distinguished from "bachelor" in "bachelors congregate on rocks near the edge of the sea" by ascribing the semantic markers "human" and "male" to the one, and "animal" and "male" to the other. The definition is completed by an expression called a distinguisher which in the first case is "who has never married," in the other case "young fur seal when without a mate during the breeding time."

In constructing a sentence, one would presumably select words with the appropriate syntactic and semantic markers in order to produce a sentence with the desired sense. In analyzing a sentence, one would presumably invoke some principle of semantic congruity which would rule out not only words with nonmating syntactic markers but also those which, although linked in syntactically acceptable constructions, have incongruous semantic markers. Thus in "the young bachelor married Jane," "bachelor" as "seal" would be ruled out by the incongruity of "animal" in its semantic marker with "human" in that of "Jane." Such cases are clear enough.

Going beyond examples to the actual construction of such a theory for a specific language is a bleak prospect indeed. It is not surprising therefore that attempts in this direction to date have been limited rather strictly to small samples of carefully circumscribed universes, to the accompaniment of a great deal of hand waving. The task of providing adequate semantic markers for a substantial lexicon seems uncomfortably close to the problem of describing the structure of the universe.

In a recent article, Bolinger [9] has given a thorough, careful, and rather caustic critique of the approach of Katz and Fodor. At this time the situation appears stalemated, with no one making significant moves in any identifiable direction.

Oddly enough, while Bolinger comes to the conclusion that "the theory of Katz and Fodor is at best a partial theory of the semantics of a natural language," he leaves open the possibility that "it may be a very good theory of how to program for mechanical translation." This preserves linguistic purity and tosses the problem to the heathens, in whose name this gambit is hereby respectfully declined.

Conclusion

One might have hoped that the problems arising at the phonemic level might have been resolved at the syntactic level. Since it is not possible to recognize a sequence of phonemes by appeal to acoustical or electrical measurements alone, one might have hoped at least to make a partial identification, leaving open a range of choices at spots where definite recognition is impossible. For example, where /s/ cannot be distinguished from /f/, both might be allowed to remain in a tentative discrete transcription of speech and the ambiguity resolved at a later stage of analysis much as the noun/verb ambiguity of "flies" is resolved by syntactic analysis.

Thus a sequence of phonemes might be accepted as a true reading only if it can be found in a dictionary. If, for example, a sequence beginning with /f/ is so found, while a sequence beginning with /s/ is not, the evidence might be deemed conclusive for /f/ over /s/. In general, of course, there will be no such luck and both types of sequences may be found. Since segmentation at the acoustic or electrical level seems impossible, a large number of potential word boundaries might then have to be explored.

The result of such a process would bring one almost, but not quite, to the point where syntactic analysis of printed material begins. Where a sentence given in printed form enters analysis at least as a unique sequence of word forms, its speech equivalent would begin as many sequences of alternative word forms. The exponential explosion problem for syntactic analysis would thus be vastly multiplied if the starting point were speech. This might be tolerable, at least in principle, if the endpoint of syntactic analysis did not touch on a semantic wall, namely, our inability to determine the unique sense of a sentence or, if the sentence is genuinely ambiguous, our inability to eliminate at least the anomalous though syntactically correct readings.

Thus our attempts to proceed from the simple to the complicated, from building block to whole structure, have been singularly unsuccessful.

One is therefore driven to question the very foundation of contemporary linguistic theories. The theories in greatest vogue have accounting for a speaker-listener's command of his language as their objective. To the extent that this objective is reached at all, it is reached only from the point of view of sentence generation, although the claim is frequently made that it is irrelevant whether the grammar is constructed from the speaker's or the listener's point of view. In any case, empirical verification of such theories is begged off as not linguistically significant.

Questions of sentence-structure recognition, psychology, or engineering, and many others that do not fit into received dogma, are dismissed as "linguistically insignificant"—a pejorative expression whose sole definition seems to be the assumption that what is linguistically significant is what is in the accepted theories.

These theories enable their builders, though not machines and not necessarily other people, to construct strings of symbols that are in a language and very few strings that are not sentences, and that fact is indeed in their favor. Yet the fact that we are unable either to analyze speech or to recover the structure of printed sentences without accepting many anomalous structures leaves room for doubt about the validity of the theories. Rejecting such empirical tests as criteria for the validity of theory is dangerously close to solipsism. Although the criterion of "linguistic significance" is also used to eliminate recourse to psychological verification, the fact that psychological evidence for or against any linguistic theory is extremely scant suggests that we are far indeed from the last word about the structure of language.

It may well be that an understanding of the meaning of a sentence is a precondition for the ascription of a syntactic structure to the sentence and for the analysis of the sentence into phonemic components. The possibility is a frightening one to face, and our attachment to working from the building block to the whole is ample testimony to this terror. Yet the schoolboy asked to parse a sentence proceeds neither like a machine nor like a generative grammar—at least there is no evidence that he does. On the contrary, the scant evidence there is suggests that he works backwards, going from meaning to structure.

We have no real idea of how people generate or understand speech. If indeed we have an ability to use a global context without recourse to formalization and if language has evolved to match this human capacity, then our optimistic discrete enumerative approach is doomed both in psychology and in computational linguistics. There is, here, a need for entirely fresh ideas.

REFERENCES

1. N. Chomsky, "Aspects of the Theory of Syntax," MIT Press, Cambridge, Mass., 1965.
2. W. V. Quine, "From a Logical Point of View," Harvard University Press, Cambridge, Mass., 1953.
3. W. Weaver, "Translation" (1949), reprinted in W. N. Lodge and A. D. Booth (eds.), "Machine Translation of Languages," John Wiley & Sons, Inc., New York, 1955.

4. R. Jakobson, C. G. M. Fant, and M. Halle, "Preliminaries to Speech Analysis," MIT Press, Cambridge, Mass., 1963.
5. R. Jakobson and M. Halle, "Fundamentals of Language," Mouton and Co., The Hague, 1956.
6. H. L. Dreyfus, "Alchemy and Artificial Intelligence," Paper P-3244, RAND Corporation, Santa Monica, Calif., 1965.
7. D. G. Bobrow, Syntactic Analysis of English by Computer—A Survey, *AFIPS Conf. Proc.*, vol. 24, Spartan, Baltimore, 1963.
8. J. J. Katz and J. A. Fodor, The Structure of a Semantic Theory (1963), in J. A. Fodor and J. J. Katz (eds.), "The Structure of Language," Prentice-Hall, Englewood Cliffs, N.J., 1964.
9. D. Bolinger, The Atomization of Meaning, *Language,* **41**(4):555–573 (1965).

CHAPTER TWO

Perception of the Speech Code[1]

A. M. LIBERMAN,[2] F. S. COOPER,
D. P. SHANKWEILER,[2] and M. STUDDERT-KENNEDY[3]

The Basic Theme

Man could not perceive speech well if each phoneme were cued by a unit sound. In fact, many phonemes are encoded so that a single acoustic cue carries information in parallel about successive phonemic segments. This reduces the rate at which discrete sounds must be perceived, but at the price of a complex relation between cue and phoneme: cues vary greatly with context, and there are, in these cases, no commutable acoustic segments of phonemic size. Phoneme perception therefore requires a special decoder. A possible model supposes that the encoding occurs below the level of the (invariant) neuromotor commands to the articulatory muscles. The decoder may then identify phonemes by referring the incoming speech sounds to those commands.

[1] Reprinted from *Psychological Review,* **74**(6) (November 1967). The research reported here was aided at its beginning, and for a considerable period afterward, by the Carnegie Corporation of New York. Funds have also come from the National Science Foundation and the Department of Defense. The work is currently supported by the National Institute of Child Health and Human Development, the National Institute of Dental Research, and the Office of Naval Research.

[2] Also at the University of Connecticut.

[3] Also at Queens College, the City University of New York.

Our aim is to identify some of the conditions that underlie the perception of speech. We will not consider the whole process, only the part that lies between the acoustic stream and a level of perception corresponding roughly to the phoneme.[4] Even this, as we will try to show, presents an interesting challenge to the psychologist.

The point we want most to make is that the sounds of speech are a special and especially efficient code to the phonemic structure of language, not a cipher or alphabet. We use the term "code,"[5] in contrast to "cipher" or "alphabet," to indicate that speech sounds represent a very considerable restructuring of the phonemic "message." The acoustic cues for successive phonemes are intermixed in the sound stream to such an extent that definable segments of sound do not correspond to segments at the phoneme level. Moreover, the same phoneme is most commonly represented in different phonemic environments by sounds that are vastly different. There is, in short, a marked lack of correspondence between sound and perceived phoneme. This is a central fact of speech perception. It is, we think, the result of a complex encoding that makes the sounds of speech especially efficient as vehicles for the transmission of phonemic information. But it also poses an important question: By what mechanism does the listener decode the sounds and recover the phonemes?

In this paper we will (1) ask whether speech could be well perceived if it were an alphabet or acoustic cipher, (2) say how we know that

[4] For our purposes the phoneme is the shortest segment that makes a significant difference between utterances. It lies in the lowest layer of language, has no meaning in itself, and is, within limits, commutable. There are, for example, three such segments in the word "bad"—/b/, /æ/, and /d/—established by the contrasts with "dad," "bed," and "bat." As commonly defined, a phoneme is an abstract and general type of segment, represented in any specific utterance by concrete and specific tokens, called *phones,* that may vary noticeably as a function of context. The distinguishable variants so produced are referred to as *allophones.*

We do not mean to imply that every phoneme is necessarily perceived as one listens to speech. Linguistic constraints of various kinds make it possible to correct or insert segments that are heard wrongly or not at all. Phonemes can be perceived, however, and some number of them must be perceived if the listener is to discover which constraints apply.

[5] We borrow the terms "cipher" and "code" from cryptography. A cipher substitutes a symbol for each of the units (letters, usually) of the original message. In a code, on the other hand, the units of the original and encoded forms do not correspond in structure or number, the encoded message typically containing fewer units. Since these distinctions are relevant to our purpose here, we have adopted the terms "cipher" and "code" as a convenient way to refer to them. We should add, however, that the arbitrary relation between the original and encoded forms of a message, so usual in cryptography, is not a feature of the encoding of phonemes into syllables.

speech is, in fact, a complex code, (3) describe some properties of the perceptual mode that results when speech is decoded, (4) consider how the encoding and decoding might occur, and (5) show that the speech code is so well matched to man as to provide, despite its complexity, a uniquely effective basis for communication.

Could Speech Be Alphabetic?

There are reasons for supposing that phonemes could not be efficiently communicated by a sound alphabet—that is, by sounds that stand in one-to-one correspondence with the phonemes. Such reasons provide only indirect support for the conclusion that speech is a code rather than an alphabet. They are important, however, because they indicate that the encoded nature of speech may be a condition of its effectiveness in communication. More specifically, they tell us which aspects of the code are likely to be relevant to that effectiveness.

Phoneme Communication and the Properties of the Ear

Of the difficulties we might expect to have with a sound alphabet, the most obvious concerns rate. Speech can be followed, though with difficulty, at rates as high as 400 words per minute [1]. If we assume an average of four to five phonemes for each English word, this rate yields about 30 phonemes per second. But we know from auditory psychophysics [2] that 30 sounds per second would overreach the temporal resolving power of the ear: discrete acoustic events at that rate would merge into an unanalyzable buzz; a listener might be able to tell from the pitch of the buzz how fast the speaker was talking, but he could hardly perceive what had been said. Even 15 phonemes per second, which is not unusual in conversation, would seem more than the ear could cope with if phonemes were a string of discrete acoustic events.

There is at least one other requirement of a sound alphabet that would be hard to satisfy: a sufficient number of identifiable sounds. The number of phonemes, and hence the number of acoustic shapes required, is in the dozens. In English there are about 40. We should, of course, be able to find 40 identifiable sounds if we could pattern the stimuli in time, as in the case of melodies. But if we are to communicate as rapidly as we do, the phoneme segments could last no longer than about 50 ms on the average. Though it is not clear from research on auditory perception how many stimuli of such brief duration can be accurately identified, the available data suggest that the number is considerably less than 40 [3–7]. We will be interested, therefore, to see whether any features of the encoding and decoding mechanisms are calculated to enhance the identifiability of the signals.

Results of Attempts to Communicate Phonemes by an Acoustic Alphabet

That these difficulties of rate and sound identification are real we may see from the fact that it has not been possible to develop an efficient sound alphabet despite repeated and thoroughgoing attempts to do so. Thus international Morse code (a cipher as we use the term here) works poorly in comparison with speech, even after years of practice. But Morse is surely not the best example; the signals are one-dimensional and therefore not ideal from a psychological standpoint. More interesting, if less well known, are the many sound alphabets that have been tested in the attempt to develop reading machines for the blind [8–14]. These devices convert print into sound, the conversion being made typically by encipherment of the optical alphabet into one that is acoustic. The worth of these devices has been limited, not by the difficulty of converting print to sound, but by the perceptual limitations of their human users. In the 50-year history of this endeavor, a wide variety of sounds has been tried, including many that are multidimensional and otherwise appropriately designed, it would seem, to carry information efficiently. Subjects have practiced with these sounds for long periods of time, yet there has nowhere emerged any evidence that performance with these acoustic alphabets can be made to exceed performance with Morse, and that is little more than a tenth of what can be achieved with speech.

Reading and Listening

We hardly need say that language can be written and read by means of an alphabet, but we would emphasize how different are the problems of communicating phonemes by eye and by ear and how different is their relevance to a psychology of language. In contrast to the ear, the eye should have no great difficulty in rapidly perceiving ordered strings of signals. Given the eye's ability to perceive in space, we should suppose that alphabetic segments set side by side could be perceived in clusters. Nor is there reason to expect that it might be difficult to find identifiable optical signals in sufficient number. Many shapes are available, and a number of different alphabets are, indeed, in use. Thus written language has no apparent need for the special code that will be seen to characterize language in its acoustic form. In writing and reading it is possible to communicate phonemes by means of a cipher or alphabet: indeed, there appears to be no better way.

Spoken and written language differ, then, in that the former must be a complex code while the latter can be a simple cipher. Yet perception of speech is universal, though reading is not. In the history of the race, as in the development of the individual, speaking and listening come first; writing and reading come later, if at all. Moreover, the most efficient way of writing and reading namely, by an alphabet—is nevertheless so unnatural that it has apparently been invented only once in all history [15]. Perceiving the complex speech code is thus basic to language, and to man, in a way that reading an alphabet is not. Being concerned about language, we are therefore the more interested in the speech code. Why are speech sounds, alone among acoustic signals and in spite of the limitations of the ear, perceived so well?

Acoustic Cues: A Restructuring of Phonemes at the Level of Sound

To know in what sense speech sounds are a code on the phonemes, we must first discover which aspects of the complex acoustic signal underlie the perception of particular phonemes. For the most part, the relevant data are at hand. We can now identify acoustic features that are sufficient and important cues for the perception of almost all the segmental phonemes.[6] Much remains to be learned, but we know enough to see that the phonemic message is restructured in the sound stream and from that knowledge we can make certain inferences about perception.

An Example of Restructuring

To illustrate the nature of the code, we will describe an important acoustic cue for the perception of the voiced stop /d/. This example is important in its own right and also broadly representative. The phoneme /d/, or something very much like it, occurs in all the languages of the world.[7] In English, and perhaps in other languages, too, it carries a heavy load of information, probably more than any other single

[6] For the discussion that follows we shall rely most heavily on the results of experiments with synthetic speech carried out at Haskings Laboratories. The reader will understand that a review of the relevant literature would refer to many other studies, including, in particular, those that rest on analysis of real speech. For recent reviews and discussions, see Ref. 16 and chap. 6 of Ref. 17.

[7] Some form of a voiceless unaspirated stop having a place of production in the alveolar-dental region is universal [18, 19]. The particular example, /d/, used here is a member of that class in almost all important respects. Even in regard to voicing, it is a better fit than might at first appear, since it shares with the voiceless unaspirated stop of, say, French or Hungarian the same position on the dimension of voice-onset time, which is a most important variable for phonemic differences in voicing [20, 21].

phoneme [22], and it is among the first of the phonemelike segments to appear in the vocalizations of the child [23, p. 84]. The acoustic cue we have chosen to examine—the second-formant transition[8]—is a major cue for all the consonants except, perhaps, the fricatives /s/ and /ʃ/, and is probably the single most important carrier of linguistic information in the speech signal [24–33].

Context-conditioned Variations in the Acoustic Cue

Figure 2.1 displays two highly simplified spectrographic patterns that will, when converted into sound, be heard as the syllables /di/ and /du/ [30]. They exemplify the results of a search for the acoustic cues in which hand-drawn or "synthetic" spectrograms were used as a basis for experimenting with the complex acoustic signal [34–37]. The steady-state formants, making up approximately the right-hand two-thirds of each pattern, are sufficient to produce the vowels /i/ and /u/ [38, 39]. At the left of each pattern are the relatively rapid changes in frequency of the formants—the formant transitions—that are, as we indicated, important acoustic cues for the perception of the consonants. The transition of the first, or lower, formant, rising from a very low frequency to the level appropriate for the vowel, is a cue for the class of voiced stops /b,d,g/ [26, 40]. It would be exactly the same for /bi,bu/ and /gi,gu/ as for /di,du/. Most generally, this transition is a cue for the perception of manner and voicing. The acoustic feature in which we are here interested is the transition of the second formant, which is, in the patterns of Fig. 2.1, a cue for distinguishing among the voiced stops /b,d,g/; that is to say, the second-formant transition for /gi/ or /bi/, as well as /gu/ or /bu/, would be different from those for /di/ and du/ [30]. In general, transitions of the second formant

[8] A formant is a concentration of acoustic energy within a restricted frequency region. Three or four formants are usually seen in spectrograms of speech. In the synthetic, hand-painted spectrograms of Figs. 2.1 and 2.2, only the lowest two are represented. Formants are referred to by number, the first being the lowest in frequency, the second, the next higher, and so on. A formant transition is a relatively rapid change in the position of the formant on the frequency scale.

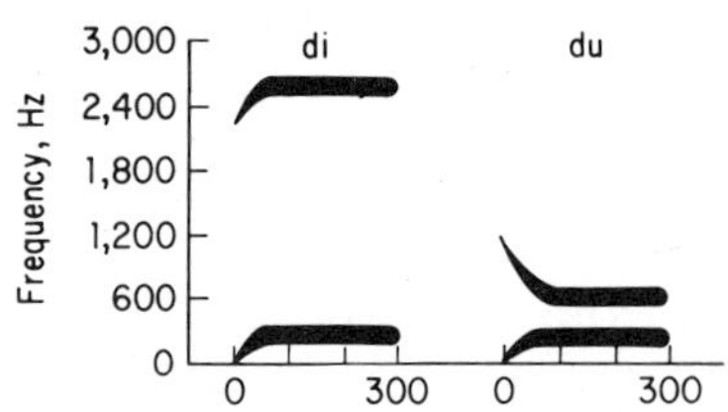

Fig. 2.1. Spectrographic patterns sufficient for the synthesis of /d/ before /i/ and /u/. (*Psychological Review, November 1967.*)

carry important information about the place of production of most consonants [24, 29, 30].

It is, then, the second-formant transitions that are, in the patterns of Fig. 2.1, the acoustic cues for the perception of the /d/ segment of the syllables /di/ and /du/. We would first note that /d/ is the same perceptually in the two cases, and then see how different are the acoustic cues. In the case of /di/ the transition rises from approximately 2,200 to 2,600 Hz; in /du/ it falls from about 1,200 to 700 Hz. In other words, what is perceived as the same phoneme is cued, in different contexts, by features that are vastly different in acoustic terms. How different these acoustic features are in nonspeech perception can be determined by removing them from the patterns of Fig. 2.1 and sounding them in isolation. When we do that, the transition isolated from the /di/ pattern sounds like a rapidly rising whistle or glissando on high pitches, the one from /du/ like a rapidly falling whistle on low pitches.[9] These signals could hardly sound more different from each other. Furthermore, neither of them sounds like /d/ nor like speech of any sort.

The Disappearance of Phoneme Boundaries: Parallel Transmission

We turn now to another, related aspect of the code: the speech signal typically does not contain segments corresponding to the discrete and commutable phonemes. There is no way to cut the patterns of Fig. 2.1 so as to recover /d/ segments that can be substituted one for the other. Nor can we make the commutation simply by introducing a physical continuity between the cut ends as we might, for example, if we were segmenting and recombining the alphabetic elements of cursive writing.

Indeed, if we could somehow separate commutability from segmentability, we should have to say that there is no /d/ segment at all, whether commutable or not. We cannot cut either the /di/ or the /du/ pattern in such a way as to obtain some piece that will produce /d/ alone. If we cut progressively into the syllable from the right-hand end, we hear /d/ plus a vowel, or a nonspeech sound; at no point will we hear only /d/. This is so because the formant transition is, at every instant, providing information about two phonemes, the consonant and the vowel—that is, the phonemes are being transmitted in parallel.

[9] This is true of the patterns shown in Fig. 2.1 as converted to sound by the pattern playback. When the formants correspond more in their various constant features to those produced by the human vocal apparatus, the musical qualities described above may be harder to hear or may disappear altogether. So long as the second-formant transitions of /di/ and /du/ are not heard as speech, however, they do not sound alike.

The Locus: An Acoustic Invariant?

The patterns of Fig. 2.2 produce /d/ in initial position with each of a variety of vowels, thus completing a series of which the patterns shown in Fig. 2.1 are the extremes. If one extrapolates the various second-formant transitions backward in time, he sees that they seem to have diverged from a single frequency. To find that frequency more exactly, and to determine whether it might in some sense be said to characterize /d/, we can, as in Fig. 2.3, pair each of a number of straight second formants with first formants that contain a rising transition sufficient to signal a voiced stop of some kind. On listening to such patterns, one hears an initial /d/ most strongly when the straight second formant is at 1,800 Hz. This has been called the /d/ "locus" [26]. There are, correspondingly, second-formant loci for other consonants, the frequency position of the locus being correlated with the place of production. In general, the locus moves somewhat as a function of the associated vowel,

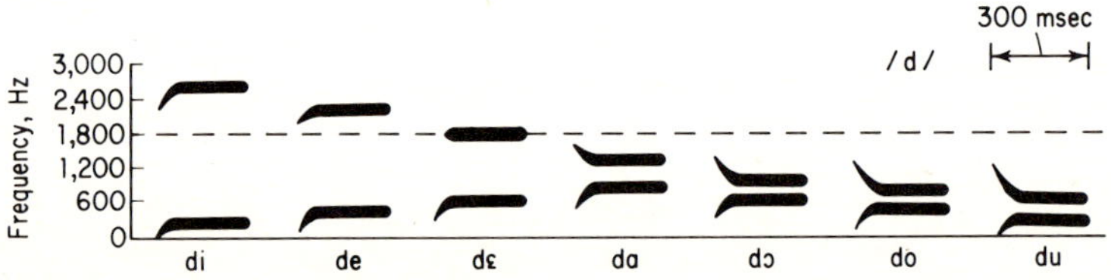

Fig. 2.2. Spectrographic patterns sufficient for the synthesis of /d/ before vowels. Dashed line at 1,800 cps shows the "locus" for /d/. (*Psychological Review, November 1967.*)

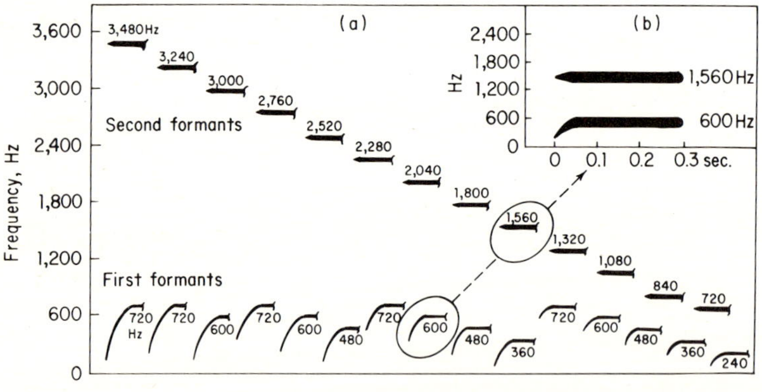

Fig. 2.3. Schematic display of the stimuli used in finding the second-formant loci of /b/, /d/, and /g/. (*a*) Frequency positions of the straight second formants and the various first formants with which each was paired. (*b*) A typical test pattern, made up of the first and second formants circled in (*a*). The best pattern for /d/ was the one with the straight second formant at 1,800 Hz. (*Delattre, Liberman, and Cooper, 1955,* Ref. 26.)

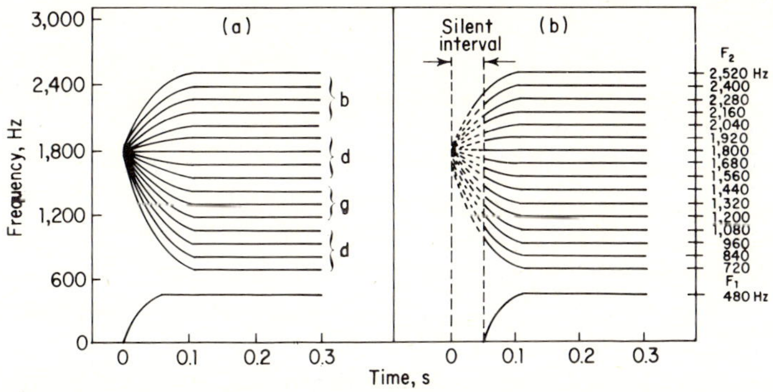

Fig. 2.4. (*a*) Second-formant transitions that start at the /d/ locus. (*b*) Comparable transitions that merely "point" at it, as indicated by the dotted lines. Those of (*a*) produce syllables beginning with /b/, /d/, or /g/, depending on the frequency-level of the formant; those of (*b*) produce only syllables beginning with /d/. (*Delattre, Liberman, and Cooper, 1955,* Ref. 26.)

but except for a discontinuity in the case of /k,g,ŋ/ the locus is more nearly invariant than the formant transition [26, 41, 42].

Is there, then, an invariant acoustic cue for /d/? Consider the various second formants that all begin at the 1,800-Hz locus and proceed from there to a number of different vowel positions, such as are shown in Fig. 2.4. We should note first that these transitions are not superimposable, so that if they are to be regarded as invariant acoustic cues, it could only be in the very special and limited sense that they start at the same point on the frequency scale. But even this very limited invariance is not to be had. If we convert the patterns of Fig. 2.4 to sound, having paired each of the second formants in turn with the single first formant shown at the bottom of the figure, we do not hear /d/ in every case. Taking the second formants in order from the top down, we hear first /b/, then /d/, then /g/, then once again /d/, as shown. In order to hear /d/ in every case, we must erase the first part of the transition as shown in Fig. 2.4*b*, so that it "points" at the locus but does not actually begin there. Thus the 1,800-Hz locus for /d/ is not a part of the acoustic signal, nor can it be made part of that signal without grossly changing the perception [26].

Though the locus can be defined in acoustic terms—that is, as a particular frequency—the concept is more articulatory than acoustic, as can be seen in the rationalization of the locus by Stevens and House [42]. What is common to /d/ before all the vowels is that the articulatory tract is closed at very much the same point. According to the calculations of Stevens and House, the resonant frequency of the cavity at the instant of closure is approximately 1,800 Hz, but since no sound emerges until some degree of opening has occurred, the locus frequency is not radiated as part of the acoustic signal. At all events it seems clear that though the locus is more nearly invariant with the phoneme than is the transition itself, the invariance is a derived one, related more to articulation than to sound. As we will see later, however, the locus is only a step toward the invariance with phoneme perception that we must seek; better approximations to that invariance are probably to be had by going further back in the chain of articulatory events, beyond the cavity shapes that underlie the locus, to the commands that produce the shapes.

How General Is the Restructuring?

Having dealt with the restructuring of only one phoneme and one acoustic cue, we should say now that with several interesting exceptions yet to be noted, it is generally true of the segmental phonemes that they are drastically restructured at the level of sound.[10] We will briefly summarize what is known in this regard about the various types of cues and linguistic classes or dimensions.

Transitions of the Second Formant

For the second-formant transition—the cue with which we have been concerned and the one which is perhaps the most important for the perception of consonants according to place of production—the kind of invariance lack we found with /d/ characterizes all the voiced stops, voiceless stops, and nasal consonants [30, 46]. Indeed, the invariance problem is, if anything, further complicated in these other phonemes. In the case of /k,g,ŋ/, for example, there is a sudden and considerable shift in the locus as between the unrounded and rounded vowels, creating a severe lack of correspondence between acoustic signal and linguistic perception that we mentioned earlier in this paper and that we have dealt with in some detail elsewhere [29].

With the liquids and semivowels /r,l,w,j/ the second-formant transition originates at the locus—as it cannot in the case of the stop and nasal consonants—so the lack of correspondence between acoustic signal and phoneme is less striking, but even with these phonemes the transition

[10] Somewhat similar complications arise in the suprasegmental domain. For data concerning the relation between the acoustic signal and the perception of intonation see Refs. 43 and 44. Lieberman [45] has measured some of the revelant physiological variables and on the basis of his findings has devised a hypothesis to account for the perception of intonation, in particular the observations of Hadding-Koch and Studdert-Kennedy. Lieberman's account of perception in the suprasegmental domain fits well with our own views about the decoding of segmental phonemes, discussed later in this paper.

cues are not superimposable for occurrences of the same consonant in different contexts [33, 47].

Transitions of the Third Formant

What of third-formant transitions, which also contribute to consonant perception in terms of place of production? Though we know less about the third-formant transitions than about those of the second, such evidence as we have does not suggest that an invariant acoustic cue can be found here [33, 47, 48]. In fact, the invariance problem is further complicated in that the third-formant transition seems to be more or less important (relative to the second-formant transition, for example) depending on the phonemic context. In the case of our /di,du/ example (Fig. 2.1), we find that an appropriate transition of the third formant contributes considerably to the perception of /d/ in /di/ but not at all to /d/ in /du/. To produce equal—that is, equally convincing—/d/'s before both /i/ and /u/, we must use acoustic cues that are, if anything, even more different than the two second-formant transitions we described earlier in this section.

Constriction Noises

The noises produced at the point of constriction—as in the fricatives and stops—are another set of cues for consonant perception according to place of production, the relevant physical variable being the frequency position of the band-limited noise. When these noises have considerable duration—as in the fricatives—the cue changes but little with context. Since the cue provided by these noises is of overriding importance in the perception of /s/ and /ʃ/, we should say that these consonants show little or no restructuring in the sound stream [28, 49]. (This may not be true when the speech is rapid.) They therefore constitute an exception to the usual strong dependence of the acoustic signal on its context—that is, to the effects of a syllabic coding operation.

On the other hand, the brief noise cues—the "bursts," so called—of the stop consonants display as much restructuring as do the transitions of the second formant [50]. Bursts of noise that produce the best /k/ or /g/ vary over a considerable frequency range depending on the following vowel. The range is so great that it extends over the domain of the /p,b/ burst, creating the curiosity of a single burst of noise at 1,440 Hz that is heard as /p/ before /i/ but as /k/ before /a/.[11] We should also note that the relative importance of the bursts, as of the transitions, varies greatly for the same stop in different contexts. For example, /g/ or /k/, which are powerfully cued by a second-formant transition

[11] This result was obtained in the experiment [50] with synthetic speech referenced above and verified for real speech in a tape-cutting experiment by Schatz [51].

before the vowel /æ/, will likely require a burst at an appropriate frequency if they are to be well perceived in front of /o/.[12] Thus the same consonant is primarily cued in two different contexts by signals as physically different as a formant transition and a burst of noise.

Manner, Voicing, and Position

In describing the complexities of the relation between acoustic cue and perceived phoneme, we have so far dealt only with cues for place of production and only with consonants in initial position in the syllable. A comparable lack of regularity is also found in the distinctions of manner and voicing and in the cues for consonants in different positions [21, 24, 26, 29, 30, 32, 40, 41, 47, 52, 53]. We will not consider these cues in detail, since the problems they present are similar to those already encountered. Indeed, the cues we have discussed as examples of encoding are merely a subset of those that show extensive restructuring as a function of context: it is the usual case that the acoustic cues for a consonant are different when the consonant is paired with different vowels, when it is in different positions (initial, medial, or final) with respect to the same vowels, and for all types of cues (manner or voicing, as well as place). Thus, for example, the cues for manner, place, and voicing of /b/ in /ba/ are acoustically different from those of /b/ in /ab/, the transitional cues for place being almost mirror images; further, the preceding set of cues differs from corresponding sets for /b/ with each of the other vowels.

The Vowels

We should remark, finally, on the acoustic cues for the vowels. For the steady-state vowels of Figs. 2.1 and 2.2, perception depends primarily on the frequency position of the formants [38, 39]. There is, for these vowels, no restructuring of the kind found to be so common among the consonant cues and, accordingly, no problem of invariance between acoustic signal and perception.[13]

However, vowels are rarely steady-state in normal speech; most commonly these phonemes are articulated between consonants and at rather rapid rates. Under these conditions vowels also show substantial re-

[12] This can be seen in the results of experiments on the bursts and transitions as cues for the stops [30, 50]. It is confirmed whenever one attempts, by using all possible cues, to synthesize the best stops.

[13] The absolute formant frequencies of the same vowel are different for men, women, and children, and for different individuals, partly as a consequence of differences in the sizes of vocal tracts. This creates an invariance problem very different from the kind we have been discussing and more similar, perhaps, to the problems encountered in the perception of nonspeech sounds, such as the constant ratios of musical intervals.

structuring—that is, the acoustic signal at no point corresponds to the vowel alone, but rather shows, at any instant, the merged influences of the preceding or following consonant [54–57].

In slow articulation, then, the acoustic cues for the vowels—and, as we saw earlier, the noise cues for fricatives—tend to be invariant. In this respect they differ from the cues for the other phonemes, which vary as a function of context at all rates of speaking. However, articulation slow enough to permit the vowels and fricatives to avoid being encoded is probably artificial and rare.

Phoneme Segmentation

We return now to the related problem of segmentation, briefly discussed above for the /di,du/ example. We saw there that the acoustic signal is not segmented into phonemes. If one examines the acoustic cues more generally, he finds that successive phonemes are most commonly merged in the sound stream. This is, as we will see, a correlate of the parallel processing that characterizes the speech code and is an essential condition of its efficiency. One consequence is that the acoustic cues cannot be divided on the time axis into segments of phonemic size.[14]

The same general conclusion may be reached by more direct procedures. Working with recordings of real speech, Harris [60] tried to arrive at "building blocks" by cutting tape recordings into segments of phoneme length and then recombining the segments to form new words. "Experiments indicated that speech based upon one building block for each vowel and consonant not only sounds unnatural but is mostly unintelligible . . ." (p. 962). In a somewhat similar attempt to produce intelligible speech by the recombination of parts taken from previously recorded utterances, Peterson, Wang, and Sivertsen [61] concluded that the smallest segments one can use are of roughly half-syllable length. Thus it has not been possible, in general, to synthesize speech from prerecorded segments of phonemic dimensions. Nor can we cut the sound stream along the time dimension so as to recover segments that will be perceived as separate phonemes. Of course, there are exceptions. As we might expect, these are the steady-state vowels and the long-duration noises of certain fricatives in which, as we have seen, the sounds show minimal restructuring.

[14] This is not to say that the sound spectrogram fails to show discontinuities along the time axis. Fant [58, 59] discusses the interpretation to be given these abrupt changes and the temporal segments bounded by them. He warns [58, p. 9]: "Sound segment boundaries should not be confused with phoneme boundaries. Several adjacent sounds of connected speech may carry information on one and the same phoneme, and there is overlapping in so far as one and the same sound segment carries information on several adjacent phonemes."

Apart from these exceptions, however, segments corresponding to the phonemes are not found at the acoustic level.

We shall see later that the articulatory gestures corresponding to successive phonemes—or, more precisely, their subphonemic features—are overlapped, or shingled, one onto another. This parallel delivery of information produces at the acoustic level the merging of influences we have already referred to and yields irreducible acoustic segments of approximately syllabic dimensions. Thus segmentation also exhibits a complex relation between linguistic structure or perception on the one hand and the sound stream on the other.

Perception of the Restructured Phonemes: The Speech Mode

If phonemes are encoded syllabically in the sound stream, they must be recovered in perception by an appropriate decoder. Perception of phonemes that have been so encoded might be expected to differ from the perception of those that have not and also, of course, from nonspeech. In this section we will suggest that such differences do, in fact, exist.

We have already seen one example of such a difference in the transition cues for /d/ in /di/ and /du/. Taken out of speech context, these transitions sound like whistles, the one rising through a range of high pitches and the other falling through low pitches; they do not sound like each other, nor even like speech. This example could be multiplied to include the transition cues for many other phonemes. With simplified speech of the kind already shown, the listener's perception is very different depending on whether he is, for whatever reason, in the speech mode or out of it [62].

Even on the basis of what can be heard in real speech, one might have suspected that the perception of encoded and unencoded phonemes[15] is somehow different. One has only to listen carefully to some of the latter in order to make reasonably accurate guesses about the auditory and acoustic dimensions that are relevant to their perception. The fricatives /s/ and /ʃ/, for example, obviously differ in manner from other phonemes in that there is noise of fairly long duration; moreover, one can judge by listening that they differ from each other in

[15] There is a need, in much that follows, for a convenient way to refer to classes of phonemes that show much—or little—restructuring of their acoustic cues as a function of context. The former are, indeed, encoded. We shall refer to the latter as "unencoded phonemes," implying only that they are found at the other end of a continuum on degree of restructuring; we do not wish to imply differences in the processes affecting these phonemes, whether or not such differences can be inferred from their perceptual characteristics.

the "pitch" of the noise—that is, in the way the energy is distributed along the frequency scale. Consider, on the other hand, the encoded phonemes /b,d,g/. No amount of listening, no matter how careful, is likely to reveal that an important manner cue is a rapidly rising frequency at the low end of the frequency scale (first formant), or that these stops are distinguished from each other primarily by the direction and extent of a rapid frequency glide in the upper frequency range (second and third formants).

These observations of perceptual differences between speech and nonspeech sounds, and even among classes of phonemes, do not stand alone. Controlled experiments can show more accurately, if sometimes less directly, the differences in perception. We will next consider some of these experiments.

Tendencies Toward Categorical and Continuous Perception

Research with some of the encoded phonemes has shown that they are categorical, not only in the abstract linguistic sense but as immediately given in perception. Consider, first, that in listening to continuous variations in acoustic signals, one ordinarily discriminates many more stimuli than he can absolutely identify. Thus we discriminate about 1,200 different pitches, for example, though we can absolutely identify only about seven. Perception of the restructured phonemes is different in that listeners discriminate very little better than they identify absolutely; that is to say, they hear the phonemes but not the intraphonemic variations.

The effect becomes clear impressionistically if one listens to simplified, synthetic speech signals in which the second-formant transition is varied in relatively small, acoustically equal steps through a range sufficient to produce the three stops /b/, /d/, and /g/. One does not hear steplike changes corresponding to the changes in the acoustic signal, but essentially quantal jumps from one perceptual category to another.

To evaluate this effect more exactly, various investigators have made quantitative comparisons of the subjects' ability to identify the stimuli absolutely and to discriminate them on any basis whatsoever. For certain consonant distinctions it has been found that the mode of perception is, in fact, nearly categorical: listeners can discriminate only slightly better than they can identify absolutely. In greater or lesser degree, this has been found for /b,d,g/ [63–67], /d,t/ [68],[16] /b,p/ in intervocalic position [69], and presence or absence of /p/ in slit *vs.* split [70–72].

[16] Studies of this distinction (and of the corresponding ones for the other stops) in 11 diverse languages indicate that it tends to be categorical also in production [20, 21, 52].

The perception of unencoded steady-state vowels is quite different:[17] one need only listen to synthetic vowels that vary, as in the example of the stops, in relatively small and acoustically equal steps through a range sufficient to produce three adjacent phonemes—say /i/, /I/, and /ɛ/. As heard, these vowels change step by step, much as the physical stimulus changes: the vowel /i/ shades into /ɪ/, and /ɪ/ into /ɛ/. Immediate perception is more nearly continuous than categorical, and the listener hears many intraphonemic variations. More precise measures of vowel perception indicate that, in contrast to the stops, listeners can discriminate many more stimuli than they can identify absolutely [73–75]. Similar studies of the perception of vowel duration [79] and tones in Thai [80], both of which are phonemic in that language, have produced similar results. We should suppose that steady-state vowels, vowel duration, and the tones can be perceived in essentially the same manner as continuous variations in nonspeech signals. The results of a direct experimental comparison by Eimas [63] suggest that this is so.

We emphasize that in speaking of vowels we have so far been concerned only with those that are isolated and steady-state. These are, as we have said, unencoded and hence not necessarily perceived in the speech mode. But what of the more usual situation we described earlier, that of vowels between consonants and in rapid articulation? Stevens [81] has supposed that the rapid changes in formant position characteristic of such vowels would tend to be referred in perception to the speech mode, and he has some evidence that this is so, having found that perception of certain vowels in proper dynamic context is more nearly categorical than that of steady-state vowels. Inasmuch as these rapidly articulated vowels are substantially restructured in the sound stream, Stevens' results may be assumed to reflect the operation of the speech decoder.

Lateral Differences in the Perception of Speech and Nonspeech

The conclusion that there is a speech mode, and that it is characterized by processes different from those underlying the perception of other sounds, is strengthened by recent indications that speech and nonspeech sounds are processed primarily in different hemispheres of the brain. Using Broadbent's method of delivering competing stimuli simultaneously

[17] In experiments with mimicry, Ludmilla Chistovich and her colleagues have obtained differences between vowels and consonants that are consistent with the differing tendencies toward categorical and continuous perception described here [17, 76–78].

to the two ears [82], investigators have found that speech stimuli presented to the right ear (hence, mainly to the left cerebral hemisphere) are better identified than those presented to the left ear (hence, mainly to the right cerebral hemisphere), and that the reverse is true for melodies and sonar signals [83–88]. In the terminology of this paper, the encoded speech signals are more readily decoded in the left hemisphere than in the right. This suggests the existence of a special left-hemisphere mechanism different from the right-hemisphere mechanism for the perception of sounds not similarly encoded. It is of interest, then, to ask whether the encoded stops and the unencoded steady-state vowels are, perhaps, processed unequally by the two hemispheres. An experiment [89] was carried out designed to answer this question, using synthetic speech syllables that contrasted in just one phoneme. A significantly greater right-ear advantage was found for the encoded stops than for the unencoded steady-state vowels. The fact that the steady-state vowels are less strongly lateralized in the dominant (speech) hemisphere may be taken to mean that these sounds, being unencoded, can be, and presumably sometimes are, processed as if they were nonspeech. In another experiment [90], the consonant and vowel comparisons were made with real speech. Different combinations of the same set of consonant-vowel-consonant (CVC) syllables were used for both tests. As before, a decisive right-ear advantage was found for contrasting stop consonants, and again there was no difference for vowels, even though these were here articulated in dynamic context between consonants. We will be interested to determine what happens to lateral differences in vowel perception when the vowels are very rapidly articulated. Such vowels are, as has been said, necessarily restructured to some extent and may be correspondingly dependent on the speech decoder for their perception.

Perception of Speech by Machine and by Eye

If speech is, as we have suggested, a special code, its perception should be difficult in the absence of an appropriate decoder such as we presumably use in listening to speech sounds. It is relevant, therefore, to note how very difficult it is to read visual transforms of speech or to construct automatic speech recognizers.

Consider, first, a visual transform—for example, the spectrogram. As we have already seen, the spectrographic pattern for a particular phoneme typically looks very different in different contexts. Furthermore, visual inspection of a spectrogram does not reveal how a stretch of speech might be divided into segments corresponding to phonemes, or even how many phonemes it might contain: the eye sees the transformed acoustic signal in its undecoded form. We should not be surprised, then, to discover that spectrograms are, in fact, extremely difficult to read.

Some part of the difficulty may be attributed to inadequacies of the transform or to lack of training. But an improved transform, if one should be found, would not by itself suffice to make spectrograms readable, since it would not obviate the need to decode. Nor is training likely to overcome the difficulty. Many persons have had considerable experience with spectrograms, yet none has found it possible to read them well.[18] Ideally, training in "reading" spectrograms should cause the transitions for /d/ in /di/ and /du/ to look alike. The speech decoder, after all, makes them sound alike when speech is perceived by ear; moreover, it seems obvious that if the decoder did not do this, speech would be much more difficult to perceive. If, as we suspect, training alone cannot make the acoustic cues for the same phoneme look alike, then we should, perhaps, conclude that the speech decoder, which makes them sound alike, is biologically tied to an auditory input.

How, then, do machines fare in recognizing the encoded sounds of speech? If speech were a cipher, like print, it would be no more difficult to build a speech recognizer than a print reader. In fact, the speech recognizer has proved to be more difficult, and by a very wide margin, largely because it needs an appropriate decoder, as a print reader does not, and because the design of that decoder is not easily accomplished—a conclusion confirmed by two decades of intensive effort. We might repeat, in passing, that for human beings the difficulty is the other way around: perceiving speech is far easier than reading.

Encoding and Decoding: From Phoneme to Sound and Back

Conversions from Phoneme to Sound

Having considered the evidence that speech is a code on the phonemes, we must ask how the encoding might have come about. The schema in Fig. 2.5 represents the various conversions that presumably occur as speech proceeds from the sentence through the empty segments at the phoneme level to the final acoustic signal. The topmost box, labeled "syntactic rules," would, if properly developed, be further broken down into phrase-structure rules, transformation rules, morphophonemic rules, and the like. (See, for example, Ref. 92.) These processes would be

[18] Fant says, "As a matter of fact I have not met one single speech researcher who has claimed he could read speech spectrograms fluently, and I am no exception myself" [58, p. 4]. Spectrograms are, even so, less difficult to read than oscillograms—whence their popular name, "visible speech," and much of the early enthusiasm for them [91].

of the greatest interest if we were dealing with speech perception in the broadest sense. Here, however, we may start with the message in the form of an ordered sequence of phonemes (or, as we will see, their constituent features) and follow it through the successive converters that yield, at the end, the acoustic waveform.

Subphonemic Features: Their Role in Production

First we must take account of the fact that the phonemes are compounded of a smaller number of elements, and, indeed, shift the emphasis from the phoneme to these subphonemic features.[19] The total gesture in the articulation of /b/, for example, can be broken down into several distinctive elements: (1) closing and opening of the upper vocal tract in such a way as to produce the manner feature characteristic of the stop consonants; (2) closing and opening of the vocal tract specifically at the lips, thus producing the place feature termed *bilabiality;* (3) closing the velum to provide the feature of orality; and (4) starting vocal-fold vibration simultaneously with the opening of the lips, appropriate to the feature of voicing. The phoneme /p/ presumably shares with /b/ features 1, 2, and 3, but differs as to feature 4, in that vocal-fold vibration begins some 50 or 60 ms after opening of the lips; /m/ has features 1, 2, and 4 in common with /b/, but differs in feature 3, since the velum hangs open to produce the feature of nasality; /d/ has features 1, 3, and 4 in common with /b/, but has a different place of articulation; and so on.

That subphonemic features are present both in production and perception has by now been quite clearly established.[20] Later in this paper

[19] The term "feature" has varied uses, even in this paper. Thus, in this paragraph, we describe a particular speech gesture in conventional phonetic terms, referring to how the articulators move and where the constrictions occur as the manner and place features that, taken together, characterize the gesture. Two paragraphs later, the description of a possible model for speech production identifies subphonemic features as implicit instructions to separate and independent parts of the motor machinery. Viewed in this way, the distinctive features of a phoneme are closely linked to specific muscles and the neural commands that actuate them.

Destinctive features of this kind are clearly different from those so well known from the work of Jakobson and his colleagues. See Ref. 93 and the various revisions proposed by the several authors [94–97]. We are, nevertheless, deeply indebted to them for essential points—in particular, that the phonemes can be characterized by sets of features which are few in number, limited to a very few states each, and maintained throughout several phonemes. Other important characteristics for an ideal system of distinctive features include mutual independence, clear correspondences with physiological—or acoustic—observables, and as much universality across languages as parsimony for a single language will allow.

[20] For discussions of the psychological reality of phoneme segments and subphonemic features, see Refs. 16, 17, and 98.

we will discuss some relevant data on production. Here we merely note that we must deal with the phonemes in terms of their constituent features because the existence of such features is essential to the speech code and to the efficient production and perception of language. We have earlier remarked that high rates of speech would overtax the temporal resolving power of the ear if the acoustic signal were merely a cipher on the phonemic structure of the language. Now we should note that speaking at rates of 10 to 15 phonemes per second would as surely be impossible if each phoneme required a separate and distinct oral gesture. Such rates can be achieved only if separate parts of the articulatory machinery—muscles of the lips, tongue, velum, etc.—can be separately controlled, and if the linguistic code is such that a change of state for any one of these articulatory entities, taken together with the current state of the others, is a change to another element of the code—that is, to another phoneme. Thus dividing the load among the articulators allows each to operate at a reasonable pace, and tightening the code keeps the information rate high. It is this kind of parallel processing that makes it possible to get high-speed performance with low-speed machinery. As we will see, it also accounts for the overlapping and intermixing of the acoustic signals for the phonemes that is characteristic of the speech code.

A Model for Production

The simplest possible model of the production process would, then, have the phonemes of an utterance represented by sets of subphonemic features, and these in turn would be assumed to exist in the central nervous system as implicit instructions[21] to separate and independent parts of the motor machinery. The sequence of neural signals corresponding to this multidimensional string of control instructions may well require, for its actualization, some amplitude adjustments and temporal coordination in the box labeled "neuromotor rules" in order to yield the neural impulses that go directly to the selected muscles of articulation and cause them to contract. If we are to continue to make the simplest possible assumption, however, we must suppose that reorganization of the instructions at this stage would be limited to such coordination and to providing supplementary neural signals to insure

[21] These instructions might be of two types, "on-off" or "go to," even in a maximally simple model. In the one case, the affected muscle would contract or not with little regard for its current state (or the position of the articulator it moves); in the other, the instruction would operate via the γ-efferent system to determine the degree of contraction (hence, the final position of the articulator, whatever its initial position). Both types of instruction—appropriate, perhaps, to fast and slow gestures, respectively—may reasonably be included in the model.

cooperative activity of the remainder of the articulatory apparatus; there would be no reorganization of the commands to the "primary" actuators for the selected features. In that case, the neural signals that emerge would bear still an essentially one-to-one correspondence with the several dimensions of the subphonemic structure. Indeed, this is a necessary condition for our model, since total reorganization at this stage would destroy the parallel processing, referred to earlier, on which high-speed reception depends, or else yield a syllabic language from which the phoneme strings could not be recovered.

The next conversion, from neural command (in the final common paths) to muscle contraction, takes place in the box labeled "myomotor rules." If muscles contract in accordance with the signals sent to them, then this conversion should be essentially trivial, and we should be able not only to observe the muscle contractions by looking at their electromyographic (EMG) signals but also to infer the neural signals at the preceding level.

It is at the next stage—the conversion from muscle contraction to vocal-tract shapes by way of articulatory rules—that a very considerable amount of encoding or restructuring must surely occur. If we take into account the structure and function of the articulatory system, in particular the intricate linkages and the spatial overlap of the component parts, we must suppose that the relation between contraction and resulting shape is complex, though predictable. True encoding occurs as a consequence of two further aspects of this conversion; the fact that the subphonemic features can be, and are, put through in parallel means that each new set of contractions (1) starts from whatever configuration then exists (as the result of the preceding contractions) and (2) typically occurs before the last set has ended, with the result that the shape of the tract at any instant represents the merged effects of past and present instructions. Such merging is, in effect, an encoding operation according to our use of that term, since it involves an extensive restructuring of the output—in this case, the shape of the tract. The relation of message units to code becomes especially complex when temporal and spatial overlaps occur together. Thus the conversion from muscle contraction to shape is, by itself, sufficient to produce the kinds of complex relation between phoneme and sound that we have found to exist in the overall process of speech production, that is, a loss of segmentability together with very large changes in the essential acoustic signals as a function of context. Given the structure of the articulatory apparatus, these complexities appear to be a necessary concomitant of the parallel processing that makes the speech code so efficient.

The final conversion, from shape to sound, proceeds by what we have in Fig. 2.5 called acoustic rules. These rules, which are now well under-

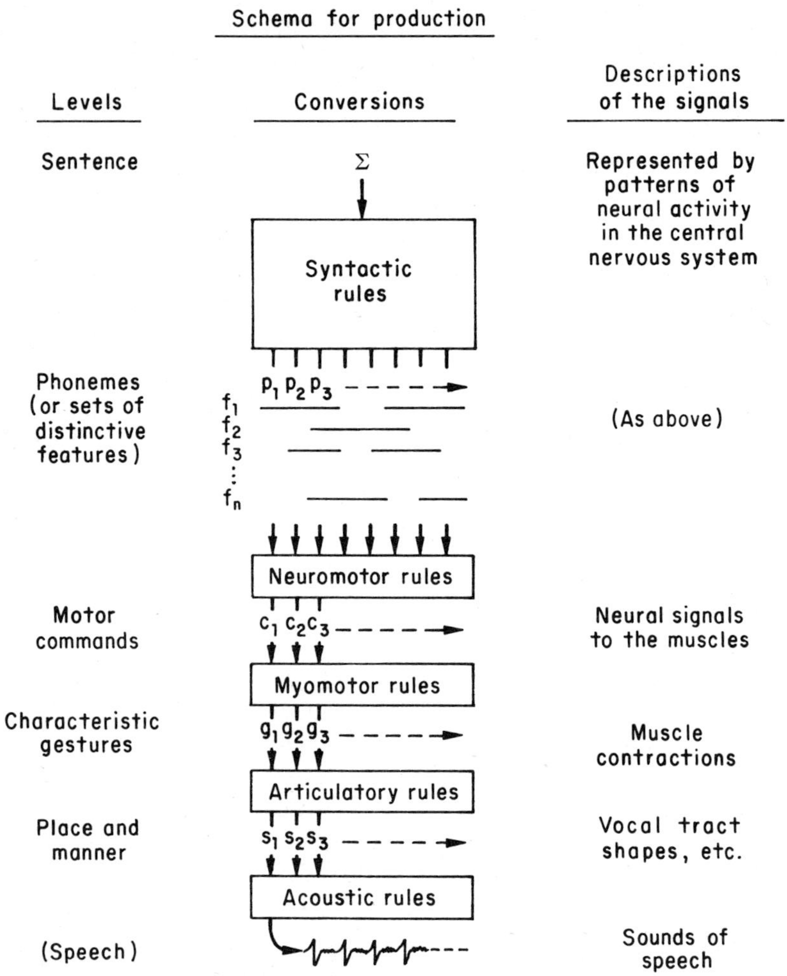

Fig. 2.5. Schematic representations of assumed stages in speech production. (*Psychological Review, November 1967.*)

stood,[22] are complex from a computational standpoint, but they operate on an instant-by-instant basis and yield (for the most part) one-to-one relations of shape to sound.

Does the Encoding Truly Occur in the Conversion from Command to Shape?

We have supposed that, of the four conversions between phoneme and sound, one at least—the conversion from contractions to tract shape—is

[22] The dependence of speech sound on vocal-tract shape (and movement) has, of course, been studied by many workers and for many years. A landmark in this field, and justification for our statement, is Ref. 99.

calculated to produce an encoding of the kind we found when earlier we examined the acoustic cues for phoneme perception. But does it, in fact, produce that encoding, and if so, does it account for all of it? Downstream from this level there is only the conversion from shape to sound, and that, though complex, does not appear to involve encoding. But what of the upstream conversions, particularly the one that lies between the neural representations of the phonemes and the commands to the articulatory muscles? We cannot at the present time observe those processes, nor can we directly measure their output—that is, the commands to the muscles. We can, however, observe some aspects of the contractions—for example, the electromyographic correlates—and if we assume, as seems reasonable, that the conversion from command to contractions is straightforward, then we can quite safely infer the structure of the commands.[23] By determining to what extent those inferred commands (if not the electromyographic signals themselves) are invariant with the phoneme we can, then, discover how much of the encoding occurs in the conversion from contraction to shape (articulatory rules) and how much at higher levels.

Motor Commands as Presumed Invariants

Before discussing the electromyographic evidence, we should say what kind of invariance with the subphonemic features (hence, with the phonemes) we might, at best, expect to find. It should be clear from many of the data presented in this paper that language is no more a left-to-right process at the acoustic level than it is syntactically. As we have seen, the acoustic representations of the successive phonemes are interlaced. Some control center must therefore "know" what the syllable is to be in order that its component subphonemic features may

[23] For commands of the "on-off" type (see footnote 21), we would expect muscle contractions—and EMG potentials—to be roughly proportional to the commands; hence the commands will be mirrored directly by the EMG potentials when these can be measured unambiguously for the muscles of interest. All these conditions are realizable, at least approximately, for a number of phoneme combinations—for example, the bilabial stops and nasal consonants with unrounded vowels, as described in later paragraphs.

Commands of the "go to" type, which may well be operative in gestures that are relatively slow and precise, would presumably operate via the γ-efferent system to produce only so much contraction of the muscle as is needed to achieve a target length. The contraction—and the resulting EMG signal—would then be different for different starting positions, that is, for the same phoneme in different contexts. Even so, the significant aspects of the command can be inferred, since presence *vs.* absence and sequential position (if not the relative timing) of the EMG signal persist despite even large changes in its magnitude.

For general discussions of the role of electromyography in research on speech, see the reviews by Cooper [100] and Fromkin and Ladefoged [101].

be appropriately combined and overlapped. There are other grounds than the data we have cited for inferring such syllabic organization. Temporal relations between syllables may be adjusted for slow or rapid speech and for changes in syllable duration such as Lindblom has reported for a given syllable placed in different polysyllabic contexts. But these changes in syllable duration do not affect all portions of the syllable equally: timing relations within the syllable are also adjusted according to context [102], and this must entail variation in the relative timing of the component subphonemic features, as is suggested by Kozhevnikov and Chistovich's [17] analysis of the articulatory structure of consonant clusters. Ohman [41, 103] has proposed a model for syllable articulation consistent with this analysis. Such contextual variations preclude the invariance of all the features that make up a phoneme in a particular context. The most that we can expect is that some subset of these features, and so of the neural signals to the muscles (after operation of the neuromotor rules of Fig. 2.5), will be invariant with the phoneme; there will then be for each subphonemic feature characteristic neuromotor "markers," implicating only one or a few component parts of the system, perhaps only the contraction of a single specific muscle. These characteristic components of the total neural activity we will refer to as "motor commands."[24] We should also emphasize that we refer here to the phoneme as perceived, not as an abstract linguistic entity serving primarily a classificatory function.

Indications from Electromyography

What, then, do we find when we look at the electromyographic correlates of articulatory activity? Recent research in our laboratory and several others has been directed specifically to the questions raised in the preceding paragraphs, but the data are, as yet, quite limited. As we see these data, they do, however, permit some tentative conclusions.

When two adjacent phonemes are produced by spatially separate groups of muscles, there are essentially invariant EMG tracings from the characteristic gestures for each phoneme, regardless of the identity of the other.[25] This has been found for /f/, for example, followed by /s/, /t/, /ts/, /θ/, or /θs/ and preceded by /i/, /il/, or /im/ [107].

[24] Thus the motor commands are, in one sense, abstract "-eme" type entities, with invariance assumed and observation directed to their discovery and enumeration; in another sense, and to the degree that observation justifies the assumption about invariance, motor commands constitute the essential subset of real neural signals with which a general model of production and perception should be principally concerned.

[25] It is not, of course, necessary that the EMG signals be precisely the same, since invariance is expected only of the motor commands inferred from them. In the minimally complicated cases cited in this paragraph, the commands do transform

Similarly, invariance has been found for /b/, /p/, and /m/ regardless of the following vowel [101, 105]. Here it is easy to associate the place and manner features with the contractions of specific muscles, and to equate the EMG signals for a specific feature wherever it occurs, at least within this limited set of phonemes. We should emphasize that corresponding invariance is not to be found in the acoustic signal: for /f/ the duration of the noise varies over a range of two to one in the contexts listed above; the vast differences in acoustic cue for /b/ or /p/ before various vowels were described in an earlier section.

When the temporally overlapping gestures for successive phonemes involve more or less adjacent muscles that control the same structures, it is of course more difficult to discover whether there is invariance or not.[26] This is the situation for the /di,du/ examples we used earlier. In our own studies of such cases we find essentially identical EMG signals from tongue-tip electrodes for the initial consonant; however, the signal for a following phoneme that also involves the tongue-tip may show substantial changes from its characteristic form [108, 109]. Such changes presumably reflect the execution of position-type commands (see footnotes 21 and 23) rather than reorganization at a higher level. True reorganization of the neural commands is not excluded by such data—indeed, we have some data that might be so interpreted [110]—but the evidence so far is predominantly on the side of invariance.

If the commands—or, indeed, signals of any kind—are to be invariant with the phonemes, they must reflect the segmentation that is so

---

into EMG potentials that are essentially the same (in different contexts), aside from some differences in magnitude.

Magnitude differences do occur, however, variously for the individual and context, and may have linguistic significance attributed to them. Thus Fromkin [104] concludes, mainly from EMG data on the lip-closing gestures of her principal speaker:

> The results of the present investigation do not support the hypothesis that a simple one-to-one correspondence exists between a phoneme and its motor commands. For the bilabial stops /b/ and /p/ different motor commands produce different muscular gestures for these consonants occurring in utterance initial and final positions [p. 195].

Harris, Lysaught, and Schvey [105] report, on the contrary, that differences in EMG signal for the lip-closing gesture did not reach statistical significance for two groups of five subjects each in two experiments, one of which overlapped Fromkin's study. They noted, though, that each of the subjects showed an individual pattern of small but consistent variations of EMG signal with context. (For a discussion of these differences in the interpretation of basically similar data, see Ref. 106.)

[26] A practical difficulty exists in allocating observed EMG potentials to specific muscles when more than one muscle is close to a surface electrode. Needle electrodes will often resolve such ambiguities, but they pose other problems of a practical nature.

conspicuously absent at the acoustic level. Do we, then, find such segmentation in the EMG records? Before answering that question, we should remind ourselves that the activity of a single muscle or muscle group does not, in any case, reflect a phoneme but only a subphonemic feature, and that a change from one phoneme to another may require a change in command for only one of several features. We should not expect, therefore, that all the subphonemic features will start and stop at each phoneme boundary, and, in fact, they do not. We do find, however, in the onsets and offsets of EMG activity in various muscles a segmentation like that of the several dimensions that constitute the phoneme. One can see, then, where the phoneme boundaries must be.[27] This is in striking contrast to what is found at the acoustic level. There, as we have earlier pointed out, almost any segment we can isolate contains information about—and is a cue for—more than one phoneme. Thus in the matter of segmentation, too, the EMG potentials—and even more the motor commands inferred from them—bear a simpler relation to the perceived phonemes than does the acoustic signal.

In summary we should say that we do not yet know precisely to what extent motor commands are invariant with the phonemes. It seems reasonably clear, however, that they are more nearly invariant than are the acoustic signals, and we may conclude, therefore, that a substantial part of the restructuring occurs below the level of the commands. Whether some significant restructuring occurs also at higher levels can only be determined by further investigation.

Decoding: From Sound to Phoneme

If speech were a simple cipher one might suppose that phoneme perception could be explained by the ordinary principles of psychophysics and discrimination learning. In that view, which is probably not uncommon among psychologists, speech consists of sounds, much like any others, that happen to signal the phoneme units of the language. It is required of the listener only that he learn to connect each sound with the name of the appropriate phoneme. To be sure, the sounds must be discriminably different, but this is a standard problem of auditory psychophysics and poses no special difficulty for the psychologist. It would follow that perception of speech is not different in any funda-

[27] In some cases the boundaries are sharply marked by a sudden onset of EMG signal for a particular muscle. Usually, though, the onsets are less abrupt and activity persists for a few hundred milliseconds. This might seem inadequate to provide segmentation markers for the rapid-fire phoneme sequences; indeed, precise time relationships may be blurred in normal articulation, but without obscuring the sequential order of events and the separateness of the channels carrying information about the several features.

mental way from perception of other sounds (assuming sufficient practice), and that, as Lane [111] and Cross, Lane, and Sheppard [112] suppose, no special perceptual mechanism is required.

The point of this paper has been, on the contrary, that speech is, for the most part, a special code that must often make use of a special perceptual mechanism to serve as its decoder.[28] On the evidence presented here we should conclude, at the least, that most phonemes cannot be perceived by a straightforward comparison of the incoming signal with a set of stored phonemic patterns or templates, even if one assumes mechanisms that can extract simple stimulus invariances such as, for example, constant ratios. To find acoustic segments that are in any reasonably simple sense invariant with linguistic (and perceptual) segments—that is, to perceive without decoding—one must go to the syllable level or higher. Now the number of syllables, reckoned simply as the number of permissible combinations and permutations of phonemes, is several thousand in English. But the number of acoustic patterns is far greater than that, since the acoustic signal varies considerably with the speaker and with the stress, intonation, and tempo of his speech [31, 61, 113–116]. To perceive speech by matching the acoustic signal to so many patterns would appear, at best, uneconomical and inelegant. More important, it would surely be inadequate, since it must fail to account for the fact that we do perceive phonemes. No theory can safely ignore the fact that phonemes are psychologically real.

How, then, is the phoneme to be recovered? We can imagine, at least in general outline, two very different possibilities: one, a mechanism that operates on a purely auditory basis, the other, by reference to the processes of speech production.

The Case for an Auditory Decoder

The relevant point about an auditory decoder is that it would process the signal in *auditory* terms—that is, without reference to the way in which it was produced—and successfully extract the phoneme string. On the basis of what we know of speech, and of the attempts to build an automatic phoneme recognizer, we must suppose such a device would have to be rather complex. There is, to be sure, some evidence for the existence of processing mechanisms in the auditory system that il-

[28] We referred earlier to perception in the speech mode and indicated that it was not operative—or, at least, not controlling—for some speech sounds as well as all nonspeech sounds. It need hardly be said, then, that the speech decoder provides only one pathway for perception; nonspeech sounds obviously require another pathway, which may serve adequately for the unencoded aspects of speech as well.

lustrate at a very simple level one kind of thing that an auditory decoder might have to do. Thus Whitfield and Evans [117] have found single cells in the auditory cortex of the cat that respond to frequency changes but not to steady tones. Some of these cells responded more to tones that are frequency-modulated upward and others to tones modulated downward. Such specificity of response also exists at lower levels in the auditory nervous system [118]. These findings are examples of a kind of auditory processing that might, perhaps, be part of a speech decoder, but one that would have to go beyond these processes—to more complex ones—if it were to deal successfully with the fact that very different transitions will, in different contexts, cue the same phoneme. But if this could be accomplished, and if it were done independently of motor parameters, we should have a purely auditory decoder.

The Case for Mediation by Production

Though we cannot exclude the possibility that a purely auditory decoder exists, we find it more plausible to assume that speech is perceived by processes that are also involved in its production. The most general and obvious motivation for such a view is that the perceiver is also a speaker and must be supposed, therefore, to possess all the mechanisms for putting language through the successive coding operations that result eventually in the acoustic signal.[29] It seems unparsimonious to assume that the speaker-listener employs two entirely separate processes of equal status, one for encoding language and the other for decoding it. A simpler assumption is that there is only one process, with appropriate linkages between sensory and motor components.[30]

Apart from parsimony, there are strong reasons for considering this latter view. Recall, for example, the case of /di,du/. There we saw that the acoustic patterns for /d/ were very different, though the perception of the consonantal segment was essentially the same. Since

[29] We have noted that training in reading speech spectrograms has so far not succeeded in developing in the trainee a visual decoder for speech comparable to the one that works from an auditory input. This may well reflect the existence of special mechanisms for the speech decoder that are lacking for its visual counterpart. In general, a theory about the nature of the speech decoder—and, in particular, a motor theory—must be concerned with the nature of the mechanism, though not necessarily with the question of how it was acquired in the history of the individual or the race. This is an interesting, but separate, question and is not considered here.

[30] We should suppose that the links between perception and articulation exist at relatively high levels of the nervous system. For information about, or reference to, motor activity, the experienced organism need not rely—at least not very heavily and certainly not exclusively—on proprioceptive returns from the periphery, for example, from muscular contractions. (See Ref. 119.)

it appears that the /d/ gesture—or, at least, some important "diagnostic" part of it—may also be essentially the same in the two cases, we are tempted to suppose that one hears the same /d/ because perception is mediated by the neuromotor correlates of gestures that are the same. This is basically the argument we used in one of our earliest papers [50] to account for the fact that bursts of sound at very different frequencies are required to produce the perception of /k/ before different vowels. Extending the argument, we tried in that same paper to account for the fact that the same burst of sound is heard as /p/ before /i/ but as /k/ before /a/, the point being that, because of temporal overlap (and consequent acoustic encoding), very different gestures happen to be necessary in these different vowel environments in order to produce the same acoustic effect (the consonant burst). The argument was applied yet again to account for a finding about second-formant transitions as cues: that the acoustic cues for /g/ can be radically different even when the consonant is paired with closely related vowels (i.e., in the syllables /ga/ and /gɔ/), yet the perception and the articulation are essentially the same [29]. But these are merely striking examples of what must be seen now as a general rule: there is typically a lack of correspondence between acoustic cue and perceived phoneme, and in all these cases it appears that perception mirrors articulation more closely than sound.[31] If this were not so, then for a listener to hear the same phoneme in various environments, speakers would have to hold the acoustic signal constant, which would in turn require that they make drastic changes in articulation. Speakers need not do that—and in all probability they cannot—yet listeners nevertheless hear the same phoneme. This supports the assumption that the listener uses the inconstant sound as a basis for finding his way back to the articulatory gestures that produced it and thence, as it were, to the speaker's intent.

The categorical perception of stop consonants also supports this assumption.[32] As described earlier in this paper, perception of these sounds is categorical, or discontinuous, even when the acoustic signal is varied continuously. Quite obviously, the required articulations would also be discontinuous. With /b,d,g/, we can vary the acoustic cue along a continuum, which corresponds, in effect, to closing the vocal tract at various points along its length. But in actual speech the closing is accomplished by discontinuous or categorically different gestures: by the lips for /b/, the tip of the tongue for /d/, and the back of the tongue for /g/. Here, too, perception appears to be tied to articulation.

The view that speech is perceived by reference to production is receiv-

[31] For further discussion of this point, see Refs. 29, 120–122.

[32] For further discussion of this point, see Ref. 123.

ing increased attention. Researchers at the Pavlov Institute in Leningrad have adduced various kinds of evidence to support a similar hypothesis [76, 77]. Ladefoged [124] has presented a motor-theoretical interpretation of some aspects of speech perception. More recently, Ladefoged and McKinney [125] have found in studies of stress that perception is related more closely to certain low-level aspects of stress production than it is to the acoustic signal. And in a very recent study Lieberman [45] has found interesting evidence for a somewhat similar conclusion in regard to the perception of some aspects of intonation.

The Role of Productive Processes in Models for Speech Perception

In its most general form, the hypothesis being described here is not necessarily different in principle from a model for speech perception called "analysis by synthesis" that has been advanced by Stevens [126] and by Halle and Stevens [97, 127] following a generalized model proposed by MacKay [128]. In contrast, perhaps, to the computer-based assumptions of analysis by synthesis, we would rather think in terms of overlapping activity of several neural networks—those that supply control signals to the articulators and those that process incoming neural patterns from the ear—and to suppose that information can be correlated by these networks and passed through them in either direction. Such a formulation, in rather general terms, has been presented elsewhere [129].

The most general form of the view that speech is perceived by reference to production does not specify the level at which the message units are recovered. The assumption is that at some level or levels of the production process there exist neural signals standing in one-to-one correspondence with the various segments of the language—phoneme, word, phrase, etc. Perception consists in somehow running the process backward, the neural signals corresponding to the various segments being found at their respective levels. In phoneme perception—our primary concern in this paper—the invariant is found far down in the neuromotor system, at the level of the commands to the muscles. Perception by morphophonemic, morphemic, and syntactic rules of the language would engage the encoding processes at higher levels. The level at which the encoding process is entered for the purposes of perceptual decoding may, furthermore, determine which shapes can and cannot be detected in raw perception. The invariant signal for the different acoustic shapes that are all heard as /d/, for example, may be found at the level of motor commands. In consequence, the listener is unaware, even in the most careful listening, that the acoustic signals are, in fact, quite radically different. On the other hand, a listener can readily hear the difference between tokens of the morphophoneme

{S} when it is realized as /s/ "in cats" and as /z/ "in dogs," though he also "knows" that these two acoustic and phonetic shapes are in some sense the same. If the perception of that commonality is also by reference to production, the invariant is surely at a level considerably higher than the motor commands.

The Efficiency of the Speech Code

Speech can be produced rapidly because the phonemes are processed in parallel. They are taken apart into their constituent features, and the features belonging to successive phonemes are overlapped in time. Thus the load is divided among the many largely independent components of the articulatory system. Within the phonological constraints on combinations and sequences that can occur, a speaker produces phonemes at rates much higher than those at which any single articulatory component must change its state.[33]

In the conversion of these multidimensional and overlapping articulatory events into sound, a complex encoding occurs. The number of dimensions is necessarily reduced, but the parallel transmission of phonemic information is retained in that the cues for successive phonemes are imprinted on a single aspect of the acoustic signal. Thus the movement of articulators as independent as the lips and the tongue both affect the second formant and its transitions: given an initial labial consonant overlapped with a tongue shape appropriate for the following vowel, one finds, as we have already shown, that the second-formant transition simultaneously carries information about both phonemic segments.[34]

If the listener possesses some device for recovering the articulatory events from their encoded traces in the sound stream, then he should

[33] The phonological constraints may, in fact, play an essential part in making the decoding operation fast and relatively free of error. Since the set of phonemes and phoneme sequences that is used in any particular language is far smaller than the possible set of feature combinations—smaller even than the combinations that are physiologically realizable—information about the allowable combinations of features could be used in the decoding process to reestablish temporal relationships that may have been blurred in articulation (see footnote 27). Such a "recutting" operation would ease the requirements on precision of articulation and so allow faster communication; also, it would make unambiguous the segmentation into phonemes, thereby qualifying them as units of immediate perception. One may speculate, further, that the serial string of reconstituted phonemes is useful—perhaps essential—in the next operation of speech reception, namely, gaining immediate access to an inventory of thousands of syllable- or word-size units.

[34] Fant [58, p. 5] makes essentially the same point: The rules relating waves to speech production are in general complex, since one articulation parameter, e.g., tongue height, affects several of the parameters of the spectrogram. Conversely, each of the parameters of the spectrogram is generally influenced by several articulatory variables.

perceive the phonemes well and, indeed, evade several limitations that would otherwise apply in auditory perception. As we pointed out early in this paper, the temporal resolving power of the ear sets a relatively low limit on the rate at which discrete acoustic segments can be perceived. To the extent that the code provides for parallel processing of successive phonemes, the listener can perceive strings of phonemes more rapidly than he could if the acoustic signals for them were arranged serially, as in an alphabet. Thus the parallel processing of the phonemes is as important for efficient perception as for production.

We also referred earlier to the difficulty of finding a reasonable number of acoustic signals of short duration that can be readily and rapidly identified. This limitation is avoided if the decoding of the acoustic signal enables the listener to recover the articulatory events that produced it, since perception then becomes linked to a system of physiological coordinates more richly multidimensional—hence more distinctive—than the acoustic (and auditory) signal.

Having said of the speech code that it seems particularly well designed to circumvent the shortcomings of the ear, we should consider whether its accomplishments stop there. As we pointed out earlier, these shortcomings do not apply to the eye, for example, and we do indeed find that the best way to communicate language in the visual mode is by means of an alphabet or cipher, not a code. But we also noted that the acoustic code is more easily and naturally perceived than is the optical alphabet. Perhaps this is due primarily to the special speech decoder, whose existence we assumed for the conversion of sound to phoneme. We would suggest an additional possibility: the operations that occur in the speech decoder—including, in particular, the interdependence of perceptual and productive processes—may be in some sense similar to those that take place at other levels of grammar. If so, there would be a special compatibility between the perception of speech sounds and the comprehension of language at higher stages. This might help to explain why, so far from being merely one way of conveying language, the sounds of speech are, instead, its common and privileged carriers.

REFERENCES

1. D. B. Orr, H. L. Friedman, and J. C. C. Williams, Trainability of Listening Comprehension of Speeded Discourse, *J. Ed. Psychol.*, **56**:148–156 (1965).
2. G. A. Miller and W. G. Taylor, The Perception of Repeated Bursts of Noise, *J. Acoust. Soc. Am.*, **20**:171–182 (1948).
3. G. A. Miller, The Magical Number Seven, Plus or Minus Two, or, Some Limits on Our Capacity for Processing Information, *Psychol. Rev.*, **63**:81–96 (1956).
4. G. A. Miller, The Perception of Speech, in M. Halle (ed.), "For Roman Jakobson," pp. 353–359, Mouton and Co., The Hague 1956.

5. P. W. Nye, Aural Recognition Time for Multidimensional Signals, *Nature,* **196:**1282–1283 (1962).
6. I. Pollack, The Information of Elementary Auditory Displays, *J. Acoust. Soc. Am.,* **24:**745–749 (1952).
7. I. Pollack and L. Ficks, Information of Elementary Multidimensional Auditory Displays, *J. Acoust. Soc. Am.,* **26:**155–158 (1954).
8. J. L. Coffey, The Development and Evaluation of the Battelle Aural Reading Device, *Proc. Intern. Congr. Technol. Blindness 1,* pp. 343–360, American Foundation for the Blind, New York, 1963.
9. F. S. Cooper, Research on Reading Machines for the Blind, in P. A. Zahl (ed.), "Blindness: Modern Approaches to the Unseen Environment," pp. 512–543, Princeton University Press, Princeton, N.J., 1950.
10. J. Freiberger and E. F. Murphy, Reading Machines for the Blind, *IRE Trans. Human Factors Electron.,* **HFE-2:**8–19 (1961).
11. P. W. Nye, Reading Aids for Blind People—A Survey of Progress with Technological and Human Problems, *Med. Electron. Biol. Eng.,* **2:**247–264 (1964).
12. P. W. Nye, "An Investigation of Audio Outputs for a Reading Machine," Autonomics Division, National Physical Laboratory, Teddington, England, February 1965.
13. M. Studdert-Kennedy and F. S. Cooper, High-performance Reading Machines for the Blind: Psychological Problems, Technological Problems, and Status, in R. Dufton (ed.), "Sensory Devices for the Blind," pp. 317–342, St. Dunstan's, London, 1966.
14. M. Studdert-Kennedy and A. M. Liberman, Psychological Considerations in the Design of Auditory Displays for Reading Machines, *Proc. Intern. Congr. Technol. Blindness,* 289–304 (1963).
15. I. J. Gelb, "A Study of Writing," University of Chicago Press, Chicago, 1963.
16. K. N. Stevens and A. S. House, Speech Perception, in J. Tobias (ed.), "Foundations of Modern Auditory Theory," Vol. II, pp. 3–62, Academic Press, New York, 1971.
17. V. A. Kozhevnikov and L. A. Chistovich, "Rech' Artikuliatsia i vospriiatie," Moscow-Leningrad, 1965; trans. in "Speech: Articulation and Perception," Joint Publications Research Service, Washington: **30:**543 (1966).
18. C. F. Hockett, "A Manual of Phonology," Waverly Press, Baltimore, 1955.
19. Joseph Greenberg, personal communication, November 1966.
20. L. Lisker and A. S. Abramson, A Cross-language Study of Voicing in Initial Stops: Acoustical Measurements, *Word,* **20:**384–422 (1964).
21. L. Lisker and A. S. Abramson, Stop Categories and Voice Onset Time, *Proc. 5th Intern. Congr. Phonetic Sci.,* Munster, August 1964.
22. P. B. Denes, On the Statistics of Spoken English, *J. Acoust. Soc. Am.,* **35:**892–904 (1963).
23. E. Whetnall and D. B. Fry, "The Deaf Child," Heinemann, London, 1964.
24. P. C. Delattre, Les indices acoustiques de la parole: Premier rapport, *Phonetica,* **2:**108–118, 226–251 (1958).
25. P. C. Delattre, Le jeu des transitions des formants et la perception des consonnes, *Proc. 4th Intern. Congr. Phonetic Sci.,* Helsinki, 1961; pp. 407–417, Mouton and Co., The Hague, 1962.
26. P. C. Delattre, A. M. Liberman, and F. S. Cooper, Acoustic Loci and Transitional Cues for Consonants, *J. Acoust. Soc. Am.,* **27:**769–773 (1955).
27. P. C. Delattre, A. M. Liberman, and F. S. Cooper, Formant Transitions and Loci as Acoustic Correlates of Place of Articulation in American Fricatives, *Studia Linguistica,* **18:**104–121 (1964).

28. K. S. Harris, Cues for the Discrimination of American English Fricatives in Spoken Syllables, *Language Speech,* **1**:1–7 (1958).
29. A. M. Liberman, Some Results of Research on Speech Perception, *J. Acoust. Soc. Am.,* **29**:117–123 (1957).
30. A. M. Liberman, P. C. Delattre, F. S. Cooper, and L. J. Gerstman, The Role of Consonant-Vowel Transitions in the Perception of the Stop and Nasal Consonants, *Psychol. Monographs,* **68** (8, Whole No. 379) (1954).
31. A. M. Liberman, F. Ingemann, L. Lisker, P. C. Delattre, and F. S. Cooper, Minimal Rules for Synthesizing Speech, *J. Acoust. Soc. Am.,* **31**:1490–1499 (1959).
32. L. Lisker, Closure Duration and the Voiced-Voiceless Distinction in English, *Language,* **33**:42–49 (1957).
33. J. D. O'Connor, L. J. Gerstman, A. M. Liberman, P. C. Delattre, and F. S. Cooper, Acoustic Cues for the Perception of Initial /w,j,r,l/ in English, *Word,* **13**:25–43 (1957).
34. F. S. Cooper, Spectrum Analysis, *J. Acoust. Soc. Am.,* **22**:761–762 (1950).
35. F. S. Cooper, Some Instrumental Aids to Research on Speech, *Rept. 4th Ann. Round Table Meeting Linguistics Language Teaching,* Monograph Series No. 3, pp. 46–53, Georgetown University Press, Washington, 1953.
36. F. S. Cooper, P. C. Delattre, A. M. Liberman, J. Borst, and L. J. Gerstman, Some Experiments on the Perception of Synthetic Speech Sounds, *J. Acoust. Soc. Am.,* **24**:597–606 (1952).
37. F. S. Cooper, A. M. Liberman, and J. M. Borst, The Inter-conversion of Audible and Visible Patterns as a Basis for Research in the Perception of Speech, *Proc. Nat. Acad. Sci.,* **37**:318–325 (1951).
38. P. C. Delattre, A. M. Liberman, and F. S. Cooper, Voyelles synthétiques à deux formants et voyelles cardinales, *Le Maître Phonétique,* **96**:30–37 (1951).
39. P. C. Delattre, A. M. Liberman, F. S. Cooper, and L. J. Gerstman, An Experimental Study of the Acoustic Determinants of Vowel Color: Observations on One- and Two-formant Vowels Synthesized from Spectrographic Patterns, *Word,* **8**:195–210 (1952).
40. A. M. Liberman, P. C. Delattre, and F. S. Cooper, Some Cues for the Distinction Between Voiced and Voiceless Stops in Initial Position, *Language Speech,* **1**:153–167 (1958).
41. S. E. G. Ohman, Coarticulation in VCV Utterances: Spectrographic Measurements, *J. Acoust. Soc. Am.,* **39**:151–168 (1966).
42. K. N. Stevens and A. S. House, Studies of Format Transitions Using a Vocal Tract Analog, *J. Acoust. Soc. Am.,* **28**:578–585 (1956).
43. K. Hadding-Koch and M. Studdert-Kennedy, An Experimental Study of Some Intonation Contours, *Phonetica,* **11**:175–185 (1964).
44. K. Hadding-Koch and M. Studdert-Kennedy, Intonation Contours Evaluated by American and Swedish Test Subjects, *Proc. 5th Intern. Congr. Phonetic Sci.,* Munster, August 1964.
45. P. Lieberman, "Intonation, Perception and Language," MIT Press, Cambridge, Mass., 1967.
46. A. Malecot, Acoustic Cues for Nasal Consonants, *Language,* **32**:274–284 (1956).
47. L. Lisker, Minimal Cues for Separating /w,r,l,j/ in Intervocalic Production, *Word,* **13**:257–267 (1957).
48. K. S. Harris, H. S. Hoffman, A. M. Liberman, P. C. Delattre, and F. S. Cooper, Effect of Third-formant Transitions on the Perception of the Voiced Stop Consonants, *J. Acoust. Soc. Am.,* **30**:122–126 (1958).

49. G. W. Hughes and M. Halle, Spectral Properties of Fricative Consonants, *J. Acoust. Soc. Am.*, **28:**303–310 (1956).
50. A. M. Liberman, P. C. Delattre, and F. S. Cooper, The Role of Selected Stimulus Variables in the Perception of the Unvoiced Stop Consonants, *Am. J. Psychol.*, 65:497–516 (1952).
51. C. Schatz, The Role of Context in the Perception of Stops, *Language,* **30:**47–56 (1954).
52. A. S. Abramson and L. Lisker, Voice Onset Time in Stop Consonants: Acoustic Analysis and Synthesis, *Rept. 5th Intern. Congr. Acoust.*, Ia, Paper A51 (1965).
53. A. M. Liberman, P. C. Delattre, L. J. Gerstman, and F. S. Cooper, Tempo of Frequency Change as a Cue for Distinguishing Classes of Speech Sounds, *J. Exptl. Psychol.*, **52:**127–137 (1956).
54. B. Lindblom and M. Studdert-Kennedy, On the Role of Formant Transitions in Vowel Recognition, *J. Acoust. Soc. Am.*, **42:**830–843 (1967).
55. L. Lisker, Anatomy of Unstressed Syllables, *J. Acoust. Soc. Am.,* **30:**682 (1958). (Abstract)
56. J. N. Shearme and J. N. Holmes, An Experimental Study of the Classification of Sounds in Continuous Speech According to Their Distribution in the Formant 1–Formant 2 Plane, *Proc. 4th Intern. Congr. Phonetic Sci.*, Helsinki, 1961; pp. 234–240, Mouton and Co., The Hague, 1962.
57. K. N. Stevens and A. S. House, Perturbation of Vowel Articulations by Consonantal Context: An Acoustical Study, *J. Speech Hearing Res.*, **6:**111–128 (1963).
58. C. G. M. Fant, Descriptive Analysis of the Acoustic Aspects of Speech, *Logos,* **5:**3–17 (1962).
59. C. G. M. Fant, Sound Spectrography, *Proc. 4th Intern. Congr. Phonetic Sci.*, Helsinki, 1961; pp. 14–33, Mouton and Co., The Hague, 1962.
60. C. M. Harris, A Study of the Building Blocks in Speech, *J. Acoust. Soc. Am.*, **25:**962–969 (1953).
61. G. E. Peterson, W. S.-Y. Wang, and E. Sivertsen, Segmentation Techniques in Speech Synthesis, *J. Acoust. Soc. Am.*, **30:**739–742 (1958).
62. P. T. Brady, A. S. House, and K. N. Stevens, Perception of Sounds Characterized by a Rapidly Changing Resonant Frequency, *J. Acoust. Soc. Am.*, **33:**1337–1362 (1961).
63. P. D. Eimas, The Relation Between Identification and Discrimination along Speech and Non-speech Continua, *Language Speech,* **6:**206–217 (1963).
64. B. C. Griffith, A Study of the Relation Between Phoneme Labeling and Discriminability in the Perception of Synthetic Stop Consonants, unpublished doctoral dissertation, University of Connecticut, 1958.
65. A. M. Liberman, K. S. Harris, H. S. Hoffman, and B. C. Griffith, The Discrimination of Speech Sounds Within and Across Phoneme Boundaries, *J. Exptl. Psychol.,* **54:**358–368 (1957).
66. M. Studdert-Kennedy, A. M. Liberman, and K. N. Stevens, Reaction Time to Synthetic Stop Consonants and Vowels at Phoneme Centers and at Phoneme Boundaries, *J. Acoust. Soc. Am.,* **35:**1900 (1963). (Abstract)
67. M. Studdert-Kennedy, A. M. Liberman, and K. N. Stevens, Reaction Time During the Discrimination of Synthetic Stop Consonants, *J. Acoust. Soc. Am.,* **36:**1989 (1964). (Abstract)
68. A. M. Liberman, K. S. Harris, J. A. Kinney, and H. Lane, The Discrimination of Relative Onset Time of the Components of Certain Speech and Nonspeech Patterns, *J. Exptl. Psychol.,* **61:**379–388 (1961).

69. A. M. Liberman, K. S. Harris, P. D. Eimas, L. Lisker, and J. Bastian, An Effect of Learning on Speech Perception: The Discrimination of Durations of Silence with and without Phonemic Significance, *Language Speech,* **4:**175–195 (1961).
70. J. Bastian, P. C., Delattre, and A. M. Liberman, Silent Interval as a Cue for the Distinction Between Stops and Semivowels in Medial Position, *J. Acoust. Soc. Am.,* **31:**1568 (1959). (Abstract)
71. J. Bastian, P. D. Eimas, and A. M. Liberman, Identification and Discrimination of a Phonemic Contrast Induced by Silent Interval, *J. Acoust. Soc. Am.,* **33:**842 (1961). (Abstract)
72. K. S. Harris, J. Bastian, and A. M. Liberman, Mimicry and the Perception of a Phonemic Contrast Induced by Silent Interval: Electromyographic and Acoustic Measures, *J. Acoust. Soc. Am.,* **33:**842 (1961). (Abstract)
73. D. B. Fry, A. S. Abramson, P. D. Eimas, and A. M. Liberman, The Identification and Discrimination of Synthetic Vowels, *Language Speech,* **5:**171–189 (1962).
74. K. N. Stevens, S. E. G. Ohman, and A. M. Liberman, Identification and Discrimination of Rounded and Unrounded Vowels, *J. Acoust. Soc. Am.,* **35:**1900 (1963). (Abstract)
75. K. N. Stevens, S. E. G. Ohman, M. Studdert-Kennedy, and A. M. Liberman, Cross-linguistic Study of Vowel Discrimination, *J. Acoust. Soc. Am.,* **36:**1989 (1964). (Abstract)
76. L. A. Chistovich, Classification of Rapidly Repeated Speech Sounds, *Akust. Zh.,* **6:**392–398 (1960); translated in *Soviet Phys.-Acoust. New York,* **6:**393–398 (1961).
77. L. A. Chistovich, Y. A. Klaas, and Y. I. Kuz'min, The Process of Speech Sound Discrimination, *Vopr. Psikhol.,* **8:**26–39 (1962). (Research Library, Air Force Cambridge Research Laboratories, Bedford, Mass. TT-64-13064 35-P.)
78. V. I. Galunov and L. A. Chistovich, Relationship of Motor Theory to the General Problem of Speech Recognition (review), *Akust. Zh.,* **11:**417–426 (1965), trans. in *Soviet Phys.-Acoust. New York,* **11:**357–365 (1966).
79. J. Bastian and A. S. Abramson, Identification and Discrimination of Phonemic Vowel Duration, *J. Acoust. Soc. Am.,* **34:**743 (1962). (Abstract)
80. A. S. Abramson, Identification and Discrimination of Phonemic Tones, *J. Acoust. Soc. Am.,* **33:**842 (1961). (Abstract)
81. K. N. Stevens, On the Relations Between Speech Movements and Speech Perception, *Z. Phonetik Sprachwiss. Kommunikationsforsch.,* **21:**102–106 (1968).
82. D. E. Broadbent, The Role of Auditory Localization in Attention and Memory Span, *J. Exptl. Psychol.,* **47:**191–196 (1954).
83. D. E. Broadbent and M. Gregory, Accuracy of Recognition for Speech Presented to the Right and Left Ears, *Quart. J. Exptl. Psychol.,* **16:**359–360 (1964).
84. M. P. Bryden, Ear Preference in Auditory Perception, *J. Exptl. Psychol.,* **65:**103–105 (1963).
85. R. B. Chaney and J. C. Webster, Information in Certain Multi-dimensional Acoustic Signals, *U.S. Navy Electron. Lab. Rept.,* No. 1339, San Diego, Calif., 1965.
86. D. Kimura, Cerebral Dominance and Perception of Verbal Stimuli, *Can. J. Psychol.,* **15:**166–171 (1961).
87. D. Kimura, Left-Right Differences in the Perception of Melodies, *Quart. J. Exptl. Psychol.,* **16:**355–358 (1964).

88. D. Kimura, Functional Asymmetry of the Brain in Dichotic Listening, *Cortex,* **3:**163–179 (1967).
89. D. Shankweiler and M. Studdert-Kennedy, Identification of Consonants and Vowels Presented to Left and Right Ears, *Quart. J. Exptl. Psychol.,* **19:**59–63 (1967).
90. D. Shankweiler and M. Studdert-Kennedy, An Analysis of Perceptual Confusions in Identification of Dichotically Presented CVC Syllables, *J. Acoust. Soc. Am.,* **41:**1581–1967 (1967). (Abstract)
91. R. K. Potter, G. A. Kopp, and H. C. Green, "Visible Speech," Van Nostrand, New York, 1947.
92. N. Chomsky, Current Issues in Linguistic Theory, in J. A. Fodor and J. J. Katz (eds.), "The Structure of Language," pp. 50–118, Prentice-Hall, Englewood Cliffs, N.J., 1964.
93. R. Jakobson, G. Fant, and M. Halle, Preliminaries to Speech Analysis: The Distinctive Features and Their Correlates, *Tech. Rept.* No. 13, Acoustics Laboratory, MIT, 1952; MIT Press, Cambridge, Mass., 1963.
94. C. G. M. Fant, Theory of Distinctive Features, *Speech Transmission Lab. Quart. Progr. Status Rept. Roy. Inst. Technol. Stockholm,* pp. 1–14, January 15, 1967.
95. M. Halle, On the Bases of Phonology, in J. A. Fodor and J. J. Katz (eds.), "The Structure of Language," pp. 324–333, Prentice-Hall, Englewood Cliffs, N.J., 1964.
96. R. Jakobson and M. Halle, "Fundamentals of Language," Mouton and Co., The Hague, 1956.
97. K. N. Stevens and M. Halle, Remarks on Analysis by Synthesis and Distinctive Features, *Proc. AFCRL Symp. Models Perception Speech Visual Form,* Boston, November 1964; pp. 88–102, MIT Press, Cambridge, Mass., in press.
98. W. A. Wickelgren, Distinctive Features and Errors in Short-term Memory for English Consonants, *J. Acoust. Soc. Am.,* **39:**388–398 (1966).
99. C. G. M. Fant, "Acoustic Theory of Speech Production," Mouton and Co., The Hague, 1960.
100. F. S. Cooper, Research Techniques and Instrumentation: EMG, *Am. Speech Hearing Assoc. Rept.,* **1:**153–158 (1965).
101. V. A. Fromkin and P. Ladefoged, Electromyography in Speech Research, *Phonetica,* **15:**219–242 (1966).
102. B. Lindblom, Articulatory Activity in Vowels, *J. Acoust. Soc. Am.,* **36:**1038 (1964). (Abstract)
103. S. E. G. Ohman, Numerical Model for Coarticulation, Using a Computer-simulated Vocal Tract, *J. Acoust. Soc. Am.,* **36:**1038 (1964). (Abstract)
104. V. A. Fromkin, Neuro-muscular Specification of Linguistic Units, *Language Speech,* **9:**170–199 (1966).
105. K. S. Harris, G. Lysaught, and M. M. Schvey, Some Aspects of the Production of Oral and Nasal Labial Stops, *Language Speech,* **8:**135–147 (1965).
106. F. S. Cooper, Describing the Speech Process in Motor Command Terms, *J. Acoust. Soc. Am.,* **39:**1221 (1966) (Abstract); *Status Rept. Speech Res. Haskins Lab.,* **SR-5/6:**2.1–2.27 (1966). (Text)
107. P. F. Macneilage, Electromyographic and Acoustic Study of the Production of Certain Final Clusters, *J. Acoust. Soc. Am.,* **35:**461–463 (1963).
108. K. S. Harris, Behavior of the Tongue in the Production of Some Alveolar Consonants, *J. Acoust. Soc. Am.,* **35:**784 (1963). (Abstract)
109. K. S. Harris, D. A. Huntington, and G. N. Sholes, Coarticulation of Some

Disyllabic Utterances Measured by Electromyographic Techniques, *J. Acoust. Soc. Am.*, **39:**1219 (1966). (Abstract)

110. P. F. Macneilage, J. L. DeClerk, and S. I. Silverman, Some Relations between Articulator Movement and Motor Control in Consonant-Vowel-Consonant Monosyllables, *J. Acoust. Soc. Am.*, **40:**1272 (1966). (Abstract)
111. H. Lane, Motor Theory of Speech Perception: A Critical Review, *Psychol. Rev.*, **72:**275–309 (1965).
112. D. V. Cross, H. L. Lane, and W. C. Sheppard, Identification and Discrimination Functions for a Visual Continuum and Their Relation to the Motor Theory of Speech Perception, *J. Exptl. Psychol.*, **70:**63–74 (1965).
113. F. S. Cooper, A. M. Liberman, L. Lisker, and J. Gaitenby, Speech Synthesis by Rules, *Proc. Speech Commun. Seminar,* Stockholm, 1962; F2, Royal Institute of Technology, Stockholm, 1963.
114. B. Lindblom, Spectrographic Study of Vowel Reduction, *J. Acoust. Soc. Am.*, **35:**1773–1781 (1963).
115. G. E. Peterson and E. Sivertsen, Objectives and Techniques of Speech Synthesis, *Language Speech,* **3:**84–95 (1960).
116. E. Sivertsen, Segment Inventories for Speech Synthesis, *Language Speech,* **4:**27–61 (1961).
117. I. C. Whitfield and E. F. Evans, Responses of Auditory Cortical Neurons to Stimuli of Changing Frequency, *J. Neurophysiol.*, **28:**655–672 (1965).
118. P. G. Nelson, S. D. Erulkar, and S. S. Bryan, Responses of Units of the Inferior-colliculus to Time-varying Acoustic Stimuli, *J. Neurophysiol.*, **29:**834–860 (1966).
119. E. Von Holst and H. Mittelstadt, Das Reafferenzprinzip, *Naturwiss.*, **37:**464–476 (1950).
120. F. S. Cooper, A. M. Liberman, K. S. Harris, and P. M. Grubb, Some Input-Output Relations Observed in Experiments on the Perception of Speech, *Proc. 2d Intern. Congr. Cybernetics,* 1958; pp. 930–941, Association Internationale de Cybernétique, Namur, Belgium.
121. L. Lisker, F. S. Cooper, and A. M. Liberman, The Uses of Experiment in Language Description, *Word,* **18:**82–106 (1962).
122. A. M. Liberman, F. S. Cooper, K. S. Harris, P. F. Macneilage, and M. Studdert-Kennedy, Some Observations on a Model for Speech Perception, *Proc. AFCRL Symp. Models. Perception Speech Visual Form,* Boston, November 1964; pp. 68–87, MIT Press, Cambridge, Mass., in press.
123. A. M. Liberman, F. S. Cooper, K. S. Harris, and P. F. Macneilage, A Motor Theory of Speech Perception, *Proc. Speech Commun. Seminar,* Stockholm, 1962; D3, Royal Institute of Technology, Stockholm, 1963.
124. P. Ladefoged, The Perception of Speech, in "Mechanization of Thought Processes," pp. 397–409, H. M. Stationery Office, London, 1959.
125. P. Ladefoged and N. P. McKinney, Loudness, Sound Pressure, and Subglottal Pressure in Speech, *J. Acoust. Soc. Am.*, **35:**454–460 (1963).
126. K. N. Stevens, Toward a Model for Speech Recognition, *J. Acoust. Soc. Am.*, **32:**47–55 (1960).
127. M. Halle and K. N. Stevens, Speech Recognition: A Model and a Program for Research, *IRE Trans. Inform. Theory,* **IT-8**(2):155–159 (1962).
128. D. M. MacKay, Mindlike Behavior in Artefacts, *Brit. J. Phil. Sci.*, **2:**105–121 (1951).
129. A. M. Liberman, F. S. Cooper, M. Studdert-Kennedy, K. S. Harris, and D. P. Shankweiler, Some Observations on the Efficiency of Speech Sounds, paper presented at the XVIII International Congress of Psychology, Moscow, August 1966; *Z. Phonetik Sprachwiss. Kommunikationsforsch.*, **21:**21–32 (1968).

CHAPTER THREE

The Quantal Nature of Speech: Evidence from Articulatory-Acoustic Data

KENNETH N. STEVENS

Introduction

The past 10 or 20 years have witnessed a significant advance in our understanding of the acoustic properties of the sounds that can be generated by the human speech production mechanism. The ideas of Dudley [1] with regard to the carrier nature of speech have been refined and quantified by Chiba and Kajiyama [2], by Dunn [3], by Fant [4], and by others [5, 6] to the point where the acoustic spectra of many speech sounds can be described in an analytic manner. The concept underlying such a description is that of an acoustic source, which has relatively simple and invariant properties, acting as the excitation of a linear distributed acoustic system—the vocal tract.

The acoustic system is often described, in part, in terms of an area function which specifies the cross-sectional area at each point along the vocal tract between the vocal cords and the lips. The acoustic excitation for this nonuniform tube is either a quasiperiodic source at the glottal end or acoustic noise which may be generated in the vicinity of a constriction in the tube as a consequence of turbulence in the air flow. If this acoustic system is perturbed in some way, such as through modification of a parameter that is used to describe the area function, it is to be expected that the properties of the acoustic output will also be perturbed. One might suppose that there would be smooth and monotonic relations between the parameters describing the articulation on the one hand and the acoustic output on the other.

Closer examination reveals, however, that these relations are far from being linear. There are certain articulatory conditions for which a small change in some parameter describing the articulation gives rise to an apparently large change in the acoustic characteristics of the output; there are other conditions for which substantial perturbations of certain aspects of the articulation produce negligible changes in the characteristics of the acoustic signal.

The situation can be visualized in the manner shown in Fig. 3.1. We suppose that some acoustic measurement can be made to provide an indication of the magnitude of a particular attribute of the signal, and we plot this measurement on the ordinate. On the abscissa is plotted the value of a parameter that specifies one aspect of the articulation. The graph shows a region (labeled I) in which, for a range of articulations, the acoustic signal essentially does not possess the attribute in question. Adjacent to this region there are relatively narrow ranges of the articulatory parameter (region II) within which the acoustic characteristics change abruptly. In region III there is a substantial range of values of the articulatory parameter for which the signal possesses the particular acoustic attribute.

The existence of relations of this type between articulation and sound output has certain implications with regard to the inventory of articulatory and acoustic properties that are used as codes for signaling linguistic information. An acoustic property that is a suitable candidate for such a code is presumably one that can be generated by the articulatory apparatus without requiring precise positioning or maneuvering of the articulatory structures, as in region III of Fig. 3.1. Thus region III delineates a set of conditions that could potentially represent the articulatory and acoustic correlates of some phonetic feature.

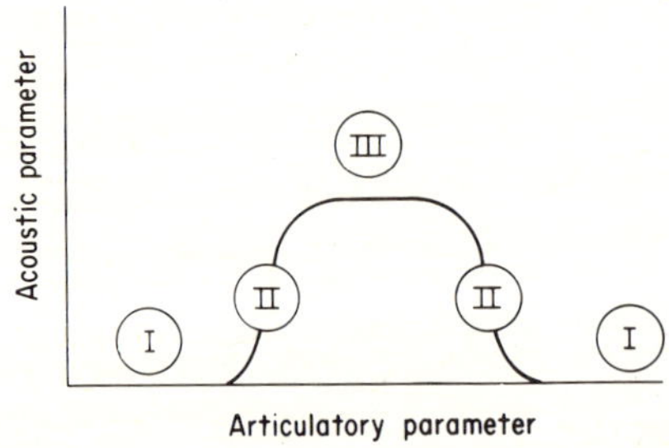

Fig. 3.1. Schematized relation between an acoustic parameter of speech and a parameter that describes some aspect of the articulation. Regions I, II, and III are discussed in the text.

In the following sections we shall present several examples of relations between articulatory and acoustic representations of speech that exhibit behavior of the type shown in Fig. 3.1. No attempt is made to provide an exhaustive inventory of the features. The objective is instead to give examples of features that occur rather extensively across many languages, and to demonstrate through these examples that there is some justification on a purely physical basis for a characterization of phonemes in terms of discrete properties or features. The acoustic correlates of some of the features have been described previously, particularly by Jakobson, Fant, and Halle [7] and by Fant [4]. For other features, some reformulation of the acoustic and articulatory correlates has been developed, motivated in part by the book by Chomsky and Halle [8], but more particularly through numerous discussions with Morris Halle.

Degree of Vocal-tract Constriction

One method that has been used to categorize speech sounds is to describe them in terms of the degree of vocal-tract constriction that is used in the generation of the sounds. It is reasonable to suppose that the degree of constriction can be ordered along a scale on which low vowels are generated with the largest vocal-tract opening and high vowels, glides, fricatives, and stops are characterized by successively more constricted vocal-tract configurations. Examination of the aerodynamic and acoustic aspects of the speech-generating process reveals, however, that the introduction of successively greater degrees of constriction introduces sharp discontinuities in the performance of the system.

The open vocal-tract configuration of low and mid vowels permits unimpeded flow of air through the vocal tract, and the lowest resonant frequency is still sufficiently high that there is negligible interaction between the vocal-cord vibrations and the supraglottal acoustic system; that is, the vocal cords can vibrate in a "natural" manner during production of such vowels. As a greater constriction is imposed on the vocal tract, corresponding to the configuration for the high vowels /i/ and /u/ or for the semivowels /w/ or /j/, theoretical considerations predict that a marked and rather sudden change should occur in the acoustic interaction between the vibrating vocal cords and the supraglottal system.* For such configurations, the constriction is sufficiently great that

* An understanding of the exact nature of this interaction effect must await the development of techniques that will permit glottal activity to be examined experimentally. There is some question as to whether the high vowels should be classified with /w,j,r,l/ and the nasals or with the low and mid vowels.

the first formant drops below about 300 Hz (for an adult male), and regular vocal-cord vibration can be maintained only through an adjustment in the mode of vibration. The waveform of a vibration cycle must be broadened considerably if the magnitude of the sound-pressure fluctuation above the glottis is to be kept well below the subglottal pressure. It can be shown that this effect comes about rather suddenly as the degree of vocal-tract constriction is increased to correspond to that for a high vowel [9]. The broadening of the glottal pulse causes a downward shift in the spectral energy concentration centered on the low-frequency first formant.

Within the range of constrictions corresponding to high vowels there is a tendency for the first-formant frequency to be relatively insensitive to the degree of constriction. This effect arises as a consequence of the acoustic shunting of the vocal-tract walls. The effective mass of these walls causes the first-formant frequency to be higher than it would be for a vocal tract with rigid walls [10]. Thus as the size of the vocal-tract constriction in this region is decreased, the lowering of the first-formant frequency that would be expected for a rigid-walled tube is offset in part by the acoustic shunting of the walls, and the first-formant frequency does not change appreciably over a range of constriction sizes.

As the area of the orifice at the vocal-tract constriction is decreased beyond that corresponding to a high vowel or a semivowel or glide, another discontinuous change occurs, this time as a consequence of aerodynamic processes in the supraglottal system. When the air flow in the orifice becomes sufficiently large, turbulent flow occurs [11]. This onset of turbulence is accompanied by an abrupt increase in the dc resistance to flow in the orifice, causing a substantial rise in the mouth pressure posterior to the orifice. It also results, of course, in the generation of random noise in the vicinity of the orifice. As the area of the constriction is gradually decreased, a point is reached where the noise generated by the turbulent flow is a maximum. For a vocal tract that is still more constricted, the noise decreases as the flow velocity becomes smaller. Thus in the vicinity of the maximum there is a range of constriction sizes within which the characteristics of the noise are relatively fixed.

One further degree of constriction leads to complete closure of the vocal tract, giving rise to another discontinuous change. There is no airflow through the mouth, pressure builds behind the constriction, and, of course, no random noise is generated.

It is quite evident, therefore, that different degrees of vocal-tract constriction give rise to sound-generating processes that have separate and distinct properties. From the point of view of speech-signal generation these can in no way be regarded as greater or smaller amounts of a given attribute. Sounds generated with an open vocal-tract configuration, with the vocal cords vibrating in a normal manner, have been classified as *nonhigh* or *nondiffuse* vowels. All sounds that do not have turbulence or closure are classified as *sonorants,* the opposite class being *nonsonorants* or *obstruents.* Nasal consonants in English would be classified as sonorants, as would /w,j,r,l/ and, of course, all vowels. Sounds whose generation requires substantial pressure rise behind the constriction would therefore be obstruents, and those generated with a complete closure would be classified in terms of still another feature.

Degree of Glottal Constriction

Through adjustment of the positions of the arytenoid cartilages and of other laryngeal muscles, the vocal cords can be maneuvered to a variety of configurations, from an abducted position in which the cords are wide apart to an adducted position in which the cords are tightly approximated. Again, however, this apparent continuum of vocal-cord positions gives rise to grossly distinct modes of glottal activity, and there are discontinuous jumps from one mode to the next as the vocal cords are gradually positioned more closely together.

The open position permits air to flow through the glottis with a minimum of resistance. There is, however, a constriction at the glottis, and the flow through this constriction gives rise to turbulence noise if the velocity of air flow is sufficiently great. This condition occurs in the generation of speech sounds with aspiration noise, such as /h/, or voiceless stop consonants in English.

As the vocal cords are moved together, a point is reached where the Bernoulli effect at the glottal orifice is sufficient to draw the cords together. This inward force, alternating with the outward force due to the subglottal pressure, causes vocal-cord vibration. The onset of this condition appears to be reasonably well defined, and occurs over a narrow range of vocal-cord configurations. As the vocal cords are adducted still further, a point is reached when the subglottal pressure is no longer sufficient to separate the vocal cords and thus to maintain vibration. This condition obtains during a glottal stop or for glottalized sounds that occur in various languages.

Within the range of configurations for which glottal vibration occurs, there may, of course, be a variety of modes and frequencies of vibration. Some of these play a role in providing additional features that are used in some languages. For example, some languages utilize a so-called "breathy voice" in opposition to the normal mode of vocal-cord vibration. Breathy voice is thought to be generated by vibrating the vocal cords in a more or less normal way but by bypassing a portion of the air flow through a chink between the arytenoid cartilages, causing turbulence and noise generation simultaneous with glottal vibration [12].

Place of Articulation for Vowels

The parameters governing the production of vowels as well as their acoustic properties are generally regarded as lying along continua. Various attempts have been made to describe the articulation of vowels in terms of a small number of parameters, and empirical relations between these parameters and the vowel formant frequencies have been derived or measured with the aid of models [4, 13]. Careful analysis of these relations, together with data from acoustic analysis of vowels and examination of the acoustic theory of vowel production, demonstrates, however, that vowels fall naturally into discrete categories instead of being identifiable as points on a continuum. We shall review here only the properties that characterize the vowels /i/, /a/, and /u/, both because they are best understood and because they occur almost universally in the languages of the world. Theories of vowel production and perception are not yet sufficiently well developed to enable us to state the correlates of all the features for vowels.

Consider first the production of the low back vowel /a/. As Fant [4] has pointed out, the cavity shape used in the production of this vowel can be approximated by a two-tube resonator of the type shown in Fig. 3.2*a*. The posterior portion of the vocal tract is constricted, and the oral cavity is relatively large. To a first approximation, the first two formants can be calculated as simple quarter-wavelength resonances of these two tubes, since the coupling between the two will be small as long as the cross-sectional areas are substantially different. For a given overall vocal-tract length $d_1 + d_2$, adjustment of these two lengths to be equal yields the highest possible first-formant frequency and at the same time causes the first and second formants to be close together in frequency. The important acoustic property associated with the output of such a vocal-tract configuration is the spectral energy concentration in the middle frequency range resulting from these two closely spaced formants. The spectrum envelope has the gross shape depicted in Fig. 3.2*b*. Analysis of the natural frequencies of the configuration of Fig. 3.2*a* shows that adjustment of the lengths d_1 and d_2 and of the cross-sectional areas A_1 and A_2 over a comparatively wide range does not greatly alter the position and shape of this central energy peak. Only when d_1 and d_2 deviate appreciably from being equal, or when A_1 and A_2 become somewhat less than an order of magnitude different, does the central energy concentration become broader and separate into two well-defined spectral peaks.

The relative insensitivity of the first- and second-formant frequencies to changes in the length d_1 is illustrated in Fig. 3.3, which shows calculated values of these frequencies for various lengths d_1, assuming an overall length $d_1 + d_2$ of 17 cm.* There is a range of about 2 cm in the middle of the curves within which the second formant varies over only 50 Hz and the first formant changes even less. Within this region the two formants are relatively close together and combine to form a major spectral prominence. In contrast, for the 2-cm range from $d_1 = 11$ cm to $d_1 = 13$ cm, the second-formant frequency changes by about 400 Hz. Thus there is a range of articulatory shapes of this type over which the gross spectral shape of Fig. 3.2*b* is obtained, but outside this range there is a pronounced change in the spectral characteristics. A vowel with this property is classified as a *compact* or *low* vowel. Vowels that do not have this central energy concentration are, of course, categorized as —*compact* or —*low*.

* These calculations were made with the aid of a computer program developed by William Henke. Professor Henke's assistance in obtaining these data is gratefully acknowledged.

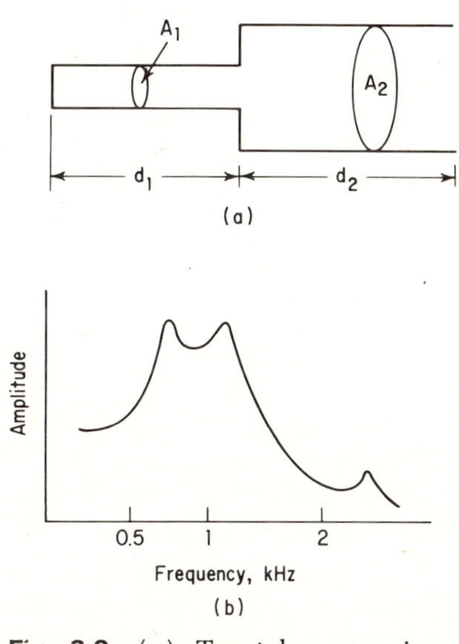

Fig. 3.2. (*a*) Two-tube approximation of vocal-tract configuration for the vowel /a/. (*b*) Approximate form of spectrum envelope of vowel generated by configuration in (*a*).

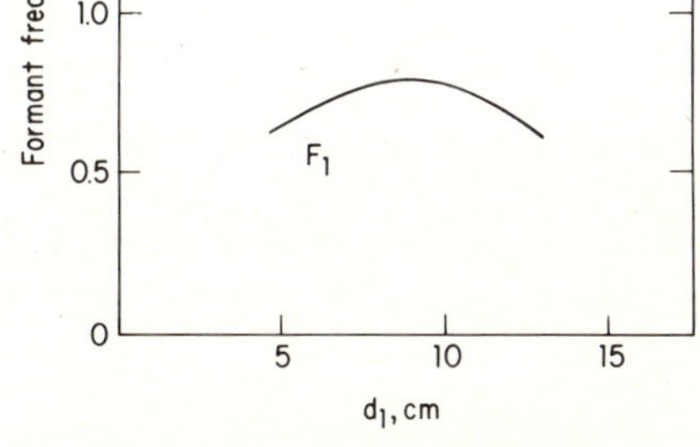

Fig. 3.3. Example of relation between frequencies of first and second formants (F_1 and F_2) and the length d_1 of the back tube of the two-tube resonator in Fig. 3.2a. The areas A_1 and A_2 are, respectively, 0.2 and 3.0 cm², and the overall length of the tube is 17 cm.

The acoustic and articulatory attributes of the vowels /i/ and /u/ can be described in a similar fashion. For both of these vowels there is a low first-formant frequency, while for /a/ the first formant is relatively high. The rapid changes in acoustic characteristics that occur at the boundary between high vowels such as /i/ and /u/ and nonhigh vowels such as /a/ have been noted above in the discussion of the effects of degree of constriction.

The area function for the vowel /i/ can be approximated by a two-tube resonator of the type shown in Fig. 3.4*a*. The lowest resonance for this system is at a relatively low frequency, but the second and third resonances are at high frequencies and are approximately half-wavelength resonances of the two sections of the vocal tract. If the two lengths d_1 and d_2 are roughly equal, these two resonances will be close together and will give rise to a high-frequency spectral energy concentration of the type shown in Fig. 3.4*b*. It is evident that these two natural frequencies do not change appreciably when d_1 and d_2 are perturbed over a substantial range (keeping the total length fixed) or when the cross-sectional areas A_1 and A_2 are modified, provided that A_1 remains several times larger than A_2. Thus the spectrum envelope is relatively insensitive to such changes in the articulatory configuration. A vowel with this high-frequency spectral prominence is classified as a *front* vowel or as *nongrave* or *acute*.

For the vowel /u/ the area function is roughly that of a double resonator of the type shown in Fig. 3.5*a*. The two lowest natural frequencies of this system are sufficiently low that they can be calculated approximately using lumped-circuit concepts. When the two constrictions have sufficiently small cross-sectional area and the volumes of the two cavities are approximately equal, the two natural frequencies are low and relatively close together, giving rise to a gross spectrum shape of the type shown in Fig. 3.5*b*. Once again it is possible to vary the distance d_1 and the volume ratio V_1/V_2 over reasonable ranges without appreciably altering the form of the spectrum. When there is a low-frequency spectral prominence of this kind, the vowel is classified as a *back* or *grave* vowel.

We can conclude, then, that there are preferred regions for vowel production in which particular acoustic attributes are realized over a range of articulatory configurations. There is some physical basis, therefore, for classifying vowels in terms of discrete or quantal features.

It is, of course, of some interest to perform a systematic exploration of a wide variety of articulatory configurations to determine whether there is a set of vowel configurations for which the properties of the acoustic output are relatively insensitive to perturbations in the articulation. Such an exploration could be carried out experimentally, using

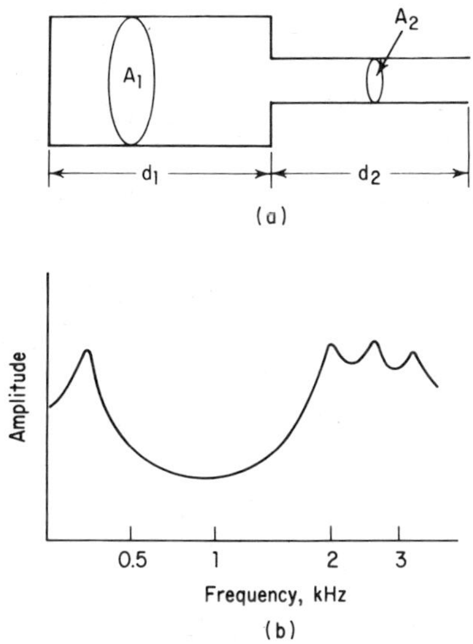

Fig. 3.4. (*a*) Two-tube approximation of vocal-tract configuration for the vowel /i/. (*b*) Approximate form of spectrum envelope of vowel generated by configuration in (*a*).

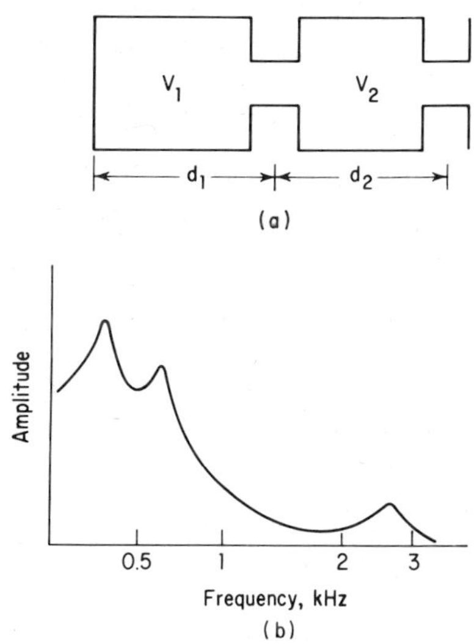

Fig. 3.5. (*a*) Approximation of vocal-tract configuration for the vowel /u/. V_1 and V_2 represent the volumes of the two cavities. (*b*) Approximate form of spectrum envelope of vowel generated by configuration in (*a*).

a model (either analog or computer-simulated) to determine acoustic data from articulatory shapes, or could make use of the elegant theoretical procedures derived by Heinz [14] and by Schroeder [15] and Mermelstein [16].

Place of Articulation for Consonants

From a purely articulatory point of view, one can postulate what amounts to a continuum of places of articulation for consonants, from labials and labiodentals to consonants generated with a constriction in the pharynx. In terms of a simple articulatory model, this range of places of articulation corresponds to a range of positions for a constriction in a tube. An idealized model of such a tube is shown schematically in Fig. 3.6. The glottis is at the left-hand end of the tube, which is considered to be almost closed, and, in order to simplify the example, a constriction has been placed in an acoustic tube that is otherwise uniform in cross-sectional area. The position of this constriction is adjusted to represent different places of articulation of a consonant.

In the case of stop or nasal consonants, the small opening of the constriction might represent an instant of time just after the release of

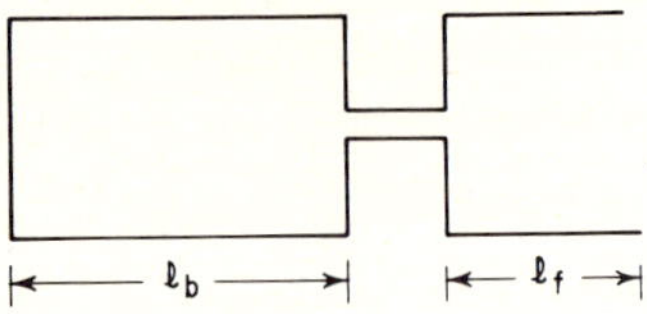

Fig. 3.6. Idealized model of constricted vocal-tract configuration corresponding to a consonant. The constriction is adjusted to different positions to represent different places of articulation.

the consonant. For voiced stops and nasals, there would be vocal-cord vibration from the instant of release and possibly preceding the release. In the case of voiceless stops in English, glottal vibration would commence some tens of milliseconds after the release. The constricted configuration shown in Fig. 3.6 might also be regarded as a simplified model for the production of a fricative consonant, in which case turbulence noise would be generated in the vicinity of the constriction or anterior to the constriction.

That the acoustic outputs of a set of idealized configurations with different constriction positions do not lend themselves to descriptions in terms of continuously changing parameters can be seen from some simple calculations of the acoustic properties of the outputs. Calculations of the natural frequencies of acoustic tubes like those in Fig. 3.6 can easily be made, assuming that the constriction has a very high acoustic impedance compared with the characteristic impedance of the uniform tube, i.e., assuming essentially no coupling between front and back sections of the tube. The lowest natural frequency for the system in which the constriction has a very small cross-sectional area is, in the limit, at zero frequency. Other natural frequencies, corresponding to the second and higher formants, are computed as simple organ-pipe resonances of a uniform tube that is closed at one end and either open (for the front section) or closed (for the back section) at the other end.

For the back portion of the tube, which is essentially closed at both ends, the natural frequencies are given by

$$f_b = \frac{nc}{2l_b} \qquad (3\text{-}1)$$

where c = velocity of sound
l_b = length of back cavity
n = any integer

The front portion of the tube, which is open at one end and closed at the other, has a series of natural frequencies given by

$$f_f = \frac{(2m - 1)c}{4l_f} \tag{3-2}$$

where l_f = length of front cavity
m = any integer

neglecting end effects.

The frequencies of the lowest few resonances for such a tube are plotted as a function of the position of the constriction in Fig. 3.7. Here we assume a total tube length of 16 cm, corresponding roughly to the vocal-tract length of an adult male speaker, and we assume that the length of the contriction is 3 cm. The abscissa on the graph is the distance l_b from the glottal end of the tube to the left-hand edge of the constriction, as shown. The dashed lines represent the lowest two

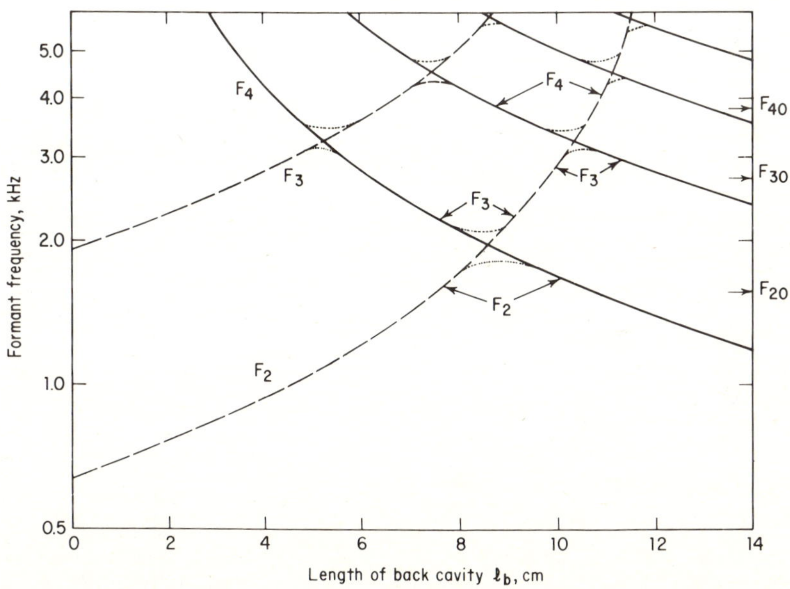

Fig. 3.7. Relations between natural frequencies and the position of the constriction for the configuration shown in Fig. 3.6. The overall length of the tube is 16 cm and the length of the constriction is 3 cm. The dashed lines represent the lowest two resonances of the front cavity (anterior to the constriction); the solid lines represent the lowest four resonances of the back cavity. The dotted lines near the points of coincidence of two resonances represent the resonant frequencies for the case where there is a small amount of coupling between front and back cavities. The resonances of a 16-cm tube with no constriction are shown by the arrows at the right. The curves are labeled with the appropriate formant numbers.

resonances of the front cavity, corresponding to $m = 1$ and $m = 2$ in Eq. (3-2), while the solid lines represent the resonances of the back cavity [$n = 1$, 2, 3, and 4 in Eq. (3-1)]. These frequencies are, of course, computed assuming no losses. For high frequencies, above about 4,000 Hz, the front-cavity resonances will be highly damped, since the radiation impedance of the mouth orifice at these frequencies has a large resistive component. The natural frequencies for a 16-cm uniform tube with no constriction are shown by arrows at the right of Fig. 3.7.

For a given value of the distance l_b from the glottis to the constriction, the formant frequencies are numbered (starting with the second formant) by drawing a vertical line and observing successive points of intersection between this line and the solid and dashed curves. When there is a small amount of coupling between front and back cavities, the situations for which two formant frequencies are identical (corresponding to points of intersection of the dashed and solid curves) are not realized exactly. The two resonances will spread apart at these points, and the actual resonant frequencies would be represented more closely by the dotted lines.

Close to a point of intersection of the solid and dashed lines, the resonances for the coupled cavities (dotted lines) cannot be assigned to either front or back cavities. Immediately to the left of such a point, the *lower* resonance is associated with the front cavity, and just to the right, the *higher* resonance is a front-cavity resonance. Thus as l_b increases through a point of intersection, there is a change in the formant number assigned to the front-cavity resonance and a rather abrupt shift in the frequency of that resonance. Since the front cavity is excited by a turbulence noise source at the constriction, this shift in the resonance produces a shift in a spectral peak in the sound output.

Constriction positions corresponding to $l_b < 8$ cm in Fig. 3.7 represent configurations for uvular or pharyngeal consonants, which do not occur in English. For l_b less than about 6 cm, the back cavity becomes sufficiently short that the first formant can no longer be assumed to be very low and close to zero, and hence the natural frequencies for this region of Fig. 3.7 must be modified. A detailed analysis of sounds produced with constrictions in this region [17] indicates two classes of sounds with well-defined but distinctively different acoustic properties—a pharyngeal consonant, corresponding to $l_b \cong 3$ cm, and a uvular consonant, corresponding to $l_b \cong 6$ cm.

In the vicinity of $l_b = 8.5$ cm, there is a region in which F_2 and F_3 are close together. Immediately to the left of this point the front-cavity resonance is the second formant, whereas to the right it is the third formant. Thus as the constriction position moves through the point $l_b = 8.5$ cm in Fig. 3.7, there is a rather abrupt shift in the frequency of the spectral peak, resulting from excitation of the front-cavity resonance by turbulence noise, as well as a change in the formant number assigned to this peak. When the constriction is in this region, increasing the size of the constriction (simulating the release of a consonant and movement toward a more open vowel configuration) would result in a separation of F_2 and F_3 from their proximate positions. All of these characteristics are observed in velar consonants: to the left of $l_b = 8.5$ cm, the acoustic characteristics are those of the consonant /g/ or /k/ before a back vowel, or the velar fricative /x/; to the right of this point, the corresponding consonant is /g/ or /k/ before a front vowel, or the fronted velar fricative /ç/.

Similar abrupt shifts in the acoustic attributes of stop and fricative consonants are observed at other points of intersection of the curves in Fig. 3.7. For example, at $l_b \cong 10.4$ cm, F_3 and F_4 are close together, and depending on whether l_b is less than or greater than this value, turbulence noise at the constriction will produce a spectral peak in the output that is coincident with either F_3 or F_4 of an adjacent vowel. The third formant tends to be excited for the fricative consonant /š/ (*sh*oe), whereas the fourth formant (or a higher formant) is excited for /s/. A similar abrupt shift occurs in principle for larger values of l_b, where formants at higher frequencies are involved. These points of intersection of back- and front-cavity resonances probably do not define boundaries between phonetic categories, since the high-frequency resonances tend to be rather broad, and since the frequency discrimination of the auditory system becomes rather poor at high frequencies.

Contrasting acoustic characteristics are obtained when the constriction is positioned at a more anterior location, beyond $l_b = 13$ cm in the model. There is now resonance of the front cavity, and hence there is no high-frequency spectral peak in the output when turbulence noise occurs at the constriction. All formants are below the frequencies of the unconstricted vocal tract, and consequently there are rising formant frequencies during transitions from such a consonant to a following vowel. These attributes characterize the labial and labiodental consonants.

A simple model like that of Fig. 3.6 and the corresponding curves in Fig. 3.7 cannot account in detail for the acoustic characteristics of consonants produced with constrictions at various points along the vocal tract and cannot predict all the possible phonetic categories that are encountered in different languages. For example, some consonants, particularly those with a constriction produced by the tongue blade (corresponding to the range $l_b = 10$–13 cm in Fig. 3.7), are characterized by a vocal-tract shape that widens gradually rather than abruptly behind the constriction. Acoustic theory predicts that, for such a tapered configuration, a turbulence noise source near the constriction would tend to excite certain high-frequency back-cavity resonances as well as the front-cavity resonances, with a resulting marked influence on the spectrum of the sound output. Furthermore, the values of F_2 and F_3 for the tapered configuration would be higher than those shown in Fig. 3.7 and would lead to falling transitions of these formants during movement of the vocal tract from the consonantal to the following vowel configuration. Thus the simplified analysis given in connection with Fig. 3.7 cannot be considered as quantitative. It demonstrates the principle that there are changing cavity affiliations of the formants and shifts in the spectrum characteristics of consonants at certain critical constriction positions, and thus provides a broad indication of the possible classes of speech sounds that can be produced with a constricted vocal-tract configuration.

Discussion

The examples that have been presented here suggest that, at least for some types of articulatory parameters, there are ranges of values of these parameters for which the acoustic signal has well-defined attributes, and these ranges are bounded by regions in which the properties of the signal are relatively sensitive to perturbations in the articulation. The acoustic attributes of the signal within one of these plateau-like regions appear to define the acoustic correlates of a phonetic feature.

We would suggest as a working hypothesis that all phonetic features occurring in language have their roots in acoustic attributes with these characteristics. Language seeks out these regions, as it were, and from them assembles an inventory of phonetic elements that are used to form the code for communication by language. This view has, of course, been expressed or implied by several authors [7, 18, 19].

The acoustic attributes defining such preferred regions of articulation must be attributes that are in some sense matched to the auditory mechanism. Thus the requirement for such a region of articulation must be that the attributes of the signal be relatively insensitive to articulatory perturbations *after the signal is transformed by the auditory mechanism.*

In fact, it is not unreasonable to suggest that the transformations imposed on the signal by the auditory mechanism accentuate the plateau-like character of the regions in which sensitivity to articulatory change is low. Data from experiments on the identification and discrimination of various classes of synthetic speech sounds support such a view. These experiments use as stimuli series of synthetic speechlike sounds with acoustic characteristics that span a range of values encompassing several phonemes. The data demonstrate that these stimuli tend to be perceived in categorial fashion. Over some portions of the stimulus range, corresponding to phoneme centers, the stimuli sound alike; over regions that span phoneme boundaries, perception changes rapidly [20–23].

There is evidence, therefore, to support the notion that the features forming the smallest units of language are anchored in the characteristics of both the generative mechanism and the auditory system. As the examples we have presented here suggest, the talker manipulates his speech-generating mechanism to select sounds with well-defined acoustic attributes that are relatively insensitive to small perturbations in articulation. Psychoacoustic data demonstrate that the auditory mechanism is predisposed to perceive sounds with these attributes in a categorial fashion, such that small perturbations in the acoustic attributes cause little change in the perception.

Acknowledgment

This work was supported in part by the U.S. Air Force Cambridge Research Laboratories, Office of Aerospace Research, and in part by the National Institutes of Health (Grant NB-04332). The substantial influence of Morris Halle in the formulation of these ideas is gratefully acknowledged.

REFERENCES

1. H. Dudley, The Carrier Nature of Speech, *Bell System Tech. J.*, **19**:495–515 (1940).
2. T. Chiba and M. Kajiyama, "The Vowel, Its Nature and Structure," Tokyo-Kaiseikan Pub. Co., Tokyo, 1941.
3. H. K. Dunn, The Calculation of Vowel Resonances, and an Electrical Vocal Tract, *J. Acoust. Soc Am.*, **22**:740–753 (1950).
4. G. Fant, "Acoustic Theory of Speech Production," Mouton and Co., The Hague, 1960.
5. K. N. Stevens and A. S. House, An Acoustical Theory of Vowel Production and Some of Its Implications, *J. Speech Hearing Res.*, **4**:303–320 (1961).
6. J. L. Flanagan, "Speech Analysis Synthesis and Perception," Academic Press, New York, 1965.
7. R. Jakobson, C. G. M. Fant, and M. Halle, "Preliminaries to Speech Analysis," MIT Press, Cambridge, Mass., 1963.
8. N. Chomsky and M. Halle, "The Sound Pattern of English," Harper and Row, New York, 1968.
9. K. N. Stevens and M. Halle, On the Mechanism of Glottal Vibration for Vowels and Consonants, *MIT Quart. Progr. Rept. Res. Lab. Electron.*, No. 85, pp. 267–277, April 1967.
10. G. Fant and B. Sonesson, Speech at High Ambient Air-pressure, *Speech Transmis-*

sion Lab. Quart. Progr. Status Rept. Roy. Inst. Technol., No. 2, pp. 9–21, Stockholm, 1964.

11. K. N. Stevens, Airflow and Turbulence Noise for Fricative and Stop Consonants: Static Considerations, *J. Acoust. Soc. Am.,* **50:**1180–1192 (1971).
12. P. Ladefoged, Linguistic Phonetics, *Working Papers in Phonetics,* No. 6, Phonetics Laboratory, UCLA, June 1967.
13. K. N. Stevens and A. S. House, Development of a Quantitative Description of Vowel Articulation, *J. Acoust. Soc. Am.,* **27:**484–493 (1955).
14. J. M. Heinz, Perturbation functions for the determination of vocal-tract area-functions from vocal-tract eigenvalues, *Speech Transmission Lab. Quart. Progr. Status Rept Roy. Inst. Technol., Stockholm,* No. 1, pp. 1–14, 1967.
15. M. R. Schroeder, Determination of the Geometry of the Human Vocal Tract by Acoustic Measurements, *J. Acoust. Soc. Am.,* **41:**1001–1010 (1967).
16. P. Mermelstein, Determination of the Vocal-tract Shape from Measured Formant Frequencies, *J. Acoust. Soc. Am.,* **41:**1283–1294 (1967).
17. D. H. Klatt and K. N. Stevens, Pharyngeal Consonants, *MIT Quart. Progr. Rept. Res. Lab. Electron.,* No. 93, pp. 207–216, April 1969.
18. M. Halle, On the Bases of Phonology, in J. A. Fodor and J. Katz (eds.), "The Structure of Language," pp. 324–333, Prentice-Hall, Englewood Cliffs, N.J., 1964.
19. K. N. Stevens and M. Halle, Remarks on Analysis by Synthesis and Distinctive Features, in Weiant Wathen-Dunn (ed.), "Models for the Perception of Speech and Visual Form," MIT Press, Cambridge, Mass., 1967.
20. A. M. Liberman, K. S. Harris, H. S. Hoffman, and B. C. Griffith, The Discrimination of Speech Sounds Within and Across Phoneme Boundaries, *J. Exptl. Psychol.,* **54:**358–368 (1957).
21. L. Chistovich, G. Fant, A. de Serpa-Leitão, and P. Tjernlund, Mimicking of Synthetic Vowels, *Speech Transmission Lab. Quart. Progr. Status Rept. Roy. Inst. Technol. Stockholm,* No. 2, pp. 1–18, 1966.
22. L. Chistovich, G. Fant, and A. de Serpa-Leitão, Mimicking and Perception of Synthetic Vowels, Part II, *Speech Transmission Lab. Quart. Progr. Status Rept. Roy. Inst. Technol. Stockholm,* No. 3, pp. 1–3, 1966.
23. K. N. Stevens, A. M. Liberman, M. Studdert-Kennedy, and S. Öhman, Crosslanguage Study of Vowel Perception, *Language and Speech,* **12:**1–23 (1969).

CHAPTER FOUR

Psychological Representation of Speech Sounds

ROGER N. SHEPARD*

Introduction

Since few of us have the time or interest to read more than a small fraction of the printed information with which we are increasingly bombarded, speech still carries the greatest burden of human communication. Under normal circumstances, then, communication is a primarily oral-aural transaction. For, as our great reliance upon the telephone attests, such communication can be effectively carried on in the complete absence of all but purely auditory cues, whereas (except in the special case of highly skilled lip readers) it begins to deteriorate as soon as the auditory signal is degraded by attenuation, distortion, or noise.

* The analyses reported here owe much to my former coworkers S. C. Johnson for the development of the algorithm for hierarchical clustering and Mrs. J.-J. Chang for programming the exponential method of proximity analysis [1]. Extensive assistance in carrying out the analyses and preparing the figures was provided by Carolyn Brown, Maureen Sheenan, and, particularly, Christine Feng. This work was supported by Bell Laboratories and the National Science Foundation (Grants GS-1302 and GS-2283).

If, now, we turn to a study of this auditory signal upon which most communication so critically depends, we find that it, in turn, can be analyzed into a sequence of distinguishable, psychologically elementary components—the *phonemes*. These are the smallest units, the individual vowels and consonants, that we intuitively recognize as separately producible speech sounds. In terms of the articulatory organs (lips, tongue, glottis, etc.), they correspond to more or less identifiable configurations or simple changes (openings, closures, etc.). In terms of the resulting acoustic signal, they correspond to more or less identifiable energy patterns in the time-frequency domain.

Basic to human communication, then, is the ability to recognize or identify these individual phonemes as they follow one another in the auditory stream of speech. This is not to say that the understanding of connected discourse consists solely in the separate recognition of each phoneme as it occurs. For, unlike the identification of isolated phonemes in the laboratory, the recognition of those very same sounds in the course of connected speech is typically aided by additional processes of a rather different kind, viz., processes of segmentation and utilization of semantic and syntactic cues from context. Still, the process of recognition of individual phonemes must be regarded as fundamental in the sense that it can be shown to operate in the absence of the context upon which these higher-level processes depend; whereas any context that is in fact present consists largely, itself, of at least partially recognized phonemes.

For these reasons, investigators concerned with the perception of speech have devoted considerable effort to the study of the human listener's ability to identify vowel and consonant phonemes—even when these are presented without context. Typically in these studies, individual phonemes (i.e., phonemes that have been either uttered in isolation or excerpted in some way from context) are presented in random order to listeners who indicate, after each presentation, which phoneme they think has been presented. The data from such an *absolute-identification experiment* are most conveniently cast in the form of an $n \times n$ matrix showing, for each of the n phonemes studied, how often it was identified correctly and how often it was misidentified as each of the $n - 1$ other phonemes. The hope is that the numbers in such a *confusion matrix* will reveal something about how these speech sounds are processed within the listener.

Further information can be gained by repeating an experiment of this kind while systematically masking or filtering the acoustic signal in some way. Indeed, the capabilities for processing speech have attained such a level of perfection in humans that, under favorable conditions, confusions between phonemes occur only rarely—even when they are presented without context. In order to ensure a rate of confusion that is sufficiently revealing of the underlying perceptual mechanism, therefore, it is often helpful to degrade the stimulus deliberately, e.g., by the addition of noise. Moreover, by examining the changes in the patterns of confusion that result when we selectively mask or filter out particular ranges of audio frequency, we can obtain more direct evidence on how the process of identification depends upon the physically measurable parameters of the stimuli.

It is important to recognize, though, that any one confusion matrix is based solely upon the responses of the listeners and can, therefore, be constructed without any knowledge of the physical properties of the stimuli. In this respect any structure or pattern that may be discerned in such a matrix of numbers represents the interrelations among the stimuli as they are perceived psychologically—not as they are measured physically. Once such a purely psychological structure has been identified in this way, however, we are in a favorable position to turn to the *psychophysical* problem of then relating this structure to any independently measured physical parameters.

If we are lucky, the results might even lead to more sophisticated devices for the automatic recognition or for the efficient compression and transmission of speech (technological goals that are discussed in Chapter 11). Here, however, we shall focus primarily on the more purely psychological problem, viz., the problem of discovering the psychological structure of a set of speech sounds as that structure is revealed solely in the responses of listeners.

This substantive problem will also serve as a vehicle for demonstrating the advantages of some recent methodological innovations, namely some computer-based techniques for transforming patterns hidden in large matrices of empirical data into a readily assimilable pictorial form. In this respect, there will be a close connection with some of the later chapters (e.g., Chapters 7 and 8) that are also concerned with the use of machines to convert raw data into a more usable form.

Confusion Data as a Source of Information about Psychological Structure

Let us turn now to a more detailed consideration of the nature of a confusion matrix of the sort we have been considering, and to the problem of discovering and characterizing whatever pattern or structure may lay hidden in its numbers. Following the usual convention, let us suppose that these are arranged in such a way that the entry at the intersection of the *i*th row and *j*th column tells us how often the *i*th stimulus led to the response that would be correct for the *j*th stimulus. Thus correct responses appear in the diagonal entries only, while all errors of identification contribute to the off-diagonal pattern.

The problem with which we are immediately faced, then, is one of getting hold of this pattern in some useful way. If the matrix is of any size, this is by no means a trivial problem. In a number of experiments to be considered here, for example, 16 different phonemes were simultaneously investigated and, for each such experiment, the resulting confusion matrix contains 256 different numbers. Yet our eyes, which are the evolutionary product of a natural environment, are ill-equipped to assimilate subtle patterns from such large arrays of artificial symbols. We may be able to pick out certain pairs in which the stimuli seem especially susceptible to mutual confusion, and we may even learn something from an examination of how the stimuli in these pairs differ physically. But we have thereby advanced very little toward our goal of discovering the overall psychological structure hidden in the data.

Attempts have been made to recast the numerical data in some form in which their magnitudes will appeal more directly to the eye. Thus the magnitude of the number that was in each cell can be represented, instead, by the size of a black circle [2, 3] or by the density of shading or cross-hatching in that cell [4; 5, p. 179]. Even so, the eye responds best to connected configurations—configurations, in this case, in which similarly filled-in cells are juxtaposed rather than scattered across the matrix [6]. For this reason, some attempt is usually also made to permute the rows and columns of the matrix so as to bring highly confused stimuli together as clusters and thus to achieve the desired condition of contiguity. However, it is not clear how this is to be done in general, particularly with large matrices. Indeed, speech sounds differ from the unidimensional stimuli studied in classical psychophysics in that their psychological interrelations cannot be adequately represented by arranging them in a simple, one-dimensional series. In this case, the desired condition of connectivity within the matrix will not, in general, be fully attainable. We may still be left, then, without any very clear overall picture of the psychological structure of the stimuli.

It therefore appears that more powerful techniques are needed if we are to recover the underlying psychological structure with enough fidelity to advance, in a material way, our understanding of the processing that must underlie the recognition performances that we observe. In what follows, two new techniques will be described and applied to existing data on confusions among vowel and among consonant phonemes. These techniques, particularly when used in combination, seem to expose the underlying structures in an especially meaningful form. Indeed, when these techniques are applied to data that have previously existed in published form for many years, some stable and orderly patterns emerge that evidently have not themselves been previously reported.

Spatial Representation of Confusion Data by "Proximity Analysis"

The first of the two types of methods to be described here is based on the notion that the underlying structure that we are seeking in our data can be treated as a *spatial* structure. Specifically, we seek a representation of the stimuli (e.g., phonemes) as points in a Euclidean space such that the spatial proximity between two points represents the frequency with which the two corresponding stimuli were actually confused; that is, the more frequently listeners tend to give to one stimulus the response belonging to another stimulus, the closer together the points representing those two stimuli should be in terms of the Euclidean metric. Moreover, we seek such a representation in a space of the smallest number of dimensions in which this desired condition of a monotonic relation between confusion frequency and interpoint distance can be achieved—at least to a satisfactory degree of approximation.

As the analyses to be presented here are intended to show, such a spatial representation has three desirable features. First, it preserves essentially all the reliable information contained in the original data. Second, it presents this information in such a way as to render the initially obscure underlying structure immediately apparent to the human eye. And third, it provides rather direct evidence as to the number of dimensions underlying the psychological relations among the stimuli which in the case of complex sounds such as phonemes is not entirely clear in advance.

Various methods have in fact previously been available for constructing spatial representations on the basis of certain types of psychological data. In addition to the widely known methods of "factor analysis" [7, 8], there have been the methods of "multidimensional scaling" first made practical by Torgerson [9] and then developed along several different lines by a number of others as well (e.g., see Refs. 10–13). Indeed, some methods of these sorts have even been used to construct psychological representations of speech sounds [14–20]. However, the method to be presented here is of a different type developed by the author and his colleagues at Bell Laboratories [21–25]. This approach provides what is felt to be the first satisfactory general solution to the problem of achieving well-defined spatial representations on the basis of measures of the degree of similarity, confusability, association, or, in general, psychological "proximity" among stimuli.

A noteworthy property of this new approach is that, except in certain "degenerate" cases [22, p. 240], nothing need be known about the form of the function relating the given data to the Euclidean distances to be recovered (except, of course, that this function is monotonic). This initially unknown form can nevertheless be essentially recovered, and to the extent that it is recovered, the spatial solution is determined to within the "extended" group of similarity transformations [26]. Since the "degenerate" exceptions have arisen only rarely in practice, much can be accomplished without assuming more than monotonicity.

Even so, any additional knowledge that we may have about the functional form of the underlying relation can be used to increase the precision of the spatial representation and to decrease its susceptibility to the sometimes troublesome "degeneracies" [27, 28]. It is therefore of some potential import that in the specific case of confusion data, the relation in question—even though assumed to be no more than monotonic—has in fact consistently turned out to have a very particular, well-defined form. With the exception of occasional degenerate cases, that is, the relation between the frequencies with which stimuli are confused and the corresponding distances among points in the recovered spatial solution has invariably been found to be closely approximated by a simple exponential decay function.

The particular method for the "proximity analysis" of confusion data to be illustrated here takes advantage of this empirical result and—instead of seeking the spatial representation that best fits the merely monotonic hypothesis—seeks the representation that best fits the stronger, exponential hypothesis. Although an analysis of this sort was originally proposed over 15 years ago [12, 29–32], it was not until the more recent implementation of appropriate numerical methods on a digital computer [21, 22, 24, 25] that it has become clear just how such an analysis should be achieved. The procedure described here follows Kruskal's [24] lead of using a variant of the method of "steepest descent" to minimize an explicitly defined measure of departure from the desired relation—in this case an exponential decay function. The computer program itself was developed primarily by Mrs. J.-J. Chang in collaboration with the present author [1].

We start with the empirically given confusion matrix in which the entry p_{ij} is the relative frequency with which the ith stimulus led to the response belonging to the jth stimulus. In this raw form, however, the entries p_{ij} are not entirely suitable as measures of proximity, for whereas we require that the proximity between i and j (like the distance between any two points) be the same in both directions, it will not in general be the case that $p_{ij} = p_{ji}$. Moreover, whereas the proximity (or distance) between a point and itself always takes on the same limiting value, it will not usually happen that $p_{ii} = p_{jj}$ for different stimuli i and j.

Before proceeding to the analysis itself, then, we first define for every pair *i* and *j* a derived estimate of the psychological proximity or similarity S_{ij} between them in terms of the four relevant numbers from the empirically given confusion matrix, viz., p_{ij}, p_{ji}, p_{ii}, and p_{jj}. A definition that has been found serviceable for this purpose is, simply, the total number of confusions between *i* and *j* divided by the total number of correct responses to these same two stimuli or, formally,

$$S_{ij} = \frac{p_{ij} + p_{ji}}{p_{ii} + p_{jj}}$$

Although there are theoretical arguments for other, slightly different definitions [30, 31], the formula just given has typically led to essentially the same results in practice and, moreover, has seemed to be somewhat less affected by statistical fluctuations in the four *p* components. In any case we have, by means of this formula, achieved the desired condition of symmetry, $S_{ij} = S_{ji}$, and equality of the diagonal entries, $S_{ii} = S_{jj} = 1$ for all *i* and *j*.

The iterative process itself is applied to the resulting symmetric matrix of these proximity measures, S_{ij}, to find a configuration of points and a set of values for the parameters of the postulated exponential that provide, jointly, an optimum fit to the S_{ij}. Specifically, we seek to minimize

$$\sum_{i>j} \{S_{ij} - (ae^{-bD_{ij}} + c)\}^2$$

where D_{ij} = distance between points *i* and *j* in recovered configuration
a = intercept of recovered exponential decay function
b = slope of recovered exponential decay function
c = asymptote of recovered exponential decay function

The D_{ij} are in turn computed from the coordinates for the points recovered during each iteration by the Euclidean formula

$$D_{ij} = \sqrt{\sum_k (x_{ik} - x_{jk})^2}$$

where x_{ik} is the coordinate for the *i*th point on the *k*th orthogonal dimension of the underlying space.

Actually, in the analyses of proximity measures derived specifically from confusion matrices in the manner indicated above, we always have $S_{ii} = 1$ for all *i*. Since the distance D_{ii} between a point and itself is zero, it is natural to ensure that the fitted exponential function intercepts the *S* axis at unit height. In the analyses to be reported here, therefore, the parameter *a* is not allowed to vary along with *b* and *c* but is constrained instead to the fixed value 1. Also, in order to facilitate convergence (and to avoid merely local minima), we have found it helpful to add two further refinements to this method: (1) a procedure for choosing starting values for the x coordinates and the variable parameters b and c on a rational rather than a purely arbitrary basis; and (2) a second-order variant of the gradient method in which the adjustments during each iteration are based upon estimates of the second, as well as the first, partial derivatives of the expression to be minimized with respect to the variable coordinates and parameters. Additional refinements have also been introduced to ensure that the variable parameters b and c will end up with appropriate signs. These and other details of the computing algorithm are somewhat tangential to our present focus on substantive problems of speech perception and so will be reserved for fuller presentation elsewhere.

Spatial Representation Based on Confusions Among 16 Consonant Phonemes

The data with which we shall be most extensively concerned, here, are from the classical study of confusions among 16 English consonants by Miller and Nicely [33]. Basically, the listeners in their experiments attempted to identify each of 16 different syllables as these were pronounced from a randomized list. All syllables terminated in the same vowel /a/ (as in f*a*ther). They differed only in the consonant that preceded this vowel, which was always one of the 16 following: /p/, /t/, /k/, /f/, /θ/, /s/, /ʃ/, /b/, /d/, /g/, /v/, /ð/, /z/, /ʒ/, /m/, and /n/.

Altogether, Miller and Nicely obtained 17 complete 16 × 16 confusion matrices, each under a different condition of filtering or signal-to-noise ratio, and, very fortunately for our present purposes, these were presented in full in their published report. To start with, however, we shall confine our attention to just one matrix, obtained by pooling their tables I through VI for those six conditions in which bandwidth was maintained at 200 to 6,500 Hz and in which deviations from the best listening condition were imposed only by manipulating signal-to-noise ratio (S/N). Combining data in this way permits the recovery of a spatial representation of greater stability without entailing any untoward biases. For, as we shall later see, although variations in S/N do affect the overall *number* of confusions, they have little or no effect on the internal *pattern* of those confusions. Table 4.1, then, presents the below-diagonal half of the 16 × 16 symmetric matrix of proximity measures obtained from the pooled confusion matrix by means of the formula for S_{ij} set forth above.

The problem is to convert into explicit form whatever pattern already exists implicitly in the data of this table. This is essentially achieved

Table 4.1 Measures of Confusion Among Sixteen Consonants (Based upon Miller and Nicely's data for their six unfitered or "flat" conditions I–VI.)

p	—															
t	.229	—														
k	.432	.241	—													
f	.101	.057	.077	—												
θ	.124	.079	.084	.423	—											
s	.052	.050	.063	.066	.157	—										
ʃ	.038	.050	.047	.030	.048	.115	—									
b	.022	.013	.018	.046	.045	.024	.012	—								
d	.025	.022	.020	.025	.041	.031	.033	.058	—							
g	.013	.016	.030	.015	.039	.033	.021	.069	.342	—						
v	.016	.022	.020	.035	.040	.023	.020	.210	.059	.054	—					
ð	.028	.016	.018	.032	.031	.026	.018	.145	.094	.120	.338	—				
z	.025	.023	.025	.018	.033	.035	.017	.055	.106	.139	.080	.161	—			
ʒ	.019	.017	.019	.007	.017	.022	.012	.027	.089	.125	.029	.033	.136	—		
m	.025	.022	.021	.016	.019	.017	.012	.038	.024	.032	.030	.034	.021	.016	—	
n	.017	.018	.020	.012	.018	.013	.011	.024	.032	.030	.022	.028	.016	.030	.151	—
	p	t	k	f	θ	s	ʃ	b	d	g	v	ð	z	ʒ	ɱ	ŋ

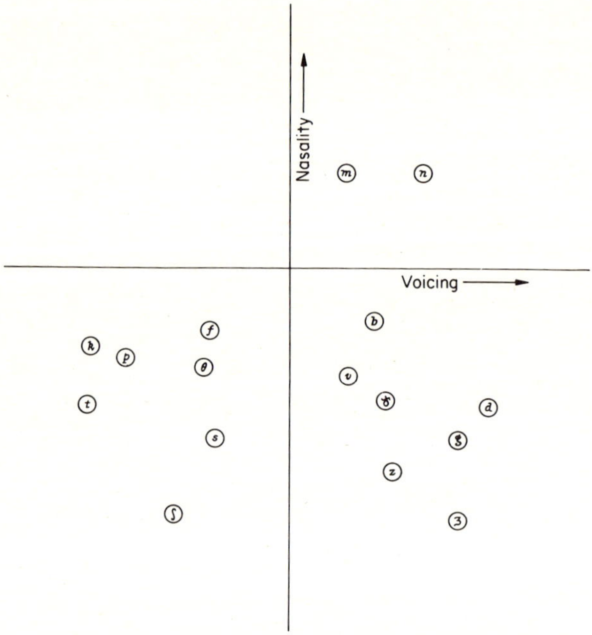

Fig. 4.1. Two-dimensional spatial representation for 16 consonant phonemes (based on the pooled data from Miller and Niceley's six flat-frequency-response conditions).

in Fig. 4.1, which presents the two-dimensional spatial representation obtained by applying the method of "exponential analysis of proximities" to the empirical proximity measures of Table 4.1.

The recovered configuration has been rigidly rotated so that the vertical and horizontal axes of the figure partition the 16 points into those representing the unvoiced stops and fricatives /ptkfθsʃ/, the corresponding voiced stops and fricatives /bdgvðzʒ/, and the (voiced) nasals /mn/. Now, by an entirely different method, Miller and Nicely had already demonstrated that among the so-called "distinctive features" that linguists have invoked as a basis for classifying consonant phonemes, those of voicing and nasality go the furthest toward accounting for these data. The emergence of the three-way grouping noted in Fig. 4.1 does not therefore provide in itself any new insight into these data. Still, it does at least attest to the potential validity of the gross features of spatial representation of this type.

Moreover, in view of the fact that these consonants were considered by Miller and Nicely to differ with respect to as many as *five* different distinctive features (viz., affrication, duration, and place of articulation, as well as voicing and nasality), it is noteworthy that 99.4 percent of the variance of the data in Table 4.1 can be accounted for solely on the basis of the two dimensions of Fig. 4.1. The residual departures of the original proximity measures S_{ij} from the reconstructed exponential decay function of the distances D_{ij} in this recovered two-dimensional space are displayed in Fig. 4.2. (Each point in this plot corresponds, of course, to a pair of the consonants.)

The fact that we can obtain such a good fit in two dimensions does not, however, mean that these dimensions must be interpreted as reflecting variations in two distinctive features only. On the contrary, as we move from left to right across the lower half of Fig. 4.1, we encounter four discernible vertically oriented groups consisting, successively, of the unvoiced stops /ptk/, the unvoiced fricatives /fθsʃ/, the voiced fricatives /vðzʒ/, and, not entirely separated from the preceding group, the voiced stops /bdg/. So the distinction of affrication is at least partially preserved. Further, the parallelism between the unvoiced and voiced fricatives with respect to place of articulation (and possibly duration) is maintained in the parallel vertical ordering of the two series of corresponding points for /fθsʃ/ and /vðzʒ/. Evidently it would be an oversimplification, then, to describe this space solely in terms of the distinctive features of voicing and nasality.

Of course, we can always seek a new best-fitting solution in a space of higher dimensionality, and the fraction of variance accounted for

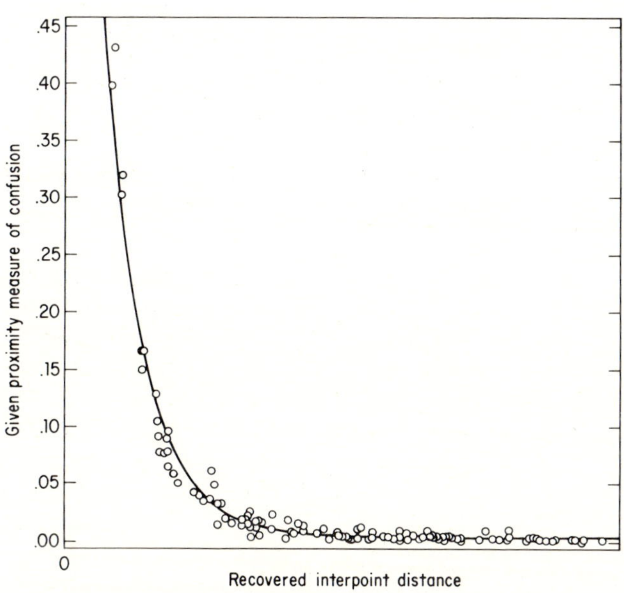

Fig. 4.2. Goodness of fit of the confusion data for 16 consonants to an exponential decay function of interpoint distance in the two-dimensional representation of Fig. 4.1.

in the given proximity data can only be increased thereby. Indeed, previous attempts have been made to extract as many as four spatial dimensions from these same data [20]. So the two-dimensional results shown in Figs. 4.1 and 4.2 do not fully settle the question of the true psychological dimensionality of these stimuli. Still, with less than 1 percent of the variance remaining to be accounted for, relatively little psychological importance could be attached to any additional spatial dimension that might be extracted. Indeed the error variability inherent in the S-measures themselves may well amount to as much as 1 percent. If so, the determination of the projections of the points on a third axis—with a concomitant increase, by half again, in the total degrees of freedom of the configuration—is not likely to possess much reliability.

A more promising alternative for evincing further structure in these data will be described in a subsequent section. An attempt will then be made to show how that alternative technique can be used in combination with the spatial type of solution just discussed to reveal further regularities in the data of Miller and Nicely. Already, however, it should be clear that the spatial solution by itself can furnish a useful reduction of the original confusion data. It is a reduction in that all 120 of the S-values originally given in Table 4.1 can now be reconstructed (except, of course, for the approximately ½ percent residual variance) from just 34 numbers (viz., the 2×16 spatial coordinates together with the two parameters of the fitted exponential). It is a *useful* reduction in that the information or structure, which was only implicit in Table 4.1, has been converted in Fig. 4.1 into an immediately accessible, explicit form.

Spatial Representation Based on Confusions Among 10 Vowel Phonemes

Before presenting the second of the two methods of analysis to be described here, it may be helpful to consider a second illustrative application of the first method—this time to vowel rather than consonant phonemes. In a well-known study by Peterson and Barney [34], ten monosyllabic words differing only in the vowel were presented aurally in random order to a group of listeners who were requested to indicate after each presentation which of the ten words they thought had been pronounced. The words ("heed," "hid," "head," "had," "hod," "hawed," "hood," "who'd," "hud," and "heard") were alike with respect to the initial and terminal consonants /h/ and /d/ but differed with respect to the interpolated vowel, /i/, /I/, /ɛ/, /æ/, /a/, /ɔ/, /ʊ/, /u/, /ʌ/, or /ɝ/, respectively. The difficulty of the task was partly determined by the further circumstance that in different presentations the same word was pronounced by different speakers (who varied in both age and sex).

A 10×10 symmetric matrix of proximity measures was computed from the resulting confusion matrix [34, table I], and was then subjected to the exponential analysis of proximities as before. Best-fitting configurations were sought in both two-dimensional and three-dimensional space. The resulting three-dimensional solution is shown in Fig. 4.3, where an attempt has been made to encode variations in the third dimension (depth) by variations in the sizes of the spheres representing the ten points. The obtained three-dimensional structure has some face validity. At least, words that seem similar in sound (like "hod" and "hawed") are close together, whereas words that seem relatively different (like "heed" and "hud") are far apart.

The extent to which the distances among the ten points can be used to account in this way for the actual frequencies with which these words were confused is indicated in Fig. 4.4. This time the exponential decay function, with which the distances were brought into a mutual best fit, accounts for 99 percent of the variance of the given proximity data. (Actually, however, because so many of the S-values are essentially zero, this is somewhat less impressive than the 99.4 percent reported in connection with Fig. 4.2.)

Further evidence for the validitiy of such a spatial representation can be sought in its relations with other, external variables. In this connection, it should be noted that it is only the internal structure of the configuration itself that is uniquely determined by the data; the orientation of the recovered configuration with respect to the reference axes is wholly arbitrary. There is, therefore, no reason to suppose that any given external variable (such as the physically measured frequency of a particular formant) will be especially related to the projections

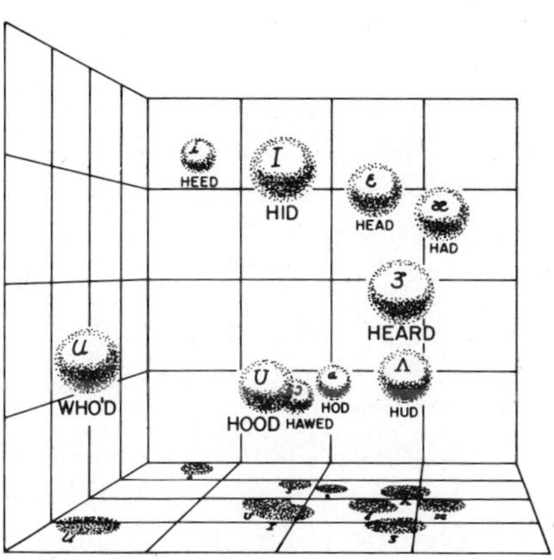

Fig. 4.3. Three-dimensional spatial representation for 10 vowel phonemes (based on the data of Peterson and Barney).

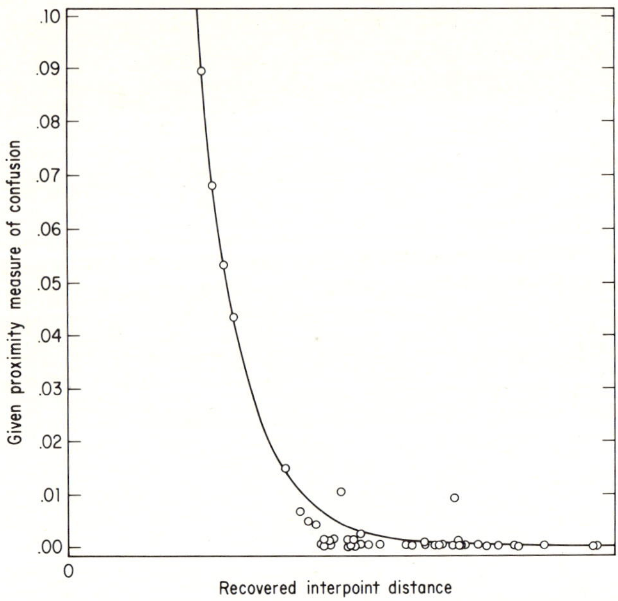

Fig. 4.4. Goodness of fit of the confusion data for 10 vowels to an exponential decay function of interpoint distance in the three-dimensional representation of Fig. 4.3.

x_{ik} of the recovered points on any one reference axis k. This consideration has often been overlooked in interpreting multidimensional scaling solutions (e.g., see Ref. 35). Actually, for the purpose of interpretation, it is quite permissible—indeed preferable—to seek for each such external variable a new axis on which the projections of the points are optimally correlated with that variable [36, 37].

In general, of course, to provide a specification of a speech sound that is complete *physically* would require a very large number of parameters. Even if we disregard phase relations, we would still need to partition the time-frequency plane into a vast number of small compartments and then specify the amount of acoustic energy contained within each such compartment. In the case of vowels, however, it is only the center frequencies of the lowest two or three formants (peaks in the energy spectrum) that have been thought to be critical *psychologically*—i.e., for recognition (see, e.g., Refs. 38 and 39). Accordingly, the method reported by Miller, Shepard, and Chang [37] was used to find three new axes through the configuration shown in Fig. 4.1 such that each would best agree with the average center frequency of a different one of the first three formants of these vowels as measured by Peterson and Barney [34, table II]. In the average formant frequencies used for this purpose, the values given by Peterson and Barney, separately, for each of their three types of speakers (viz., men, women, and children) were weighted according to the number of each type in their total sample of 76 speakers (viz., 33, 28, and 15, respectively).

The resulting product-moment correlations with the projections on the new, rotated axes were .88, .98, and .82 for the first, second, and third formants, respectively. As is to be expected, these relations between the purely physical variables and the recovered psychological structure were appreciably nonlinear. To this extent, the true strengths of these relations are even greater than indicated by the obtained linear correlations.

The angles between the new directions corresponding to these three formants were 99° for one and two, 104° for one and three, and 49° for two and three. That the first axis is nearly orthogonal (close to 90°) to the other two indicates that the psychological effect of the first formant is nearly independent of the other two. The substantially smaller angle between the second and third directions, on the other hand, suggests that the psychological effects of these two higher formants are to some extent interdependent.

In Fig. 4.3 the three-dimensional configuration is pictured as viewed normal to the plane of the first two rotated axes. Indeed, horizontal and vertical axes through the pictured structure would, as nearly as possible, agree with the frequencies of the first and second formants, respectively. This is why the picture reproduces something resembling the traditional "vowel loop" (starting with the "high front" vowel /i/ at the upper left and proceeding around the U-shaped curve through the "lower" vowels at the right and back to the "high back" vowel /u/ at the lower left). The rotated axis that best relates to the frequency of the third formant points both away (into the depth of the picture) and upward (since it is also correlated with the second).

Because the 10 recovered points fall roughly on a U-shaped "loop" and because the axes corresponding to the second and third formants are appreciably correlated, a good approximation to the original data can also be achieved in a reduced space of just two dimensions. In fact, 97 percent of the variance of the given S-values can still be accounted for by the best-fitting two-dimensional solution. In appearance this reduced configuration is rather similar to the projection of the three-dimensional configuration on the plane of the first two axes. That is, it is not very different from the pattern already shown in Fig. 4.3—but with all ten spheres reduced to the same size.

In either case, a rather clear relationship emerges between certain physically measured properties of these stimuli and a "psychological" structure that was obtained entirely independently of those physical measurements. The existence of this relationship provides a different kind of support for the psychophysical notion that it is the frequencies of the first three formants—and particularly of the first two—that are critical for the identification of spoken vowels. At the same time, it furnishes further evidence of the validity of such spatial representations of psychological structure.

Hierarchical Representation of Confusion Data by Cluster Analysis

The representation of stimuli as points in an underlying continuous space seems particularly natural when the psychologically relevant physical variables are themselves inherently continuous, as in the case of the formant frequencies of the vowels. In cases of this kind there is reason to suppose that the psychological space is a continuous (and probably differentiable) deformation of the space defined by the basic physical variables [30, 31]. It is therefore understandable that, when we have recovered such a psychological space, the existence of relevant and measurable physical variables can, as in the case of the vowels, greatly facilitate the interpretation of that space.

Sometimes, however, as in the case of the consonants, we do not yet have a good hold on the relevant physical variables. Perforce, in attempting interpretations of any psychological structure that may be recovered in this latter case, we tend to fall back on the traditional "distinctive features," which (like the earlier linguistic classifications of vowels as "high" or "low" and "front" or "back") derive more from qualitative considerations of how these sounds are articulated by the speaker than from quantitative measurements of how the resulting acoustic wave actually strikes the ear of the listener. Moreover, each such distinctive feature, being merely qualitative, defines not a quantitative spacing of the consonants on some underlying continuum but only a discrete classification into two (or sometimes three) separate groups.

In cases of this type, it is not wholly obvious that the most valid psychological representation of the stimuli will be as points in a continuous space. Perhaps, instead, they should simply be represented as grouped into a certain number of discrete "clusters," each of which contains those stimuli that are most frequently confused with each other. Accordingly, we turn now to a second general type of method that does achieve a clustering representation of this general sort. In fact it divides the stimuli, not only into clusters, but also into subclusters and sub-subclusters, according to that overall hierarchical scheme that best agrees, in a certain sense, with the matrix of symmetrized confusion measures S_{ij} as a whole.

Pictorially, the recovered hierarchical clustering takes a form that is known among combinatorial mathematicians as a "rooted tree." The stimuli, instead of appearing as points in a continuous space, now appear as the discrete, terminal nodes of their associated tree. The inclusion relations among the clusters and subclusters of these stimuli are represented by the way in which the branches of the tree converge from these terminal nodes toward the base or "root."

Interestingly, one method for yielding this sort of representation was proposed over 20 years ago for application to problems of biological taxonomy [5, p. 181; 40]. However, the present exposition and results are based on a more elegant formulation and computer algorithm recently developed at Bell Laboratories by S. C. Johnson [41]. Actually, Johnson's general approach (which is based on the unifying concept of an "ultrametric") subsumes two somewhat different methods: one that constructs clusters that are in a certain well-defined sense optimally "compact," and another that constructs clusters that are in a similar sense optimally "connected" (i.e., free of gaps). Here, however, we shall be concerned with only the former ("compactness") method. So far that method has seemed to provide the most uniformly interpretable results in the analysis of data on confusions among speech sounds.

The type of tree representation recovered by this method is best explained by reference to a specific example. Figure 4.5, then, presents the structure that was recovered when Johnson's program was applied to the matrix of S-values already computed from Miller and Nicely's [33] data and presented in Table 4.1 above. The 16 consonants are listed across the top of the tree. At that level, each stimulus is regarded as constituting its own separate "cluster." But as we move down through the tree, what were previously separate clusters successively join together to form fewer, larger clusters until we finally reach the base of the tree, where all 16 stimuli have finally merged into one grand cluster.

Any horizontal section through this tree defines a particular partitioning of the 16 stimuli into a certain number of mutually exclusive and exhaustive classes. Moreover, the total system of distinct classifications obtained by taking such sections at all possible levels in the tree is necessarily strictly hierarchical in the sense that classifications can always be obtained, at any higher level, merely by splitting and, at any lower level, merely by combining the component classes or "clusters."

Figure 4.5 has been constructed such that the precise height at which any particular cluster splits into two or more branching subclusters (as indicated by the numerical scale at the left of the tree) reflects the internal cohesiveness or "strength" of that particular cluster. Trees constructed with this feature have sometimes been called "dendrograms"

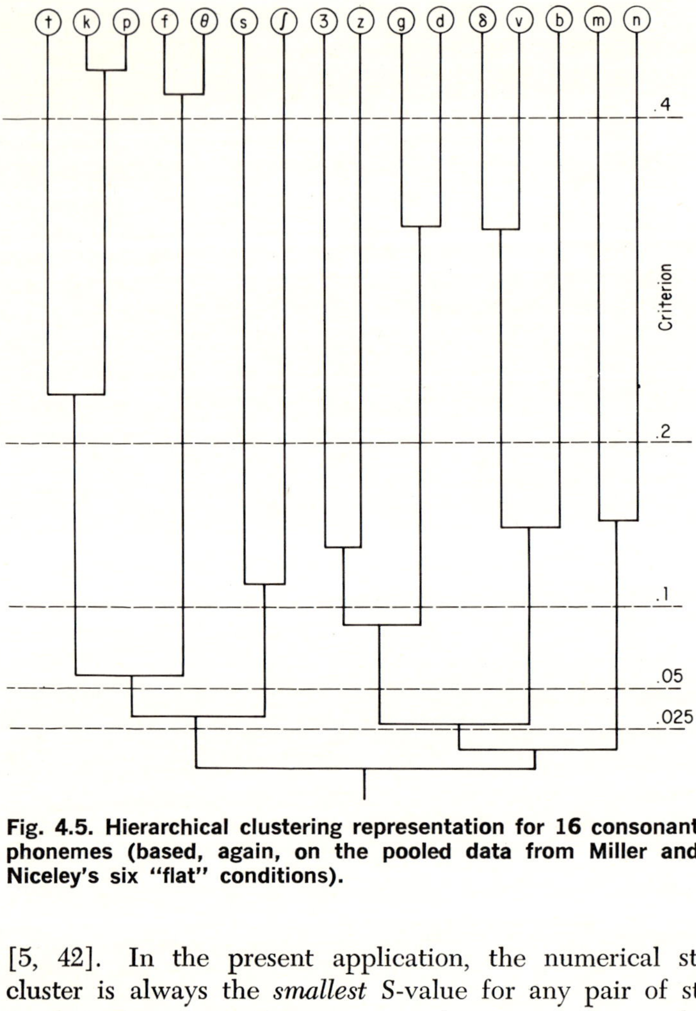

Fig. 4.5. Hierarchical clustering representation for 16 consonant phonemes (based, again, on the pooled data from Miller and Niceley's six "flat" conditions).

[5, 42]. In the present application, the numerical strength of any cluster is always the *smallest* S-value for any pair of stimuli included in that cluster. It thus corresponds, in a sense, to the weakest link holding that cluster together.

The algorithm for finding such a representation is quite simple. At each stage of the process, any two (or more) objects that are connected by the largest remaining value in the S-matrix are simply combined into a new object or "cluster." A new S-matrix is then constructed for the reduced set of objects in which the S-value connecting a new, combined object to any other object is defined to be the *smallest* of the S-values that previously connected the components of this new object to that other, external object. The process is then repeated until (after not more than $n - 1$ stages) all n of the original objects have been incorporated into one final object. The resulting overall hierarchical scheme has the property that, for the clustering defined by the horizontal section corresponding to a specified number of clusters, the within-cluster S-values are all kept above the highest possible bound. Since the S-values are inversely related to "ultrametric" distances [41], this amounts to minimizing the "diameters" of the clusters and hence to maximizing "compactness."

The resulting hierarchical clustering (as it is revealed in the topological structure of the tree) is strictly invariant under monotonic transformations of the given S-values. The numerical values of the clusters as reflected in the vertical heights of the branch points, however, do not possess this degree of invariance. Still, we usually have some confidence in more than just the rank order of the given values of S; and, to this extent these S-values can guide us in selecting particular horizontal sections through the tree. Certainly, the clustering associated with a cut (at .34 in Fig. 4.5) that just leaves /g/ and /d/ clustered while just separating /ð/ from /v/ would not be very reliable. The most stable clusterings would be those resulting from a cut (like that shown at .2) that can be moved up and down over an appreciable range without changing the clustering.

For some purposes it is convenient to plot the numerical values associated with different cuts through the tree as a function of the number of resulting clusters, as shown in Fig. 4.6. Here, the more reliable

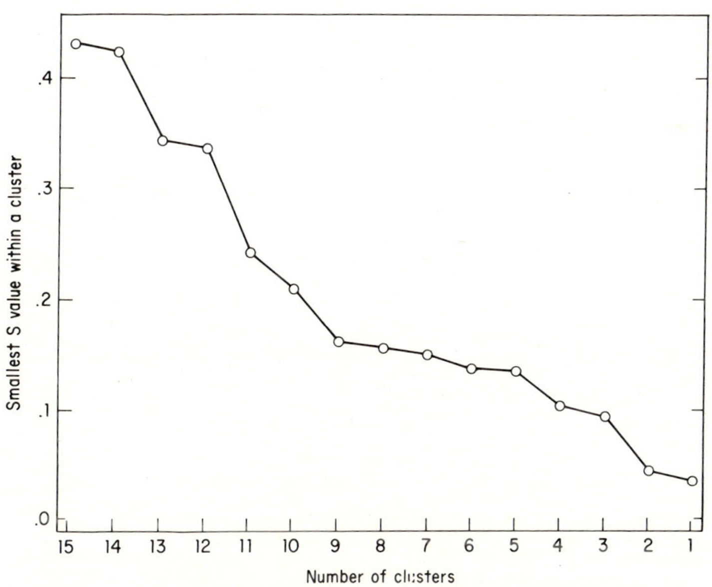

Fig. 4.6. Dependence of the smallest level of confusion within a cluster upon the number of clusters (for the pooled data from the six "flat" conditions).

clusterings correspond to points on this graph immediately followed by an abrupt drop in the curve. Thus we see, for example, that the division of the 16 consonants into 11 clusters is probably more reliable than their division into 10 clusters.

Combined Hierarchical-Spatial Representation and Its Relation to Distinctive Features

Figure 4.5, despite its radically different appearance from Fig. 4.3, actually contains much of the same information. The consonants /p/ and /k/, for example, are first to join in Fig. 4.5 and are also closest together in Fig. 4.3. Next comes the pair /f/ and /θ/ in both figures. Likewise, at a level near the bottom of the tree we find a division into the three major groups already noted in Fig. 4.3; namely, the groups /ptkfθsʃ/, /bdgvðzʒ/, and /mn/, which are distinguished solely on the basis of voicing and nasality.

That this agreement holds up throughout the whole hierarchical structure can be verified by representing that structure on top of the earlier spatial solution itself. This has been done in Fig. 4.7 by drawing closed curves around those points (of the earlier Fig. 4.3) that are grouped together by taking horizontal slices through the tree (in Fig. 4.5). In

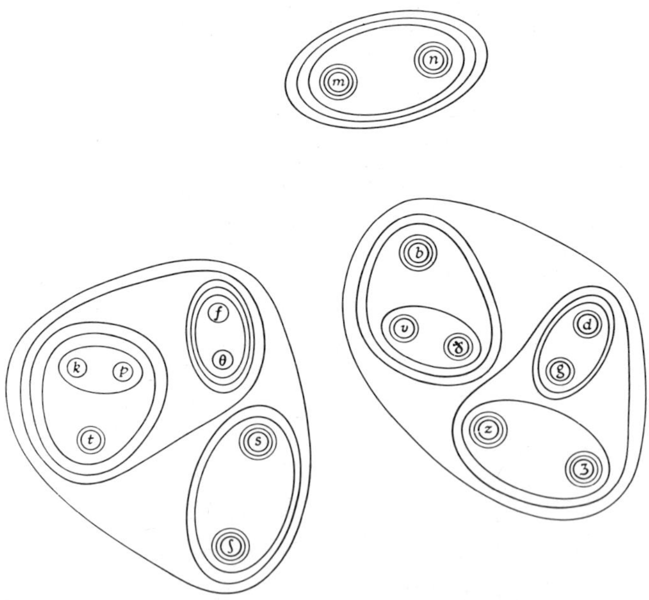

Fig. 4.7. Combined spatial and hierarchical representation (in which the hierarchical clusters of Fig. 4.5 are embedded into the spatial configuration of Fig. 4.1).

order to keep the combined figure from becoming too crowded with these added curves, the horizontal slices have been taken only at certain representative heights; specifically, at the geometrically decreasing levels .4, .2, .1, .05, and .025 (as indicated by the dashed lines in Fig. 4.5).

The lowest level (.025) divides the consonants into just the three major clusters indicated by the three outermost curves. The next level (.05) then subdivides the consonants into the five clusters indicated by the five curves just inside the earlier three. Finally, for the highest level (.4), there are 14 separate clusters indicated by the 14 innermost curves, and only the pairs /pk/ and /fθ/ still remain enclosed together. The overall agreement between the spatial representation and the hierarchical clustering consists in the fact that points that are enclosed together within more curves are generally closer together too. It is this fact, of course, that permits these curves to assume such simple, convex forms.

By embedding the hierarchical clustering scheme within the two-dimensional spatial solution in this way, we obtain a picture that seems particularly revealing of the underlying structure of the original confusion data. Certainly Fig. 4.7 is more immediately informative than the matrix of numerical data with which we began (Table 4.1). Moreover, the two types of representations that have been combined in Fig. 4.7 are to some extent complementary. The spatial representation contains some information that is not preserved in the hierarchical clustering, e.g., that within the cluster /bvð/ it is /v/ and /ð/ that are closest to the nearby cluster /zʒ/. The clustering, on the other hand, may be more readily related to other discrete classifications such as those based upon the traditional distinctive features. (Then, too, the clustering solution can serve as a partial confirmation that the spatial solution corresponds to the absolute optimum, not just to one of several merely local optima.)

An important feature of Fig. 4.7 is that it was obtained solely on the basis of the empirical data (Table 4.1). We have not, that is, provided any opportunity for theoretical preconceptions about the structure or grouping of these 16 consonants to insinuate themselves into the final picture. This approach is, in this sense, purely psychological. It differs from more *psychophysical* approaches, in which one starts with a definite preconception as to what variables are relevant and then tries to quantify the relation of the data to just these variables.

Miller and Nicely [33], in particular, began with a system of five distinctive features (voicing, nasality, affrication, duration, and place of articulation), and then analyzed their data specifically with respect to these five variables. This approach did enable them to assess the relative importance of each of these five variables in accounting for the confusion data. But as we shall see, it did not provide a very sensitive test of possible departures of their data from the structural requirements of their distinctive-feature system as a whole.

Figure 4.8 is a pictorial representation of the particular system of distinctive features considered by Miller and Nicely [33]. The three orthogonal dimensions of either the upper or the lower rectangular box are used to distinguish the consonants with respect to the three features of voicing, affrication, and place of articulation. The further feature of nasality, then, is encoded in the separation of the upper from the lower box. The final feature, duration, is not explicitly represented in the picture. It simply distinguishes the four "longer" fricatives /sʃzʒ/, at the lower front corners of the box, from the other 12 consonants. (Without this last feature there would, of course, be no basis for distinguishing /θ/ from /s/ or /ð/ from /z/.)

This particular system of distinctive features is just one of several that have been proposed for the consonants. Halle [43], for example, has advanced a system of eight features that are all purely dichotomous, while Wickelgren [44] has advocated a system of only four features that, however, can take on as many as four values on one feature (place). Nevertheless, these three systems are essentially alike in the properties that will be of primary interest here. They all distinguish the consonants in exactly the same way with respect to voicing and nasality and share the further important property of a complete structural parallelism between the unvoiced consonants /ptkfθsʃ/ and their corresponding voiced analogs /bdgvðzʒ/. That is, for each consonant

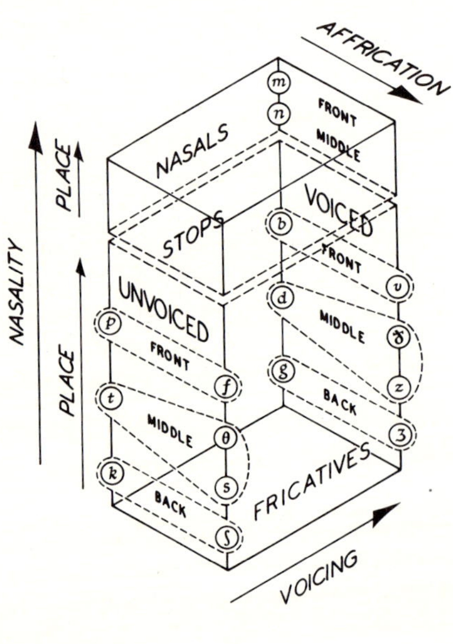

Fig. 4.8. Representation of the 16 consonants in terms of five distinctive features.

in the unvoiced group, the corresponding consonant in the voiced group has exactly the same value with respect to all features except (of course) voicing. In Fig. 4.8 this shows up in the isomorphism between the arrangement of the unvoiced and voiced consonants on their two opposing faces of the lower box.

Let us turn then to a comparison of these common properties of the various distinctive-feature systems with the independently determined empirical structure exhibited in Fig. 4.7. There is, first of all, the important agreement (already noted) between the unanimous classification of these consonants on the basis of the distinctive features of voicing and nasality and the clear-cut division of these consonants into the three major groups shown in Fig. 4.7. On the other hand, the unanimously postulated parallelism between the voiced consonants and their corresponding unvoiced consonants does *not* hold up in this figure. Instead, the unvoiced consonants tend to split into three rather strong subgroups /ptk/, /fθ/, and /sʃ/, whereas the corresponding voiced consonants tend to split, quite differently, into a strong subgroup /bvð/ and a separate group consisting of the two weakly linked subgroups /dg/ and /zʒ/. None of the proposed distinctive-feature systems appear to provide any basis for understanding why /b/ should group so strongly with /v/ and /ð/, while /p/ groups equally strongly—not with /f/ and /θ/—but with /t/ and /k/.

Of course, no evidence has yet been adduced to show that the empirical groupings exhibited in Fig. 4.7 are statistically reliable. In the ensuing sections, however, we shall find rather compelling evidence of their reality in the fact that these same groupings emerge again and again when the individual and independently collected confusion matrices reported by Miller and Nicely are analyzed separately.

We seem to have, then, an empirical basis for constructing a classificatory scheme for the consonants. In addition to its firmer foundation in data, such a scheme would come closer to representing these sounds as they are actually heard by a listener (rather than as they are thought to be articulated by a speaker). Presumably, such a listener-oriented scheme would be more useful for attempts to build automatic devices for the recognition of speech or for the compression and transmission of speech.

Effect of Variations in Signal-to-Noise Ratio

Figure 4.7 was based on the pooled data for the first six of Miller and Nicely's 17 different conditions. Since these first conditions differed only with respect to signal-to-noise ratio, it is of some interest to analyze the data for each condition separately and, thus, to determine the effect

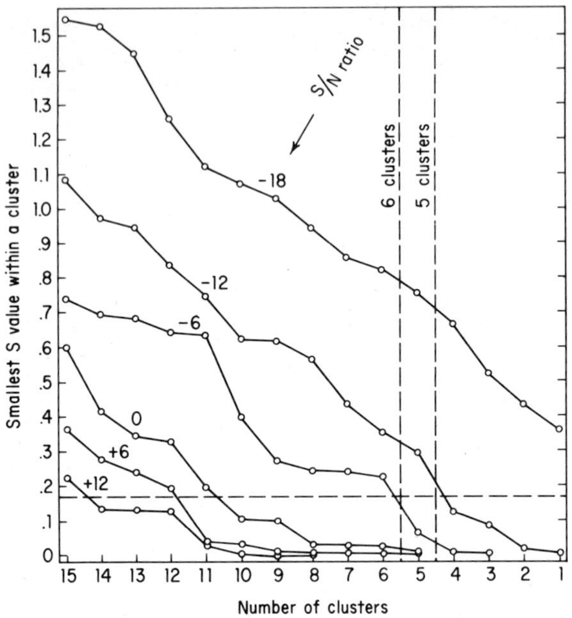

Fig. 4.9. Dependence of the smallest level of confusion within a cluster upon the number of clusters, plotted separately for each of the six "flat" conditions. (*Miller and Niceley, tables I–VI.*)

of that variable on the pattern of the resulting confusions. As a first step toward this end, Johnson's clustering algorithm was applied to a matrix of S-values (like the present Table 4.1) computed separately for each of Miller and Nicely's Tables I through VI.

Figure 4.9 includes, for each of the six resulting clustering solutions, a curve of the type previously introduced in Fig. 4.6. The curves show how the level of confusion within clusters (the smallest within-cluster S-value) decreases as the clusters are merged into fewer and fewer clusters. The signed number over each curve indicates the S/N ratio of the condition to which that curve applies. Naturally, lower S/N ratios lead to higher frequencies of confusion and hence to higher curves.

Now an informative way of looking at the clustering results is to specify some fixed level of confusion and then look at the clustering defined by the slice through each of the six trees at that specified level. For this purpose, the S-value of .17 (indicated by the horizontal dashed line in Fig. 4.9) seemed to establish a level with two desirable properties: (1) it cuts through as many of the six curves as possible, and yet (2) it cuts through each at a point of relatively abrupt decline in that curve. We can see from the figure that, at the S/N ratio of —18 dB, the curve remains above a confusion level of .17 even when we get down to a single cluster; evidently all 16 consonants are confused with each other at this level. Under the optimum condition of +12 dB, at the other extreme, we find that there are 15 different clusters that can be distinguished from each other at this level. (Only /f/ and /θ/ are still confused with an S-value of .17.)

The specified level of .17 thus defines six distinct clusterings—one for each of the six *S/N* conditions. Given a spatial representation of the consonants as 16 points in a plane, then, we can embed any or all of these six clusterings in this plane in the manner previously illustrated in Fig. 4.5. Perhaps the most reasonable spatial representation to use for this purpose is the one that was based on the combined data for all six conditions; that is, the one already presented in Figs. 4.1 and 4.5. This has been done in Fig. 4.10 where the signed number associated with a closed curve designates the *S/N* ratio of the condition upon which that curve is based. Thus for —18 dB, all 16 consonants form one confused group, as we already noted. For —12 dB, then, this group divides into five different groups that can be discriminated from each other at the specified level (.17), and so on for the higher *S/N* ratios.

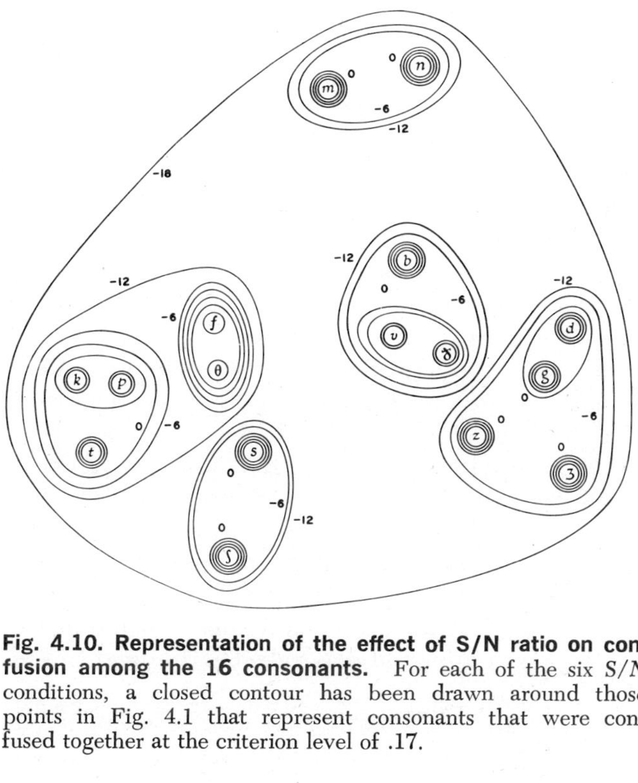

Fig. 4.10. Representation of the effect of S/N ratio on confusion among the 16 consonants. For each of the six *S/N* conditions, a closed contour has been drawn around those points in Fig. 4.1 that represent consonants that were confused together at the criterion level of .17.

This combined picture reveals a gratifying degree of consistency in Miller and Nicely's data, for in this figure the different curves (i.e., curves for different S/N ratios) are based upon independent sets of data. One consequence is that Fig. 4.10—unlike the earlier Fig. 4.7—is not necessarily constrained to a hierarchical pattern. It could, for example, happen that the cluster /fθ/ would group with the cluster /ptk/ at −12 dB, but would group with the cluster /sʃ/ at −6 dB. If this happened, Fig. 4.10 could not be constructed without one curve actually cutting across another. It is the remarkable consistency of the data obtained under the different S/N ratios that permits the curves to assume this strictly nested or hierarchical structure.

This in turn permits us to think of these curves as level curves like the elevation contours on a topographical map. Concretely, we might think of the 16 consonants as situated at the lowest points of 16 depressions in an uneven terrain. Added noise, then, might picturesquely be likened to muddy water welling up in these depressions. As we infuse more and more noise, more and more of the previously separate puddles lose their identity by merging into fewer, larger pools. At −12 dB just five separate "pools" (i.e., distinguishable sounds) are left; and at −18 dB everything has finally run together, so to speak, in one big muddy confusion.

An even more striking demonstration of the consistency of the data is afforded by taking vertical rather than horizontal cuts through the six curves in Fig. 4.9. Whereas a horizontal cut corresponds to a fixed level of confusion (or S-value), a vertical cut corresponds to a fixed number of clusters. We can, that is, move down each hierarchical tree until we find the consonants grouped into some prespecified number of clusters and then see just what those clusters are. In the present case, cuts of this sort were taken at both five and six clusters, as indicated by the two vertical dashed lines in Fig. 4.9. We shall not consider the two most extreme conditions in any detail; at +12 dB there are insufficient confusions to define a grouping into fewer than eight clusters, and at −18 dB the data are to nearly random to define *any* very stable groupings. For all four of the intermediate conditions (−12, −6, 0, +6 dB), however, the data are completely consistent. In each case the grouping into five clusters leads to exactly the *same* five clusters. These are indicated by the dashed curves in Fig. 4.11. Moreover, in all four cases, the change from five to six clusters comes about by a split of the same cluster, /ptkfθ/, into the same two subclusters, /ptk/ and /fθ/, as indicated by the solid curves in the figure. Evidently the patterns to which attention was called in the earlier Fig. 4.7 are indeed reliable.

Indeed, although the +12-dB condition did not lead to enough confusions to define fewer than eight clusters, the eight-cluster solution for that extreme condition is completely consistent with the six-cluster solutions exhibited in Fig. 4.11 and, in fact, can be derived from that six-cluster pattern merely by splitting /ʃ/ off from the cluster /sʃ/ and by splitting /ʒ/ off from the cluster /dgzʒ/. Hence, /bvð/ emerges once again as a coherent grouping. Even in the almost random data of the very noisiest, —18-dB condition, /b/ was more often confused with /v/ than with any other phoneme. This initially unexpected grouping of the voiced stop /b/ with certain voiced fricatives rather than with the other voiced stops has thus recurred, now, in each of Miller and Nicely's first six independent sets of data.

The remarkable regularity summarized in Fig. 4.11 has an interesting consequence. It suggests that, although *S/N* is a powerful determiner of overall level of confusion (as indicated in the overall heights of the curves in Fig. 4.9), it has little or no effect on the internal pattern of confusion, for over a range from —12 to +6 dB we find that the consonants that are most confused together constitute exactly the same groups; and this is true even though the absolute level of confusion associated with these groups changes over a 50-fold range from .352

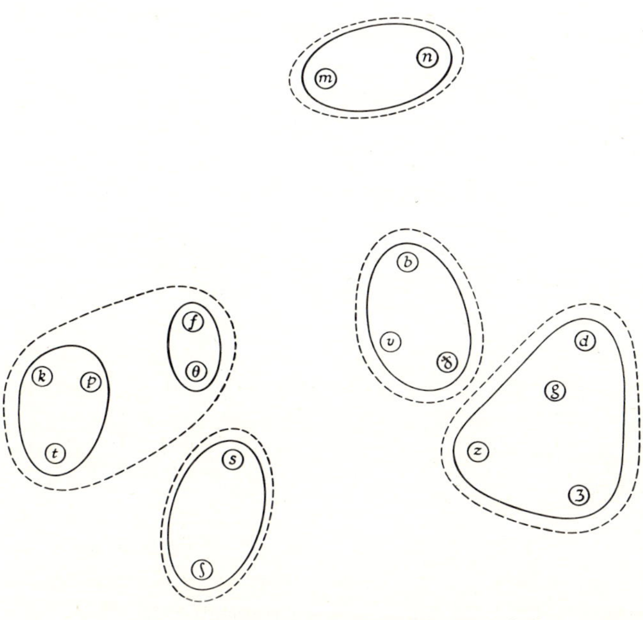

Fig. 4.11. Representation of the invariance of the pattern of confusion over different S/N ratios. The broken contours represent the five-cluster solutions and the solid contours represent the six-cluster solutions for all but the most extreme *S/N* conditions.

(for six groups at —12 dB) to .006 (for the same six groups at +6 dB). The strictly nested pattern of the contours in the earlier Fig. 4.10 (for all six S/N conditions) can of course be adduced, too, as evidence for such an invariance under wide shifts in S/N ratio.

This same invariance can also be demonstrated by obtaining a spatial solution like that already shown in Fig. 4.1—but for each of the six S/N conditions separately. For this purpose the assumed exponential relation between probability of confusion and interpoint distance has the nice property that the "slope" parameter b enters into a purely symmetric, multiplicative relation with the distances D_{ij}. Thus we are free to fix b at any arbitrary value (e.g., unity), and differences in overall level of confusion should then be accommodated merely by changes in the overall size of the resulting spatial configuration.

Essentialy, this is what in fact happened when spatial solutions were separately obtained for each of the individual matrices. For the worst (—18-dB) condition, all 16 points were crowded together in one tight little clump. With improvements in S/N, however, each consonant became perceptually more distinct or "distant" from all others, and so the 16 points spread further and further apart. During this overall expansion of scale, moreover, the relational structure (as defined by the *relative* distances among the 16 points) remained quite stable—at least until +6 or +12 dB. (At these highest S/N, the spatial solution tended to become somewhat indeterminate owing to the small number of nonzero entries in the resulting confusion matrices.)

In order to evaluate this conjectured invariance throughout the entire range of S/N ratios, we evidently need more stable estimates of the frequencies of confusion—particularly for the most dissimilar pairs at high S/N. Toward this end, the 120 pairs of consonants were partitioned into four groups on the basis of the S-measure previously computed for the average data for Miller and Nicely's Tables I through VI. The high-similarity group contained the four pairs (/pk/, /fθ/, /dg/, and /vð/) of highest average similarity ($.250 < S \leq .500$); the medium-high group contained the nine pairs of next highest similarity ($.125 < S \leq .250$); the medium-low group contained the twelve pairs of next highest similarity ($.075 < S \leq .125$); and, finally, the low group contained the remaining 95 pairs of lowest similarity ($.000 < S \leq .075$).

Figure 4.12 shows the mean S-value for each of these four groups as computed for each of the six S/N conditions separately. As is to be expected, the mean psychological similarity declines as S/N improves for all pairs (whether of high or low average similarity). However, the shapes of the curves for the four levels of average similarity are quite different, and so the invariance we are looking for is not very evident in the untransformed S-measures of confusion themselves.

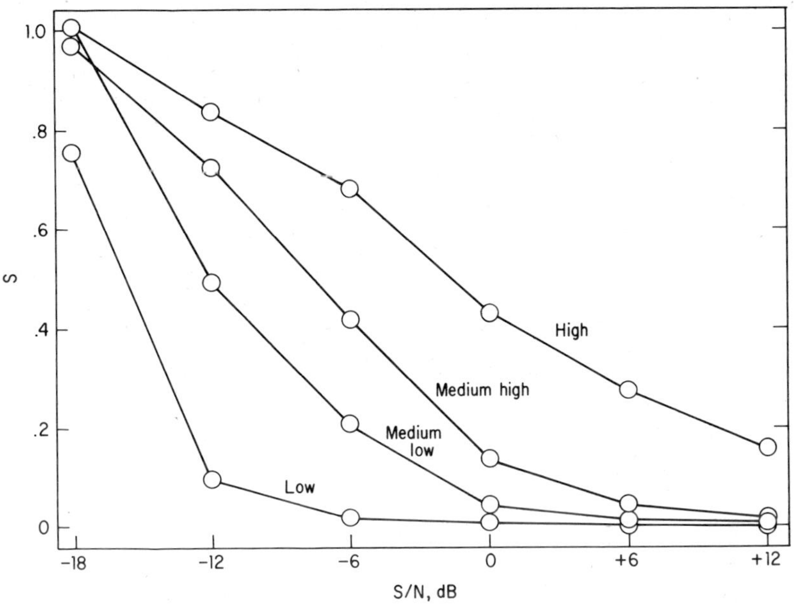

Fig. 4.12. Mean level of confusion (S) as a function of S/N ratio, for pairs of consonants of low, medium-low, medium-high, and high degrees of similarity.

The spatial model, however, suggests that the invariance should emerge in clearer form when the similarities are converted into distances. According to the exponential assumption, moreover, this is to be accomplished by applying a logarithmic transformation to the empirical S-values. In particular, since the asymptote c of the exponential will generally be greater than zero [30], the desired distance estimates should be computed as $D = -\log (S - c)$. In the present case, if we take $c = .0003$, we find the kind of invariance we are looking for. Approximately, the distances for each S/N condition then differ from the distances for any other S/N condition merely by a constant factor. Indeed, as shown in Fig. 4.13, we can then find a slightly adjusted spacing of the six S/N conditions such that, after the logarithmic transformation, the four curves which in Fig. 4.12 were highly nonlinear now radiate nearly linearly from an approximately common point (perhaps somewhat to the left of —18 dB).

We seem to have, then, a possible way of separating the intrinsic structure of the 16 consonants, which is reflected in the relational pattern of the points, and the extrinsic effect of added noise, which is primarily reflected in a compression of the overall scale of this pattern. The possibility of such a separation undoubtedly depends upon the fact that the noise added by Miller and Nicely was spectrally flat or "white." By

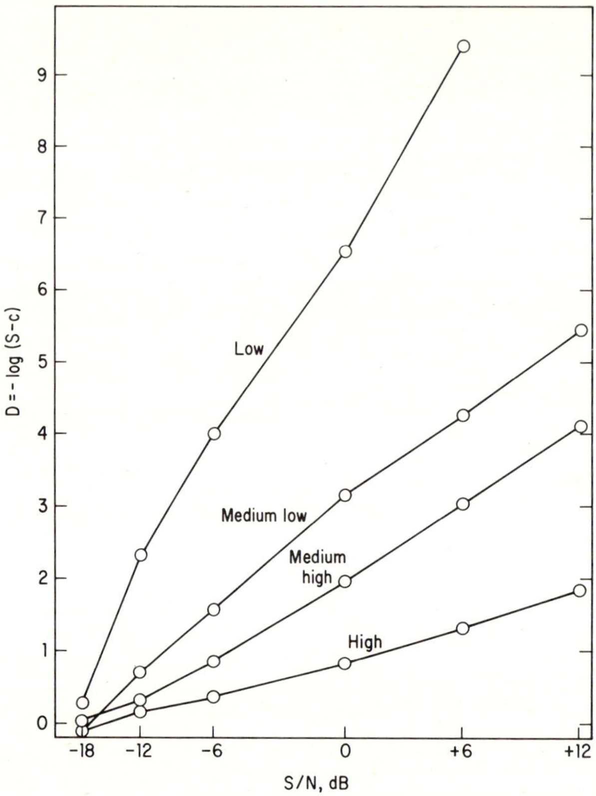

Fig. 4.13. The data of Fig. 4.12 logarithmically transformed to reveal the invariance of structure (proportionality of interconsonantal distance) over different S/N ratios.

choosing suitably band-limited noises one presumably could mask various cues or features of these sounds *differentially* [2] and thus induce nonscalar deformations of the spatial configuration.

Effects of Variations in Low-pass Filtering

The next six of the conditions reported by Miller and Nicely [33] were designed to clarify the effects of filtering out the higher frequencies. The signal-to-noise ratio (before filtering) was fixed at +12 dB, and a high-pass cutoff was maintained at 200 Hz. The low-pass cutoff, however, was varied and, in particular, took on values of 300, 400, 600, 1,200, 2,500, or 5,000 Hz (in Miller and Nicely's Tables VII through XII, in that order).

Figure 4.14 is constructed in the same manner as the earlier Fig. 4.9, but this time the number attached to each curve indicates the setting of the low-pass cutoff. As is to be expected, the overall level of confusion is higher for conditions in which more of the high frequencies have been filtered out. In order to see just how this filtering affects the pattern of confusion, a cut has again been made through these six curves at the same S-value (.17) used in Figs. 4.9 and 4.10. Fortunately, except in the case of the highest of the six curves, this cut (which is indicated by the horizontal dashed line in Fig. 4.14) again intersects each curve at a point of comparatively sharp drop.

Again as in Fig. 4.10, the spatial solution originally obtained on the basis of the first six matrices combined has been used as a framework on which to display the six clusterings that result from this specified level of confusion. The result is presented in Fig. 4.15. The picture is slightly different from that obtained before for variations only in S/N (Fig. 4.10) but, again, we find a perfect hierarchical nesting of the contours. Under the worst of these six conditions (low-pass cutoff set at only 300 Hz), only about four kinds of sounds can be discriminated at the .17 level of confusion. Under the best condition (cutoff raised to 500 Hz), as many as 14 consonants can be discriminated (and confusion at this level is now confined to just the two pairs /fθ/ and /vf/).

The fact that none of these curves are forced to cross again points to the consistency of the data. Even so, these data are not quite as homogeneous as the data from the first six conditions. In particular, there are indications of a qualitative change in the pattern of confusions

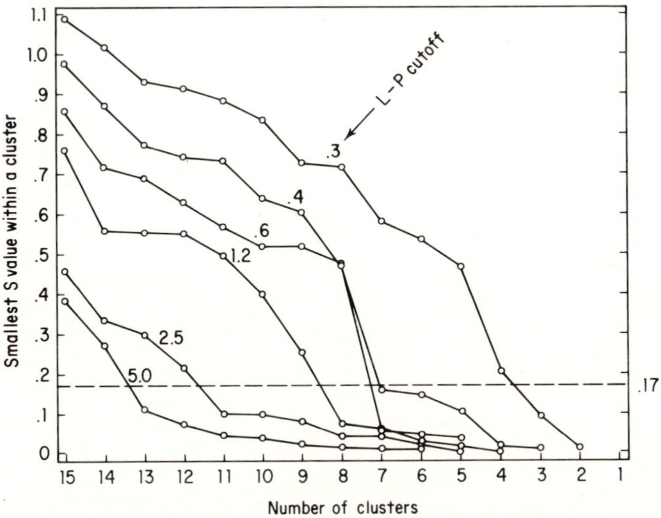

Fig. 4.14. Dependence of the smallest level of confusion within a cluster upon the number of clusters, plotted separately for each of the six low-pass conditions. (*Miller and Niceley, tables VII–XII.*)

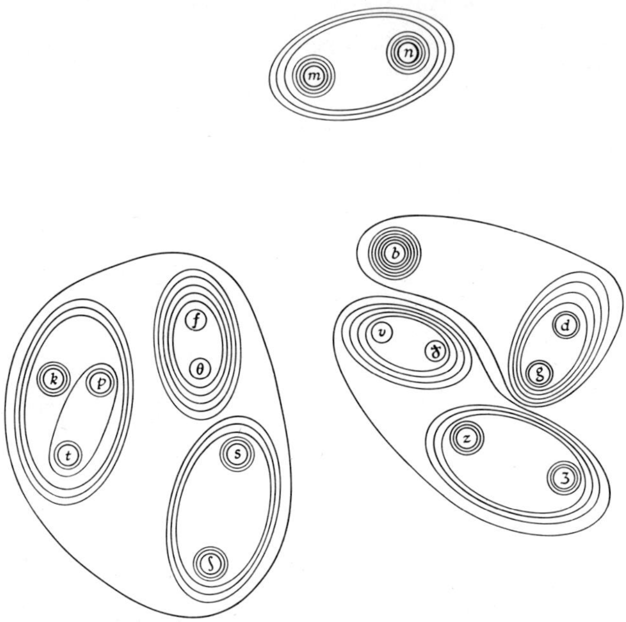

Fig. 4.15. Representation of the effect of differential filtering of high frequencies on confusions among the 16 consonants. For each of the six low-pass conditions, a closed contour has been drawn around those consonants that were confused together at the criterion level of .17.

for the condition of severest filtering—in which the low-pass cutoff is reduced to only 300 Hz. The three- and five-cluster representations for just this one condition (Miller and Nicely's Table VII) are exhibited in Fig. 4.16. (These two clustering representations both correspond to relatively sharp drops in S-value, as can be seen from the highest curve in Fig. 4.14.)

This pattern, which resulted when only the very lowest frequencies were transmitted, departs systematically from the pattern consistently obtained under all conditions of relatively "flat" transmission of frequencies (Fig. 4.11). Indeed, this lowest-frequency condition is the only one of Miller and Nicely's 17 conditions that yields a pattern in close agreement with the distinctive-feature schemes discussed earlier. As indicated by the labels added to Fig. 4.16, the clusters defined by the confusions under this one condition are precisely what we should expect on the basis of three of Miller and Nicely's distinctive features, viz., voicing, nasality, and affrication.

Of course, the spatial configuration (which was based on the six "flat" conditions) is not quite appropriate for the highly filtered condition. (This is why the clusters in Fig. 4.16 tend to be long and narrow.) If a new spatial solution is obtained for just this condition, the clusters assume the more compact form shown in Fig. 4.17. The fact that the consonants are relatively undiscriminated within each of these five inner clusters indicates that the remaining distinctive features (viz., place and duration) tend not to be preserved when all but the lowest frequencies are filtered out.

Even the remaining five of the low-pass conditions show some evidence of qualitative changes in pattern. In any event, vertical cuts (corresponding to fixed numbers of clusters) do not yield precisely the same results for all conditions (as they did for the "flat" conditions in Fig. 4.11). Still, certain of the clusters do recur in most or all of the low-pass conditions. The most ubiquitous of these are shown in Fig. 4.18. The numbers outside each contour indicate which of Miller and Nicely's conditions (VII through XII) yield that particular cluster. Thus, for example, all five of these six conditions except VII led to the cluster /bvð/, which has already been put forward as something of a puzzle for traditional distinctive-feature schemes.

Generally, the pattern resulting from low-pass filtering is remarkably like the pattern resulting from the addition of broadband noise (Fig. 4.11). (Indeed the only notable difference seems to be that /f/ and

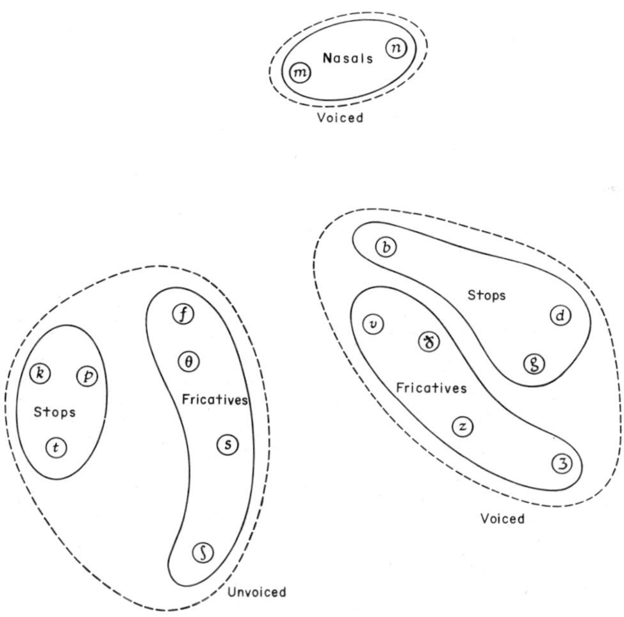

Fig. 4.16. The three-cluster and five-cluster representations for the condition in which only the lowest frequencies were passed (embedded, again, in the spatial configuration of Fig. 4.1).

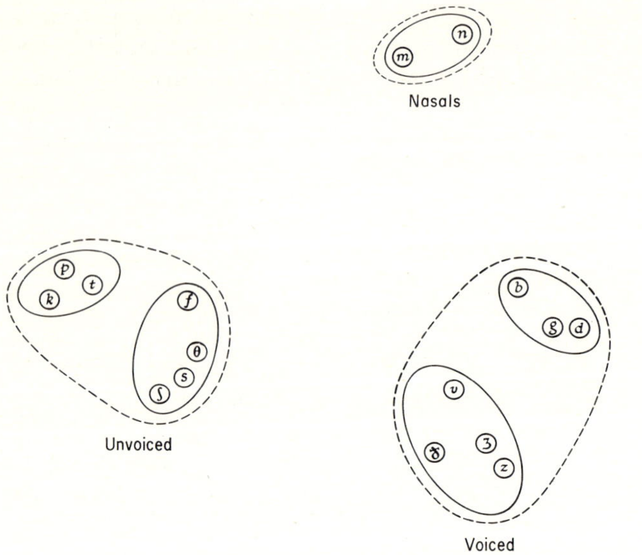

Fig. 4.17. The three-cluster and five-cluster representations of Fig. 4.16 reembedded in a new two-dimensional spatial representation based just upon the data from the condition in which only the lowest frequencies were passed.

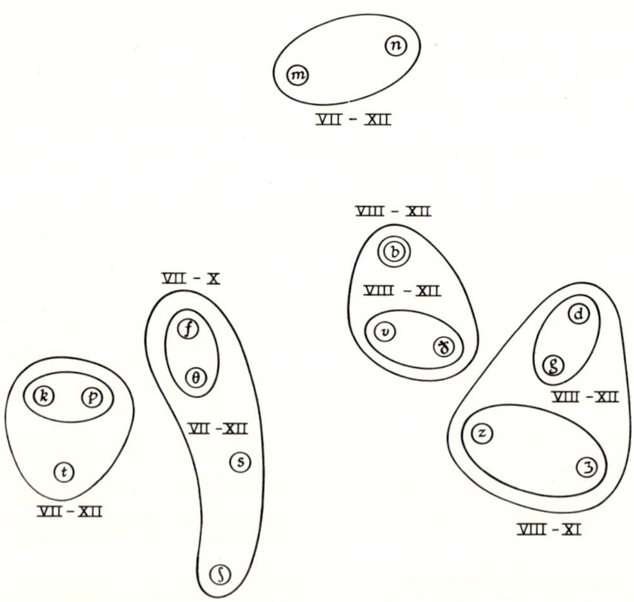

Fig. 4.18. Recurrent clusterings in the low-pass conditions (embedded, again, in the configuration of Fig. 4.1).

/θ/ group with the unvoiced stops /ptk/ in the "flat" conditions but with the other unvoiced fricatives /sʃ/ in the low-pass conditions.) Miller and Nicely also noticed the overall resemblance in the two patterns of confusion and attributed it to the relatively greater susceptibility of the high frequencies to masking by white noise [33, p. 350]. Such a differential effect of white noise needs, however, to be reconciled with the remarkable invariance in pattern already noted with changes in *S/N*.

Effects of Variations in High-pass Filtering

The five remaining conditions studied by Miller and Nicely are concerned with the effects of filtering out just the lower frequencies. Again the signal-to-noise ratio (before filtering) was fixed at +12 dB. But this time a low-pass cutoff was maintained at 5,000 Hz, while a high-pass cutoff took on values of 1,000, 2,000, 2,500, 3,000, and 4,500 Hz (in Miller and Nicely's Tables XIII through XVII, in that order).

Figure 4.19 shows the five resulting curves of the type displayed before (in Figs. 4.9 and 4.14). As expected, the overall level of confusion generally increases with the frequency of the high-pass cutoff. A horizontal cut has also been made through these curves at the S-value selected before (viz., .17). Conveniently, this again intersects most of the curves at a point of relatively steep decline.

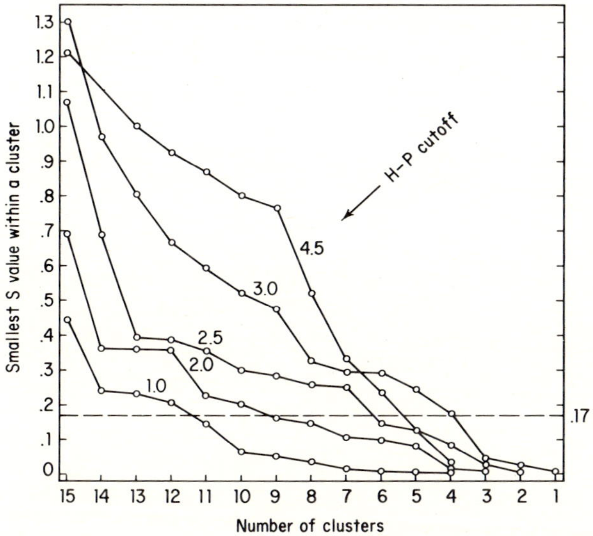

Fig. 4.19. Dependence of the smallest level of confusion within a cluster upon the number of clusters, plotted separately for each of the five high-pass conditions. (*Miller and Niceley, tables XIII–XVII.*)

In Fig. 4.20, as before, the spatial solution that was originally based upon the pooled data for the first six conditions has been used as a framework on which to display the clusterings corresponding to the .17 cut through Fig. 4.19. The contours for the least severely filtered condition (Miller and Nicely's Table XIII) are not included in the figure. Generally, these omitted contours would fall inside the others. However, as might be expected, the pattern for this nearly "flat" condition departs somewhat from the pattern for the remaining, more severely filtered conditions. At the .17 level of S, this discrepancy is confined entirely to the occurrence of the two clusters /fθ/ and /ðz/ in this relatively unfiltered condition.

With the exception of this one condition, however, Fig. 4.20 shows that the contours for the high-pass conditions form a hierarchically nested set. The pattern that thus consistently emerges for these high-pass conditions nevertheless differs radically from the patterns noted earlier for the flat conditions (Fig. 4.10) and the low-pass conditions (Fig. 4.15). This is further indicated by the most recurrent clusters, which are represented in Fig. 4.21 in the same manner as in the earlier Fig. 4.18.

Regarding these high-pass conditions, Miller and Nicely remark that

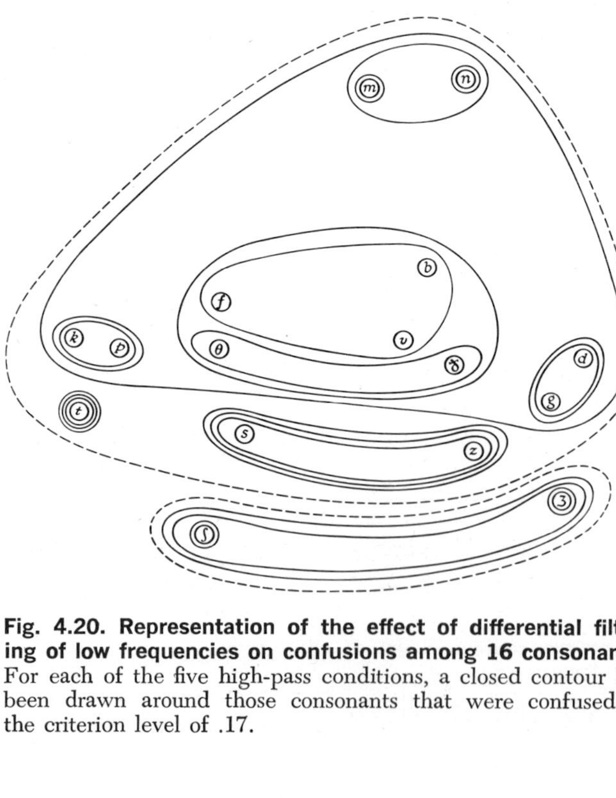

Fig. 4.20. Representation of the effect of differential filtering of low frequencies on confusions among 16 consonants. For each of the five high-pass conditions, a closed contour has been drawn around those consonants that were confused at the criterion level of .17.

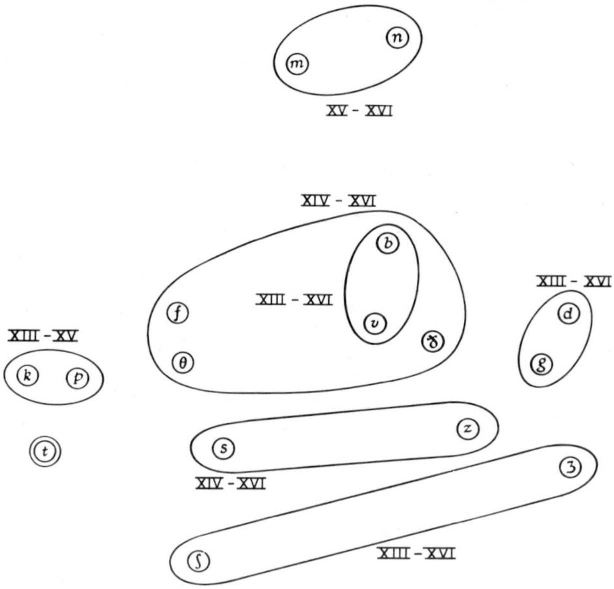

Fig. 4.21. Recurrent clusterings in the high-pass conditions.

"the errors do not cluster or fall into obvious patterns in the confusion matrix, but seem to distribute almost randomly over the matrix" [33, p. 350]. However, the present Figs. 4.20 and 4.21 do seem to reveal some definite structure in these data. Roughly speaking, we might say that, under the high-pass conditions, it is those consonants that are separated horizontally in the figure that are most confused (e.g., /s/ and /z/ or /ʃ/ and /ʒ/ in Fig. 4.21). Under the most extreme low-pass condition, on the other hand, the prevalent confusions tended to run in a roughly vertical direction (e.g., between /f/ and /ʃ/ or between /v/ and /ʒ/ in Fig. 4.16). Thus we are led to the crude interpretative conjecture that the vertical and horizontal dimensions of this space have, in part, to do with discriminations among high frequencies and among low frequencies, respectively.

Now voicing has been largely identified with the laryngeal injection of low-frequency energy. So it is not surprising that, after the low frequencies have been filtered out, the distinction of voicing is all but lost for the fricatives (as shown by the strong pairings /θð/, /sz/, and /ʃʒ/ in Fig. 4.20). Note, however, that this distinction of voicing is relatively much less dependent upon the presence of low frequencies in the case of the stops. Here, then, we seem to find a further departure from the kind of symmetry or parallelism that one tends to expect on the basis of the traditional systems of distinctive features. Moreover, we see (in Fig. 4.21) that whereas the unvoiced stops tend, as before, to group together (particularly /p/ and /k/), the voiced stop /b/ persists in its closer association with the voiced fricatives (particularly /v/).

Actually, of course, the difficulty in accounting for these aspects of the patterns in terms of distinctive features arises only to the extent that we suppose, with Miller and Niceley [33, p. 348], that "the features were perceived almost independently of one another" and, also, that just these five features were operative. The absence of parallelism in the structure of the voiced and unvoiced consonants (Figs. 4.11, 4.18, and 4.21) could, for example, be explained by assuming, instead, that whether the fricative-*vs.*-stop distinction or the place and duration distinctions take precedence critically depends upon whether the consonants are unvoiced or voiced, respectively (cf. Fig. 4.8). Likewise, the pattern in Figs. 4.20 and 4.21 could be explained by supposing simply that the salience of the voicing distinction depends strongly upon whether the consonants are stops or fricatives. The attractiveness of an account of the confusion data in terms of distinctive features is, however, somewhat reduced by the necessity of invoking such interactive complications. Perhaps the simplest and most plausible way of explaining both of these seeming anomalies in the confusion data is the one suggested by Savin [45], in which we invoke—instead of interactions among these five distinctive features—an additional, *sixth* distinctive feature, aspiration, that arises only in the case of the three syllables /pa/, /ta/, and /ka/. Such a feature would certainly account for the persistent grouping of the unvoiced stops /ptk/ even when there is no parallel grouping of the voiced stops /bdg/. At the same time, since aspiration is represented in the higher frequencies, it would account for the tendency of the unvoiced stops /ptk/ to remain distinct from the voiced stops /bdg/ even when the unvoiced fricatives /fθsʃ/ are no longer discriminated from their corresponding voiced fricatives /vðzʒ/.

In any case, the point should now be clear that it is potentially limiting to conduct one's analysis solely within the framework of any one particular a priori framework of distinctive features. Sometimes it may prove illuminating to take, as an alternative starting point, a natural grouping of the consonants (e.g., as in Fig. 4.11) determined a posteriori, purely by analysis of the empirical data.

Judged Similarities among Consonants and Their Relation to Confusion Data

So far here, we have exclusively considered, as a measure of psychological similarity, the frequency with which phonemes are actually confused with each other by human listeners. It is of course also possible to ask listeners to attempt direct subjective estimates of the similarities of pairs of stimuli. Indeed, such an experiment has been done by Peters [19] using, as stimuli, the same 16 consonants studied by Miller and Nicely. Accordingly, some comparisons can now be made between the patterns we have noted in the confusion data reported by Miller and Nicely and whatever pattern may emerge from the judgmental data subsequently collected by Peters.

In the experiment of interest here, Peters had each subject pronounce each pair of consonants aloud and then rate the pair on a nine-point scale ranging from 1 for "extreme similarity" to 9 for "extreme dissimilarity." Each consonant was pronounced as followed by the vowel /ʌ/. Thus the subject would pronounce one of the 120 possible pairs, say /pʌ-tʌ/, and then write down a number from 1 to 9 to indicate the apparent similarity (or dissimilarity) of the two consonants (e.g., /p/ and /t/). It may be a significant aspect of this procedure that the subject can respond to the consonants not merely as a listener (as in Miller and Nicely's experiments) but as a speaker as well.

For purposes of overall comparison, Johnson's [41] clustering algorithm was applied to the matrix of similarity estimates obtained simply be averaging over all nine of Peters' subjects.* Also, the spatial solution originally obtained on the basis of Miller and Nicely's "flat" conditions (Fig. 4.1) is again used to display the resulting clusters. The most salient of these have been included in Fig. 4.22. In this case many widely separated points (like /t/ and /d/) are grouped together as pairs. In order to simplify the picture such high-similarity pairs have simply been connected by a single heavy line (rather than enclosed in a surrounding curve, as before).

At the level of four clusters, we find the consonants neatly grouped into the stops /p,t,k,b,d,g/, the sibilants /s,ʃ,z,ʒ/, the remaining fricatives /f,θ,v,ð/, and the two nasals /m,n/. Then, at the level of eight clusters, we find that every voiced consonant is simply paired with its unvoiced counterpart, except for the two voiced nasals which (as in all earlier solutions) remain grouped with each other. As the greatly elongated representations of these groupings attest, the pattern here bears little resemblance to those found in the confusion data (except, perhaps, for the conditions of high-pass filtering, which did lead to such a horizontal elongation in the case of the fricatives—but not the stops).

This marked disparity between the similarity and confusion data is of some interest—particularly since earlier comparisons between the two types of data with other types of stimuli have not revealed any such

* Peters' published report does not include the matrices of data upon which his analyses were based. I am grateful to him for generously making these available to me and thus permitting me to carry out the further analysis reported here.

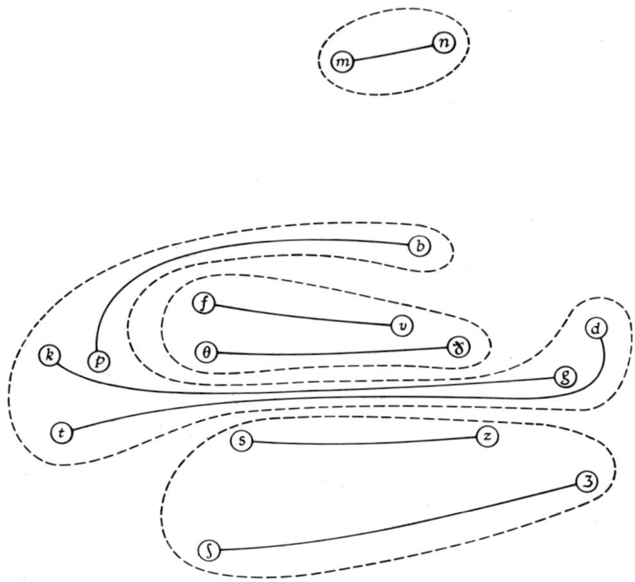

Fig. 4.22. Clusterings according to Peters' data on judged similarity of consonant phonemes.

discrepancy (e.g., Ref. 12, p. 515). In the present instance, the discrepancy may in part be due to the difference, already noted, between responding purely as listener and responding as speaker. However, a somewhat different, more cognitive hypothesis also suggests itself.

First, however, with regard to distinctive features, Peters [19, p. 1989] concluded from his analysis of these data, "In general phonemes are first sorted according to manner; voicing is next in importance, and place, for some individuals, is also important." The simplest interpretation of the very strong pairings evident in Fig. 4.22, however, seems to be that the feature of voicing was, more than any other feature, suppressed or ignored by these subjects. This is curious in view of the fact that the confusion data clearly show voicing (and, probably, nasality) to be the most easily discriminated of the distinctive features (Fig. 4.1).

One hypothesis that might explain this apparent suppression of the usually salient feature of voicing in the judgmental task is that Peters' subjects treated this task as an analogy task rather than a pure similarity task. As an illustration of the kind of possibility being suggested here, consider the 12 visual stimuli displayed in Fig. 4.23. Now the difference between the black and the white figures shown is probably at least as salient or discriminable as the differences among the various shapes. Yet subjects who are asked to judge the similarities among these figures might be most impressed by the parallelism between the structure of the set of black figures and the structure of the set of white figures. The fact, that is, that each black figure has a perfect analog among the white figures might lead them to discount the obvious difference in color between the two parallel sets and simply report that the black triangle is most like the white triangle, and so on for the other shapes.

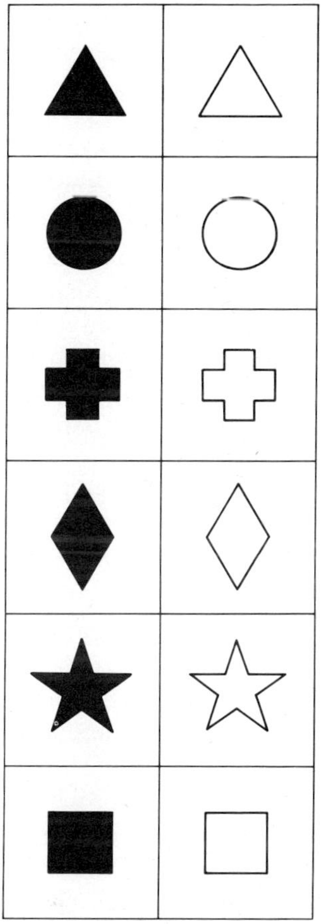

Fig. 4.23. Twelve geometrical stimuli illustrating an implicit analogical structure.

There is, of course, no certainty that Peters' subjects treated voicing in the way the hypothetical subjects were just supposed to have treated color. Still, the parallelism in the distinctive-feature structure of the voiced and unvoiced consonants was probably apparent to Peters' subjects. At least half of his subjects had had some training in phonetics and, since the distinctive-feature schemes are based primarily upon the way the consonants are articulated, the fact that the subjects pronounced the phonemes themselves might tend to focus their attention on the distinctive-feature structure of these phonemes.

In any case, the disparity between the patterns observed in the two kinds of data argues for considerable caution in generalizing from subjective judgments of similarity to the confusions actually made by listeners. Moreover, the speculations as to the possible reason for the observed disparity suggests that similarity judgments may be quite sensitive to the particular types of instructions and training given to the subjects. The primary advantage of subjective judgments of similarity, in the present connection, is that they can be collected more rapidly than comparably stable confusion data. But they also have the disadvantage that their relation to the basic processes underlying the identification of speech sounds is, as we have seen, more tenuous and uncertain.

Conclusions

1. Computer algorithms of considerable elegance and power are now available for converting patterns hidden in large arrays of empirical data into a graphical form that is much more readily interpreted by the human investigator.

2. Speech sounds, in particular, can be represented as points in a Euclidean space in such a way that the frequency with which any two phonemes are confused is, to a close approximation, a simple exponential decay function of the distance between the two corresponding points (Figs. 4.2 and 4.4).

3. Moreover, a computer algorithm designed to find the spatial configuration that provides the best (exponential) account of given confusion data can provide useful information about the dimensions or features of the phonemes that underlie the recognition of these speech sounds by human listeners. Since the spatial representation is based solely upon the given confusion data, nothing need be known or assumed about the number or nature of the relevant physical dimensions of the phonemes. In short, the psychological data are allowed to speak for themselves.

4. Applications of this new method to the data of Peterson and Barney [34] and of Miller and Nicely [33] provided further support for their earlier conclusions that the recognition of phonemes is heavily dependent upon the frequencies of the first three formants in the case of the vowels, and upon the features of voicing, nasality, and (to a lesser extent) affrication in the case of the consonants (Figs. 4.1 and 4.3).

5. Although the identification of a consonant has been thought to require discriminations along as many as five different dimensions, 99.4 percent of the variance in the confusion data can in fact be accounted for on the basis of just two underlying dimensions (Figs. 4.1 and 4.2).

6. With respect to such a two-dimensional representation obtained on the basis of the broadband or "flat" conditions, the confusions under the extreme high-pass conditions (Fig. 4.21) tended to extend across the space at right angles to the confusions under the extreme low-pass condition (Fig. 4.16). Hence the two dimensions of the spatial representation may be at least roughly interpreted as reflecting discriminations among high and low frequencies, respectively.

7. Further insight can be gained by embedding, within the spatial representation, a hierarchical clustering of the kind Sørensen [40] originally proposed for use in biological taxonomy and Johnson [41] recently supplied with an elegant mathematical rationale and computational algorithm. Closed curves are drawn around subsets of points that form natural clusters in the sense that all pairs of phonemes within each cluster exceed some criterion level of confusion (Fig. 4.7).

8. As signal-to-noise ratio ranged from —18 to +12 dB in Miller and Nicely's experiment, the overall level of confusion also changed enormously; but the recurrence of the same clusterings at each S/N level indicated that the internal *pattern* of the confusions was essentially invariant (Figs. 4.10 and 4.11). Indeed, with respect to the spatial

representation, the effect of adding a given amount of white noise seemed to be almost entirely confined to a reduction of all interpoint distances by the same, constant factor (Fig. 4.13).

9. The recurrent clusterings reveal a highly reliable difference in structure between the unvoiced consonants and corresponding voiced consonants. In particular, whereas /p/ always groups with the other unvoiced stops /t/ and /k/, /b/ groups—not with the other voiced stops /d/ and /g/—but with the voiced fricative /v/ (in 15 out of Miller and Nicely's 17 conditions) and also /ð/ (in 13 of these 15 conditions).

10. Selective removal of the high frequencies did not have much effect on the pattern of confusions until the high-frequency cutoff was lowered to 300 Hz. Above that point the only reliable difference appeared to be the tendency for /f/ and /θ/ to group with the other unvoiced fricatives /s/ and /ʃ/ rather than (as in the broadband conditions) with the unvoiced stops /p/, /t/, and /k/ (Fig. 4.18). However, when only the frequencies below 300 Hz were passed, the pattern of confusions among the voiced consonants shifted so that, for the first and only time, /b/ grouped with the other voiced stops /d/ and /g/ (Fig. 4.16).

11. Selective removal of the low frequencies, on the other hand, produced a drastic alteration in the pattern of confusions as soon as the low-frequency cutoff was raised as high as 1,000 Hz. When only the frequencies above 1,000 Hz were passed, the distinction between voiced and unvoiced consonants was largely lost for the fricatives but, interestingly, was preserved for the stops (Figs. 4.20 and 4.21).

12. The present findings of a lack of parallelism between the voiced and unvoiced consonants (see point 9, above) and between the stops and fricatives (see point 11, above) complicate attempts to account for the confusion data in terms of the traditional "distinctive feature" schemes unless, perhaps, we include the additional distinctive feature of aspiration in order to distinguish /p/, /t/, and /k/ from the other consonants.

13. Direct judgments of similarity obtained by Peters [19] for all pairs of the same 16 consonants conform to a pattern that departs radically from the patterns consistently found in the confusion data of Miller and Nicely. The fact that Peters' subjects evidently judged each unvoiced consonant to be most similar to its voiced counterpart (Fig. 4.22) suggests that certain cognitive processes (e.g., analogical reasoning) may intervene in such judgmental tasks to alter the pattern from that found in the frequencies with which listeners actually confuse these phonemes.

14. Information gained in these ways about the patterns underlying human confusions among speech sounds may prove useful for engineers

concerned with the development of devices for mechanical recognition or for compression and efficient transmission of speech.

15. Finally, the methods for extracting underlying structure, applied here primarily to data on auditory confusions among individual phonemes, may also be applicable to other quite different problems in communication science and technology. Some of the problems that currently look amenable to this approach are the following: a parallel study of visual confusions among printed letters or numbers [46, p. 90]; the study of semantic or associative structure [47, 48, 49], syntactic structure [50, 51], or, perhaps, the use of such structures for information storage and retrieval (e.g., Ref. 52); the explication of the relations among different languages [4, 53]; and the development of techniques for evaluation of the subjective quality of speech transmitted over different types of circuits [54, 55].

In the five years since this paper was completed, many of the possibilities for application of these methods that were only suggested in the references listed here have been explored much more extensively. However none of the subsequently published reports appears to alter any of the results or conclusions presented in this chapter. There has been one important methodological development that is directly related to the material presented here. This is the perfection, by my former colleague J. D. Carroll, of a powerful new method for the simultaneous analysis of multiple matrices of the sort considered here [56] and, further, the instructive application of this new method to these very data by Carroll's present colleague, M. Wish [57]. By means of Carroll's new method, Wish has been able to obtain a spatial representation for the 16 consonant phonemes with six distinct dimensions, which he has interpreted as "voiced versus voiceless," "nasality," "sibilant versus nonsibilant," "sibilant frequency," "voiceless stops versus voiceless fricatives," and "second formant transition after voiced consonants." His results, though consistent with the findings presented here, help to bring out some aspects of the underlying patterns in the data in an especially clearcut form.

REFERENCES

1. J.-J. Chang and R. N. Shepard, Exponential Fitting in the Proximity Analysis of Confusion Matrices, paper presented at the annual meeting of the Eastern Psychological Association, New York, April 14, 1966.
2. J. M. Pickett, Perception of Vowels Heard in Noise of Various Spectra, *J. Acoust. Soc. of Am.,* **29:**613–620 (1957).
3. J. M. Pickett, Perception of Compound Consonants, *Language Speech,* **1:**288–304 (1958).

4. C. D. Chretien, Word Distributions in Southeastern Papua, *Language,* **32**:88–108 (1956).
5. R. R. Sokal and P. H. A. Sneath, "Principles of Numerical Taxonomy," W. H. Freeman, San Francisco, 1963.
6. B. Julesz, Visual Texture Discrimination, *IRE Trans. Inform. Theory,* **IT-8**:84–92 (1962).
7. L. L. Thurstone, "Multiple Factor Analysis," University of Chicago Press, Chicago, 1947.
8. H. H. Harman, "Modern Factor Analysis," University of Chicago Press, Chicago, 1960.
9. W. S. Torgerson, Multidimensional Scaling: I. Theory and Method, *Psychometrika,* **17**:401–419 (1952).
10. C. H. Coombs, "A Theory of Data," John Wiley & Sons, Inc., New York, 1964.
11. G. Ekman, A Direct Method for Multidimensional Scaling, *Psychometrika,* **28**:33–41 (1963).
12. R. N. Shepard, Stimulus and Response Generalization: Tests of a Model Relating Generalization to Distance in Psychological Space, *J. Exptl. Psychol.,* **55**:509–523 (1958).
13. W. S. Torgerson, "Theory and Methods of Scaling," John Wiley & Sons, Inc., New York, 1958.
14. J. H. Greenberg and J. J. Jenkins, Studies in the Psychological Correlates of the Sound System of American English, *Word,* **20** (2) (1964).
15. G. Hanson, "Phoneme Perception," Almqvist & Wiksell, Upsala, 1962.
16. G. Hanson, A Factorial Investigation of Speech Sound Perception, *Scand. J. Psychol.,* **4**:123–128 (1963).
17. G. Hanson, A Further Factorial Investigation of Speech Sound Perception, *Scand. J. Psychol.* **5**:117–122 (1964).
18. R. W. Peters, Research on Psychological Parameters of Sound, *WADD Tech. Rept.* 60-249, Wright Air Development Division, Wright-Patterson Air Force Base, Ohio, 1960.
19. R. W. Peters, Dimensions of Perception of Consonants, *J. Acoust. Soc. Am.,* **35**:1985–1989 (1963).
20. K. V. Wilson, Multidimensional Analyses of Confusions of English Consonants, *Am. J. Psychol.,* **76**:89–95 (1963).
21. R. N. Shepard, The Analysis of Proximities: Multidimensional Scaling with an Unknown Distance Function, I, *Psychometrika,* **27**:125–140 (1962).
22. R. N. Shepard, The Analysis of Proximities: Multidimensional Scaling with an Unknown Distance Function, II, *Psychometrika,* **27**:219–246 (1962).
23. R. N. Shepard, Analysis of Proximities as a Technique for the Study of Information Processing in Man, *Human Factors,* **5**:33–48 (1963).
24. J. B. Kruskal, Multidimensional Scaling by Optimizing Goodness of Fit to a Nonmetric Hypothesis, *Psychometrika,* **29**:1–27 (1964).
25. J. B. Kruskal, Nonmetric Multidimensional Scaling: A Numerical Method, *Psychometrika,* **29**:115–129 (1964).
26. R. N. Shepard, Metric Structures in Ordinal Data, *J. Math. Psychol.,* **3**:287–315 (1966).
27. E. T. Klemmer and N. W. Shrimpton, Preference Scaling via a Modification of Shepard's Proximity Analysis Method, *Human Factors,* **5**:163–168 (1963).
28. R. N. Shepard, Polynominal Fitting in the Analysis of Proximities, *Proc. 17th Intern. Congr. Psychol.,* pp. 345–346, North Holland Publishing Co., Amsterdam, 1964. (Abstract)

29. R. N. Shepard, Stimulus and Response Generalization During Paired-associates Learning, unpublished doctoral dissertation, Yale University, 1955.
30. R. N. Shepard, Stimulus and Response Generalization: A Stochastic Model Relating Generalization to Distance in Psychological Space, *Psychometrika,* **22:**325–345 (1957).
31. R. N. Shepard, Stimulus and Response Generalization: Deduction of the Generalization Gradient from a Trace Model, *Psychol. Rev.,* **65:**242–256 (1958).
32. R. N. Shepard, Similarity of Stimuli and Metric Properties of Behavioral Data, in H. Gulliksen and S. Messick (eds.), "Phychological Scaling, Theory and Applications," pp. 33–43, John Wiley & Sons, Inc., New York, 1960.
33. G. A. Miller and P. E. Nicely, An Analysis of Perceptual Confusions among some English Consonants, *J. Acoust. Soc. Am.,* **27:**338–352 (1955).
34. G. E. Peterson and H. L. Barney, Control Methods Used in a Study of the Vowels, *J. Acoust. Soc. Am.,* **24:**175–184 (1952).
35. R. W. Peters, Dimensions of Quality for the Vowel [æ], *J. Speech Hearing Res.,* **6:**239–248 (1963).
36. J. D. Carroll and J.-J. Chang, A General Index of Nonlinear Correlation and Its Application to the Interpretation of Multidimensional Scaling Solutions, *Am. Psychologist,* **19:**540 (1964). (Abstract)
37. J. E. Miller, R. N. Shepard, and J.-J. Chang, An Analytic Approach to the Interpretation of Multidimensional Scaling Solutions, *Am. Psychologist,* **19:**579–580 (1964). (Abstract)
38. M. Joos, Acoustic Phonetics, supplement to *Language* (Monograph No. 23), **24:**1–136 (1948).
39. R. K. Potter and G. E. Peterson, The Representation of Vowels and Their Movements, *J. Acoust. Soc. Am.,* **20:**528–535 (1948).
40. T. Sørensen, A Method of Establishing Groups of Equal Amplitude in Plant Sociology Based on Similarity of Species Content and Its Application to Analyses of the Vegetation on Danish Commons, *Biol. Skrifter,* **5**(4):1–34 (1948).
41. S. C. Johnson, Hierarchical Clustering Schemes, *Psychometrika.* 32:241–254 (1967).
42. E. Mayr, E. G. Linsley, and R. L. Usinger, "Methods and Principles of Systematic Zoology," McGraw-Hill Book Company, New York, 1953.
43. M. Halle, On the Bases of Phonology, in J. A. Fodor and J. J. Katz (eds.), "The Structure of Language," pp. 324–333, Prentice-Hall, Englewood Cliffs, N.J., 1964.
44. W. A. Wickelgren, Distinctive Features and Errors in Short-term Memory for English Vowels, *J. Acoust. Soc. Am.,* **38:**583–588 (1965).
45. Harris Savin, personal communication.
46. E. J. Gibson, "Principles of Perceptual Learning and Development," Appleton-Century-Crofts, New York, 1969.
47. R. N. Shepard, Multidimensional Scaling of Concepts Based upon Sequences of Restricted Associative Responses, *Am. Psychologist,* **12:**440–441 (1957). (Abstract)
48. J. Deese, "The Structure of Associations in Language and Thought," The John Hopkins Press, Baltimore, Md., 1965.
49. C. E. Osgood, G. J. Suci, and P. H. Tannenbaum, "The Measurement of Meaning," University of Illinois Press, Urbana, Ill., 1957.
50. E. R. Gammon, On Representing Syntactic Structure, *Language,* **39:**369–397 (1963).
51. W. J. M. Levelt, A Scaling Approach to the Study of Syntactic Relations, in

G. B. Flores d'Arcais and W. J. M. Levelt (eds.), "Advances in Psycholinguistics," North Holland Publishing Co., Amsterdam, 1970.

52. C. Watson, Computer Generation of Word Association Maps for Man-Machine Communication, *System Development Corporation Rept.* SP-1153, March 25, 1963.
53. E. R. Gammon, personal communication.
54. B. J. McDermott, Multidimensional Analyses of Circuit Quality Judgments, *J. Acoust. Soc. Am.*, **45**:774–781 (1969).
55. V. McGee, Semantic Components of the Quality of Processed Speech, *J. Speech Hearing Res.*, **7**:310–323 (1964).
56. J. D. Carroll and J.-J. Chang, Analysis of Individual Differences in Multidimensional Scaling via an N-Way Generalization of Eckart-Young Decomposition, *Psychometrika*, **35**:283–319 (1970).
57. M. Wish and J. D. Carroll, Multidimensional Scaling with Differential Weighting of Dimensions, in D. A. Kendall, R. C. Hodson, and D. Tautu (eds.), *Mathematics in the Archaeological and Historical Sciences*, Edinburgh University Press, pp. 150–167, 1971.

CHAPTER FIVE

Decision Theory, Signal-detection Theory, and Psychophysics

H. LEVITT*

Introduction

In recent years, the concepts and techniques of decision theory have come to play an increasingly important role in psychophysics. The development of decision-theory models of sensory perception was initiated by comparisons of human signal detection with predictions from signal-detection theory. In retrospect, it is not surprising that these comparisons were made. The need to determine practical methods of signal detection in radar led engineers to compare the human observer with powerful electronic and statistical detectors, thereby discovering the relatively high efficiency of the human observer [1–3]. It was largely through the work of Peterson, Birdsall, and Fox [4] and Tanner and Swets [5], however, that the concept of modeling the human observer in terms of an analogous statistical detector was developed. Since then much experimental evidence has been gathered in support of this

* Formerly with Bell Laboratories, Murray Hill, New Jersey.

notion, and the use of decision-theory models in psychophysics is now widespread.

To an experimenter, the evolution of new theories of sensory perception poses perplexing questions. In order to measure, it is necessary to have an appropriate model of the system under study. How accurate are the various models that have been proposed? Unfortunately, earlier reviews of decision-theory models have been highly partisan, either enthusiastically in support of the theory or wholly opposed to it. One purpose of this chapter is to provide a balanced, critical review of the topic. A second aim is to provide a unified treatment of decision-theory models and to show the effect of the separate assumptions underlying different models. A third aim is to present a brief overview of the major results and to place the contributions of the decision-theory approach in perspective with other developments in psychophysics.

The chapter has been structured in keeping with the above three aims. Section 5.1 contains a brief description of the theory, Sec. 5.2 consists of a critical review of the experimental evidence,* and Sec. 5.3 contains a summary of the major conclusions. The description of the theory is intended to be brief, particularly in those areas that have been treated extensively elsewhere. Some detail, however, has been devoted to points which have not received adequate treatment in the published literature. For an excellent basic account of the theory see Swets [6, sec. 1], Green and Swets [7], and Clarke and Bilger [8]. See also Treisman and Watts [9] and Wickelgren [10] for treatments from a slightly different point of view. This review is concerned primarily with the role of decision theory and signal-detection theory in the modeling of human signal detection. The application of the theory in other areas such as learning or speech perception, for example, is not considered, although much of the material may be pertinent.

5.1 The Decision Process

5.1.1 Testing Statistical Hypotheses

Consider the *simple* hypothesis-testing situation. It is assumed that an observed event is the result of one of two mutually exclusive causes (or concomitant states of nature). The task of the observer is to decide which of the two possible causes could more reasonably have given rise to the observed event. In most signal-detection experiments the "event" is an observation of finite duration of a waveform produced by one of two possible processes, noise alone (N) or signal plus noise (SN). The source of the noise can be either external (i.e., applied

* As available to the author at the time of writing, July 1968.

with the signal) or internal (generated within the observer), or a combination of both. It is assumed that for each of the two states, N or SN, there is a fixed probability law governing the distribution of observations. One of the two alternatives is postulated as the true state of nature (the *null hypothesis* H_0). The observer is required to decide on the available evidence whether the null hypothesis H_0 is true or false. If false, the *alternative hypothesis* H_1 is accepted.

In signal-detection work the null hypothesis is usually that the observed event is due to noise alone. There are four possible outcomes to an experiment of this type:

1. *Hit:* true state is SN, observer rejects H_0 (i.e., correctly states that signal is present).
2. *False alarm:* true state is N, observer rejects H_0 (i.e., incorrectly states that signal is present).
3. *Miss:* true state is SN, observer accepts H_0 (i.e., incorrectly states that signal is absent).
4. *Correct rejection:* true state is N, observer accepts H_0 (i.e., correctly states that signal is absent).

Owing to the random nature of the observations it is not possible for the observer to decide correctly on every trial. It is possible, however, for the observer to adopt a decision rule which, on the average, will tend to produce a reasonably high proportion of correct responses. Since there are two types of errors (misses and false alarms), the most appropriate decision rule depends on the relative penalties for each type of error. The specification of relative penalties is known as the *payoff matrix.* Whereas it may be possible for the observer to reduce the probability of a false alarm, this is usually done at the expense of reducing the probability of a hit. The curve relating the probability of a hit to the probability of a false alarm (Fig. 5.1) is known as the *receiver operating characteristic* (ROC) or *isosensitivity curve* [11] and provides a convenient method of specifying an observer's performance. The "best" operating point on a given ROC curve is a matter of definition. One very common definition is the stipulation that, given the payoff matrix and the a priori probability of a signal being present, the expected loss per trial be minimized.

If the observer guesses at random but maintains a fixed proportion of *SN* responses, then the resulting operating point will fall on the positive diagonal (Fig. 5.1). Changing the proportion of *SN* responses moves the operating point to another location on the diagonal. This process is referred to as *biased guessing.* An observer can, of course, do worse than biased guessing by using a relatively good decision rule and then reversing his decisions, e.g., responding "SN" when the decision rule specifies an "N" response. An ROC curve generated in this way

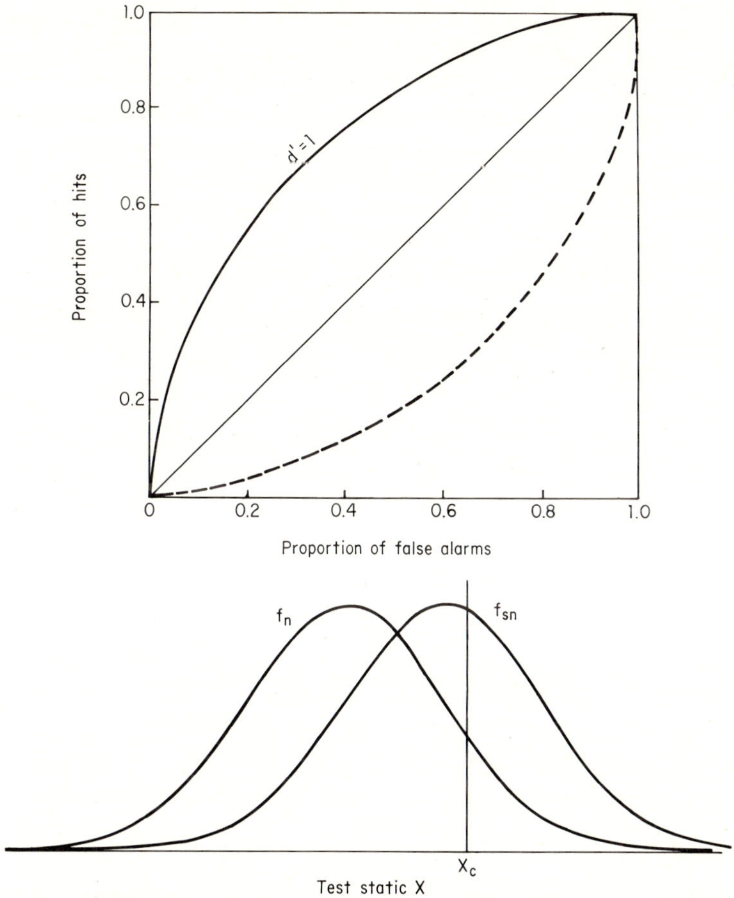

Fig. 5.1. Receiver Operating Characteristic—Single-criterion Model. The lower part of the figure shows the canonical f_n and f_{sn} distributions. The decision rule is to respond "signal present" whenever the test statistic exceeds the criterion X_c. By varying the location of X_c on the decision axis, the solid ROC curve shown in the upper part of the figure is generated. In this diagram the f_n and f_{sn} distributions are normal, of equal variance, and differ in location by one standard deviation. If the decision rule is reversed, i.e., a "no signal" response is given whenever the test statistic exceeds X_c, then the dashed ROC curve is generated. The positive diagonal corresponds to the operating characteristic that is obtained with random, biased guessing.

will lie below the positive diagonal, as shown by the dashed curve of Fig. 5.1. Obviously, the better the observer's performance, the higher the ROC curve is above the positive diagonal.

The relative performance of two or more observers (or the relative detectability of different signals for a given observer) may be gauged by comparing their respective ROC curves. It is sometimes more convenient to specify an observer's performance approximately, in terms of a single index, rather than exactly, in terms of an entire curve. One possibility is to use the area under the ROC curve as a measure of detectability [7]. Other measures of detectability are defined in terms of specific models and are discussed later.

5.1.2 Several Decision Rules

There are many possible decision rules which an observer may employ, "optimum" or otherwise. In modeling human detection it is exceedingly useful to have as a basis a simple, generalized procedure which, by suitable choice of parameters, is equivalent to most decision procedures of practical interest. One such procedure is the *single-criterion* rule described below. It is important to bear in mind that the human observer is being modeled in terms of an equivalent statistical detector. That is, although it is not known exactly how the human observer makes decisions, it is possible to specify a mathematically concise model which, on average, provides essentially the same responses as the human observer.

5.1.2.1 Single-criterion Rule

The information obtained during a given observation interval is reduced in some way to a single number, referred to as the *test statistic.* Methods for deriving the test statistic are discussed shortly. For simple hypothesis testing there are two possible probability distributions for the test statistic, f_n and f_{sn}, depending on whether the observation is of noise alone (N) or of signal plus noise (SN), respectively. The decision rule is for the observer to accept the null hypothesis (i.e., respond "N") whenever the test statistic falls below a critical value X_c, referred to as the *criterion,* and to reject the null hypothesis if the test statistic exceeds X_c. Using this decision rule, the area under f_{sn} to the right of X_c (see Fig. 5.1) is the probability of a hit and the area under f_n to the right of X_c is the probability of a false alarm. The ROC curve may thus be generated by varying the criterion X_c over the entire range of X and plotting the probability of a hit against that of a false alarm.

An important property of the single-criterion rule is that, provided the ROC curve is monotonic (i.e., an increase in the false-alarm rate is always accompanied by an increase in the hit rate), then two probability distributions f_n and f_{sn} can always be derived which will generate the specified ROC curve. There is, however, an infinite number of f_n and f_{sn} distributions which will satisfy these conditions and, to eliminate ambiguity, a further restriction may be imposed. Typically, the f_n distribution is given a convenient mathematical form. For example, f_n

may be defined to be normal with zero mean and unit variance. The f_n and f_{sn} distributions are then both uniquely defined and are referred to as *canonical* distributions, being the simplest or most convenient distributions for generating a given ROC curve.

A common measure of detectability d' is defined in terms of the single-criterion model and is equal to the distance between the means of the f_n and f_{sn} distributions divided by the standard deviation of the f_n distribution. Another parameter of interest is the ratio of the standard deviations of the two distributions (i.e., $r = \sigma_n/\sigma_{sn}$). If the canonical distributions are both normal, then the ROC curve plotted on normal-normal probability paper (see Fig. 5.7) is a straight line with slope equal to σ_n/σ_{sn}. It has also been proposed that twice the value of the abscissa (in transformed coordinates) at the point of intersection between the ROC curve and the negative diagonal be used as a measure of detectability [12]. This measure is commonly referred to as d'_e or d_s. A discussion of these and other measures of detectability is contained in Green and Swets [7, chap. 4].

5.1.2.2 Fixed Criterion Plus Biased Responses*

According to this rule the criterion remains fixed throughout, but the hit and false-alarm rates can nevertheless be varied by introducing a response bias. If, for example, the observer is motivated to increase the hit rate (e.g., the payoff matrix may favor hits) he does so by responding SN for a proportion u of those trials (chosen at random) which would otherwise have been N decisions. As u is varied from 0 to 1 both the hit and false alarm rates increase proportionately, as shown by the upper limb of the solid ROC curve in Fig. 5.2. If the observer wishes to decrease the hit rate below P_0 he does so by responding N for a proportion v of those decisions which would otherwise have been SN. As v is varied from 0 to 1 the lower limb of the solid ROC curve in Fig. 5.2 is generated. The point at which the two limbs meet represents the operating point with no response bias present. Such an ROC curve could, of course, be generated by the previously described single-criterion model having rectangular canonical distributions of the form shown in the lower part of Fig. 5.2. The values of $X_{\max}$ $X_{\min}$ are chosen arbitrarily. A characteristic feature of these distributions is the existence of a discontinuity in at least one of the distributions corresponding to the join point (p_0,P_0) in the ROC curve. A very special case is that in which $p_0 = 0$, that is, the false-alarm rate is zero if there is no response bias. An ROC curve of this type is shown by the dashed

* The decision rule described here is based on Luce's [13] two-state threshold model.

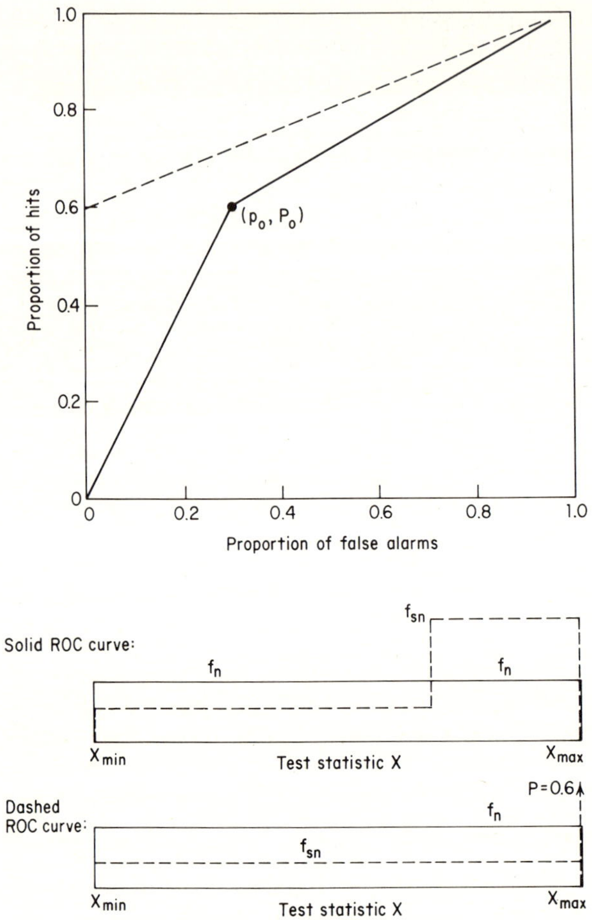

Fig. 5.2. Receiver Operating Characteristics—Fixed Threshold plus Biased Responses. If X_c is fixed, the observer can nevertheless adjust the hit and false-alarm rates by manipulating the response mechanism; e.g., if the payoff matrix strongly favors hits over false alarms then a proportion of the "no signal" responses is reversed to "signal present" responses. If the payoff matrix favors a low false-alarm rate, then the bias is reversed and a proportion of the "signal present" responses is reversed. The ROC curve generated in this way consists of two straight-line segments. The join point (p_0,P_0) corresponds to the operating point with no biased responses. If $p_0 = 0$, as in the high-threshold model, the resulting ROC curve is a single straight line. Rectangular canonical distributions for the equivalent single-criterion models are shown in the lower part of the figure. The maximum and minimum values of X are chosen arbitrarily.

line of Fig. 5.2. The corresponding canonical distributions for the single-criterion rule are shown at the bottom of the figure. Note that in this case the f_{sn} distribution contains a dirac pulse, the area under which is equal to the probability of a hit when the probability of a false alarm is zero.

5.1.2.3 Single-criterion Rule with Random Fluctuations

In certain situations the criterion selected by the observer may be subject to random fluctuations beyond the observer's control. For example, on trial j with X_j as the test statistic, the criterion used by the observer may be $X_{cj} = \bar{X}_c + e_j$, where $\bar{X}_c$ is the expected value of the criterion and e_j is a random variable.

The effect of variability in X_{cj} on the observer's performance may be illustrated by considering the simple case where $e_j = +\Delta X$ on a proportion q of the trials and $e_j = -\Delta X$ on the remaining $(1-q)$ trials. Let the ROC curve obtained with $e_j = 0$ be that shown in Fig. 5.3. Point A represents the operating point for the criterion $\bar{X}_c + \Delta X$, B represents the operating point for the criterion $\bar{X}_c - \Delta X$. If responses based on a criterion of $\bar{X}_c + \Delta X$ are combined with responses based on a criterion of $\bar{X}_c - \Delta X$, the resulting operating point will fall on the straight line joining A and B. In particular, if the criterion $\bar{X}_c + \Delta X$ is used as often as $\bar{X}_c - \Delta X$, i.e., $q = 0.5$, then the operating point will fall midway between A and B, as shown by point C. It may be noted that if the ROC curve is convex upwards, the effect of randomly mixing two or more criteria results in poorer performance, i.e., the straight line AB lies below that section of the ROC curve joining A and B.

The preceding example considers the case in which the distribution of e_j is binomial. For the general case, where $g(e)$ is the probability distribution of e_j, the effect of the random fluctuation in X_{cj} may be evaluated by assuming a fixed criterion $\bar{X}_c$ and using $X_j - e_j$ rather than X_j as the test statistic on trial j. If e_j and X_j are statistically independent, the canonical distributions of $X_j - e_j$ may be obtained from the convolution of $g(-e)$ with f_n and f_{sn}, respectively. In general, the variances of these new distributions will be greater than the respective variances of f_n and f_{sn}, but the variance ratio will be closer to unity.* An analysis of the fluctuating-criterion model is given by Smith and Wilson [14] and by Wickelgren [10] for the case where e_j is normally distributed.

* The variances of the new canonical distributions are $\sigma_n^2 + \sigma_e^2$ and $\sigma_{sn}^2 + \sigma_e^2$, respectively, where σ_e^2 is the variance of $g(e)$. It is easily shown that

$$\left|1 - \frac{\sigma_n^2}{\sigma_{sn}^2}\right| > \left|1 - \frac{\sigma_n^2 + \sigma_e^2}{\sigma_{sn}^2 + \sigma_e^2}\right|.$$

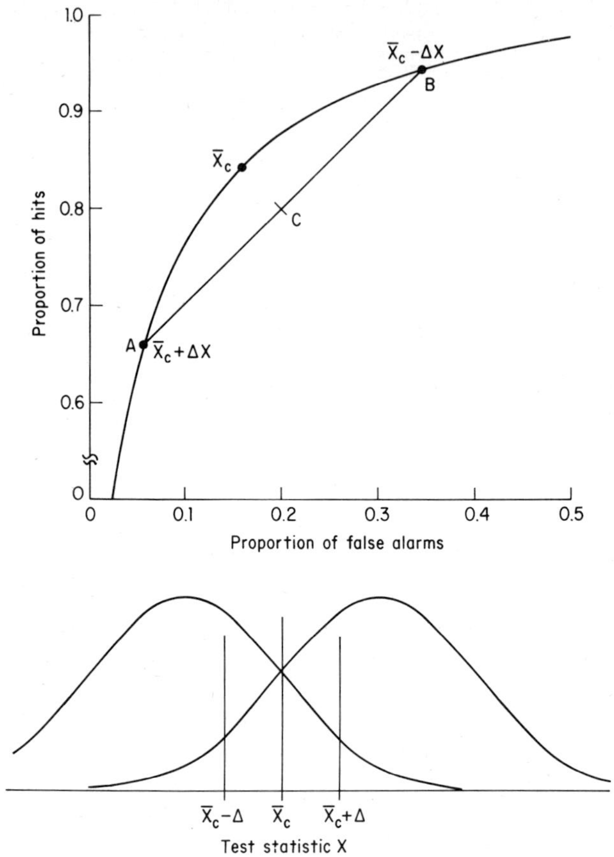

Fig. 5.3. Derivation of Equivalent Operating Point for Fluctuating Criterion. The criterion on trial j is assumed to be $X_{cj} = \bar{X}_c + e_j$, where $\bar{X}_c$ is the expected value of the criterion and e_j is a random variable. In this example, e_j is assumed to be binary, i.e., e_j equals $+\Delta X$ on a proportion q trials and $-\Delta X$ on the remaining $(1 - q)$ trials. A is the operating point for $\bar{X}_c + \Delta X$, i.e., for $q = 1$; B is the operating point for $\bar{X}_c - \Delta X$, i.e., for $q = 0$. The operating point for any other value of q lies on the straight line joining A and B. The operating point C corresponds to $q = 0.5$. If the ROC curve generated by the fixed-criterion model is convex upward, then the equivalent operating point for a fluctuating criterion lies below this curve.

One consequence of the random fluctuations in $\bar{X}_c + e_j$ is that the curve relating the probability of rejecting the null hypothesis to the value of the test statistic is not a step function at X_c, as originally postulated, but an ogive which is the cumulative distribution of $\bar{X}_c + e_j$. Although not of direct interest in the discussion to follow, it may be noted that certain learning effects may be accounted for by allowing this ogive to vary systematically as a function of feedback or reinforcement. The interrelationship between detection theory and mathematical learning theory is discussed in Atkinson, Bower, and Crothers [15] and Lee [16].

5.1.2.4 Dual-criterion Rule

Under certain circumstances the observer can improve his performance over the single-criterion rule by using a dual criterion. For example, consider the case where the canonical f_n and f_{sn} distributions are both normal, but differ in location and variance. Figure 5.4 shows a pair of such distributions where $\sigma_{sn}/\sigma_n = 1.5$ and $d' = 0.2$. The ROC curve generated by the single-criterion rule is shown by curve A. Note that at high false-alarm rates the curve falls below the positive diagonal, indicating that the observer could do better in this region simply by biased guessing (i.e., guessing at random but maintaining a high proportion of SN responses).

Much better performance can be obtained, however, if the observer uses a dual criterion. That is, two separate criteria are chosen, X_{c_1} and X_{c_2}. If the test statistic either exceeds X_{c_2} or is less than X_{c_1}, the decision is SN; if the test statistic lies between X_{c_1} and X_{c_2}, the decision is N.

A particularly good strategy for choosing X_{c_1} and X_{c_2} is to introduce the restriction that the ratio of f_{sn}/f_n is the same at both X_{c_1} and X_{c_2}. Thus for every choice of X_{c_1} a value of X_{c_2} is uniquely defined. By varying X_{c_1} and X_{c_2} over their entire range and maintaining the restriction of a common ratio for f_{sn}/f_n, the receiver operating characteristic has the form shown by curve B in Fig. 5.4. Note that this curve is uniformly higher than the ROC curve generated by the single-criterion rule. Since X_{c_1} and X_{c_2} are functionally dependent, it is possible to define a new test statistic which incorporates the restriction that the ratio f_{sn}/f_n is the same at both X_{c_1} and X_{c_2}. A convenient way of doing this is to use the ratio f_{sn}/f_n as the test statistic, although any monotonic transformation of this ratio will do. Thus for any observation X_i there corresponds a specific value to the ratio f_{sn}/f_n, referred to as L_i, and which like X_i is a random variable specified by one of two probability distributions depending on whether the observation was of signal plus noise or noise alone. Figure 5.5 shows two such distributions of L_i corresponding to the X_i distributions of Fig. 5.4. The criterion in this case is defined as L_c, and by varying L_c over its entire range ($L_{\min}$ to ∞) the upper ROC shown in Fig. 5.4 is generated. $L_{\min}$ is the lowest value of the ratio f_{sn}/f_n and is dependent on the specific distributions and parameter values assumed for f_n and f_{sn}.

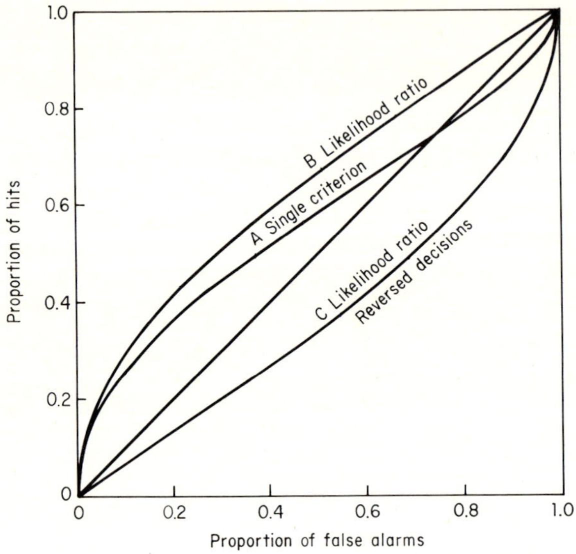

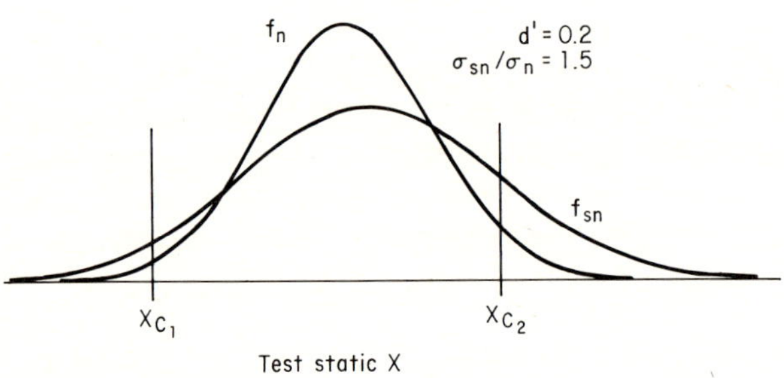

Fig. 5.4. Dual-criterion Model. The canonical f_n and f_{sn} distributions are normal, but of unequal variance ($d' = 0.2$; $\sigma_{sn}/\sigma_n = 1.5$). The resutling ROC curve generated by the single-criterion model is uniformly lower than that which could be generated by a dual-criterion model. At high false-alarm rates, in particular, the single-criterion ROC curve falls below the positive diagonal, indicating that better performance could be obtained in this region by biased guessing. The best possible performance is obtained by using a dual-criterion model subject to the constraint that f_{sn}/f_n is the same at both X_{c_1} and X_{c_2}. This model is equivalent to using a single-criterion model with likelihood ratio as the test statistic.

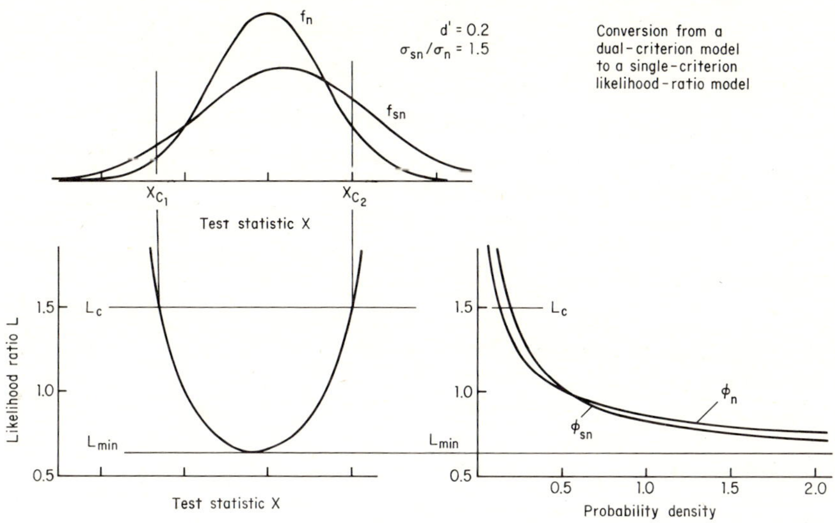

Fig. 5.5. Relation Between Dual-criterion Model and Likelihood-ratio Criterion. The upper left-hand section of the diagram shows the canonical f_n and f_{sn} distributions for a dual-criterion model. The distributions are both normal with $d' = 0.2$ and $\sigma_{sn}/\sigma_n = 1.5$. The lower left-hand section shows the relation between the likelihood-ratio L $(= f_{sn}/f_n)$ and the test statistic X. The probability distributions of L corresponding to f_n and f_{sn}, respectively, are shown in the bottom right-hand section. Note that the criterion L_c is the value of the likelihood ratio at both X_{c_1} and X_{c_2}.

Thus far, the test statistic L_i has been treated as no more than a number computed from the observed X_i. The algebraic manipulation, however, requires a knowledge of the two distributions governing the X_i. In statistical terms, the ratio f_{sn}/f_n is known as the *likelihood ratio** and has very special properties, as discussed in the next section.

5.1.3 Derivation of the Test Statistic

In principle, any combination of the observed data can be used as a test statistic. The detection performance of the observer is, of course, critically dependent on how the test statistic is derived. It can be shown, for example, that if the likelihood ratio is used as the test statistic (the single-criterion rule is implied) then the hit rate at any given false-alarm rate will be either equal to or better than that obtained by any other decision rule [17]. This important result, however, holds only for simple hypothesis testing, i.e., deciding on one of two alternatives.

An example of a likelihood ratio was given in the preceding section

* The likelihood of an event may be thought of as the probability which can be assigned to that event on the assumption a given hypothesis is true.

in which the observation X_i was a single number. The observation could, of course, be a vector **X**, in which case the probability distribution of **X** is multidimensional. However, since both the numerator and denominator of the likelihood ratio are obtained by integrating over the same incremental volume in multidimensional space, the ratio always reduces to a single number and is independent of the dimensionality of **X**.

Since the likelihood ratio L, like any other test statistic, is computed from the data, it is itself a random variable and is distributed according to one of two possible probability laws depending on whether the observation was of noise only or signal plus noise. It is thus possible to compute the likelihood ratio of L, yielding the quantity LL which is itself a random variable and which in turn may be used as the test statistic. The process can be repeated *ad infinitum.* However, it should be apparent that nothing can be gained by this process, since the likelihood of an observation cannot be changed by any amount of algebraic manipulation and hence the likelihood ratio L cannot be any different from the likelihood ratio LL. The reader may ascertain this relationship numerically from Fig. 5.5; the likelihood ratio ϕ_{sn}/ϕ_n at any value of L should equal L. As Green and Swets [7] have aptly put it, "The likelihood ratio of the likelihood ratio is the likelihood ratio." A proof of this result may be found in Birdsall [18].

The ROC curve generated with the likelihood ratio as the test statistic has several important properties. The curve represents an upper limit of performance which cannot be exceeded on the average. Random-sampling errors, however, will lead to observed operating points lying either just above or just below this curve. Conversely, the mirror image of this curve (Fig. 5.4, curve C), obtained by reversing decisions, represents a lower limit of average performance. The area between curves B and C represents the region of attainable performance. The slope of the single-criterion ROC curve at any point is equal to f_{sn}/f_n at the criterion corresponding to that point. If f_{sn}/f_n is used as the test statistic, then the slope and the criterion are equal. As a result, the slope of the likelihood-ratio ROC curve always decreases monotonically with false-alarm rate.

The computation of the likelihood ratio is not always a simple matter, nor is it necessarily the most appropriate test statistic to assume in modeling human detection. Of great practical interest are those test statistics which are either easy to compute or which reflect some physical property of the stimulus but which nevertheless give rise to reasonably good performance. A good example of such is the use of short-term energy as the test statistic [19]. Another approach is to use an appropriate physiological quantity as the test statistic. FitzHugh [20], for example, uses as the test statistic the number of impulses during a critical

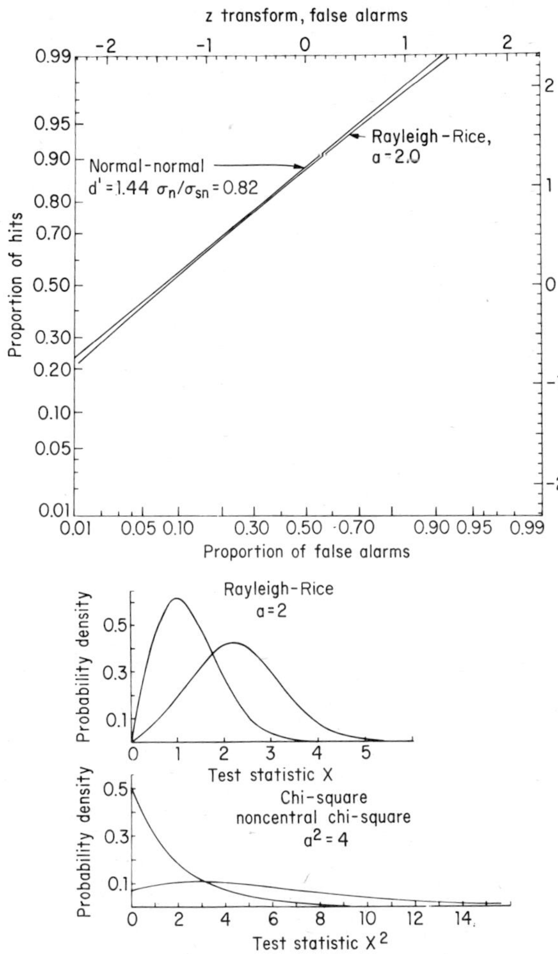

Fig. 5.6. Rayleigh-Rice ROC Curve and a Close-fitting Normal-Normal Curve. The lower ROC curve is generated by a single-criterion model with canonical distributions belonging to the Rayleigh-Rice family of distributions. The Rayleigh distribution f_n has unit variance and the Rice distribution f_{sn} has unit variance and noncentrality parameter 2. If the test statistic is squared, the resulting disributions are chi-square and noncentral chi-square (2 degrees of freedom). Since X is always positive, the squaring operation represents a monotonic transformation and the receiver operating characteristic is the same for both pairs of distributions. The upper ROC curve is that obtained with a single-criterion model and normal distributions of unequal variance ($d' = 1.44$; $\sigma_n/\sigma_{sn} = 0.82$). Normal-normal axes are used in plotting these curves in order to show up the small differences between them. Also, a normal-normal curve lying just above the Rayleigh-Rice curve was chosen for purposes of illustration. Plotted on linear axes a pair of close-fitting curves would be virtually indistinguishable by eye.

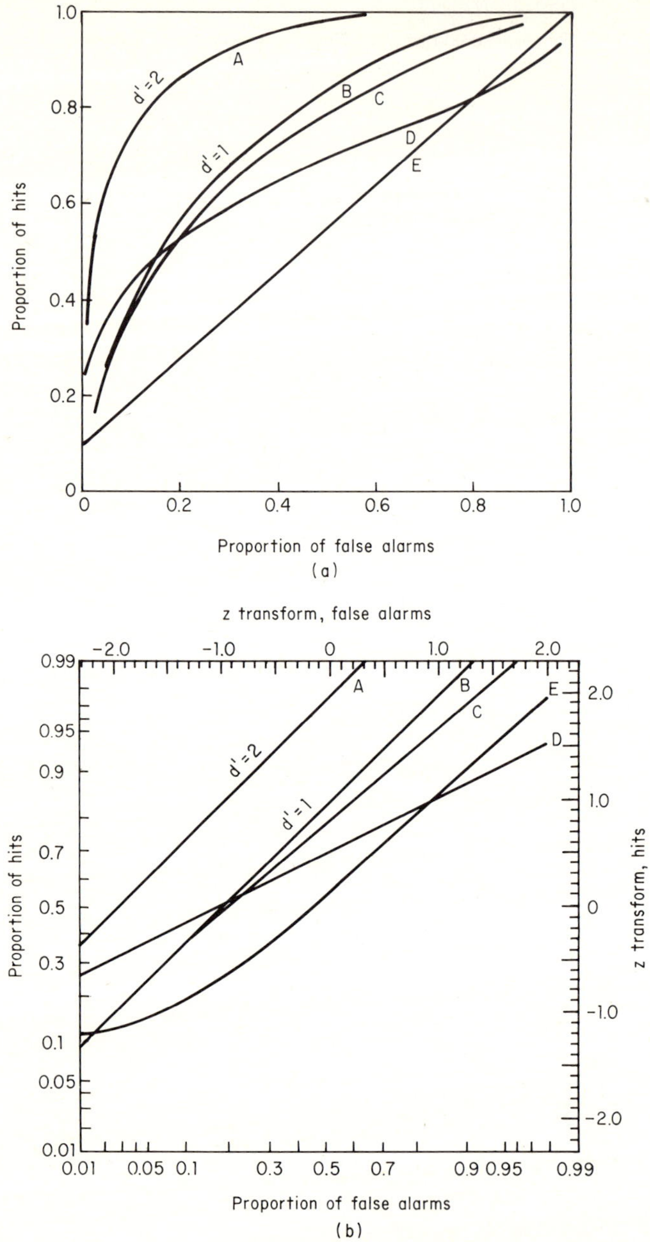

Fig. 5.7. Typical ROC Curves on Linear and Normal-Normal Axes. The effect on several typical ROC curves of transforming the hit and false-alarm axes to normal coordinates is shown. A single-criterion model is assumed throughout. For curve A the canonical distributions f_n and f_{sn} are both normal and of equal variance, with $d' = 2$. For curve B, f_n and f_{sn} are normal, and of equal variance, with $d' = 1$. For curve C, f_n and f_{sn} are Rayleigh-Rice with noncentrality parameter 2. For curve D, f_n and f_{sn} are normal with $\sigma_{sn}/\sigma_n = 2$ and $d' = 1$. Curve E is the ROC curve for a high-threshold model.

time period as recorded in single ganglion cells from the eye (of decerebrate cats).

Throughout this discussion, the derivation of the test statistic has been treated as a process that is separate from, and presumably independent of, the subsequent decision rule. The distinction is important. The derivation of the test statistic is essentially an algebraic operation. Statistical inference only enters at the stage where the observer uses the test statistic in making decisions. Furthermore, in many decision-theory models of sensory perception the test statistic reflects the coding properties of the peripheral sensory system, whereas the decision-making stage is assumed to occur at a much higher level in the system. If, however, the observer is required to satisfy certain idealized requirements, then the distinction between the derivation of the test statistic and the subsequent decision rule may be redundant since the two stages are highly interdependent.

At this point a substantial difference in emphasis may already be apparent between conventional applications of decision theory, such as in signal-detection theory, and its application in psychophysics. In the former application, the emphasis is on maximizing efficiency or some other desirable property. In the latter application the emphasis is on modeling an actual observer, one who may be relatively inefficient.

5.1.4 Optimum Procedures

The use of likelihood ratio as the test statistic has many desirable features and has often been referred to as the *optimum* procedure, and an observer using this procedure has been termed the *ideal* observer. For the simple detection problems considered thus far, the use of the term "optimum" appears to be reasonable, since average detection performance using the likelihood-ratio procedure is either equal to or uniformly better than that obtained by any other procedure. The situation is very different, however, in the testing of compositie hypotheses (i.e., deciding on one of several alternatives). With more than two alternatives, there is more than one type of incorrect decision, usually with different losses associated with each. There is no obvious definition in this case as to what constitutes a "best" procedure and there is a wide diversity of opinion on suitable testing procedures. At least two approaches are widely favored: one is to minimize the average expected loss per trial, the other is to minimize the largest expected loss per trial (the "mini-max" procedure).

A second problem concerns the nature of the data available to the observer. If the data are discrete, i.e., if each observation is represented by a finite set of numbers, then there is no difficulty, in principle, in deriving the likelihood ratio for that observation (simple hypothesis testing is assumed), and an ROC curve specifying the upper limit of detectability can be derived. If, however, the observation is of a continuous waveform, then difficulties arise in specifying an upper bound on detectability. Under certain conditions, depending on the nature of the stimulus, there may be no theoretical upper limit, and the "ideal" observer would never make an error.

A good illustration of this point is provided by the case of a narrow-band signal centered in random noise of bandwidth W. The stimulus that is presented to the observer may consist of either noise alone or signal plus noise and is observed over a finite interval T. The nature of the signal is known to the observer, who is required to determine whether or not the signal is present. If the observed waveform (N or SN) is of the type described as Fourier-series band-limited [4], it may be fully specified by $2WT$ independent samples. An example of such a waveform is one that is band-limited and periodic in time, where the observation interval T equals one period. The waveform can thus be represented by a Fourier series consisting of $2WT$ terms (excluding the dc term). If the logarithm of the likelihood ratio is used as the test statistic, then the underlying f_n and f_{sn} distributions are both approximately normal and equal in variance. The distributions, however, differ in location by an amount proportional to the signal intensity, and since there is some overlap between the distributions, detectability is limited.

If, however, band-limited stationary Gaussian noise is assumed, then the stimulus cannot be fully characterized by a finite number of samples. Slepian [21] and Martel and Mathews [22], for example, have shown for stimuli of this type that if there is no limit on the precision of measurement during the observation interval T, there is no upper bound on detectability. This result is critically dependent on the assumption of stationary, band-limited noise. Such critical dependence on an assumption which at best is no more than a good approximation is obviously unrealistic. In discussing "ideal" or "perfect" observers, however, it is relevant to know that perfect detection is at least theoretically possible. Furthermore, in those cases for which detectability is bounded, the limit is crucially dependent on the noise process that is assumed.

An intuitive explanation of why detectability should be unbounded for band-limited, Gaussian noise may be obtained by considering the process of analytic continuation. According to Taylor's theorem [23, p. 35] any point on an analytic function (i.e., the function and all its derivatives are continuous) can be determined from a series expansion involving derivatives of the function at any other point. The waveform generated by a narrow-band, Guassian process satisfies the necessary conditions for analyticity, and hence by successive differentiation at any point within the observation interval the waveform outside of the interval can, in principle, be predicted. Having extrapolated the waveform over all time there is no difficulty in obtaining its spectrum and hence determining whether or not a signal is present. The precision of measurement necessary for this operation is, of course, totally unrealistic. Also, even if a few derivatives could be obtained with some precision, truncating the Taylor series results in a very poor approximation. More practical methods of extrapolation using observations over a finite time interval rather than at a single point are described in Ref. 24, pt. I.

The preceding comments on the limited applicability of the $2WT$ representation may seem surprising in view of Shannon's well-known sampling theorem [25]. In essence the theorem states that a function of bandwidth W can be fully characterized by independent samples taken at an average rate of $1/2W$ samples per second. It is assumed, however, that the waveform is specified over all time. If only a section T of the waveform is considered, unless the waveform is periodic with period T, the theorem does not apply. Defining the waveform to be zero outside the observation interval renders the theorem inapplicable, since a time-limited waveform cannot at the same time be band-limited. It is sometimes argued that since the observer does not see the waveform outside the interval T, the function may just as well be periodic. This argument is fallacious in that by assuming the waveform to be periodic, additional frequency components are implicitly assumed which lie beyond the range of the original band-limited signal.

To a good *approximation*, however, it is possible to characterize a band-limited waveform over an interval T by $2WT$ independent samples. The quality of the approximation is, of course, dependent on how the waveform is reconstructed, and for this purpose the prolate spheroidal wave functions are recommended rather than the familiar $\sin x/x$ sampling function [26]. For T much greater than $1/W$ the approximation is sufficiently good for most practical purposes. The approximation, however, does not define the theoretical upper bound to detectability.

5.1.5 Data Analysis

Three well-known psychophysical procedures are analyzed directly within the context of a decision-theory model. The most obvious procedure is the *yes-no* method, in which the subject is required to state directly whether or not a signal is present. Typically, it is assumed that the observer computes an appropriate test statistic with each observation, and if the test statistic exceeds a predetermined criterion, a "yes" response (i.e., signal present) is given; otherwise the response is "no" (i.e., signal absent). The criterion is assumed to be held constant during a single test, but may be varied between tests. The subject can be induced to change his criterion either by direct instruction or by altering relevant parameters such as the payoff matrix or a priori probabilities. For each criterion that is used, a separate point on the ROC curve is obtained. In analyzing the data obtained in this way it is common practice to plot observed hit and false-alarm rates on normal-normal probability paper and to fit a straight line to the plotted points (i.e., normal canonical distributions are assumed). Difficulties arise, however, in that both coordinates of each data point are subject to sampling errors; furthermore, the error variances differ for each coordinate of each point. Appropriate statistical procedures for fitting such curves are described in Dorfman and Alf [27], Ogilvie and Creelman [28], and Abrahamson and Levitt [29].

In the *forced-choice* procedure, two or more intervals are marked out (e.g., by light flashes in an auditory experiment) and a presentation is made in each interval. The subject is required to identify the interval containing the signal. The experiment can take one of two forms. If no distinction between intervals is made (symmetric forced choice), then there are only two possible outcomes to each trial; either the interval containing the signal is correctly identified, or it is not. In analyzing such data it is usually assumed that the observer computes a test statistic for each of the several intervals and selects that interval for which the test statistic is greatest. The index d' is usually estimated on the assumption that the f_n and f_{sn} distributions are both normal and of equal variance, differing only in location. The equal-variance assumption is not always tenable, and Fig. 5.10*a* to *d* shows the relation between proportion correct P_c and detectability d' for different values of the ratio σ_{sn}/σ_n. In using these curves to obtain an estimate of d', the standard error of the d' estimate is equal to the binomial sampling error of the proportion correct $(= \sqrt{P_c(1 - P_c)/\text{No. of trials}})$ divided by the slope of the curve in the region of P_c.

In the asymmetric forced-choice technique, one interval is selected as the "target" interval and the equivalent of hits and false alarms are computed for that interval, i.e., correct identification of signal in the target interval is a "hit" and correct identification of signal in a nontarget interval is a "correct rejection." The method of testing is analogous to the yes-no technique, but since information in several intervals is available to the observer, the measured d' should be correspondingly higher.

A third well-known method of measurement is the rating-scale procedure. Several variants of this method have been proposed. In essence, the technique takes the following form:* With each presentation of

* A similar method for analyzing rating-scale data in the context of Thurstonian scaling is given by Attneave [30]; see also Lee [31].

the stimulus the subject rates his confidence that a signal is present by selecting a number within a given range. For example, the range between 1 and 9 may be used, where 1 indicates that the subject is certain that the signal is present and 9 indicates that the subject is equally certain that the signal is absent. The data may be analyzed by assuming that had the subject been restricted to simple binary responses, the resulting data would have been equivalent to that obtained by dividing the rating scale into two parts; all ratings above a given value being defined as *N* responses and all ratings below this critical value as *SN* responses. The critical value used in dividing the rating scale corresponds to the criterion used by the subject in the hypothetical binary-choice experiment. By regrouping the rating-scale data about a second critical value, another set of binary data is generated corresponding to a different criterion. Several points on the ROC curve may thus be estimated within a single experiment. The estimated points, however, are not statistically independent.

Other detection situations, such as vigilance tasks, have also been analyzed within a decision-theory framework [32–35]. Unfortunately, space limitations do not allow a discussion of these methods.

5.1.6 Choice Theory*

Although this chapter is primarily concerned with decision theory, a brief description of choice theory as applied to signal detection and recognition is nevertheless appropriate. Basically, choice theory provides a mathematical summary of empirical findings. A convenient method of summarizing detection and recognition data is the confusion matrix (Table 5.1). The rows identify the different stimuli used in an experiment and the columns the subject's responses. The entries within each cell may be either the frequency f_{sr} of response r to stimulus s or the proportion $p(r/s) = f_{sr} / \sum_{r'} f_{sr'}$ of r responses to stimulus s. The summation is taken over all possible responses to stimulus s.

According to choice theory, the true probability of response r to stimulus s is given by

$$p(r/s) = \frac{\gamma[s,i(r)]b(r)}{\sum_{r'} \gamma[s,i(r')]b(r')} \tag{5-1}$$

where $\gamma[s,i(r)]$ is a measure of similarity between stimulus s and stimulus $i(r)$ for which r is the correct response, and where $b(r)$ is a measure of response bias. As before, the summation is taken over all possible responses to the stimulus s.

* The description of choice theory as applied to signal detection and recognition is based on the model described by Luce [11].

In its present form, Eq. (5-1) contains more free parameters than entries in the confusion matrix. Several simplifying assumptions are obviously necessary, and three basic assumptions are:

1. $\gamma(S_xS_y) = \gamma(S_yS_x)$
2. $\gamma(S_xS_x) = \gamma(S_yS_y) = 1$
3. $\gamma(S_xS_z) \geq \gamma(S_xS_y) \cdot \gamma(S_yS_z)$

where S_x, S_y, and S_z are any of the stimuli used in defining the confusion matrix. The *constant-ratio rule* [36] may be seen to be a special case of Eq. (5-1) provided no bias is present, i.e., $b(r)$ is the same for all r.

As an example of the application of choice theory, consider the simple detection experiment described earlier. Let γ be a measure of the similarity between the N and SN conditions, and let b be a measure of the subject's bias towards giving an N response. The matrices defining the similarity measure and response bias are shown in Table 5.2. The confusion matrix is obtained by applying Eq. (5-1) to the composite similarity-bias matrix $\gamma[s,i(r)]b(r)$.

As in the decision-theory model, there are two independent parameters to account for two independent variables: γ may be regarded as analogous to d' and b as analogous to the criterion X_c. Predictions of forced-choice data using the choice-theory model are slightly more complex and require the use of a transformation for the $\gamma[s,i(r)]$ measure as well as an additional assumption; see Luce [11] for details.

TABLE 5.1 Typical Confusion Matrix

The rows refer to stimuli and the columns to responses. The entry f_{sr} indicates the frequency with which the response r occurs with stimulus s. Proportions may be used in place of frequencies; i.e., in place of f_{sr} use $p(r/s) = f_{sr} \Big/ \sum_{r'} f_{sr'}$, where the summation is taken over all possible responses to stimulus s.

		Responses						
		1	2	3	. . .	r	. . .	. . .
Stimulus	1	f_{11}	f_{12}	f_{13}	. . .	f_{1r}	. . .	. . .
	2	f_{21}	f_{22}	f_{23}	. . .	f_{2r}	. . .	. . .
	3	f_{31}	.	.		f_{3r}	. . .	. . .
	4	f_{41}	.	.		.		
	.	.						
	.	.			.			
	.	.			.			
	.	.			.			
	s	f_{s1}	f_{s2}	.	.	f_{sr}	. . .	. . .
	.	.			.			
	.	.			.			
	.	.			.			

TABLE 5.2 Choice-theory Analysis of Stimulus-response Matrix
The stimulus-response matrix corresponding to a typical detection experiment is considered. The upper left-hand corner shows the similarity matrix; the row matrix alongside indicates the response bias. The composite similarity-bias matrix is shown in the upper right-hand corner. The stimulus-response matrix, shown at the bottom center, was derived using the rule given in Sec. 5.1.6 for predicting the probability of response r to stimulus s.

Similarity measure:

Stimulus	Response: Yes	Response: No
SN	1	γ
N	γ	1

Response bias:

Response: Yes	Response: No
1	b

Composite $\gamma[s,i(r)]b(r)$ matrix:

Stimulus	Response: Yes	Response: No
SN	1	γb
N	γ	b

Stimulus-response Matrix:

Stimulus	Response: Yes	Response: No
SN	$\dfrac{1}{1+\gamma b}$	$\dfrac{\gamma b}{1+\gamma b}$
N	$\dfrac{\gamma}{\gamma+b}$	$\dfrac{b}{\gamma+b}$

5.2 Experimental Evidence

5.2.1 Basic Assumptions

The central assumption in any decision-theory model of sensory perception is that there exists, at some stage in the process, a responsible statistical decision mechanism. Thus, for example, if the relative cost of a false alarm is increased, the observer tends to give fewer false alarms; similarly, if the a priori probability of signal plus noise is increased, the observer increases the proportion of SN responses accordingly. There is a good deal of experimental evidence in support of this aspect of the theory.

Most decision-theory models of sensory perception, however, claim far more than that a statistical decision mechanism exists at some stage in the system. Detailed models have been proposed and far-reaching assumptions have been made regarding the nature of the observer, the statistical properties of the internal noise, and the type of decision rule that is employed. The experimental evidence in support of these models is, as may be expected, the subject of much controversy. It is the purpose of this section to consider several of the more important assumptions that have been made (implicitly or explicitly) and the extent to which these assumptions are consistent with experimental data.

Typically, a single-criterion model of the type described in Sec. 5.1.2.1 is assumed. This assumption is in itself not unduly restrictive since, as yet, nothing has been assumed regarding the form of the underlying f_n and f_{sn} distributions. A very wide range of data on human signal detection can be interpreted in terms of such a model provided a suitable choice is made for the f_n and f_{sn} distributions.

5.2.2 Intersessional Fluctuations

Concomitant with the assumption of a single-criterion model (or, for that matter, any of the simple models discussed in Sec. 5.1.2) is the assumption that the probability distributions f_n and f_{sn} are fixed, i.e., there is no change in the relative location or shape of f_n and f_{sn} during an experiment. Assumptions of stability are, of course, not unique to decision-theory models of sensory perception. Experience has shown that the assumption of fixed probability laws governing an observer's responses should be regarded as no more than a useful first approximation. Decision-theory models, however, are particularly sensitive to this assumption in that the procedure for generating an ROC curve using the yes-no or asymmetric forced-choice method requires that observations from separate test sessions be combined to provide an estimate of the curve. Since a separate point is obtained in each session, differences between points may be due not only to changes in the observer's criterion but also to intersessional differences in the underlying f_n and f_{sn} distributions.

In a direct attack on this problem, Gray [37] showed that it is possible to limit the intersessional variability of measured points in ROC space by careful experimental design. Several stimulus-presentation paradigms were considered, and it was found that for at least one paradigm* the measured hit and false-alarm rates for identical experimental conditions did not differ between sessions by an amount significantly greater than that which could be attributed to chance. This result implies that both the criterion and the f_n and f_{sn} distributions remain relatively fixed from session to session (unless, of course, both variables interact in such a way as to leave the hit and false-alarm rates unchanged, but this possibility seems highly unlikely). Gray was concerned with

* The recommended procedure was an asymmetric, two-alternative forced-choice technique in which the two alternatives (*A* and *B*) were presented in an *AB*, *BA* sequence.

frequency discrimination, and it is not clear to what extent these results hold for the typical signal-detection experiment. Nevertheless, the demonstration that intersessional variability can be virtually eliminated by careful experimental design is important.

An analysis of published data, however, indicates that in many cases intersessional variability can be substantial. The degree of variability also appears to depend on the criterion adopted by the observer. In a study on tonal detection, for example, Emmerich [38, 39] obtained data in which the criterion was adjusted by instruction only, i.e., the subject was instructed to use either a "lax," "medium," or "strict" criterion, where a "strict" criterion results in a low false-alarm rate. The a priori probability of a signal was 0.5 throughout. Four subjects were tested on two separate days with three sessions of 80 trials per day for each of the three detection criteria. An analysis of Emmerich's data shows that variations in the measured hit and false-alarm rates were not significant from session to session for the strict criterion, but that there were statistically significant differences between sessions for the lax criterion. The estimated variability for the medium criterion, although greater than that obtained for the strict criterion, did not exceed the expected sampling error by a statistically significant amount. It would thus appear that subjects are more able to maintain a repeatable strict criterion than the presumably less natural lax criterion.

Intersessional differences between plotted points in ROC space may be attributed either to variability in the choice of criterion or to changes in the underlying f_n and f_{sn} distributions,* or to some combination of these two effects. Intersessional fluctuations in the choice of criterion are readily interpreted within the framework of conventional decision-theory models, and much of the published data in human signal detection is consistent with this interpretation. The data of Tanner, Swets, and Green [40] provide a good illustration of the situation where criterial variability (between sessions) is high but detectability is relatively invariant. A yes-no technique was used for the detection of a tone in Gaussian noise. Sessions were paired under identical experimental conditions where the a priori probability of a signal being presented was varied systematically for each pair of sessions over the range 0.1, 0.3, 0.5, 0.7, and 0.9. The payoff matrix was held constant throughout, the relative cost of a false alarm being equal to that for a miss. Some of the data obtained in this experiment are shown in Fig. 5.8. A single ROC curve was fitted to the five pairs of points obtained with each subject [29]. Although the differences between pairs of points are sta-

* It is assumed, unless stated otherwise by the experimenter, that intersessional differences due to equipment instability are negligibly small.

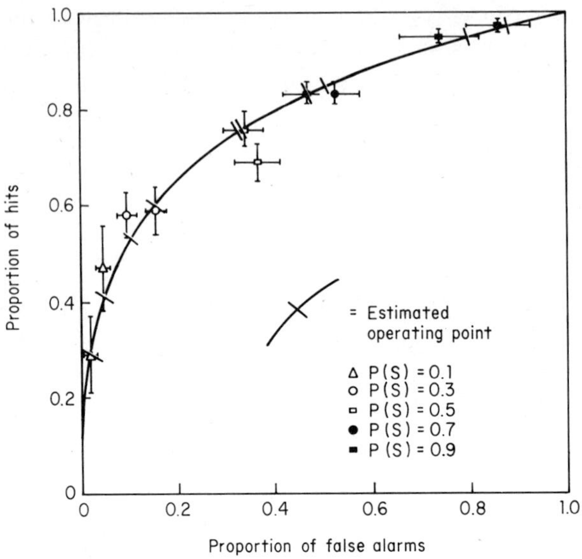

Fig. 5.8. Fitted ROC Curve and Estimated Operating Points. The ROC curve has been fitted to the data of Tanner, Swets, and Green [40] for the detection of a 500-Hz tone in Gaussian noise. A single-criterion model is assumed with normal canonical distributions. Estimates of d', σ_{sn}/σ_n, and each of the ten operating points used by the observer were obtained using the method of maximum likelihood. Response probabilities were varied by manipulating the a priori probability $P(S)$ of a signal presentation. Two replications were obtained at each of five values of $P(S)$. The vertical and horizontal bars show the estimated standard errors for each observed point on both the hit and false-alarm axes.

tistically significant,* particularly for the very high and very low a priori probabilities, the observed points do not differ significantly from their estimated positions on the fitted ROC curve. The differences between the paired sessions could thus be attributed to fluctuations in the choice of criterion rather than to any changes in the location or shape of the underlying f_n and f_{sn} distributions.

A more serious problem is that situation in which intersessional variability cannot be explained solely by changes in criterion between sessions. An example is provided by data obtained by Norman [41].

* A simple significance test for the difference between two points in ROC space may be obtained by considering the statistic $\chi^2 = (P_1 - P_2)^2/\text{var}\,(P_1 - P_2) + (p_1 - p_2)^2/\text{var}\,(p_1 - p_2)$, where $(P_1 - P_2)$ and $(p_1 - p_2)$ are the differences between the hit and false-alarm probabilities, respectively, for the two points. Var (x) is the variance of x and may be estimated in each case from the binomial sampling distributions of P and p. If the observed difference between two points is due to sampling errors only, then χ^2 is approximately distributed as chi-square with two degrees of freedom.

In a series of experiments on incremental tonal detection, subjects were required to detect a change in the intensity of a 1,000-Hz tone at a 60-dB sensation level. A yes-no paradigm was used. The a priori probability of an increment (i.e., the SN condition) was 0.5 throughout the experiment. Response probabilities were varied by manipulating the payoff matrix. Several sessions of approximately 100 trials each were repeated for each payoff matrix. Tests on the homogeneity of the data from repeated sessions showed that in rougly 90 percent of all tests the variability in the measured hit and false-alarm rates was not significantly greater than that to be expected from binomial sampling. Of those cases showing significant intersessional variability, about half could be attributed to criterion variability. The remaining 5 percent of cases, however, indicated significant intersessional variations in sensitivity.

Two illustrative sets of data are shown in Fig. 5.9*a* and *b*. The plotted points are the measured hit and false-alarm rates for five individual sessions having the same payoff matrix. The ROC curves, however, have been fitted to all the data of their respective experiments, and the plotted points represent only a fraction (less than one-sixth) of the total number of observations. In Fig. 5.9*a*, the spread of points is indicative of a substantial variation in the observer's criterion between sessions. In Fig. 5.9*b*, the spread of points is indicative of a substantial variation in sensitivity between sessions. It may be that for this case the basic model needs to be modified so as to take into account intersessional fluctuations in sensitivity. It should be noted that Norman used tonal stimuli without external noise and that detectability was limited solely by the observer's internal noise.

The problem of intersessional variability is not critical for the rating-scale experiment, since sufficient data to generate an ROC curve can be obtained within a single session. The problem, however, is replaced by that of instability between category boundaries within a test. Although several experimental investigations of the single-interval rating-scale method in human signal detection [12, 42, 43] indicate that the decision-theory treatment of this experiment is reasonably consistent with experimental data, the variability of category boundaries has not been investigated in great detail. The effect of wrongly assuming fixed boundaries when they are in fact variable leads to an overestimate of the internal sensory noise. Experimental comparisons between the rating-scale method and other procedures are considered in Sec. 5.2.8.

5.2.3 Regular Trends

Apart from the problem of intersessional variability, there is also the question of regular trends between sessions. For simple signals against

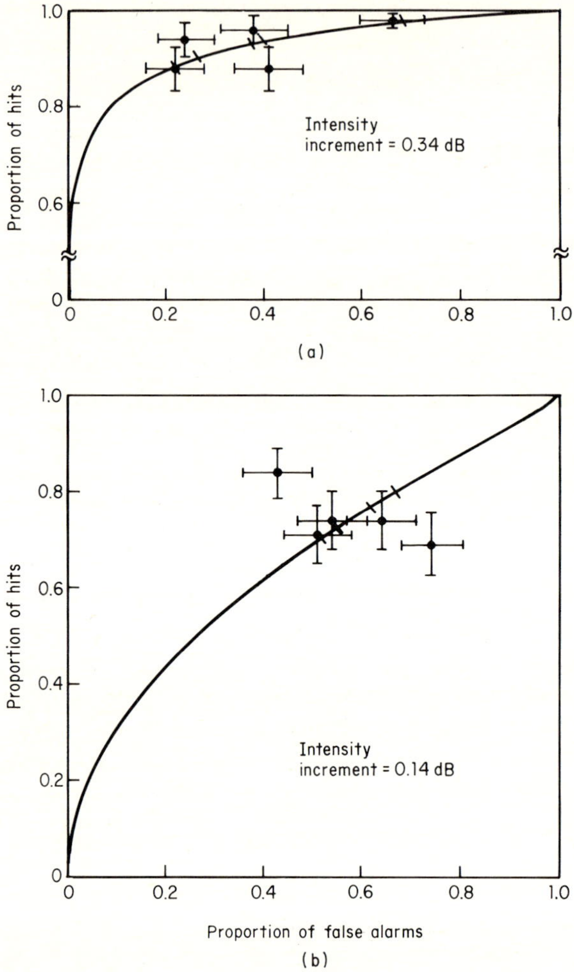

Fig. 5.9. Two Forms of Intersessional Variability. A yes-no technique was used in detecting intensity increments in a 1,000-Hz tone at a 60-dB sensation level [41]. Response probabilities were varied by manipulating the payoff matrix. The ROC curve in (*a*) was fitted to data obtained at six different values of the payoff matrix, and the ROC curve of (*b*) was fitted to data obtained at eleven different values of the payoff matrix. Several sessions of approximately 100 trials each were repeated at each value of the payoff matrix. The plotted points are the measured hit and false-alarm rates for five individual sessions having the same payoff matrix. In (*a*) the spread of the plotted points is indicative of a variation in the observer's criterion between sessions. In (*b*) the spread of the points is indicative of a variation in sensitivity between sessions. The vertical and horizontal bars show the estimated standard errors for each observed point on the hit and false-alarm axes.

a background of fixed, high-level noise, detectability appears to be relatively invariable except for adaptation effects which occur at the start of an experiment or with naive observers [44–46]. Gradual, long-term improvements in detectability, however, have been observed for tones in quiet [47, 48], in vigilance studies [49], and in experiments where the observer's task is not strictly one of signal detection. Tanner and Rivette [50], for example, have reported long-term learning effects in an experiment on time-interval estimation.

Gradual changes in detectability must involve changes in the canonical f_n and f_{sn} distributions, in which case the assumption of fixed distributions is violated. If the change is sufficiently gradual, then there is no difficulty in extending decision-theory models to take such trends into account. If, however, the change is relatively rapid, leading to significant differences between successive test sessions, then difficulties arise in interpreting the data.

Apart from changes in detectability, there is also the question of regular trends in the choice of criterion over repeated tests. Although this consideration has not received much attention (it is not crucial to the validity of decision-thoery models) there is nevertheless some experimental evidence of a gradual adjustment to extreme conditions. Norman [51] describes an experiment in which repeated tests were carried out using a highly asymmetric payoff matrix. In one set of six tests, the payoff matrix greatly favored a hit over a false alarm. In a second set of six tests, the relative costs were reversed and the cost of a false alarm greatly exceeded the value of a hit. For both cases, the observer showed a trend towards reducing the response bias induced by the payoff matrix, i.e., the measured points on the ROC curve tended to approach each other with time. It would appear that the observer gradually adjusted his criterion as he adapted to the payoff matrix. Although the existence of gradual drifts in the choice of criterion does not conflict with the assumption of fixed distributions, it does present difficulties for a subsequent postulate, that the observer uses a well-defined rule in deriving the criterion.

Gradual changes in parameter values is a central theme in the modeling of learning processes, and in view of the preceding discussion it may seem that decision-theory models are basically unsuitable for this purpose. This is not the case, however, if the model is designed specifically for the learning process. Schoeffler [52] has developed a learning model in which classical conditioning principles are superimposed on a decision-theory framework. An additional stage is introduced, however, specifying a probabilistic relation between the observer's responses and the test statistic which is the perceived stimulus magnitude. The model makes some novel predictions about the effect of feedback.

In particular, if the a priori probabilities of signal occurrence are unequal and feedback is provided, the response criterion is gradually adjusted so as to improve average performance. If, however, there is no feedback, the criterion shifts so as to degrade average performance. Both these predictions have found experimental support [53]. A detailed discussion of learning and adaption effects, including the role of information feedback, is beyond the scope of this work. There is, however, some overlap between decision-theory models and pertinent theories in this area [54–56; see also Sec. 5.1.2.3].

5.2.4 Sequential Dependencies

Closely allied to the assumption of fixed distributions is that of statistical independence between successive responses. There is considerable experimental evidence showing the existence of response dependencies in the signal-detection situation (see Ref. 57 for a general review). Unfortunately, the data do not exhibit a consistent pattern. To complicate matters, it would appear that not only are response dependencies affected by a variety of experimental variables (e.g., signal level and presentation schedule), but also that different subjects tend to show different response dependencies. In terms of decision-theory models, a response dependency may take several forms. Either only the criterion is affected or the observer's sensitivity is affected, or both.

It is, of course, entirely proper to limit the field of inquiry to those conditions under which sequential dependencies do not exist, provided the implications of this restriction are realized and there is sufficient evidence to show that the assumption is consistent with the data. A useful practical approach is to use an experimental paradigm designed to eliminate response dependencies and then to include a check within the experiment to test whether the assumption of statistical independence is, in fact, valid [58].

5.2.5 The Threshold Concept

An assumption implicit in virtually all decision-theory models is that the f_n and f_{sn} probability distributions are true density functions and overlap over their entire range. Although not usually stated in this form, this assumption characterizes the difference between the conventional decision-theory model and the traditional high-threshold model. According to the latter model, there is a critical stimulus level (corresponding to the *threshold*) below which the stimulus has no effect. Above this critical level, however, the stimulus is always observed. Variability in the subject's responses is accounted for by trial-by-trial fluctuations in the value of the threshold. The observer can also give biased responses for a certain proportion of trials and may do so if the payoff matrix warrants such a strategy (see Fig. 5.2). In terms of this model, false alarms are a result of response bias and do not reflect any sensory mechanism. Accordingly, a simple "correction" for false alarms may be carried out in which the hit rate is reduced to that which would have been observed in the absence of a response bias (i.e., at zero false alarms).

There is a good deal of experimental evidence contrary to the high threshold for signals in noise. Swets, Tanner, and Birdsall [59] and Tanner, Swets, and Green [40], for example, obtained empirical ROC curves for both visual and auditory detection (against high-level background noise) which differ substantially from the predicted ROC curves of the high-threshold model. In addition, a strong correlation was observed between the "corrected" hit rate and the false-alarm rate, an effect clearly contrary to predictions of the high-threshold model. The nonindependence of the "corrected" hit and false-alarm rates was in fact shown experimentally at an earlier date by Smith and Wilson [14]. Perhaps the most elegant experiment illustrating the inadequacy of a high-threshold theory is that proposed by R. Z. Norman and carried out by Swets, Tanner, and Birdsall [42, 59], in which the observer was allowed a second choice in a multiple-alternative forced-choice experiment. Given an incorrect first choice, the hit rate for second choices was significantly better than that which could have arisen by chance.* According to the high-threshold model, second-choice responses should be no better than random guessing.

The preceding evidence does not imply that the notion of a threshold is entirely without foundation, but only that the assumption of a simple, high threshold is inadequate—at least for simple signals against a high-level background noise. Luce [13], for example, provides an example of a two-state threshold model which is consistent with a wide range of data. The model is of the form described in Sec. 5.1.2.2. Most of the published data on empirical ROC curves appears to be fitted as well by the two-state threshold model as by the conventional decision-theory model, assuming normal distributions. There have also been relatively few experimental comparisons between decision-theory and high-threshold models for signals in quiet. In one investigation using visual signals against low-level background illumination [61], it was found that predictions based on a two-parameter decision-theory model

* Kincaid and Hamilton [60] repeated this experiment and found that, unlike the subjects in the Swets, Tanner, and Birdsall investigation, their subjects tended to confuse first- and second-choice responses, thereby contributing in part to the better-than-chance performance with the nominal "second-choice" responses. Even with this effect taken into account, however, the Kincaid and Hamilton data could not be adequately accounted for by a simple, high-threshold model.

(normal distributions, $\sigma_n \neq \sigma_{sn}$) were only marginally superior to those based on the simpler, high-threshold model. Nachmias and Steinman [62] have obtained data on absolute visual detection using a rating-scale procedure, but although their data are consistent with the conventional decision-theory interpretation, the two-state threshold model is not necessarily refuted, since the response mechanism for rating-scale data is not uniquely defined [63–66]. However, the response mechanism of a two-state threshold model that will account for rating-scale data may turn out to be fairly intricate since, as shown by Nachmias and Steinman [62], predictions based on a simple extension of the two-state threshold model to account for rating data are not in good agreement with experimental data.

Even if decision-theory models are found to provide adequate predictions of absolute, incremental, and signal-in-noise detections, it should not be assumed that the relevant test statistics are necessarily the same for all three situations. Different perceptual mechanisms may be involved, in which case the relevant physical variables contributing to detectability may be quite different. Although some signal-detection models have treated absolute detection as a special case of incremental detection, this assumption is not essential to the theory. In a model of visual detection, for example, Barlow [67] assumes that differential sensitivity is limited by fluctuations in the number of quanta absorbed from the background light and that absolute sensitivity is limited by retinal noise. For signals against a low-level background illumination the two sources of noise are assumed to add. Although this model accounts for a wide range of data, Baumgardt and Smith [68] have shown that if the area of the background illumination is small, then the addition of a low-level background increases rather than decreases probability of detection; i.e., the two sources of noise are different and are not necessarily additive.*

5.2.6 Distributional Assumptions

Various distributional assumptions have been made regarding the f_n and f_{sn} distributions, the most common being that of normality. In order to test this assumption, normal ROC curves have been fitted to several published sets of yes-no data using appropriate statistical procedures [29]. Reasonable fits were obtained in most cases, provided both the location and scale of the f_n and f_{sn} distributions are free parameters to be estimated from the data. The results for auditory detection are summarized in Table 5.3. In those instances where the fit was poor, the discrepant points did not show a regular pattern indicative of an

* Certain aspects of the Baumgardt and Smith experiment have been challenged by Nachmias. See Nachmias [69] and Nachmias and Kocher [70] for details.

TABLE 5.3 Typical Auditory Detection Data

Several sets of yes-no data in auditory detection have been analyzed to obtain estimates of d, σ_n/σ_{sn}, the standard errors of these estimates, and the chi-square goodness-of-fit statistic. The estimates were obtained using the method of maximum likelihood. A single-criterion model with normal canonical distributions was assumed. Estimates of σ_n/σ_{sn} were almost always less than 1 and usually by a statistically significant amount. In most cases the underlying model provided an adequate fit to the data.

Source	Description	Subject	Signal-to-noise ratio,* dB	Signal frequency, Hz	d'	SE(d')†	σ_n/σ_{sn}	SE(σ_n/σ_{sn})†	Goodness-of-fit test: Chi-square	Degrees of freedom	Signif. level
Tanner, Swets, and Green [40]	Tone in noise; varied a priori prob.	1	6.5	1,000	1.33	0.12	0.73	0.07	6.2	8	
		2	6.5	1,000	0.83	0.08	1.01	0.11	4.9	8	
Green and Swets [7]	Tone in noise; varied payoff matrix	1	6.5	1,000	0.81	0.06	0.89	0.06	9.2	3	<.05
Lindner [112]	Tone in noise; criterion varied by instruction	1	11	500	1.08	0.10	0.81	0.07	0.3	1	
		2	11	500	1.27	0.31	0.83	0.08	0.1	1	
		3	11	500	0.80	0.07	0.91	0.11	0.5	1	
		4	11	500	0.90	0.08	0.96	0.08	3.5	1	
		1	13	1,100	1.03	0.08	0.69	0.06	0.3	1	
		2	13	1,100	1.14	0.09	0.84	0.08	0.0	1	
		3	13	1,100	1.58	0.14	0.58	0.09	3.6	1	
		4	13	1,100	1.59	0.13	0.63	0.06	0.6	1	
Emmerich [38]	Tone in noise; criterion varied by instruction	Day‡									
		1 1	10	400	1.56	0.19	0.96	0.20	16.7	7	<.05
		1 2	10	400	2.05	0.34	0.57	0.13	8.3	7	
		2 1	10	400	1.72	0.21	1.08	0.23	6.3	7	
		2 2	10	400	1.76	0.24	0.98	0.22	4.9	7	
		3 1	10	400	1.26	0.18	0.71	0.11	7.5	7	
		3 2	10	400	0.62	0.11	1.48	0.33	11.9	7	
		4 1	10	400	1.87	0.28	0.68	0.16	5.1	7	
		4 2	10	400	2.26	0.41	0.55	0.14	14.8	7	<.05

* Signal-to-noise ratio expressed as signal energy over noise power per unit bandwidth.

† SE(x) = standard error of x.

‡ Data pooled for each day; 3 sessions obtained with each of three sets of instructions (strict, medium, or lax criterion). Choice of criterion varied significantly between sessions and data were not averaged over sessions, hence seven degrees of freedom available in fitting each curve.

incorrect distributional assumption, but rather appeared to be the result of overly large intersessional variations. The quality of fit was measured by a chi-square goodness-of-fit test.

One alternative to the normal assumption is that of Rayleigh-Rice distributions [71, 72]. The difference between ROC curves generated by Rayleigh-Rice distributions as opposed to normal distributions of unequal variance is relatively small (see Fig. 5.6), and it would require a considerable amount of experimental data to discriminate reliably between the two cases. In a Monte Carlo study [73] in which normal ROC curves were fitted to data generated by a Rayleigh-Rice model, it was found that the average value of the chi-square goodness-of-fit statistic was only marginally greater than its expected value (3.5 as opposed to 3). A typical experimental design was used with five roughly equally spaced groups of 200 observations. Even when the data were generated by a high-threshold model ($P_{\text{hit}} = 0.7$ at zero false alarms), the chi-square goodness-of-fit test led to a rejection at the 0.1 significance level only 17 times out of 100 sets of data. Decision-theory models based on normal distributions are obviously highly robust in that adequate fits for the ROC curves may be obtained even when there are gross departures from the distributional assumptions.

5.2.7 The Equal-variance Assumption

An important assumption in many decision-theory models is that the f_n and f_{sn} distributions are of equal variance. Referring once again to Table 5.3, it is seen that few sets of data show an equal-variance solution. In most cases the estimates of σ_n/σ_{sn} were less than unity and usually by an amount significantly greater than the standard error of the estimate. It is evident from these and other data in auditory and visual detection that the equal-variance assumption is untenable except in a few cases. This conclusion is, of course, based on an analysis of published data of the yes-no type. Rating-scale data were not considered with the same precision since at the time of writing the necessary statistical analysis had not been completed. Graphical analyses of single-interval rating-scale data, however, also show estimated variance ratios which differ consistently from unity [12, 74, 75].

5.2.8 Comparisons Between Different Psychophysical Procedures

5.2.8.1 Yes-No and Forced-choice Procedures

There have been a number of experimental comparisons between measures of detectability obtained by different psychophysical procedures. These comparisons are important in that they provide an overall test of the decision-theory approach as well as emphasizing the practical value of the theory in providing a basis for such comparisons. One of the more obvious comparisons is that between the yes-no and the symmetrical forced-choice procedure. Several investigations have been reported showing the similarity of d' estimates for these two methods [5, 40, 76]. In each of these studies, however, the forced-choice estimates of d' were obtained on the assumption that the variance ratio σ_n^2/σ_{sn}^2 is unity. As pointed out in the preceding section, this assumption is not always tenable. Curves showing the relation between proportion correct and d' for several different variance ratios are shown in Fig. 5.10*a* to *d*. The differences between predicted d' values for different variance ratios can be quite substantial, particularly at high values of proportion correct. For lower values of proportion correct and for cases involving more than two alternatives, the curves tend to overlap leading to similar predictions of d'.

The experimental comparisons that have been carried out between the yes-no and symmetric forced-choice techniques have generally involved d' estimates on the order of 1.5, and the effect of an incorrectly assumed variance ratio in this region, although substantial, is not critical. A reanalysis of Swets's [76, expt. I] data, for example, using variance ratios typical of those obtained experimentally for similar stimuli (Table 5.3) does not alter the conclusion reached earlier by Swets that the different techniques yield similar estimates of d'. The differences between the separate estimates, although small for practical purposes, were nevertheless significantly larger than their estimated sampling errors. These differences may have been due to intersessional fluctuations in detectability, an effect which is not adequately taken into account by the theory.

In some cases, a higher degree of consistency is obtained between the d' estimates from separate procedures if an appropriate value is used for the variance ratio. Thus, for example, in the experimental comparison reported by Tanner, Swets, and Green [40], estimates of both d' and σ_n/σ_{sn} were obtained from the yes-no data using the method of maximum likelihood [29]. Estimates of d' for the forced-choice data were then obtained from curves of the type shown in Fig. 5.10, assuming a variance ratio equal to that obtained for the yes-no case. The results are summarized in Table 5.4. As may be seen, the differences between the d' estimates for the two procedures do not differ significantly. The forced-choice data for observer 2 have not been pooled, since interreplication differences were statistically significant. However, the average value of d' for the three forced-choice sessions was not significantly different from the average value of d' for the yes-no experiment.

Swets [76] describes a comparative experiment on the symmetrical

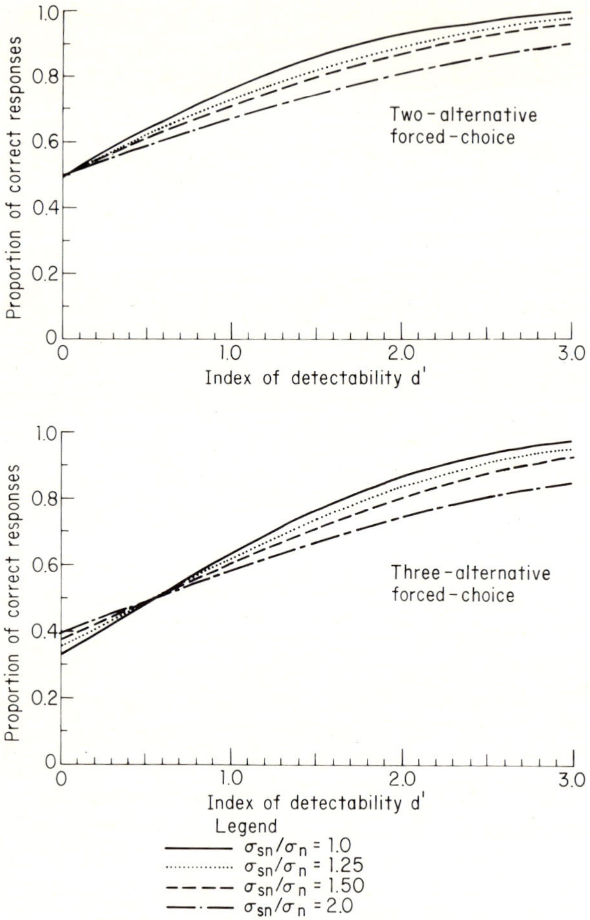

Fig. 5.10. Relation Between Proportion Correct and d′ for the Forced-choice Experiment. A family of curves is shown for each of the 2-, 3-, 4-, 6-, and 8-alternative forced-choice experiments. The conventional interpretation of the forced-choice experiment is assumed, in which the interval containing the largest test statistic is selected by the observer. The underlying distributions are assumed to be normal, but not necessarily of equal variance. The parameter for each family of curves is the ratio σ_{sn}/σ_n.

forced-choice procedure in which the number of alternatives was varied from two to eight. Although the equal-variance model was found to provide an adequate fit to these data, better predictions are obtained if a variance ratio other than unity is assumed. The data of this experiment are summarized in Fig. 5.11. Predictions of proportion correct for specified values of *d′* are shown for variance ratios of $(1.0)^2$, $(1.25)^2$,

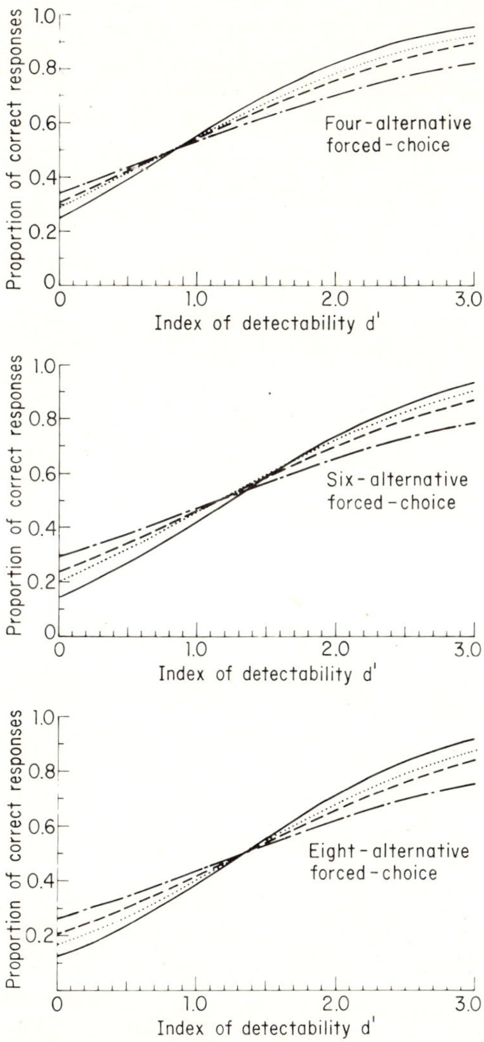

Fig. 5.10. Continued

and $(1.5)^2$, respectively. The value of d' for each curve is such that the mean square deviation between observed and predicted values is minimized. Although each of the three curves provides relatively good predictions of proportion correct, the best fit is obtained with a variance ratio of $(1.25)^2$. From Table 5.3 it is seen that a value of $\sigma_n/\sigma_{sn} = 1/1.25$ is fairly typical of auditory detection data. Although the model appears to be relatively insensitive to changes in the variance ratio, the value of d' necessary to obtain a good fit can change substantially.

TABLE 5.4 Comparison Between Forced-choice and Yes-No Procedures
The data were obtained by Tanner, Swets, and Green [40]. The signal consisted of a 500-Hz tone against a background of high-level Gaussian noise. Forced-choice data are shown in the upper half of the table and yes-no data in the lower half. The estimates for the forced-choice experiment were derived using information on the ratio σ_n/σ_{sn} obtained in the yes-no experiment. The differences between the yes-no and forced-choice d' estimates are not statistically significant.

Four-Alternative Forced Choice

	OBSERVER 1				OBSERVER 2			
	N	P_c*	d'	SE(d')†	N	P_c*	d'	SE(d')†
Replication 1	99	.62	1.31	.20	99	.58	1.09	.16
Replication 2	99	.55	1.03	.19	99	.49	.80	.16
Replication 3	99	.64	1.39	.20	99	.63	1.26	.16
Average	...	...	1.25	.19‡	...	...	1.05	.23‡
Pooled Data	297	.60	1.24	.11	§	§	§	§

Yes-No Experiment

	σ_n/σ_{sn}	SE(σ_n/σ_{sn})	d'	SE(d')†	σ_n/σ_{sn}	SE(σ_n/σ_{sn})	d'	SE(d')†
Replication 1	0.68	0.10	1.47	.19	1.06	0.19	.83	.12
Replication 2	0.78	0.11	1.20	.15	0.96	0.14	.82	.10
Average	0.73	0.07	1.34	.19‡	1.01	0.07	.83	.01‡
Pooled Data	0.73	0.07	1.33	.12	1.01	0.11	.83	.08

* P_c indicates proportion correct.
† SE(x) indicates standard error of x.
‡ Computed across replications.
§ Data not pooled since interreplication differences statistically significant.

Experimental comparisons between the yes-no and asymmetric forced-choice techniques have not been as extensive as with the symmetric forced-choice procedure, possibly because both of these procedures are extremely time-consuming. Of the comparisons that have been reported, the asymmetric forced-choice d' has usually been found to be greater than the corresponding yes-no d', although the ratio between the two is not always close to $\sqrt{2}$ as predicted for the equal-variance case [75, 77, 78]. Markowitz and Swets [75], in particular, obtained ROC curves for both the yes-no and asymmetric forced-choice experiment and found that, although the ROC curves were all of unit slope which is consistent with current theories, the differences in detectability were systematically less than the theoretical ratio of $\sqrt{2}$ by about 20 percent. Since the precision of the slope estimates is not known, it is not clear to what extent these differences represent a significant departure from theory.

An interesting apparent inconsistency in the interpretation of yes-no and asymmetrical forced-choice data has been reported by McFadden

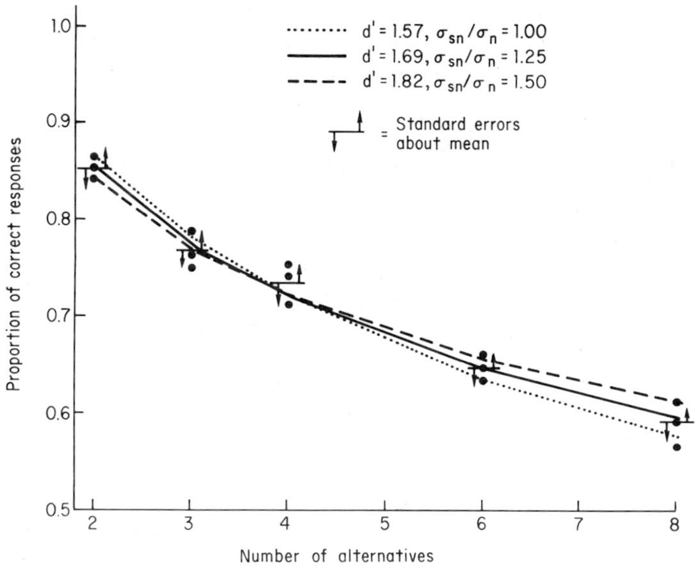

Fig. 5.11. Comparison of Data from Multiple-alternative, Forced-choice Experiments. Swet's [76] data on tonal detection for the 2-, 3-, 4-, 6-, and 8-alternative forced-choice experiments are shown. Three subjects were tested and separate points are plotted for each subject. The arrows show the binomial sampling error about the mean for each of the five experiments. Predictions of proportion correct for three values of the ratio σ_{sn}/σ_n are shown. In each case the value of d' was chosen so as to minimize the mean square deviation between observed and predicted values. Of the three curves, the best fit to the data is obtained with $\sigma_{sn}/\sigma_n = 1.25$ and $d' = 1.44$.

[79], who, in an experiment in auditory detection with signal and noise binaurally out of phase, obtained estimates of detectability that appeared to be both a function of experimental technique and of the type of noise used (burst or continuous). For signal and noise binuarally in phase, however, consistent estimates of detectability were obtained for the two techniques. McFadden implicitly assumed normal distributions of equal variance in analyzing his data, and it is not clear whether the apparent inconsistencies between the yes-no and forced-choice d' estimates were due to a change in the observer's decision strategy, or whether the out-of-phase binaural condition leads to a markedly different form for the canonical f_n and f_{sn} distributions. Current theories on binaural signal detection [80, 81] and the nature of relevant stimulus distributions [82] suggest that the latter explanation is more plausible. Emmerich [38, 83] also provides evidence of consistent differences in the slope of ROC curves for different interaural conditions.

5.2.8.2 Rating-scale Data

Experimental comparisons between the rating-scale method and other procedures have been fairly extensive, and here again a reasonable degree of consistency between methods has been observed. Egan, Shulman, and Greenberg [12], in one of the earliest comparative studies, obtained essentially the same estimates of d' using a three-category rating scale and a yes-no procedure with three separate choices of criterion. Although an unweighted least-squares procedure was used in fitting their ROC curves (and hence reliable information on precision of estimation is not available), the variation in the d' estimates across subjects and methods of measurement did not appear to differ substantially from that shown in Table 5.3. Emmerich [38, 39, 83] has also obtained comparable ROC curves for the yes-no and rating-scale methods as well as data showing that the estimated area under a single-interval rating-scale ROC curve is not significantly different from the proportion of correct responses in a two-interval forced-choice experiment. In addition, Schulman and Mitchell [84], in a rating-scale analog of the yes-no and asymmetric forced-choice procedures, obtained consistent estimates of detectability for these two procedures. The slope of the two-interval rating-scale ROC curve was found not to differ significantly from the predicted value of unity. The effect of signal probability on rating-scale ROC curves has been investigated by Nachmias [85], who obtained essentially the same ROC curves with signal probabilities of 0.25, 0.5, and 0.75, respectively. A four-category scale was used. Nachmias also found that the rating-scale ROC curve was essentially the same as that obtained with yes-no data.

Not all comparisons, however, have been entirely favorable. Markowitz and Swets [75], for example, have observed consistent differences between binary and rating-scale ROC curves. Their binary ROC curves, plotted on normal-normal coordinates, exhibited a slope of unity, whereas the rating-scale curves showed slopes of less than unity, the deviation from unity increasing with an increase in signal-to-noise ratio. One possible explanation for these differences may be due to variations in experimental technique. Markowitz and Swets obtained changes in criterion for the yes-no experiment by varying the a priori probability of a signal presentation, whereas Egan, Schulman, and Greenberg and Emmerich did not alter the experimental paradigm in any way but obtained changes in criterion (strict, medium, or lax) by instructions only. Presumably the correspondence between the category boundaries of the rating scale and the subject's own choice of criterion (strict, medium, and lax) is closer than if the criterion changes are imposed on the subject by the experimenter's choice of a priori probabilities. Also, if stability of the criterion is a factor and the yes-no procedure may have had a less stable criterion, a variance ratio closer to unity is to be expected (see Sec. 5.1.2.3). Despite the differences in slope that were observed, however, the estimates of detectability d'_e were found to be very similar for both the rating-scale and binary-choice procedures.

Markowitz and Swets also obtained ROC curves for a two-interval rating-scale procedure in which the slopes, contrary to theory, were not unity. These data conflict with corresponding observations by Schulman and Mitchell [84], who obtained slopes close to unity. To complicate matters further, Leshowitz [86, 87] obtained slopes slightly greater than unity using a two-interval rating-scale procedure. Leshowitz also found that the improvement in detectability for the two-interval procedure over the single-interval procedure was not always $\sqrt{2}$ as predicted. On average, the measured detectability ratio for tones in continuous noise was less than $\sqrt{2}$, whereas for pedestal detection in gated noise it was greater than $\sqrt{2}$. No explanation resolving these discrepancies has been proposed.

5.2.9 Optimal Decision Rules

One of the more controversial aspects of decision-theory models is the question of optimization. Although it is evident that the subject can adjust his criterion in a responsible manner depending on relative penalties and a priori probabilities, it is not clear to what extent the subject is utilizing a rule that may be regarded as optimum.

The evidence in support of the human observer as an optimum or near-optimum detector is based largely on observations showing a high average return in expected-value experiments [42, 88] and on a high positive correlation between the measured and theoretically optimum criteria [42, 89]. Whereas these data show that the adjustment of the criterion is in the right direction, they do not necessarily prove that the observer is using an optimum decision rule; a good but far from optimum decision rule could yield similar data. Green [89], for example, points out that the function relating expected gain to criterion value is relatively flat and that substantial deviations from the theoretically optimum criterion can be tolerated with only a small loss in expected gain.

Ideally, the criterion is determined according to a well-defined rule and should remain unchanged within a session, and also between sessions if there is no change in the payoff matrix or a priori probabilities. However, there is no direct evidence that the criterion remains fixed within sessions, and, as discussed earlier, there is evidence of substantial variations between sessions, particularly for a priori probabilities in the vicinity of 0.1 or 0.9 (see Fig. 5.8). There is also a consistent tendency for the observed criterion to be less extreme than the optimal. Further evidence of this effect is provided by Norman [51], who observed that for a highly asymmetric payoff matrix the observer tends to adjust the criterion in consecutive tests towards a less extreme value. Finally, the observed criterion appears to depend on whether the payoff matrix or a priori probabilities are manipulated, although the theoretically optimum criterion may be the same for both cases [7, chap. 4].

A significant feature of the data reported by Green and Swets [7, chap. 4] is that the observed criterion is not very different from the predicted criterion for the balanced payoff matrix where neither the a priori probabilities nor relative costs favor either a yes or no response. It may be that the decision process approximates an optimal strategy for only a limited set of conditions. Siebert [90], for example, has conjectured that "the stochastic coding or neural noise in the primary units is in *simple signal situations* [italics added] the dominant or principal limitation on the auditory discrimination performance of a human observer, i.e., that the more central parts of the nervous system behave in an effectively optimum manner in such situations." Although there is no direct experimental evidence to support this conjecture, predictions based on a neurophysiological model employing this principle are very similar in form to those obtained with human observers (see Sec. 5.2.10).

If, as may be inferred from experimental data, the canonical f_n and f_{sn} distributions for a single-criterion model are normal and of unequal variance, then the additional assumption that the observer uses an optimum decision strategy introduces a theoretical inconsistency. If the canonical probability distributions cross at more than one point (as is the case for normal distributions of unequal variance), then the test statistic is clearly not the likelihood ratio, or any monotonic function of the likelihood ratio, and the observer is therefore not using the optimal strategy (see Fig. 5.5). Either the distributional assumptions are incorrect or the observer is using a less-than-ideal decision strategy.

The concept of optimality also enters at the initial coding stage, e.g., in defining the "best" statistic for representing a continuous waveform observed over a finite interval of time. One type of encoder which is frequently assumed in audition* but which is not necessarily optimum is the $2WT$ sampling detector using a likelihood-ratio criterion (see Sec. 5.1.4). Experimental data show that not only is the human ob-

* Although an upper bound on visual detection is readily defined owing to the quantal nature of light [91] idealized visual detectors have not been studied to the same extent as idealized auditory detectors, despite the theoretical difficulties encountered with the latter in converting from a continuous waveform to a discrete representation.

server less efficient than this detector, but that the relative efficiency of the human observer is highly dependent on the stimuli used and the type of experiment. Marill [92], in a direct comparison between the two, showed that for the detection of tones (phase unknown) in Gaussian noise the human observer required a signal roughly 14 dB greater in intensity to match the performance of the $2WT$ sampling detector. For experiments in which an increment in signal intensity is to be detected, the human observer requires progressively larger increments in intensity to maintain the same level of detection as the background level is increased, although the $2WT$ sampling detector is presumably independent of signal level. In addition, human detectability is critically dependent on the relative phase of the stimulus increment and background tone [19]. Finally, the idealized detector does not take into account the relative onset times of signals and noise, although this has been found to be an important variable for the detection of tone bursts in gated noise [93, 94].

5.2.10 Stimulus Encoding

A much better approximation to the human observer can be obtained if a less-than-ideal coding procedure is assumed. The predictions may also be very much simpler to derive even if there is no difference in form from the idealized case [95]. The problem of choosing the most appropriate test statistic in a decision-theory model reduces essentially to the perennial problem of determining the appropriate physical correlate of the sensory effect. Unless questions of optimality arise, which appears not to be the case, the coding and decision processes are basically independent, and there is no theoretical reason for favoring one form of coding over any other.

Space does not allow a detailed discussion of the various coding procedures that have been proposed, and only a few of the more important models are briefly described. The simplest approach has been to assume that the sensory effect is directly proportional to stimulus intensity giving rise to a class of models in which the normalized distance between the f_n and f_{sn} distributions increases linearly with signal intensity. Predictions of the psychometric function based on this simple model differ substantially from observation, unless it is also assumed that the internal noise changes with stimulus intensity [96, 97]. Some elaboration of the theory is also required in order to account for the psychometric functions obtained with comparison rather than detection judgments [96].

Relatively good predictions of auditory and visual signal detection have been obtained by assuming that f_n and f_{sn} belong to distributional families which show an increase in variance with an increase in distance between distributions. Both the Poisson and chi-square distributions exhibit the property that the variance increases linearly with expected value, and several auditory and visual-detection models employing these distributions have been proposed. Direct application of a Poisson counting process, for example, has met with comparative success in the modeling of visual intensity discrimination [67, 98–100] where a square-root law between detectability and stimulus energy holds over a wide range. The use of counting processes in auditory modeling is more subtle, in that the relationship between detectability and intensity in decibels is more nearly linear (Weber's law). Auditory counting models which have been proposed [90, 101, 102] include an additional transformation which together with the counting process produces the linear or near-linear relationship.

A related class of models is that in which the test statistic is defined as the short-term energy of the stimulus. For the case of tonal signals in band-limited noise, the derived f_n and f_{sn} distributions are approximately chi-square and noncentral chi-square, respectively. By a suitable choice of averaging time and effective bandwidth, relatively good fits to experimental data have been obtained for the pedestal effect, Weber's law, integration effects, and other data [7, 19, 103]. Each of the models referred to, however, accounts for only a portion of the data. At present there is still no single, universal model which will account for all these effects.

Another type of stimulus encoding is that of the neural quantum model wherein the sensory effect is assumed to change in large, discrete steps, presumably as a result of discreteness in the peripheral neural system [104]. A characteristic feature of these models is that the quanta are few in number and the discrete nature of the process is not obscured by variability within the system. In terms of decision-theory models, a quantal coding process gives rise to f_n and f_{sn} distributions that are discrete and which in turn generate ROC curves and psychometric functions showing distinct join points.

The evidence in support of the neural quantum model in audition is not overwhelming. The quantal response curves observed by Stevens, Morgan, and Volkmann [104] have not always been observed by others, presumably as a result of differences in experimental technique. Data reported by Larkin and Norman [105] and Norman [77] tend to satisfy a quantum model, but predictions based on conventional decision-theory models assuming continuous rather than discrete distributions also provide an adequate fit to their data [106]. Although there is some evidence of quantal effects in vision, this is due to the quantum nature of light rather than any discreteness caused by neural coding. Furthermore, the evidence showing that the visual system can be stimulated by a single quantum of light is primarily physiological [107], and unambiguous evidence of perceptual discreteness has yet to be obtained. Blackwell [96, 108] has studied this problem extensively, and although in a few individual experiments psychometric functions were obtained which were consistent with a quantum model, most of the data were not consistent with this interpretation. If very many quanta are required for discrimination, then the model more appropriately belongs to the class of counting models discussed earlier. For a more detailed review of the quantum model see Corso [109].

Perhaps the most promising approach to the modeling of sensory systems is to base the coding process on available neurophysiological data. In the auditory model proposed by Siebert [90] the relevant physiological variable is assumed to be the time interval between successive spikes in single, primary afferent neurons in the VIIIth nerve. The probability distributions governing interpulse intervals were obtained by direct measurement (in cats) and were found to approximate a gamma distribution with a simple scale adjustment to adjust for differences in frequency or intensity. An optimal decision rule using a likelihood-ratio criterion is assumed which for this particular model reduces to using the total number of spikes during each tone burst as the test statistic. Predictions based on this model of the difference limen for frequency and intensity of high-frequency tones parallels data obtained with human observers, including an effect similar to Weber's law.

5.2.11 Detection and Recognition

An important class of experiments is that in which the subject is required to identify which of several stimulus alternatives was presented. A central feature of recognition experiments is that, generally, more than two stimulus and more than two response alternatives are involved. The conventional detection experiment may be formally treated as a special type of recognition experiment in which there are only two stimulus alternatives, but this is essentially a case of redefining terms. It is of greater interest to consider how decision-theory models may apply to recognition experiments which are only slightly more complex than the conventional detection experiment.

A classic experiment is that in which the stimulus may be either one of two signals in noise, or noise alone. The observer is required both to detect whether or not a signal is present and also to recognize which of the two signals may have been presented [110, 111]. Initially, data obtained by Shipley [110] indicated that if no signal was detected, the recognition decision was no better than chance. Two tones of different frequency (500 and 1,100 Hz) were used as the signals in a background of broadband, Gaussian noise. This result implies either the existence of a simple sensory threshold (contrary to other evidence), or that there may be a recognition threshold although there is no detection threshold. It has been suggested by Lindner [112, 113], however, that the subjects in Shipley's investigation were not highly motivated to make a correct recognition. Lindner's data and additional data obtained by Shipley [114, p. 304, footnote 2] show that, given sufficient motivation, the recognition responses after a miss are better than chance. Although these data do not support a simple threshold theory, they do not necessarily support the conventional decision-theory interpretation.

Tanner [115] proposed an extension of the conventional decision-theory model to account for simple recognition data. A spatial representation is used for the separate signal and noise conditions where each point locates the mean of a bivariate normal distribution. The normalized distance between any two points represents the relative discriminability between the conditions corresponding to the two points. The line joining the two points is used as the decision axis, and the decision rule is to set a criterion on this axis and to consider the projection of each observation on the axis, deciding in favor of that condition which is on the same side of the criterion as the observation. As before, the operating characteristic for a pair of conditions is obtained by varying the criterion along the decision axis. Both Tanner [115] and Swets and Birdsall [88] have found a model of this sort adequate for describing their data on the detection and recognition of tones in noise. Their experiments, however, did not provide a critical test of their respective models; Swets and Birdsall were concerned with detection only, and Tanner did not consider motivational variables.

A more exacting test of Tanner's model is provided by Lindner's [112] data, in which the role of motivational variables for both detection and recognition is considered. The model fails to account for a substantial portion of these data. For two of the four subjects tested the model was inapplicable in that recognition responses were well beyond predictions based on their detection data; the data of the remaining two subjects, although analyzable within the framework of the model, showed a substantially higher proportion of correct recognitions when using a strict detection criterion than predicted by the model. Lindner has proposed a more sophisticated version of Tanner's model yielding substantially better predictions in which the recognition rule depends on the location of the test statistic on each of the detection axes. More data are required, however, for an adequate evaluation of this model. In contrast with the difficulties encountered with the decision-theory formulation, models based on choice theory account for recognition data reasonably well. Lindner [112, chap. 5] found relatively minor deviations between the recognition data and predictions based on Shipley's [114] choice model.

A factor not to be overlooked in modeling both detection and recognition is that stimulus uncertainty reduces detectability. For example, the probability of detecting a tone in noise is reduced if the observer is uncertain of the frequency of the tone [116]. This uncertainty appears to affect the perceptual rather than the response mechanism, since, as shown by Swets and Sewall [117], information on the signal frequency improves detection if presented before a trial, but not if presented immediately after a trial. Experimental data on the detection of tones of uncertain frequency suggest some form of frequency filtering prior to the detection mechanism, where the mode of filtering may be mediated by a central process [118]. The implication is that the modeling of the sensory mechanism is strongly affected by such nonsensory factors as number of stimulus alternatives or frequency of occurrence. Whereas for the simple detection experiment the decision-theory approach provides a simple basis for separating sensory from nonsensory variables, the interaction of these variables is considerably more complicated in the detection-recognition problem.

A common feature of both the decision-theory and choice models is the use of a spatial representation in defining the relative discriminability between pairs of conditions. In most decision-theory models the test statistic is related to some physical (or physiological) parameter of the stimulus. Thus if the test statistic is multidimensional, then each dimension is presumably related to a different parameter of the stimulus. If, however, the spatial representation is no more than a convenient mathematical summary, then the decision-theory model may not differ from the choice-theory model in any important sense. Furthermore, if the locations of the points are to be estimated solely from the data, with no constraints on their configuration, then a relatively unstructured approach such as that of choice theory, or Shepard's [119] analysis of proximities, has obvious advantages.

Sperling [120] provides a good example of the need for a relatively unstructured approach to the analysis of detection-recognition data. An experiment was performed in which the signal consisted of a light source against background illumination of fixed intensity. The signal intensity could take one of 11 values from −5 units below the background illumination to +5 units above the background. The observer was required to identify which of the 11 signal levels was used on each trial. The results are summarized schematically in Fig. 5.12. Each of the possible signals is represented by a point in a two-dimensional space where the distance between pairs of points is monotonically related to the frequency of confusion between the signals represented by the

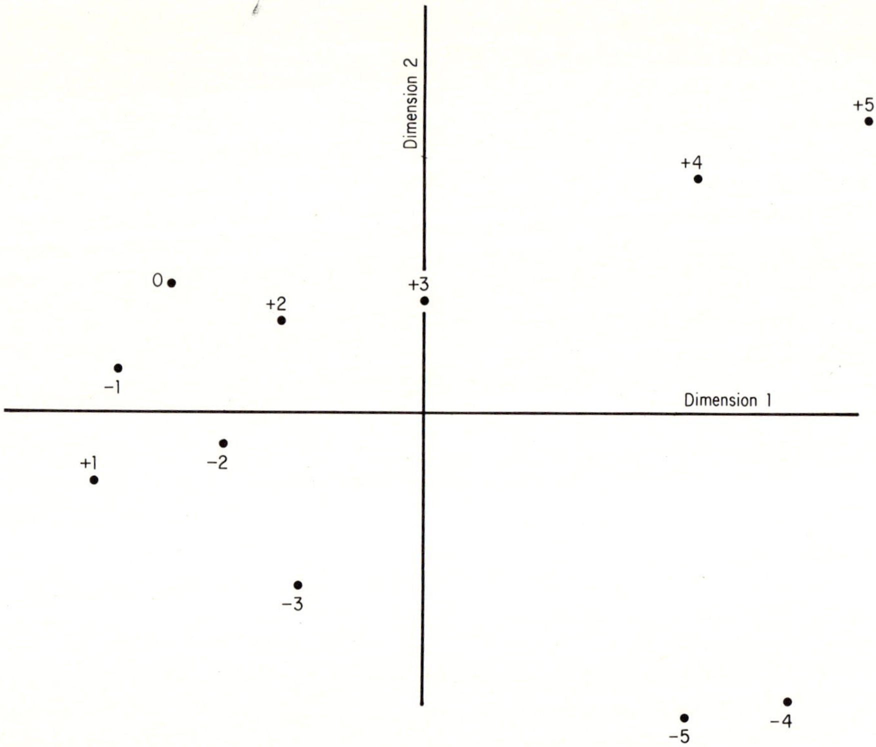

Fig. 5.12. Analysis of Proximities: Sperling's Detection-Recognition Data. In a visual experiment involving both detection and recognition [120], the signal intensity could take one of 11 values from −5 units below the background illumination to +5 units above the background. The observer was required to identify which of the 11 signal levels was used on each trial. The data were analyzed using an improved version of the analysis of proximities [121]. Each of the possible stimuli is represented by a point in a multidimensional space where the distance between pairs of points is monotonically related to the frequency of confusion between the conditions represented by the two points. The closer the points the greater is the frequency of confusion. In the case of Sperling's [120] data, an adequate fit to the data was obtained using two dimensions. Note that the frequency of confusion tends to be greater for very large differences in intensity as opposed to moderately large differences.

two points. The closer the points, the greater the frequency of confusion. The data were analyzed using an improved version of Shepard's analysis of proximities devised by Kruskal [121].

It is apparent from the analysis that two factors play a prominent role, signal intensity and the direction of the difference between the signal intensity and the background illumination. In particular, the frequency of confusion for moderate differences in intensity involving signals that are either both above or both below the background illumination is smaller than the frequency of confusion for very large differences in intensity where the signal levels straddle the background illumination. Prior to the experiment it was not known that these two factors would be of importance, or would interact in this way. Having used a relatively unstructured approach to isolate the relevant perceptual variables, a concise mathematical model can be developed to account for recognition data of this type.

5.3 Discussion

5.3.1 Applicability of Decision-theory Models

It is clear from the preceding section that no single decision-theory model can account for the wide diversity of data that have been considered. The overall picture, rather, appears to be one in which a family of decision-theory models can be used to describe a substantial range of sensory phenomena with varying degrees of success. The areas in which decision-theory models appear to be most successful involve the detection of simple auditory or visual signals against a background of fixed, high-level noise. The theory has not been validated as extensively with signals in quiet where the subject's internal noise is a dominant factor. Also, decision tasks involving complex response mechanisms are not always amenable to a simple decision-theoretic formulation. Presumably the assumption of a simple decision rule confounds factors relating to the response mechanism with factors relating to the perceptual process. An example of such is the change in the equivalent f_n and f_{sn} distributions resulting from instability of the criterion.

Despite the success of the theory in predicting receiver operating characteristics for simple detection tasks, the prediction of psychometric functions has not been as successful. The emphasis of much recent work in psychoacoustics has been directed to this problem as well as to questions relating to the systematic decrease in sensitivity with signal strength (Weber's law). Current developments indicate that these effects can be accounted for within a decision-theory framework, provided a suitable choice is made for the test statistic. Other areas which present a challenge to the decision-theory approach are the analysis of sequential response dependencies, learning effects, and, in particular, recognition.

Another overall view may be obtained by considering the key assumptions underlying the theory and the conditions under which these are inconsistent with experimental data. The joint assumptions of fixed distributions and of a criterion determined solely by the payoff matrix or specified a priori probabilities appear to hold only under very special circumstances. A more realistic situation is that of fixed distributions and a criterion that is reasonably stable within a test session but varies slightly about its mean value between sessions. Well-designed auditory and visual detection experiments using a random, high-level background noise appear to satisfy these conditions. Apart from initial adaptation effects, long-term trends have not been observed in these experiments, although sequential response dependencies have occasionally been reported. The detection of signals without a fixed external noise has not received the same degree of experimental investigation, but the available evidence suggests that the above-mentioned difficulties (instability, gradual trends, sequential dependencies) are far more common. Whereas intersessional differences in criterial variables are adequately handled by the theory, intersessional variations in sensitivity pose a serious problem. This difficulty is not unique to decision-theory models.

Distributional assumptions have in many cases favored the normal distribution. The assumption appears consistent with the data for virtually all modalities (vision, audition, touch, smell), provided the variance ratio is a free parameter to be estimated from the data. For most sets of data, the variance of the f_{sn} distribution tends to be greater than that for the f_n distribution. An adequate fit using normal distributions does not imply that this assumption is necessarily the correct or the most accurate one; good fits to several sets of auditory and visual data have also been obtained using the Poisson or gamma family of distributions (including the chi-square and Rayleigh-Rice distributions as special cases).

Assumptions of optimal performance have not found strong experimental support, although the possibility that the decision process may be near-optimum under favorable experimental conditions should not be ruled out. The experimental evidence indicates that the observer does adjust his criterion in a responsible manner, but that the choice of criterion differs consistently from the predicted optimum values and also depends on whether the payoff matrix or a priori probabilities are manipulated. There is, in addition, a good deal of evidence showing an element of randomness in the observer's choice of criterion. Furthermore, the assumption of normal distributions of unequal variance is inconsistent with the use of likelihood ratio as a test statistic (the single-criterion model is implied), and at least one of these assumptions is in error.

The coding of sensory stimuli differs substantially between modalities, and there is little evidence of a general, "optimal" coding principle. In particular, there is no strong evidence to show that the coding processes used by a human listener are comparable to that of the $2WT$ sampling detector. Whereas the basic concepts of decision theory are eminently well suited for the modeling of human signal detection, detailed models based on highly structured and efficient statistical detectors are both unnecessarily complicated and not always consistent with experimental data.

5.3.2 Relative Merits of the Decision-theory Approach

Basically, the decision-theory approach provides a convenient and consistent framework for the modeling of sensory systems. The suitability of decision theory in this context is perhaps not surprising, since in most of the basic experiments the task of the human observer is essentially that required of an electronic or statistical detector. The modeling process thus reduces essentially to finding that statistical detector which approximates the human observer most closely. Modeling the human observer in terms of a statistical detector, however, does more than redefine old problems in a new terminology. Whereas previously it was known, albeit imprecisely, that an observer's performance could be affected by a variety of nonsensory factors, such as motivation, knowledge of a priori probabilities, and relative costs, it was not clear how these effects could be quantified. The value of the decision-theory approach thus lies not only in the insight brought to bear on old problems by the concepts and techniques of a new and relevant theory, but also in providing a quantitative basis for attacking these problems.

To the experimentalist, one of the most valuable features of decision-theory models is the separation of certain criterial variables from the inherent sensitivity of the sensory system. Whereas criterial variables may depend on experimental technique, sensitivity should be independent of method. As pointed out earlier, however, only certain criterial variables can be isolated in this way. An unstable criterion, for example, results in an ROC curve lying below that which would be obtained using a fixed criterion, thereby resulting in a lower measure of sensitivity. A relatively stable criterion represents a desirable goal which can be achieved by careful experimental design but which should never be taken for granted.

The generality of the decision-theory approach also allows for a meaningful comparison to be drawn between data obtained by different psychophysical procedures. Comparative experiments with the yes-no, forced-choice, and single-interval rating-scale procedures show comparable estimates of detectability for all three methods. Estimates of the variance ratio, however, do not show the same degree of consistency. Also, in order to estimate d' accurately using the symmetric forced-choice method, it is necessary to have additional information on the variance ratio. Rough estimates can be obtained, however, by arbitrarily setting this ratio at some reasonable value. Bounds on the error obtained in this way may be derived from the curves shown in Fig. 5.10*a* to *d*.

Perhaps the most celebrated result to follow from the application of decision theory in psychophysics has been the virtual demolition of the simple, high-threshold concept. Although high-threshold models have seldom been assumed explicitly, the conventional "correction" procedure for false alarms clearly implies such a model. Furthermore, the traditional view of false alarms being solely a nuisance effect for which a "correction" is necessary had a profound effect on experimental design. Great care was taken to keep the false-alarm rate as low as possible; subjects were trained to avoid false alarms, and in some cases tests with too high a false-alarm rate were rejected as unreliable. The specification of performance in terms of hits and false alarms does not, of course, necessarily imply a decision-theory model, but it was largely through the application of decision theory that the value of the false alarm as a relevant experimental variable was realized. In terms of the ROC or isosensitivity curve it is seen that a low false-alarm rate restricts data unnecessarily to a narrow region of the curve and much pertinent information is lost. The possibility of a low sensory threshold is not incompatible with a decision-theory formulation, and a hybrid model of this type may be well worth further investigation.

In deciding on the merit of a theory it is essential, as in any decision task, to consider the alternatives. At least two competing theories provide a serious challenge: choice theory [11, 114] and multiple-state threshold models, a classic example of which is Luce's [13] two-state model. Although choice theory appears unrivaled in certain areas, such as recognition, decision-theory models appear to be superior in the modeling of human signal detection where the judgmental task required of the observer is relatively simple. The choice-theory model discussed by Luce [11], for example, does not account for asymmetric ROC curves and makes inaccurate predictions for the proportion of correct responses in the multiple-alternative, symmetrical forced-choice experiment. For more complex experimental paradigms, however, such as the multiple-look multiple-alternative experiment [Swets et al., 1959, quoted in Ref. 11], predictions of proportion correct based on choice theory appear superior to those based on a decision-theory model. It could be that neither model is accurate, since, as pointed out by Luce in the same chapter, there is reason to doubt the assumption of independent observations implicit in both models.

The two-state threshold model has not been studied as extensively as decision-theory models, and hence a comprehensive comparison is not possible. However, for the simple yes-no experiment the two-state model provides good predictions of the isosensitivity function, although it does not provide an adequate link between the observed operating points and the payoff matrix [13]. Predictions of proportion correct for the symmetrical forced-choice experiment do not tax the model, owing to the large number of free parameters. The two-state threshold model was not designed to handle rating-scale data, and it is not clear what decision rule the observer might be using. As Wickelgren [66] has pointed out, there are many possible decision rules, and none stands out as being appreciably more likely than the others.

A characteristic feature of decision-theory models is that the manipulation of response probabilities reflects the perceptual process (assuming a simple response mechanism). Since the modeling process, at best, can yield no more than an approximation of reality, it is not surprising that those experiments which have been designed to concentrate on the peripheral system and which simplify the response task as far as possible have tended to yield data favorable to a decision-theory formulation. More complicated experimental paradigms, however, which tax the observer's response mechanism appear to favor the more flexible choice-theory analysis. Thus, although the theories overlap, the decision-theory approach may perhaps be regarded as more appropriate within its intended area of applicability.

Although a proper understanding of perception entails a detailed knowledge of both perceptual and response mechanisms, the current trend in experimental psychophysics is largely stimulus-oriented. The underlying reason, presumably, is the belief that a deeper understanding of the peripheral sensory system will ultimately lead to a proper understanding of response mechanisms. New developments in physiology underscore this belief where in recent years a substantial body of data on the peripheral auditory and visual systems has been obtained. Since the neurophysiology of sensory systems is of a stochastic nature, a signal-detection approach appears eminently well suited for the modeling of such systems.

5.3.3 Shortcomings of the Decision-theory Approach

The shortcomings to be discussed relate more to the interpretation accorded to the theory rather than inadequacies of the theory per se. Perhaps the most serious criticism that can be leveled is the rigidity with which the initial decision-theory models were interpreted, leading to highly structured models based on a multiplicity of assumptions, not all of which were adequately supported by experimental data. In particular, little effort was made to distinguish between assumptions pertaining to separate aspects of these models. Whereas, for example, assumptions relating to the decision process appear to be reasonably consistent with experimental data, many of the early assumptions pertaining to the stimulus encoding process have found little experimental support.

Another criticism is that of treating assumptions that have been shown to be acceptable for one type of experiment as being generally valid. Thus for example, most of the basic data supporting a decision-theory formulation were obtained with signals superimposed on high-level background noise. It is not clear to what extent these results are applicable to situations in which no external noise is applied. There is a dearth of experimental evidence in this area. No investigator can afford to place unquestioned reliance on assumptions underlying any method of measurement, and in psychophysics, in particular, generalizations across different types of stimuli require continual experimental verification.

One consequence of the uncritical acceptance of the early, highly structured decision-theory models has been the development of performance indices which are highly theory-dependent. At present, at least half a dozen different indices of sensitivity have been proposed, nearly all of which make some distributional assumption (usually normality) for f_n and f_{sn}. Fortunately, there now appears to be a trend towards non-parametric and to some extent theory-independent measures of performance [122, 123]. The index proposed by Green [124], that the area under the ROC curve* be used as a measure of sensitivity, is a particularly good candidate, since it is independent of the underlying model. If, however, it is assumed that the ROC curve is generated by a single-criterion decision-theory model, this index has the additional property of being equal to the expected proportion of correct responses in the symmetric two-alternative forced-choice experiment.

The method of measuring detectability using the yes-no or asymmetric forced-choice methods poses serious practical problems. The technique is extremely time-consuming, in that separate test sessions are required for each point on the ROC curve and considerable care in experimental design is needed to ensure that intersessional differences in sensitivity are negligible. In addition, the analysis of data obtained in this way is not trivial. In fitting ROC curves, for example, it is necessary to take into consideration that measurements on both axes (hit rate and false-alarm rate) are subject to sampling errors and that the error variance varies along each axis. The usual method of fitting straight lines by eye or by a crude least-squares procedure to data plotted on transformed coordinates is not always satisfactory. These procedures provide no reliable information on precision of estimation or of the criterial values used by the observer. Crude estimates of the criterion have

* The use of the area under an operating characteristic as a measure of the quality of a statistical test has also been proposed by Subrahamanya [125] in the context of acceptance sampling.

been obtained by estimating the slope of the ROC curve in the region of the observed operating point. Apart from the practical difficulties of slope estimation, it is also unclear at exactly which point on the curve the slope should be estimated. Adequate methods of data analysis have only recently been developed.

A very practical psychophysical technique is the symmetric forced-choice procedure, but this method, in turn, is not designed to provide information on motivational variables. There is also a need for additional information on the variance ratio in order to estimate d' accurately from the observed proportion of correct responses. The rating-scale procedure offers several advantages over both the yes-no and forced-choice techniques, but this method is also not without its shortcomings. Although highly efficient in that several points on the ROC curve may be estimated within a single session, the estimated points are not independent. Apart from the difficulties encountered in the statistical analysis of these data, the nature of this dependency is such that the estimated points always appear to fall on a monotonically increasing ROC curve. There is a danger that smooth curves obtained in this way may be taken as evidence of the consistency of an underlying sensory model when they more accurately reflect the method of data analysis. It should also be noted that data obtained using a two-interval rating-scale procedure have not been in complete accord with predictions based on the usual decision-theory analysis.

One feature of the decision-theory approach which is both an advantage and a disadvantage is the similarity of ROC curves for a wide range of models. Thus, for example, the two ROC curves shown in Fig. 5.6 relate to different models, yet do not differ appreciably from each other. In some respects robustness is a distinct advantage and tends to mitigate the effect of selecting the wrong model. On the other hand, the task of discriminating experimentally between models is difficult. Even if an observed ROC curve could be obtained with complete accuracy, the f_n and f_{sn} distributions generating the ROC curve cannot be determined uniquely. Any monotonic transformation of the decision axis will alter the shape of the f_n and f_{sn} distributions without affecting the ROC curve. The difficulty of discriminating between models may be lessened by considering features other than the ROC curve. The use of second-choice responses, for example, provides an elegant method of testing the high-threshold model. It is interesting to note that the use of second-choice responses in this context predates the first decision-theory models [126].

Finally, one of the most controversial topics associated with the application of decision theory in psychophysics is that of the so-defined "ideal" observer. Whereas it may be convenient to compare the human observer with an idealized, statistical detector, the concept of idealness should be treated with great caution. The definition of "ideal" or "optimum" must necessarily be arbitrary, thus substituting one form of arbitrariness for another less obvious form [127]. A more insidious danger, however, is that the definition of the "ideal" observer may imply constraints which are either unrealistic or restrict unnecessarily the applicability of the model. For example, the likelihood-ratio detector operating on $2WT$ independent samples can be thought of as representing an upper limit of detectability only if the stimulus can be fully characterized by $2WT$ independent samples. The range of stimuli which satisfy this constraint, however, is severely limited. It should also be remembered that the likelihood-ratio procedure is uniformly more efficient than other procedures only in the testing of *simple* hypotheses.

Acknowledgment

I would like to thank Drs. E. L. R. Corliss, W. A. Lindner, J. Nachmias, E. F. Shipley, W. P. Tanner, M. Treisman, and my many colleagues at the Bell Telephone Laboratories for their helpful comments and criticisms. I am particularly grateful to David Emmerich, Don Norman, and George Sperling, who, in addition to many valuable discussions, graciously allowed me access to their unpublished data.

REFERENCES

1. A. Rose, The Relative Sensitivities of Television Pickup Tubes, Photographic Film, and the Human Eye, *Proc. IRE,* **30:**293–300 (1942).
2. J. H. Van Vleck and D. Middleton, A Theoretical Comparison of the Visual, Aural, and Meter Reception of Pulsed Signals in the Presence of Noise, *J. Appl. Phys.,* **17:**940–971 (1946).
3. C. S. Sherwin, F. Kodman, Jr., J. J. Kovaly, W. C. Prothe, and J. Melrose, Detection of Signals in Noise: A Comparison Between the Human Detector and an Electronic Detector, *J. Acoust. Soc. Am.,* **28:**617–622 (1956).
4. W. W. Peterson, T. G. Birdsall, and W. C. Fox, The Theory of Signal Detectability, *IRE Trans. Inform. Theory,* **PGIT-4:**171–212 (1954).
5. W. P. Tanner, Jr., and J. A. Swets, A Decision-making Theory of Visual Detection, *Psychol. Rev.,* **60:**401–409 (1954).
6. J. A. Swets (ed.), "Signal Detection and Recognition by Human Observers," John Wiley and Sons, Inc., New York, 1964.
7. D. M. Green and J. A. Swets, "Signal Detection Theory and Psychophysics," John Wiley and Sons, Inc., New York, 1966.
8. F. R. Clarke and R. C. Bilger, The Theory of Signal Detectability and the Measurement of Hearing, in J. Jerger (ed.), "Modern Developments in Audiology," Academic Press, New York, 1963.
9. M. Treisman and T. R. Watts, Relation Between Signal Detectability Theory and the Traditional Procedures for Measuring Sensory Thresholds: Estimating

d′ from Results Given by the Method of Constant Stimuli, *Psychol. Bull.*, **66:**438–454 (1966).

10. W. A. Wickelgren, Unidimensional Strength Theory and Component Analysis of Noise in Absolute and Comparative Judgments, *J. Math. Psychol.*, **5:**102–122 (1968).
11. R. D. Luce, Detection and Recognition, in R. D. Luce, R. R. Bush, and E. Galanter (eds.), "Handbook of Mathematical Psychology," pp. 103–189, John Wiley and Sons, Inc., New York, (1963).
12. J. P. Egan, A. I. Schulman, and G. A. Greenberg, Operating Characteristics Determined by Binary Decisions and by Ratings, *J. Acoust. Soc. Am.*, **31:**768–773 (1959).
13. R. D. Luce, A Threshold Theory for Simple Detection Experiments, *Psychol. Rev.*, **70:**61–70 (1963).
14. M. Smith and E. A. Wilson, A Model of the Auditory Threshold and Its Application to the Problem of the Multiple Observer, *Psychol. Monographs,* **67**(9) (Whole No. 359) (1953).
15. R. C. Atkinson, G. H. Bower, and E. J. Crothers, "An Introduction to Mathematical Learning Theory" John Wiley and Sons, Inc., New York, 1965.
16. W. Lee, Detection Theory Micromatching, and the Constant-ratio Rule, *Perception Psychophys.*, **4:**217–219 (1968).
17. J. Neyman and E. S. Pearson, On the Problem of the Most Efficient Tests of Statistical Hypotheses, *Phil. Trans. Roy. Soc. London,* **A:**289 (1933).
18. T. G. Birdsall, The Theory of Signal Detectability: ROC Curves and Their Character, Ph.D. Thesis, University of Michigan, 1966.
19. S. M. Pfafflin and M. V. Mathews, Energy Detection Model for Monaural Auditory Detection, *J. Acoust. Soc. Am.*, **34:**1842–1852 (1962).
20. R. FitzHugh, The Statistical Detection of Threshold Signals in the Retina, *J. Gen. Physiol.*, **40:**925–948 (1957).
21. D. Slepian, Some Comments on the Detection of Gaussian Signals in Gaussian Noise, *IRE Trans. Inform. Theory,* **PGIT-4:**65 (1958).
22. H. C. Martel and M. V. Mathews, Further Results on the Detectability of Known Signals in Gaussian Noise, *Bell System Tech. J.*, **40:**423–451 (1961).
23. L. P. Smith, "Mathematical Methods for Scientists and Engineers," Prentice-Hall, Inc., New York, 1953.
24. D. Slepian, H. O. Pollack, and H. J. Landau, Prolate Spheroidal Wave Functions, Fourier Analysis and Uncertainty, *Bell System Tech. J.*, **40:**43–84 (1961).
25. C. E. Shannon and W. Weaver, "The Mathematical Theory of Communication," University of Illinois Press, Urbana, Illinois, 1949.
26. H. J. Landau and H. O. Pollack, Prolate Spheroidal Wave Functions, Fourier Analysis and Uncertainty—III, *Bell System Tech. J.*, **41:**1295–1336 (1962).
27. D. D. Dorfman and E. Alf, Jr., Maximum Likelihood Estimation of Parameters of Signal Detection Theory—A Direct Solution, *Psychometrika,* **33:**117–124 (1968).
28. J. C. Ogilvie and C. D. Creelman, Maximum Likelihood Estimation of ROC Curve Parameters, *J. Math. Psychol.*, **5:**377–391 (1968).
29. I. G. Abrahamson and H. Levitt, Analysis of Data from Experiments on Human Signal Detection, *J. Math. Psychol.*, **6:**391–417 (1969).
30. F. Attneave, A Method of Graded Dichotomies for the Scaling of Judgments, *Psychol. Rev.*, **56:**334–340 (1949).
31. W. Lee, Relationships between Thurstone Category Scaling and Signal Detection Theory, *Psychol. Bull.*, **71:**101–107 (1969).
32. J. P. Egan, G. Z. Greenberg, and A. I. Schulman, Operating Characteristics,

Signal Detectability, and the Method of Free Response, *J. Acoust. Soc. Am.*, **33:**993–1007 (1961).

33. D. E. Broadbent and M. Gregory, Vigilance Considered as a Statistical Decision, *Brit. J. Psychol.*, **54:**309–322 (1963).
34. J. F. Mackworth and M. M. Taylor, *d′* Measure of Signal Detectability in Vigilance-like Situations, *Canad. J. Psychol.*, **17:**302–325 (1963).
35. P. A. Lucas, Human Performance in Low Signal-probability Tasks, *J. Acoust. Soc. Am.*, **42:**158–178 (1967).
36. F. R. Clarke, Constant-ratio Rule for Confusion Matrices in Speech Communication, *J. Acoust. Soc. Am.*, **29:**715–720 (1957).
37. P. R. Gray, A Design Philosophy for Psychophysical Experiments, M.S. thesis, Massachusetts Institute of Technology, 1963.
38. D. S. Emmerich, Receiver Operating Characteristics Determined under Several Interaural Conditions of Listening, *Tech. Rept.* AF-AFOSR-548-567, Air Force Office of Scientific Research, Directorate of Information Sciences, 1967. (See also Refs. 39 and 83.)
39. D. S. Emmerich, ROCs obtained with Two Signal Intensities Presented in Random Order, and a Comparison between Yes-No and Rating ROCs, *Perception Psychophys.*, **3:**35–40 (1968).
40. W. P. Tanner, Jr., J. A. Swets, and D. M. Green, Some General Properties of the Hearing Mechanism, *Tech. Rept.* No. 30, Electronic Defense Group, University of Michigan, 1956.
41. D. A. Norman, Sensory Thresholds and Response Biases in Detection Experiments: A Theoretical and Experimental Analysis, Ph.D. thesis, University of Pennsylvania, 1962.
42. J. A. Swets, W. P. Tanner, Jr., and T. G. Birdsall, Decision Processes in Perception, *Psychol. Rev.*, **68:**301–340 (1961).
43. C. S. Watson, Signal Detection and Certain Physical Characteristics of the Stimulus During the Observation Interval, Ph.D. thesis, Indiana University, 1962.
44. J. P. Egan, A. I. Schulman, and G. Z. Greenberg, Memory for Waveform and Time Uncertainty in Auditory Detection, *J. Acoust. Soc. Am.*, **33:**779–781 (1961).
45. R. F. Gundy, Auditory Detection of an Unspecified Signal, *J. Acoust. Soc. Am.*, **33:**1008–1012 (1961).
46. J. A. Swets and S. T. Sewall, Invariance of Signal Detectability over Stages of Practice and Levels of Motivation, *J. Exptl. Psychol.*, **66:**120–136 (1963).
47. J. Zwislocki, F. Maire, A. S. Feldman, and H. Rubin, On the Effect of Practice and Motivation on the Threshold of Audibility, *J. Acoust. Soc. Am.*, **30:**254–262 (1958).
48. J. S. Lukaszewski and D. N. Elliot, Auditory Threshold as a Function of Forced-choice Techniques, Feedback, and Motivation, *J. Acoust. Soc. Am.*, **34:**223–228 (1962).
49. J. R. Binford and M. Loeb, Changes within and over Repeated Sessions in Criterion and Effective Sensitivity in an Auditory Vigilance Task, *J. Exptl. Psychol.*, **72:**339–345 (1966).
50. W. P. Tanner, Jr., and C. L. Rivette, Learning in Psychophysical Experiments, *J. Acoust. Soc. Am.*, **35:**1896 (1963). (Abstract)
51. D. A. Norman, Sensory Thresholds and Response Bias, *J. Acoust. Soc. Am.*, **35:**1432–1441 (1963).

52. M. S. Schoeffler, Theory for Psychophysical Learning, *J. Acoust. Soc. Am.*, **37:**1124–1133 (1965).
53. M. S. Schoeffler, personal communication, 1968.
54. R. C. Atkinson, A Variable Sensitivity Theory of Signal Detection, *Psychol. Rev.*, **70:**91–106 (1963).
55. M. P. Friedman, E. C. Carterette, L. Nakatani, and A. Ahumada, Comparisons of Some Learning Models for Response Bias in Signal Detection, *Perception Psychophys.*, **3:**5–11 (1968).
56. W. Lee and T. R. Zentall, Factorial Effects in the Categorization of Externally Distributed Stimulus Samples, *Perception Psychophys.*, **1:**120–124 (1966).
57. G. S. Tune, Response Preferences: A Review of Relevant Literature, *Psychol. Bull.*, **61:**286–302 (1964).
58. H. Levitt, Testing for Sequential Dependencies, *J. Acoust. Soc. Am.*, **43:**65–69 (1968).
59. J. A. Swets, W. P. Tanner, Jr., and T. G. Birdsall, The Evidence for a Decision Making Theory of Visual Detection, *Technical Rept.* No. 40, Electronic Defense Group, University of Michigan, 1955.
60. W. M. Kincaid and C. E. Hamilton, An Experimental Study of the Nature of Forced-choice Responses in Visual Detection, *Rept. Proj.* Michigan, 2144-295-T, Vision Research Laboratories, University of Michigan, 1959.
61. R. H. Hohle, Detection of a Visual Signal with Low Background Noise: An Experimental Comparison of Two Theories, *J. Exptl. Psychol.*, **70:**459–463 (1965).
62. J. Nachmias and R. M. Steinman, Study of Absolute Visual Detection by the Rating-scale Method, *J. Opt. Soc. Am.*, **53:**1206–1213 (1963).
63. W. D. Larkin, Rating Scales in Detection Experiments, *J. Acoust. Soc. Am.*, **37:**748–749 (1965).
64. C. S. Watson and W. T. Bourbon, Rating Scales and Two-state Threshold Models, *J. Acoust. Soc. Am.*, **38:**667–668 (1965).
65. D. E. Broadbent, Two-state Threshold Model and Rating-scale Experiments, *J. Acoust. Soc. Am.*, **40:**244–245 (1966).
66. W. A. Wickelgren, Testing Two-state Theories with Operating Characteristics and A Posteriori Probabilities, *Psychol. Bull.*, **69:**126–131 (1968).
67. H. B. Barlow, Increment Thresholds at Low Intensities Considered as Signal/Noise Discriminations, *J. Physiol.*, **136:**469–488 (1957).
68. E. Baumgardt and S. W. Smith, Facilitation Effect of Background Light on Target Detection: A Test of Theories of Absolute Threshold, *Vision Res.*, **5:**299–312 (1965).
69. J. Nachmias, Photosensitization and Intrinsic Noise in the Visual System, *Vision Res.*, **6:**113–115 (1966).
70. J. Nachmias and E. C. Kocher, Visual Detection and Discrimination of Luminance Increments, *J. Opt. Soc. Am.*, **60:**382–389 (1970).
71. L. A. Jeffress, Stimulus-oriented Approach to Detection, *J. Acoust. Soc. Am.*, **36:**766–774 (1964).
72. L. A. Jeffress, Stimulus-oriented Approach to Detection Reexamined, *J. Acoust. Soc. Am.*, **41:**480–488 (1967).
73. I. G. Abrahamson, H. Levitt, and L. Landgraf, Statistical Estimation of Parameters of Decision-theory Models, *J. Acoust. Soc. Am.*, **42:**1195 (1967). (Abstract)
74. C. S. Watson, M. E. Rilling, and W. T. Bourbon, Receiver-operating Character-

istics Determined by a Mechanical Analog to the Rating Scale, *J. Acoust. Soc. Am.,* **36:**283–288 (1964).

75. J. Markowitz and J. A. Swets, Factors Affecting the Slope of Empirical ROC Curves: Comparison of Binary and Rating Responses, *Perception Psychophys.,* **2:**91–100 (1967).
76. J. A. Swets, Indices of Signal Detectability Obtained with Various Psychophysical Procedures, *J. Acoust. Soc. Am.,* **31:**511–513 (1959).
77. D. A. Norman, Sensory Thresholds, Response Biases, and the Neural Quantum Theory, *J. Math. Psychol.,* **1:**88–120 (1964).
78. J. P. Egan and W. Benson, Lateralization of a Weak Signal Presented with Correlated and with Uncorrelated Noise, *J. Acoust. Soc. Am.,* **40:**20–26 (1966).
79. D. McFadden, Masking-level Differences with Continuous and with Burst Masking Noise, *J. Acoust. Soc. Am.,* **35:**1206–1218 (1966).
80. N. Durlach, Equalization and Cancellation Theory of Binaural Masking-level Differences, *J. Acoust. Soc. Am.,* **35:**1206–1218 (1963).
81. L. A. Jeffress, H. C. Blodgett, T. T. Sandel, and C. L. Wood, Masking of Tonal Signals, *J. Acoust. Soc. Am.,* **28:**416–426 (1956).
82. H. Levitt and E. A. Lundry, Some Properties of the Vector Model for Binaural Hearing, *J. Acoust. Soc. Am.,* **39:**1323 (1966). (Abstract)
83. D. S. Emmerich, Receiver-operating Characteristics Determined under Several Interaural Conditions of Listening, *J. Acoust. Soc. Am.,* **43:**298–307 (1968).
84. A. I. Schulman and R. R. Mitchell, Operating Characteristics from Yes-No and Forced-choice Procedures, *J. Acoust. Soc. Am.,* **40:**473–477 (1966).
85. J. Nachmias, Effects of Presentation Probability and Number of Response Alternatives on Simple Visual Detection, *Perception Psychophys.,* **3:**151–155 (1968).
86. B. Leshowitz, Receiver Operating Characteristics and Psycho-Metric Functions Determined under Several Conditions, Ph.D. dissertation, Brooklyn College, City University of New York, 1968.
87. B. Leshowitz, A Comparison of ROC Curves from One- and Two-interval Rating-scale Procedures, *J. Acoust. Soc. Am.,* **46:**399–402 (1969).
88. J. A. Swets and T. G. Birdsall, The Human Use of Information III: Decision-making in Signal Detection and Recognition Situations Involving Multiple Alternatives, *IRE Trans. Inform. Theory.* **PGIT-2:**138–165 (1956).
89. D. M. Green, Psychoacoustics and Detection Theory, *J. Acoust. Soc. Am.,* **32:**1189–1203 (1960).
90. W. M. Siebert, Some Implications of the Stochastic Behavior of Primary Auditory Neurons, *Kybernetik,* **2:**206–215 (1965).
91. A. Rose, A Unified Approach to the Performance of Photographic Film, Television Pickup Tubes, and the Human Eye, *J. Soc. Motion Picture Eng.,* **47:**273–294 (1946).
92. T. M. Marill, Detection Theory and Psychophysics, *Tech. Rept.* No. 319, Research Laboratories of Electronics, Massachusetts Institute of Technology, 1956.
93. J. M. Pickett, Backward Masking, *J. Acoust. Soc. Am.,* **31:**1613–1615 (1959).
94. L. L. Elliot, Backward Masking: Monotic and Dichotic Conditions, *J. Acoust. Soc. Am.,* **34:**1108–1115 (1962).
95. W. J. McGill, Variations on Marill's Detection Formula, *J. Acoust. Soc. Am.,* **43:**70–73 (1968).
96. H. R. Blackwell, Neural Theories of Simple Visual Discriminations, *J. Opt. Soc. Am.,* **53:**129–160 (1963).

97. J. M. Thijssen and A. J. H. Vendrik, Internal Noise and Transducer Function in Sensory Detection Experiments: Evaluation of Psychometric Curves and of ROC Curves, *Perception Psychophys.*, **3**:387–400 (1968).
98. H. L. de Vries, The Quantum Character of Light and Its Bearing Upon the Threshold of Vision, the Differential Sensitivity, and Acuity of the Eye, *Physica,* **10**:553–564 (1943).
99. V. Cane, Some Statistical Problems in Experimental Psychology, *J. Roy. Statist. Soc.,* **18B**:177–201 (1956).
100. M. Treisman, A Statistical Decision Model for Sensory Discrimination which Predicts Weber's Law and Other Sensory Laws: Some Results of a Computer Simulation, *Perception Psychophys.,* **1**:203–230 (1966).
101. J. R. Pierce, Proposal for an Explanation of Limens of Loudness, *J. Acoust. Soc. Am.,* **30**:418–420 (1958).
102. W. J. McGill and J. P. Goldberg, Pure Tone Intensity Discrimination and Energy Detection, *J. Acoust. Soc. Am.,* **44**:576–581 (1968).
103. W. J. McGill, Neural Counting Mechanisms and Energy Detection in Audition, *J. Math. Psychol.,* **4**:351–376 (1967).
104. S. S. Stevens, C. T. Morgan, and J. Volkmann, Theory of the Neural Quantum in the Discrimination of Loudness and Pitch, *Am. J. Psychol.,* **54**:315–335 (1941).
105. W. D. Larkin and D. A. Norman, An Extension and Experimental Analysis of the Neural Quantum Theory, in R. C. Atkinson (ed.), "Studies in Mathematical Psychology I," Stanford University Press, 1964.
106. M. M. Taylor, Comments on "Sensory Thresholds and Response Bias," *J. Acoust. Soc. Am.,* **36**:599 (1964).
107. H. B. Barlow, Retinal Noise and the Absolute Threshold, *J. Opt. Soc. Am.,* **46**:634–639 (1956).
108. H. R. Blackwell, Evaluation of the Neural Quantum Theory in Vision, *Am. J. Psychol.,* **66**:397–408 (1953).
109. J. F. Corso, "The Experimental Psychology of Sensory Behavior," Holt, Rinehart and Winston, Inc., New York, 1967.
110. R. D. Luce, Detection Thresholds: A Problem Reconsidered, *Science,* **132**:1495 (1960).
111. E. F. Shipley, A Model for Detection and Recognition with Signal Uncertainty, *Psychometrika,* **25**:273–289 (1960).
112. W. A. Lindner, The Detection-Recognition Problem and Its Theoretical Implications, Ph.D. thesis, Indiana University, 1966.
113. W. A. Lindner, Recognition Performance as a Function of Detection Criterion in a Simultaneous Detection-Recognition Task, *J. Acoust. Soc. Am.,* **44**:204–211 (1968).
114. E. F. Shipley, Detection and Recognition: Experiment and Choice Models, *J. Math. Psychol.,* **2**:277–311 (1965).
115. W. P. Tanner, Jr., A Theory of Recognition, *J. Acoust. Soc. Am.,* **28**:882–888 (1956).
116. D. M. Green, Detection of Auditory Sinusoids of Uncertain Frequency, *J. Acoust. Soc. Am.,* **33**:877–903 (1961).
117. J. A. Swets and S. T. Sewall, Stimulus versus Response Uncertainty in Recognition, *J. Acoust. Soc. Am.,* **33**:1586–1592 (1961).
118. J. A. Swets, Central Factors in Auditory-frequency Selectivity, *Psychol. Bull.,* **60**:429–460 (1963).
119. R. N. Shepard, The Analysis of Proximities: Multidimensional Scaling with

an Unknown Distance Function, I and II, *Psychometrika,* **27:**125–140, 219–246 (1962).

120. G. Sperling, personal communication, 1967.
121. J. B. Kruskal, Nonmetric Multidimensional Scaling: A Numerical Method, *Psychometrika,* **29:**115–129 (1964).
122. I. Pollack, D. A. Norman, and E. Galanter, An Efficient Non-parametric Analysis of Recognition Memory, *Psychol. Sci.,* **1:**327–328 (1964).
123. G. W. Wilcox, Inter-observer Agreement and Models of Monaural Auditory Processing in Detection Tasks, *Rept.* MMPP 68-4, Michigan Mathematical Psychology Program, University of Michigan, October 1968.
124. D. M. Green, General Prediction Relating Yes-No and Forced-choice Results, *J. Acoust. Soc. Am.,* **36:**1042 (1964). (Abstract)
125. M. T. Subrahamanya, Error Areas Under the Operating Characteristic Curves, *Sankhya: Indian J. Statist.,* **A:**71–86 (1966).
126. P. D. Bricker and A. Chapanis, Do Incorrectly-perceived Tachistoscopic Stimuli Convey Some Information?, *Psychol. Rev.,* **60:**181–188 (1953).
127. L. A. Zadeh, What is Optimal?, *IRE Trans. Inform. Theory,* **PGIT-4:**3 (1958).

CHAPTER SIX

Signal Analysis in the Auditory System

J. L. FLANAGAN

6.0 Introduction

Much scientific effort has aimed to formulate viable theories of human hearing, but no theory, so far, has succeeded in achieving generality. The reason is simple: Most theorizing has concerned specific behavioral functions and, as such, represents analytical organization (albeit sophisticated) of bodies of data relating to specific phenomena. Customarily physiological details of the hearing mechanism are bypassed to achieve functional descriptions of subjective behavior. Good examples are models that have been applied to binaural unmasking, threshold detection of signals in noise, and pitch perception.‡ To proceed otherwise—with the paucity of physiological knowledge presently at hand—would serve poorly to bring order into observed auditory phenomena. Even though specific models may have little generality, they often have immense usefulness when wisely applied in limited areas.

‡ The author can hold these up because he, along with others, has formulated analytical structures for such effects.

For any theory of hearing to attain a measure of generality, it must account, at least functionally, for the major transformations performed on acoustic signals received and processed by the auditory system. One such transformation is the conversion of mechanical motion in the inner ear into electrical activity in the first-order fibers of the auditory nerve. Present physiological knowledge does not permit an adequate functional description of this process. Nevertheless, the mechanical operation of the ear is relatively well understood (thanks to the brilliant experiments of von Békésy) and information is being accumulated rapidly about neural mechanisms. A relevant view, therefore, might be: "Given the physiological knowledge available, how many of the voluminous observations of psychoacoustic behavior can at least be interpreted (not necessarily explained) in terms of this physiological knowledge?" Any effort to draw together physiological facts on the one hand and psychophysical data on the other should serve to sharpen those areas where functional descriptions are lacking. Such an effort in itself requires speculation and hypothesis, but it still may serve to establish a basis for the eventual understanding of signal analysis in the auditory system. To hope that such effort might go as far as to encompass central perceptual mechanisms is too much for the present. But to expect that unifying relations may emerge about signal processing at the ear's periphery is not too much.

Why dream about an ultimate theory of hearing? One obvious motivation is simply the gratification of knowing what "makes the mechanism tick." A less academic one, which is the primary motivation for this chapter, is to determine those constraints imposed upon communication by the auditory system. If we could learn what signal features are important to audition and how the system processes and preserves these features, speech communication systems might exploit the same process to conserve channel capacity. It is quite reasonable to suppose that transmission economies might be realized fully as much through auditory and perceptual phenomena as through physical properties of the vocal tract.‡

The burden of this chapter is hence taken to be the correlating of certain measured psychoacoustic behavior with the meager physiological facts at our disposal—in other words, the interpreting (not explaining) of certain subjective responses in terms of peripheral ear physiology. Without in any way attempting to be exhaustive, we would like to put forward some examples of how this correlating can provide insight into signal processing in the auditory system.

‡ Other important and well-known motivations are those which aim to alleviate deafness and to understand the mechanism of the brain and human perception.

6.1 Functions of the Ear

To establish a common point of departure, we can recall a few rudimentary points about the ear, as shown in Fig. 6.1. Sound waves falling on the auricle are led down the external canal and set the eardrum into vibration. This motion is transmitted via the ossicular bones (malleus, incus, and stapes) into the cochlea. The cochlea, a fluid-filled chamber in the temporal bone, is wound in a spiral of two and one-half turns. It is partitioned into two chambers over almost its whole length by a complex structure, bounded on one side by the basilar membrane and on the other by Reissner's membrane. The partition terminates short of the end (apex), and the two chambers communicate there. A section taken through the cochlea is shown in Fig. 6.2.

The basilar membrane is a mechanical frequency analyzer of sorts, being light and stiff at the basal (stapes) end and more massive and compliant at the apical end. If the sound wave impinging on the ear contains high frequency energy (say a 10,000-Hz tone), the basilar membrane vibrates maximally near the basal (or stapes) end. If the signal is of a low frequency (say a 100-Hz tone) then the far (or apical) end vibrates maximally. Motion along the membrane is propagated as a traveling wave. The dispersive nature of the membrane is to act as a low-pass filter and delay the wave progressively as it traverses from base to apex.

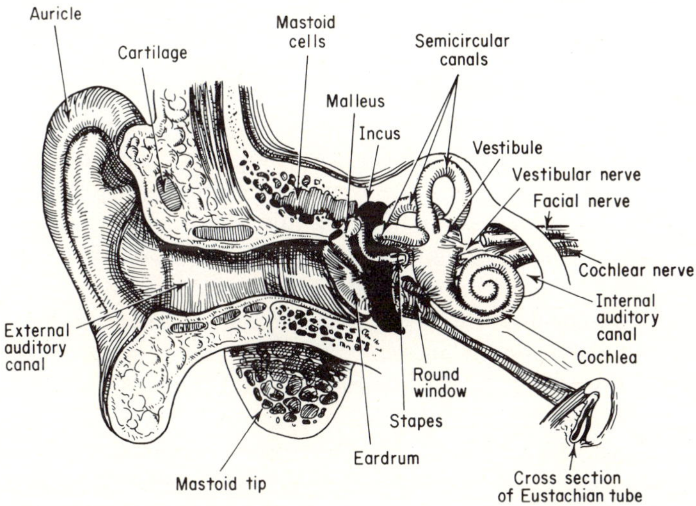

Fig. 6.1. Diagram of the peripheral auditory system. (*After H. Davis, ed., "Hearing and Deafness: A Guide for Laymen," Rinehart, New York, 1947.*)

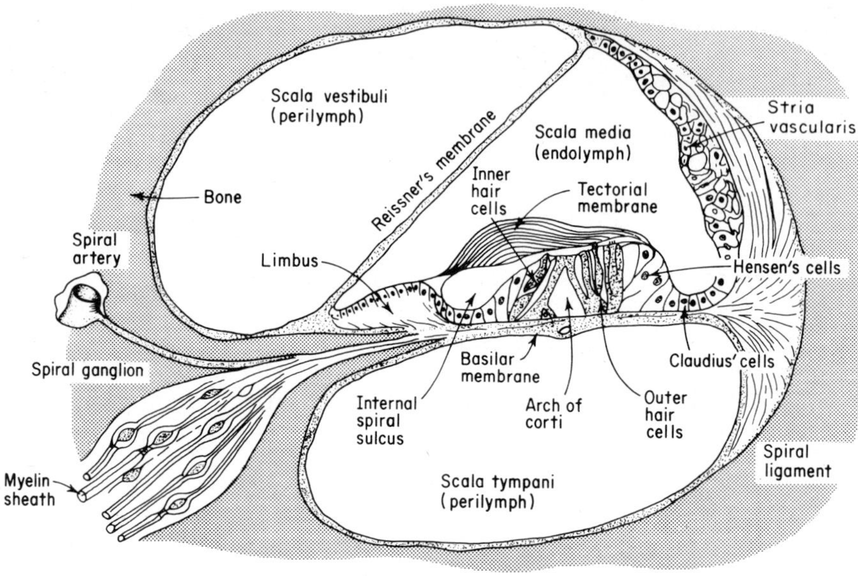

Fig. 6.2. Cross section of the cochlear canal. (*Adapted from Davis, 1947.*)

Situated along the basilar membrane is the spiral organ of Corti, which contains some 30,000 sensory cells (hair cells). Tiny hairs protrude from the cells and contact the tectorial membrane. A comparable number of first-order fibers of the auditory nerve terminate either multiply or singly upon these cells. Local deformation of the basilar membrane is believed to produce a shearing force on the hairs of the sensory cells. The shear is transduced in an unknown manner to trigger an on-off type of electrical activity in the fibers of the auditory nerve. This activity is propagated by the nerve over about 5 mm into the lower brain stem (medullar level). Here the first nerve junctions in the ascending auditory neural system occur. From this point, neural connections exist with several other sites, including the auditory cortex of both hemispheres and the sensory cells of the opposite ear.

The major transformations which an acoustic signal must undergo in eliciting an auditory response are now evident. First, there is the acoustomechanical processing of the middle ear and cochlea, resulting in signal representation in terms of basilar membrane motion. Second, the mechanical motion stimulates the sensory cells to produce a transducer potential, the details of which are unknown. Third, the transducer potentials trigger two-state electrical activity in the first-order fibers of the auditory nerve. Finally, the central nervous system receives and processes this aggregate neural activity and registers an appropriate percept.

Little is known about the details of the first three stages, and virtually nothing of a quantitative nature is known about the last. In our present effort, we wish to correlate psychoacoustic behavior with knowledge about these first three steps and, if possible, suggest how behavioral response to specific signals may be manifest at these stages. Toward this end, it is worthwhile to outline present understanding of the nature of these transformations. The next four sections summarize this understanding. The remaining part of the chapter points up examples of psychoacoustic behavior which can be interpreted in terms of this known physiology.

6.2 Acoustomechanical Properties of the Ear

The mechanical response of the basilar membrane has been measured over its apical extent by von Békésy. These data exist as amplitude-*vs.*-frequency and phase-*vs.*-frequency plots of membrane displacement for known displacements of the stapes. Similarly, the middle-ear transmission has been measured as the amplitude and phase of stapes displacement in response to known sound pressure at the eardrum.

Taking these physiological data, it is possible to fit mathematical functions to them to achieve analytically tractable descriptions of the mechanical behavior. This can be done in two steps: first, by making a functional description of eardrum-to-stapes transmission; and second, by making a functional description of stapes-to-membrane transmission. The idea is illustrated in Fig. 6.3. In the lower part of the diagram, the transfer function $G(s)$, written as a Laplace transform, relates the sound pressure at the eardrum $p(t)$ to the stapes displacement $x(t)$. The function $F_l(s)$, also written in Laplace notation, relates the membrane displacement $y_l(t)$ at some distance l from the base to the stapes motion $x(t)$. To the approximations which are possible in the physiological data, we consider that the transmission functions of Fig. 6.3 characterize a linear, passive, non-time-varying system.

In earlier work [1, 2] we derived forms for $G(s)$ and $F_l(s)$ which appear appropriate to the known physiological data. The results can be summarized for use here. The characteristics of middle-ear transmission can be described relatively well by the third-degree function

$$G(s) = \frac{c_0}{(s+a)[(s+a)^2+b]^2}$$

where $s = \sigma + j\omega =$ the complex frequency

$c_0 =$ a positive, real constant relating absolute values of eardrum pressure and stirrup displacement

$b = 2a = 2\pi(1{,}500)$ rad/s

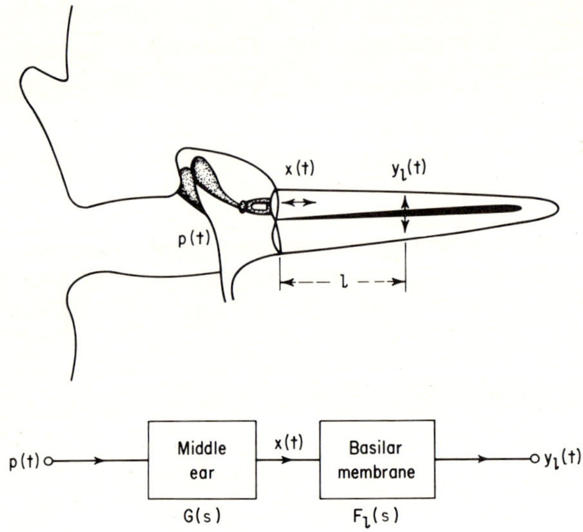

$$\frac{Y_l(s)}{P(s)} = \frac{X(s)}{P(s)} \cdot \frac{Y_l(s)}{X(s)} = G(s) \cdot F_l(s)$$

Fig. 6.3. Functional relations between eardrum pressure p(t), stapes displacement x(t), and basilar membrane displacement y_l(t). (*After Flanagan, 1962.*)

This function, with a single real-axis pole and two complex conjugate poles, has the relative amplitude and phase response shown in Fig. 6.4. The function is essentially low-pass in character and exhibits a lagging phase which monotonically increases.

One function which has been found to be a reasonable fit to von Békésy's data for stapes-to-membrane transmission is the fifth-degree function

$$F_l(s) = c_1 \beta_l^4 \left(\frac{2{,}000\pi\beta_l}{\beta_l + 2{,}000\pi} \right)^{0.8} \left(\frac{s}{s + \beta_l} \right) \left[\frac{1}{(s + \alpha_l)^2 + \beta_l^2} \right]^2 e^{-3\pi s/4\beta_l}$$

where c_1 = positive, real constant defining absolute value of displacement
β_l = radian frequency to which point l distance from the stapes responds maximally
α_l = constant approximately equal to $\beta_l/2$
$e^{-3\pi s/4\beta_l}$ = delay factor which accounts for traveling wave transit delay to membrane point l, over and above the group delay of the rational term

The function $F_l(s)$ exhibits five poles and one zero, as shown in Fig. 6.5*a*, and its relative amplitude and phase response is shown in Fig. 6.5*b*.‡

The curves of Fig. 6.5*b* are plotted in terms of normalized frequency,

‡ Note that the analytical model shows a phase response approaching $(+\pi/2)$ at low frequencies. This behavior is at variance with von Békésy's data but is predicted by calculations described in Ref. 28. The $(+\pi/2)$ response has been confirmed in later experiments. See "Notes Added in Proof," p. 220.

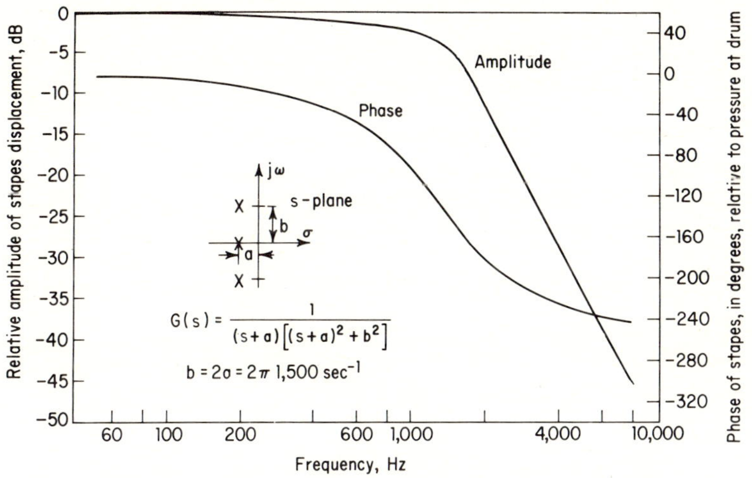

Fig. 6.4. Functional approximation to middle-ear transmission.

$\zeta = \omega/\beta_l$. Since the existing physiological data indicate that the mechanical response of the basilar membrane is constant-percentage bandwidth in nature (i.e., constant Q, as reflected by the constant relation between β_l and α_l), the curves of Fig. 6.5*b* are appropriate to all membrane places embraced by the functional approximation. Thus, the function $F_l(s)$ is completely specified by β_l, the radian frequency that produces maximum response of the point distance l from the base.

The stapes-to-membrane transmission is hence seen to be bandpass in nature, with a shallow low-frequency skirt and a steep high-frequency cutoff.‡

A rational-function formulation of the middle-ear and basilar-membrane transformations permits simulation of these relations in terms of lumped-parameter electrical networks. Using these formulations, electrical networks representing the properties of a number of points along the membrane have been constructed [1, 2]. Even more convenient the rational-function form permits digital simulation of the basilar membrane response on a computer. Sampled values of the continuous behavior at any point can be calculated by noting the relation between the z transforms and Laplace transforms for that point. The following section expands on this relation and illustrates a simulation.

6.3 Computer Simulation of Basilar-membrane Motion

The transmission from eardrum to a point l distance along the basilar membrane is characterized by the product function $H(s) = G(s) \cdot F_l(s)$.

‡ Von Békésy's physiological data should now be modified in accordance with Mössbauer measurements of basilar membrane motion, especially as concerns the steepness of the high-frequency cutoff. See "Notes Added in Proof," p. 220.

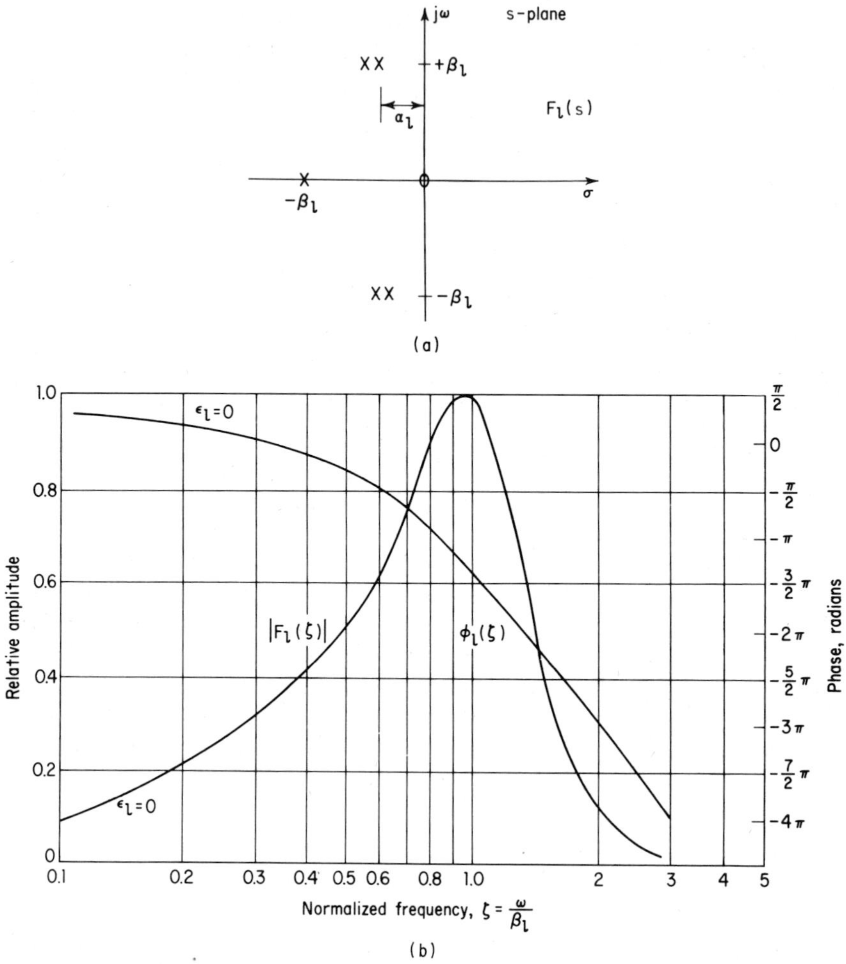

Fig. 6.5. Analytical model for basilar-membrane displacement. (*After Flanagan, 1962.*)

The inverse transform $\mathfrak{L}^{-1}[H(s)]$ is the response of this point to an impulse of sound pressure at the eardrum. Call this impulse response $h(t)$. Its sampled values $h\dagger(t)$ can be described as a sequence of impulses having areas equal to the value of $h(t)$ at the sampling instants, or

$$h\dagger(t) = \sum_n h(t)\,\delta(t - nD)$$

where $\delta(t)$ is a unit area impulse and D is the sampling interval. Then the transform of the sampled function is the complex convolution

$$\mathfrak{L}[h\dagger(t)] = H\dagger(s) = H(s) * \mathfrak{L}\left[\sum_n \delta(t - nD)\right]$$

Application of the residue theorem—and recognizing that the poles of $H(s)$ lie in the left half of the complex-frequency plane—leads to the result

$$H\dagger(s) = \sum_k \left(\frac{1}{1 - e^{-D(s-\lambda_k)}}\right) \text{res}\,[H(\lambda)]_{\lambda=\lambda_k}$$

where the λ_k are the poles of $H(\lambda)$ and the residue notation res $[H(\lambda)]_{\lambda=\lambda_k}$ means $\lim_{\lambda \to \lambda_k} (\lambda - \lambda_k)H(\lambda)$. Using the substitution $e^{-sD} = z^{-1}$, $H\dagger(s)$ can be written

$$H(z^{-1}) = \sum_k \left(\frac{1}{1 - e^{\lambda_k D} z^{-1}}\right) \text{res}\,[H(\lambda)]_{\lambda=\lambda_k}$$

But now, the temporal correlate (inverse transform) of $z^{-1} = e^{-sD}$ is simply the unit delay operator, with delay equal the sampling interval D. Therefore, the sampled values $h(nD)$ of the continuous response $h(t)$ can be calculated from $H(z^{-1})$ simply from a knowledge of the complex poles of $H(s)$ and by application of unit-sample delays. For any arbitrary input (excitation) to $H(s)$—not necessarily a single impulse—the sampled values of the response are related to sampled values of the input by the discrete operations specified by $H(z^{-1})$. In addition, if the input and transmission functions are band-limited, and if the sampling rate $1/D$ exceeds twice their bandwidth, the continuous response can be reconstructed exactly by low-pass-filtering the response samples.

These relations permit calculation of sample values of $y_l(t)$ for any arbitrary $p(t)$ simply from a knowledge of the rational-function forms $G(s)$ and $F_l(s)$ for middle-ear and stapes-to-membrane transmission, respectively. In earlier work, a computer program was written to compute the basilar membrane displacement at 40 successive points, in response to an arbitrary input $p(t)$ sampled at a rate of 20 kHz and quantized to 11 bits [3]. When the input sound pressure at the eardrum is a single-sample rarefaction pulse, the basilar membrane displacement calculated by the program is as shown in Fig. 6.6. Several features are apparent. Motion at the low-frequency (apical) end exhibits long latency and relatively slow oscillation. Conversely, at the high-frequency (basal) end the latency is short and the oscillatory motion is fast. Near the basal end the tendency is for the waveform of the pulse response not to be highly dependent upon place. The reason is the controlling influence of the middle-ear low-pass characteristic. In fact, the basal-end motion is very similar in waveform to the time derivative of the stapes displacement.

If alternate rarefaction (positive) and condensation (negative) pulses of 100-μs duration and repetition frequency 200 s^{-1} are delivered to the eardrum, the buildup of membrane motion is as shown in Fig. 6.7. The input signal is initiated at time zero. Since in this instance the fundamental frequency of the input acoustic signal is 100 Hz the fundamental component of the signal is resolved in frequency and the motion at the 100-Hz membrane place builds up sinusoidally. At the high-frequency end, individual pulses continue to be resolved temporally, and the membrane executes complete pulse responses at these basal places. At all places, this mechanical motion is converted into electrical activity by the sensory cells in the organ of Corti. This mechanism is considered next.

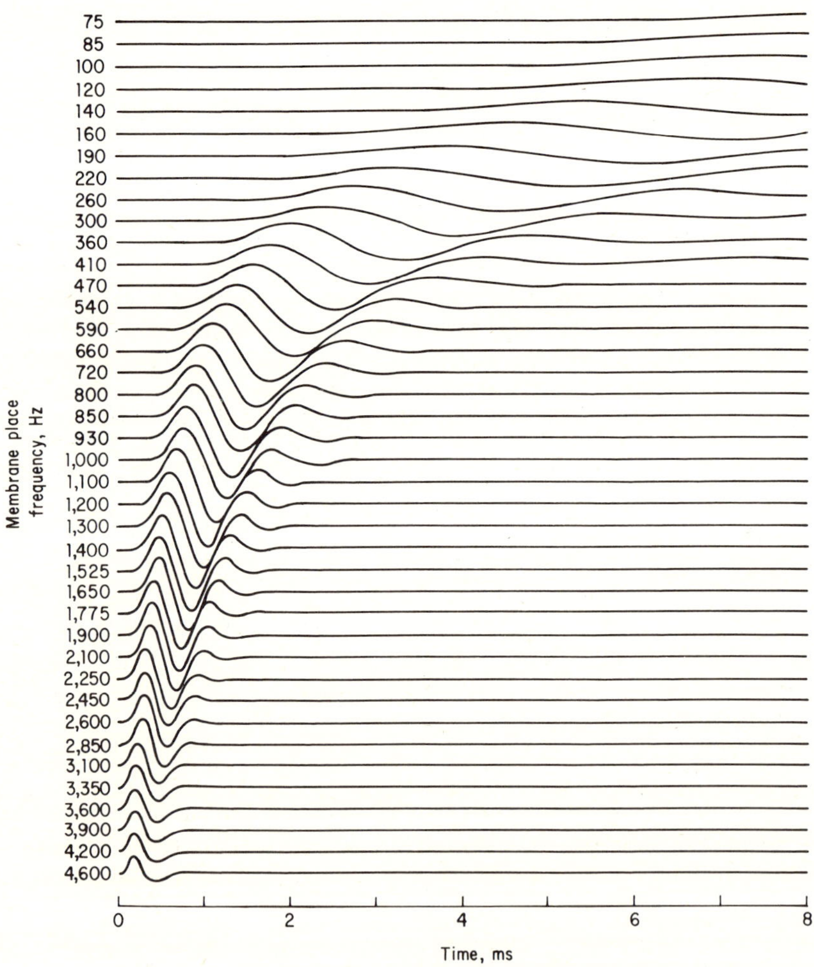

Fig. 6.6. Computer model of basilar-membrane displacement. Response to a single rarefaction impulse of sound pressure at the eardrum.

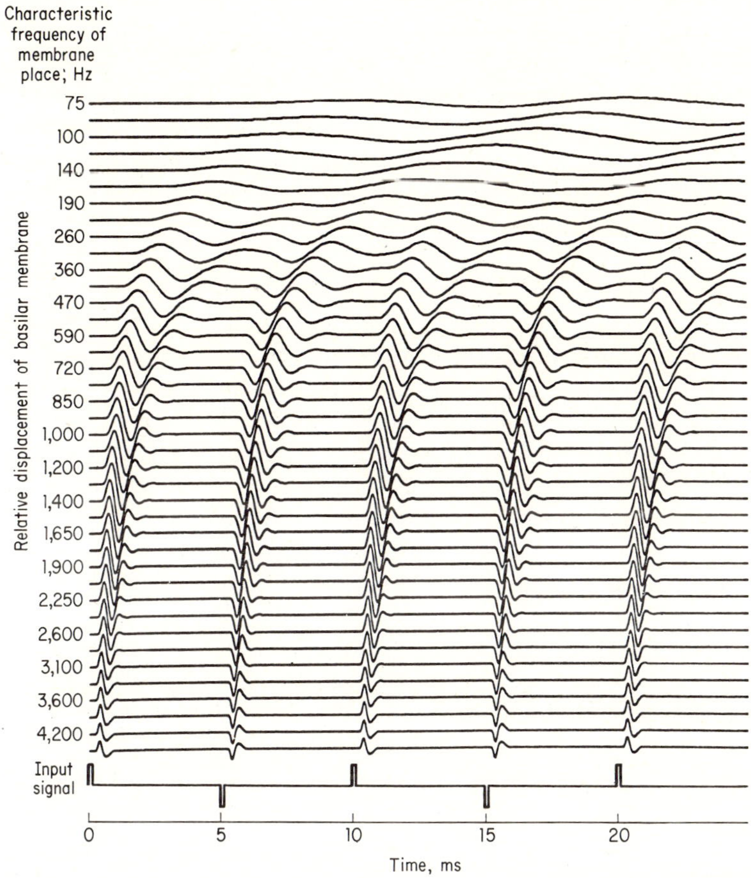

Fig. 6.7. Response of the computer model to alternate rarefaction and condensation pulses delivered at a rate of 200 s^{-1}. (*After Flanagan, 1962.*)

6.4 Transducer Action in the Cochlea

As mentioned earlier, the nature of the conversion of membrane displacement into first-order neural activity is not known. Neither does there exist a substantiated, quantitative picture of the functional relations involved. Qualitatively, however, several deductions seem now to be generally accepted. First, the hairs of the sensory cells, in experiencing a lateral shear owing to relative motion of basilar membrane and tectorial membrane (see Fig. 6.2), generate local electrical potentials which represent the local basilar-membrane displacement (rather than its velocity or higher derivatives of displacement) [4]. More precisely the shearing forces on the sensory hairs "modulate" (as would a variable resistor) a current passing between the scala media and the base of the hair cell.

Second, this facsimile alternating potential, acting at the base of the hair cell, modulates the liberation of a chemical mediator about some quiescent rate. The mediator, in sufficient quantity, stimulates the dendritic endings of the first-order nerve fibers and causes the fibers to fire. Because of its quiescent bias rate, the hypothesized chemical mediator is secreted more on one phase of the sensory potential than on the other, or a rectifying function is implied in triggering the nerve fiber.

Lastly, the chemical stimulation of the nerve endings produces an all-or-none electrical firing, which is propagated axonally to subsequent higher-order fibers in the central nervous system.

There are two basic electrical phenomena in the cochlea: the resting (dc) polarization of the parts, and the ac output of the organ of Corti (which, as stated, reflects the displacement of the cochlear partition). Current thinking [5] holds that the cochlear microphonic‡ is a potential produced by the sensory or receptor cells and is derived from the preexisting resting polarization of the receptor cells by a change in the ohmic resistance of a mechanically sensitive portion of the cell membrane: "This change in resistance is presumably brought about by a deformation, however slight, of a critical bit of the polarized surface. [The negative summating potential (—SP), which may also be a receptor potential, may be produced in this way as well as the cochlear microphonic.]" [5]

Energy considerations argue for an active (power-amplifying) type of transduction, as in a carbon microphone. The biasing current (power supply) for the transducer is produced by the biological battery which is the resting polarization of the hair cell. The mechanical energy of the basilar membrane is not transduced into electricity; rather it controls or modulates the flow of electricity across the interface (cell membrane) which separates the negative polarization inside the hair cell from the positive, endocochlear potential of the endolymph inside the cochlear partition.

A map of the cochlear resting potential is shown in Fig. 6.8. The scala tympani is taken as the reference potential, and regions of similar potential are often found within the organ of Corti. Other areas, presumably intracellular, are strongly negative. The endolymphatic space (scala media) is strongly positive. (See Fig. 6.2 for more details on the organ of Corti.)

If a microelectrode penetrates upward through the basilar membrane, recording simultaneously the dc potentials (which serve to locate the

‡ The ac potential observed by a gross electrode.

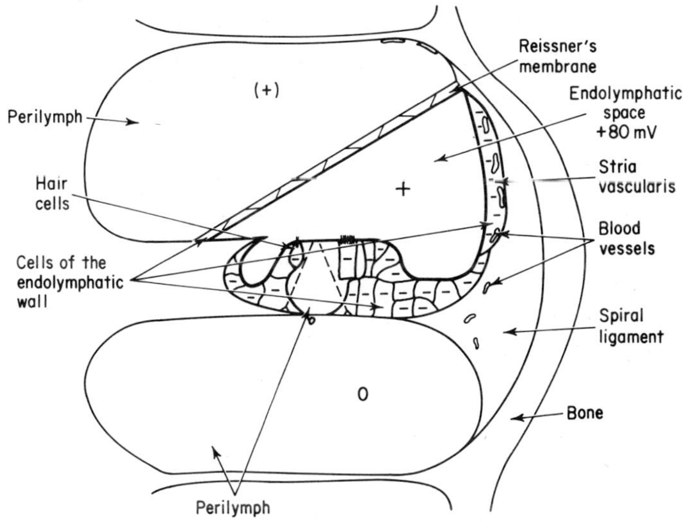

Fig. 6.8. Diagram showing the distribution of resting potentials in the cochlea. The scala tympani potential is chosen as the reference. The scala vestibuli potential is weakly positive, and the interiors of all cells are strongly negative. (*After Tasaki, Davis, and Eldredge, 1954.*)

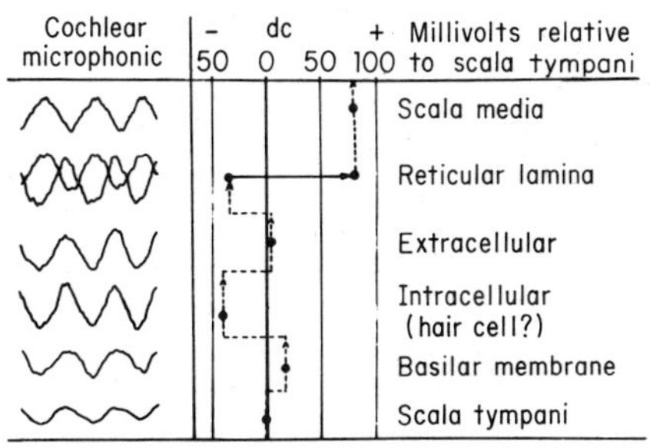

Fig. 6.9. The dc potential and the ac cochlear microphonic recorded by a microelectrode as it penetrates the basilar membrane and organ of Corti from the scala tympani side. The acoustic signal at the ear-drum is a 500 Hz sinusoid. (*After Davis, 1965.*)

electrode tip) and the cochlear microphonic response to a 500-Hz tone, the result is shown in Fig. 6.9. The conclusion is that the electrical interface at which the phase reversal of the cochlear microphonic occurs is the hair-bearing surface of the hair cell (although one cannot differentiate between the surface and base locations of the hair cell).

Two biological batteries therefore act in series: the internal (negative) polarization of the hair cells and the (positive) dc polarization of the endocochlear voltage (which is probably generated by the stria vascularis). This action leads to the conception of the equivalent circuit for cochlear excitation shown in Fig. 6.10.

The cochlear microphonic, as already mentioned, is viewed as the fluctuating voltage drop across the cell membrane due to alternating

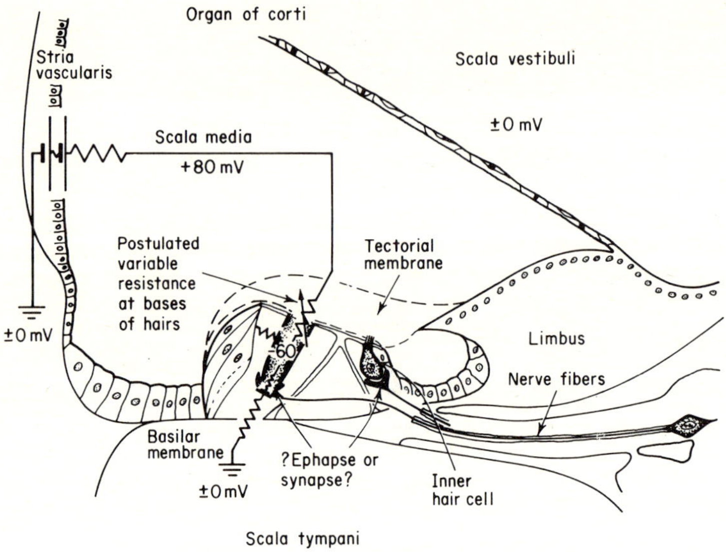

Fig. 6.10. Diagram illustrating Davis' "resistance microphone" theory of cochlear excitation. The primary "battery" is in the hair cell, and an accessory series battery is in the stria vascularis. The leakage current through the hair cells is assumed to be modulated by an increase and decrease of ohmic resistance due either to bending or shearing of the hairs. The change in leakage current is assumed to either (1) stimulate the nerve ending directly (ephapse), or (2) cause liberation of a chemical mediator which excites the nerve ending (synapse). Chemical mediation seems the more probable. (*After Davis, 1965.*)

increase or decrease in its ohmic resistance. It appears to be a facsimile representation of the local displacement of the basilar membrane. Using a differential electrode technique and recording between scalas, Teas et al. [6] have measured the cochlear microphonic at different places along the cochlear partition in guinea pigs. The input signal was a transient pulse produced from the step response of a filter set to match the earphone transducer (so that the acoustic signal corresponded well with the electrical input). Using the relatively broadband signal shown in Fig. 6.11, the cochlear microphonic recorded in the first turn is found to be a relatively close facsimile. For the same signal, the microphonics observed in the four turns‡ are shown in Fig. 6.12. The change in oscillatory character and amplitude with place and the increase in latency as the apex is approached are reminiscent of the calculated displacements shown previously in Fig. 6.6. (Account must be taken, of course, for the differences in input signals.)

‡ The guinea pig cochlea has four turns in contrast to two and one-half turns for the human.

From measurements such as those of Fig. 6.12, a spatial pattern for the cochlear microphonic can be constructed. Such a pattern is shown in Fig. 6.13 for six successive time instants, separated by 0.1 ms. The acoustic input signal is a transient similar to that of Fig. 6.11, but with about twice the duration. Time increases from thinner to thicker lines on the diagram. This spatial pattern of the cochlear microphonic is strikingly similar to the traveling wave of displacement that has been observed by von Békésy and which can be calculated by transforming data such as given in Fig. 6.6.

In addition, the dynamic range of the microphonic is relatively large. Its range and linearity are illustrated in Fig. 6.14 for the same input signal as given in Fig. 6.11.

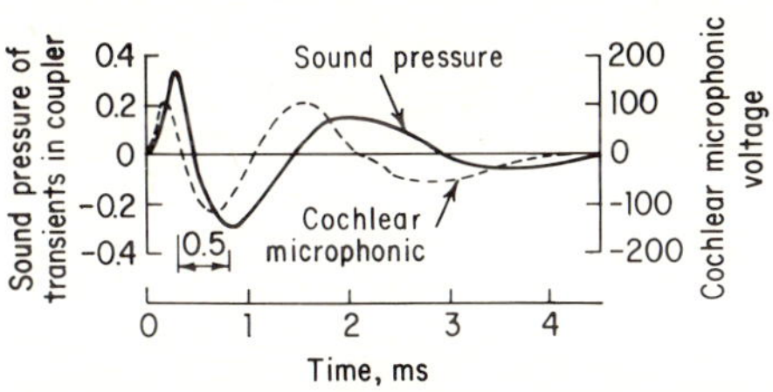

Fig. 6.11. Sound pressure waveform and the cochlear microphonic voltage measured in the first turn of the cochlea. *(After Teas et al., 1962.)*

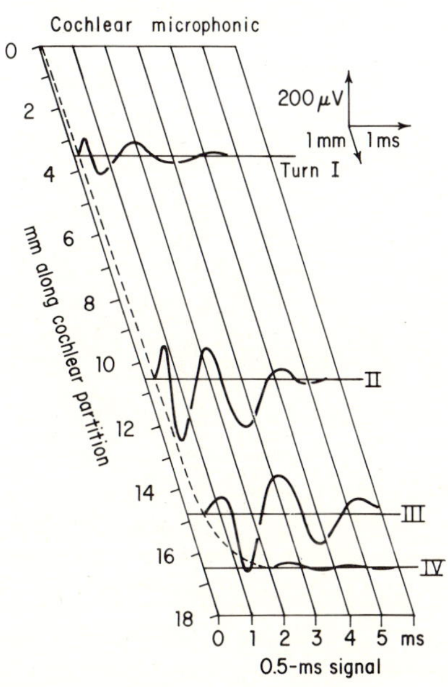

Fig. 6.12. Waveforms of the cochlear microphonic voltages as a function of location along the basilar membrane. The input sound pressure is the pulsive signal shown in Fig. 6.11. (*After Teas et al., 1962.*)

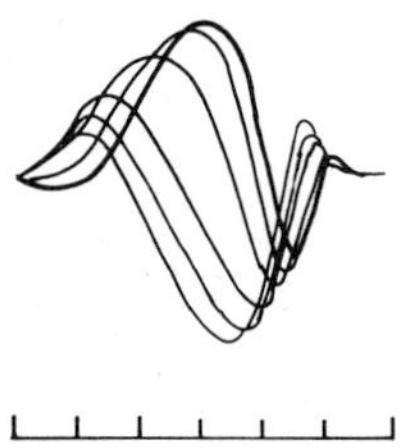

Fig. 6.13. Values of the cochlear microphonic voltage, as a function of distance along the cochlear partition, measured at 0.1 ms intervals. Thicker lines represent more recent times. The input acoustic signal is a filtered transient pulse. (*After Teas et al., 1962.*)

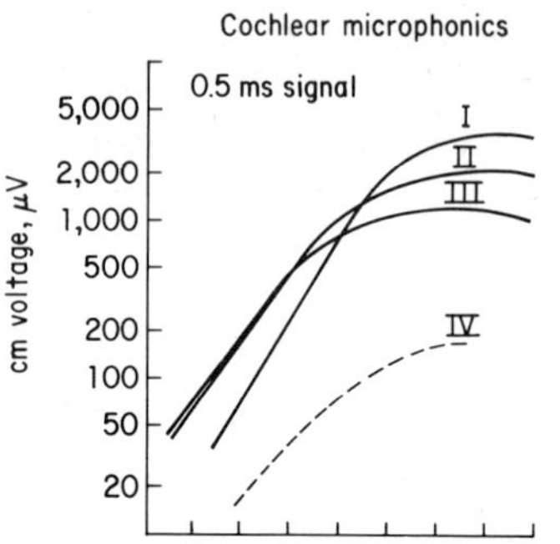

Fig. 6.14. Amplitude of the cochlear microphonic voltages as a function of input sound-pressure amplitude. Data are shown for all four turns of the cochlea. The input acoustic signal is the pulse shown in Fig. 6.11. (*After Teas et al., 1962.*)

The next link in the chain of functional description is the relation between the cochlear microphonic (or the facsimile membrane displacement) and the all-or-none electrical activity in the first-order fibers of the auditory nerve. As already mentioned, the nature of the process is not known at present, although chemical mediation has been implicated. Operations equivalent to rectification, amplitude compression, and temporal inhibition (refractory behavior) also appear to be involved. In the absence of details about these operations, the next positive step is to examine the electrical behavior of the nerve and relate it to the mechanical response of the basilar membrane.

6.5 Electrical Activity in Single Auditory-nerve Fibers

The fibers of the auditory nerve terminate at different places along the cochlear partition. Starting at the point (apex) of the cochlea, they are progressively collected in the internal auditory meatus until, at the base, the whole nerve trunk is formed. Because the basilar membrane is a mechanical frequency analyzer, it is not surprising that individual fibers exhibit frequency specificity. Owing to the way in which the fibers are collected and the trunk formed, those fibers which have greatest sensitivity to high frequencies lie on the outer part of the whole nerve, while those more sensitive to low frequencies tend to be found toward the core. This "tonotopic" organization of the auditory system (that is, its place-frequency-preserving aspect) seems to be maintained at least to some degree all the way to the cortical level [7].

As mentioned earlier, the electrical response of individual fibers is a standard pulse. Characteristically, the pulse exhibits a duration on the order of a millisecond. The activity is statistical in two senses: first, the firing patterns of an individual fiber are not identical in successive repetitions of a given stimulus; second, individual fibers exhibit spontaneous firing (electrical output) of a random nature. The latter appears to be much the same for all first-order fibers.

Comprehensive investigation of first-order electrical behavior in cats has been carried out by Kiang and his associates [8]. Since the structure of the cochlea and auditory nerve follows the same general plan in all mammals, data from these studies should give valuable insight into the human auditory system.

Typical microelectrode recordings from single fibers are illustrated in Fig. 6.15. In this instance, the signal comprises 50-ms tone bursts of a 2.3-kHz frequency. The upper recording is from a fiber that is maximally sensitive to this frequency, while the lower is from a fiber maximally sensitive to 6.6 kHz. The electrical output of the former is highly correlated with the stimulus, while the electrical output of the latter is not. The nerve response potential is recorded with respect to a convenient reference potential, in this case the head holder for the preparation, and a positive voltage is indicated by a downward deflection.

By choosing a suitable criterion of response, the frequency characteristic (tuning curve) of an individual fiber can be measured. Results

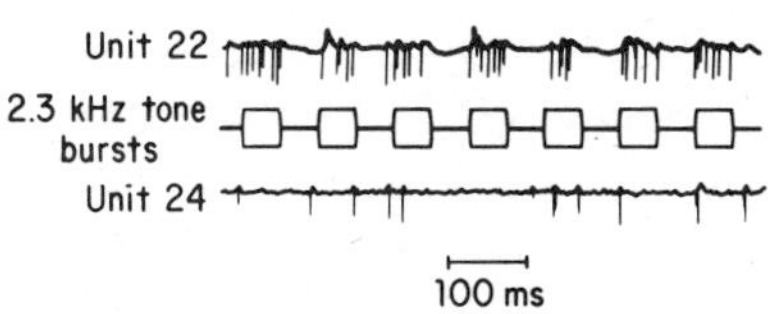

Fig. 6.15. Electrical responses from two auditory nerve fibers (units 22 and 24). The middle line shows the simulus signal; namely, 50 ms bursts of 2.3 kHz tone. Characteristic frequencies (CF's) are: Unit 22, 2.3 kHz; Unit 24, 6.6 kHz. (*After Kiang et al., 1965.*)

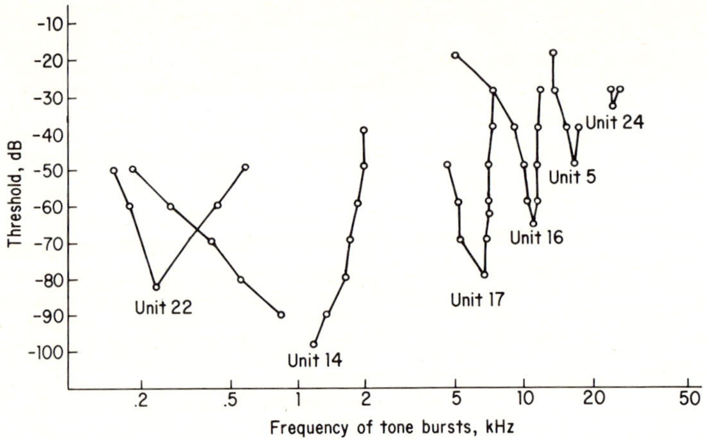

Fig. 6.16. Thresholds of electrical response, or tuning curves, measured for six auditory nerve fibers. (*After Kiang et al., 1965.*)

of such measurements are illustrated for several fibers in Fig. 6.16. The frequency for which the threshold is lowest (the minimum of each curve) is called the *characteristic frequency* of the fiber (unit). These minima appear to match well the shape of the audiogram determined from behavioral measurements. An interesting aspect of these data is that while over the low-frequency range the shapes of the tuning curves appear to be nearly constant-percentage bandwidth in character (constant Q) and display a bandwidth which correlates reasonably well with von Békésy's mechanical responses, the tuning curves of high-frequency cells are much sharper and display Q increasing with frequency. [von Békésy's observations on the human basilar membrane were, of course, limited to the low end of the spectrum—2,400 Hz and down.]

Kiang et al. have also observed the electrical response of primary units to punctate signals, namely, broadband clicks. Individual responses to 10 successive rarefaction clicks of 100-μs duration are plotted in Fig. 6.17. The time origin is taken as the time the pulse is delivered to the earphone. The characteristic frequency (CF) of the unit in this figure is 540 Hz. The pattern of firing differs in successive presentation, but the responses show a consistent periodic aspect. Multiple firings in response to a single click are apparent.

A convenient way to analyze this periodic feature is, in successive presentations of the signal, to measure the number of times the fiber fires at a prescribed time after the signal onset. This number plotted against the time of firing forms the post-stimulus time (PST) histogram. Some quantization of the time scale is implied and this quantization (or "bin width") is made sufficiently small to resolve the periodicities of interest (in Kiang's studies [8], a bin width of 0.063 ms was customarily used.) A digital computer is a valuable tool for calculating and displaying the histogram. One minute of data from the conditions in Fig. 6.17 produces the histogram of Fig. 6.18. (The clicks are delivered at a rate of 10 s^{-1}; therefore this histogram is the result of 600 signal presentations.) The times of firings show a periodic structure, or "preferred" times for firing. In the mid-frequency range for the animal, the histogram may exhibit as many as five or six distinct peaks or preferred times. At the upper end of the animal's frequency range, the tendency is for the histogram to display a single major peak.

The preferred times for firing appear to be intimately linked to the characteristic frequency of the unit, and the interval between peaks in the PST histogram is approximately equal to 1/CF. Higher-frequency units consequently show smaller intervals between the PST histogram peaks. The relation between the interval between peaks and 1/CF for 56 different units is shown in Fig. 6.19.

The multiple responses of single primary units to single clicks almost certainly reflect the mechanical response of the cochlea. The calculations shown previously in Fig. 6.6 (based on von Békésy's data for humans) show that the oscillatory displacement responses depend strongly upon place in the apical extent of the cochlea. In the extreme basal end, the waveform of displacement has a tendency to become constant, being controlled primarily by the middle-ear low-pass characteristic, and is somewhat more damped. Intervals between peaks in the histograms seem to correspond with the calculated oscillatory behavior, and the absence of multiple peaks at high frequencies is also consistent with this picture.‡ One noticeable difference, however, is the appearance of more multiple peaks in the histogram than the displacement behavior suggests. This could point toward some amplitude-compressing operation as has been suggested for the functional link between mechanical displacement and primary units response [9].§

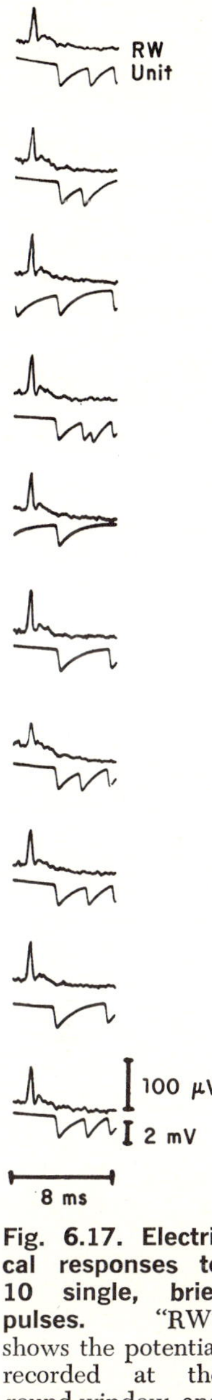

Fig. 6.17. Electrical responses to 10 single, brief pulses. "RW" shows the potential recorded at the round window, and "Unit" shows the single-unit potential recorded by a microelectrode. CF for the unit is 540 Hz. (*Adapted from Kiang et al., 1965.*)

‡ Also figuring in the absence of multiple peaks at high frequencies is the refractory characteristic of the fiber.

§ More likely, now, the multiple peaks reflect sharper mechanical selectivity in the basilar membrane. See "Notes Added in Proof," p. 220.

Besides reflecting the preferred times for firing, the PST histogram also indicates the latency of the first electrical response (that is, the time to the first peak in the histogram). If the neural firings are closely linked to the mechanical deflection of the basilar membrane, then not only should the preferred times of firing reflect the oscillatory characteristics of the membrane, but the latency to the first peak should correspond with the traveling-wave transit time down the membrane (see Fig. 6.6). This does in fact seem to be the case. When the CFs for 102 different units are plotted against the latency of the first peak in the PST histogram, for rarefaction clicks, the result is as shown in

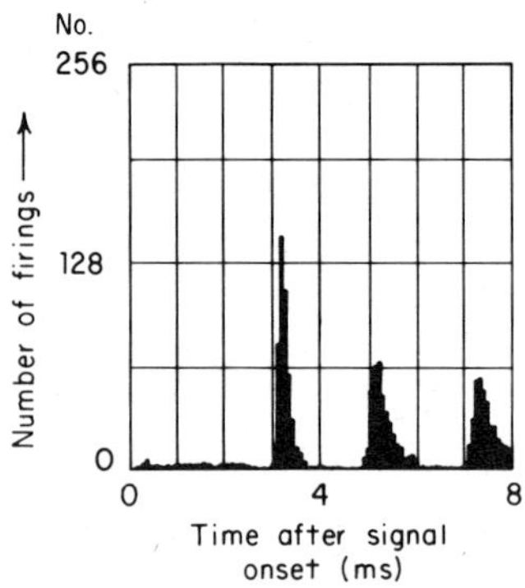

Fig. 6.18. Poststimulus time (PST) histogram for the nerve fiber of Fig. 6.17. The histogram is produced from approximately 600 unit responses. (*After Kiang et al., 1965.*)

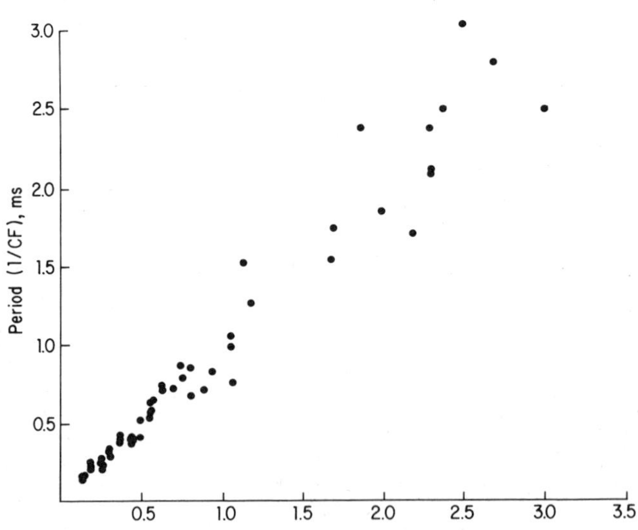

Fig. 6.19. Characteristic period (1/CF) for fifty-six auditory units plotted against the interpeak interval measured from PST histograms. (*After Kiang et al., 1965.*)

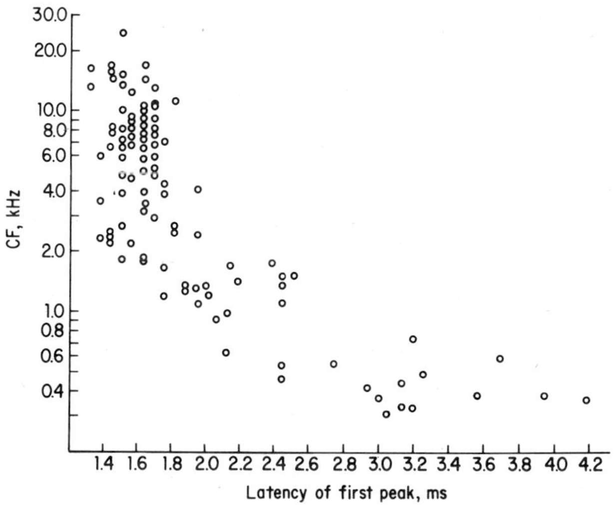

Fig. 6.20. The characteristic frequency (CF) for 102 units plotted against the latency of the first peak in their PST histograms. (*After Kiang et al., 1965.*)

Fig. 6.20. In comparing these data with the latencies suggested by the calculations of Fig. 6.6, it should be pointed out that the time reference for the PST histogram is the onset of the electrical signal to the transducing headphone. Any electrical and acoustic delay between headphone input and eardrum pressure must therefore be corrected for. As a rough estimate, a time reference corresponding to onset of stapes motion should lie slightly to the left of the 1.4-ms point on the abscissa of Fig. 6.20.

6.6 Models of Electrical Activity in First-order Fibers

As already emphasized, the mechanism of conversion of basilar membrane displacement into electrical activity remains to be firmly established. Nevertheless, enough information (of the type described in the preceding section) is available to postulate models for linking the mechanical and electrical behavior. Such models for the conversion process could help organize existing data and suggest critical questions for further experiment. At least two such formulations have recently been put forward [10, 11]. Both make use of digital simulation techniques. One of these [11] serves to illustrate the insight that can be gained from such an organization.

The fundamental assumption is that deformation of the hairs protruding from the hair cells modulates the chemical mediator that fires the nerve. The excitatory chemical is assumed to be released in uniformly

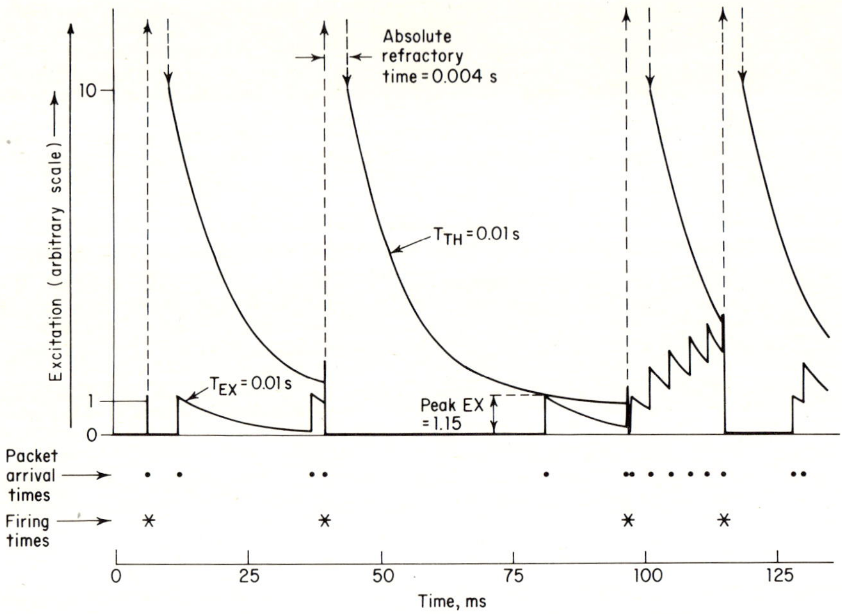

Fig. 6.21. Computer model for the spontaneous firing of auditory nerve fibers. (*After Lummis, 1968.*)

sized "packets" with an average rate which is a function of the hair deformation and hence the basilar membrane deflection. Rarefaction-going displacements increase the release rate and condensation-going displacements decrease the release rate. In the absence of acoustic stimulation, packets are released at random intervals and at a mean rate which characterizes the spontaneous behavior of the nerve fiber. A Poisson random process is an appropriate law for the packet release, and one number specifies the process; namely, the mean rate.

When an excitatory packet is released in the model, it does not produce an action potential directly, but produces a postsynaptic potential which may or may not trigger the fiber. Each packet initiates an excitation function, which jumps to a peak value and then decays back to zero exponentially. The peak value and decay time constant are variable parameters in the model. When packets are released in rapid succession, separate excitation functions are added linearly to give the total excitation of the nerve fiber. When the total excitation exceeds a time-varying threshold, a firing occurs. The excitation function is immediately reset to zero, and the threshold goes to infinity for the duration of the refractory time of the fiber. The threshold is then assigned some initial recovered value from which it decays exponentially to its resting value. The refractory time, the initial recovered threshold, and the threshold time constant are three more parameters that must be established in the model.

The excitation and threshold functions are diagramed in Fig. 6.21, where, for illustrative purposes, the parameters are chosen as follows: excitatory time constant 10 ms, threshold time constant 10 ms, refractory time 4 ms, resting threshold (relative) value 1, initial recovered threshold value 10, and peak excitation 1.15. Packet-release times are represented by the dots, and firing epochs are represented by the asterisks.

Physiological data from Kiang on spontaneous activity in first-order fibers are summarized in Fig. 6.22. To a first approximation first-order firing characteristics can be described very simply. The intervals between adjacent firings are independent random variables. The interval histogram shows an absence of very short intervals, then a rapid increase

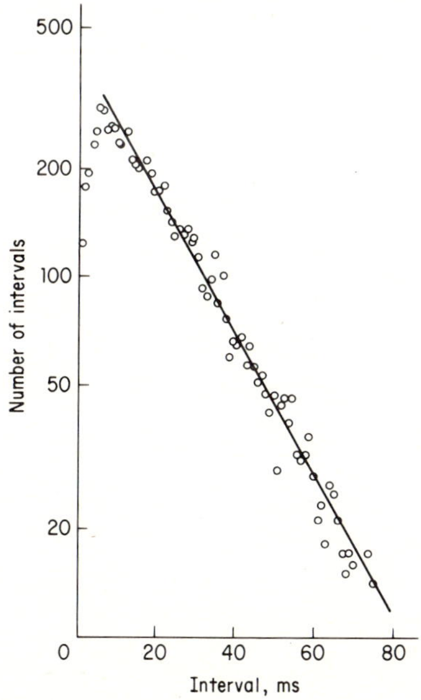

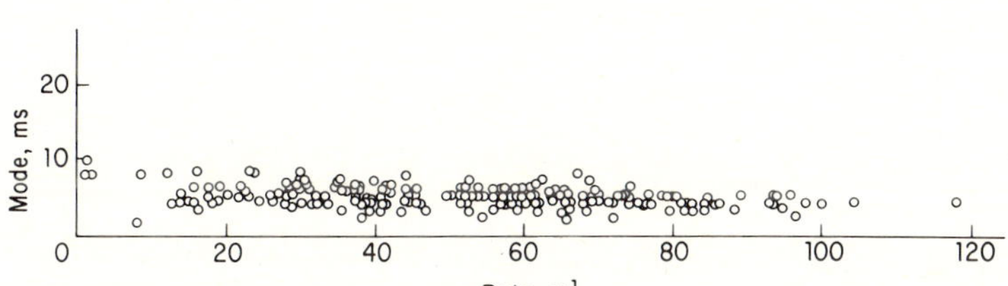

Fig. 6.22. Physiological data determined by Kiang et al. for spontaneous firing. Top: Interval histogram. Bottom: Histogram mode versus firing rate. (*After Lummis, 1968.*)

in the number of intervals to a maximum at about 5 ms, and then a nearly exponential tail. The lower graph shows the modes of the histograms for a large number of fibers of widely differing mean firing rates. The mode (that is, the most frequently occurring interval) is always less than 10 ms and there is no substantial variation of mode with firing rate. Requiring the model to have similar characteristics places rigorous constraints on certain of the parameter values.

Without analyzing the detailed results, the spontaneous firing behavior of the model can be made similar to that of cat nerve fiber when the stimulation time constant is equal to or smaller than the threshold time constant. Further, to make the modal interval independent of firing rate (as found in cat fibers) the stimulation produced by each packet must be larger than the resting threshold (shown as value 1 in Fig. 6.21) and still further, the stimulation time constant must not be greater than 1.0 ms. This means that the nerve can be fired by a single packet, although accumulated effects of successive packets can and do influence the distribution of intervals between firings. The important point here is that even starting with a fairly general model, with many variable parameters, requiring the model to conform to only the observed spontaneous behavior of real nerves places strong constraints on the parameters involved.

Other computer simulations indicate that this approach has potential for describing acoustically stimulated behavior. Further, efforts to incorporate lateral inhibition may extend the generality as well as define other relevant parameters. The ultimate aim, of course, is to predict the pattern of nerve firings generated by any arbitrary sound waveform. This accomplishment would be a notable step toward understanding the neural processing of acoustic signals, and it essentially represents the frontier in auditory physiology.

6.7 Relations Between Psychoacoustic Behavior and Physiological Response

There now arises the question "Can some of the important aspects of psychoacoustic behavior be interpreted in terms of the mechanical and electrical features of auditory physiology?" Any success in bridging the gap between behavior and physiology would be a step in the direction of generality.

Two specific areas are representative of some success in this respect. They deal with binaural lateralization and pitch perception for relatively academic, analytically tractable signals; namely, trains of periodic pulses. In these instances temporal detail in membrane motion, and hence in timing of neural firings, can be related to auditory behavior.

6.7.1 Binaural Lateralization

Binaural lateralization is the subjective ability to locate a sound image at a particular point inside the head. The phenomenon is conventionally observed in earphone listening. If identical clicks (impulses of sound pressure) are produced simultaneously at the two ears, the average listener hears a sound image in the center of his head. If one click is produced a little earlier (or with slightly greater intensity) than the other, the sound image shifts toward the earlier (or more intense) signal. This shift increases with increasing time difference until the image moves entirely to one side of the head and eventually breaks apart. One then hears individual clicks located at the two ears.

Naïvely we suppose the subjective position of the image to be determined by a computation of coincidence between neural firings. Volleys of neural firings originate at the periphery and travel to higher centers via synaptic connections. The superior olivary complex of the cochlear nucleus is the first center in the ascending auditory pathway where cross-connections exist between primary fibers from the two ears. In view of the auditory system's sensitivity to interaural differences, it seems reasonable to conjecture that temporal and intensity detail of the signal are neurally represented with considerable precision, at least to the cochlear nucleus level. The volley initiated earliest progresses to a point in the cochlear nucleus where a coincidence occurs with the later volley from the other ear to produce a subjective image appropriately off center. This view has been used in several models for binaural interaction [12–14].

Suppose one produces impulses of pressure at the two ears, of equal intensity but of opposite polarity (i.e., one a rarefaction and the other a condensation). How would a listener adjust the times of occurrence of such pulses so that he hears the sound image exactly in the center of his head? We can consider what the basilar membrane displacement waveforms and the mechanical-to-neural conversion model would predict.

An impulse of pressure rarefaction draws the eardrum and stapes initially outward and causes the membrane displacement to be initially upward (i.e., toward the tectorial membrane). A condensation pulse, on the other hand, causes an initially inward displacement of drum and stapes and consequently an initially downward movement of the membrane. At any given point on the membrane the waveforms of displacement produced by these two stimuli differ only in sign; that is, one is the negative of the other. Calculated displacements of apical and basal points caused by rarefaction and condensation pulses are shown in Fig. 6.23. (These traces are essentially reproduced from the

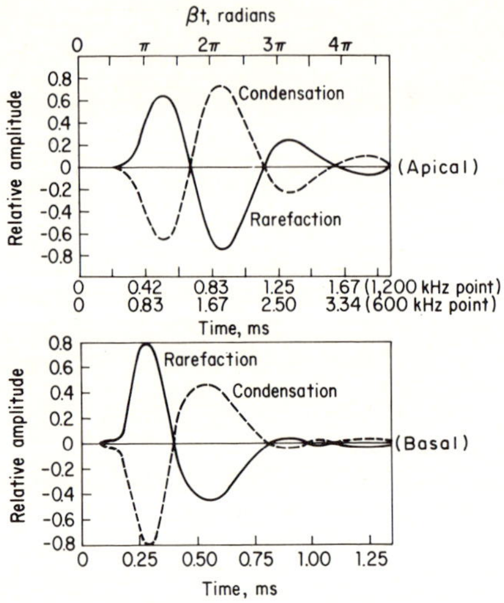

Fig. 6.23. Basilar membrane displacements calculated from a computer model. (*After Flanagan, 1962.*)

computer results shown in Fig. 6.6. They of course represent data for man.)

The top diagram in Fig. 6.23 is representative of points in the apical (low-frequency) half of the membrane. The solid curve is the displacement for a rarefaction pulse, the dashed for a condensation. The abscissa at the top is in terms of the product $\beta_l t$, where β_l is the radian frequency of maximal response for the apical point l distance from the stapes. The lower abscissa on the top graph shows time scales appropriate to the specific points maximally responsive to 1,200 and 600 Hz, respectively. The lower graph shows the displacement appropriate to points in the basal (high-frequency) half of the membrane. As discussed earlier, this waveform has nearly the same shape and time scale for all basal points.

In accordance with the earlier discussion of mechanical-to-neural transduction, we suppose that release of the chemical mediator at the hair cell is modulated by the membrane deflection, and that neural firings take place at some amplitude level corresponding to the upward (rarefaction-going) deflections of the membrane. A first-order fiber, terminating at a given place, should reflect in its electrical activity (1) the latency to that place, (2) the polarity of the stimulating pulse, and (3) the characteristic frequency of that place. Are such relations found in the auditory nerve activity? Measurements by Kiang show that they are.

PST histograms for a single unit of CF = 1.65 kHz, responding to rarefaction and condensation clicks at 10 s^{-1} and at an intensity of about 40 dB above threshold, are shown in Fig. 6.24. For a lower CF (470 Hz) and at about 10 dB above threshold, the result is shown in

Fig. 6.25. For a high-frequency CF (6.61 kHz), the result at about 40 dB above threshold is shown in Fig. 6.26.

These data suggest, therefore, that a difference in latency should exist between the firings for a rarefaction pulse and those for a condensation pulse. The difference should be about one-half cycle of the displace-

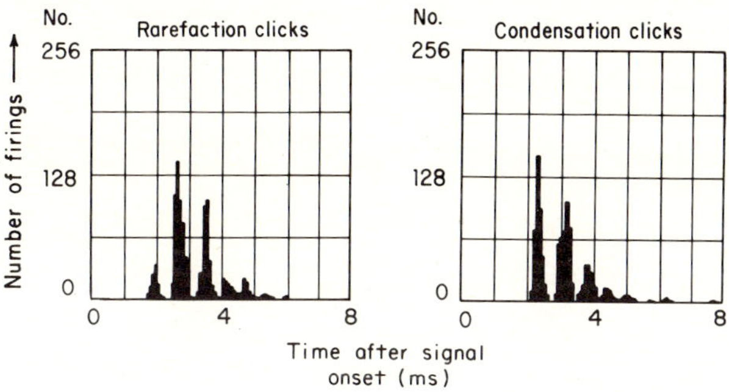

Fig. 6.24. PST histogram for single fiber responses to rarefaction and condensation clicks. CF: 1.65 kHz. (*After Kiang et al., 1965.*)

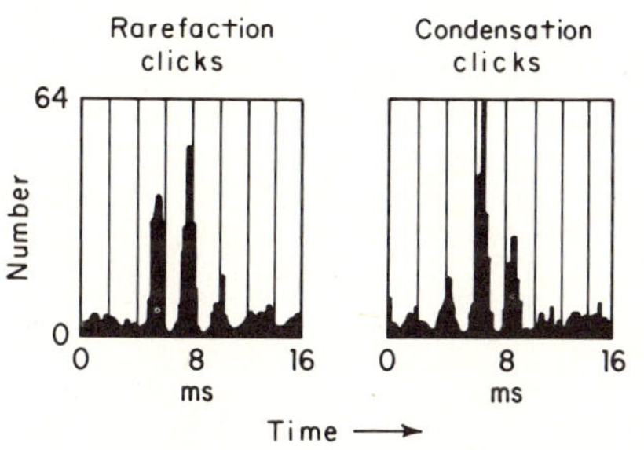

Fig. 6.25. PST histogram for single fiber responses to rarefaction and condensation clicks. CF: 0.47 kHz. (*After Kiang et al., 1965.*)

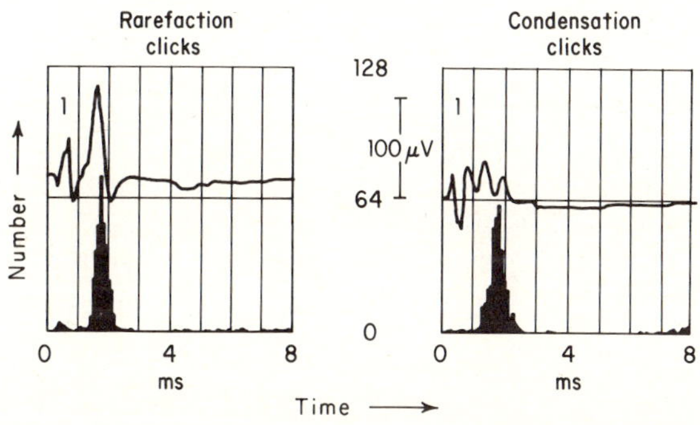

Fig. 6.26. PST histograms for a unit with high CF (6.61 kHz) to rarefaction and condensation clicks. Superposed on the histograms are averaged round-window responses. The early events (less than 1-ms latency) in the round-window records are cochlear microphonic potentials. (*After Kiang et al., 1965.*)

ment waveforms. The computed responses of Figs. 6.6 and 6.7 indicate that for broad-spectrum excitation the greatest deflections occur near the middle of the membrane, in the vicinity of the region maximally responsive to 1,000 to 2,000 Hz. For such a place, the half-cycle intervals are of the order of 250 to 500 μs. The time scale for the 1,200-Hz point in the top graph of Fig. 6.23 is indicative of this magnitude.

Assuming that simultaneity of neural firings at the two ears produces a centered sound image, a rarefaction pulse and a condensation pulse should produce a centered image if the condensation is advanced in time to bring its positive (rarefaction-going) displacement peak approximately into coincidence with that of the rarefaction pulse. This means advancing the condensation, or letting it lead, by about 250 to 500 μs. Furthermore, the periodic nature of the displacements suggests that secondary fusions of the sound image might occur by virtue of neural firings triggered at secondary positive excursions. These fusions should occur for interaural times which are full-cycle increments of the principal fusion, either lead or lag. A half-cycle lead of the condensation pulse would represent a principal fusion; a half-cycle lag would be a secondary fusion.

If cophasic pulses are delivered to the two ears, that is, rarefaction-rarefaction or condensation-condensation, the same argument says that the principal fusion should obtain for zero interaural time differences, and secondary fusions for full-cycle shifts, either lead or lag.

The preceding remarks relate to broadband, unmasked pulses, where the dominant neural response is likely to originate near the central portion of the basilar membrane. Suppose the dominant response were elicited from some other place on the membrane. The interaural time difference for lateralization ought to change in accordance with what the responses in Fig. 6.6 imply.

Band-filtering of the pulse stimuli is an obvious means for confining membrane activity to specific regions. This has the disadvantage, however, that the stimulus signal is contaminated with the impulse response of the filter, so that it is inconvenient, if not difficult, to analyze the membrane displacement. The objective can be achieved more conveniently by selectively masking the membrane response with filtered random noise. That is, the significant neural information can be made to originate from a normally less responsive region by obscuring the maximally responding place with noise.

The top graph in Fig. 6.23 suggests that if the disparity between the interaural times for lateralizing cophasic and antiphasic pulses is to be increased, the dominant response must be made to originate nearer the apex, that is, from points that respond maximally at lower frequencies. In such a case high-pass noise should be used to obscure activity in the basal part of the membrane. Low-pass noise, on the other hand, causes the dominant information to arise from the basal section. Here, because of the nature of the pulse response, the disparity between cophasic and antiphasic fusions is predicted to be roughly constant with place along the membrane, and should be on the order of 250 μs. This, too, ought to be about the minimum interaural disparity that can be produced for the antiphasic situation.

An experiment was performed to determine whether these predicted phenomena are in fact manifest [15]. The arrangement to measure the effects is shown in Fig. 6.27. A pair of pulse generators produced identical 0.1-ms rectangular pulses in separate channels at a sensation level of 40 dB. The repetition rate of the pulses was 10 s^{-1}. Random noise from two independent generators was filtered by identical filters and added to the signal channels. The level of the filtered noise was set to completely mask that portion of the pulse spectrum equal in frequency range to the noise band. High-pass and low-pass noise cutoff frequencies of 600, 1,200, and 2,400 Hz were used in addition to no masking. Condenser microphones fitted with ear-insert plugs were used as earphones to provide good transduction of the pulse signals. The subject was provided a delay control which permitted continuous adjustment of the time of occurrence of one pulse relative to the other over

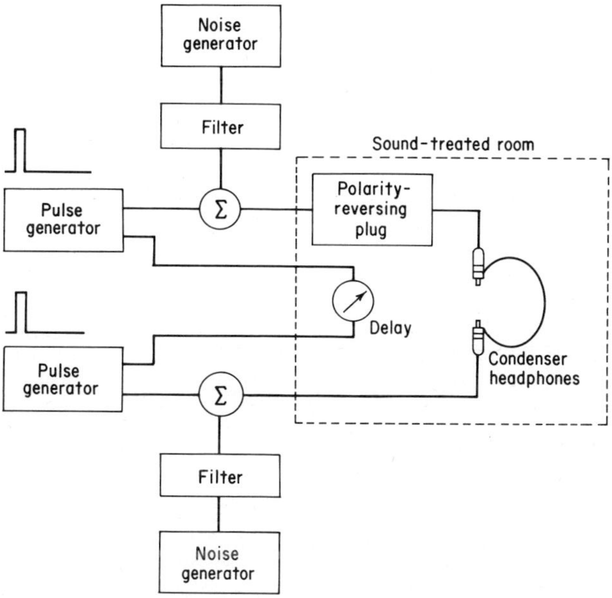

Fig. 6.27. Experimental arrangement for measuring the binaural lateralization of pulses. *(After Flanagan, David, and Watson, 1964.)*

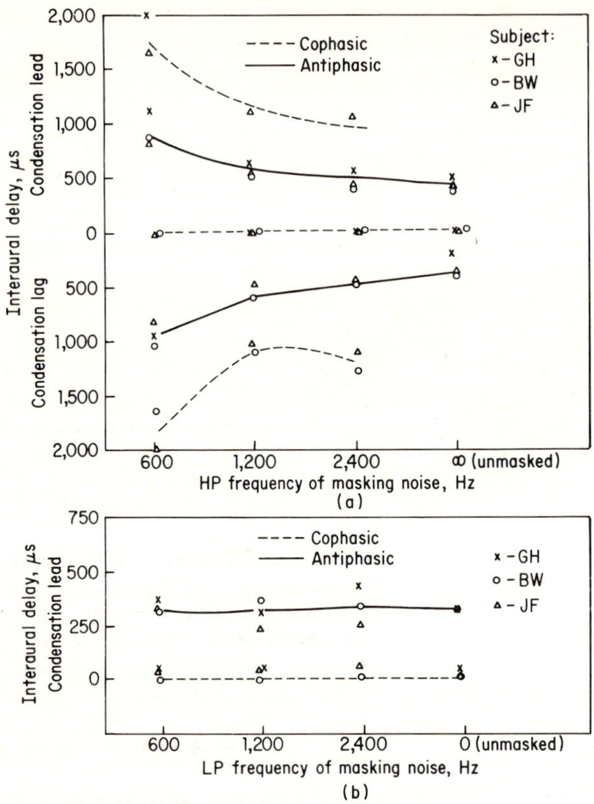

Fig. 6.28. Binaural fusion of pulsive signals. The data are consistent with interaural times predicted from the computer model of Fig. 6.6. (*After Flanagan, David, and Watson, 1964.*)

the range ±5 ms. A switch could reverse the polarity of the pulse delivered to one earphone.

The results of this experiment are summarized in Fig. 6.28. Median responses are shown for three listeners. For high-pass masking (Fig. 6.28*a*), the interaural time for the principal antiphasic lateralizations is seen to increase as the cutoff frequency of the high-pass noise is lowered. For these conditions the maximally responding unmasked place on the membrane should be that just below the cutoff frequency f_c of the filter. The interaural time for the antiphasic fusion ought then to be about $\pm 1/2f_c$. The data follow this value reasonably well.

The secondary antiphasic fusions (condensation lag) show a time separation between the principal and secondary points approximately equal to the predicted full-cycle shift, or about $1/f_c$. The principal cophasic fusions fall along the x axis for zero interaural times, and the secondary cophasic fusions (highest and lowest curves) fall at about the right value for the full-cycle shift.

The results for the low-pass masking (Fig. 6.28*b*) indicate that the hypotheses about fusions of basal-end information are essentially sustained. The cophasic-antiphasic disparity is roughly constant at about 300 μs. Secondary images, however, are not easily heard because the low-pass noise is a more potent out-of-band masker. Both masking conditions make it clear that the significant neural timing information can be made to originate from different points along the membrane and that the neural timing is intimately related to the individual excursions of the membrane displacement.

6.7.2 Pitch Perception

A number of studies on the pitch of complex sounds point up the important link between the temporal detail of the basilar membrane motion in a specific region and the psychoacoustic percept. Data from three of these studies provide a particularly convenient vehicle to emphasize further this link.

Consider a signal $s_a(t)$, periodic in T and composed of identical brief pulses $p(t)$ of alternating polarity,

$$s_a(t) = \sum_{m=-\infty}^{\infty} \left\{ p(t - mT) - p\left[t - \left(\frac{2m+1}{2}\right)T\right]\right\}$$

If the pulse $p(t)$ is sufficiently brief (that is, if its reciprocal duration is great compared with the frequency range of interest), it may be considered an impulse. The amplitude spectrum of $s_a(t)$ is therefore composed of odd harmonics all having the uniform amplitude $2/T$. The phase spectrum of $s_a(t)$ is identically zero at all these odd harmonics. The signal and its spectrum are shown in Fig. 6.29*a*.

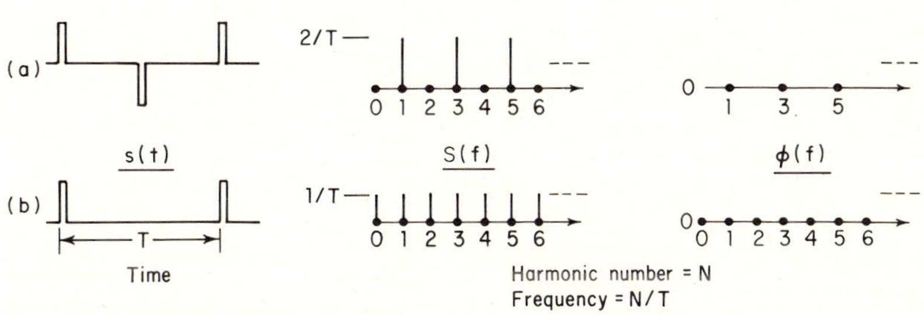

Fig. 6.29. Waveforms, amplitude, and phase spectra of periodic pulse signals. Each pulse is of uniform amplitude and 0.1-ms duration. The fundamental period is T, and the harmonic number is N.

Similarly, a periodic unipolar pulse signal $s_b(t)$ can be described as

$$s_b(t) = \sum_{m=-\infty}^{\infty} p(t - mT)$$

The amplitude spectrum of $s_b(t)$ has all even and odd harmonics in uniform amplitude $1/T$, and its phase spectrum is also identically zero, as shown in Fig. 6.29*b*.

6.7.2.1 Gross Perception of Pulse Pitch

If a listener is required to adjust (match) the pitch of s_b to that of s_a at moderate listening levels, his response behavior is indicated in Fig. 6.30 [16, 17]. At low pulse rates of s_a, the match is effected to equate pulse rates, that is, the pulses of s_a and s_b are aligned without regard to polarity. At the high pulse rates of s_a, on the other hand, the signals are equated in fundamental frequency and the pulse rates differ by a factor of 2. The transition between these pitch modes occurs in the range of 100 to 400 pulses per second. In this transition region the tendency is to match neither the pulse rate nor the fundamental.

This gross, two-mode behavior is explicable in terms of the mechanical resolution of the basilar membrane and the corresponding first-order electrical activity discussed previously. At very low pulse rates (say, 20 s^{-1}), the membrane resolves each pulse temporally, with the greatest amplitude of motion occurring in the central region of the membrane. Except for the half-period disparity in the pulse response (which

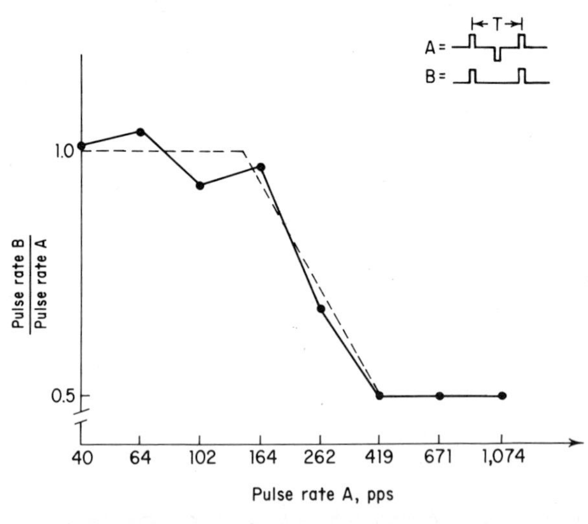

Fig. 6.30. Experimental data for adjusting the pulse rate of pulse train B to equal the pitch of pulse train A. (*Adapted from Flanagan and Guttman, 1960.*)

is a very small percentage of the pulse period), the neural firings occur essentially at the pulse rate. It is the interval between these firings which the subject apparently equates to pitch.

At high pulse rates (say, 1,000 s^{-1}), the prominent membrane displacement becomes sinusoidal at the fundamental frequency. That is, the frequency resolution of the membrane is such as to resolve the fundamental component of s_a. The corresponding neural firings from this dominant place now exhibit the interval of the fundamental, and the pitch match is made accordingly.

6.7.2.2 Fine Structure in the Perception of Pulse Pitch

In the transition zone, the situation is somewhat more complicated. Pitch matches are more difficult, and are commonly made at frequencies corresponding to neither the pulse rate nor the fundamental. Near the pulse rate side of the range, the distribution of matches is frequently bimodal about the pulse rate value. The basilar membrane mechanics for this situation are nicely reflected in Fig. 6.7 (given previously). Here the signal is periodic 100-μs rectangular pulses of alternating polarity. The pulse rate is 200 s^{-1}. One immediately sees from the figure at least two conflicting pitch cues. In the basal (high-frequency) end of the membrane, individual pulses are resolved, leading presumably to neural spikes whose intervals correspond closely to the pulse rate. In the apical (low-frequency) end, the fundamental is just beginning to be resolved (at the place of 100 Hz) and the deflection here is sinusoidal at the fundamental rate. Neural firings on fibers originating in this region should reflect the fundamental period. In the central region, however, say around 600 to 1,000 Hz, the displacement impulse response has an oscillatory period comparable to the pulse-repetition period, and the half-period time of the pulse response is a significant percentage of the repetition pulse period. Still assuming that the neural firings occur on positive deflections of the membrane, the intervals between neural spikes on fibers originating from this region should be alternately long and short, as illustrated by the intervals T_1 and T_2 in Fig. 6.31. Also it is in this general region that the membrane displacement has the greatest amplitude. One might, therefore, expect at least some bimodality in the pitch percept, corresponding to these long and short intervals. This is in fact found [16–19].

Assuming the dominance of a membrane place characterized by frequency f_m, the perceived pitch f_p should correspond to

$$f_p = \left(\frac{1}{r} \pm \frac{1}{2f_m}\right)^{-1}$$

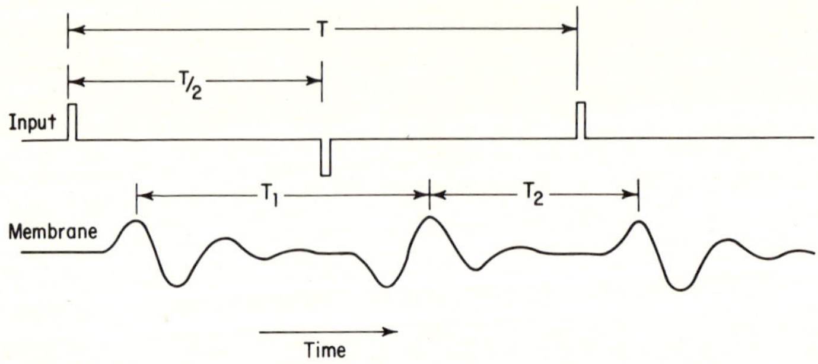

Fig. 6.31. Basilar membrane response to pulses of alternating polarity. See also Fig. 6.7.

where r is the pulse rate of the alternating-polarity signal. By the same argument, if f_p is the perceived pitch, the membrane place giving rise to this response is implied by

$$f_m = \left| \frac{rf_p}{2} (r - f_p)^{-1} \right|$$

As a specific example, if a listener is given s_a at a rate of 100 pulses per second, the s_b matches which he makes correspond approximately to the bimodal responses

$$f_p \cong \left[\frac{1}{100} \pm \frac{1}{2(600)} \right]^{-1} \cong \begin{cases} 92 \\ 109 \end{cases} \text{Hz}$$

That is, for this case, the dominant membrane frequency f_m is in the vicinity of 600 Hz. As pulse rate increases, the frequency of the dominant place also increases up to the point where the fundamental pitch mode takes over (above about 250 Hz or 500 pulses per second) and the responses cease to reflect a bimodality. A plot of f_m calculated from the above formula versus the s_a pulse rate is given in Fig. 6.32. Data are shown for two subjects [19]. The sensation level (SL) of the signals is 30 dB.

In this mode-transition range the bimodal responses and the dominant membrane place can be influenced by masking noise. For example, if the s_a signal of 100 pulses per second is masked by high-passed broadband noise, the dominant place is determined by the membrane characteristics of those places which are unobscured. As the cutoff frequency of the noise is made progressively lower (below 750 Hz), the dominant frequency f_m follows the noise cutoff frequency and the value of $1/2f_m$ becomes increasingly larger. For noise cutoffs above about 750, $1/2f_m$

is not much affected. This behavior with high-pass masking is illustrated in Fig. 6.33.

In similar fashion, high-pass and low-pass masking can influence the central frequency f_m, as illustrated in Fig. 6.34.

While these behavioral results can be interpreted directly in terms of calculated displacement of the basilar membrane, we have no direct electrophysiological measurements with which to compare them. Presumably for the situations reflected by Fig. 6.33, an interval histogram would display intervals corresponding to both $[(1/r) + (1/2f_m)]$ and $[(1/r) - (1/2f_m)]$. It would be interesting to see such electrical measurements on single primary fibers.

6.7.2.3 Tone Complexes

The preceding discussion has considered examples of links which can be established between perception and physiological response for periodic pulses. Can similar links be established for tone complexes? Such signals, though spectrally discrete, may not be as punctuate in time as pulses. Consider a superposition of cosine components

$$s(t) = \sum_{n=1}^{N} a_n \cos(\omega_n t + \theta_n)$$

In general $s(t)$ is aperiodic unless the ω_n are in the ratio of whole numbers. It often is convenient to characterize such complexes in terms

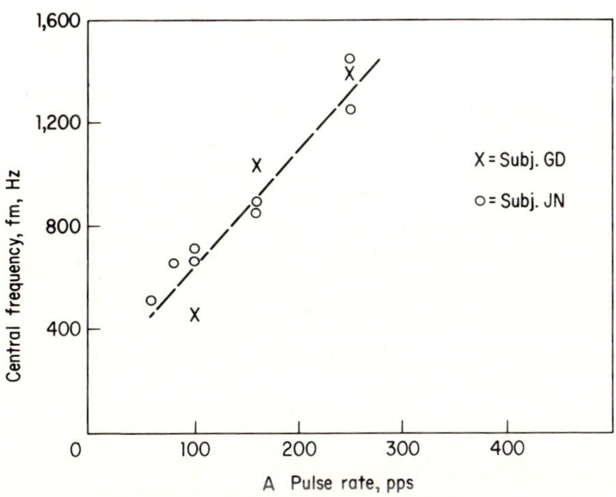

Fig. 6.32. Characteristic frequency of basilar membrane place (f_m) which is dominant in the pitch matches for the pulse signals shown in Fig. 6.29. The data are for a sensation level of 30 dB. (*After Ritsma, 1967.*)

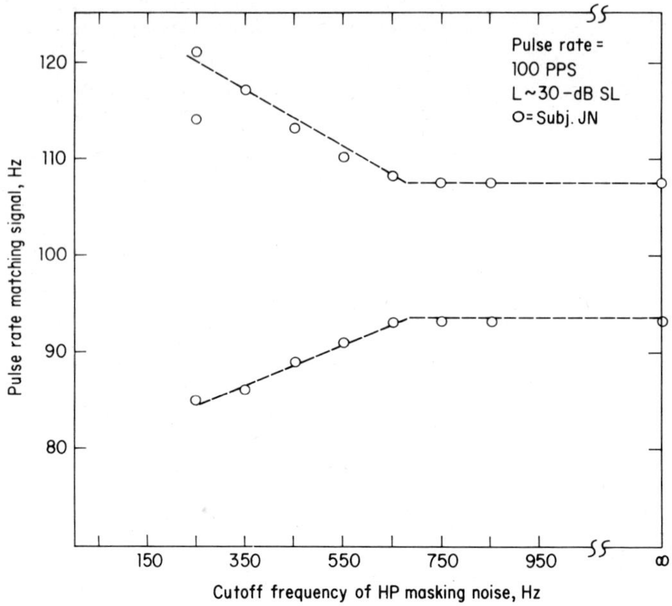

Fig. 6.33. Influence of high-pass masking noise upon the pitch of a pulse train of alternating polarities when matched by a uniform-polarity train. The signal level is 30 dB SL. (*After Ritsma, 1967.*)

of an envelope function $A(t)$ and an instantaneous phase function $\varphi(t)$ so that

$$s(t) = A(t) \cos \varphi(t)$$

where
$$\begin{aligned} A(t) &= (s^2 + \hat{s}^2)^{1/2} \\ \varphi(t) &= \tan^{-1} \hat{s}/s \\ \hat{s}(t) &= \text{Hilbert transform of } s(t) \end{aligned}$$

In the present case

$$\hat{s}(t) = \sum_{n=1}^{N} a_n \sin(\omega_n t + \theta_n)$$

Alternatively, the signal can be described in terms of its envelope and instantaneous frequency:

$$s(t) = A(t) \cos \left[\int_0^t \dot{\varphi}(t)\, dt + \varphi_0 \right]$$

where $\dot{\varphi}(t) = d/dt\ \varphi(t) = \dfrac{s\dot{\hat{s}} - \dot{s}\hat{s}}{s^2 + \hat{s}^2}$ and φ_0 is the instantaneous phase at the instant from which time is reckoned.

For the tone complex then

$$A^2(t) = \sum_{n=1}^{N} a_n{}^2 + 2 \sum_{n=1}^{N-1} \sum_{m=n+1}^{N} a_n a_m \cos\,[(\omega_n - \omega_m)t + (\theta_n - \theta_m)]$$

$$\dot{\varphi}(t) = \frac{1}{A^2(t)} \sum_{n=1}^{N} a_n{}^2 \omega_n + \sum_{n=1}^{N-1} \sum_{m=n+1}^{N} a_n a_m (\omega_n + \omega_m) \cos\,[(\omega_n - \omega_m)t + (\theta_n - \theta_m)]$$

Notice from this that $A^2(t)$ and $[A^2(t)\dot{\varphi}(t)]$ are band-limited to the same bandwidth as $s(t)$, but that nothing comparable can be said about $A(t)$, $\varphi(t)$, and $\dot{\varphi}(t)$.

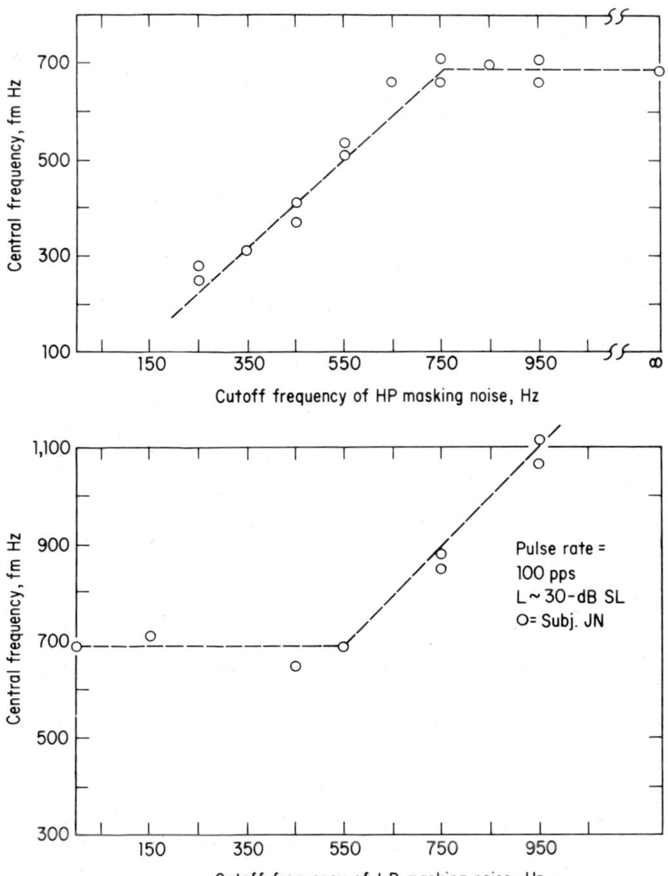

Fig. 6.34. Characteristic frequency of dominant basilar membrane place (f_m) for pulse-train pitch matches masked by filtered noise. (*After Ritsma, 1967.*)

If $s(t)$ is composed of nothing more than a single sinusoid, it is characterized by three parameters, namely a, ω, and θ. The subjective attributes loosely associated with the first two parameters are loudness and pitch, and we have seen in the previous discussion that these are reflected at the neural level by the number and interval of single-fiber firings. For monaural perception, θ is of no importance.

If $s(t)$ is composed of two cosine components, the relations for $A(t)$ and $\dot{\varphi}(t)$ are considerably simplified:

$$A^2(t) = a_1^2 [1 + \alpha^2 + 2\alpha \cos(\Delta\omega t + \Delta\theta)]$$

$$\dot{\varphi}(t) = \omega_1 + \alpha\Delta\omega \left[\frac{\alpha + \cos(\Delta\omega t + \Delta\theta)}{1 + 2\alpha \cos(\Delta\omega t + \Delta\theta) + \alpha^2} \right]$$

where $\alpha = a_2/a_1$

$\Delta\omega = \omega_1 - \omega_2$

$\Delta\theta = \theta_1 - \theta_2$

For the particular case of $a_1 = a_2 = a_0$, $A(t) = \sqrt{2}a_0$, $|\cos(\Delta\omega t + \Delta\theta)/2|$ and $\dot{\varphi}(t) = (\omega_1 + \omega_2)/2$, which is a familiar result (describing a double-sideband, suppressed-carrier modulation).

If such a complex of two equal-amplitude tones is presented to the ear at a relatively low level (for example, in the range of 40 to 50 dB sensation level), and one is asked to attend critically to the pitch attributes as the components are individually shifted in frequency, the multidimensional features of the perceived sound are truly impressive.‡ If the two frequencies are relatively close (say less than 100 Hz apart) and the lower one is decreased in frequency, there is a clear pitch attribute which increases. Also, if the frequency interval is less than about $\omega_2/\omega_1 = 1.5$, and the higher component is increased in frequency, there is a clear pitch attribute which decreases. In general these attributes are present along with others directly associated with the individual ω_1 and ω_2 components. Can these behavioral attributes be found in the physiology?

In the case of close frequency spacing and low level, one pronounced attribute is a periodicity or beat corresponding to $\Delta\omega = \omega_2 - \omega_1$. For small $\Delta\omega$, the basilar membrane response does not significantly alter the a's and θ's of the input signal (as described above) and hence this attribute arises from the periodicity of the envelope $A(t)$. [The instantaneous frequency is constant at $(\omega_2 + \omega_1)/2$.]

This beat percept or envelope periodicity is clearly reflected in the electrical activity of the first order fibers of cats. For example, Fig. 6.35 shows the spike activity of a single fiber responding to a two-tone complex of small frequency separation. The difference frequency beats

‡ In the interest of maintaining a healthy respect for nonlinearities of the ear, I periodically go in the lab and listen to a "simple" two-tone complex. I recommend the multidimensional percept associated with changes in a_1 and a_2 and ω_1 and ω_2 as an effectively humbling experience.

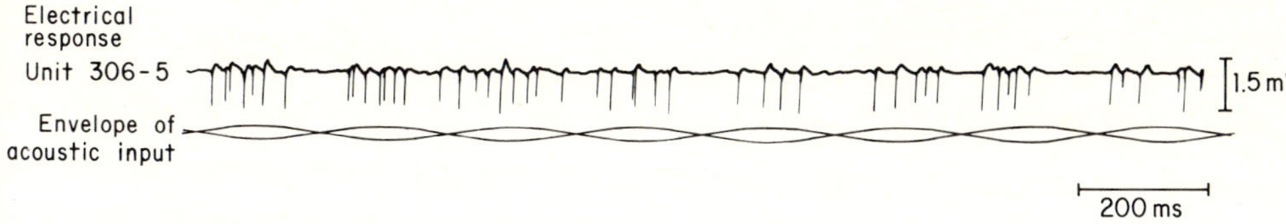

Fig. 6.35. Response of an auditory nerve fiber to two tones that beat at five cycles/sec. The input sinusoids are 1,532 and 1,527 Hz. The CF for the unit is 1,400 Hz. (*After Kiang et al., 1965.*)

are clearly identified in the electrical behavior. A lowering in frequency of the lower component increases the difference frequency and hence the perceived periodicity. The percept is of a tone at frequency $(\omega_1 + \omega_2)/2$ modulated in amplitude at a rate of $\Delta\omega$. To the extent that the monaural-pitch percept is dominated by the envelope function, the values of θ_n cannot influence the percept. [For tone complexes with more than two components, however, the waveshape of $A(t)$ is influenced by the θ_n.]

If we follow the membrane displacement at the place of the lower component, the filtering action of this place (as the lower component is decreased in frequency) is such as to attenuate fairly rapidly the influence of the higher component, in accordance with the characteristics discussed earlier (Sec. 6.2). The net effect is to diminish the amplitude ratio α so that eventually, at the place of the lower component, the membrane motion is simply of amplitude a_1 and frequency ω_1. The descending lower component then becomes more prominent than the ascending difference frequency in the pitch percept, and the tendency is to describe the pitch attribute as a descending one. In this extreme, the $\dot{\varphi}(t)$ at the place of the lower component dominates the pitch percept.

The periodicity associated with the difference frequency at small frequency separation and low level can be accounted for in terms of an envelope periodicity in the linear response of the ear. The difference component is not energetically present. Another strong pitch attribute of the same two-tone complex cannot be accounted for on linear grounds. It is one in which an increase in the frequency of the ω_2 component leads to a decrease in the pitch attribute. Its origin is a combination tone which is a "cross" difference of the input frequencies (particularly $2\omega_1 - \omega_2$). These components are also produced at relatively low (normal) listening levels and indicate some important things about the conversion of mechanical displacement into neural activity. They have received renewed emphasis in the work of Goldstein [20] and of Goldstein and Kiang [21].

Psychoacoustic measurements on two-tone complexes reveal several important aspects about combination tones. Combination tones higher in frequency than the primaries are not heard, whereas those lower in frequency are heard. The latter are of the form $[\omega_1 - n(\omega_2 - \omega_1)]$, and their audibility decreases sharply with increasing n. The most prominent component is $2\omega_1 - \omega_2$. Its perceived level falls sharply as the frequency interval $(\omega_2 - \omega_1)$ increases. The perceived combination tone can be canceled by an objective tone of the same frequency and appropriate amplitude and phase, and hence its equivalent level can be measured.

The $2\omega_1 - \omega_2$ tone is perceived over a wide range of stimulus levels, from about 20-dB sensation level (SL) to over 60-dB SL. The level of the combination tone relative to the objective stimulus level tends to be constant over this range. For a frequency interval $\omega_2/\omega_1 = 1.10$, the perceived combination tone is typically a constant 15 dB or so below the stimulus level. For an interval $\omega_2/\omega_1 = 1.20$, the combination tone level is on the order of 20 to 25 dB below the objective tones.

Figure 6.36 shows the variation of combination tone level as the level of equal-amplitude objective tones is varied. The data are for $\omega_2/\omega_1 = 1.20$ and for two values of ω_1. Figure 6.37 shows the variation of perceived combination tone level as a function of the frequency ratio ω_2/ω_1. Figure 6.38 shows the combination tone behavior as the level of the higher objective tone is varied.

By contrast, the difference tone $(\omega_2 - \omega_1)$ is not heard at levels below 50 dB SL, and grows to a level about 15 dB below the objective tones

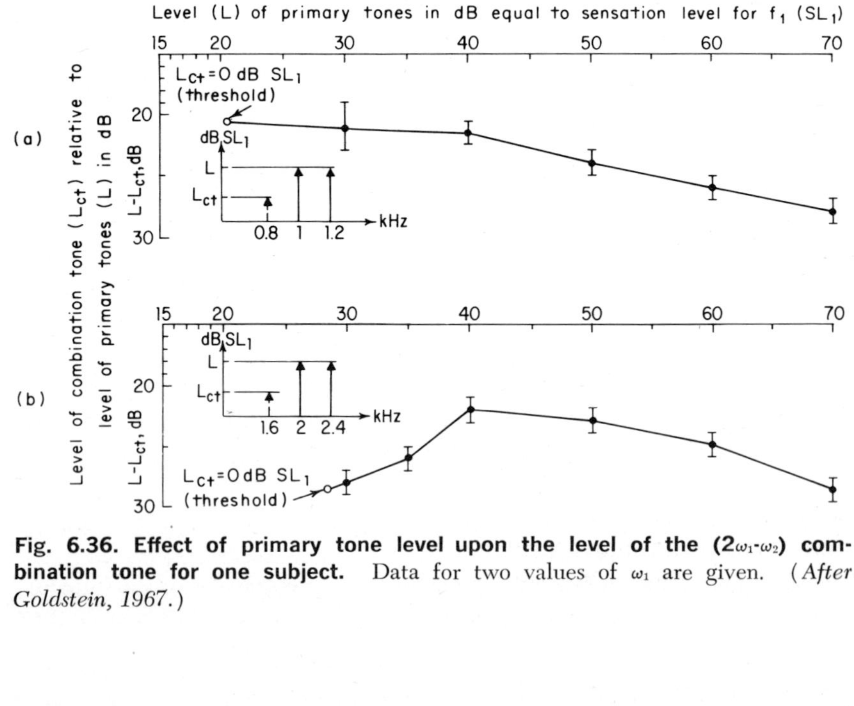

Fig. 6.36. Effect of primary tone level upon the level of the $(2\omega_1\text{-}\omega_2)$ combination tone for one subject. Data for two values of ω_1 are given. (*After Goldstein, 1967.*)

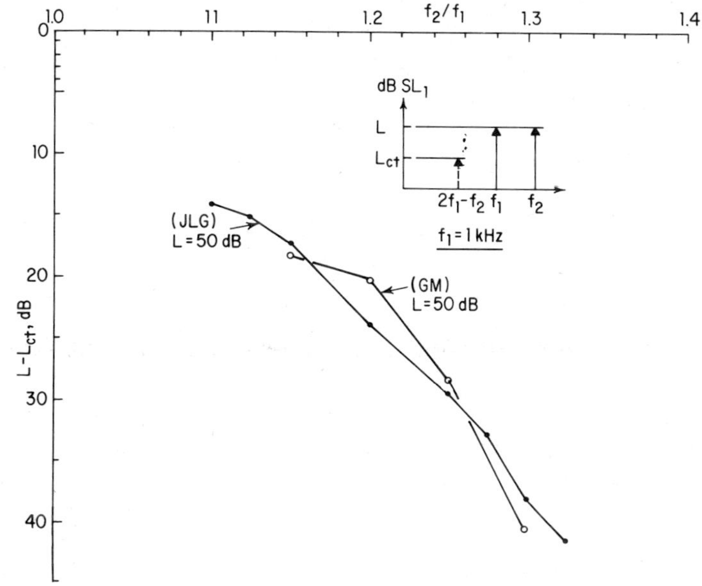

Fig. 6.37. Variation of combination tone level with frequency spacing of primary tones. Data are shown for two subjects. (*After Goldstein, 1967.*)

only for intense inputs exceeding 100 dB SL.‡ In addition, the difference tone is relatively insensitive to frequency interval. The difference and combination frequencies appear therefore to be produced by distinctly different mechanisms.

A square-law distortion is adequate to explain the difference frequency and its behavior with level. Because of the insensitivity of the difference tone to frequency interval, the most attractive candidate for the seat of this distortion is mechanical nonlinearity in the middle ear, as proposed by Helmholtz nearly a century ago. The components of a distortion with a square-law term are

$$\begin{aligned} s^2(t) &= (a_1 \cos \omega_1 t + a_2 \cos \omega_2 t)^2 \\ &= \left\{ \frac{(a_1^2 + a_2^2)}{2} + \frac{a_1^2}{2} \cos 2\omega_1 t + \frac{a_2^2}{2} \cos 2\omega_2 t \right. \\ &\qquad + a_1 a_2 [\cos (\omega_2 - \omega_1)t + \cos (\omega_2 - \omega_1)t] \end{aligned}$$

In this process the amplitude of the difference frequency $(\omega_2 - \omega_1)$ depends directly upon the amplitudes of the objective components. No

‡ In contrast to the linear, difference-tone envelope periodicity (beat) discussed previously, this difference frequency is one which is energetically present on the basilar membrane. It can be canceled by an objective tone of the same frequency, and its relative level can be measured.

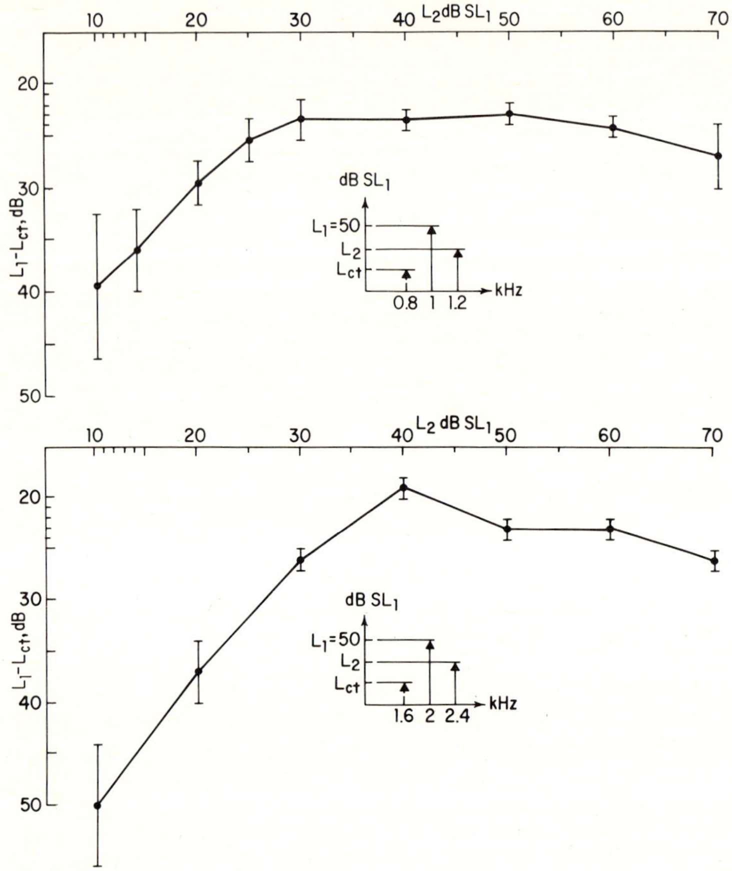

Fig. 6.38. Effect of level of higher-frequency primary tone upon the combination tone level. (Top) Subject JG, $f_1 = 1{,}000$ Hz. (Bottom) Subject GM, $f_1 = 2{,}000$ Hz. (*After Goldstein, 1967.*)

components corresponding to combination tone frequencies are produced.

Production of combination frequencies, on the other hand, requires a distortion characteristic that is at least cubic. In this case

$$\begin{aligned} s^3(t) = {} & \frac{a_1^3}{4} \cos 3\omega_1 t + \frac{a_2^3}{4} \cos 3\omega_2 t \\ & + \left(\frac{3a_1^3}{4} + \frac{3a_1a_2^2}{2}\right) \cos \omega_1 t + \left(\frac{3a_2^3}{4} + \frac{3a_1^2a_2}{2}\right) \cos \omega_2 t \\ & + \frac{3a_1a_2^2}{4} [\cos (2\omega_2 - \omega_1)t + \cos (2\omega_2 + \omega_1)t] \\ & + \frac{3a_1^2a_2}{4} [\cos (2\omega_1 - \omega_2)t + \cos (2\omega_1 + \omega_2)t] \end{aligned}$$

The psychoacoustic observations on the combination tones require several other factors in a suitable model. First, combination tones are produced at relatively low objective levels, and combination tones higher in frequency than the objective tones ω_1 and ω_2 are not heard. Second, the amplitude of the most prominent combination tone $(2\omega_1 - \omega_2)$ relative to the amplitude of equal-intensity objective tones is nearly constant as shown in Fig. 6.36. For varying intensity of ω_2, however, the behavior is as shown in Fig. 6.38. Finally, the audibility of the most prominent tone $(2\omega_1 - \omega_2)$ diminishes sharply as the frequency interval becomes large, as indicated in Fig. 6.37.

These facts seem consistent with the following views: The basilar membrane displacement, in response to two objective tones, is a linear superposition of the individual responses, as von Békésy's measurements indicate. The conversion of basilar membrane motion into first-order electrical activity involves a distortion which includes at least a cubic term. The conversion distortion could be of mechanical, electrical, or chemical origin. A mechanical candidate might be peak limiting in hair-cell shear, caused by the manner in which the tectorial membrane "rides" over the organ of Corti when the basilar membrane deflects. The distortion is produced at the place of the primaries and propagates from there to its characteristic place on the membrane. The behavior with frequency interval suggests that the primaries must be close enough to be well "embraced" by the mechanical response of the membrane at their place. The behavior with level indicates that a peak normalization is involved. The amplitude of the $2\omega_1 - \omega_2$ term in the cubic distortion above is proportional to $a_1{}^2a_2$, but the observed behavior with level suggests that the generated $2\omega_1 - \omega_2$ component is nearly a constant number of decibels below equal-amplitude objective tones. Also the behavior with level a_2 suggests that to a first approximation the perceived combination tone is normalized in peak amplitude similar to a function such as $a_1{}^2a_2/(a_1 + a_2)^2$.

Finally, the inability to hear distortion products higher than the primaries seems not so much a question of masking as one that the distortion products, generated at the place of the primaries, cannot propagate to higher frequency places. Peterson and Bogert [21] have modeled the complex propagation constant of the basilar membrane and show that a high-frequency displacement applied to the low-frequency end of the membrane will not propagate "backwards" on the membrane but will rapidly attenuate.

A logical question in the quest to find counterparts of these behavioral observations in the physiology is whether primary fibers of the auditory nerve display combination tone responses (that is, a neural response whose time pattern resembles that of a single tone at frequency

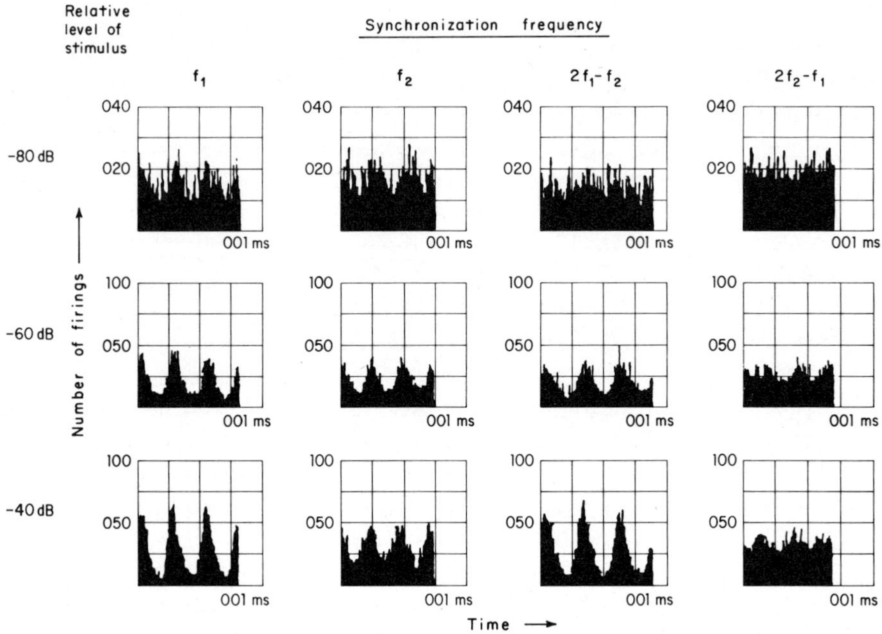

Fig. 6.39. PST histograms for a single auditory-nerve fiber with characteristic frequency CF = 3.20 kHz. The input signal is two sinusoids: f_1 = 3.66 kHz and f_2 = 3.99 kHz. The histograms are synchronized to four different reference frequencies shown. Data are shown for three intensity levels of the input signal. (*After Goldstein and Kiang, 1968.*)

$2\omega_1 - \omega_2$). Electrophysiological measurements by Goldstein and Kiang [22] show that they do.

Goldstein and Kiang measured the electrical response in single fibers of the cat's auditory nerve for two-tone stimulation. In particular they examined PST histograms‡ for fibers whose characteristic frequency (CF) corresponds to the $2\omega_1 - \omega_2$ combination tone. A typical result is shown in Fig. 6.39. Each histogram is one minute of data and shows responses to three cycles of the reference signal. The PSTs are synchronized to the reference frequencies indicated. For this fiber, a sound-pressure level (SPL) of 40 dB resulted in essentially spontaneous behavior, although a slight amount of synchrony is detectable. When the level is increased to 60 and then to 80 dB SPL, the stimulated firings show: very pronounced synchrony with the combination tone ($2\omega_1 - \omega_2$); strong synchrony with the lowest objective component (ω_1);

‡ For the sinusoidal signals, the PST histogram shows the number of neural spikes per unit time (1 bin width) after a reference time which is determined by a synchronizing signal. The synchronizing signal is periodic and produces one sweep of the quantized time axis in each of its periods.

moderate synchrony with ω_2; and virtually no synchrony with the higher combination tone $(2\omega_2 - \omega_1)$. These and other data indicate that increases in stimulus level increase the firing rate of the fiber (tuned to the combination tone) in a manner very similar to that obtained with a single objective tone at the combination-tone frequency. (A typical dynamic range for a fiber's firing rate is about 30 dB in stimulus level.)

Further experiments show that the stimulus tones can be chosen so that the fiber responds only to the combination tone $(2\omega_1 - \omega_2)$ when ω_1 and ω_2 are outside the fiber's tuning curve, although the fiber responds to all three tones when all frequencies are all within the tuning curve. Also, behavior of neural response with level indicates the combination tone amplitude is nearly proportional to the stimulus amplitude over a broad range of objective level. Further, the neural response at the combination-tone frequency decreases when the interval between the stimulus frequencies is increased. All these indications are consistent with the psychophysical observations discussed earlier.

The nonlinearity involved in producing the combination tone must be at least of third order, and it operates over the normal listening range of sound intensities. This nonlinearity therefore seems to be a fundamental characteristic of the mechanism for converting basilar membrane motion into nerve activity. The nonlinear operation is approximately level-normalized and is frequency-dependent. It cannot be accounted for by any known characteristics of the middle-ear structure, and hence with high probability is located in the cochlea. No direct evidence has been found that the nonlinearity is mechanical, electrical, or chemical, or any combination of such processes. A tempting speculation, however, is that the mechanical shear in the sensory cell hairs is a nonlinear function of the linear basilar membrane motion. Only direct detailed studies of cochlear mechanics will resolve the question. Even so, the psychoacoustic and physiological experiments on combination tones provide further instances where insight can be gained by drawing together psychophysical behavior and the relevant physiology.

6.8 Conclusions

This discussion has aimed to make the single point that research in auditory physiology and psychoacoustics should be designed to be complementary. Work in one field often provides answers or, perhaps more important, critical questions which lead to progress in the other. While a complete theory of hearing is not on the horizon, efforts to coalesce physiological and behavioral knowledge into models of some generality serve a vital purpose in organizing data and suggesting key experiments.

It is in the latter area that the signal theorist, who may be neither physiologist nor psychoacoustician, can make important contributions.

Even at present the known mechanical and electrical properties of the ear provide a valuable framework within which much of the psychoacoustic data compiled over the years can be interpreted. Moreover, these data should be interpreted within this frame of reference, for any other is likely to be spurious and misleading. Conversely, psychoacoustic experiments often indicate fundamental physiological relations which should be searched for. Cases in point are the binaural lateralization phenomena and the monaural fine-pitch structure associated with pulsive signals, as discussed in Sec. 6.7. Electrophysiological correlates of this behavior must exist. It would be valuable to establish how the information is represented neurally.

An omnipresent danger in auditory experimentation, as in any science, is that the effort can fall into an aimless measuring of many effects in the hope that the results will eventually form themselves into a pattern, and hence into an understanding of hearing. This result could obtain, but most people do not live long enough to see it. A more significant approach for the psychoacoustician who is designing a new experiment is not only to ask himself what the measurements will tell him about auditory behavior, but also to ask what questions his experiment might suggest to the physiologist (particularly questions that the physiologist has a hope of answering). Reciprocal effort in this direction probably would result, on the one hand, in the psychoacoustician dealing with signals more deterministic and analytically tractable, and on the other, in the physiologist getting interested in signals somewhat more complicated than single clicks and tones. Hopefully, too, it would aid in establishing a firm understanding of the mechanical-to-neural transduction mechanism and of the behavior of first-order fibers, the details of which are basic to a general theory and model of hearing.

This view is not intended to slight interests in central mechanisms and behavioral responses to complex signals such as speech. It is, however, put forward as the most likely route to understanding how information is processed in the auditory system. Certainly a significant transformation and recoding of acoustic signals is performed even at the periphery of the auditory system. An understanding of this recoding—what signal attributes are preserved, what discarded—could have important implications for communication.

Notes Added in Proof

This chapter was written upon invitation in 1966. It was revised and additional material supplied in 1967–68. Since that time a number of new and significant research results have emerged. Many of these results deserve emphasis and prominent comment in any exposition of auditory function. This note is added to partially bridge the time gap and to point the direction to several of these later and important works.

(a) Mössbauer Measurements of Basilar Membrane Motion (1967–71)

B. M. Johnstone and his associates [23, 24, 25] achieved pioneering successes in applying the Mössbauer effect to the measurement of basilar membrane velocity. Pursuing this direction, Rhode [26] and Rhode and Geisler [27] conducted comprehensive experiments on squirrel monkeys. They established several new findings which bear upon and modify the views put forward in the preceding discussions of this chapter.

First, their observations confirm in a broad sense the classical discoveries of von Békésy. But their differences in detail add important new information about basilar membrane properties. In brief, Rhode employed realistic acoustic levels and observed the following about the amplitude versus frequency and phase versus frequency responses of the membrane displacement. For a given place, the amplitude versus frequency response grows at about +6 dB/oct up to frequencies just below the maximum response, where the response slope increases to about +24 dB/oct. At frequencies above the maximum response, the displacement amplitude drops at approximately —100 dB/oct. The response did not drop off indefinitely but tended to level off. Further, a nonlinear aspect was found in membrane displacement at its largest deflections. The response curve was sharper at low levels (70 dB SPL) than at higher levels (90 dB SPL).

The measured phase of the basilar membrane displacement was found to lead the malleus displacement by $+90^\circ$ at low frequencies, and the total phase lag at high frequencies approaches -7π to -9π.

Several points are important here. The mechanical frequency selectivity, particularly the high-frequency skirt of the response, is more acute than found by von Békésy. This increased selectivity could easily be incorporated into the computer model discussed earlier by increasing the order of the approximating function. Also, von Békésy noted no significant nonlinear behavior in membrane displacement at sound levels much higher than 90 dB SPL.

Further, the phase indicated by von Békésy does not correspond to the $+\pi/2$ lead measured by Rhode at low frequencies. That this $+\pi/2$ lead should exist was predicted some years earlier, solely on analytical grounds, by Flanagan and Bird [28]. Needless to say, the eventual experimental confirmation was gratifying to this author. This leading phase characteristic was incorporated into the earlier computer model just on analytical bases, despite the (then) absence of experimental support.

(b) Psychophysics of Pitch Perception (1970–72)

Several new aspects of periodicity pitch, similar to those described in the chapter text, have been carefully quantified and related to residue phenomena and auditory frequency analysis. Comprehensive review is not possible in this note, but two important collections of papers in this area have been published: Plomp and Smoorenburg, eds., "Frequency Analysis and Periodicity Detection in Hearing," Sijthoff, Leiden, 1970 [29], and Tobias (ed.), "Foundations of Modern Auditory Theory," Academic, New York, 1970 [30]. These writings, by many leading auditory scientists, give data vital to a current assessment of pitch perception.

Further, at least one other new pitch effect derives from E. Zwicker's discovery of the "negative afterimage" [31]. This phenomenon has been quantified in comprehensive experiments by Lummis and Guttman [32].

(c) Neural Modeling in the Peripheral Auditory System (1968–72)

As indicated in the chapter text, a research frontier is exemplified by the problems of analytically characterizing the transducer action involved in converting membrane motion into electrical neural behavior, and in characterizing the subsequent processing of peripheral neural signals. Efforts similar to those of Weiss and of Lummis, mentioned previously, have been expanded in several significant directions. Siebert's work [33, 34] gives further insight into probabilistic models of neural signals. The work of Goldstein, Baer, and Kiang [35] gives new theories for accounting for observed nerve responses. All these data, plus others, are brought together into a model for the "transfer characteristics of the peripheral auditory system" by Duifhuis [36] and subjected to computer tests. Careful study of all these writings is a mandatory continuation to where the preceding chapter leaves off.

REFERENCES

1. J. L. Flanagan, Models for Approximating Basilar Membrane Displacement, *Bell System Tech. J.*, **39:**1163–1191 (September 1960); **41:**959–1009 (May 1962).
2. J. L. Flanagan, "Speech Analysis, Synthesis and Perception," Springer Verlag, New York, 1965.
3. J. L. Flanagan, Computer Simulation of Basilar Membrane Displacement, Proceedings Fourth International Congress on Acoustics, Copenhagen, August 21–28, 1962.

4. G. von Békésy, The Gap between the Hearing of External and Internal Sounds, *Symp. Soc. Exptl. Biol. Great Britain,* vol. 16: Biological Receptor Mechanisms, 1962.
5. H. Davis, A model for Transducer Action in the Cochlea, *Cold Spring Harbor Symp. Quant. Biol.,* **30:**181–189 (1965).
6. D. C. Teas, D. H. Eldredge, and H. Davis, Cochlear Responses to Acoustic Transients: An Interpretation of Whole-nerve Action Potentials, *J. Acoust. Soc. Am.,* **34:**1438–1459 (1962).
7. A. R. Tunturi, Analysis of Cortical Auditory Responses with the Probability Pulse, *Am. J. Physiol.,* **181:**630–638 (1955).
8. N. Y. S. Kiang et al., Discharge Patterns of Single Fibers in the Cat's Auditory Nerve, *Res. Monograph* No. 35, MIT Press, Cambridge, Mass., 1965.
9. T. Weiss, Model for Firing Patterns of Auditory Nerve Fibers, *MIT Quart. Progr. Rept. Res. Lab. Electron.,* April 15, 1963.
10. T. F. Weiss, A Model for Firing Patterns of Auditory Nerve Fibers, *MIT Tech. Rept.* 418, March 2, 1964.
11. R. C. Lummis, The Secret Code of Hearing, *Bell Lab. Record,* pp. 261–266, September 1968.
12. J. C. R. Licklider, Three Auditory Theories, in "Psychology: A Study of a Science," McGraw-Hill, New York, 1959.
13. L. A. Jeffress et al., Making of Tonal Signals, *J. Acoust. Soc. Am.,* **28:**416 (May 1956).
14. B. McA. Sayers and E. C. Cherry, Mechanism of Binaural Fusion in the Hearing of Speech, *J. Acoust. Soc. Am.,* **29:**973 (September 1957).
15. J. L. Flanagan, E. E. David, Jr., and B. J. Watson, Binaural Lateralization of Cophasic and Antiphasic Clicks, *J. Acoust. Soc. Am.,* **36**(11):2184–2193 (November 1964).
16. J. L. Flanagan and N. Guttman, On the Pitch of Periodic Pulses, *J. Acoust. Soc. Am.,* **32:**1308–1319 (1960).
17. J. L. Flanagan and N. Guttman, Pitch of Periodic Pulses without Fundamental Component, *J. Acoust. Soc. Am.,* **32:**1319–1328 (1960).
18. A. E. Rosenberg, Effect of Masking on the Pitch of Periodic Pulses, *J. Acoust. Soc. Am.,* **38**(5):747–758 (November 1965).
19. R. J. Ritsma, Frequencies Dominant in the Perception of the Pitch of Complex Sounds, *J. Acoust. Soc. Am.,* **42**(1):191–198 (July 1967).
20. J. L. Goldstein, Auditory Nnolinearity, *J. Acoust. Soc. Am.,* **41**(3):676–689 (March 1967).
21. L. C. Peterson and B. P. Bogert, A Dynamical Theory of the Cochlea, *J. Acoust. Soc. Am.,* **22:**369–381 (1950).
22. J. L. Goldstein and N. Y. S. Kiang, Neural Correlates of the Aural Combination Tone $2f_1$-f_2, *Proc. IEEE,* **56**(6):981–992 (June 1968).
23. B. M. Johnstone and A. J. Boyle, Basilar Membrane Vibration Examined with the Mössbauer Technique, *Science,* **158:**389–390 (1967).
24. B. M. Johnstone and K. J. Taylor, Mechanical Aspects of Cochlear Function, in "Frequency Analysis and Periodicity Detection in Hearing," R. Plomp and G. F. Smoorenburg (eds.), Sijthoff, Leiden, 1970.
25. B. M. Johnstone, K. J. Taylor, and A. J. Boyle, Mechanics in the Guinea Pig Cochlea, *J. Acoust. Soc. Am.,* **47:**504–509 (1970).
26. W. Rhode, Observations of the Vibration of the Basilar Membrane in Squirrel Monkeys Using the Mössbauer Technique, *J. Acoust. Soc. Am.,* **49:**1218–1231 (1971).
27. W. Rhode and C. D. Geisler, Measurements of the Amplitude and Phase of the

Basilar Membrane Using Mössbauer Effect, *J. Acoust. Soc. Am.,* **47:**69(A) (1970).

28. J. L. Flanagan and C. M. Bird, Minimum Phase Responses for the Basilar Membrane, *J. Acoust. Soc. Am.,* **34:**114–118 (1962).
29. R. Plomp and G. F. Smoorenburg (eds.), "Frequency Analysis and Periodicity Detection in Hearing," Sijthoff, Leiden, 1970.
30. J. V. Tobias (ed.), "Foundations of Modern Auditory Theory," Academic, New York, 1970.
31. E. Zwicker, "Negative Afterimage" in Hearing, *J. Acoust. Soc. Am.,* **36:**2413–2415(L) (1964).
32. R. C. Lummis and N. Guttman, Exploratory Studies of Zwicker's "Negative Afterimage" in Hearing, to appear in *J. Acoust. Soc. Am.,* **51** (1972).
33. W. M. Siebert, Stimulus Transformations in the Peripheral Auditory System, in P. A. Kolers and M. Eden (eds.), "Recognizing Patterns," MIT Press, Cambridge, Massachusetts, 1968.
34. W. M. Siebert, Frequency Discrimination in the Auditory System: Place of Periodicity Mechanisms?, *Proc. IEEE,* **58:**723–730 (1970).
35. J. L. Goldstein, T. Baer, and N. Y. S. Kiang, A Theoretical Treatment of Latency, Group-Delay and Tuning Characteristics for Auditory-Nerve Responses to Clicks and Tones, *Proc. Johns Hopkins Symposium on Physiology of the Auditory System,* Johns Hopkins Medical Institutes, 25–26 (June 1971).
36. H. Duifhuis, Perceptual Analysis of Sound, doctoral thesis, Technical University of Eindhoven, Grene N. V., Eindhoven, 1972.

NOTE: References 23 through 36 were added in proof. See "Notes Added in Proof," p. 220.

CHAPTER SEVEN

Practicing Digital Spectrum Analysis

B. P. BOGERT

Introduction

In this paper we will discuss the practical aspects of spectrum (frequency) analysis of data streams by digital computation. There is no question that analysis and interpretation of data, after transformation into the frequency domain, generally yields more useful insight into the mechanism generating the original data than does analysis in the time domain in which the data is taken. For example, the frequency analysis of speech waveforms, carried out so successfully by the sound spectrograph, has been largely responsible for our present knowledge of speech mechanism and has guided our studies for efficiently coding the information bearing elements of speech. Another example of the power of spectrum analysis to delineate the mechanism underlying the data arose recently in seismology. Digital recordings of seismic waves originating from very energetic earthquakes yielded the periods of the free vibrations of the earth as a whole, excited by the earth tremors as a bell would be when struck by a hammer. The observed values of the periods of the various overtones have, in turn, helped choose between possible values of the elastic constants of the earth's deep interior.

Although our emphasis will be on digital spectral analysis, we must start with considerations of the conversion of analog data into sampled and quantized digital data streams suitable for manipulation in a digital computer. We will be concerned with prefiltering of the analog data and the effects of periodic time sampling to get a sequence of equispaced instantaneous data values. We will discuss the effects of quantization—conversion of the continuum of possible values of the instantaneous samples to one of a finite number corresponding to a fixed-length binary number suitable for digital computation. In any digital data-acquisition system occasional errors or overloads may occur, and we must consider how to recognize and correct or ameliorate these errors. In many situations one must deal with several data streams at once and search for interrelations among them. This means the multichannel data must be sampled so that either all channels are sampled simultaneously or the time lags between channel sample times must be accounted for in subsequent processing. We are not yet prepared to analyze our data; it is profitable to remove the mean value and any linear trend in the stretches to be analyzed, as so doing will ease the burden on subsequent frequency analysis.

In most instances, the data to be processed may be considered to be a sample of a random process, and the particular stretch represents a segment of finite length lifted from an unending data stream. To avoid the effects of a sudden start and stop in the data stretch, it is sometimes made to start and end smoothly by tapering the beginning and end appropriately. Although we have removed the mean and a linear trend (which may be loosely thought of as the zero frequency cosine and sine components), there may be sufficiently strong periodic (or otherwise) components in the data which ought to be removed by filtering—a linear convolutary operation on the data. This procedure, called *prewhitening*, will reduce the spectrum analytical equivalent of interstation interference on a radio receiver. With all the procedures and preparation mentioned above, and with considerations of the length of data to be processed, we are ready to proceed.

What we choose to call data processing includes the calculation of Fourier transforms; covariances and cross-covariances; the estimation of power density spectra and cross-spectra; coherence; the estimation of transfer functions; and some further extensions of spectrum analysis including the bispectrum and the cepstrum. It should be obvious that the division we have chosen between data preparation and data processing is somewhat arbitrary, and merely reflects our particular viewpoint.

Basic to this kind of data processing are the Fourier transform and the Fourier series. They provide a representation of a given data stream in terms of sinusoidal components for the aperiodic and periodic case, respectively; and, indeed, a suitable generalization of the Fourier transform is applicable to random processes as well. For data which are considered to be representative of a random process, covariances give useful insights in their own right and form the starting point for the calculation of power-density spectra by the indirect method. The recent formulation of methods for rapid calculation of Fourier series on a digital computer leads us to consider the direct calculation of power-density spectra. We then consider cross-spectra, which give useful information on the interrelations between two data streams. Related to the cross-spectrum are coherence and phase, which provide another viewpoint. It may be that of two pieces of data one represents the input to a linear transformation or filter, and the other the output. From these two one can estimate the transfer function (frequency response) of the filter. We will consider the bispectrum, which is an extension of the power spectrum to higher-order relations between frequency components in data streams and is a means to characterize intermodulation between two frequencies and their sum or difference frequencies. Situations may arise when it is thought that the data contains a delayed version of itself, so we will discuss the cepstrum: a processing technique which looks for the ripple in the power-density spectrum produced by the echo and determines the amplitude and delay thereof.

With this summarizing overview of the preparation and processing of digital data, we proceed now to a detailed discussion from the viewpoint of the practicing analyst.

Data Preparation

We assume that the reader has some acquaintance with the Fourier transform $F(\nu)$ of the time function $f(t)$:

$$F(\nu) = \int_{-\infty}^{\infty} f(t)e^{-2\pi i\nu t}\,dt \tag{7-1}$$

and its inverse

$$f(t) = \int_{-\infty}^{\infty} F(\nu)e^{2\pi i\nu t}\,d\nu \tag{7-2}$$

where ν is the frequency. The Fourier series for a periodic function

$f(t)$ with period T is

$$a_0 + 2 \sum_{k=1}^{\infty} \left(a_k \cos \frac{2\pi k}{T} t + b_k \sin \frac{2\pi k}{T} t \right) \tag{7-3}$$

with

$$a_k = \frac{1}{T} \int_0^T f(t) \cos \frac{2\pi kt}{T} \, dt \tag{7-4a}$$

and

$$b_k = \frac{1}{T} \int_0^T f(t) \sin \frac{2\pi kt}{T} \, dt \tag{7-4b}$$

Observe that the Fourier integral applies to a time function of finite energy, that is, if $f(t)$ represents the voltage across a 1-ohm resistance, the total energy is

$$E = \int_{-\infty}^{\infty} f^2(t) \, dt < \infty \tag{7-5a}$$

and by Parseval's theorem, the energy is expressible as the integral over all frequencies of the squared modulus of the Fourier transform:

$$E = \int_{-\infty}^{\infty} |F(\nu)|^2 \, d\nu \tag{7-5b}$$

We also recall the convolution theorem, which relates the product of two Fourier transforms to the convolution of the original time function. Let $f_1(t)$, $f_2(t)$, and $f_3(t)$ have the Fourier transforms $F_1(\nu)$, $F_2(\nu)$, and $F_3(\nu)$, respectively, if

$$\begin{aligned} f_3(t) &\equiv \int_{-\infty}^{\infty} f_1(\tau) f_2(t-\tau) \, d\tau = \int_{-\infty}^{\infty} f_1(t-\tau) f_2(\tau) \, d\tau \\ &\equiv f_1(t) * f_2(t) \end{aligned} \tag{7-6a}$$

That is, if $f_3(t)$ is the convolution of $f_1(t)$ and $f_2(t)$, then

$$F_3(\nu) = F_1(\nu) F_2(\nu) \tag{7-6b}$$

Similarly, if

$$\begin{aligned} F_3(\nu) &= \int_{-\infty}^{\infty} F_1(\nu-\lambda) F_2(\lambda) \, d\lambda = \int_{-\infty}^{\infty} F_1(\lambda) F_2(\nu-\lambda) \, d\lambda \\ &\equiv F_1(\nu) * F_2(\nu) \end{aligned} \tag{7-7a}$$

then

$$f_3(t) = f_1(t) f_2(t) \tag{7-7b}$$

The concept of a "band-limited" function is very important in data preparation, as it enters in an essential way in the *sampling theorem*. If a time function $f(t)$ has a Fourier transform which is zero for $|\nu| > W$, then equally spaced instantaneous samples of the function, if taken often

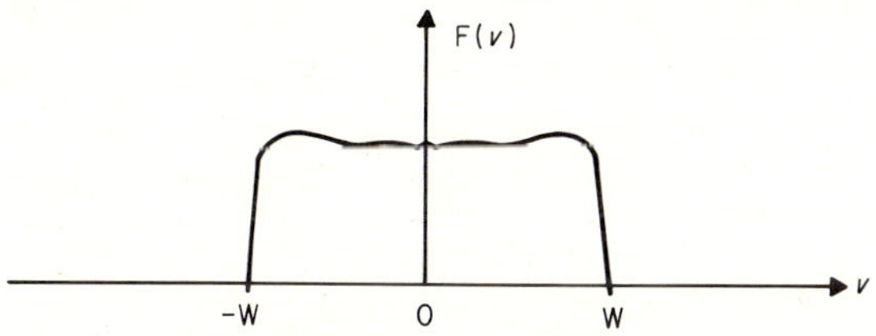

Fig. 7.1. A band-limited function $f(t)$ has its transform $F(\nu) = 0$ for $|\nu| > W$.

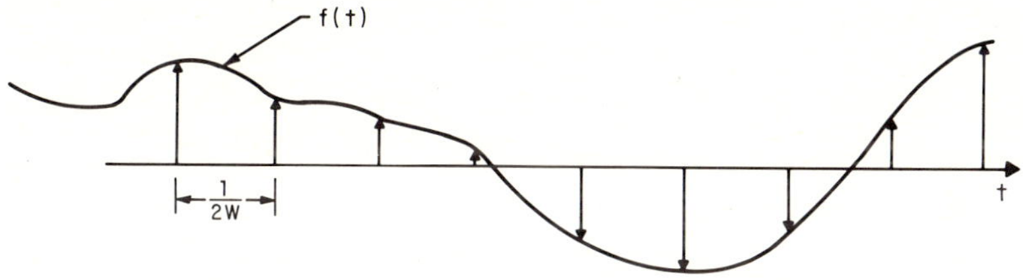

Fig. 7.2 Sampling the time function $f(t)$.

enough, are sufficient to reconstruct the function precisely:

$$f(t) = \sum_{k=-\infty}^{\infty} f\left(\frac{k}{2W}\right) \frac{\sin \pi(2Wt - k)}{\pi(2Wt - k)} \tag{7-8}$$

for $-\infty < t < \infty$. The sampling theorem requires the samples to be taken at most $1/2W$ second apart. This frequency, $2W$, the Nyquist

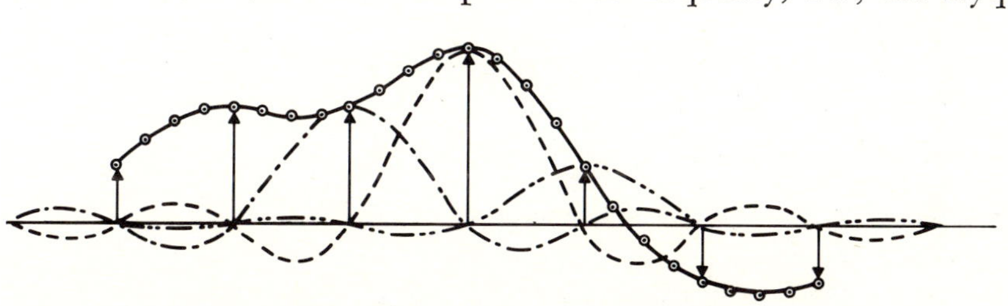

Fig. 7.3. Representation of a band-limited function by its samples.

frequency, is the lowest sampling frequency permissible: a higher $2W_1$ ($W_1 > W$) is equivalent to assuring that the function $f(t)$ is band-limited to a higher frequency W_1 which naturally includes the band up to W.

The product of the data length T and the sampling frequency gives the number of points in that stretch of data, and is at least $2WT$. If the data gatherer is careful and the instrumentation he uses is above suspicion, he may not need to examine the data for errors, either visually or by a suitable computer program. In this case, it would be sufficient to sample at the Nyquist rate $2W$. Usually, however, there will be reason to examine data after sampling and to correct bad points, and so it may be worthwhile to oversample. Sampling at a rate from 1.5 to 3 times the Nyquist rate will provide enough redundancy so that graphs of the data are easy to follow visually, and if special programs are written to correct isolated bad points, the redundancy can be used to advantage.

The sampling theorem, therefore, makes it essential to provide suitable low-pass filtering to the data before sampling. Often the physical source of the data, or the sensors used to collect it, provide of themselves the equivalent of adequate low-pass filtering for the desired sampling rate, but much more often this is not the case. Let us consider what happens if the signal $f(t)$ is sampled at a rate $2W$ samples per second. Let, for example, $f(t)$ be a sinusoid of frequency $2W$ with an arbitrary phase φ:

$$f(t) = A \sin (4\pi Wt + \varphi)$$

At times given by

$$t_k = \frac{k}{2W}$$

$$f(t_k) = A \sin (2\pi k + \varphi) = A \sin \varphi$$

a constant; and the result is identical to that obtained from sampling

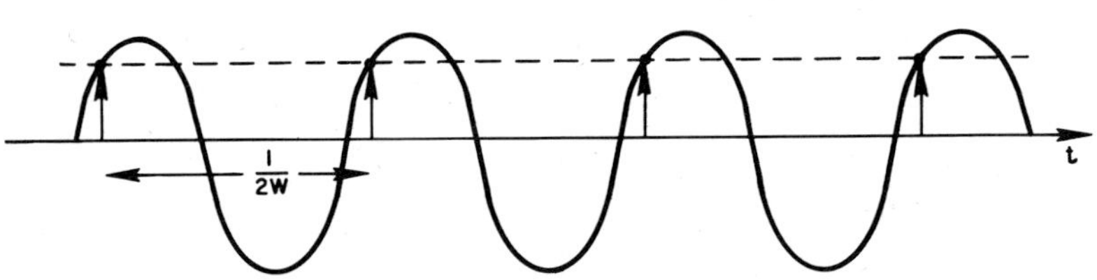

Fig. 7.4. Sampling a sinusoid of frequency 2W.

a "dc" or constant term of amplitude $A \sin \varphi$. More generally, a frequency $2kW \pm \nu$, when sampled at a rate $2W$ samples per second, will be indistinguishable from a frequency ν. This is called *aliasing*, and means that unless the analog data is low-pass-filtered so that frequencies above W are stopped, energy at frequencies thought to lie between zero and W will actually contain energy from other frequencies folded into the zero-to-W frequency band. It may be helpful to consider the (positive) frequency range from zero to very high frequencies to lie on a strip which is folded upward at frequencies W, $3W$, $5W$, . . . , and downward at $2W$, $4W$, ... When the data is sampled it is equivalent to accordion-folding the whole frequency strip down into the zero-to-W frequency range.

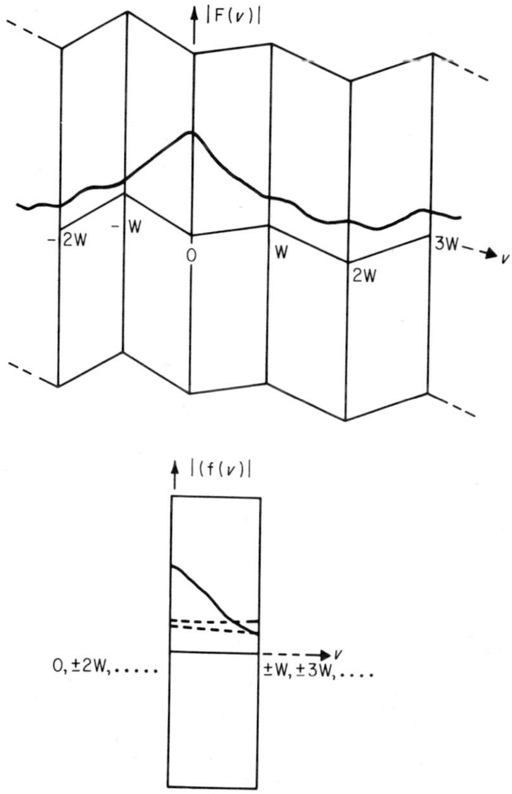

Fig. 7.5. Effects of sampling a non-band-limited function.

Filtering for Band Limiting

We now consider the problems associated with assuring that the data we wish to process is properly band-limited before sampling. We suppose, for definiteness, that we plan to perform a digital spectrum analysis of our data. We must assume, a priori, some upper frequency of interest, either based on knowledge of the properties of the source of data or based on limitations of our data-gathering and digitizing equipment. We will now determine the pertinent characteristics of a smoothing or low-pass filter placed in the analog data stream before sampling.

We characterize the low-pass filter in terms of its frequency response; the amplitude and phase of the sinusoid at the output of the filter when a sinusoid of unit amplitude and zero phase is applied at the input: if the input signal $e_i(t)$ of frequency $\omega = 2\pi\nu$ is

$$e_i(t) = \sin 2\pi\nu t$$

the output signal $e_o(t)$ (for a linear filter) will be

$$e_o(t) = A \sin (2\pi\nu t + \varphi)$$

where the amplitude A and the phase φ depend on the frequency ν. We usually write A and φ as the magnitude and phase of a complex function of frequency $H(\nu)$ called the *transfer function:*

$$H(\nu) = A(\nu)e^{i\varphi(\nu)} \tag{7-9}$$

whose Fourier transform is called the *impulse response* $h(t)$ of the filter, since if the input $e_i(t)$ is a sharp spike or impulse which vanishes except at $t = 0$ but has finite area, then the output $e_o(t)$ is

$$e_o(t) = h(t)$$

An ideal low-pass filter has a transfer function $H(\nu)$ which is unity for frequencies less than the cutoff frequency ν_0; and is zero for frequencies greater than ν_0:

$$\begin{aligned} H(\nu) &= 1 \qquad |\nu| \leq \nu_0 \\ &= 0 \qquad |\nu| > \nu_0 \end{aligned}$$

Such an ideal filter, however, cannot be realized exactly, since its impulse response $h(t)$ is nonzero for $t < 0$, which implies a response before the stimulus. In fact, for this ideal filter

$$h(t) = 2\nu_0 \frac{\sin 2\pi\nu_0 t}{2\pi\nu_0 t}$$

which has the same form as the kernel of the sampling theorem if $\nu_0 = W$. Practical low-pass filters will approximate the ideal filter behavior more or less. We may characterize a practical filter by dividing the (positive) frequency interval into three segments. In the *passband* segment we require $|H(\nu)|$ to fall between the limits

$$1 - \delta \leq |H(\nu)| \leq 1 + \delta \qquad 0 \leq |\nu| \leq \nu_1$$

In the third segment, the *stop band,* we require

$$|H(\nu)| \leq \epsilon \qquad |\nu| > \nu_2$$

In the second segment, or *transition band,* for which $\nu_1 \leq |\nu| \leq \nu_2$, we would like the filter amplitude response to fall from its value in the passband to that in its stop band approximately uniformly. The constants δ and ϵ are small and to be determined by requirements on accuracy for the spectrum or whatever is to be computed. An example

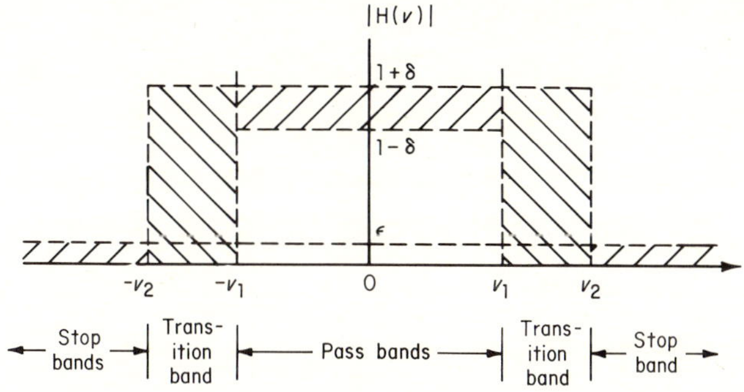

Fig. 7.6. Characterization of a practical low-pass filter.

of the determination of ϵ will be given after we discuss quantizing noise. In any case, it is clearly seen that alias frequencies will be attenuated by the factor ϵ and we must assure ourselves that the total energy contained in the alias frequencies is appropriately limited. Ordinarily δ might be in the neighborhood of 0.06, whch corresponds to uniformity in the passband of about 1 dB. Alternatively, a specification of the passband response of the filter can be made by giving the functional form of $|H(\nu)|$, and corrections for it may be made in the computer after digitization. The form of $|H(\nu)|$ in the passband may be determined by requirements for prewhitening, a subject to be considered later on.

The electrical complexity of a realizable low-pass filter depends strongly on δ, ϵ, and the ratio $(\nu_2 - \nu_1)/\nu_1$, the complexity increasing as each approaches zero. It is particularly desirable to keep the relative width of the transition band as large as possible. The specification for the filter can be approached as follows. The passband cutoff frequency ν_0 is set equal to or greater than the highest frequency of interest in the data. The value of ϵ is chosen to assure that energy at alias frequencies is sufficiently small. The lower edge of the stop band ν_2 is chosen to be near W, where $2W$ is the digitized sampling rate. If it is possible to choose W to be about 1.5 to 2.5 times ν_1, the transition band will be wide enough to lead to relatively simple realizations of the band-limiting filter. If there are compelling reasons to keep the sampling rate near $2\nu_1$, either the band-limiting filter will necessarily become complicated or alias frequencies near the folding frequency may cause trouble.

The phase in the passband of the band-limiting filter is of some interest, particularly if an accurate replica of the analog waveform is desired. To preserve the waveform, the phase φ must be proportional to frequency. This will be approximately true in the passband of a low-pass filter except near the cutoff frequency ν_1, and the departure from linearity increases as the relative width of the transition band becomes smaller. Allowing a reasonable ratio for the sampling frequency to the cutoff frequency, as discussed above, the phase shift and its associated distortions should be tolerable. If more precision is required, the actual phase shift $\varphi(\nu)$ can be measured or calculated and allowances made in subsequent digital processing. For digital power-spectrum analysis, the phase shift introduced by the filter is immaterial and is usually ignored.

Sampling and Quantization

In the sampling theorem we have assumed that the value of the analog data was sampled by specifying the value of the function at equally spaced time instants. This is accomplished by electrical circuits which require a small but finite time to measure the value of the analog wave. Because of the finite time required, in fact, the electrical wave is averaged over the sampling time and the value so obtained will be the average of the voltage wave over the small time interval. In most cases for acoustic waveforms the sampling time is so short that it may be regarded as instantaneous. For more rapid sampling of higher-frequency waveforms, however, this effect will be significant; but it can be taken into account by regarding the sampling waveform of finite width as the impulse response of a low-pass filter, and a transfer function for the sampling waveform can be calculated and used to correct the digitized data.

A possible source of error in sampling an analog waveform is variations in the sampling rate which causes nonuniformity in the spacing between successive samples. The effect of this jitter is to smear out the frequency components originally present in the sampled waveform, and it may be regarded as a form of phase modulation. Ordinarily this effect is insignificant with modern sampling and digitizing circuitry and is likely to be negligible compared to similar effects produced by analog recording means. Experience with digital cross-spectral analysis between two playbacks of an analog recording has shown that the higher-frequency coherence between two successive playbacks can be greatly affected by the time variations produced by the analog recording facility.

Multichannel Sampling

When N data streams are to be analyzed concurrently, it is desirable to sample each stream simultaneously. Although this can be done by using N sampling circuits each followed by its quantizer, the usual practice is to *sample* the N data streams at the same instant and *hold* the instantaneous sample values before quantization. The values need only be held until the next sample time. A single higher-speed quantizer can then be connected successively to each of the N held samples to provide a quantized data stream at a rate of $2NW$ quantized values

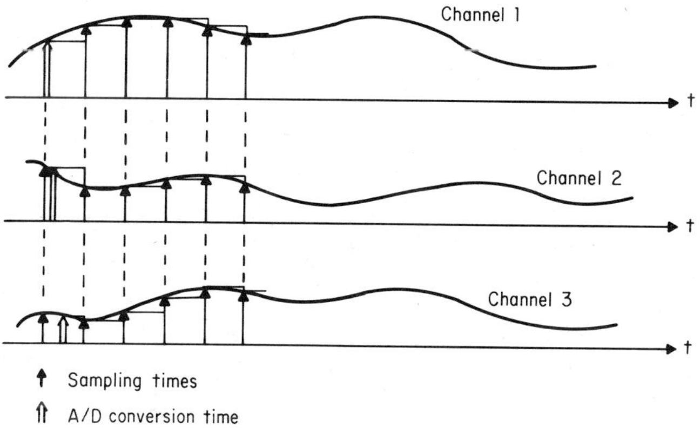

Fig. 7.7. Multichannel sampling, holding, and A/D conversion.

per second. If sample-and-hold techniques are not used, the N analog data streams are sampled successively, with a sample interval $1/2W$, by a commutator circuit. The net effect of this is to introduce a small constant time delay between different data streams, the delay being different for each stream. The maximum delay is less than $1/2W$ seconds—one sampling interval—and could be accounted for in subsequent digital processing by interpolation, applying the sampling theorem given previously. This complication is most easily overcome by providing sample-and-hold circuitry in the data-acquisition system to begin with.

Quantization

Fundamental to digital data processing is the conversion of the continuous range of data sample values into a finite number of discrete values. These discrete values form the *quantized* representation of the continuum of original values, and are generally represented by a binary number. Usually the interval between the (algebraically) smallest and the largest instantaneous values of the sampled data stream is divided into 2^m equal intervals, and an m-bit binary number is then assigned to each interval: for example, 0000 . . . 0 might be assigned to the interval corresponding to the smallest (most negative) value and 1111 . . . 1 to the interval corresponding to the largest value. It is clear that any value of the analog signal sample falling within a given interval will be assigned the same binary number. If we associate with each binary number a particular value for the sample—say the value

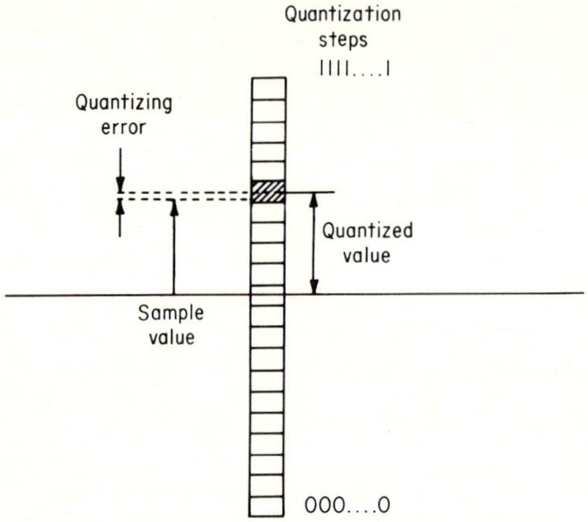

Fig. 7.8. Quantization.

corresponding to the midpoint of the interval—we can regard the difference between the actual sample value and the assumed value as *quantizer error,* which can be made as small as desired by providing more quantized intervals to which corresponds a larger value of m. Typical values of m range from 6 to 14, although under special conditions, where sinusoidal frequency components in white noise are to be estimated, it is possible to use but a single bit ($m = 1$) with some loss (about 1 dB) in performance.

If the data quantized to more than five or six bits (32 or 64 quantizing intervals), the quantizing noise is approximately uniformly distributed in amplitude between plus and minus one-half the quantizer interval, and the noise values between successive sample values are substantially uncorrelated. Thus the quantizing noise can be considered to be an additive white noise, but non-Gaussian. The ratio in decibels between the rms value of the largest sinusoid which can be digitized without overload to the rms value of the quantizing noise is given by

$$(1.8 + 6m) \qquad \text{dB}$$

Since 6 dB corresponds to a factor of 4 in power, adding one more bit to the quantizer (doubling the number of intervals) reduces the quantizing error power by 4.

In addition to the reduction of quantizing noise afforded by an increase in the number of bits, one gains an increase in the dynamic range of the input data for a given tolerable quantizing noise power. It may be desirable to use several additional bits in the quantizer to increase the allowable tolerance in the input data level—each bit is equivalent to 6 dB of tolerance. However, increasing the number of bits increases the accuracy requirements of the quantizer and analog-to-digital converter circuits, which in turn increases the cost or increases the time required to make a conversion. Such increased time requirement may limit the data sampling rate.

Another possible limitation in the value of m is made by a desire to have an integral number of data-sample words in the word length of the digital computed used to process the data. If, for example, the computer uses 36-bit words, then one might use 6-, 9-, or 12-bit data words so that 6, 4, or 3 words fit nicely into one computer word. Whether a nice fit is important may depend on how long a stretch of uninterrupted data needs to be recorded and stored, as well as the amount to be processed in the computer.

Considering together the two sources of noise in the digitized data—(1) aliasing due to imperfection in the low-pass filter, and (2) quantizing noise—we can design the low-pass filter performance in its stop band and the number of quantizing levels 2^m so that the sum of the alias power and quantizing-noise power is held to some design level. It is most likely that the alias-frequency power is statistically independent of the desired signal, and if the quantization is fine enough, the quantizing noise is also statistically independent of the signal; hence the two noise powers are additive. Suppose, for example, we want to process an analog Gaussian data signal having approximately uniform frequency content out to a frequency—say $3W$—and zero beyond. W, as usual, denotes the folding or Nyquist frequency. Since we are interested in frequencies between zero and W, the power in the W-to-$3W$ band which will alias into the zero-to-W band is twice the power on the desired band. If we want the total alias and quantizing-noise power to be 10^{-4} (—40 dB) of the desired signal power, and if we split the contributions equally between the two sources, it is clear† that we must

† $$|H(\nu)|^2 = 1 \qquad 0 \le \nu \le W$$

Let the signal power per unit frequency band be

$$\begin{aligned} S(\nu) &= a \qquad 0 \le \nu \le 3W \\ &= 0 \qquad \nu > 3W \end{aligned}$$

Our (ideal) low-pass filter has the power transfer function

$$\begin{aligned} |H(\nu)|^2 &= 1 \qquad 0 \le \nu \le W \\ &= \epsilon \qquad W \le \nu \le 2W \end{aligned}$$

After filtering, the total desired power is

$$\int_0^W |H(\nu)|^2 S(\nu)\, d\nu = aW$$

and the total aliased power is

$$\int_W^{3W} |H(\nu)|^2 S(\nu)\, d\nu = 2\epsilon a W$$

If the ratio of desired to undesired power is to be 2×10^4, we have $aW/2\epsilon W = 2 \times 10^4$, and get the result stated.

have $|H(\nu)|^2$ in the stop band equal 2.5×10^{-5} if $|H(\nu)|^2 = 1$ in the passband.‡

To compute the number of bits required to keep the ratio between signal power and quantizing noise power $\geq 2 \times 10^4$ (43 dB), we first observe that a Gaussian random signal may occasionally attain very high peak sample values. We must then decide how often we will tolerate an instantaneous sample value which might exceed the limiting value for the quantizer. If we set the signal level at such a point that about 1 in 10,000 sample values of the signal may exceed the overload limits, the rms signal voltage must be ≤ 0.257 (-11.8 dB) of the overload value, so that the required ratio now reads $(6m - 7.0)$ dB. For our example, $m = 9$ is sufficient while $m = 8$ might be barely adequate. To get the same ratio of sinusoidal signal power to quantizing noise power will only require seven-bit quantization and the additional bits for the Gaussian signal are needed because of the higher peak factor. Although the example given here may seem artificial, it gives an idea of the requirements for the digitizing parameters needed in a typical situation.

Monitoring and Error Corrections

Most modern digitizing equipment provides, soon after analog-to-digital conversion, for an additional bit added to the data bits to provide error detection. The additional bit is usually a *parity bit* whose value is such that the total number of ones in a data word is even or odd. In this way subsequent processing and recording within the digitizer will include the parity bit; and errors that may occur subsequent to analog-to-digital conversion can be detected. However, errors in the quantization or in the level setting of the data-input analog are not accounted for in this way; and it is usually desirable to monitor for such errors. After the digitized data has been introduced into the digital computer, it may be a good idea to plot the data by some graphing procedure, such as a microfilm plotter, on such a scale that the waveforms can be examined visually. Prior knowledge and experience of the appearance of the data will then help decide if the digitization was faithful to the input. Occasional overloads may be seen and a decision may be made as to whether these overloads are tolerable, whether they may be corrected by interpolation from the neighboring values, or whether a rerun of the experiment will be necessary. One of the virtues of oversampling is that the occasional error can be discovered by differencing the data values and observing the distribution of the differ-

‡ We suppose an ideal filter without a transition band.

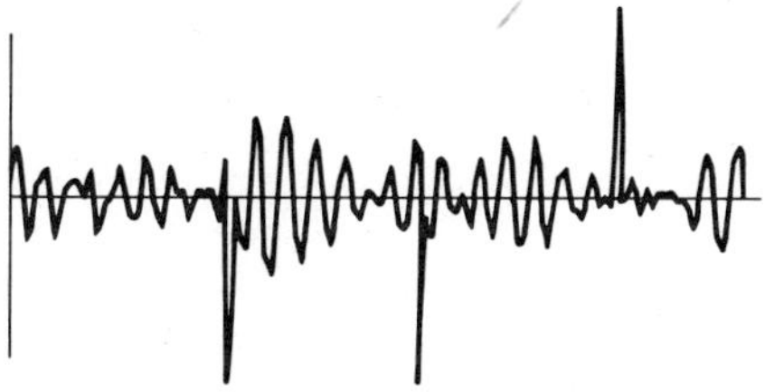

Fig. 7.9. Plotted data showing isolated gross errors correctable by interpolation.

ences. Visual inspection of the data sample values corresponding to the tails of the distribution can be used to determine if the data points are likely to be in error. Appropriate error detection and correction methods cannot easily be listed, but need to be invented when the peculiarities of the actual data at hand are observed.

Demeaning and Detrending

Much time-series data has as its source the output of a transducer which does not respond to zero-frequency components in the input signals, and a nonzero mean in the data then indicates some imbalance in the data-acquisition apparatus. On the other hand, the mean value of the data may be a significant parameter which must be estimated. In either case, since the presence of a nonzero mean value may affect the results of further processing, it is usually estimated and then subtracted from each data stretch, the mean value itself being of interest or not as the case may be. The mean is estimated in the obvious way by forming the sum of the N data values and dividing it by N:

$$\bar{x} = \frac{1}{N} \sum_i x_i \tag{7-10}$$

and the residuals $y_i = x_i - \bar{x}$ form the basis for further processing. Roughly, extraction of the mean may be regarded as removal of the "zero frequency" cosinusoidal Fourier component from the data.

In addition to a possible nonzero mean in the data, there may be significant linear trends due to gradual drift in the data-acquisition apparatus. That is, the output of the apparatus with no input may be nonzero, as discussed above, and further, the nonzero output may change slowly with time. Over the time of the data stretch this drift may be closely approximated by a linear trend. This trend can then be estimated by a least-squares procedure, subtracted from the data stretch, and the residual utilized in further processing. A convenient formula to compute the linear trend of a zero-mean data stretch $y_i(i = 1,N)$ is

$$w_i = \frac{12 \sum_{k=1}^{N} k y_k}{N(N^2 - 1)} \left(i - \frac{N+1}{2} \right) \qquad (7\text{-}11)$$

and the trend-free residual $z_i = y_i - w_i$. It will be observed that $\Sigma w_i = 0$, so that z_i has zero mean as well as zero average slope.

By demeaning and detrending, we minimize the chance for a large discontinuity at the end points of the data stretches. In computing the Fourier transforms of the data, we regard the given data stretch as being periodic. A large difference between the initial and the final data value would then show up in the Fourier transform as harmonics decreasing roughly inversely with frequency. These harmonics may well interfere with an interpretation of the spectrum of the data itself.

Tapering

Continuing the above line of thought, if by chance the initial and final data values are substantially different from zero, and possibly from each other, the discontinuity so produced may be in reality associated with the precise instants at which one started and stopped taking the data. We can minimize this effect by "tapering" a fraction of the points near the start and end. A useful taper for this purpose is a raised cosine; the tapered time series y_k in terms of the untapered x_k is

$$\begin{aligned} y_k &= \frac{1}{2}\left(1 - \cos \pi \frac{k}{M+1}\right) x_k & 1 \le k \le M \\ y_k &= x_k & M+1 \le k \le N-M \qquad (7\text{-}12) \\ y_k &= \frac{1}{2}\left(1 - \cos \pi \frac{N-k+1}{M+1}\right) x_k & N-M+1 \le k \le N \end{aligned}$$

If N is the number of data points, M/N is the fraction of the points tapered both at the start and at the end. $M = 0.05N$ or $M = 0.1N$ are not unreasonable values to use in practice.

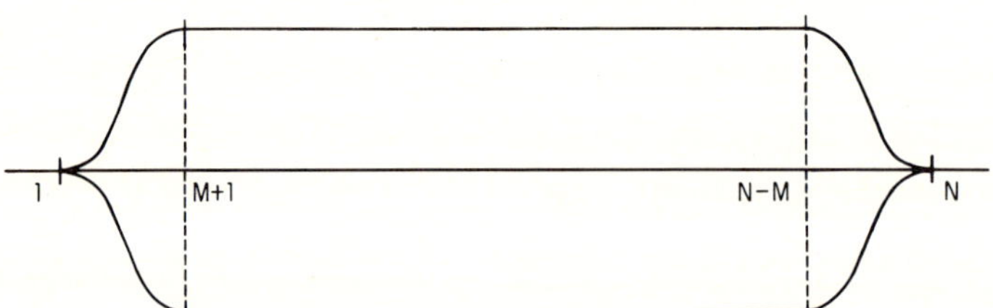

Fig. 7.10. Cosine tapering.

Fourier Transforms

Looking at data in the frequency domain by way of the Fourier transform or its various derived functions, often gives a great deal more insight than does examination and study in the time domain. Furthermore, filtering and smoothing in the time domain involve convolution, which may be time-consuming on the digital computer because of the large number of computer operations needed, while its counterpart in the frequency domain is point-by-point multiplication, a much faster process. Until recently, the complexity of the computation of the Fourier transform has been such that rapid and economical transfer between the time and frequency domains has been impossible, and there was certainly no advantage in the second method shown in Fig. 7.11 over the first. The rediscovery and development of computer algorithms to speed the computation of Fourier transforms, in particular the work of Cooley and Tukey, have made a profound change in this situation. In may cases, particularly where the data stretch is long and the filter impulse response is complicated, it may now be quicker to filter in the frequency domain. Furthermore, to smooth a spectrum by convolution in the frequency domain may be slower than transforming the raw spectrum, multiplying by the "lag window," and transforming back again.

We must first establish a relation between the Fourier transform for a continuous or unsampled wave and for the Fourier transform of its sampled and digitized counterpart. It is the latter with which we must

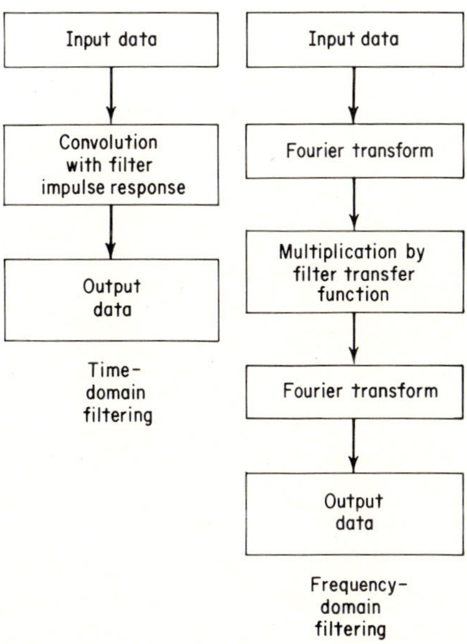

Fig. 7.11. Filtering in the time and frequency domains.

deal on a computer and it is important to understand the relation between our computations and the equivalent operations we might do with the analog signal from which the digitized version was derived. In our data preparation we start with a stretch of data, of finite but large extent. This analog data stretch will be filtered, sampled, and digitized, and will result in a time series of a finite number of equispaced data points. Let us now regard the sampled data stretch of N points as being derived from an analog stretch T seconds long, sampled each $1/2W$ seconds, so that $N = 2WT$. If we imagine these data points to be samples of a band-limited function $f(t)$, then by the sampling theorem [Eq. (7–8)] we have

$$f(t) = \sum_{k=0}^{2WT-1} f\left(\frac{k}{2W}\right) \frac{\sin \pi(2Wt - k)}{\pi(2Wt - k)} \tag{7-13}$$

which says that given the N sample points we can construct a band-limited function having these sample values. We now may ask what the Fourier transform of $f(t)$ is in terms of the sample values $f(k/2W)$. What function of the $f(k/2W)$ should be chosen to represent the Fourier transform? Let us write down a (complex) Fourier representation of the form

$$C_m = \frac{1}{2WT} \sum_{k=0}^{2WT-1} f\left(\frac{k}{2W}\right) e^{-\pi ikm/WT} \qquad m = 0, 1, \ldots, 2WT - 1 \tag{7-14}$$

and observe that the Fourier transform of $f(t)$ can be expressed in terms of the C_m as follows. Using Eqs. (7-1) and (7-13), we have

$$\begin{aligned} F(\nu) &= \int_{-\infty}^{\infty} f(t)e^{-2\pi i\nu t}\,dt \\ &= \int_{-\infty}^{\infty} \sum_{k=0}^{2WT-1} f\left(\frac{k}{2W}\right) \frac{\sin \pi(2Wt - k)}{\pi(2Wt - k)} e^{-2\pi i\nu t}\,dt \end{aligned}$$

$$\begin{aligned} F(\nu) &= \sum_{k=0}^{2WT-1} f\left(\frac{k}{2W}\right) e^{-\pi ik\nu/W} \int_{-\infty}^{\infty} e^{-2\pi i\nu x} \frac{\sin 2\pi Wx}{2\pi Wx}\,dx \\ &= \frac{1}{2W} \sum_{k=0}^{2WT-1} f\left(\frac{k}{2W}\right) e^{-\pi ik\nu/W} \qquad |\nu| < W \\ &= \frac{1}{4W} \sum_{k=0}^{2WT-1} f\left(\frac{k}{2W}\right) e^{-\pi ik\nu/W} \qquad |\nu| = W \\ &= 0 \qquad |\nu| > W \end{aligned} \tag{7-15}$$

Comparing the expressions for $F(\nu)$ and C_m, we see that

$$C_m = \frac{1}{T} F\left(\frac{m}{T}\right) \qquad m < WT \tag{7-16}$$

so that the C_m are proportional to the Fourier transform $F(\nu)$, evaluated at frequency intervals $1/T$ apart. Such a spacing corresponds to the harmonic spacing for a periodic time function of period T, and, if one regards the original function $f(t)$ as both band-limited and periodic, the Fourier coefficients C_m are the coefficients of that band-limited and periodic function. We see that the coefficients are equispaced fre-

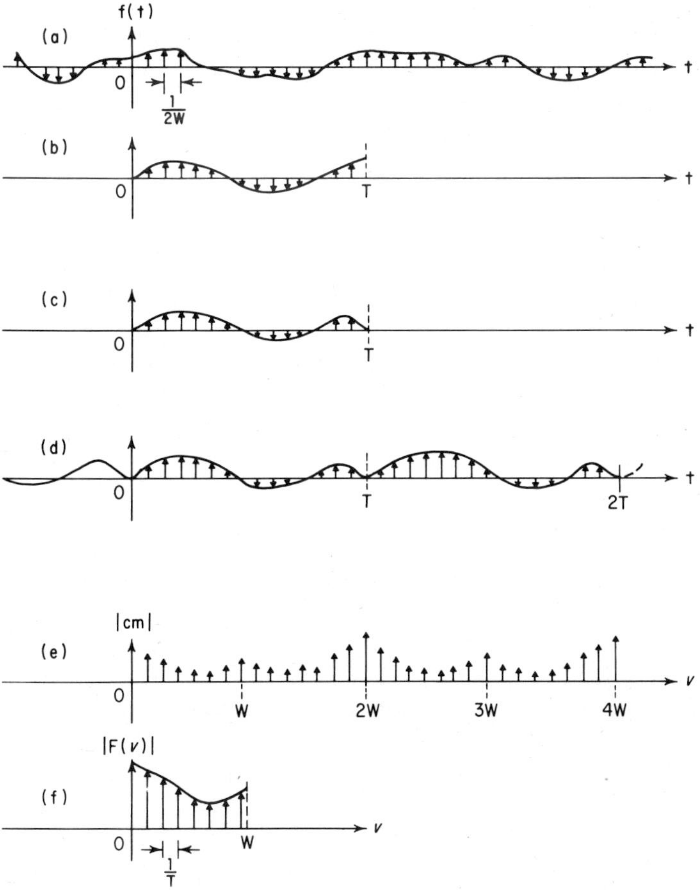

Fig. 7.12. Fourier transforming a stretch of data: (*a*) $1/2W$ continuous data stream; (*b*) truncated version of (*a*); (*c*) tapered version of (*b*); (*d*) periodic version of (*c*); (*e*) Fourier series of (*d*); (*f*) in $|\nu| < W$, (*e*) samples the Fourier transform of (*b*).

quency samples of the continuous Fourier transform of the original analog function, and thus in the frequency domain as well as in the time domain we have represented our original data in terms of a finite number of equispaced samples.

The Fast Fourier Transform

The complex Fourier transform gives $N = 2WT$ complex values of C_m, each of which is made up of a sum of N products of the form $f(k/2W) \exp\{-\pi ikm/WT\}$. There are then about N^2 operations required to obtain the transform in this way, where an operation consists of a complex multiplication and addition. Let the number of points in the transform be factorable so that $N = rc$ (r, c integers). We can imagine the N data points $f_k \equiv f(k/2W)$, $k = 0, \ldots, N$ written out in a rectangular array of r rows and c columns. It turns out, but it is by no means obvious, that we can calculate r parallel Fourier transforms, each of length c, and combine them appropriately to get the final result. By so doing, we cut down on the number of operations needed over the naive approach, and, by extending the idea to the case when N has a large number of factors, make a very substantial improvement in computational efficiency. If N is a power of two, for example $N = 2^n$, then we need about $2N \log_2 N$ operations to evaluate the Fourier coefficients. For $N = 8{,}192$ points, the saving is about 300 to 1!

To sketch out the basic idea, let us suppose N is factored into the integers r and c. We want to calculate

$$C_m = \frac{1}{N} \sum_{k=0}^{N-1} f_k e^{-2\pi ikm/N} \qquad m = 0, \ldots, N-1$$

We factor the index k in the following way:

$$k = \alpha_1 + \alpha_2 r \qquad \begin{array}{l} \alpha_1 = 0, \ldots, r-1 \\ \alpha_2 = 0, \ldots, c-1 \end{array}$$

We can then write the single summation as two, in the variables α_1 and α_2, as

$$C_m = \frac{1}{N} \sum_{\alpha_1=0}^{r-1} e^{-2\pi im\alpha_1/N} \sum_{\alpha_2=0}^{c-1} f_{\alpha_1+\alpha_2 r} e^{-2\pi im\alpha_2/c}$$

In the same way as we wrote k, we now write m in the form

$$m = \beta_1 c + \beta_2 \qquad \begin{array}{l} \beta_1 = 0, \ldots, r-1 \\ \beta_2 = 0, \ldots, c-1 \end{array}$$

and have

$$C_{\beta_1 c+\beta_2} = \frac{1}{N} \sum_{\alpha_1=0}^{r-1} e^{-2\pi i(\beta_1 c+\beta_2)\alpha_1/N} \sum_{\alpha_2=0}^{c-1} f_{\alpha_1+\alpha_2 r} e^{-2\pi i\beta_1 c\alpha_2} e^{-2\pi i\beta_2\alpha_2/c}$$

but since $e^{-2\pi i} = 1$, $e^{-2\pi i\beta_1\alpha_2} = 1$ as well, and

$$C_{\beta_1 c+\beta_2} = \frac{1}{N} \sum_{\alpha_1=0}^{r-1} e^{-2\pi i(\beta_1 c+\beta_2)\alpha_1/N} \sum_{\alpha_2=0}^{c-1} f_{\alpha_1+\alpha_2 r} e^{-2\pi i\beta_2\alpha_2/c}$$

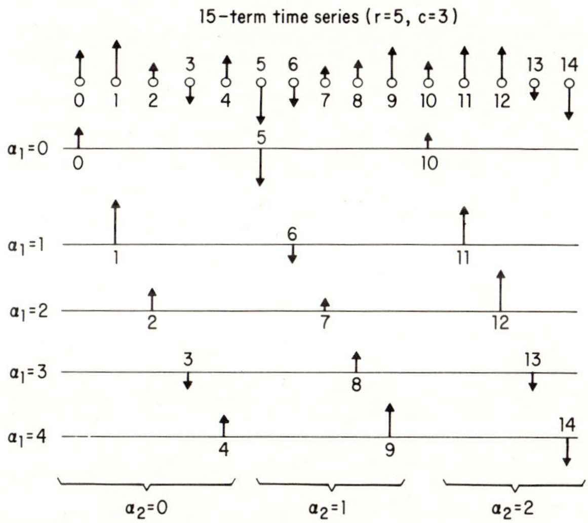

Fig. 7.13. Factoring a time series to apply FFT.

We note that the second sum has c terms, and must be evaluated for r values of α_1 and for c values of β_2, so we have rc^2 multiplications in all. The first summation has r terms, and must be evaluated for all $N = rc$ terms for a total of r^2c multiplications. Thus the total number of multiplications is then $(r + c)N$, rather than $N^2 = rcN$ needed for the naïve method. If we look at the second sum, we note, for a given value of α_1, that it is a Fourier series of length c with α_2 as the "time" index and β_2 as the "frequency" index. Then, if c, in turn, can be written as

$$c = c_1 c_2$$

we need but $(c_1 + c_2)c_1c_2$ multiplications to evaluate it for fixed α_1, and $rc_1c_2(c_1 + c_2)$ multiplications to evaluate the second sum. Hence, we need $(r + c_1 + c_2)N$ multiplications in all, to evaluate the entire Fourier series. Thus, if $N = 2^n$, we need about $nN = N \log N$ multiplications.

Although there are $N = 2WT$ Fourier coefficients C_m associated with the real or complex time series $f_k = f\left(\frac{k}{2W}\right)$, we find that if the f_k are real, the coefficients C_{N-m} are the complex conjugates of the C_m:

$$C_{N-m} = C_m^* = A_m - iB_m$$

and we need only calculate C_m for $m = 0, 1, \ldots, WT - 1$.

Another way of looking at this is to observe that we calculate the transform for frequencies from zero to $2W$, and that the transform is periodic in frequency over this frequency interval. Hence the transform in the frequency range from W to $2W$ is actually the alias of the transform from $-W$ to zero. If a time function is real, its transform for negative frequencies is the complex conjugate of the values for positive frequencies, and the preceding result follows. Since we deal mostly with real data streams, we will generally think in terms of positive frequencies only.

If we want the inverse Fourier transform to go from the frequency domain back to the time domain, we have

$$f_k = \sum_{m=0}^{2WT-1} C_m e^{\pi ikm/WT} \qquad k = 0, \ldots, 2WT - 1 \tag{7-17}$$

Apart from the $1/2WT$ factor, the inverse transform has a positive exponent instead of a negative one, and its computation is the same. A simple way to compute the inverse transform, using the direct transform algorithm, is to use the complex conjugates C_m^* of the coefficients C_m in the direct transform, and the complex conjugate of the result will be the desired inverse. The coefficients C_m are usually complex, so of course the entire range of values must be computed to get all the values of the resultant time series f_k.

Let us rewrite the complex Fourier representation [Eq. (7-14)] of a real data stretch explicitly in terms of real and imaginary parts:

$$C_m = A_m + iB_m = \frac{1}{2WT} \sum_{k=-WT+1}^{WT} f\left(\frac{k}{2W}\right)\left\{\cos\frac{\pi km}{WT} - i\sin\frac{\pi km}{WT}\right\} \tag{7-14a}$$

For convenience, we have moved the origin for the index k to the approximate midpoint of the data stretch. Suppose now $f(t)$ is real, and that $f\left(\frac{k}{2W}\right) = f\left(\frac{-k}{2W}\right)$, that is, $f(t)$ is even around the midpoint of the data stretch. Then the *cosine transform* A_m is

$$A_m = \frac{1}{2WT}\left\{f(0) + 2\sum_{k=1}^{WT-1} \cos\frac{\pi km}{WT} f\left(\frac{k}{2W}\right) + (-1)^m f\left(\frac{T}{2}\right)\right\} \quad (7\text{-}18)$$

and $B_m = 0$.

On the other hand, if $f(t)$ is odd, so $f(k/2W) = -f(-k/2W)$, we have for the *sine transform* B_m

$$B_m = \frac{-1}{WT}\sum_{k=1}^{WT-1} f\left(\frac{k}{2W}\right) \sin\frac{\pi km}{WT} \quad (7\text{-}19)$$

and $A_m = 0$.

These contracted formulas are useful when data stretches are known to be either even or odd, in which case the computation of Fourier coefficients can be simplified considerably, since only half the data stretch is needed. An example occurs whenever a power spectrum density is computed indirectly by taking the transform of a covariance. Since the covariance function of a stationary random process is even, we need only compute the covariance for positive time lags and take its cosine transform using the contracted formula.

We also see, by direct substitution, that the sine transform of the sine transform of an odd function brings us back to the original data points divided by $WT/2$, and that the cosine transform of a cosine transform of an even function recovers the original data points, divided by $WT/2$, and that the cosine transform of a cosine transform of an even function recovers the original data points, divided by $WT/2$, except that the first and last data points $f(0)$ and $f(T/2)$ are divided by WT.

Deterministic and Random Waveforms

We must now recognize the essentially statistical character of most data we want to analyze. We will occasionally need to observe well-defined waveforms, such as square waves or damped sinusoids, and our objective will be to determine certain easily defined properties: for example, the duration of a square wave or the frequency of the sinusoid. In these cases, the data may be replicated by simply repeating the experiment, as there may be negligible differences in the data between replications. Having one set of waveform data, additional sets tell us nothing new, and indeed we can predict the results of experimental replication as well as we please.

In most cases, however, our data is unpredictable, and is but representative of a phenomenon in which we are interested. The more often we might repeat an experiment, the more useful information we would gain and the more accurately we could determine significant properties.

Each experiment produces data which may be regarded as a sample drawn from the universe of possible sets of data. The object of the analysis of the given data is to deduce properties of the universe as a whole, which is done by assuming a statistical model which usually assumes given probability distributions for the data. Data analysis then determines the parameters of the assumed model.

Suppose, for example, we record a stretch of analog data: the voltage across a pair of terminals of a "black box." For each replication of the experiment producing the data, we get a different function $x(t)$. The family of possible data stretches $x(t)$ is called a *random process*. At particular instants of time $t = t_1$, the same for each experiment, a distribution of values of $x(t_1)$ would be observed. The term $x(t_1)$ is called a *random variable*. We associate a *probability density* $p(x_i,t_i)$ for the

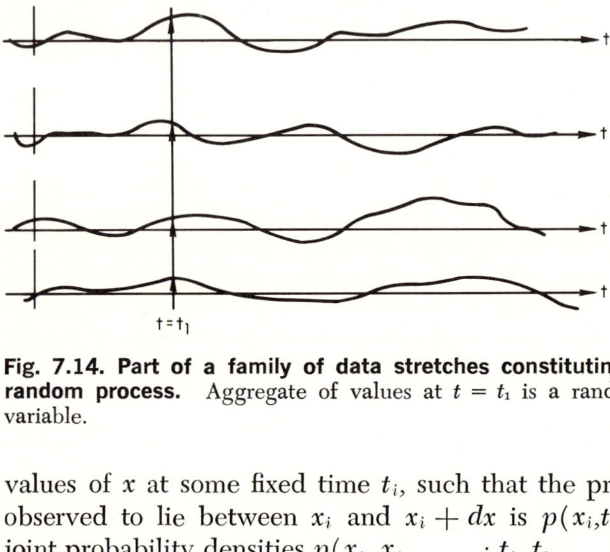

Fig. 7.14. Part of a family of data stretches constituting a random process. Aggregate of values at $t = t_1$ is a random variable.

values of x at some fixed time t_i, such that the probability that $x(t_i)$ is observed to lie between x_i and $x_i + dx$ is $p(x_i,t_i)\ dx$. Similarly, the joint probability densities $p(x_1, x_2, \ldots ; t_1, t_2, \ldots)$ give the probability that $x(t_1) = x_1$, $x(t_2) = x_2$, . . . and so forth. Given the probability densities, we can define the *expectation* of a function of x:

$$E\{f(x(t_1))\} = \int_{-\infty}^{\infty} f(x)p(x,t_1)\ dx \tag{7-20}$$

which includes the mean: ave$\{x\} = E\{x(t_1)\}$, for which $f(x) = x$; and the *variance* var$\{x\}$, for which $f(x) = [x - Ex]^2$. That is, var$\{x\} = E\{x^2(t_1)\} - [E\{x(t_1)\}]^2$: the expectation of x^2 minus the square of the mean. The *autocorrelation* of $x(t)$ is

$$\begin{aligned} R(t_1,t_2) &= E\{x(t_1)x(t_2)\} \\ &= \int_{-\infty}^{\infty}\int_{-\infty}^{\infty} x_1x_2p(x_1,x_2,t_1,t_2)\ dx_1\ dx_2 \end{aligned} \tag{7-21}$$

and the autocovariance $C(t_1,t_2)$ is

$$C(t_1,t_2) = E\{[x(t_1) - \text{ave}\{x(t_1)\}][x(t_2) - \text{ave}\{x(t_2)\}]\}$$
$$= R(t_1,t_2) - \text{ave}\{x(t_1)\}\text{ ave}\{x(t_2)\} \tag{7-22}$$

and we see that

$$\text{var}\{x(t_1)\} = C(t_1,t_1)$$

A very important class of random processes are those for which a time translation does not change any of the joint probability densities, that is, $p(x_1,x_2, \ldots t_1,t_2 \ldots) = p(x_1,x_2 \ldots t_1 + \Delta, t_2 + \Delta, \ldots)$ for any Δ. In particular, the first-order probability density $p(x_1,t_1)$ must be independent of t: $p(x_1,t_1) = p(x)$, and furthermore the mean and variance do not depend on t. It is also true that the autocorrelation function $R(t_1,t_2)$ depends only on $t_1 - t_2 = \tau$. This class of random processes is called *strict-sense stationary.*

A process is called *wide-sense stationary* if the mean is a constant and the autocorrelation depends only on $t_1 - t_2$. If a process is strict-sense stationary, it is also wide-sense stationary, but the converse is not true, as wide-sense stationary is conditioned only by the mean and correlation, not by the higher-order joint probability distributions.

As an extension of the idea of a single random process, one considers joint processes $x(t)$ and $y(t)$ such that appropriate probability distributions are defined as before for y as well as x, and, in addition, joint distributions for $x(t)$ and $y(t)$ together are given. From the joint probability density $p(x_1,y_1;\ t_1,t_2)$ we can define the cross-correlation

$$R_{xy}(t_1,t_2) = E\{x(t_1)y(t_2)\}$$
$$= \int_{-\infty}^{\infty}\int x_1(t_1)y_1(t_2)p(x_1,y_1;\ t_1,t_2)\,dx_1\,dy_1 \tag{7-23}$$

and the cross-covariance

$$C_{xy}(t_1,t_2) = R_{xy}(t_1,t_2) - \text{ave}\{x(t_1)\}\text{ ave}\{y(t_2)\} \tag{7-24}$$

If x and y are jointly stationary, we have $R_{xy}(t_1,t_2) = R_{xy}(\tau)$ and $C_{xy}(t_1,t_2) = C_{xy}(\tau)$.

Gaussian or normal processes, for which the probability densities are normal to all orders, are particularly important because all higher-order densities are determined from the mean and the covariance. Further, if a normal process is subjected to a linear operator, such as a filter, the output process is also normal. Because of these desirable properties, much of the theoretical work on signal and data analysis is carried out for Gaussian processes, and if there is reason to believe that real data may come from a Gaussian process, such an assumption is gladly made.

Time Averages and Ergodicity

Our discussion of random processes has been concerned with *ensemble averaging,* that is, we can regard our averages in the following way. We line up a large number of realizations of the random process one above the other so that a given value of the time parameter t lines up vertically. Then we can think of ave $\{x\}$ as an average vertically among all the realizations at a given instant of time. On the other hand, most experiments yield but a few realizations of a time series, so ensemble averaging is not feasible. However, there is a large class of stationary random processes for which ensemble averaging and time averaging yield the same result. That is to say, for these processes, time or "horizontal averaging" is equivalent to "vertical averaging." Such processes are called *ergodic,* and for them we can obtain, from one (sufficiently long) realization of the process, all the information we need about the process. We define time averages as follows. We define the mean

$$m(x) = \lim_{T \to \infty} \frac{1}{2T} \int_{-T}^{T} x(t)\, dt \tag{7-25}$$

and the autocorrelation

$$r(\tau) = \lim_{T \to \infty} \frac{1}{2T} \int_{-T}^{T} x(t)x(t + \tau)\, dt \tag{7-26}$$

and so on. Then for an ergodic process ave $\{x\} = m(x)$, $r(\tau) = R(\tau)$.

Generalized Harmonic Analysis—The Fourier-Stieltjes Integral

In previous discussions involving the Fourier transform, we have assured that we had a finite stretch of data, so the energy in the whole signal was finite, and so its Fourier transform existed. We would now like to consider the generalization of the Fourier transform which can be defined for a stationary random process. Since the power associated with the stationary process $x(t)$ is ave $\{x^2(t)\}$, which does not depend on time, the total energy of a realization of the process in infinite, and its ordinary Fourier transform cannot be defined. This difficulty can be gotten around by using generalized harmonic analysis, in which we define a *generalized transform* $G(\nu)$, which is itself a complex stochastic process, by the relation

$$G(\nu_1) - G(\nu_2) = i \int_{-\infty}^{\infty} \frac{e^{-2\pi i \nu_1 t} - e^{-2\pi i \nu_2 t}}{t}\, x(t)\, dt \tag{7-27}$$

which defines $G(\nu)$ apart from an additive constant, since the definition is given only in terms of the difference between values of $G(\nu)$ at two distinct frequencies ν_1 and ν_2. If $x(t)$ should in fact have an ordinary Fourier transform $X(\nu)$, then it turns out that

$$2\pi X(\nu) = \frac{dG(\nu)}{d\nu} \tag{7-28}$$

and since [Eq. (7-2)]

$$x(t) = \int_{-\infty}^{\infty} e^{2\pi i\nu t} X(\nu)\, d\nu$$

we will write

$$x(t) = \frac{1}{2\pi}\int_{-\infty}^{\infty} e^{2\pi i\nu t}\, dG(\nu) \tag{7-29}$$

which holds even when $X(\nu)$ cannot be defined. Equation (7-29) is the *Fourier-Stieltjes integral,* which can be used to express a random process in terms of the generalized transform $G(\nu)$. The term $dG(\nu)$ may be regarded crudely as the elementary frequency component at the frequency ν in the narrow band $d\nu$ wide. Now if $x(t)$ is a wide-sense stationary process, the average of $dG(\nu)$ vanishes except for $dG(0)$, which represents the mean of the process $x(t)$:

$$\begin{aligned} \text{ave } dG(\nu) &= 0 & \nu &\neq 0, \\ &= \text{ave } \{x(t)\} & \nu &= 0. \end{aligned} \tag{7-30}$$

Furthermore, the average of the squared absolute value of $dG(\nu)$ represents the power in the process $x(t)$ in a narrow frequency band $d\nu$ wide centered at the frequency ν:

$$\text{ave } \{|dG(\nu)|^2\} = 4\pi^2 S(\nu)\, d\nu \tag{7-31}$$

where $S(\nu)$ is the *power spectrum* or power spectral density of $x(t)$. It also turns out that

$$\text{ave } \{dG(\nu_1)\, dG^*(\nu_2)\} = 0 \qquad \nu_1 \neq \nu_2 \tag{7-32}$$

unless $\nu_1 = \nu_2$, for which Eq. (7-31) holds. Equation (7-32) tells us that the complex process $G(\nu)$ has orthogonal and uncorrelated increments, and so disjoint bands of elementary frequencies are uncorrelated. With the provision that ave $\{G(\nu)\}$ is continuous away from $\nu = 0$, the converse is also true that $x(t)$ is wide-sense stationary if its generalized transform $G(\nu)$ is a process with orthogonal increments.

If the process $x(t)$ is Gaussian, then so is $G(\nu)$, since $G(\nu)$ is obtained by a linear operation on $x(t)$. If $x(t)$ has zero mean, then $dG(\nu)$ is also zero mean, and differing elementary frequency components $dG(\nu_1)$

and $dG(\nu_2)$ are statistically independent, and the variance of $dG(\nu)$ is $4\pi^2 S(\nu)\,d\nu$.

Suppose now we filter a stationary process $x(t)$ with a band-pass filter with transfer function $H(\nu)$:

$$\begin{aligned} H(\nu) &= 2\pi \qquad \nu_1 \leq \nu \leq \nu_2 \\ &= 0 \qquad \text{otherwise} \end{aligned}$$

The resultant filtered process $Y(t)$ has a value at time $t = 0$ of

$$y(0) = G(\nu_2) - G(\nu_1)$$

and so its average squared magnitude ave $\{|y(0)|^2\}$, which since $y(t)$ is stationary is its average power, is

$$\text{ave}\ \{|y(0)|^2\} = \text{ave}\ \{|G(\nu_2) - G(\nu_1)|^2\} = 4\pi^2 \int_{\nu_1}^{\nu_2} S(\nu)\,d\nu$$

Thus the average power (for an ergodic process we can equate ensemble and time averages) measured at the output of a band-pass filter will give the value of the power spectrum averaged in frequency across the filter band. If the spectrum $S(\nu)$ is smooth, and if $\nu_2 - \nu_1 = \Delta\nu$ is small, we have

$$\text{ave}\ \{|G(\nu + \Delta\nu) - G(\nu)|^2\} = 4\pi^2 S(\nu)\,\Delta\nu \tag{7-33}$$

and we can estimate the power spectrum by using a set of narrow band-pass filters which span the frequency range in interest, each feeding a square law detector. Each detector output is then averaged over the length of the data, or is averaged over a number of experiments.

Effect of Finite Data Stretches

The orthogonality of the generalized transform process $G(\nu)$ hinges on the stationarity of $x(t)$. If we have only a finite stretch of $x(t)$, say running from $t = -T/2$ to $t = T/2$, then there is a slight smearing of the elementary frequency components $dG(\nu)$. This *leakage* means that as we make the bandwidth $\Delta\nu$ of the analyzing filter $H(\nu)$ much less than $1/T$, even if we average over many realizations of the process, we will not measure $4\pi^2 S(\nu)\,\Delta\nu$, but rather $4\pi^2 S_B(\nu)\,\Delta\nu$, which is the convolution of $S(\nu)$ with the square of the Fourier transform of the data window. For the rectangular window T seconds long,

$$S_B(\nu) = \frac{1}{T} \int_{-\infty}^{\infty} \frac{\sin^2 \pi T(\nu - \lambda)}{\pi^2(\nu - \lambda)^2}\, S(\lambda)\, d\lambda \tag{7-34}$$

We recall that the Fourier representation C_m for sampled and band-limited data is given at discrete frequencies $\nu = m/T$ where T is the length of the data. We find from the sampling theorem and the definition of the generalized transform that

$$G\left(\frac{m+1/2}{T}\right) - G\left(\frac{m-1/2}{T}\right) \cong 2\pi C_m \tag{7-35}$$

so that

$$\text{ave}\left\{\left|G\left(\frac{m+1/2}{T}\right) - G\left(\frac{m-1/2}{T}\right)\right|^2\right\} = 4\pi^2 S\left(\frac{m}{T}\right)\cdot\frac{1}{T}$$
$$= 4\pi^2 \text{ ave } \{|C_m|^2\}$$

Hence the power spectrum $S(\nu)$ of the process $x(t)$ is approximately

$$S\left(\frac{m}{T}\right) \cong T \text{ ave } \{|C_m|^2\} \tag{7-36}$$

where [Eq. (7-14) modified]

$$C_m = \frac{1}{2WT}\sum_{k=-WT+1}^{WT} x\left(\frac{k}{2W}\right) e^{-\pi ikm/WT} \tag{7-37}$$

Because of the finite stretch of data, the smearing between neighboring elementary frequency intervals given by Eq. (7-34) amounts to about 10 percent from each of the adjacent intervals and about 1.8 percent from the next-to-adjacent ones. The rate of dropoff with frequency difference of the smearing is increased by using cosine-tapered leading and trailing edges on the data window, as we discussed before.

It also turns out that the frequency components are approximately uncorrelated so that

$$\text{ave } \{C_m C_m^*\} \cong 0 \qquad m \neq n \tag{7-38}$$

and indeed, writing $C_m = A_m + iB_m$ it can be shown further that approximately

$$\text{ave } \{A_m B_m\} = 0 \tag{7-39}$$
$$\text{ave } \{A_m A_n\} = \text{ave } \{B_m B_n\} = 0 \qquad m \neq n \tag{7-40}$$

while

$$\text{ave } \{A_m{}^2\} = \text{ave } \{B_m{}^2\} = \frac{1}{2} \text{ ave } \{|C_m|^2\} \tag{7-41}$$

The Power Spectrum

We have just introduced the power spectrum by way of the generalized Fourier transform $G(\nu)$, of a stationary random process. For a finite portion of a realization of the process, the squared magnitude of $G(\nu_2) - G(\nu_1)$, itself a random process, gives an estimate of the power spectrum integrated between the frequencies ν_1 and ν_2. The effect of the finite piece of data is to smear the components of the power spectrum slightly in frequency; the longer the time interval of the realization, the less smearing takes place. For a stretch of a band-limited stationary process, we can get an estimate of the power spectrum by squaring the magnitude of the Fourier coefficients obtained from the $2WT$ data samples.

If we average the spectrum estimates obtained in this way, the average gives us the spectrum, even though an estimate from one realization will depart from the true spectrum because of statistical fluctuations. The averaging referred to may be an ensemble average, or, for an ergodic random process, an average over time. For that matter, some of both may be used. Before discussing the behavior of spectrum estimates in enough detail to determine their variability, let us discuss some of the properties of the power spectrum which make it a useful representation of random data. In the first place, for a stationary random process the power spectrum is the Fourier transform of the correlation function $R(\tau)$. Since $R(\tau)$ is real if the process is real, the power spectrum is even in ν and we can write it using the Fourier cosine transform:

$$S(\nu) = \int_{-\infty}^{\infty} R(\tau) \cos 2\pi\nu\tau \, d\tau \tag{7-42}$$

and conversely

$$R(\tau) = \int_{-\infty}^{\infty} S(\nu) \cos 2\pi\nu\tau \, d\nu \tag{7-42a}$$

If we consider a hierarchy of statistics to characterize a random process, the first would be the mean value ave $\{x\}$, and the next would be the correlation $R(t_1,t_2) = E\{x(t_1)x(t_2)\}$. Further ones would be $E\{x(t_1)x(t_2)x(t_3)\}$ and so on. Hence the power spectrum, which is a linear transformation of $R(\tau)$, characterizes the second-order statistic of a stationary process, with the desirable property that (aside from leakage due to finite lengths of data) estimates of $S(\nu)$ for different elementary frequencies are uncorrelated. On the other hand, estimates for the correlation function at different lag times τ are interrelated in a complicated way.

If the stationary process is Gaussian, then all its statistics can be derived from the mean and the correlation or spectrum, so naturally, the power spectrum takes a particular importance for this situation.

A second important property of the power spectrum, which we have already used, is that if a random process $x(t)$, having a power spectrum $S_x(\nu)$, is passed through a linear filter with a transfer function $H(\nu)$, the output is another random process $y(t)$ with the power spectrum $S_y(\nu)$, where

$$S_y(\nu) = |H(\nu)|^2 S_x(\nu) \tag{7-43}$$

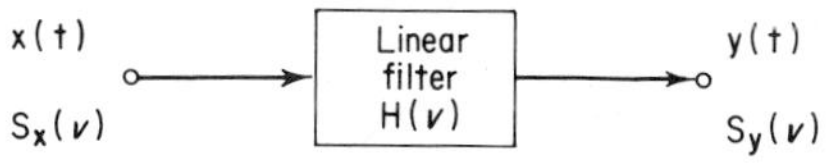

$S_y(\nu) = |H(\nu)|^2 S_x(\nu)$

Fig. 7.15. Effect of a linear operation on the power spectrum of a signal.

Thus if signals are passed through linear filters or transducers, their power spectra are modified in an easily calculated way. Hence if the power spectrum is estimated from the signal at an accessible point in a system, the spectrum of the signal at an unaccessible point may easily be found. For example, measuring sound pressure with a microphone and a preamplifier with known frequency-response characteristics enables us to determine the spectrum of the sound pressure. We divide the power spectrum of the preamplifier output signal by the squared absolute value of the transfer function of the microphone and preamplifier. If the transfer function has stop bands or nulls, then obviously the spectrum of its input cannot be determined from measurements on its output in the frequency regions where the stop bands occur.

Estimation of the Power Spectrum

There are two methods of power-spectrum estimation in use. The *direct method* uses the squared magnitude of the Fourier coefficients, as we have discussed in connection with the generalized transform. The *indirect method* computes the cosine transform of an estimate of the autocorrelation function. Prior to the application of efficient algorithms to compute Fourier coefficients on digital computers (the fast Fourier transform algorithms) the indirect method was used as it involved less computation. The situation has changed now, and for many applications the direct method is preferable. We will discuss the direct method first and then consider the indirect one.

Estimating the spectrum directly, the naïve approach might be to take a data stretch T seconds long and compute its Fourier coefficients C_m. The estimate of the spectrum would then be $T|C_m|^2$, which estimates the spectrum at the elementary frequencies $1/T$ Hz apart. The problem is that as we take a longer and longer stretch of data, we get a more fine-grained spectrum estimate having elementary frequencies spaced closer and closer together, and the stability of the estimates (as characterized by var $\{|C_m|^2\}$) does not improve.

Now the distributions of the real and imaginary parts of C_m for a zero-mean Gaussian process are Gaussian, (almost) independent, with zero means, and the variance of each is equal to half the power spectrum for that elementary frequency. Hence the distribution of $|C_m|^2$ for the Gaussian case is that of the sum of the square of two independent Gaussian variates, that is, a scaled chi-square distribution with two degrees of freedom. Suppose now we sum $2k+1$ adjacent values of $|C_m|^2$ and regard the sum as an estimate of the value of the spectrum at the center of the band of elementary frequencies. That is, the estimate $S(n/T)$ is:

$$\hat{S}\left(\frac{n}{T}\right) = \frac{T}{2k+1}\sum_{n-k}^{n+k} |C_m|^2 \qquad (7\text{-}44)$$

and we can let n run over values corresponding to the elementary frequencies from zero to the folding frequency. What we have done in fact is to smooth the raw spectral estimates $T|C_m|^2$ to get another estimate which is the spectrum average over a band $(2k+1)/T$ Hz wide. Since $\hat{S}(n/T)$ is the sum of $2(2k+1)$ independent Gaussian variables, of zero mean and approximately equal variance (if the spectrum does not change much across the averaging band), its statistic is then approximately scaled chi-square with $2(2k+1)$ degrees of freedom. The expected value of $\hat{S}(n/T)$ is $S(n/T)$, if the approximation of constant S holds over the elementary frequencies summed. Since the variance of a chi-square statistic is twice the square of the mean divided by the number of degrees of freedom, we have,

$$\text{var}\,\{\hat{S}(n/T)\} = S^2(n/T)/(2k+1) \qquad (7\text{-}45)$$

We see that for a smooth spectrum, for which $S(\nu)$ does not vary much over the bandwidth $B = (2k+1)/T$, the estimate S is unbiased (the expected value of $\hat{S}$ is S), and that the variance of $\hat{S}$ is proportional to the square of S and inversely proportional to the number of elementary frequency bands composing the bandwidth B.

From this we observe the essential fact that the price we pay for stability (low variance) in the smoothed spectral estimates is a large time-bandwidth product BT. Either we take larger amounts of data (large T), or we agree to poorer frequency resolution (large B). From the chi-square distribution, we can determine the number of degrees of freedom to assure that the resultant smoothed spectral estimates represent the spectrum to the desired accuracy. For example, if we want 90 percent of the estimates to lie within a ± 1 dB range of the true value, we need 104 degrees of freedom. For a range of values of ± 2.5 dB and the same confidence level (90 percent), we need only 18 degrees of freedom, and for ± 5 dB we need but five. Thus we see that we must pay heavily for high accuracy in the estimates, and relaxing the requirement from ± 1 dB to ± 2.5 dB reduces the time-bandwidth product almost sixfold.

Rather than using equal weight for smoothing the $|C_m|^2$, one often uses tapering coefficients F_m, symmetrical about the midpoint, so that

$$\hat{S}\left(\frac{n}{T}\right) = T \sum_{m=0}^{2WT-1} F_{n-m}|C_m|^2 \tag{7-46}$$

where $F_l = F_{-l}$, $F_l = 0$ for $|l| > k$, and, to keep the estimate reasonably unbiased, $\Sigma F_l = 1$. The tapering is in the form of a convolution, with the F_l acting as filtering coefficients on the $|C_m|^2$. The aggregate of coefficients F_l is called the *spectral window* and appropriately smooths the *raw estimates* $|C_m|^2$ to give the smoothed estimate $\hat{S}(n/T)$. In the simple case first discussed, the spectral window is called the *Daniell window*, and is rectangular in shape. It has the advantage of having a chi-square distribution for $\hat{S}$, and the disadvantage that if the spectrum is irregular, the smoothed estimates become biased. That is, that if one

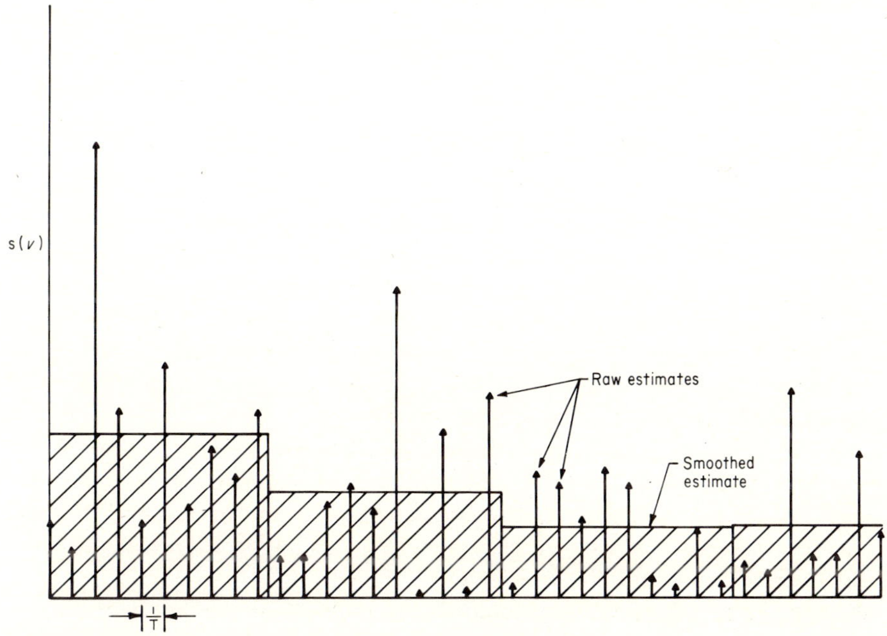

Fig. 7.16. Raw spectral estimates of a constant (white) spectrum and smoothing with a Daniell window for twenty degrees of freedom.

or more of the raw estimates are much larger than the others, they will increase the value of the smoothed estimate as long as they lie in the frequency band of the smoothing.

The variance for the smoothed spectrum estimate (of a smooth spectrum) is now

$$\text{var}\ \{\hat{S}\} = S^2\left(\frac{n}{T}\right)\sum_{l=-k}^{k} F_l^2 \tag{7-47}$$

which reduces to the previous case when $F_l = 1/2(2k+1)$.

We can define an equivalent number of degrees of freedom, when we use a spectral window other than the Daniell, by supposing the statistics to be approximately chi-square. Since twice the square of the mean divided by the variance equals the number of degrees of freedom for a chi-square distribution, we can write the equivalent degrees of freedom as

$$n = \frac{2S^2}{\text{var}\ \{\hat{S}\}} = \frac{2}{\sum\limits_{l} F_l^2} \tag{7-48}$$

Now noting the constraint that $\Sigma F_l = 1$, and that $F_l = 0$ for $|l| > k$, we seek the values of F_l which minimize the variance. Schwartz's inequality specialized to this problem tells us that

$$(2k+1)\Sigma\ F_l^2 \geq 1$$

and equality holds if $F_l = 1/(2k+1)$. Hence for a fixed number of elementary frequency bands, the Daniell window minimizes the variance of the smoothed estimate of a smooth spectrum.

But spectra are not necessarily smooth, and the Daniell window has, for the given number of elementary frequencies within it, poor frequency resolution. We can compromise between stability of the estimates and the frequency resolution of the smoothed estimates by using a window having one of a number of bell shapes, the choice being dependent on factors not closely related to either stability or resolution. Since application of a spectral window is a convolution operation, and if the window spans a substantial number of elementary frequencies, the computation required may be considerable. It may then prove better to Fourier-transform the raw spectral estimates, which gives us the *circular autocovariance,* and to multiply the circular autocovariance by the Fourier transform of the spectral window. The Fourier transform of the result is the smoothed spectrum. The transform f_l of the spectral window F_k is called the *lag window,* as it modifies the autocovariance, which is a function of time difference τ, or *lag.*

The reason the Fourier transform of the raw spectral estimates is called the circular autocovariance is this: We recall that the Fourier transform we use in digital computation is equivalent to the Fourier transform of a periodic, band-limited function of period T and bandwidth W. When we estimate the raw power spectrum by squaring the amplitude of the Fourier coefficients C_m, we obtain the Fourier transform of the convolution of the data stream with a backward version of itself. That is, C_m is the (complex) transform of a periodic, band-limited version of the data, and the complex conjugate C_m^* is the transform of the *time-reversed* periodic and periodic, band-limited version; hence the raw spectrum, $|C_m|^2 = C_m C_m^*$, is the convolution of the two. Because of the periodicity implicit in the digital transform, the convolution will include close interaction between the beginning and ends of the data which takes place because of the overlap introduced by the periodicity. This means that the circular autocovariance, which is the transform of $|C_m|^2$, is not precisely the autocovariance, unless steps are taken to avoid the overlap. This can be done by surrounding the data with $2WT$ zeros and taking the transform of the augmented data stretch. The transform of the $|C_m|^2$ so obtained will then be free of the overlap and will represent the autocovariance.

There have been several spectral windows developed, notable among them being the Hanning, the Parzen, and the Gaussian. The Hanning window is named after the Austrian meteorologist Julius von Hann, and has the three nonzero spectral window coefficients $F_0 = \frac{1}{2}$ and $F_{-1} = F_1 = \frac{1}{4}$. It has the desirable property of easy application in the frequency domain. Parzen's window is usually applied in the time domain, and the lag-window coefficients are

$$\begin{aligned} f_l &= 1 - \frac{6l^2}{l_m{}^2} + \frac{6|l|^3}{l_m{}^3} && |l| < \frac{l_m}{2} \\ &= 2\left(1 - \frac{|l|}{l_m}\right)^3 && \frac{l_m}{2} \leq |l| \leq l_m \\ &= 0 && |l| > l_m \end{aligned} \tag{7-49}$$

The lag window is limited to nonzero values over the lag range $-l_m$ to $+l_m$, and the value of the largest lag l_m is to be determined by the amount of spectral smoothing desired. To be sure that $\Sigma F_l = 1$ so that estimates are unbiased, we must have $f_0 = 1$. We shall consider this in more detail shortly when we discuss the indirect method of power spectrum estimation. The Gaussian spectral window has also a Gaussian-shaped lag window, since the Fourier transform of a Gaussian function is Gaussian. It has the desirable property that the product of its frequency resolution and time resolution is minimum and is therefore useful in analysis of nonstationary data, particularly using analog equipment. In digital analysis, the additional computational complexity outweighs such advantages as the Gaussian window may have.

Another technique to smooth spectrum estimates is to divide the data stretch into nonoverlapping or slightly overlapping intervals of a length inversely proportional to the frequency resolution desired in the smoothed estimates. The raw power spectrum is computed after tapering the data slightly within each interval. The smoothed estimates are obtained by averaging the raw estimates so obtained. By averaging the raw spectra from $2k+1$ nonoverlapping data intervals, we get smoothed estimates having chi-square statistics with $2(2k+1)$ degrees of freedom, and the bandwidth is $(2k+1)/T$ Hz wide, just as if we averaged over frequency $2k+1$ adjacent raw spectrum estimates of the entire stretch of data. This procedure is approximately equivalent to forming an ensemble average over the realizations of the data for each interval. It is approximate insofar as the data in the intervals are statistically independent, which become nearer the truth the more uniform or "white" the spectrum may be. In any event, it is a reasonable procedure, as examination of the behavior of the raw spectra in successive data intervals may give insight into the nonstationarity of the data.

The Indirect Method

In the indirect method of power spectrum estimation we first form estimates of the covariance function $R(\tau)$ using either the relation

$$\hat{R}\left(\frac{l}{2W}\right) = \frac{1}{2WT} \sum_{k=-WT+1}^{WT-l} f\left(\frac{k}{2W}\right) f\left(\frac{k+l}{2W}\right) \qquad l = 0, 1, \ldots, l_m \tag{7-50a}$$

or

$$\hat{R}\left(\frac{l}{2W}\right) = \frac{1}{2WT-l} \sum_{k=-WT+1}^{WT-l} f\left(\frac{k}{2W}\right) f\left(\frac{k+l}{2W}\right) \tag{7-50b}$$

These two forms differ only in the divisors $2WT$ or $(2WT-l)$. For the second form, the expected value of $\hat{R}$ is the autocovariance $R(l/2W)$, and therefore forms an unbiased estimate. On the other hand, it is equivalent to multiplying the first form of $\hat{R}$ by a lag window $f_l = 2WT/(2WT-l)$, a function which increases with lag number out to the maximum lag. Its Fourier transform has negative lobes which may, in turn, introduce negative smoothed spectral estimates, a situation to be avoided. For this reason, the first form is preferred if the autocovariance is calculated to compute spectra, and the second if we are interested in the covariances themselves.

When the spectral window is relatively complicated, as is the Parzen window, the power spectrum is computed by taking the cosine transform of the product of the lag window f_l and the autocovariance estimates $R(l/2W)$. If the spectral window is simple, as is the Hanning window, we set $f_l = 1$ and smooth the resultant raw spectral estimates. For a stationary process, the autocovariance is even, so we can use positive lags only in the cosine transform formula [Eq. (7-18)]:

$$\hat{S}_m = \frac{1}{2l_m} f_0\hat{R}(0) + 2 \sum_{k=1}^{l_m-1} f_k\hat{R}\left(\frac{k}{2W}\right) \cos \frac{\pi k_m}{l_m} + (-)^m f_{l_m}\hat{R}\left(\frac{l_m}{2W}\right) \tag{7-51}$$

The smoothed spectral estimates obtained in this way provide $l_m + 1$ values of the spectrum spaced uniformly over the frequency range from zero to the folding frequency W with spacing $\Delta\nu = W/l_m$. The frequency resolution is also controlled by the value of l_m, as the bandwidth is approximately $2\Delta\nu$.

The equivalent number of degrees of freedom n associated with each smoothed estimate is

$$n = \frac{2N}{\sum_k f_k{}^2} = \frac{2N}{l_m} K_e \tag{7-52}$$

where $N = 2WT$ is the number of data points, and K_e is a coefficient which depends on the particular lag window. Table 7.1 gives the

TABLE 7.1

Window	f_l		K_e
Periodogram	$f_l = 1$	$\lvert l\rvert \leq l_m$	½
	$= 0$	$\lvert l\rvert > l_m$	
Bartlett	$f_l = 1 - \dfrac{\lvert l\rvert}{l_m}$	$\lvert l\rvert \leq l_m$	3⁄2
	$= 0$	$\lvert l\rvert > l_m$	
Parzen	$f_l = 1 - \dfrac{6l^2}{l_m{}^2} + \dfrac{6\lvert l\rvert^3}{l_m{}^3}$	$\lvert l\rvert < \dfrac{l_m}{2}$	1.85
	$= 2\left(1 - \dfrac{\lvert l\rvert}{l_m}\right)^3$	$\dfrac{l_m}{2} \leq \lvert l\rvert \leq l_m$	
	$= 0$	$\lvert l\rvert > l_m$	
Hanning	$f_l = \dfrac{1}{2}\left(1 + \cos \dfrac{\pi l}{l_m}\right)$	$\lvert l\rvert \leq l_m$	4⁄3
	$= 0$	$\lvert l\rvert > l_m$	

values of K_e for several lag windows; for the Hanning window $K_e = 4/3 \approx 1$, and for the Parzen window $K_e = 1.85 \approx 2$. The gross approximations are not unreasonable in the simple calculations needed to determine appropriate data-processing parameters.

The decision to use the direct or indirect method of estimation depends on the frequency resolution desired. For a fine-grained spectrum estimate, the direct method will be easiest, while for a very coarse-grained one, with high stability, the indirect method is to be preferred. If we want intermediate resolution, for which the estimates have perhaps 20 to 50 degrees of freedom, the modified direct approach may be best. In this case, the covariances are computed from the transform of the squared Fourier coefficients of the demeaned, detrended, and tapered data surrounded by as many zeros as data points.

To use the fast Fourier transform we need data in blocks of specific size. The number of data points ought to be of the form $2^p \cdot 3^q$, where p and q are integers (with $q = 0$ usually). Data stretches which are not of requisite length are made so by adding an appropriate number of zeros to each end. This should be done after demeaning, detrending, and tapering. The direct or modified direct approach to estimating the spectrum can then be applied.

When the indirect method is used, negative spectral estimates may occur, particularly if one attempts fine resolution with estimates having few degrees of freedom. The reason for these negative estimates is unclear. Theoretically, estimates using an appropriate spectral window, such as the Parzen, are necessarily positive, so the explanation must lie in round-off error in the digital computation. However, in computer experiments using double precision computations of the covariances and the cosine transform, negative estimates still occurred. Happily, negative estimates seem to appear just in the situation where for other reasons it is most profitable to use the direct method of estimation.

Log Spectrum Estimates

There are several reasons why the logarithm of the estimates power spectrum is more useful than the spectral estimates themselves. In the first place, the range of power within which a spectrum may lie is often great enough that the display of the spectrum itself is difficult to interpret, particularly in the regions of extreme values. Displaying the log spectrum brings out the local behavior more uniformly throughout the range. Secondly, with appropriate scaling, the log spectrum is easily expressed in decibels, which in most applications is easier to work with. Another reason to employ log spectrum estimates follows from a consideration of their variance. We recall that the variance of spectrum estimates is proportional to the square of the spectrum. It turns out that the variance of the logarithm of the estimates is approximately independent of the spectrum itself. This means that the amplitude of the sampling fluctuations of the log estimates is approximately constant, no matter whether the spectrum is large or small. We have implicitly used this property when we considered the confidence bands for the estimates and expressed the result in terms of their range in decibels. Plots of spectral estimates look "noisy," the "noise" being superimposed on the "true" spectrum. The "noise" associated with the spectral estimates themselves becomes larger as the spectrum is larger, but the "noise" associated with log spectral estimates forms a band uniformly wide.

Display of Spectral Estimates

It is almost impossible to get a grasp of the spectrum behavior from a direct computer printout. The trends and fluctuations of the spectral estimates are obscure in the uniform rows of numbers. This is particularly the case if exponential notation is used; i.e., .72570 *E*-02 for the number .007257 and .84300 E-03 for 843. If there is no alternative for numerical printout, it is considerably easier to interpret the spectrum expressed in decibels 10 log $\hat{S}$ rather than $\hat{S}$ itself. It may also be worthwhile to scale the log spectrum additively so the largest log estimate is a convenient multiple of 10, and all others are then easily relatable to the largest. That is, if the scaled log spectrum is denoted by $\hat{D}$, we have

$$\hat{D} = 10 \log \hat{S} - 10 \log \hat{S}_{\max} + 10k$$

where k is an integer determined by the expected range of the spectrum.

Much the best display of spectra is by microfilm graphic output generated directly by the computer. There are well-developed techniques of drawing titled and labeled graphs with the printed matter as well as the graphs under program control. Since one may plot a large number of graphs including log spectra, covariances, etc., it is advisable to title each graph adequately so little or no additional information is needed to interpret it. A very large amount of computation can be completely wasted if the analyst is unable to identify precisely the output some time after the analysis was done.

Prewhitening and Filtering

In our discussion of power spectrum estimation, we have often assumed the spectrum was smooth, particularly within the bandwidth of the smoothed estimate. If there are very strong single-frequency components in the data, they will influence neighboring smoothed spectrum estimates through the spectral window. The sidelobes of the windows, although very small, can allow contributions from very strong components to leak into other estimates and affect the results. In particular, the zero-frequency component can be very troublesome unless it is removed by demeaning and detrending.

If the spectrum has regions of high energy, there may be leakage by way of the spectral window, and possibly through round-off error in the digital computation. Steep slopes in the spectrum may cause bias in the estimates. It may be desirable to reduce these effects by *prewhitening*, i.e., filtering or equalizing the data by appropriate digital filters, before estimating the spectrum. The filter should equalize the resultant spectrum to make it as smooth and flat as possible. Often prior information or experience with similar data will be enough to enable one to design an appropriate filter, but perhaps one must first make a pilot estimation of the spectrum, using coarse frequency resolution, to estimate what the filter characteristics should be. Filter design can then be carried out by one of a large number of techniques, and the final spectrum analysis can be made on the filtered data. The effect of the filter transfer function is then taken into account by dividing the prewhitened spectrum estimates by the squared absolute value of the filter transfer function, yielding the desired spectrum of the original data.

Should we need simple filters with simple transfer functions, as will generally be the case for prewhitening, we can use convolution type filters having only a few coefficients h_k in the filter's impulse response. To produce a digital filter with no phase shift, we use a symmetrical filter having an odd number of terms. A phaseless filter is particularly useful if we want to look at the filtered data itself, or if we wish to process it by other than power spectrum techniques. Let the $2K + 1$ symmetrical filter coefficients be h_0, $h_1 = h_{-1}$, $h_2 = h_{-2}$, . . . , $h_K = h_{-K}$. Then the transfer function of the filter is

$$H\left(\frac{m}{T}\right) \equiv H_m = \frac{1}{2K+1}\left\{h_0 + 2\sum_{k=1}^{K} h_k \cos\frac{\pi k m}{WT}\right\} \tag{7-53}$$

and if we use H_m to filter the data, the unfiltered data's power spectrum $S(m/T)$ will be multiplied by the power transmission $|H_m|^2$. The resultant prewhitened power spectrum $S_W(m/T)$ will be

$$S_W\left(\frac{m}{T}\right) = |H_m|^2 S\left(\frac{m}{T}\right) \tag{7-54}$$

If there are few filter coefficients h_k, symmetrical or not, it is usually better to filter in the time domain by a convolution operation. On the other hand, if the filter is complicated, operating in the frequency domain may prove more practical.

An example of a simple low-pass filter is the Hanning type, which we introduced for smoothing spectral estimates. Its coefficients are $h_0 = \frac{1}{2}$ and $h_{-1} = h_1 = \frac{1}{4}$. Its transfer function is

$$H_m = \frac{1}{6}\left(1 + \cos\frac{\pi m}{WT}\right) = \frac{1}{3}\cos^2\frac{\pi m}{2WT}$$

This transfer function has a maximum at zero frequency ($m = 0$), and has a double zero at the folding frequency $W = m/T$. Its effect on the power spectrum is to attenuate the higher frequencies and produce a fourth-order zero in S_W at the folding frequency. Since we estimate $S_W(m/T)$ and deduce $S(m/T)$ from

$$S\frac{m}{T} = \frac{S_W m/T}{|H_m|^2}$$

we would like to avoid dividing by zero. This can easily be done by adding a small amount to h_0, say 0.1, and using the modified filter

$$H_m = \frac{1}{3}\left(0.1 + \cos^2\frac{\pi m}{2WT}\right)$$

which is always positive. The ratio between the maximum and minimum power transmission $|H_m|^2$ is 21 dB. By changing the constant added to h_0, we can change this ratio at will.

The high-pass filter which complements the preceding one has the filter coefficients $h_{-1} = h_1 = -\frac{1}{4}$, $h_0 = \frac{1}{2}$, and the transfer function

$$H_m = \frac{1}{3}\sin^2\frac{\pi m}{2WT}$$

with a double zero at zero frequency. As before, we can remove the zero by increasing h_1 appropriately, and if $h_0 = 0.6$,

$$H_m = \frac{1}{3}\left(0.1 + \sin^2\frac{\pi m}{2WT}\right)$$

A simple filter like this may be useful to flatten a spectrum which drops off rapidly with increasing frequency.

There is a considerable body of theory on the design of digital filters, especially useful for problems in digital data processing when the filter transfer function must have carefully controlled properties. Such problems arise in the design of filters for Vocoders, where contiguous band-pass filters, which form a coarse spectrum analyzer, must have their phase shifts controlled properly. Design considerations of this sort are beyond the scope of this paper, and for much exploratory data analysis, including power-spectrum estimation, it is not necessary at first to go to complex design procedures to get adequate digital filters. With the fast Fourier transform algorithms now available, we can do fairly complicated filter design in the frequency domain, multiply the transformed data by the filter transfer function H_m, and transform back again. This technique is particularly useful if we want to extract bands of frequencies from the data. Suppose we want to extract the band from ν_1 to ν_2, where $0 \leq \nu_1 < \nu_2 \leq W$. Let the desired filter transfer function be

$$\begin{aligned} H(\nu) &= 1 \qquad \nu_1 \leq \nu \leq \nu_2 \\ &= 0 \qquad \text{elsewhere} \end{aligned}$$

We compute the transform of the data to get the $C_m = F(m/T)$, and write

$$\begin{aligned} D_m &= C_m \qquad m_1 = [\nu_1 T] \leq m \leq m_2 = [\nu_2 T] \\ &= 0 \qquad \text{otherwise} \end{aligned}$$

and transform the D_m back to the time domain to get the filtered output data. (The notation $[x]$ means "integer part of x.")

This technique is particularly useful to low-pass-filter digital data. It sometimes happens that the most interesting part of the data is at low frequencies relative to the Nyquist frequency. This may have come about because we did not know to what frequency the spectrum was significant, and we filtered and digitized the data at a much higher Nyquist frequency than turned out to be necessary. As as matter of economy in data storage, we would like to filter and resample at a lower sampling rate. This can be easily done by Fourier-transforming the data stretch and transforming back to the time domain only the coefficients C_m for $0 \leq m \leq 2WT/K$. By doing this, we have low-pass-filtered the data to an upper frequency of W/K and recreated a time series, still of length T seconds, but with a sampling frequency $2W/K$. In other words, the original data, sampled at $2W$ samples per second, has been *decimated* by the factor K, and we now have $2WT/K$ data points.

Cross-spectra

Loosely speaking, the cross-spectrum gives the relation between elementary frequency components at the same frequency in a pair of time series. It is a complex function of frequency, which if expressed in terms of magnitude and phase gives the relative phase between the components and the magnitude of their product. Writing the cross-spectrum as $S_{xy}(\nu) = C_{xy}(\nu) + iQ_{xy}(\nu)$, we denote the real part $C_{xy}(\nu)$ as the *cospectrum* and the imaginary part $Q_{xy}(\nu)$ as the *quadrature spectrum.* The cross-spectrum is usually defined as the Fourier transform of the cross-correlation $R_{xy}(\tau)$:

$$S_{xy}(\nu) = \int_{-\infty}^{\infty} e^{-2\pi i\nu\tau} R_{xy}(\tau)\, d\tau \tag{7-55}$$

Since $R_{xy}(\tau) = R_{yx}(-\tau)$, we find that $S_{xy}(\nu) = S^*_{yx}(\nu)$. We can regard the cross-spectrum as a frequency analysis of the cross correlation and thus gives us a measure, frequency by frequency, of how the random processes $x(t)$ and $y(t)$ relate to one another.

In terms of the generalized transform $G_x(\nu)$ and $G_y(\nu)$ of $x(t)$ and $y(t)$, we find that

$$\text{ave}\,\{dG_x(\nu)\, dG_y^*(\nu)\} = (4/\pi^2) S_{xy}(\nu)\, d\nu \tag{7-56}$$

and using this relation, we can compute by a direct method cross-spectral estimates in the same way as for the power spectrum.

To get the cross-spectrum by the direct method, we compute the Fourier transforms of the demeaned, detrended, and tapered data stretches of $x(t)$ and $y(t)$. This gives us the Fourier coefficients X_m and Y_m:

$$X_m = \frac{1}{2WT} \sum_{k=-WT+1}^{WT} x\left(\frac{k}{2W}\right) e^{-\pi ikm/WT} \tag{7-57a}$$

$$Y_m = \frac{1}{2WT} \sum_{k=-WT+1}^{WT} y\left(\frac{k}{2W}\right) e^{-\pi ikm/WT} \tag{7-57b}$$

and we find that

$$S_{xy}\left(\frac{m}{T}\right) \cong T\ \text{ave}\,\{X_m Y_m^*\} \tag{7-58}$$

The "raw" cross-spectral estimates X_mY can then be smoothed by averaging over neighboring frequencies (the spectrum window), or by breaking up the data stretch into smaller segments of length reciprocal to the desired frequency resolution and averaging the individual estimates. While the statistics of the power-spectrum estimates of a Gaussian process are chi-square, the statistics of cross-spectral estimates of joint Gaussian processes are much more complex, as there are interrelations between $\hat{S}_{xy}(\nu)$ and the two power spectra $S_{xx}(\nu)$ and $S_{yy}(\nu)$. For smoothed estimates with a large number of degrees of freedom, we give the approximate variances and covariances of the estimates $\hat{S}_{xx}$, $\hat{S}_{yy}$, $\hat{C}_{xy}$, and $\hat{Q}_{xy}$ in Table 7.2.

TABLE 7.2

$$\text{var}\ \{\hat{S}_{xx}\} = \frac{2S_{xx}^2}{n} \qquad \text{var}\ \{\hat{S}_{yy}\} = \frac{2S_{yy}^2}{n}$$

$$\text{var}\ \{\hat{C}_{xy}\} = \frac{1}{n}\,[S_{xx}S_{yy} + C_{xy}^2 - Q_{xy}^2]$$

$$\text{var}\ \{\hat{Q}_{xy}\} = \frac{1}{n}\,[S_{xx}S_{yy} + Q_{xy}^2 - C_{xy}^2]$$

$$\text{cov}\ \{\hat{S}_{xx},\hat{S}_{yy}\} = \frac{2}{n}\,[C_{xy}^2 + Q_{xy}^2]$$

$$\text{cov}\ \{\hat{S}_{xx},\hat{C}_{xy}\} = \frac{2}{n}\,S_{xx}C_{xy} \qquad \text{cov}\ \{\hat{S}_{xx},\hat{Q}_{xy}\} = \frac{2}{n}\,S_{xx}Q_{xy}$$

$$\text{cov}\ \{\hat{S}_{yy},\hat{C}_{xy}\} = \frac{2}{n}\,S_{yy}C_{xy} \qquad \text{cov}\ \{\hat{S}_{yy},\hat{Q}_{xy}\} = \frac{2}{n}\,S_{yy}Q_{xy}$$

$$\text{cov}\ \{\hat{C}_{xy},\hat{Q}_{xy}\} = \frac{2}{n}\,C_{xy}Q_{xy}$$

Since the cross-spectrum is complex and each component can range from positive through zero to negative values, we are unable to use the log cross-spectrum and get the advantages of display we get with the log power spectrum.

The indirect method for cross-spectral estimation is similar to the indirect method for the power spectrum and need not be elaborated. It may be comforting to observe that if $y(t) = x(t)$, we see that $S_{xx}(\nu) = S_{yy}(\nu) = C_{xy}(\nu)$ and that $Q_{xy}(\nu) = 0$. It also can be seen that the co-spectrum relates the in-phase elementary components and the quadrature spectrum the components 90° out of phase in the two time series.

Coherence and Transfer-function Estimation

A more satisfying measure of the relation between frequency components of two time series is given by the *coherence* $\rho(\nu)$, which is a normalized cross-spectrum, defined by

$$\rho(\nu) = \gamma(\nu)e^{i\varphi(\nu)} = \frac{S_{xy}(\nu)}{\sqrt{S_{xx}(\nu)S_{yy}(\nu)}} \qquad 0 \le \gamma(\nu) \le 1 \tag{7-59}$$

The squared magnitude of the coherence ζ is usually called the *coherency* $W(\nu) = \gamma^2(\nu)$. The phase φ of the coherence is the phase of the cross spectrum and can be calculated from

$$\varphi(\nu) = \tan^{-1}\frac{Q_{xy}(\nu)}{C_{xy}(\nu)} \tag{7-60}$$

The coherence is a better measure of the correlation between x and y at the frequency ν than is the cross-spectrum as it is invariant with respect to a scale change in either x or y.

Suppose we have an input signal $x(t)$ which is simultaneously applied to two filters. The transfer function of the filters are $H_1(\nu)$ and $H_2(\nu)$, and the output signals are $y(t)$ and $z(t)$, respectively. If $S_{xx}(\nu)$ is the power spectrum of x, the cross-spectrum between y and z is

$$S_{yz}(\nu) = H_1(\nu)H_2^*(\nu)S_{xx}(\nu) \tag{7-61}$$

and by putting $H_2(\nu) \equiv 1$, so that $z(t) = x(t)$, we see that the cross-spectrum between the input and output of the H_1 filter is

$$S_{xy}(\nu) = H_1^*(\nu)S_{xx}(\nu) \tag{7-62}$$

and the power spectrum of y is [Eq. (7-43)]

$$S_{yy}(\nu) = |H_1(\nu)|^2 S_{xx}(\nu)$$

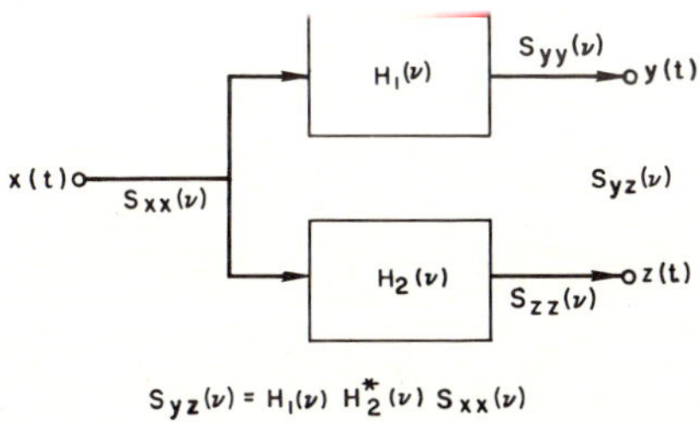

Fig. 7.17. The cross-spectrum between the outputs of two filters.

The coherency W between x and y is then

$$W(\nu) = \frac{|S_{xy}(\nu)|^2}{S_{xx}(\nu)S_{yy}(\nu)} = \frac{|H_1(\nu)|^2 S_{xx}{}^2(\nu)}{S_{xx}(\nu)|H_1(\nu)|^2 S_{xx}(\nu)} \equiv 1 \tag{7-63}$$

corresponding to perfect coherence ($\lambda = 1$). If the output $y(t)$ should be contaminated with another signal (or noise) $n(t)$, independent of $x(t)$, we find that

$$S_{yy}(\nu) = |H_1(\nu)|^2 S_{xx}(\nu) + S_{nn}(\nu) \tag{7-64}$$

where $S_{nn}(\nu)$ is the power spectrum of the noise. Then the coherency is

$$W = \frac{1}{1 + S_{nn}/|H_1|^2 S_{xx}} < 1 \tag{7-65}$$

so we may regard the coherency as a measure of the commonality between input and output.

We can use the cross-spectrum to estimate the transfer function of a network or filter if we have data taken simultaneously at its input and output, even if the input is not under our direct control. If $x(t)$ is the input and $y(t)$ the output, since $S_{xy}(\nu) = H^*(\nu)S_{xx}(\nu)$, we have

$$\hat{H}^*(\nu) \equiv \hat{A}(\nu)e^{-i\hat{\varphi}(\nu)} = \frac{\hat{S}_{xy}(\nu)}{\hat{S}_{xx}(\nu)} \tag{7-62a}$$

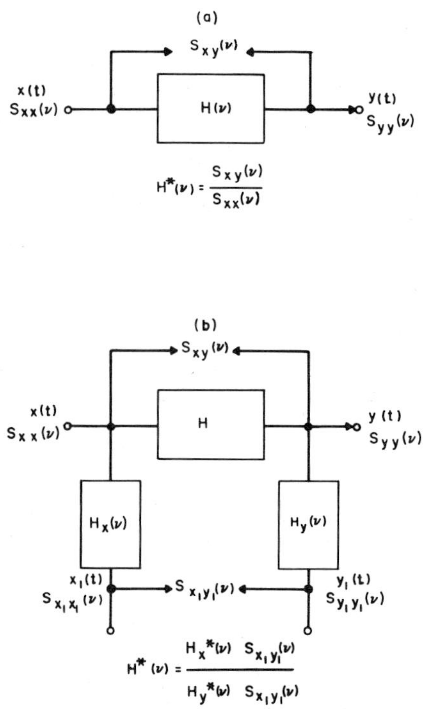

Fig. 7.18. Estimating the transfer function of a filter: (a) direct access to filter terminals; (b) indirect access to filter terminals.

If we are unable to measure the waveforms directly at the input and output terminals of the filter whose transfer function we want, we can get it indirectly if we know the transfer function of the intervening networks. This situation often arises when the sensors used to acquire the data have nonuniform but calibrated responses. Figure 7.18 shows the situation in which the accessible signals are $x_1(t)$ and $y_1(t)$, which are modified versions of the desired $x(t)$ and $y(t)$. If we know the transfer function $H_x(\nu)$ and $H_y(\nu)$ we can still get $H(\nu)$ from measurements on x_1 and y_1 through the relation

$$H^*(\nu) = \frac{H_x^*(\nu)S_{x_1y_1}(\nu)}{H_y^*(\nu)\ S_{x_1x_1}(\nu)} \tag{7-66}$$

Before giving an example of a design for digital-spectrum and transfer-function analysis, we need expressions for the variances of the estimates of coherency $W(\nu)$ and of amplitude $\hat{A}(\nu)$ and phase $\hat{\varphi}(\nu)$. Approximate expressions for these variances are

$$\text{var}\,\{\hat{W}(\nu)\} = \frac{1}{n}[1 - W^2(\nu)]^2 \tag{7-67}$$

$$\text{var}\,\{\hat{A}(\nu)\} = \left(\frac{A^2(\nu)}{n}\right)\left(\frac{1}{W^2(\nu)} - 1\right) \tag{7-68}$$

and

$$\text{var}\,\{\hat{\varphi}(\nu)\} = \frac{1}{n}\left(\frac{1}{W^2(\nu)} - 1\right) \tag{7-69}$$

It is interesting that the variance of A is proportional to A^2 and so exhibits similar behavior to power-spectrum estimates. One is led then to estimate $\log \hat{A}$, whose variance is

$$\text{var}\,\{\log \hat{A}(\nu)\} = \frac{1}{n}\left(\frac{1}{W^2(\nu)} - 1\right) \tag{7-70}$$

which is the same as the variance for the phase $\hat{\varphi}(\nu)$ and depends only on the coherency. Since to the approximation used in these calculations the covariance between $\hat{A}$ and $\hat{\varphi}$ is zero, we can regard $\log \hat{A}(\nu)$ (naturally expressed in nepers) and $\hat{\varphi}(\nu)$ as independent, and to be sensible estimators of the transfer function $H(\nu)$. As the coherency $W(\nu)$ drops from unity to zero, the variance of the estimates for $\log A$ and φ goes from zero to infinity, hence the coherency is an important factor in determining the accuracy of the estimates. We must estimate $W(\nu)$ before we can determine appropriately the parameters for estimating the transfer function.

The coherency $W(\nu) = \gamma^2(\nu)$ is necessarily positive, and so even if $\gamma = 0$, the estimate $\hat{W}(\nu)$ will always be positive, hence

$$W(\nu) = \frac{\hat{C}_{xy}{}^2(\nu) + \hat{Q}_{xy}{}^2(\nu)}{\hat{S}_{xx}(\nu)\hat{S}_{yy}(\nu)} \tag{7-71}$$

is a biased estimate of W. $\hat{W}$ is biased most near zero, and for Gaussian signals, it turns out that the expected value of $\hat{W}$ when $\gamma = 0$ is

$$\text{ave}\,\{\hat{W}(\nu)\} = \frac{1}{n} \qquad (\gamma = 0) \tag{7-72}$$

where n is the equivalent number of degrees of freedom of the spectral estimates. As γ gets larger the bias decreases. If, for example, for $n = 20$, we have

$\|\gamma\|$	W	ave $\{\hat{W}\}$	Bias
0	0	0.05	0.05
0.2	0.04	0.0863	0.0463
0.5	0.25	0.279	0.029
0.7	0.49	0.504	0.014
0.8	0.64	0.647	0.007
0.9	0.81	0.812	0.002

An Example

Let us consider an experiment to determine the spectra of voiced sounds, both at the glottis and just outside the mouth, and to estimate the transfer function of the articulatory mechanism. We will need two input channels to the digitizer so the two signals can be handled simultaneously. We must first decide on an upper frequency of interest so we can determine the digital sampling rate. Let us choose 4 kHz as the upper frequency; and to make our low-pass filter design simple let us choose the channel sampling rate to be 12 kHz. We would like the quantizing noise and the aliased spectrum to be at least 40 dB below the signal. Since the power in a voiced speech signal above 6 kHz is small, it should be sufficient for the low-pass filters before the sampler to have a 43 dB stop-band attenuation. In the pass band, the filter should be flat to within 1 dB ($|H(\nu)| = 1 \pm .06,\ 0 \leq \nu \leq 4$ kHz), and $|H(\nu)| \leq 7 \times 10^{-3}$ for frequencies above 6 kHz. As we pointed out on page 238, these requirements are not particularly demanding. It would be desirable to keep the phase shift between the two low-pass filters within 5 or 10 degrees of each other, so their effect on the estimation of the cross spectrum is minimized. To keep the quantizing noise within bounds, we should use nine bits in the digitizer.

In estimating the power spectrum let us consider two possibilities. First, we might want enough frequency resolution so that we resolve the pitch harmonics. To do this, let us suppose we need 25-Hz resolution. If we want our estimates (with 90 percent confidence) to lie in a ± 1 dB band we need 104 degrees of freedom ($n = 104$). We then need 52 elementary frequencies in the 25-Hz resolution band, so $\Delta\nu = \frac{1}{2}$ Hz. If we use the direct method, we must have the record length $T = 2$ s and the number of data points $N = 2WT = 24{,}000$ points. If an accuracy of ± 2.5 dB is sufficient, $n = 18$ and $\Delta\nu = 3$ Hz, so the record length $T = \frac{1}{3}$ s, and we need 4,000 data points. Since it is unlikely that the subject can maintain sufficiently constant pitch and phonemic value over the 2-s record length, and since the resulting

4,000 data points is nicely compatible with a fast Fourier transform calculation using 4,096 data points, it might be better to take eight 4,096-point data stretches and average their spectra to increase n to 104.

If we would be satisfied with only enough resolution to delineate the format structure, we might use a frequency resolution of 200 Hz. For ± 1 dB accuracy with $n = 104$, our elementary frequency bandwidth need be only 4 Hz, so the record length need be only ¼ of a second, requiring 3,000 data points. It might be preferable to use 4,096 so that we can employ the fast Fourier transform.

Our experiment then consists of a probe microphone to measure the sound pressure near the glottis and another microphone placed near the lip. As a preliminary we need to calibrate the sensors and digitizing low-pass filters, both in amplitude and phase. If the frequency response of the sensors is not reasonably uniform (say within 10 dB from zero to 4,000 Hz) it would be advisable to design networks which will equalize their response before digitizing the data. Using a two-channel multiplexer we collect ten 4,096-point data stretches for each channel. We play back one data stretch for each channel and monitor on an oscilloscope for evidence of overload or digitization errors. If we are satisfied with the quality of our data we demean and detrend, taper the first and last 5 percent, and compute the spectra. We use either the fast Fourier transform followed by smoothing with an appropriate spectral window, or we use the indirect method of spectral estimation, choosing a number of lags in the covariance and a lag window (Parzen or Hanning) which will yield the desired number of degrees of freedom for the smoothed estimates.

To estimate the transfer function we need first estimate the coherence W, as W enters into the variance of the estimate of the transfer function. To get an idea of what values of W are tolerable, let us suppose that we will allow the factor $\frac{1}{W^2} - 1 \leq 2$ so that var $\{\hat{A}\} \cong \frac{A^2}{n}\cdot$ Since var $\{\hat{A}\}$ looks much like the variance of the power spectra, and since A is always positive, it is not unreasonable to assume that A is distributed approximately chi-square (although it really is not), and for a given accuracy in the $\hat{A}$ estimate we can use the same number of degrees of freedom as we used for the power spectra. The nearer W approaches unity the poorer the approximation that A is chi-square but the more accurate our estimates will be. Hence, for experimental design purposes it is reasonable to assume a chi-square distribution with n degrees of freedom. Our requirement on W is that it be larger than 0.58 or that $\hat{W} \geq 0.6$. This must be verified by computation on the data itself. If the noise added to the signals of interest were due only to quantizing and aliasing, W would be very close to one. On the other hand, other noise sources exist, including the noise introduced by roundoff in computing the spectra, and we would be foolish not to measure W itself. We compute $\hat{A}$ and $\hat{\varphi}$ from the estimates of the spectra and cross-spectra. Assuming a frequency resolution of 200 Hz we can assume that $\hat{A}$ will be within a ± 1 dB band if we use 3,000 data points.

Plotting of the phase $\hat{\varphi}$ will be a problem, as determining the appropriate angle from $\tan^{-1} \hat{Q}_{xy}/\hat{C}_{xy}$ is troublesome. We must appeal to continuity in phase to determine what multiple of 2π must be added when the phase shows large discontinuities.

If we use the direct method to compute spectra, the effect of the frequency response of the sensors is best taken into account by modifying the Fourier coefficients of each data stretch by dividing them by the complex (voltage) transfer function of the appropriate sensors. This can be done by evaluating the sensor transfer function at each elementary frequency and incorporating the division in the computer program. The resultant Fourier coefficients can then be used to determine the smoothed spectra and cross-spectra.

The Bispectrum

On page 248 we discussed various statistics characterizing a random process $x(t)$, and mentioned a hierarchy starting with the mean value $E\{x(t)\}$, followed by the correlation $R(t_1,t_2) = E\{x(t_1)x(t_2)\}$. In this sequence, the next one would be $E\{x(t_1)x(t_2)x(t_3)\}$.† Just as the power spectrum, the Fourier transform of $R(t_1,t_2)$, is a more desirable statistic characterizing the second-order properties of $x(t)$, so we might expect the Fourier transform of $E\{x(t_1)x(t_2)x(t_3)\}$ to be a correspondingly desirable characterization of the third-order statistics of $x(t)$. This function is called the *bispectrum* of x.

The development of the bispectrum parallels closely that of the power spectrum. If the random process $x(t)$ is stationary, the expected value of the triple depends only on two time differences, and we can write

$$E\{x(t_1)x(t_2)x(t_3)\} = P(\tau_1,\tau_2) \tag{7-73}$$

where $\tau_1 = t_2 - t_1$ and $\tau_2 = t_3 - t_1$, and where $P(\tau_1,\tau_2)$ is a two-variable analog to $R(\tau)$. Then the bispectrum $B(\nu_1,\nu_2)$ is the two-dimensional Fourier transform of $P(\tau_1,\tau_2)$:

$$B(\nu_1,\nu_2) = \int_{-\infty}^{\infty} \int_{-\infty}^{\infty} P(\tau_1,\tau_2) e^{-2\pi i\nu_1\tau_1 - 2\pi i\nu_2\tau_2}\, d\tau_1\, d\tau_2 \tag{7-74}$$

† More accurately, the sequence of cumulant functions is the appropriate one. For zero-mean processes, up to the third order the two characterizations are identical.

We recall that if $x(t)$ is real and stationary, then the power spectrum $S(\nu)$ is real and $S(\nu) = S(-\nu)$. On the other hand, the bispectrum of a real stationary process is complex, and we have $B(\nu_1,\nu_2) = B^*(-\nu_1,-\nu_2)$. In terms of the Fourier-Stieltjes representation of $x(t)$ [Eq. (7-29)], we pointed out in Eqs. (7-31) and (7-32) that

$$\begin{aligned} \text{ave } \{dG(\nu_1)\, dG^*(\nu_2)\} &= 4\pi^2 S(\nu_1)\, d\nu_1 && \text{if } \nu_1 = \nu_2 \\ &= 0 && \text{if } \nu_1 \neq \nu_2 \end{aligned}$$

which, since $dG^*(\nu_2) = dG(-\nu_2)$, can be written

$$\begin{aligned} \text{ave } \{dG(\nu_1)\, dG(\nu_2)\} &= 4\pi^2 S(\nu_1)\, d\nu_1 && \text{if } \nu_1 + \nu_2 = 0 \\ &= 0 && \text{if } \nu_1 + \nu_2 = 0 \end{aligned} \qquad (7\text{-}75)$$

The bispectrum can be defined similarly:

$$\begin{aligned} \text{ave } \{dG(\nu_1)\, dG(\nu_2)\, dG(\nu_3)\} &= 8\pi^3 B(\nu_1,\nu_2)\, d\nu_1\, d\nu_2 && \text{if } \nu_1 + \nu_2 + \nu_3 = 0 \\ &= 0 && \text{if } \nu_1 + \nu_2 + \nu_3 \neq 0 \end{aligned} \qquad (7\text{-}76)$$

and we can use this result to compute bispectral estimates in terms of the Fourier coefficients $C_m = A_m + iB_m$. Assuming the data is real, and that we will use negative indices to represent negative elementary frequencies, we have

$$\begin{aligned} A_m &= A_{-m} \\ B_m &= -B_{-m} \end{aligned} \qquad (7\text{-}77)$$

From Eqs. (7-38) to (7-40) we see that

$$\begin{aligned} \text{ave } \{(A_i + iB_i)(A_j + iB_j)\} &= \frac{1}{T} S\left(\frac{i}{T}\right) && \text{if } i + j = 0 \\ &= 0 && \text{if } i + j \neq 0 \end{aligned} \qquad (7\text{-}78)$$

and similarly, we find that

$$\begin{aligned} \text{ave } \{(A_i + iB_i)(A_j + iB_j)(A_k + iB_k)\} &= \frac{1}{T^2} B(i/T,j/T) \equiv Bi(i,j) \\ & \qquad \text{if } i + j + k = 0 \\ &= 0 \qquad \text{if } i + j + k \neq 0 \end{aligned} \qquad (7\text{-}79)$$

The resultant raw bispectral coefficients $Bi(i,j)$ must be smoothed just as is done in power-spectrum estimation, and for the same reason, since without smoothing, the variance of the bispectral estimates does not decrease as T increases. The smoothing function $F(m,n)$ used should be symmetrical in m, n, $-m$, and $-n$, and the smoothed bispectral estimates are

$$\hat{Bi}(i,j) = \sum_m \sum_n F(i - m,\, j - n) Bi(m,n) \qquad (7\text{-}80)$$

where

$$F(m,n) = F(n,m) = F(-m,-n) = F(m,-m,-n) \tag{7-81}$$

and

$$\sum_m \sum_n F(m,n) = 1 \tag{7-82}$$

The detailed properties of the statistics of smoothed bispectral estimates have not yet been investigated, so we are unable to specify the amount of smoothing or length of data needed to achieve appropriate stability of the estimates. It appears that 5 to 10 times as much data is needed to get comparable stability as is needed for ordinary power-spectrum estimates.

There are important symmetries in the bispectrum which can be taken advantage of. The bispectral coefficients $Bi(i,j)$ are symmetric in i and j, and since all the indices i, j, and k range from $-WT$ to $+WT$ and are periodic beyond, we can limit $i + j = -k \leq WT$. The bispectrum is then defined by its values in the truncated octant bounded by the lines $i = 0$, $i = j$, and $i + j + j = WT$, as shown in Fig. 7.19. Although this seems like a significant reduction in size over the whole plane, the order of $(WT)^2/8$ complex points must still be plotted in an insightful manner, and this may not be easy.

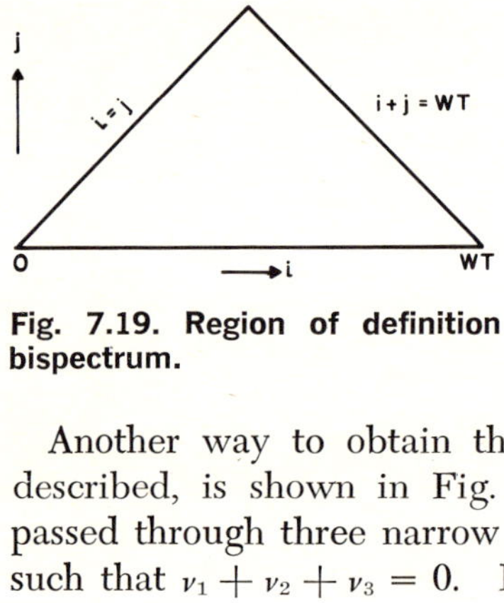

Fig. 7.19. Region of definition of bispectrum.

Another way to obtain the bispectrum, related to the method just described, is shown in Fig. 7.20. The signal $x(t)$ to be analyzed is passed through three narrow band-pass filters centered on ν_1, ν_2, and ν_3, such that $\nu_1 + \nu_2 + \nu_3 = 0$. In practice with real data, of course, since positive and negative frequencies amount to the same thing, we set $\nu_3 = \nu_1 + \nu_2$. To get the real part of the bispectrum, we multiply the three band-pass-filter outputs together and integrate over the duration of the signal. To get the imaginary part, we insert a 90° phase shifter in the output of the ν_3 band-pass filter only, multiply the three together, and integrate. Before the fast Fourier transform was available, this method was employed on a digital computer, by constructing appropriate digital band-pass filters.

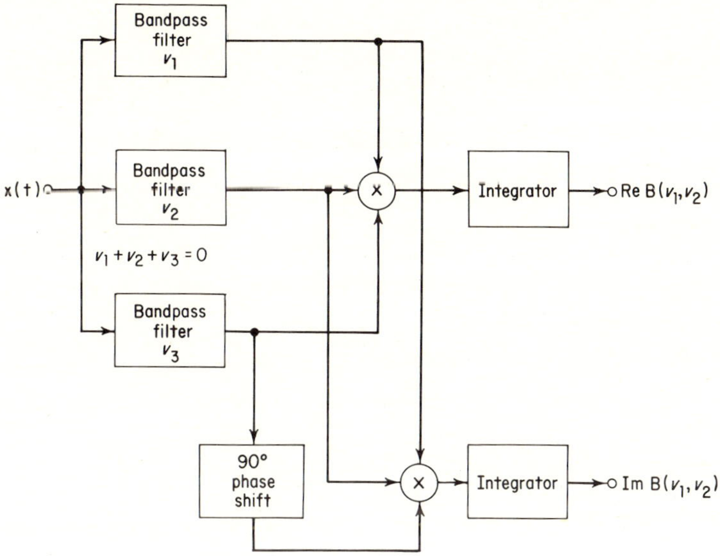

Fig. 7.20. Obtaining the bispectrum with band-pass filters, a phase shifter, multipliers, and integrators.

The bispectrum of a zero-mean stationary Gaussian process vanishes because the average of a triple of a Gaussian process is proportional to the mean. If we pass a stationary Gaussian signal through a *linear* network or filter, the output is also Gaussian, so the output bispectrum is still zero. If, on the other hand, we pass a signal with zero bispectrum through a nonlinear network, the nonlinearity will produce interactions between frequency pairs leading to the generation of sum and difference frequencies, whose phase relative to the original elementary frequency components is determined by the type of nonlinearity. The bispectrum of the result will be nonzero, since elementary frequency components will exist which sum to zero and process definite phase relation. Thus, the bispectrum is a way to reveal the presence of nonlinearity in a network or system whose input is Gaussian. A deterministic signal may have a nonzero bispectrum; for example, a pulse train is the resultant of a number of harmonics of the basic pulse rate, and the definite phase relation between the harmonics will lead to nonzero bispectral estimates.

The Cepstrum

Another kind of higher order data processing of interest resulted from an ad hoc approach to find echoes in time series. The techniques developed, usually lumped under the name "cepstrum," include, among others, the pseudocovariance as well as the cepstrum itself. While the bispectrum is a natural formal extension of the power spectrum, cepstral techniques were based chiefly on the results of experimentation on a digital computer, and while they were motivated by seismological studies, they have turned out to be most useful in determining the pitch of voiced sounds.

Briefly, the cepstrum is the power spectrum of the log power spectrum, and the pseudoautocovariance is the cosine transform of the log power spectrum. Suppose we have a signal $x(t)$ which in passing through some transmission medium acquires an echo $\alpha x(t-\tau)$, where α is the echo amplitude and τ is the echo delay. We want to analyze the echoed signal

$$s(t) = x(t) + \alpha x(t-\tau)$$

for its echo. If the power spectrum of $x(t)$ is $G_x(\nu)$, then the power spectrum $G_s(\nu)$ of $s(t)$ is

$$G_s(\nu) = G_x(\nu)(1 + \alpha^2 + 2\alpha \cos 2\pi\tau\nu)$$

We see that the echo modifies the spectrum of x by "modulating" it with a cosinusoidal term $\cos 2\pi\tau\nu$. The periodicity of the ripples in the spectrum of the echoed signal is $1/\tau$, so the longer the echo time the closer together in frequency are the ripples. Suppose we consider the logarithm of $G_s(\nu)$. We see that

$$\log G_s(\nu) = \log G_x(\nu) + \log (1 + \alpha^2 + 2\alpha \cos 2\pi\tau\nu)$$

and if the echo amplitude is small compared to unity, we can expand the second term and get

$$\log G_s(\nu) \cong \log G_x(\nu) + 2\alpha \cos 2\pi\tau\nu$$

where we have used the approximation $\log(1+x) = x$. Thus, the ripple due to the echo is *additive* in the log spectrum, and to find the echo means now to find a cosinusoidal term in the frequency series of $\log G_x(\nu)$. If $G_x(\nu)$ is rather smoothly varying in frequency, that is, smooth compared to the echo ripple, we can search the frequency series with a "filter" tuned to the echo delay τ. One way to "filter," particularly if the phase of the ripple is unknown, is to take the power spectrum of $\log G_s(\nu)$, and by so doing, we get the cepstrum of the time series $s(t)$. On the other hand, if the phase of the ripple is known a priori, as it is for the echo ripple, it is better to cross-correlate $\log G_s(\nu)$ with a cosine wave of the same periodicity as the echo ripple. This can be accomplished by taking the Fourier cosine transform of $\log G_s(\nu)$, which gives us the pseudoautocovariance.

One might ask why we need to go to such lengths to determine if an echo is present in $s(t)$. Why not look for the echo in the autocorrelation function $R_s(\lambda)$, since in terms of the autocorrelation $R_x(\mu)$ of x we have

$$R_s(\lambda) = (1 + \alpha^2)R_x(\lambda) + \alpha[R_x(\lambda - \tau) + R_x(\lambda + \tau)]$$

The effect of the echo is to add α times the autocorrelation of x, displaced by τ on either side of $(1 + \tau^2)R_x(\lambda)$. If there is a significant peak at $\lambda = 0$, and if $R_x(\lambda)$ is nearly zero away from $\lambda = 0$, the autocorrelation is a good way to find the echo. Unfortunately, however, the autocorrelation function for a process with a nonflat power spectrum may be quite substantial for nonzero x, and the peaks due to the echo can be obscured more or less, depending on the spectrum of $x(t)$.

It turns out that the cepstrum and the pseudoautocovariance are much less affected by the spectrum shape, for reasons related to the nonlinearity of the logarithm. In fact, processing the data by the pseudoautocovariance technique but without taking the logarithm of the spectrum produces the autocorrelation! The logarithm does two things. The first, already discussed, is to make the echo ripple additive. The second has to do with the effects of the spectrum "noise" associated with estimates of the spectrum from a finite stretch of data, which we discussed in the section on log spectrum estimates. The echo ripple can be obscured by corresponding ripple components as the spectrum of the unechoed signal, and, of course, we can do nothing about this. It can also be obscured by the log spectrum estimation "noise," which is a random process in the frequency variable ν. We recall [Eq. (7-45)] that the variance of power-spectrum estimates is proportional to the square of the spectrum, whereas the variance of the log spectrum does not depend on the spectrum, but only on the smoothing used in the estimation procedure. Hence by looking for the echo ripple on the log spectrum, we have isolated the effect of the echo as much as possible from the shape of the spectrum itself; so it is not surprising that the cepstrum and pseudoautocovariance can be much more effective than ordinary autocorrelation. Computer experimentation has shown that the cepstrum is invariant to the shape of the spectrum of $x(t)$ so long as it is sufficiently smooth.

In application of cepstrum techniques to vocal-pitch detection, the problem is somewhat different. We are looking for the fundamental period of the voiced speech wave, possibly without the lowest harmonics, and in the face of a highly variable spectrum due to the changes in the articulatory mechanism. We use the cepstrum then to determine the pitch harmonic spacings rather than to find a ripple due to an echo. The harmonics are likely to be prominent, although their spacing may not be uniform because of the phase-shifting caused by the formants. The frequency resolution of the log power spectrum must be good

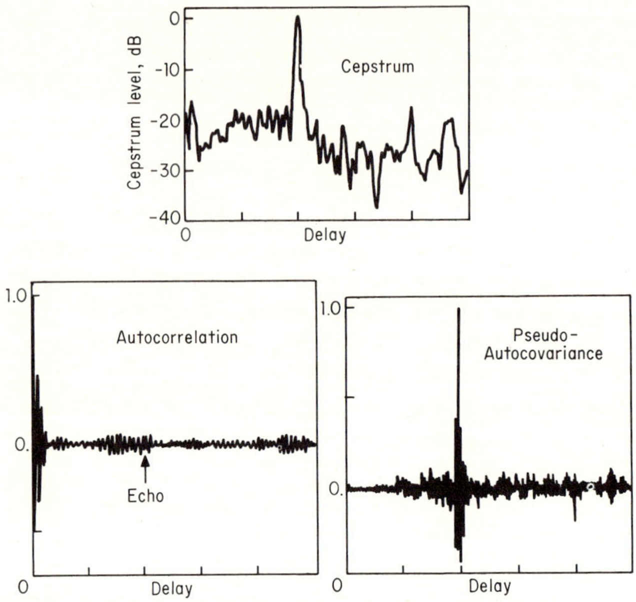

Fig. 7.21. The cepstrum, autocorrelation, and pseudoautocovariance of an echoed signal having a nonsmooth spectrum. Note the positive peak in the cepstrum and the negative one in the pseudoautocovariance at twice the delay of the echo. They correspond to the second term in the expression of $\log(1 = x) = x - x^2/2 + \cdot \cdot \cdot$.

enough to yield at least two estimates per harmonic spacing for the lowest pitch of interest. To get a reasonable equivalent number of degrees of freedom in the spectrum estimates we may need to average over a number of data stretches. If we want the cepstrum, we should use little smoothing for the cepstral estimates, as we want the best "frequency" resolution we can get to pick the harmonic periodicity out of the long spectrum estimation "noise."

Conclusion

From a reasonably practical point of view, we have tried to discuss ways to process digitized time series meaningfully. We have stressed the frequency analytic approach and have been quite explicit about the collection and digitization of the data and about the importance of quality assurance in data preparation. We have discussed, in a nonrigorous way, the concepts of frequency analysis of random data as related to the Fourier-Stieltjes representation of a random process, as this is meaningfully related to digital Fourier analysis, an approach made much more practical by fast Fourier transform algorithms. We mentioned the importance of proper display of the results of data analysis but did not go into as much detail as we would like, because it is closely related to the particular computer-user output interface. Time spent on usable graphical display instrumentation and programming is time well spent.

Data from the real world is seldom precisely stationary, or Gaussian, or zero mean, etc., and the theories of data analysis may not strictly apply. To study their applicability is best accomplished by computer experimentation: trial and error, changing data processing parameters, replication of the experiment, trial with computer-generated data stream, and so forth. For example, belief in the validity of the assumption that spectral estimates are close to chi-square-distributed is greatly strengthened by experience and computer experimentation.

Computer experimentation can be made much more effective by breaking the data-analysis procedures into relatively simple building blocks which are incorporated into subroutines, each having a simple and convenient calling sequence. An example of this approach is the TISER (TIme SERies) subroutine package, which includes detrending and tapering routines, filtering (convolution), auto- and cross-covariance, Fourier sine and cosine transforms, scaling routines, complex modulation and demodulation, and rectangular-polar coordinate conversion. A complicated data-processing program can be made up from these subroutines, with the largest part of the programming effort spent in input/output and display.

R. W. Hamming said, "The purpose of computing is insight—not numbers." Insight comes from experience, and that requires a willingness to try new techniques and see what happens, to replicate, to try different kinds of data, to use a different set of parameters, and so on. From the insight may come enough understanding to form a theoretical basis, which in turn will lead to better and more purposeful data analysis.

BIBLIOGRAPHY

Blackman, R. B., and J. W. Tukey, "The Measurement of Power Spectra," Dover Publications, Inc., New York, 1959.

Healy, M. J. R., and B. P. Bogert, FORTRAN Subroutines for Time Series Analysis, *Commun. ACM*, **6**:32–34 (January 1963).

Oppenheimer, Schafer, and Stockham, *Proc. IEEE*, **56**:1264–1291 (August 1968). Discussion of an extension and generalization of the cepstrum, homomorphic filtering.

Papoulis, A., "Probability, Random Variables, and Stochastic Processes," McGraw-Hill Book Company, New York, 1965.

Rosenblatt, M. (ed.), "Time Series Analysis," John Wiley & Sons, Inc., New York, 1963. See particularly chap. 18 on cross-spectra, chap. 8 on the bispectrum, and chap. 15 on cepstrum techniques.

Various authors, *IEEE Trans. Audio Electroacoust.*, **AU-15**(2) (June 1967). See particularly the papers by Bingham, Godfrey, and Tukey on the fast Fourier transform and the paper by Cooley, Lewis, and Welch on the relationships between the Fourier transform and discrete Fourier series.

Various authors, *IEEE Trans. Audio Electroacoust.*, **AU-16**(3) (September 1968); **AU-18**(2) (June 1970). Designing digital filters.

Various authors, *IEEE Trans. Audio Electroacoust.*, **AU-17**(2) (June 1969). The fast Fourier transform and its applications.

Various authors, Technometrics, **3**(2) (May 1961). See particularly the papers by Jenkins and Parzen.

CHAPTER EIGHT

Visual and Auditory Perception—An Essay of Comparison

BELA JULESZ
IRA J. HIRSH

Introduction

The purpose of this study was to find analogies between visual and auditory pattern perception. This comparison was limited to relatively simple perceptual processes, since the higher symbolic processes exhibit features that are general properties of cognition rather than common properties of visual and auditory processing. Except for the influence of cognition and especially of language on perception [1], we will hold our discussion to more properly perceptual phenomena.

A few comments might be appropriate since it is now four years since this chapter was completed. While some visual and auditory parameters—such as brightness and loudness, or spatial extent in one dimension and time—lent themselves to comparisons, the inherently two- and three-dimensional spatial patterns in vision are very different from the one-dimensional temporal patterns in audition. In order to make such pattern comparisons more meaningful, we tried to draw analogies between two-dimensional brightness distributions on the retinae (and beyond) and the two-dimensional loudness distributions of time and pitch on cochlear levels (and beyond). The analogies which we have found between these patterns may be of some interest and have not been repudiated in the four ensuing years.

There is, however, a second approach for comparing patterns of the two modalities. Instead of trying to add a second dimension in audition, one can reduce visual patterns to one dimension. This can be done by varying the luminance distribution of a pattern in only one direction while keeping it constant in the perpendicular direction. We briefly mentioned the use of such patterns in the form of sinusoidal vertical gratings in vision and their visibility threshold as a function of spatial frequency and brightness contrast (modulation) in Sec. 8.3.2.3. However, it was not clear at the time that these modulation transfer functions in vision would mean more than the mathematical fact that any linear system (and many systems are linear near threshold) can be described as the sum of a set of orthonormal functions.

That the visual system *actually* performs spectral decomposition by spatial-frequency-tuned filters—and thus exhibits remarkable similarities to auditory spectral decomposition—is a new finding, obtained in recent years. Evidence for visual spectral decomposition comes from the pioneering work of Robson, Campbell, Pantle, Sekuler, Blakemore, and Sutton [2–5]. From frequency-dependent adaptation to critical bands [6] we can find similar phenomena for both modalities. Since much of auditory spectrum analysis is the result of the mechanical properties of the basilar membrane while its visual counterpart is carried out by neural processing, the many similarities might be just coincidental. However, the mechanical frequency tuning of the basilar membrane is very shallow, and early neural processes are sharpening the tuning by lateral inhibition (similarly to the Mach bands in vision). Furthermore, the phenomenon of residue (periodicity) pitch is based on auditory neural processes, and for this case the visual analogy might be genuine [7]. Some of these novel findings and their possible implications are discussed in a recent book by one of us [8].

Interestingly, while visual researchers are turning to the neglected aspects of visual frequency analysis, auditory neural experts in turn start to discover neural processes that take place in the temporal domain (and not in the frequency domain as previously thought).

If some of these new findings, particularly the auditory and visual spectral decomposition, were to be shown as being a fundamental principle of the central nervous system, we would have to reconsider the basic conclusions of this chapter. Until then, we present it almost in the same form as written four years ago. The only departure from the original is that we shortened it considerably and deleted an entire section on neurophysiology. Even now, so much more is known about the neurophysiology underlying visual perception than about its auditory counterpart that it is premature to draw parallels between them. While we regret that we could not update this chapter completely, we hope that it will inspire some of our readers to engage in their own comparative studies.

8.1 Orientation

Perception is the process whereby a living organism receives and interprets information about the surrounding world. The reception and interpretation are based upon an interaction between patterns of stimulation and patterns of neural activity, the latter being dependent on the sensory modality and various physiological states that are either genetically given or result from previous experience. In this section we wish to ask generally how perception works and whether in some ways it works similarly in vision and hearing. Perhaps there are special rules of perception depending on whether the perception is visual or auditory. The difference in modality is clear in sensory processes where elements are labeled with such terms as brightness, hue, and saturation, or loudness, pitch, and timbre. On the other hand, some of the higher-order patterns in the perception of form, space, melody, harmony, and speech may exhibit analogies in spite of the differences in their constituent parts.

8.1.1 On Perceptual Theory

Among the many theories of perception, summarized, for example, by F. H. Allport [9], one is impressed at how few arguments there appear to be concerning the same subject treated by different theorists and how many theories there are that do not concern the same subject. Some theoreticians seek to explain perceptual phenomena by appealing either to the character of elements in the stimulus array or to relations inherent in the structure of the array. Others are concerned with the influence of motivation on perception, almost to the exclusion of the stimulus. Still others devote themselves exclusively to the underlying physiological mechanisms. To find a general source from which to draw perceptual principles has been impossible. Most perceptual theory concerns vision: perception of color, form, motion, and depth. But, as has been pointed out [10], theory in hearing for a long time dealt only with loudness and pitch until Licklider [11] broadened the base of auditory theory to include auditory spatial localization, masking, speech perception, and signal detection.

We shall begin with visual theory, and especially those aspects that concern general properties of pattern perception as related to features of the stimulus configuration. What are some of the important concepts and "rules"? Can we progress from such concepts to audition, either directly or through some analogy? This procedure involves some difficulties because the vocabulary used in visual-perception theories is often special to vision. For example, while concepts like *figure, ground, form,* and *grouping* may be immediately applicable to several modalities of perception, others like *closedness, area,* and *object* have definite spatial properties that may be out of bounds for a theory about nonspatial patterns. In this latter case, we will have to invent some analogies or systems of translation.

Although the paucity of theory in audition makes the attempt to go in the reverse direction less promising (that is, from auditory concepts to their visual counterparts), one recent development in speech perception is interesting. Remember that in psychology the structuralists sought to understand perception by trying to decompose complex percepts into simple sensory attributes. The important contribution of the gestalt psychologists was to emphasize that the whole is more than the sum of its parts; a final percept is always more than the simple combination of the sensory elements. The global perception arose from local interrelations in the physical stimulus pattern according to some organizational principles.

Now the theory of speech perception has undergone a similar history. Very little attention was paid to speech perception during an epoch rich in studies on sensory attributes in hearing. An implicit faith in our ability to predict speech perception from knowledge of acoustical analysis of the speech sounds and the psychophysics of the analyzed acoustic dimensions expressed a structuralist attitude [12]. More recently, however, speech perception has been influenced by the considerable work of the linguists, and we are told that simple properties like loudness and pitch will not suffice, and even that facts related to the intelligibility of single words are insufficient. Speech perception must be understood within the framework of the global structural properties of the language being spoken [13, 14].

The visual analog is now becoming evident also. Those who want to build machines to recognize patterns find inadequate those perceptual theories based on lists of properties of patterns [15]. They seem to require a scheme more like that of a language in which the principles of pattern recognition are generated like those of a grammar.

8.1.2 Visual and Auditory Processes Compared

There have been many previous attempts to compare vision and hearing, at least with respect to sensory processes at a peripheral level [16–18].

There are clear differences with respect to specialized cells for transducing either light or sound energy, and also with respect to the specific attributes associated with light and sound. But Stevens [19] has called our attention to similarities as well, including the generation of electrical potentials at the sensory receptors, the sensitivities of these receptors which come close to theoretical quantal efficiency, the comparable dynamic ranges, and even the phenomenon of brightness or loudness recruitment under special conditions. He has also shown [20] how ubiquitous is the psychophysical power law that relates sensory magnitude to stimulus intensity, not only for several modalities but also for several psychological dimensions within modalities. Both vision and audition include sensory attributes that exemplify *prothetic* and *metathetic* psychophysical scales (like brightness or loudness and visual area or pitch), the former varying according to the increasing or decreasing of the number of elements stimulated and the latter according to the stimulation of different sensory elements.

The phenomenon of masking is yet another instance where data and theoretical work related to physiological mechanisms have shown striking similarities between the two senses. The sensory surfaces of eye and ear, on which visual space and one aspect of auditory pitch seem to be laid out, are characterized by zones, subsequently sharpened to the requirements of visual acuity or pitch discrimination by neural excitatory and inhibitory mechanisms [21, 22]. Such sharpenings exhibit similar time courses, which are revealed in measurements of metacontrast and backward masking [23] as minimum separable distances in vision or as critical bands in audition. (Further analogies to critical bands were given in the introduction to this chapter.)

We note, anticipating our discussion of the figure-ground phenomenon, that the theory of signal detectability, derived from the field of statistical communication theory, has been applied, tested, and found fruitful as a generator of models for both auditory and visual detection of signals in noise [24].

Information theory provides another link between sensory processes. Since the auditory and optic nerves have many properties in common, it is not surprising that several studies have compared the rate of information for the two modalities [17, 25, 26]. These rates are much higher than any practical value obtained for the entire processing chain. Information theory has been useful to students of perception, both as a model and as a guide in experimentation [18].

In short, there are already many bases for comparing and for distinguishing vision and audition on the level of sensory processing. Our present concern, however, directs us to that somewhat higher and more complex level which psychologists have called *perception*.

8.1.2.1 Visual and Auditory Perceptual Processes Compared

In spite of similarities discussed above, the differences between the two modalities are more characteristic. In the preceding comparison, the sensory surfaces of eye and ear were regarded as neural arrays which process the information in *parallel.* Many of the more central processes appear to operate *sequentially,* and perhaps one fundamental difference between vision and audition is that visual processes occur in parallel much further along the chain than do auditory processes. However, at the processing level, where stimuli are discriminated along several dimensions, some recent work by Egeth suggests that even visual discrimination involves the processing of features serially [27].

Some other fundamental modality differences and their implications are more obvious. For instance, the fact that the eyes can be closed whereas the ears cannot indicates that hearing can act as an "early warning system," alerting and orienting the visual system before an object can be sighted. The small spatial angle of visual resolution requires complete attention for viewing, whereas listening does not. Complicated kinesthetic and proprioceptive feedback systems are used to keep the target of interest fixated (converged and focused on the foveas). Even entire auditory pathways are committed to serve visual attention, as might be inferred from the recent anatomical study of different animals by Harrison and Irving [28], who found linear correlation between the number of cells in the nucleus of the sixth cranial nerve (one of the motor nuclei concerned with eye movement) and the number of cells in the medial superior olivary nucleus (of the auditory system), except for bat and dolphin (the echo-locating animals). Thus in diurnal animals, and in nocturnal animals with good night vision, the medial superior olivary nucleus appears to be concerned with the pointing of the head and eye in the direction of a source of sound. We shall consider further aspects of attention in Sec. 8.3.2.3.

8.1.3 Levels of Sophistication of Perceptual Models

In the foregoing orientation, we asked how perception works. Historically, what amounts to the "understanding" of a certain phenomenon may pass through several developmental levels of increasing sophistication. As an example we take perceptual closure in vision. First it was observed that small gaps and imperfections in outlined drawings were not noticed. Then it was realized that this is a general tendency and this "filling in" phenomenon was elevated to the "law of closure." At the next stage, explanations of closure were sought outside the discipline by using analogies from hydrodynamics or electromagnetic fields [29]. A next level aimed at a more plausible, general explanation within the discipline itself by using models of neural summation and propagation in neural nets. Recently some specific neural units have been found by the neurophysiologists (such as Hubel and Wiesel's hypercomplex units) which seem to account for the psychological phenomenon [30].

In this section we will try to compare visual and auditory perception on whatever level of sophistication is possible. Unfortunately only a few phenomena have reached the level of neurophysiological explanation, and they are mostly visual examples. Nevertheless, comparisons even at the level of analogies can be very revealing. We illustrate by an interesting example. Suppose we were told about a hypothetical black box that had the following properties, properties that characterize the structures underlying form perception both on a psychological and physiological level: (1) many memories for forms can be stored in the same structure without affecting each other, (2) certain memories can be associated together and evoking one of them will retrieve the others, (3) one memorized form can be retrieved by a similar stimulus at a different location and size, (4) extirpation of a large percent of the structure will not affect the performance, and (5) the more the input stimulus resembles the memorized image, the sharper the recalled function. If a black box with these properties had been presented to us, say five years ago, without hesitation we would have identified it with the brain of some higher animals. These properties seemed very mysterious and too unrelated to each other to suggest any other possibility. Recently, however, such properties have been demonstrated in hologram recordings as pointed out by Julesz and Pennington [31]. Of course, it is not suggested that brains store visual information as holograms, but it is revealing that some simple linear optical phenomena show such a striking analogy. Even the extirpation analogy holds, since any amorphic fragment of a diffusion-type hologram plate contains the original information and can be used for reconstructing the entire scene (with reduced signal-to-noise ratio). To those who think that such an analogy is useless or even comical, we would note that Lashley [32] and many neurophysiologists searched unsuccessfully for a location for the engram. It seems worthwhile, therefore, to explore any avenue, however bizarre, that indicates at least some promise.

8.2 Characteristics of Perception

Perception gives information about the world around us. Some of the differences between the spatial patterns of vision and the temporal patterns of hearing, which seem so very basic, become more easily understood as we consider the several kinds of information provided through the senses. There appear to be at least three classes of such information, in terms of its purpose or goal for the perceiver:

1. Perception gives information on the basis of which the perceiver can know the presence of and recognize *objects* in his environment.

2. Perception can part from the object per se and be concentrated on received information in the form of *signs*, as in the case of communication, whether through language or art forms.

3. Perception can also serve as a tool whereby the perceiver builds up *concepts*, not only those that are specific to certain modalities, but more importantly such general dimensions of experience as space and time, those basic aspects that form the matrix on which all perception is laid.

8.2.1 Perception of Objects

Both visual and auditory perception inform us of the presence of objects by decoding the stimulus patterns that characterize them. It is these coded patterns, usually reflected or radiated light or sound waves, that are perceived and not the objects themselves, as was pointed out centuries ago. We do not perceive an object directly; we infer its properties by decoding these patterns. Physical objects are usually covered by textured surfaces, whose grain and sharp discontinuities at the contours make visual recognition possible, as pointed out by Gibson [33]. (A patternless, uniformly illuminated surface is either invisible or visually ambiguous.) Similarly, acoustic patterns characterize for hearing certain properties of the objects from which the sounds emanate or are reflected.

We mean by "objects" things that occupy space and can be measured or specified in spatial terms. An object thus defined can be inferred by a perceiver on the basis of auditory, visual, olfactory, gustatory, or tactile patterns, or combinations of these. We have stated already that physical objects themselves are not perceived directly, but in vision the surfaces of objects can be perceived and reflect the spatial attributes of the stimulus pattern. Therefore, it is customary to regard the term "object" as the referent for a visual percept. It has seemed difficult for us, however, to use "object" in an analogous way as the referent for an auditory percept. The more appropriate stimulus configuration for auditory perception is an *event;* that is, a pattern of change in time whose physical description may not at all be a thing spatially definable [34]. In discussing this first function of perception, we do mean real, thing-like objects, and we recognize that visual perception probably exceeds the auditory with respect to this function.

Events (i.e., patterns in time) will be discussed in the next section, on sign perception. Here we note only that vision, of course, is also able to detect events. Nevertheless, the perceivable temporal changes of visual information are very limited when compared to auditory perception. For instance, speeds of Morse code perception drop by at least five times when a light signal is used instead of a buzzer [18]. The highest temporal resolution in vision is about 16 frames per second for continuous motion perception, and about 60 Hz is the flicker threshold for bright illumination. The auditory temporal resolution is about two orders of magnitude higher. For example, 1,000 interruptions per second of auditory white noise can be perceived [35], and at 5,000 Hz there is some neurophysiological evidence for traces of temporal analysis [36].

It should be emphasized that our visual environment is relatively stable in time; it is very seldom turned on or off suddenly. This is one reason why the visual phenomenological space can be built up by successive fixation motions of the eyes into a static image. On the other hand, auditory patterns are dynamic, never constant, rapidly changing in time. (In postulating that no auditory objects exist, we neglect the fact that sound sources can be found and located by hearing, and a crude estimation can be given of their size and distance. We shall return to this point later.)

Our constant awareness of sounds and auditory noises in our environment—the familiar humming of a transformer, typewriter sounds, the quiet noise of a fan, etc.—are signaling the presence of objects without our having to inspect them continuously. Nevertheless, we would not regard these familiar auditory patterns as auditory objects. We come to this distinction when the perception of signs is discussed. Our maxim of emphasizing visual objects and auditory events should be taken cautiously.

Man can distinguish an abstracted object from the coded pattern that represents it, but in lower animals the coded pattern of an object and the object itself seem inseparable. For example, the frog recognizes edible objects and potential predators by vision, but mating partners by audition. Certain simple pattern codes, like curvature, will reveal whether a bug or a snake approaches, and thus whether to attack or to escape [37]. Similarly, the presence or absence of low- or high-frequency components in a croak will give a bullfrog sufficient information about the species, sex, and age of a potential companion [38]. These acoustic and optic codes are rather simple structurally and appear to be genetically determined. This example demonstrates that for some species the different modalities can be complementary.

It is even tempting to stretch our frog story to man. The frog's vision aids his personal survival, connects him with his environment. His hearing links him to his species. A blind man is cut off in major ways from his environment, and cannot survive without some aid. He does not, however, feel cut off from his society of fellow men. A deaf man, on the other hand, while quite able to cope with his physical environment and to survive, feels alienated from his society. Of course, this analogy between frog and man is not phylogenic, since several species exist where the roles of vision and hearing are somewhat reversed (e.g., bats).

8.2.2 Perception of Signs

Let us continue our analogy. Man can cope with his physical environment if he can recognize objects and manipulate them and himself. He feels alienated from his society when he cannot communicate with others. To say that vision mediates the former function while audition mediates the latter is too simple, because contrary examples can easily be found. What is clear, however, is that processes involved in recognizing signs in the context of some language system, whether natural, mathematical, or esthetic, operate somewhat differently from those that give information concerning objects.

Auditory recognition of a particular talker is close to object perception. But we do not have to identify the talker when the task is to understand what he is saying. In perceiving a passage of music, one hears the melody, the harmony, the structure, the composer's grammar—one often does not perceive the sound-producing objects as objects. As one regards a painting he perceives what is portrayed—not the canvas, the pigments, etc. Whether one uses his eyes to receive the spatial patterns of a painting or a sculpture, or his ears to receive the temporal patterns of music or poetry, or uses both to receive the spatiotemporal patterns of the ballet, he is using perception in a manner much more like that in communication. Perhaps one essential difference between artistic communication and ordinary language communication is that in the former the codebooks and grammars are not always explicitly shared by sender and receiver, whereas in the latter they usually are.

Painters, until the nineteenth century, did try to represent objects. They were making icons, that is, signs that bore a resemblance to the things signified [39]. As painting developed, impressions became relatively more important, until recently when very abstract designs are commonly used, parting almost entirely from a physical representation of things. In music, on the other hand, early composers did not imitate real sounds of nature. Their constructions from the beginning were rather arbitrary patterns of melody and then harmony, patterns that were generated by obeying some historically developed conventions. Later on, a kind of impressionism characterized the romantic period, but it is only recently that composers have gone beyond the traditional sound-making capacities of instruments to create sounds and stochastic patterns (some of which resemble the noises of the environment). The histories are almost reversed.

Of course, there are many species (including man) that use signs, not icons, or that can be trained to use signs which originally, before some learning, did not represent the thing signified. All forms of conditioning exemplify this role of sign as a conditioned stimulus. A further distinction, made by Morris [40], is that between symbols and signs. Symbols are used in language systems. They differ from other signs in two respects: First, their use requires a grammar, and second, they are producible by the users. The requirement of producibility appears to offer another visual-auditory distinction within the perception of communication. Natural language most often involves the auditory messages of speech, while the language of gesture or of facial and bodily expression of affect and attitude employs visual patterns in addition to voice. Except for writing and reading, vision in direct interpersonal communication remains essentially passive, the receiver alone, while audition always accompanies the production of one's own speech. The feedback so important for speech, permitting precision both in sending and receiving, is carried by auditory signals. We do not ordinarily look at ourselves when we transmit gestures or facial expression. Whatever feedback exists is a very crude kinesthetic and somaesthetic one.

A particular case of visual sign processing is the reading of written symbols. Poor readers seem to convert the visual text into an "inner speech." On the other hand, there are experienced readers who can read text or musical scores without inner speech or singing, and at very high rates. Some reports by Sperry indicate that patients whose corpus collosum has been cut can read and carry out instructions with their "speechless" nondominant hemisphere [41]. Thus perception of written texts may be independent of their auditory representations.

At this point the question of dual, audiovisual signs might be discussed. Day and Beach [42] have reported a large number of retention studies which indicate that combined audiovisual presentation is superior to a simple modality for the retention of information. Also there are many examples in which the two modalities transmitted together give more information than either alone [17] and also give the feeling of reality and presence (movies, television) which to a great extent are missing in radio or silent movies. Also in emergency warning situations it is more effective to address an alarm to both sense channels simultaneously [17].

It should be noted in this context again, to quote R. Jakobson [39], that a complex visual sign involves a set of simultaneous constituents, while a complex auditory sign primarily consists of successive constituents. (Of course, written text is sequentially processed, while chords, polyphony, orchestration, and formants of speech are manifestations of simultaneity in audition. But the dominant role is assumed by the sequence in audition and simultaneity in vision.)

8.2.3 An Experiential Framework

Our discussion of figures against backgrounds, of patterns that are fixed or change with time, and of modes of processing and decoding in the nervous system presupposes a framework upon which such phenomena are laid. For such a framework we will borrow the basic dimensions of space and time from the physicist. Here, however, we note that one's conceptions of space, size, and distance and of time, duration, temporal order, and speed are constructed out of perceptual experience. Here is yet another function of perception, different from that of recognizing things and of receiving messages.

One's concept of space and of distance appears to require some coordination between the visual and the motor systems. A combination of tactile and motor patterns alone appears to generate a rather punctiform, discontinuous notion of space, at least according to such reports as those of von Senden [43] on persons who are born blind. Less anecdotally Held and Hein [44] have also suggested that the superposition of visual experience on the field in which motor behavior takes place is necessary for the creation of certain spatial notions like the distance of a surface.

One's concepts of time, duration, or speed, however, appear to be rather intimately connected with auditory patterns. Hirsh, Bilger, and Deatherage [45] showed that the apparent duration of either a sound or a light was modified considerably by the presence of background noise but was invariant with changes in ambient light. Subjective and anecdotal reports from persons who lose their hearing suggest that the dynamic, ongoing, time-varying characteristic of the environment disappears when the sounds that accompany such changes are removed. The main point here is, of course, not so much this apparent separation of visual and auditory function with respect to space and time but rather that even such basic notions as space and time in the observing individual are built out of different kinds of perceptual experience.

This section represents an attempt to delineate three different ways in which information in the external world is abstracted to a perceiving individual as (1) objects, (2) signs, and (3) concepts. The classification will be useful only insofar as it helps us present material on the ways in which this external information is received, decoded, and repatterned.

8.3 Some-thing or Not-thing: The Figure-Ground Problem

The very essence of visual perception is to find a certain object amid a vast number of unimportant ones without effort or delay. This is such an important requirement that the perceptual system has to possess inherently the ability to separate object from background. For some simple visual systems, including that of the frog, this problem is solved by feature extractors (receptive fields) most of which respond to *moving* objects. For organisms whose biological makeup permits the luxury of ignoring the still background with all its complexity this is a simple solution. The probability that more than one fly-sized moving object will enter the visual field of the frog at a given instant is small. On the other hand, the problem of finding a needle in a haystack is eliminated. Our peripheral vision is somewhat reminiscent of this ancient solution. No stationary small object can be perceived in our periphery, but a moving or flickering object is immediately detected [46].

A different mechanism must be used for *stationary* objects in human foveal vision, and this is shown by the *figure-ground* phenomenon. Here the name "figure" is somewhat deceptive. It does not refer to some recognized, familiar figure. Instead, it refers to the fact that patterns having certain properties (to be discussed below) are perceived as sharp, definite "things" and are called *figures,* while the rest is perceived as some "substance" and is the *ground.* This perceptual change is particularly noticeable when two domains have a common boundary, most often experienced in outline drawings. The more equal in strength those organizational properties are which influence figure perception for the two domains, the easier it is to reverse them perceptually. The most important aspect of figure-ground perception, whether stable or reversible, is the fact that only one perceptual organization can be experienced at a time. It is impossible to perceive both domains as two figures or as two grounds simultaneously.

This emergence of figure from ground occurs effortlessly and spontaneously. It was regarded by the gestalt psychologists and more recently by Hebb as basic for perception [47]. As we have said, "figure" in this context does not refer to a recognizable object but to a perceptual change which converts an area inside a contour into a sharp, well-defined and remembered entity, whereas areas outside the contour become indefinite, blurred and forgotten. For two-dimensional drawings the figure may even appear to be in depth in front of the ground.

8.3.1 Gestalt Rules and Visual Figure-Ground

In order to study figure-ground perception, Rubin [48] in 1915 used ambiguous stimuli, in which figure and ground perception could be reversed. These stimuli were extensively used by the gestalt school in formulating their well known "rules" of perceptual organization [49]. The five most important ones (for vision) may be ranked as follows:

1. *Proximity and similarity.* Spatially adjacent units of similar brightness, color, and shape form connected clusters. The precise meaning of similarity as it applies to cluster formation was recently clarified [50]. Only brightness or hue values which are adjacent can be "grouped" into a cluster. For instance, proximate red and yellow dots can be perceived as one cluster, and so can proximate green and blue dots, but red with green or yellow with blue dots do not form clusters.

2. *Area.* The smaller a closed region (within the limits of visual acuity), the more it tends to be seen as a figure (see Fig. 8.1); and obviously the larger the area of a region is, the more it appears to be the ground.

3. *Closedness.* Areas with closed contours tend to be perceived more often as figure than areas with open contours (see Fig. 8.2).

4. *Symmetry.* The more symmetrical a closed region is, the more likely it is to appear as figure. The greater the number of symmetries the region possesses, the stronger this tendency (see Fig. 8.3).

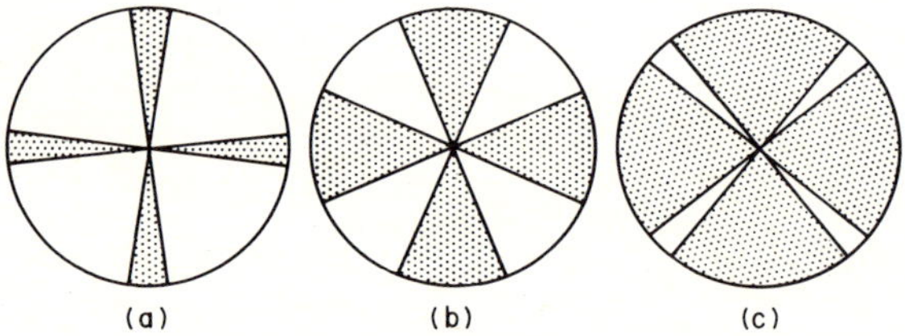

Fig. 8.1. The role of area in figure-ground perception. The smaller area tends to be perceived as the figure, thus in (*a*) the figure is a wheel with black spokes, in (*c*) it is a wheel with white spokes, and in (*b*) it is ambiguous. From J. E. Hochberg, "Perception," Prentice Hall, Inc., New York, 1964, with permission from author and publisher.

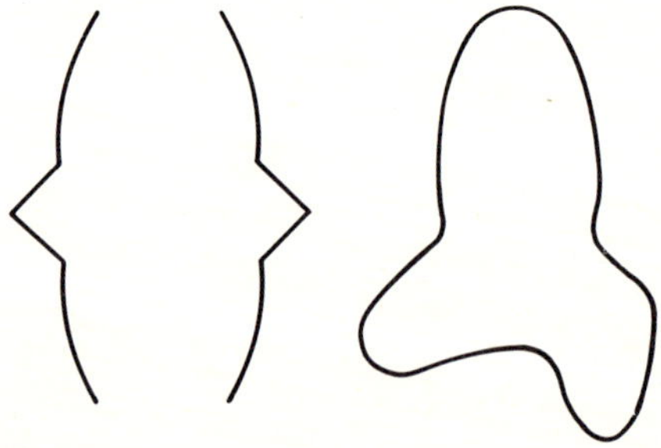

Fig. 8.2. Demonstration that the rules of closedness override the importance of symmetry. The open symmetric drawing tends less to be perceived as the figure than the closed asymmetric drawing. From J. E. Hochberg, "Perception," Prentice Hall, Inc., New York, 1964, with permission from author and publisher.

Fig. 8.3. Demonstration that the rules of area override the importance of symmetry. The symmetric white stripes are less often perceived as the figure than the asymmetric stripes of smaller areas. From J. E. Hochberg, "Perception," Prentice Hall, Inc., New York, 1964, with permission from author and publisher.

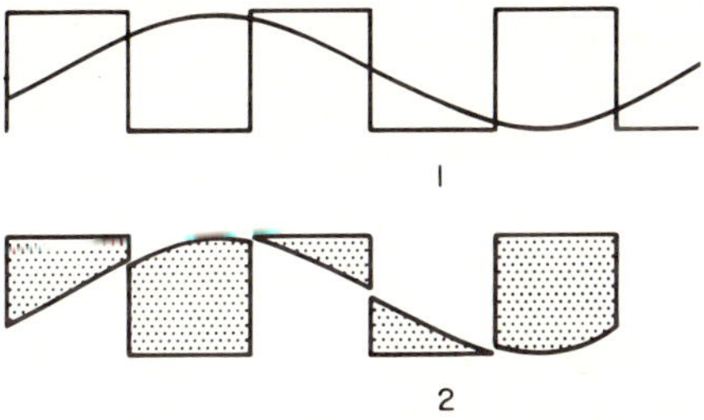

Fig. 8.4. Demonstration that the rules of area can override the importance of "good continuation." From J. E. Hochberg, "Perception," Prentice Hall, Inc., New York, 1964, with permission from author and publisher.

5. *Smooth continuation.* Among many possible perceptual organizations, those that will minimize changes or interruptions in the contours of the perceived constituents will be perceived as figures (see Fig. 8.4).

The importance of figure-ground reversal and, more generally, of ambiguous figures is that these perceptual factors can be added or juxtaposed in various amounts and their perceptual weights determined. A hierarchy of figure formation exists. First, proximate points of similar brightness or color clusters or lines. In the case of lines, the closure of lines forms outlined clusters. Smooth continuation resolves ambiguities at places where outlines cross. Both clusters and outlined clusters determine an area. The smaller the area is, the more it is perceived as a figure (provided it is above resolution limit). Other properties of the clusters, such as orientation, perimeter-to-area fraction, convexity, etc., may then be evaluated. Finally, the symmetries are observed.

This local formation of *micropatterns* can be extended to *macropatterns* as well, provided these macropatterns are the *elements* of a larger set. Textures (see below), composed of familiar objects, can be organized into figure and ground. As an example, think of a wallpaper of randomly or periodically presented familiar forms. Similar forms in proximity will be perceived as a cluster of roses or elephants or whatever the wallpaper portrays. Whether the cluster of roses or elephants will be seen as figure or ground will depend on the above discussed organizational factors. Thus if the clusters of roses are of much smaller area fraction than the clusters of elephants, then the rose-clusters will be seen as figures in the ground formed by elephant cluster. Of course, in case of familiar shapes some perceptual bias might enter, but in this context we can ignore the enigmatic processes of shape recognition.

In these examples both micropatterns and macropatterns were regarded as *local* elements out of which the perceptual organization formed *global* entities, such as figure or ground. This figure-ground dichotomy is the simplest case of perceptual organization that exhibits ambiguity. The perception of ambiguous figures in general is a more complex phenomenon than figure and ground reversal and is often studied in perception (e.g., Boring's young-wife mother-in-law figure [51]). Nevertheless the understanding of figure-ground perception in both visual and auditory perception is an ambitious enough goal, without considering the complicated ambiguous figures.

In random arrays only clusters of similar dots are perceived, whereas other combinations of nonsimilar dots occurring with even higher probability may pass unnoticed as shown by Julesz [50] and reproduced

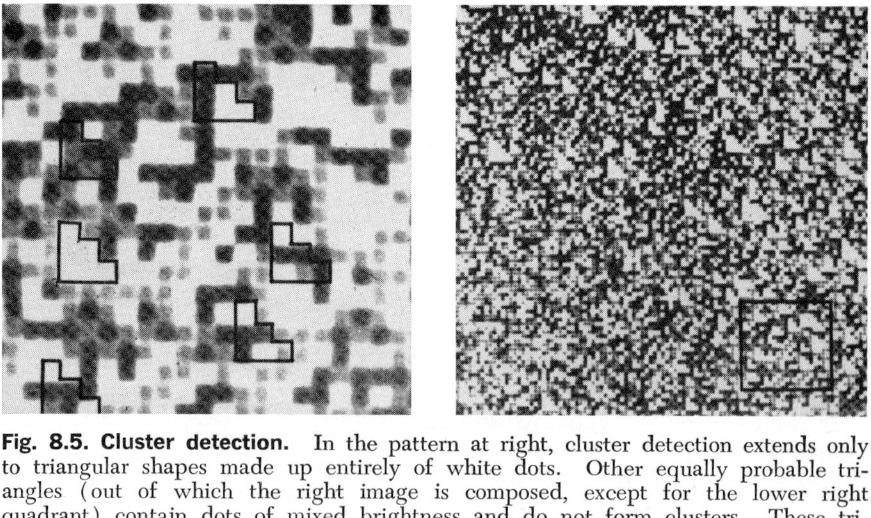

Fig. 8.5. Cluster detection. In the pattern at right, cluster detection extends only to triangular shapes made up entirely of white dots. Other equally probable triangles (out of which the right image is composed, except for the lower right quadrant) contain dots of mixed brightness and do not form clusters. These triangles are marked in the enlargement at left. From B. Julesz, Visual Pattern Discrimination, *IRE Trans. Inform. Theory,* **IT-8:**84–92, 1962, with permission of publisher.

in Fig. 8.5. In a two-dimensional random array it is impossible to attend to a given point domain which is not a cluster. In a one-dimensional array this visual task is easier. It is possible to pick out brightness or line sequences from a random background. If the two-dimensional visual patterns are not random but occur *repeatedly*, the detection of these repeated unfamiliar complex domains is possible. This will be discussed later in the context of periodicity or rhythm perception. Without recurrent sequences only simple sequences or clusters of similar elements can be detected. This statement is restricted to effortless, spontaneous perception only. If learning is permitted, sequences of high complexity might become familiar enough to emerge as figures. These higher processes of memory and learning are not reviewed here.

8.3.2 Auditory Figure-Ground

The integrity of perceived structure in spite of a change in the elements was pointed out explicitly by von Ehrenfels, who observed that a melodic form remained the same when a key change was made that changed all of the notes but kept the relations among them the same [52]. This auditory example for later gestalt theory gradually was succeeded by visual ones, and vision has been the predominant subject of gestalt theory ever since. How applicable are the rules for visual figure-ground perception in hearing?

Auditory figures or clusters stand out from auditory grounds as events or discrete occurrences. Within auditory perception, the important figure is the message, the happening—in contrast to a ground that is an ongoing accompaniment, often not even noticed. Whether or not we can find parallels in hearing to the gestalt rules listed above will depend in part on how we translate the spatial and visual terms of those rules. One possible translation is to substitute time for the horizontal dimension of visual space, and frequency for the vertical dimension, but there are some difficulties that will appear presently. This time-frequency substitution for the X and Y dimensions of space is, of course, a device that has been used by composers for a long time in musical notation, precisely a system for representing to the eye the frequency variation in time of musical tones. The more recently created visible-speech spectrogram uses the same translation.

A second representation of auditory figure-ground relations is in terms of the physical separation of sound sources in a perceived auditory space, given by the interaural time and intensity differences. This spatial separation is probably less important in hearing than in vision, since, as we suggested, object finding is a relatively unimportant process in auditory perception.

8.3.2.1 Auditory-Temporal Figure-Ground

Adopting our first rule of space-time translation, we review the visual rules.

1. *Proximity and similarity.* In visual space, elements that are close together and are similar tend to form clusters that become figures. Proximity, even along this single dimension, appears to hold for time as well. A series of clicks or bursts of tone in which elements recur with perfectly regular periodicity does not ordinarily yield figure perception. Temporal clusters compellingly appear when a subgroup of clicks occurs together, closer in time than those of the regular, background series. Although speech forms a more or less continuous sound over long times, segmentation and the identification of syllables, words, and tunes partially results from the temporal proximity of intrasyllabic elements.

In rhythmic grouping, a repeated pattern of different elements in a measure gives rise to rhythmic figures. Rhythmic groups are formed in spite of periodic regularity when, for example, every second sound is different from the others in loudness, duration, or pitch. The "accented notes" are similar to each other and are different from the unaccented ones. Musical rhythm is an excellent example of the operation of different kinds of similarity; "keeping time" is the connecting of successive beats with similar elements regularly spaced even at very long periods, and those similar elements may themselves comprise complex patterns that yield higher-order rhythms. Thus the law of proximity for grouping appears to apply to all dimensions of visual space and to the time dimension of hearing.

If, now, in hearing, we turn to the vertical or pitch dimension, the parallel is more complicated. A unidimensional vertical array of elements (a thin vertical line of dots on the spectrogram) is a very brief sound with many frequency components. Within the brief event, closer spacing of the frequency components probably does not yield figurelike clusters. (The harmonic relations among the components that give rise to concepts like consonance and dissonance conflict with simple proximity of pitch.) In speech, again, we may find the exception. The harmonics of the voice are equally separated on a linear scale of frequency, but certain groups of them get reinforced by resonant properties of the vocal tract. These "formants" do not stand out as separate figures but turn out to be the bases for identifying the spoken vowels.

2. *Area.* The smaller the relative area of a visual cluster, the easier it is to perceive it as figure. This principle holds for auditory perception as well, but mostly in the single dimension of time where a component of area corresponds to length or duration. The crack of a rifle shot

appears to be more easily heard as a figure than the longer buildup and decay of a jet airplane. If the visual pattern consists of black and white random dots in a two-dimensional tessellation, then an area fraction $\phi = 0.15$ of white dots will be perceived as white specks on a black "tabletop" by all subjects, whereas $\phi = 0.75$ will be perceived as black specks on a white tabletop [53]. Similarly, if the loudnesses of two discriminable segments A and B form a sequence, such as AAABAAAABBAABAA most subjects will perceive clusters of B as figure in a homogeneous background composed of A's. Of course, if the loudnesses are not identical, the situation changes, but this is true for vision as well, if for instance brightness or hue is also introduced.

The area principle may also be applied in the Y dimension, or pitch. Just as *brief* clusters appear as figures on longer background elements (along the time axis) so also small changes in pitch within a cluster are more easily heard as figures (parts of melody for example) than wide excursions. Miller and Taylor [35] and Heise [54] reported the perception of a simple melodic pattern in which there was a regular alternation between two frequencies. When frequencies became widely separated, however, the melodic pattern broke into two figures, each belonging to one of the frequencies used.

3. *Closedness.* This principle requires at least two dimensions in order to operate. For one-dimensional auditory patterns, such as temporal sequences of identical sounds (e.g., drumbeats), it is not possible to imagine a closed figure. In the frequency-time domain, a melodic line formed by rules of harmony, like dominant to tonic, can be regarded as a kind of closure. Here we have to assume that our space is closed by gluing together the beginning and the end of our time scale. It seems to us that the lack of real closed figures in auditory perception is not due to the features of auditory events but rather to the unidirectionality of time. As time advances, the perceptual response function rapidly decays, and the beginning and end points of a temporal event are very differently weighted and are difficult to "close."

Perceptual closure in vision—that is, the neglecting of small gaps in an outlined drawing—is often believed to belong to this category. In reality closure is a special case of smooth continuation, and will be mentioned in point 5 below.

4. *Symmetry.* The perception of symmetries contributes to figure-ground perception, although less importantly than the previous factors. The perception of geometrical symmetries is a special case of the perceptual invariances. Geometrical symmetries are defined by those transformations (rotations, translations, and reflections) which leave the stimulus invariant. Some of these symmetries can be perceived easily, others only with difficulty. The perceptual constancies or invariances are those

more general transformations of the stimulus under which the perceived gestalt stays invariant. The best known perceptual invariances in vision are brightness constancy, size constancy, and translational invariance. An object does not change perceptually as its brightness, size, or location varies within reasonable limits.

These invariances exist for auditory perception as well. A melody or a spoken word does not change perceptually if the loudness, duration, or relative pitch position is changed. The principle of duration invariance (size constancy) is less obvious, since playing back a recorded speech at higher speed produces the "Donald Duck" effect (earthquake records can be speeded up to sound like little chirps [55]), increasing the pitch as well as the speed. Playback at lower-than-recorded speeds results in the reversed effect. If the change in pitch with changed playback durations is compensated (using some complex mechanical or electronic circuitry for frequency multiplication or division), speech remains intelligible at half or double rates [162]. Melodies, like Wagner's *leitmotifs* for the young and old Siegfried, can be contracted or expanded in time (different musical tempi) without impairing their recognition.

Some other perceptual constancies prevalent in vision, such as rotational invariance and invariance under affine transformations, have no counterpart in audition. Probably, perception of these invariances has evolved because of the importance of perceiving rigid objects unchanged under the various perspective projections on the retinas. Since no auditory rigid body exists, such an auditory invariance is unlikely to be represented in the auditory system.

Whether a certain geometrical symmetry possessed by an object is directly coded by the perceptual system is an important question in perception. Fig. 8.6 shows a random-dot pattern with a horizontal axis of bilateral symmetry. This horizontal symmetry is not immediately apparent, but becomes obvious as we rotate the image by 90 degrees, and the axis of symmetry becomes vertical [57]. Thus the bilateral symmetry of the stimulus is not equally extracted by the visual system for various directions. This was first noted by Mach [58] for simple clusters, but as we just discussed, it holds for complex displays as well. This bilateral or mirror symmetry is only immediately apparent close to the axis and as we go further from the axis we have to scrutinize the stimulus for large clusters.

In auditory perception, mirror symmetry or reflection plays a far less important part, probably because events in real life are not reversible in time. A melody changes considerably if played backward (time reflection), and for the nonprofessional listener it is hard to recognize frequency reflection when it is used in the construction of a fugue.

Fig. 8.6. Demonstration that bilateral symmetry across a horizontal axis of symmetry is less well perceived than across a vertical axis. From B. Julesz, Suppression of Monocular Symmetry during Binocular Fusion without Rivalry, *Bell Syst. Tech. J.*, **46:** 1203–1221, 1967, with permission of publisher.

Repetition, on the other hand, is easily perceived both in visual and auditory patterns. Group theory of finite order describes all possible one-, two-, and three-dimensional repetitions. These groups, known as Federov groups, describe crystal structures as well as the ornamentational art. Figure 8.7 shows a simple one-dimensional repetition of a random two-dimensional array, whereas Fig. 8.8 shows the same repetition in two dimensions. There are seven linear Federov groups shown in Fig. 8.9, and 17 Federov groups in the plane. It is interesting to note that the masters of ornamentation have in practice discovered all ornamentational symmetries; it fell to the theory of groups centuries later to prove that no other forms exist. Out of the seven linear Federov groups in Fig. 8.9 only L_1 and L_3 can be generated in time alone. For the other groups a second dimension, most likely frequency, has to be included. The flags could be phonemic or melodic patterns. The abscissa corresponds to time, the ordinate to frequency. It remains to be seen whether all seven linear Federov groups (auditory ornaments) when generated from different flags (micromelodies) could be discriminated from each other by hearing alone.

L_1 discrimination was investigated with random auditory sequences of duration T periodically repeated, by Guttman and Julesz [163]. As long as $T < 1$ s the repetition can be effortlessly perceived. For periodicities: $4\text{ s} > T > 1$ s the repetition can be still perceived, but with great effort, whereas for $T > 4$ s the repeated segments sound like noise without repetition. These experiments were performed with segments of random elements. When learning is permitted, of course

Fig. 8.7. Periodicity perception of seven picture element wide horizontal stripes which are repeated in the vertical direction only.

Fig. 8.8. Periodicity perception of a 20 × 20 random-dot array repeated in two dimensions.

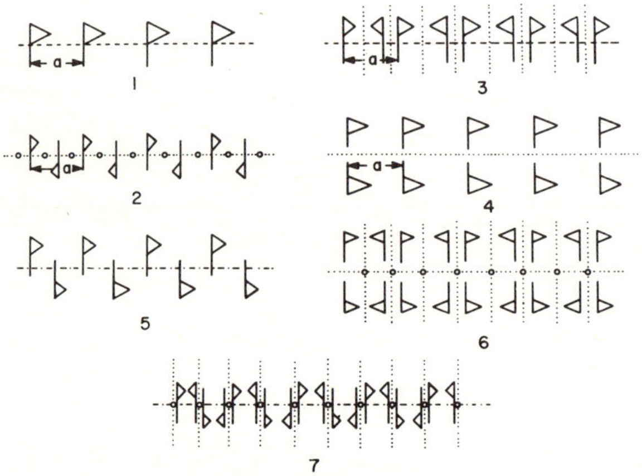

Fig. 8.9. The seven linear Fedorov groups used in ornamentation. From A. D. Aleksandrov, A. N. Kolmogorov, and M. A. Lavrent'ev, "Mathematics: Its Content, Methods, and Meaning," MIT Press, Cambridge, Mass., 1963.

complex repetitions can be perceived such as a musical theme with all its variations.

5. *Smooth continuation.* This organizational principle, like closedness, requires a two-dimensional space. In the frequency-time domain there exist good auditory analogs for smooth continuation. For instance, each of the several voices in a choral piece or a string quartet shows smooth continuation. Although the melodies often cross each other,

we can perceive the continuity of the unitary melodic lines. A higher degree of complexity appears in counterpoint where each melodic line can keep its identity, but in addition a new organization takes place and the different parts are also perceived in a larger structure.

Not only melodic lines show features of continuation in hearing. The speech of different talkers contains features like those of melody that persist over time. When we hear a number of speakers simultaneously, we can keep track of the speech of any particular one. This ability is helped by binaural hearing, but it exists monaurally as well. Even if recorded speech is periodically interrupted, and further, if the silent gaps are now filled with noise, the perception of speech proceeds in a manner analogous to the viewing of a scene through a picket fence [60]. Whether the structural features in spoken sound patterns show this continuation by virtue of properties of the stimulus configuration or of the language habits of listeners is not clear.

8.3.2.2 Auditory-Spatial Figure-Ground

We now return to our second plan for finding auditory analogs to the visual gestalt rules, namely, that in which the visual spatial dimensions are paralleled (as in the X and Y dimensions of auditory phenomenal space). We will speak now of auditory spatial figures on spatial grounds, not temporal figures on temporal backgrounds.

1. *Proximity and similarity.* Similarity rules will operate here in the same way as for temporal figures. The proximity question is: Do acoustic sources that are close together yield clusters or figures, in contrast with more widely spaced or spatially extended source surfaces? When an airport control-tower operator must listen to the voices of several pilots simultaneously, he faces a confusing and difficult task. It has been shown [61] that if each voice channel is directed to a separate loudspeaker and the several loudspeakers are located in different places, the possibility of understanding the speech of any one is much higher. Both similarity of voice and spatial proximity over time operate here in that the enhancement of a particular string of words as figure against the ground of other messages is mediated both by the consistent voice quality of a given talker and by their continued origin from a single place (see Sec. 8.3.2.4). The same principle seems to hold in listening to symphonic music. In the concert hall, the several figures that emerge as different melodic lines in different instruments seem to remain separable not only by the persisting quality of each instrument carrying its own part over time (similarity and temporal continuation), but also by the fact that these instruments are located in different places. This spatial separation gets lost in a single-channel recording, and is partially restored in a stereo recording of two or more channels.

2. *Area.* Do small sound sources stand out more clearly as figures than large ones? Although there have been some studies [62] on the apparent size or volume of artificially generated sounds like tones, there does not appear to be any quantitative information on apparent size of real acoustic sources. The question is complicated in part by the nature of the stimulus energy. All visually perceived objects and reflecting surfaces down to about the size of a virus are considerably larger than the wavelength of light. But most objects that radiate or reflect sound waves have sizes (overall or enfolded) approximating those of acoustic wavelengths. The size of a sounding body is often related to the characteristic frequencies that it produces, and thus we have an interesting tangle between spatial and temporal figure properties. We have already stated that brief events stand out as figures more clearly than longer, drawn-out ones. But extreme brevity also implies wide bandwidth with high frequencies, which in turn imply small bodies. Thus small bodies may seem to stand out as figures more clearly than large ones, both because of their area and also because of pitch. The sound of a single cricket stands out clearly from more widely distributed night sounds. He is small and generates high chirps; being small he cannot sound a low-frequency click or rumble, like that of thunder. (Note that this relation between small size and brevity in time permits translation between our two analogies only for the time dimension, not for frequency, in which brevity requires a wide bandwidth.)

3. *Closedness.* The closedness of a surface that radiates or reflects sound cannot be treated at all. Spatial gaps, defined by the eye or a ruler, simply cannot be known to a listener and so this property is as difficult to apply to sound in spatial terms as it was in temporal ones.

4. *Symmetry.* The simple spatial symmetry around an axis in the $X - Y$ plane also resists treatment in the auditory realm because listeners cannot know of this property in a sounding surface. It is demonstrable, however, that in order to sharpen the distinction between a particular signal source and a more widespread background, a listener will turn toward that source, thus centering it in phenomenal space—a kind of bilateral symmetry, sought for clearest figure.

5. *Smooth continuation.* While we have suggested how this principle might apply to temporal forms, it represents another case where a spatial feature of the sounding body or surface is probably not available to the listener. On the other hand it is easy to attend to moving sound sources if they move along a smooth trajectory. It would be more difficult to follow a sound source in an unexpected zigzag or discontinuous motion.

8.3.2.3 Signal Detection in Noise

This field of research has been extended, during the past decade, as a model for virtually all discrimination and recognition behavior. "Signal-detection theory" is thoroughly reviewed in the recent book by Green and Swets [63], who deal with applications to both auditory and visual problems, although most of the work has been in psychoacoustics. Two major contributions of detection theory have been, first, that many discrimination problems have been fruitfully analyzed in terms of an analogy with statistical decision theory—suggesting, first, that a significant portion of the variance in psychophysical responses may be related to the particular criterion or response strategy adopted by the observer rather than to his sensitivity; and, second, that the classical concept of the *threshold* may best be understood as an artifact of a given psychophysical method, rather than as a limiting sensory condition. In addition, detection theory has also motivated the development of numerous theoretical "ideal detectors" which can be thought of as setting limits on the performance of real sensory systems. While this theory may be applied to the discrimination of any stimulus from any other, it is often used in the case of the discrimination of *some*-thing from *not*-thing, and such cases may be considered to deal with a specialized figure-ground problem. Pfafflin and Mathews have suggested that auditory signal detection is much simpler than that required by the mathematical theory of the ideal observer [63, 64].

On the other hand, some modifications of the basic paradigm lead to perceptual questions. For instance Tanner, Swets, and Green [65] showed that detection becomes more difficult for the condition where the signal might be either of two frequencies as compared with the fixed-frequency condition. The decrease was small (about 3 dB) but seemed to depend on the frequency separation of the two possible signals. This dependence on a priori known information of perception is characteristic of both audition and vision.

The visual examples are similar to the auditory ones. The simplified case corresponds to the modulation transfer-function technique, in which sinusoidal or Bessel function–type gratings are measured at visibility threshold [66, 67]. The more complex conditions are the examples of hidden figures in noise (or in the context of overlapping intricate objects). The hidden objects are often sought for minutes, but the slightest hint of what is to be found reduces this time considerably. After the hidden figure is once perceived, it resists masking by increased noise. In spite of countless examples of this kind, there is a lack of careful numerical studies of how a priori information reduces visual detection or recognition threshold, error rate, latency, or reaction time. It remains to be seen whether prior knowledge of the stimulus parameters has the same effect on visual thresholds as on auditory thresholds. Anderson and Leonard [68] showed an apparent paradox that redundant figures were more difficult to detect than random ones. Since the redundancy (constraints on figure parameters) affected the occurrence of certain unique features and made the appearance of the stimuli more homogeneous, the results are understandable. Only for the reconstruction task (where each minute detail has to be recalled) did the redundant stimulus class require less time than the random one. Thus before it is known what perceptual features are attended to in complex visual and auditory stimuli, considerations based on information theory or detection theory are premature.

8.3.2.4 Attention and Figure-Ground

Still another aspect of figure-ground perception is found in the psychological treatment of attention. The ability to shift attention mechanically in vision (by moving the eyes and fixating the target) but not in audition leads to many psychophysiological differences between these modalities. In vision the problem of attention is simple, but complicated neural control and buffer systems are required for steering the eyes and integrating the small areas of fixation into an entire panoramic view. In hearing the problem is opposite. All auditory stimuli impinge on the ears, even if not equally. The problem is one of selective attention, which has to be solved by the central nervous system. At least two stages of analysis must occur, as postulated by the psychological experiments of D. E. Broadbent [69], C. Cherry [70], and Anne Treisman [71]. Simple features of multiple sources can be attended to simultaneously such as position, male or female voice, loudness, etc., but the verbal content of only one channel can be attended to at one time. Exceptions to this generalization have been found: Moray [72] showed that subjects sometimes hear their own names in the unattended channel; Treisman [71] found that even certain words could be attended to if these were highly probable in the context; Cherry [17] showed that if the irrelevant message was identical to the selected one and the interval between the same words on the two ears was gradually reduced, the identity was noticed with delays between 6 and 2 s; Treisman [73] extended Cherry's findings by showing that the delayed identity between the attended and unattended channel was noted by bilingual subjects when the two messages were in different languages.

It is interesting to note that visual attention to detail requires entire physical involvement and fixation movements of the eyes, whereas in audition this is accomplished neurally without physical restraint. This difference imposes grossly dissimilar involvement, such as the great distinction between attending to television in contrast to radio.

In spite of these differences between mechanisms of visual and auditory attention, the more central systems for selection exhibit greater similarity. The limited attention to a given auditory channel can be obtained either by concentrating on another auditory message or by reading a passage of written text. The limiting factor comes at a stage more central than visual or auditory preprocessing. Such a central processor might be responsible for weighting the various feature extractors. A typical theory based on weighting was developed by Sutherland [74], who trained a group of rats to approach a white horizontal bar and avoid a black vertical bar. He then tested them whether they were attending to orientation or color. He found that the better they did on one test, the worse they did on the other. Thus during the preliminary training they had been attending to one feature but not to both. Either the brightness analyzer or the orientation analyzer had been switched out. This *visual* example shows striking similarity to the neural feature extraction and weighting of *auditory* features discussed in the previous paragraphs.

8.3.3 Classes of Gestalt Rules

The gestalt rules discussed in the preceding sections have an intuitive appeal and, as shown in Figs. 8.1 to 8.4, are visually evident. The concepts involved are not, however, rigorously defined, nor do they seem to concern the same levels of generality. For example, the rules of proximity, similarity, and smooth continuation explicitly concern principles of structural organization. The structure may be spatial or temporal, and the applicability of such rules appears to hold both in vision and in hearing.

The rules concerning closedness and symmetry appear to be special for visually perceived spatial structures. Symmetry is probably not so restricted when its definition and mathematical treatment concern higher orders than balance around an axis in a planar array.

There have been several attempts to regard the perceptual organization rules as special cases of the general principles of *simplicity*. In the event of simultaneous presence of several perceptual organizations the one that is the simplest will prevail. Of course, the definition of simplicity or complexity is not easily given. For instance in case of two-dimensional and three-dimensional perception of line drawings, Hochberg and Brooks [75] defined two-dimensional complexity by the number of interior angles, average number of nonidentical angles and number of continuous lines in some combination. The more complex a drawing is in two dimensions the more apparent its tridimensionality becomes (see Fig. 8.10).

Finally, we summarize some of the features that characterize a figure for vision and hearing. In vision, the figure is a cluster. The cluster may be a single point seen against a homogeneous background, or it may be a cluster of proximate points of similar brightness or hue. In hearing, the figure may be a single event of brief duration, like a pitchless click or longer click with some pitch. Or the figure may be a

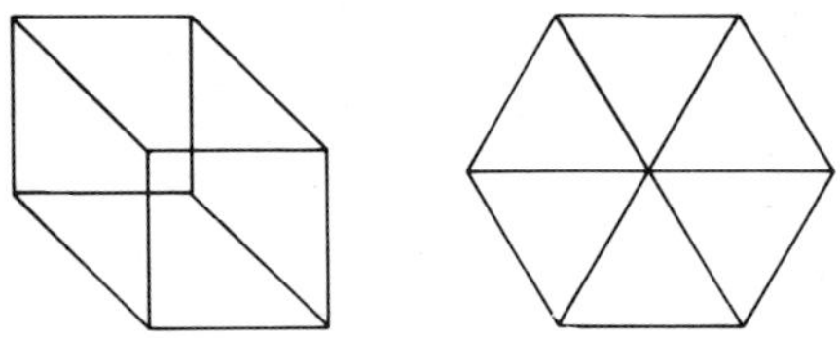

Fig. 8.10. Demonstration of how two-dimensional complexity increases the three-dimensional perception of an outlined cube. The right image is the same cube from another perspective, yet because of its two-dimensional simplicity the three-dimensional perception is difficult. After Hochberg and Brooks [75]

cluster of events; that is, a succession that reveals some structure or pattern over time, like a word or melodic phrase. The grounds against which such figures are perceived must also be characterized, and the next section attempts to analyze these textures.

8.4 Textures: Features of Grounds or Not-things

Figures are perceived against grounds, but the grounds may differ from one another. The differences for vision lie in the features of surfaces; that is their texture and grain. In hearing, the grounds are the sounds of longer duration against which the figure-events are heard. Those grounds may also be different in texture, in temporal grain. Much of early psychophysics concerned the dimensions in respect to which sustained tones differed—pitch, loudness, quality, or timbre. Similar concern in vision with brightness, hue, and saturation for illuminated, nonfigured surfaces has been supplemented by a concern for other aspects of surface by Gibson [33].

8.4.1 Visual Texture Discrimination

Even quite homogeneous surfaces may differ in texture, as shown by two painted surfaces, one glossy and the other "flat." Pieces of cloth, of the same color, show even greater differences, as between silk and an unfinished worsted. The problems of texture discrimination follow logically after those involving separation of figure from ground, even before we reach those pertaining to the recognition and discrimination of figures.

Are two textures discriminable side by side or are they perceived as a single entity? This unum-duo organization was studied by the gestaltists, but early work was restricted to real objects and surfaces where familiarity could play a role. Recently it has been investigated by mathematical treatment [50]. Two objects can be discriminated either because of differences in their surface textures or because of differences in their spatial connectively or both. These factors can be studied by using artificially generated random dot stimuli that do not have familiarity cues but possess controlled statistical and topological properties. In the following, we review a few of the findings by Julesz for monocular and binocular texture discrimination. The most important findings are as follows:

1. Texture discrimination undergoes a preprocessing consisting of cluster detection of adjacent points similar in brightness or color. (See preceding on proximity and similarity.)

2. It is only through evaluating the low-order statistics of these clusters and attending to some simple properties of these clusters (orientation, perimeter-area fraction, etc.) that texture discrimination is carried out. Figure 8.11 shows two textures with the same first-order statistics but different second-order statistics. ("First-order statistics" describes the distribution of the brightness value of each point alone, while "second-order statistics" gives the distribution of the brightness values of two simultaneously drawn points.)

3. Textures composed of clusters having the same statistics and the same simple properties are not spontaneously discriminable even if they differ in familiarity. (See Fig. 8.12, which contains a half field of En-

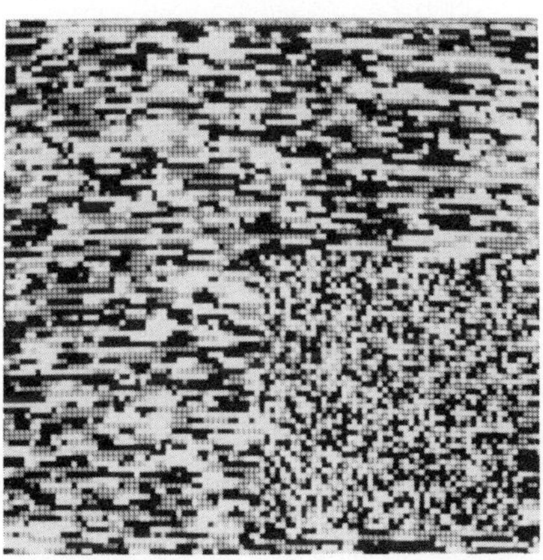

Fig. 8.11. Discrimination between two random fields having the same first-order statistics but different second-order statistics.*

METHODS SCIENCE COLUMNS NIATREC YLKCIUQ DEHCNUP
SUBJECT MERCURY GOVERNS ECNEICS YFICEPS ESICERP
COLUMNS CERTAIN QUICKLY SDOHTEM SDROCER EZIDIXO
RECORDS EXAMPLE SCIENCE STCIPED HSILGNE NIATREC
MERCURY SPECIFY PRECISE TCEJBUS DEHCNUP SNREVOG
METHODS COLUMNS MERCURY ELPMAXE YLKCIUQ YFICEPS
CERTAIN DEPICTS ENGLISH ECNEICS ESICERP ELPMAXE
QUICKLY METHODS EXAMPLE YFICEPS YRUCREM DEHCNUP
ENGLISH SUBJECT RECORDS ELPMAXE SNREVOG EZIDIXO
MERCURY PUNCHED CERTAIN SNMULOC TCEJBUS ESICERP
SUBJECT OXIDIZE GOVERNS HSILGNE SDROCER ELPMAXE
METHODS ENGLISH COLUMNS NIATREC ESICERP DEHCNUP
DEPICTS SPECIFY PRECISE EZIDIXO YLKCIUQ ECNEICS
CERTAIN RECORDS SCIENCE STCIPED ELPMAXE HSILGNE
PRECISE QUICKLY METHODS YFICEPS YRUCREM SNREVOG

Fig. 8.12. No visual discrimination between the left and right half fields, which contain English and nonsense words, respectively.*

*From B. Julesz, Visual Pattern Discrimination, *IRE Transactions on Information Theory,* **IT-8**: 84-92, 1962, with permission of publisher.

Fig. 8.13. Random-dot stereogram in which a center square is seen in vivid depth in front of a surround when viewed stereoscopically. When monocularly viewed the two images appear as a random texture. From B. Julesz, Binocular Depth Perception without Familiarity Cues, *Science* **145**: 356-362, 1964, with permission of publisher.

glish words and a half field of nonsense words of the same length, orientation, and frequency of occurrence.) Every difference that is mathematical but not perceivable we could call "numerology," a fad often applied in contemporary art. For instance, two textures which differ only in third- and higher-order statistics are not discriminable [50].

4. Objects with identical textures can be discriminated binocularly, provided they have surfaces at different depths. Such a case is shown in Fig. 8.13, where a random-dot stereo image contains two surfaces of the same texture. When viewed monocularly the two surfaces cannot be separated, but when viewed binocularly a center square jumps out in vivid depth in front of the surround [76]. Some of these points will be further discussed in Sec. 8.8.1.

8.4.2 Auditory Textures

The best examples of different auditory textures are to be found in music. The simplest homogeneous ground is probably a sustained tone composed either of a single frequency or complex tones and combinations of complex tones (the latter comprising chords) and of course also noise. Granularity and roughness of texture are produced by interruptions. Now periodic interruption of a tone changes not only the periodicities involved but also the harmonic structure, and thus the physical bases for heard changes are complicated. A white noise, however, which contains a rectangular distribution of frequencies of equal amplitudes, may be interrupted without consequent long-term spectral change [35], and the interruption or roughness is clearly an auditory effect of introducing a periodicity (and changes in the short-term spectrum). These periodicities are limited to a minimum duration of about 1 ms, a figure that represents also a limit for the detection of beats. In fact, even the earliest studies on beats included "roughness" as either a volunteered or instructed description of the change from a smooth tone.

Musical texture concerns also the differences between consonant and dissonant chords. Some chords sound smooth, harmonious, pleasant, while others sound rough, harsh, unpleasant. Helmholtz's [77] explanation was a clear analogy to visual granularity. He pointed out that certain combinations of complex tones would involve harmonics that were either very far apart or very close together (consonant), but that others would generate harmonics that might differ by thirty to several hundred hertz, and these differences would yield audible difference tones that introduce an unpleasant (dissonant) effect. His notion has recently been extended by Plomp and Levelt [78], who point out that the prediction of dissonance is more precise if the difference is specified, not in hertz, but as a fraction of the auditory critical bandwidth [79]. Without venturing into the mechanism involved, we suggest that further study of the acoustical effect of these conclusions is warranted. If one sets up combinations of tones according to the rules of Plomp and Levelt, one does indeed obtain listeners' judgments of smooth or rough, consonant or dissonant, as predicted. If now one also looks at the waveforms of the complexes or chords produced, one finds that those combinations judged consonant have smoothly undulating shapes, while those that are judged dissonant have peaks and sharp discontinuities. Informal observations suggest that auditory roughness is indeed roughness—of the complex amplitude waveform over time.

Recently, Goldstein studied complex tones with involved haromonics [80], particularly to determine the role of phase in their perception. He confirmed Helmholtz's suggestion that phase is irrelevant to perception only if each tone in a tone complex is separately resolved. He also concluded that monaural perception of phase requires that the envelope must be changed by phase. J. R. Pierce recently studied complex computer-generated tones with harmonics precisely controlled [81]. These experiments indicate that certain complex spectral changes can be perceived by frequency analysis alone.

The auditory counterpart of visual experiments on the statistical basis of texture can vary depending on whether amplitude or frequency patterns in time are used for analogy. In the preceding section we mentioned brief figure-events whose duration is just sufficient to yield pitch. If, however, instead of clusters we substitute sinusoidal tone bursts of adequate duration for pitch to be perceived, a strong analogy exists between texture discrimination in the two modalities, at least for the

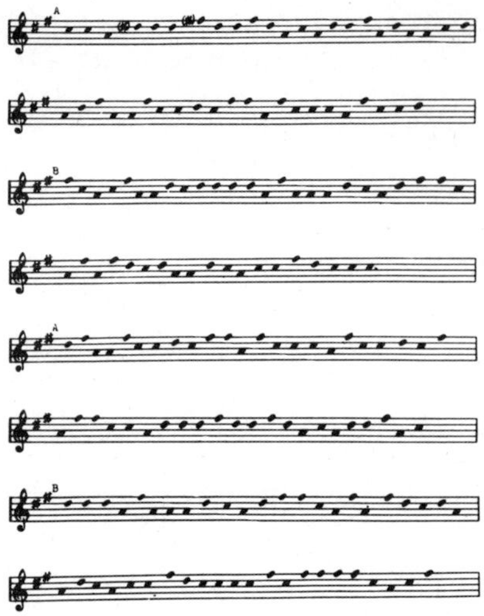

Fig. 8.14. Two melodies A and B composed of four notes such that their first- and second-order statistics are identical, but their third-order statistics are different. The two melodies are not discriminable when learning is excluded. From B. Julesz and N. Guttman, High-order Statistics and Short-term Auditory Memory, *Proc. 5th Int'l Congress on Acoustics,* Liege, Belgium, 1963.

monocular and monaural cases. It is the low-order statistics which affect the frequency and duration of the bursts in the auditory textures and thus lead to their discriminability. Differences in higher-order statistics alone are usually not discriminable and seldom allow the formation of clusters of bursts. Two random melodic sequences having the same first- and second-order statistics but with different third-order probability distributions are given in Fig. 8.14; subjects were unable to discriminate between them [82]. On the other hand, differences in second-order statistics, such as monotonically increasing or decreasing tones, would be easily perceived as two different melodic patterns.

8.5 Psychological Space: Where?

Vision and hearing not only give us information about the spatial properties of figures and grounds but also allow us to localize the object sources in space. Viewed objects or surfaces may appear to the left or right, up or down, or centered in the frontal plane, and in addition they may be located in depth. Sound sources can be localized best in the X dimension (horizontal) of the frontal plane, fairly well in the Y dimension (vertical), and poorly in the Z or depth dimension.

8.5.1 Where in the Frontal Plane?

Modern visual theory is not much concerned about the localization of objects in the $X - Y$ plane per se. Older philosophical treatises, however, frequently discussed the effects of stimuli falling on different parts of the retina, the problem of local sign and local areas of stimulation in the visual brain. In a sense, there was little to be explained, since the retina and the brain surface are spread out as is the frontal plane, and different points in space correspond to different points of stimulation. Nevertheless, the representation between retina and cortex is not one-to-one, but one-to-many and also many-to-one, and the foveal region is more densely represented than the periphery. In addition, depth perception greatly complicates localization. Even for perspective drawings in two dimensions a given point can be perceived as a point on the surface of the image but also as a three-dimensional point outside the surface of the drawings. In binocular vision, disparity (binocular parallax) further complicates matters. Finally, the problem of how the small visual samples which are collected by many rapid eye motions are integrated into a global percept has been studied by many researchers. Adaptational phenomena caused by wearing distorting prisms for periods as long as hours or days [83, 84] and change in perceived localization because of disrupted proprioceptive feedback [85] or because of changed proprioceptive perception [59] are closely related to this problem. Other phenomena like figural aftereffects [29] and changes of perceived localization during saccadic eye motions [86] should be also mentioned. In spite of all these complications relative visual localization in the $X-Y$ plane is a reasonably clear-cut problem.

In hearing, the situation is very different. "Auditory spatial localization" has meant primarily lateralization [87] in the X dimension, and more recently also elevation to give point localization in the $X-Y$ plane. No sensory surface is available on which place of stimulation corresponds to a place in space, for one thing because that function on the basilar membrane is preempted for frequency analysis. Instead, sources arrayed along the X dimension produce sounds that arrive at different times and different loudness levels at the two ears [88]. Even simple X localization is a binaural phenomenon [89].

Some recent experiments by Julesz and Levitt [90] demonstrated that the ear is able to discriminate binaurally between complex spatial patterns. They used "spatial chords" which contained five pitches (harmonically related) at equal spacings along the X axis between the two ears. When two such chords of the same constituent pitches but having different spatial locations were used, subjects could discriminate slight positional changes.

Adaptational phenomena such as changes in perceived localization can be demonstrated under a typical binaural stimulation; see Held [85] and Wien [91]. In all these situations of increased or asymmetrical binaural parallax (e.g., by displaced microphones), subjects showed adaptation.

The orders of precision are also quite different in the two senses. Trained observers can just tell the difference between two sound sources located generally in front (where auditory lateralization is best) when they are separated horizontally by 1 or 2 degrees [92]. The data on visual acuity in a similar central region, the foveal projection, indicate discriminable separations in X and Y plane for two dots of less than a minute of arc visual angle and for breaks in a line of a few seconds of arc [78]. Auditory spatial acuity is limited by subacuities for interaural time differences and intensity differences, while visual acuity is limited by the density of retinal cells and patterns of summation and inhibition at all levels of the nervous system.

Furthermore, auditory localization can be greatly influenced by conflicting visual cues. In motion pictures the sound appears to emanate from the speaker's mouth overriding wide limits of loudspeaker placement. For comprehensive reviews on auditory-visual interactions see Arnoult [93] and Jackson [94]. It seems generally true that auditory localization can be influenced by visual cues, whereas the opposite occurs less frequently. Nevertheless, stereophonic presentation can give a pseudo-three-dimensionality to two-dimensional visual presentations (as exploited in Cinerama).

The vertical or Y dimension for hearing is more complicated in that it appears to require not only the binaural information of lateralization but also a covariation between binaural cues and feedback from head movement. When a 20-degree movement of the head is accompanied by a 20-degree shift in the apparent lateralized image, then we perceive the sound source in the horizontal plane. When a 20-degree lateral rotation of the head is accompanied by no change in the auditory image, then it must be either directly above or below the head. In between, head movements accompanied by shifts in the auditory image that are greater than zero but less than the amount of head movement lead to intermediate vertical-height judgments for the sound source as shown by Wallach [95]. Auditory localization in the frontal plane seems to require more complicated processing of differences and changes of such differences with movements than does visual localization where the frontal plane corresponds more closely to a sensory or cortical surface.

The lack of feedback between binaural cues and head movements can give the illusion of internal localization, but no externalization. If a person listens to a stereophonic recording with headphones alone, he will not hear sound spread out in external space, but rather inside his head unless some artificial feedback alters the channels by retrospective tracking movement of the original sound pickups in synchrony with the listener's head [96].

8.5.2 How Far Away? Depth and Stereopsis

Depth perception represents one of the oldest concerns in the study of vision. Subjects can estimate the distance of viewed objects reasonably well, but auditorily perceived objects are judged much more crudely. Familiarity with the object perceived accounts in part for distance judgment: it interacts with size and color for vision, and with changes in the spectrum for hearing. Some monocular cues to distance require familiarity, like changes of size of known objects, effects of interposition of other objects, etc. Some other monocular cues such as motion parallax and changes in perspective are effective for unfamiliar objects as well. Even without stereopsis, such cues, along with the possible effects of changes in the accommodation of the lens, allow some distance judgment with only one eye.

In hearing, the distance of a sound source from the observer is judged through the quality of sound, which changes according to the radiation characteristics of the source and also the perceived ratio of direct to reflected sounds. In a room with reflecting walls, the echoes are weaker and later (relative to the direct sound) as the source is closer to the observer. Although all of these cues and familiarity provide reasonable accuracy, with unfamiliar sounds errors in relative distance judgment on the order of 20 percent are not uncommon [97].

In visual experiments one can eliminate familiarity cues and the role of other near objects by using uniformly illuminated surfaces in a black surround. Similarly, one can use sound sources in an anechoic chamber to eliminate reverberation effects. Under these circumstances, if secondary cues are sufficiently reduced, both vision and hearing give only rudimentary depth information.

The superiority of visual depth judgment is more marked for binocular viewing where true stereopsis is brought into play. The eyes may be turned independently until disparate images on the two retinae correspond exactly. The detailed geometric relations have been treated elsewhere [98], but the main factors are the separation between the eyes, independent turning of the eyes (convergence), and relations established through experience. The random-dot stereo image technique developed by Julesz demonstrated that no form recognition is necessary for stereopsis, and a simple cross-correlation-like operation can establish correspondence between areas in the left and right retinal projections [76]. Convergence motions of the eyes bring the images into rough registration, and the central nervous system performs the task of fine registration. There is a complex interaction between convergence motions and stereopsis, as the latest findings by Fender and Julesz indicate [56]. They used binocularly stabilized retinal images and found that binocular fusion, once established, is not lost even if the images are then considerably displaced from the "corresponding points" on the two retinae.

Binaural fusion occurs also at an early level, prior to recognition of form. Experiments using binaural noise with various degrees of temporal delay and correlation [99–101] show some remote analogies to the random-dot stereo images. Perceptual fusion of a sound arriving at the two ears occurs for temporal disparities that are nevertheless large enough to give information about left-right positions of sound sources.

Even this brief comment on spatial localization by eye and ear allows us to conclude that our concept of the space around us, in which the objects of perception are localized, is best built out of visual experience, which probably also calibrates our sense of touch and movement [59, 102]. The auditory system seems well designed for revealing that something is present, but it is the visual system that tells us precisely what it is.

8.5.3 How Much Space? Size

Size is another aspect of space which allows us to discriminate objects or patterns. Again there is a correspondence between the visual stimulus array and the area of stimulation on the retinal surface. Size discrimination has been studied as such and also used in studying the influence on visual perception of a great variety of factors. Of greater interest in visual theory is size constancy, the fact that the apparent size of an object (even an unfamiliar one) does not decrease in proportion to the size of the retinal image as the distance is changed. This is another case where the details of experiments and their interpretations have already filled many volumes and will not be treated here. We mention this aspect of space for completeness and note again that we have only a little information on the ability of listeners to judge the size of the sound sources or of surfaces that reflect sound [103]. That stereophiles prefer stereo to monophonic recordings, that listeners prefer the spatial spread of an orchestra in the concert hall as opposed to a single-source recording in the living room, or that humor results when a deep voice is made to come from a child's mouth, suggests that some judgments of the appropriateness of source size and sound can be made.

Neurophysiological and behavioral experiments on the "croak detectors" in bullfrogs indicate the existence of some kind of auditory "size" perception [38, 42]. An inhibitory frequency band exists between the low- and high-frequency excitatory regions. Only the adult can emit sounds with low enough frequency components to avoid the inhibitory region, whereas before maturity the smaller sound cavity generates higher frequencies, which stimulate the inhibitory regions.

8.6 Psychological Time: When?

Analogous to the questions "Where is it?" and "How big is it?" we have questions about objects or events in time: When did it occur? How long did it last? In considering these questions we do not have the three spatial dimensions of "Where?" and "How big?"; there is only one physical dimension and it is undirectional.

The time of occurrence of an event is judged in relation to the time of other events. The exact time of a particular event is specified by relation to a calendar for date, to a clock or watch for hour, and to a chronograph for more precise times. But always, the judgment is coincidence between the judged event and another, like the crossing of a clock hand over a marker (and so began studies on reaction). The influence of knowledge of when a detection or recognition of "when" is treated has been reviewed elsewhere [104].

8.6.1 Perceived Order of Events

The ordering of events in time appears to be independent of the sensory modalities through which the events are known. Untrained observers can reliably tell whether a light preceded a sound, or vice versa, if the events are separated by about 100 ms [105]. Well-trained observers can make such a discrimination even if the onsets of the two events are separated by as little as 20 ms. Furthermore, this temporal-order acuity obtains if the two events are two different sounds or two different lights [106].

Just as there are cases where an object cannot easily be located in space because it does not clearly stand out (insufficient contrast, blurred edges, etc.), so there are cases where individual events cannot be located in time because they do not stand out as clear, discrete events. Ordering of events implies clear changes from one state to another, but of course there are also continuous changes where transformations, movements, waxings, and wanings take place. Precision in judging temporal points for such cases is, of course, low, but judgments are made of the direction of change. Though we cannot specify a time when the light of sunrise began, we note that it has been getting brighter. We shall return to such phenomena when we consider movement.

8.6.2 Duration—How Much Time?

The temporal size of an event is its duration. Apparent duration, like order, appears also to be relatively independent of the sense modality through which the event appears. The history of study of apparent duration has included temporal intervals with onsets and ends marked by short lights or noises, intervals filled with sound or light, intervals named in seconds or reproduced in subsequent, subject-controlled intervals. In general, the ability to discriminate durations follows Weber's law in that the percentage of error is constant over a wide range of values [107].

There are two aspects of duration, however, that suggest differences between vision and hearing. The first, which is less quantitatively treated, concerns the fact that sounds ordinarily begin and end in time, whereas visual objects need not. A speech utterance, a musical melody, or a noise begins and ends and, in fact, the duration is one aspect of the figure that contributes to its recognition. But a scene, a painting, a surface remains for times beyond those during which one observes in spite of random fixations as a result of saccadic eye motions. In fact, in order to generate stimuli for studying visual duration, one must turn lights on and off, a technique that is not typical of visual patterns in nature.

Another difference concerns clock or time sense by which persons judge duration. Experiments that have employed mental arithmetic, increased body temperature, or drugs to manipulate apparent duration concern quite general effects on the passage of time [108]. But it appears also that changes in the stimulus background during an observation interval will affect the judged duration (of either light or sound) if the ground comprises sound, but not if it comprises light [45]. The judged duration of a sound or a light in the presence of noise is longer than that for the same sound or light in quiet. Whether the judgment is made in the light or in dark, however, is of no consequence. Here is another piece of evidence for the role of the auditory system as a timekeeper, perhaps complementary to the role of vision as the generator of the concept of space.

8.6.3 Successiveness versus Simultaneity

The specification of when an event occurred and how long it lasted implies that the event is separated from others, that it is a part of an ensemble of events that were successive. How far apart must two events be in order to be perceived as separate and not fused? That question is analogous to the one about visual acuity in space, and is also basic to our previous discussion of temporal texture or grain. The temporal interval that separates fused from successive pairs or longer sequences does appear to depend on the sensory modality. Visual flicker cannot be distinguished from continuous light in the fovea if the successive light events are closer than about 20 ms, whereas auditory flutter (associated with an interrupted noise) is still distinguishable from continuous noise when the successive bursts follow each other by as little as 1 or 2 ms [88]. Clearly, the temporal resolving powers of the two senses differ just as their spatial resolving powers do, but in the opposite direction.

8.7 Movement: Space-Time Interrelations

Real movement of an object in space can be perceived, and the percept is clearly different from that when the object is still. What is more, speed, orientation, and direction can be perceived. The response of a kitten to a moving ball or a swinging string is very different from that to still objects. Moving sound sources also produce different reactions than do still ones. What is more, few people have difficulty in distinguishing approaching from receding sound sources like automobiles, planes, or people who are talking.

Movement is a special case of temporal figures. We have already mentioned continuous change or transformation (in contrast to temporally ordered discrete events) where a temporal form depends upon the way in which the color or brightness of a lighted surface or the loudness, pitch, or quality of a sound changes in time. What is called movement is that subclass of such changes where that which changes in time is a spatial property like size, shape, or position. It is not entirely clear why (especially in vision) such movement has seemed to offer more of a problem in interpretation or explanation than that posed by other temporal-change phenomena. There have been many "explanations" of perceived movement, ranging from the postulation of a movement sense (like Mach's time sense) to a more parsimonious appeal to an organizing or processing center where spatial information is put into relation with that of time. We suppose that eventually the latter kind of explanation will be most satisfactory and further that it will typify all interpretations of these perceptual phenomena that concern change in time.

Apparent movement (stroboscopic or beta movement), demonstrated early by Wertheimer as a pillar for gestalt psychology [109] and applied in the cinema, is an exception to our definition of perception as that which gives information about the world around us. In one sense, apparent movement represents a failure, due to limited temporal resolving power, of perception to inform us of successive, discrete events. In a more positive sense, it gives us continuity over a sequence of such changes—desirable in the movies, inadequate where preservation of physical discontinuities is needed. The conditions for apparent movement between two lights whose temporal interrelations are manipulated but which do not themselves move are summarized in Korte's laws [110] and show dependence on intensity, distance, and timing. Since the discovery of moving-edge detectors in the visual cortex of cat and monkey by Hubel and Wiesel [30] and even at retinal level in rabbit by Barlow and Hill [111] the local constituents of apparent motion are better understood. Under laboratory conditions differences can be shown between real and apparent motion [112–114], but these are subtle differences, not to be dealt with at present.

Melodic patterns are sometimes said to display movement, not of spatial position but of pitch. While pitch change is not true spatial movement, even here it is not clear that there can be a phenomenon akin to visual phi; i.e., that one could present special timing and pitch intervals where a succession of pitches appears to be heard as continuous change. Perhaps *movement* as used in hearing is a widespread metaphor, related to the fact that the adjectives used, in many languages, to label pitches involve spatial concepts—high and low.

8.7.1 Trading of Time and Space

There are two interesting instances where time is translated into space, or vice versa. One concerns binaural auditory lateralization, perceived from the temporal and intensive disparities between the sounds arriving at the two ears. We do not believe that the range of temporal disparities involved, from 10 or 20 μs up to less than a millisecond, is handled as are longer intervals of successivity or order in some complex time-processing center. There appears to be, in fact, a trading back to space of interaural differences in time [115, 116]: First, in certain cells that respond only when time differences between the sounds at the two ears have a certain value [117], and second, in a hypothesized model of a neural structure where sets of such elements are arranged in a geometric pattern so that only one region will be active for each interaural temporal disparity [118]. A somewhat similar trading of visual depth for temporal disparity exists in the Pulfrich phenomenon [119]. A moving pendulum with a planar motion is perceived to move instead along a conic surface when the two eyes are not equally illuminated. The brightness changes are presumed to be converted into propagation time differences. The brighter optical channel carries the information faster (or the latency of retinal receptive fields is reduced), and so alters the apparent binocular disparity and the resultant experience of depth.

A second example is the so-called *tau* and *kappa* phenomena. Some 30 years ago, it was shown by Helson and King [120] that the apparent location on the forearm of three successive touches depended upon the time interval between them. If A, B, and C are equally separated spatially and the time interval between A and B is shorter than that between B and C, then B appears to be closer to A than to C. This tau effect was subsequently confirmed for visual space by Abe [121] and Cohen,

Hansel, and Sylvester [122]. In vision too, changing the time of arrival of an event relative to others changes the apparent location of the event.

More recently the reverse effect, the *kappa* effect, was shown by Cohen et al. [122] in vision. Here the subject is not asked to give a judgment about the spatial locations of three light sources, but rather is asked about their temporal relation: was the interval between A and B the same as the interval between B and C? It is shown that if light B is closer to light A than it is to C in space, it will appear to come earlier when in fact the timing between A and B was equal to that between B and C. Using an analogy between visual space and the sensory surface in hearing that has to do with pitch, the experimenters extended these studies to hearing and showed a small tau effect but no kappa effect. It would appear that the auditory sense is such a good timekeeper that changes in the spatial relations among auditory stimuli cannot modify the apparent time of occurrence as easily as they can in visual space with visual stimuli.

8.8 Pattern Recognition: What is Perceived?

8.8.1 Schemes for Visual Recognition

Visual form recognition is the highest level of visual pattern processing if we ignore the cognitive processes (which can occur without stimulation). In the hierarchy of pattern processing, the simplest process is a point-by-point comparison between two input patterns. Such processing occurs in stereopsis between a left and right retinal image or in apparent-motion perception between images that are presented in rapid temporal succession. As has been demonstrated, this level of processing—that is, the finding of corresponding point domains in the two images—does not require form recognition [76]. Figure 8.14 shows the technique of random-dot stereoscopic images as briefly discussed in Sec. 8.4.1. The two images are composed of an array of 100×100 black and white dots located at random. The positions and brightnesses of the dots in both images are identical except for a center square that has been shifted horizontally in the left image as if it were a solid sheet. When the stereo pair is viewed monocularly, the impression is of random dots having no overall form. When viewed stereoscopically, however, the center square appears vividly in front of the surround [76, 123].

The next level of complexity occurs in visual texture discrimination. Here two input patterns are compared—not point-by-point, but in some gross properties. An example is shown in Fig. 8.11 where two random-dot patterns having different statistical properties are shown in close proximity to each other. Inspection immediately discloses a difference in the granularity of the two patterns, and the textures are perceived spontaneously as distinct entities. Such experiments have shown, however, that only certain kinds of textured patterns can be identified. That is, some physically different textures are not usually discriminable. The stochastic parameters that underlie visual texture discrimination have been studied by several researchers [50, 124, 125], but few studies exist for auditory textures [82]. Julesz has suggested for both modalities that differences in first- or second-order probability distributions will yield discrimination, mainly because these simple statistics regulate the cluster formation of adjacent elements of similar brightness values or, in music, the occurrence of some simple sequences of increasing or decreasing tones.

Without cues of familiarity most differences between patterned textures pass unnoticed (provided both that the clusters occur with the same frequency and that some of their most primitive properties, like area and orientation, are kept similar). This is shown in Fig. 8.12, where the left half of the field contains English words, whereas the right half contains nonsense words of the same length [50]. We can see this is so by scrutinizing the field word by word, but it is impossible to perceive the two halves as separate entities. Thus the highest level of pattern processing—form recognition—yields the least vivid discrimination between textures. This must clearly be so, since in form recognition the stimulus is compared with the memorized version of it. The information stored in our memories has undergone a drastic reduction in detail—otherwise a limited number of stimuli would exhaust the storage capacity of our brains—so that the correlation between stimulus and the stored image of it is greatly reduced. Incidentally, this weak correlation between stimulus and memory is essential for experiencing perceptual invariances.

What these examples show is that the more primitive the perceptual process, the less memory and preprocessing it requires. At the same time, slight changes in a pattern become more apparent for the simpler processes. Similarly, gross distortions are tolerated in shape recognition (e.g., caricatures), while the slightest scratch or damage in a stereoscopic image or motion picture frame is immediately detected. As we study the higher-order processing in form recognition, we are startled by the complexity of these data reductions.

The simplest form of data reduction is the use of *contours*. E. Mach a century ago studied the "crispening" effect at spatial intensity changes (Mach bands) and suggested from his tachistoscopic presentations that this enhancement is caused by simultaneous reciprocal neural interaction [58]. Riggs, Ratliff, and Keesey [126] compared normal and retinally stabilized Mach bands. Before image fade-out (5 s after stabilization), the crispening was apparent. The Mach-band effect appears to be the result of a neurophysiological process like Kuffler units (see Sec. 8.9) and edge detectors in which antagonistic areas are connected. The importance of contours is such that often the brightness and hue of an area are determined by the brightness and hue of the surrounding contours. For instance, Yarbus [127] and J. Krauskopf [128] demonstrated that if a red disk and green annulus have a common retinally stabilized contour and the outside of the annulus is not stabilized, then the stabilized contour together with the red disk disappears and green fills in. This phenomenon can be simulated under ordinary vision if the contour between disk and annulus is blurred and the outside contour of the annulus is sharp. (The auditory analog might be the precedence effect due to the leading auditory contours in which a second similar event is perceived as originating from the first source.) The importance of contours in perception is exemplified by the frequent use of outlined drawings in communication.

Contour extraction is the first step in data reduction. The contours have orientation, position, and velocity which are discriminated by very simple visual systems. Vowles [129] showed that a wood ant can learn a T maze and visually discriminate between horizontal and vertical stripes, but not between +45° and −45° diagonal slopes. The same perceptual response for slope discrimination is shared by octopus [130–132]. Even humans perform better for horizontal and vertical direction [133]. Hassenstein and Reichardt [134] have shown that differential flicker for the two eyes can be used both for movement perception and for figure-ground discrimination in beetles. Some recent experiments by Celeste McCollough [135] indicate that edge detectors of a given orientation can be selectively adapted by a given color. Many recent experiments are designed to test the geometry of edge detectors by psychological means [136, 137].

The position of an edge is generalized for parallel translations early in the processing chain. In addition to the complex units of Hubel and Wiesel [30], which fire for a given orientation of an edge regardless of its position within a receptive field, we know from segmentation phenomena under retinal stabilization that parallel lines and segments of concentric circles fade out simultaneously, as reported by Pritchard [138] and Evans [139].

The next step of processing is the determination of the end of an edge and of corners. It is interesting that in addition to line extractors the relation of two perpendicular lines is also represented in the nervous system. The hypercomplex units of Hubel and Wiesel [30] determine end-of-lines and corners. The preponderance of these feature extractors is psychologically evident. We can perceive small deviations from perpendicularity without effort and we are constantly amused at how cats concentrate on the end of a string.

After edges, slits, ends-of-lines, corners, and cusps are extracted, the obvious question arises whether forms of higher complexity are also extracted by feature extractors. It is very unlikely that particular neural units for complex pattern extraction will exist at an early processing level. Even though the neurophysiologists have their probes already in the highest levels of the visual cortex, the hypercomplex units found there are still simple compared to shapes. Third, an experiment was performed presenting sides of pentagons and hexagons in temporal sequence [140]. It was conjectured that for polygon extractors (that is, for receptive fields built from simultaneously connected edge detectors in polygonal arrangement) the order of the presentation would be immaterial. It was experimentally found that slower rates of presentation were adequate to maintain the polygon as a gestalt when the edges were presented successively than when the sequence was not ordered. The 50 percent faster rates required for the nonsequential case indicate that "parallel" organization of higher form detectors is unlikely. Perhaps a temporal scanning mechanism follows the parallel extracted simple features. Mayzner recently showed that long words when presented letter by letter on a cathode-ray tube in ordered sequence in either direction are seen intact, but when presented out of order at the same rate certain letters disappeared from the word [141].

Segmentation phenomena in afterimages and retinally stabilized images also show how some perceptual fragments fade out differentially from global structure [138].

These phenomena have auditory counterparts and are manifestations of a general phenomenon studied at the turn of the century by Titchener's students [142, 143]. They described how a word would lose its meaning when visually fixated for longer times or auditorily repeated. Only recently were these observations followed up under the name of semantic satiation [144]. Modern research studies on such and similar phenomena are described under various rubrics like habituation, adaptation, satiation, reactive inhibition, etc. These psychological phenomena have countless neurophysiological manifestations and we only mention the EEG-wave habituation of humans listening to lists of synonyms [145] and of cats listening to repeated alternations of simple sound patterns [146]. Semantic satiation affects even related words in another language [147]. The modern explanation of these auditory phenomena might be that a word presented over and over again for several minutes may adapt certain feature extractors which then "fade out." It is not clear why only certain phonemes fade out and others are intact.

This adaptation or perceptual "bleaching" of higher functional units is specially interesting in perceptual aftereffects. The "waterfall illusion" is a well-known example, in which after prolonged viewing of a waterfall, when changing the gaze to a blank background, one sees upward motion. MacKay's orthogonal afterimages are even more striking [148]. In this illusion, if certain patterns such as concentric circles, radial lines, horizontal and vertical grids, etc., are presented for some time and are followed by visual noise, the noise seems to be organized into patterns geometrically orthogonal to the adaptation pattern. Hoffman [149] believes that these patterns are the "eigenpatterns" (eigenfunction) of the perceptual invariances. These eigenpatterns stay invariant for certain transformations: the radial lines for dilations, the concentric lines for rotations, etc. The class of operators are "bleached out" when the corresponding eigenpattern is presented and the "unbleached" orthogonal pair becomes dominant. A simpler explanation might assume neural organizations in which orthogonal units interact.

As we turn our attention to still higher form cues, our knowledge becomes more sporadic in spite of the vast literature. A large amount of experimental data exists for various form-cue discriminations collected for many species. From simple studies of square-rectangle and circle-ellipse discrimination to the complicated figural distortions of airplane windshields and television images, thousands of ad hoc aspects of form cues have been investigated. Unfortunately most of the results are for isolated cases, and we are still far from having a psychophysics of form. A recent review presents some of the difficulties [150].

In spite of the absence of a general theory, some interesting work has been done by workers in automatic pattern recognition. From their first frustrated attempts to build character-recognition machines based on template matching to the next step of using property lists, we can obtain many insights into the difficulties involved. In some recent attempts feature extractors were applied to obtain a useful set of properties, and finally a "language" was developed which describes the relations between the extracted features. A syntax is under development which has its own symbols and "grammar" with "sentences" such as "A closed figure A contains an open figure B and right next to it a closed figure C and both are under figure D, etc." [15, 151]. The combination of adjacent parts into a higher entity resembles grammatical combinations of constituents into a higher unit. The main difference is that the combination of a language structure is a one-dimensional operation whereas pictorial combination has to be undertaken in two dimensions. This pictorial syntax should not be confused with some verbal description or analysis of the stimulus since the "language" used is not like any spoken language. Nevertheless, on this level of pattern processing it is hoped that some analogies might exist between the two modalities.

8.8.2 Auditory Pattern Recognition

In discussing acoustic patterning we need to separate two functions, as was done at the outset of this chapter. What few rules there are appear to be quite different depending on whether the acoustic pattern is used to identify the *object* that was its source or whether it is interpreted as a particular signal in a communicative act.

8.8.2.1 Object Identification

We know from studies of perceptual development in children [152] that patterns of sensory stimulation are not well differentiated in the early stages, either within or between sensory modalities. This learning process is very complex, and in the preceding section we noted how difficult it is to specify precisely in what ways certain familiar objects differ from each other so that visual discrimination and recognition are possible. Take some familiar household objects, like a washing machine, an oil burner, and a vacuum cleaner. These objects are clearly discriminable on the basis of size, form, color, and surface texture. What about their sounds? One has no trouble recognizing which machine was turned on simply by virtue of the sound.

Somehow the incorrect notion has developed that acoustical spectrum analysis provides unique parametric representation of the auditory stimulus. It is true that we can measure the overall intensity, or the spectral distribution of intensity, or the oscillographic representation of the waveform, or the time-frequency representation of the spectrogram. But we do not know, any better than does the visual scientist, what are the crucial dimensions, the ones out of which the cues used by the perceiver are built. If the spectrum were crucial, then we should not be able to recognize these sounds of the machines when their acoustic output is limited in bandwidth through some filters preceding a tape recording. The spectrum does play a part, but it may be a dispensable part, like the color of these same objects—the objects can be recognized in black-and-white photographs.

In short, the cues used to discriminate common sounds and to recognize the objects that produced them are just as evasive as those that still elude definition of form in visual pattern recognition.

8.8.2.2 Speech Recognition

The first problem to be considered in speech recognition is segmentation, the establishing of temporal contours or edges. When a talker utters a phrase, there is an essentially continuous flow of sound that is interrupted only by certain stops or silences that accompany some of the brief consonant sounds. Yet tests of the intelligibility of speech reveal that listeners perceive differences in individual speech sounds that are, rather arbitrarily, the components or phonemes characteristic of a language. Thus it appears that the continuous sound of speech is perceived as a series of events each corresponding to a phoneme of the language. A strong present guess as to how listeners accomplish this feat concerns the listener's own speaking habits since the individual phonemes correspond to unique positions or movements of the various parts of the speech mechanism.

The sounds of English can be divided into two broad classes, the vowels and the consonants (though there are some intermediate cases like /l/ and /r/ that are called semivowels). The features that distinguish one speech sound from another include a great variety of acoustical cues. For example, the different vowels are discriminated on the basis of the position in frequency of two or more *formants* (i.e., peaks in the spectrum composed of the harmonics of the fundamental vocal tone). Vowel discrimination thus turns out to be discrimination on the basis of spectrum of a cue that is similar to that used to distinguish instruments in the orchestra that are playing the same note.

The consonant sounds differ from each other in more complicated ways. Some of them, like /s/ and /ʃ/, are discriminated on the same basis as vowels, namely the spectrum. On the other hand /s/ and /z/ have the same peak region in the spectrum but the former is a pure noise (continuous spectrum) and the latter is a noise with a complex tone superimposed (irregular spectrum envelope). Further, /s/ and /t/ have similar spectral distributions, but one is long and the other is short. Combinations of sounds permit still other discriminations where the cue apparently is the way in which the transition is made from one sound to another.

One interesting theory of speech perception, developed by French and Steinberg, has been summarized by Licklider [11]. Here, however, the basic relation concerns the percentage of words perceived correctly by a listener and the characteristics of the transmission system between speaker and listener. Thus we can know how much speech intelligibility is to be expected through a system with a specified bandwidth or with a specified signal-to-noise ratio. While this theory does cover an important aspect of speech perception, it does not set forth the particular cues or features that permit listeners to distinguish speech sounds one from another. In spite of all of the acoustical analyses that have been done on the sounds of speech, the basic acoustical concepts that are used are not closely related to those features that listeners apparently utilize in perceiving speech.

Another kind of theory of speech perception is part of a more general linguistic theory about the distinctions among speech sounds. This theory, advanced by Jakobson and his colleagues [153], utilizes about a dozen features, each two-valued, on the basis of which listeners could distinguish speech sounds. While there are acoustical definitions for most of these features, it is interesting to note that they arose not so much from a knowledge of acoustical phonetics as from the requirements for sound distinction within a particular language. Developed at a time when the concepts of information theory were becoming available, the system concerns itself with a finite number of choices among the speech sounds of a particular language, not an infinite number of choices among all possible sounds that could be uttered by a talker. One feature, already alluded to above, is whether the speech sound in question is vocalic or nonvocalic. The phonetician knows that there are both vocalic and nonvocalic sounds in a language; he leaves it to the student of acoustics, the student of the speech mechanism, or the student of auditory perception to specify what are the correlates of vocalic or nonvocalic in the sound, the articulation, or the perception.

Still another group of features concerns the envelope (or time course) of the waveform and the two values are called "interrupted" or "continuous." Such a distinction is required, as mentioned above, between /t/ and /s/. Another group of features concerns the spectrum and may be exemplified by a distinction between "compact" and "diffuse" sounds. A compact sound is one in which the energy peaks in the spectrum are close together in frequency, and a diffuse sound is one in which energy peaks occur in quite different regions of frequency.

The details concerning speech sounds and speech perception can be found in other chapters of this book and, concerning the feature-analysis system itself, can be found in Jakobson and Halle [153]. The major reason for introducing this system here is to suggest how a system based upon the number of alternatives that is available to the perceiver has been found useful in describing a complicated process like speech recognition. Here the perceiver does not have to create a percept out of each stimulus array but rather identifies what it is in terms of what it might have been. The features that become important in such a system are those that arise from a consideration of the requirements for communication in a particular language.

Evidence on comprehension of spoken sentences and paragraphs suggests that a theory dealing with the recognition of individual speech sounds is insufficient unless it is coupled to some features of memory and learning in the talker and the perceiver. The listener probably does not examine a series of speech-sound memories before he decides what word was said or what combination of words was said in the sentence. He listens with the same formal framework generated in his memory used by the talker who is speaking the same language. The more recent concern of psycholinguists with framework features, namely the features of grammar, emphasizes the necessity for reaching at least one level of abstraction higher in order to understand the speech perception process. That such whole-structure considerations are essential in considering speech perception is clear, and it may also be that a similar grammatical framework imposed on the task of the visual recognizer confronted with, for example, familiar objects might permit pattern-recognition theory to advance beyond the stage of pattern matching or other models that still require enormous memories.

8.8.3 Further Comparisons Based on Information Theory and Multidimensional Scaling

There are many ways to look at pattern perception; we have reviewed only a few points of view. We have not discussed the information theoretical aspects of perception, particularly the role of redundancy. Attneave studied intensively the role of redundancy in visual patterns, especially symmetric patterns, and he applied Shannon's "guessing game" to determine the important features in a figure [154]. Such attempts, originally devised by C. Shannon, were first used to determine the redundancy of languages. Pollack and Klemmer [155] demonstrated that when redundancy is defined in Shannon's sense as the set of equivalent members, then redundancy is related to perceptual performance. This is usually the case in speech communication, where for instance many allophones yield the same phoneme. On the other hand, when it is defined in terms of the characteristics of construction of each figure, then no simple relation exists between redundancy and perception. This latter case occurs in vision. (See also Ref. 156.)

As we have seen, the peculiarities of vision and audition have a great effect on the way these senses can be studied. Since no auditory object exists, the many perceptual invariances and symmetries which characterize rigid three-dimensional bodies in motion when projected onto our two-dimensional retinas do not exist for auditory perception. According to Gregory [157] most optical illusions, which are so characteristic of visual perception, are due to monocular depth cues and invariances. If we accept this view, it is not surprising that so few if any real "auditory illusions" exist. The recently devised infinite "auditory staircase" of Shepard [158] (where a compound pitch rises indefinitely) is not analogous to the classical illusions but rather to the perceptual effects of moving grids in vision (such as a rotating "barber pole").

On the other hand, information theory can be applied profitably to speech communication where both a receiver and a transmitter exist. However, in visual perception the "transmitter" is not matched to the receiver in the same way as in speech and hearing, and information theory is not as profitable. This difference is clearly demonstrated in practice as well, where auditory bandwidth reduction (by vocoders) seems more feasible than in television, even though the latter medium has a much greater redundancy.

A profitable area of comparison exists in the multidimensional factor analysis or multidimensional scaling of both auditory and visual perceptual performance, particularly since Shepard's [159] and Kruskal's [160] pioneering work. From confusion matrices in Morse code to phonemic discrimination an extensive literature exists on the underlying phenomenal "space" and its dimensions. For instance, the space of Morse code perception while it is being learned is very different from the one described after the task is mastered. Of course, the way the perceptual space changes is characteristic of perceptual learning. Moreover, when attention drifts voluntarily, the phenomenal space changes as well [161]. Also a new dimension (factor) which is possessed by only a few members in the set introduces irrelevant "noise" which may destroy a solution for the majority of the members [140]. For instance, in scaling facial similarity, complexion and ovality of faces are two strong factors. When some faces carry a beard or mustache a strong third factor (which is irrelevant for most faces) enters and reduces the tightness of the solution. In spite of these difficulties, the possibility of developing a psychophysics of form for both modalities may exist.

8.9 Conclusion

In this chapter we have sought to share with our readers the somewhat tortuous path that our thinking has taken to find grounds in which visual and auditory perception could be compared and in which we could find visual-auditory analogies. Both modalities include a two-dimensional sensory surface on which receptor cells are laid out, but those surfaces appear to subserve two different kinds of function. In the visual case different points of stimulation correspond to different points of origin of the light stimulus; and in the auditory case different regions of stimulation correspond to different pitch values of auditory sensation. In contrast to this difference between the two modalities there are units in both for which the adequate stimulation is not sound of a particular frequency or light falling on a particular point on the retina but rather change. To be sure, in the visual case, the change must occur across space, whereas in the auditory case the change occurs across time, but the neural units involved appear to treat incoming information in a somewhat similar manner.

There is a strong asymmetry between visual and auditory perception.

For *monocular* and *monaural* comparisons there are only visual objects and no auditory objects, whereas there exist both auditory and visual events. Thus while temporal events can be directly compared, visual objects and auditory events can be compared only through abstract concoctions. There is the further complication that the visual image is integrated into a visual field from small samples collected by many quasi-random fixations, capitalizing on the fact that the visual environment is relatively stable in time. On the other hand, the auditory patterns are dynamic and ordered in time.

Also, the auditory environment impinges on the ears in its entirety requiring complex neural mechanisms for attention, whereas the small visual angle of clear vision permits an easy preselection of objects using mechanical fixation.

Binocular and *binaural* comparisons can be more direct, since in this case both visual and auditory patterns can have spatial properties. The similarities are more analogies than parallelisms, since localization in vision and audition are such different experiences.

One of the hopes entertained originally when we set about this joint task was to be able to conclude that there was a kind of central processor of information that would be common to these two if not to all sensory modalities and that the major differences among the modalities would be found in the flow of information prior to that central processing. It turns out, however, that there are major differences, large when originally stated but smaller when suitable schemes of translation are inserted, that depend not only on the particular form of information brought in and processed but also on the ways in which such information will be used by the organism. Animals, from the simplest to the human, use their eyes to recognize objects, to distinguish the edible from the poisonous, to distinguish the friend from the foe. Similarly, most animals use their ears for detecting warnings of distant and as yet unrecognized things. The marked difference between humans and other animals that is characterized by the development of spoken language in humans alone maps out a whole new territory for auditory perception in communication that is quite different from visual perception.

We note that the important aspects of figure, textured grounds, and complex patterns can be characterized in similar ways, particularly when we devise a means of translating spatial aspects of visual form to temporal aspects of auditory form. Furthermore we note that the auditory and visual systems are complementary with respect to permitting us to generate general concepts about the external environment, the eyes serving best to inform us about space and the ears supporting our notions concerning ordered time.

Even though the differences appear to outweigh the similarities, and even though contrasts are more readily available than comparisons, we suggest that perceptual rules, theories of information processing, interpretations of physiological activity and theoretical models for such activity that are introduced in either the visual or the auditory domain will, more often than not, be found useful as suggestions for what is important, what might work, and what might explain in the other domain.

REFERENCES

1. L. Carmichael, H. P. Hogan, and A. A. Walter, An Experimental Study of the Effect of Language on the Reproduction of Visually Perceived Form, *J. Exptl. Psychol.,* **15:**73–86 (1932).
2. F. W. Campbell and J. G. Robson, Application of Fourier Analysis to the Visibility of Gratings, *J. Physiol.,* **197:**551–566 (1968).
3. A. Pantle and R. W. Sekuler, Size-detecting Mechanisms in Human Vision, *Science,* **162:**1146–1148 (1968).
4. C. Blakemore and F. W. Campbell, On the Existence of Neurones in the Human Visual System Selectively Sensitive to the Orientation and Size of Retinal Images, *J. Physiol.,* **203:**237–260 (1969).
5. C. Blakemore and P. Sutton, Size Adaptation: A New Aftereffect, *Science,* **166:**245–247 (1969).
6. B. Julesz and C. F. Stromeyer III, Masking of Spatial Gratings by Filtered One-dimensional Visual Noise, talk given at the 10th Annual Meeting of the Psychonomic Society, San Antonio, Texas, November 5–7, 1970.
7. B. Julesz, Critical Bands in Vision and Audition, *Proc. 7th Intern. Congr. Acoust.* (Akademiai Kiado, Budapest), **3:**445–448 (1971).
8. B. Julesz, "Foundations of Cyclopean Perception," University of Chicago Press, Chicago, 1971.
9. F. H. Allport, "Theories of Perception of the Concept of Structure," John Wiley & Sons, Inc., New York, 1955.
10. I. J. Hirsh, Audition, *Contemp. Psychol.,* **IV:**346–347 (1959). Review of Licklider, "Three Auditory Theories," Ref. 11.
11. J. C. R. Licklider, Three Auditory Theories, in Sigmund Koch (ed.), "Psychology: A Study of a Science," Study I: Conceptual and Systematic, vol. 1: Sensory, Perceptual, and Physiological Formulations, McGraw-Hill Book Company, New York, 1959.
12. H. Fletcher, "Speech and Hearing in Communication," Van Nostrand, New York, 1953.
13. M. Halle, Speech Sounds and Sequences, *Proc. 4th Intern. Congr. Phonetic Sci.* (Helsinki, 1961), pp. 428–434, Mouton and Co., The Hague, 1962.
14. M. Halle, Phonology in Generative Grammar, *Word,* **18:**54–72 (1962).
15. M. Minsky, Steps toward Artificial Intelligence, *Proc. IRE,* **49:**8–30 (1961).
16. J. D. Harris, "Some Relations Between Vision and Audition," Charles C Thomas, Springfield, Ill., 1950.
17. G. H. Mowbray and J. W. Gebhard, Man's Senses as Information Channels, Applied Physics Laboratory, Johns Hopkins University, Silver Springs, Md., AD630025, May 1958.
18. R. H. Henneman and E. R. Long, A Comparison of the Visual and Auditory Senses as Channels for Data Presentation, University of Virginia, AD61558, August 1954.

19. S. S. Stevens, Some Similarities Between Hearing and Seeing, *The Laryngoscope,* **68:**508–527 (1958).
20. S. S. Stevens, Psychophysics of Sensory Function, in W. A. Rosenblith (ed.), "Sensory Communication," MIT Press, Cambridge, Mass., 1961; John Wiley & Sons, Inc., New York, 1961.
21. F. Ratliff, "Quantitative Studies on Neural Networks in the Retina: Mach Bands," Holden-Day, San Francisco, 1965.
22. G. von Békésy, Funneling in the Nervous System and Its Role in Loudness and Sensation Intensity on the Skin, *J. Acoust. Soc. Am.,* **30:**399–412 (1958).
23. L. L. Elliott, Temporal and Spatial Parameters in Auditory and Visual Masking, paper presented to Symposium on Theory of Temporal Factors in Vision and Visual Perception, Center for Visual Science, Rochester, N.Y., 1966.
24. D. M. Green and J. A. Swets, Signal Detection Theory and Psychophysics, John Wiley & Sons, Inc., New York, 1966.
25. H. Jacobson, The Informational Capacity of the Human Ear, *Science,* **112:**143–144 (1950).
26. H. Jacobson, The Informational Capacity of the Human Eye, *Science,* **113:**292–293 (1950).
27. H. E. Egeth, Parallel versus Serial Processes in Multidimensional Stimulus Discrimination, *Perception Psychophys.,* **1:**245–252 (1966).
28. J. M. Harrison and R. Irving, Visual and Nonvisual Auditory Systems in Mammals, *Science,* **154:**738–743 (1966).
29. W. Köhler and H. Wallach, Figural After-effects, *Proc. Am. Phil. Soc.,* **88:**269–357 (1944).
30. D. H. Hubel and T. N. Wiesel, Receptive Fields, Binocular Interaction and Functional Architecture in the Cat's Visual Cortex, *J. Physiol.,* **160:**106–154 (1962).
31. B. Julesz and K. S. Pennington, Equidistributed Information Mapping: An Analogy to Holograms and Memory, *J. Opt. Soc. Am.,* **55:**64 (1965).
32. K. S. Lashley, In Search of the Engram, in "Physiological Mechanisms in Animal Behavior," *Proc. Soc. Exp. Biol. Med.,* Symposium No. 4, pp. 454–482 (1950).
33. J. J. Gibson, "The Perception of the Visual World," Houghton Mifflin, Boston, 1950.
34. I. J. Hirsh, Certain Temporal Factors in Audition, *Science,* **116:**523–524 (1952). (Abstract)
35. G. A. Miller and W. G. Taylor, Perception of Repeated Bursts of Noise, *J. Acoust. Soc. Am.,* **20:**171–182 (1948).
36. I. J. Hirsh, The Influence of Interaural Phase on Interaural Summation and Inhibition, *J. Acoust. Soc. Am.,* **20:**536–544 (1948).
37. J. Y. Lettvin, H. R. Maturana, W. S. McCulloch, and W. H. Pitts, What the Frog's Eye Tells the Frog's Brain, *Proc. IRE,* **47:**1940–1951 (1959).
38. R. R. Capranica, The Evoked Vocal Response of the Bullfrog: A Study of Communication by Sound, Research Monograph No. 33, MIT Press, Cambridge, Mass., 1965.
39. R. Jakobson, On Visual and Auditory Signs, *Phonetica,* **11:**216–220 (1964).
40. C. S. Morris, "Signs, Language and Behavior," Prentice-Hall, New York, 1946.
41. R. W. Sperry, Brain Bisection and Mechanisms of Consciousness, in J. C. Eccles (ed.), "Brain and Conscious Experience," pp. 298–313, Springer, New York, 1966.
42. W. F. Day and B. R. Beach, A Survey of Research Literature Comparing the Visual and Auditory Presentation of Information, U.S. Air Force Tech. Rept. No. 5921, November 1950.

43. M. von Senden, "Raum und Gestaltanfassung bei operierten Blindgeborenen vor und nach dem Operation," Barth, Leipzig, 1932.
44. R. Held and A. V. Hein, Adaptation of Disarranged Hand-Eye Coordination Contingent upon Re-afferent Stimulation, *Perception Motor Skills,* **8:**87–90 (1958).
45. I. J. Hirsh, R. C. Bilger, and B. H. Deatherage, The Effect of Auditory and Visual Background on Apparent Duration, *Am. J. Psychol.,* **69:**561–574 (1956).
46. S. Hecht and C. D. Verrjip, The Influence of Intensity, Color and Retinal Location on the Fusion Frequency of Intermittent Illumination, *Proc. Natl. Acad. Sci. Wash.,* **19:**522–535 (1933).
47. D. O. Hebb, "The Organization of Behavior," John Wiley & Sons, Inc., New York, 1949.
48. E. Rubin, Figure and Ground, in Beardslee and Wertheimer (eds.), "Readings in Perception," p. 194, Van Nostrand, Princeton, N.J., 1958.
49. W. Köhler, "Gestalt Psychology," Liveright, New York, 1929.
50. B. Julesz, Visual Pattern Discrimination, *IRE Trans. Inform. Theory,* **IT-8:**84–92 (1962).
51. E. G. Boring, A New Ambiguous Figure, *Am. J. Psychol.,* **42:**444 (1930).
52. E. G. Boring, "Sensation and Perception in the History of Experimental Psychology," Appleton-Century, New York, 1942.
53. H. L. Frisch and B. Julesz, Figure-Ground Perception and Random Geometry, *Perception Psychophys.,* **1:**389–398 (1966).
54. G. A. Heise, Experimental Study of Auditory Patterns, *Am. J. Psychol.,* **64:**68–77 (1951).
55. S. D. Speeth, Seismometer Sounds, *J. Acoust. Soc. Am.,* **33:**909–916 (1961).
56. D. Fender and B. Julesz, Extension of Panum's Fusional Area in Binocularly Stablized Vision, *J. Opt. Soc. Am.,* **57:**819–830 (1967).
57. B. Julesz, Binocular Disappearance of Monocular Symmetry, *Science,* **153:**657–658 (1966).
58. E. Mach, "Analysis of Sensations" (1897), republished by Dover, New York, 1959.
59. C. S. Harris, Perceptual Adaptation to Inverted, Reversed and Displaced Vision, *Psychol. Rev.,* **72:**419–444 (1965).
60. G. A. Miller and J. C. R. Licklider, The Intelligibility of Interrupted Speech, *J. Acoust. Soc. Am.,* **22:**167–173 (1950).
61. J. C. Webster and L. N. Solomon, Effects of Response Complexity upon Listening to Competing Messages, *J. Acoust. Soc. Am.,* **27:**1199–1203 (1955).
62. G. J. Thomas, Equal-volume Judgments of Tones, *Am. J. Psychol.,* **62:**182–201 (1949).
63. D. M. Green and J. A. Swets, "Signal Detection Theory and Psychophysics," John Wiley & Sons, Inc., New York, 1966.
64. S. M. Pfafflin and M. V. Mathews, Energy Detection for Human Auditory Perception, *J. Acoust. Soc. Am.,* **34:**1842–1853 (1962).
65. W. P. Tanner, J. A. Swets, and D. M. Green, Some General Properties of the Hearing Mechanism, Tech. Rept. No. 30, University of Michigan Electronic Defense Group, 1956.
66. F. W. Campbell and J. G. Robson, Application of Fourier Analysis to the Modulation Response of the Eye, *J. Opt. Soc. Am.,* **54:**581A (1964).
67. D. H. Kelly, Frequency Doubling in Visual Responses, *J. Opt. Soc. Am.,* **56:**1628–1633 (1966).
68. N. S. Anderson and J. A. Leonard, The Recognition, Naming, and Reconstruc-

tion of Visual Figures as a Function of Contour Redundancy, *J. Exptl. Psychol.*, **56:**262–270 (1958).
69. D. E. Broadbent, "Perception and Communication," Pergamon, London, 1958.
70. E. C. Cherry, Some Experiments on the Recognition of Speech with One and with Two Ears, *J. Acoust. Soc. Am.*, **25:**975–979 (1953).
71. A. Treisman, Contextual Cues in Selective Listening, *Quart. J. Exptl. Psychol.*, **12:**242–248 (1960).
72. N. Moray, Attention in Dichotic Listening: Affective Cues and the Influence of Instructions, *Quart. J. Exptl. Psychol.*, **11:**56–60 (1959).
73. A. Treisman, Monitoring and Storage of Irrelevant Messages in Selective Attention, *J. Verbal Learning Verbal Behavior*, **3:**449–459 (1964).
74. N. S. Sutherland, The Learning of Discrimination by Animals, *Endeavour*, **23:**148–152 (1964).
75. J. Hochberg and V. Brooks, The Psychophysics of Form: Reversible-perspective Drawings of Spatial Objects, *Am. J. Psychol.*, **73:**337–354 (1960).
76. B. Julesz, Binocular Depth Perception of Computer Generated Patterns, *Bell Systems Tech. J.*, **39:**1125–1162 (1960).
77. H. L. F. von Helmholtz, "On the Sensations of Tone," 4th ed., pp. 205–211, 290–350, Longmans, Green, New York, 1912.
78. R. Plomp and W. J. M. Levelt, Tonal Consonance and the Critical Bandwidth, *J. Acoust. Soc. Am.*, **38:**548–560 (1965).
79. E. Zwicker, G. Flottorp, and S. S. Stevens, Critical Bandwidth in Loudness Summation, *J. Acoust. Soc. Am.*, **29:**548–557 (1957).
80. J. L. Goldstein, Auditory Nonlinearity, *J. Acoust. Soc. Am.*, **41:**676–689 (1967).
81. J. R. Pierce, Some Aspects of Sound Quality, address to the Acoustical Society of Scandinavia, Stockholm, 1966.
82. B. Julesz and N. Guttman, High-order Statistics and Short-term Auditory Memory, *Proc. 5th Intern. Congr. Acoust.*, Liege, Belgium, 1965.
83. G. M. Stratton, Vision without Inversion of the Retinal Image, *Psychol. Rev.*, **4:**341–360 (1897).
84. I. Kohler, The Formation and Transformation of the Perceptual World, *Psychol. Issues*, **3:**28–46, 116–133 (1964), trans. by H. Tiss.
85. R. Held, Plasticity in Sensory-motor Systems, *Sci. Am.*, **213:**84–94 (1965).
86. L. Matin and D. C. Pearce, Visual Perception for Stimuli Flashed during Voluntary Saccadic Eye Movements, *Science*, **148:**1485–1488 (1965).
87. L. A. Jeffress and R. W. Taylor, Lateralization vs. Localization, *J. Acoust. Soc. Am.*, **33:**482–483 (1961).
88. H. Wallach, E. B. Newman, and M. R. Rosenzweig, The Precedence Effect in Sound Localization, *Am. J. Psychol.*, **62:**315–336 (1949).
89. B. H. Deatherage, Examination of Binaural Interaction, *J. Acoust. Soc. Am.*, **39:**232–249 (1966).
90. B. Julesz and H. Levitt, Spatial Chords, *J. Acoust. Soc. Am.*, **40:**1253 (1966).
91. G. E. Wien, A Preliminary Investigation of the Effect of Head Width on Binaural Hearing, M.S. thesis, MIT, Cambridge, Mass., June 1964.
92. A. W. Mills, On the Minimum Audible Angle, *J. Acoust. Soc. Am.*, **30:**237 (1958).
93. M. D. Arnoult, Localization of Sound during Rotation of the Visual Environment, *Am. J. Psychol.*, **65:**48–58 (1952).
94. C. V. Jackson, Visual Factors in Auditory Localization, *Quart. J. Exptl. Psychol.*, **5:**52–65 (1953).
95. H. Wallach, The Role of Head Movements and Vestibular and Visual Cues in Sound Localization, *J. Exptl. Psychol.*, **27:**339–367 (1940).

96. K. De Boer, Stereofonische Geluidsweergave, dissertation, Delft, 1940; see also N. V. Transsen, Some Considerations on the Mechanism of Directional Hearing, thesis, Tech. Hogeschool, Delft, 1960.
97. J. Fletcher, Localization of Sound in Depth, final report under Contract No. DA-49-193-MD-2088, U.S. Army Medical Research Laboratory, January 31, 1961.
98. K. N. Ogle, "Researches in Binocular Vision," Saunders, Philadelphia, 1950.
99. J. C. R. Licklider, Influence of Interaural Phase Relations upon the Masking of Speech by White Noise, *J. Acoust. Soc. Am.,* **20:**150 (1948).
100. E. C. Cherry and B. McA. Sayers, Human "Cross-correlator," *J. Acoust. Soc. Am.,* **28:**889–895 (1956).
101. E. M. Cramer and W. H. Huggins, Creation of Pitch Through Binaural Interaction, *J. Acoust. Soc. Am.,* **30:**413 (1958).
102. C. R. Hamilton, Intermanual Transfer of Adaptation to Prisms, *Am. J. Psychol.,* **77:**457–462 (1964).
103. C. E. Rice, Human Echo Perception, *Science,* **155:**656–664 (1967).
104. J. D. Frankmann and J. A. Adams, Theories of Vigilance, *Psychol. Bull.,* **59:**257–272 (1962).
105. I. J. Hirsh and P. Fraisse, Simultanéité et succession de stimuli hétérogènes, *L'Année physiol.,* **64:**1–19 (1964).
106. I. J. Hirsh and C. E. Sherrick, Jr., Perceived Order in Different Sense Modalities, *J. Exptl. Psychol.,* **62:**423–432 (1961).
107. L. W. Gregg, Fractionation of Temporal Intervals, *J. Exptl. Psychol.,* **42:**307–312 (1951).
108. P. Fraisse, "The Psychology of Time," chap. 7, Harper and Row, New York, 1963.
109. M. Wertheimer, Experimentelle Studien über das Schen von Bewegung, *Z. Psychol.,* **61:**161–265 (1912).
110. W. Korte, Kinematoskopische Untersuchungen, *Z. Psychol.,* **72:**193–296 (1915).
111. H. B. Barlow and R. M. Hill, Selective Sensitivity to Direction of Movement in Ganglion Cells of the Rabbit Retina, *Science,* **139:**412–414 (1963).
112. P. A. Kolers, Some Differences Between Real and Apparent Visual Movement, *Vision Res.,* **3:**191–206 (1963).
113. G. Sperling, Comparisons of Real and Apparent Motion, *J. Opt. Soc. Am.,* **56:**1442 (1966).
114. B. Julesz, Effects of Contour Flicker or Apparent Motion on Retinally Stabilized Images, *J. Opt. Soc. Am.,* **53:**1336 (1963).
115. B. H. Deatherage and I. J. Hirsh, Auditory Localization of Clicks, *J. Acoust. Soc. Am.,* **31:**486–492 (1959).
116. E. E. David, Jr., N. Guttman, and W. A. van Bergeijk, On the Mechanism of Binaural Fusion, *J. Acoust. Soc. Am.,* **30:**801–802 (1958).
117. R. Galambos, J. Schwartzkopff, and A. Rupert, Microelectrode Studies of the Superior Olivary Complex, *Am. J. Psychol.,* **197:**527–536 (1959).
118. L. A. Jeffress, A Place Theory of Sound Localization, *J. Comp. Physiol. Psychol.,* **41:**35–39 (1948).
119. A. Lit, The Magnitude of the Pulfrich Stereo-phenomenon as a Function of Binocular Differences of Intensity at Various Levels of Illumination, *Am. J. Psychol.,* **62:**159–181 (1949).
120. H. Helson and S. M. King, The Tau Effect: An Example of Psychological Relativity, *J. Exptl. Psychol.,* **14:**202–217 (1931).
121. S. Abe, Experimental Study on the Correlation Between Time and Space, *Tohoku Psychol. Folia,* **3:**53–68 (1935).

122. J. A. Cohen, C. E. M. Hansel, and J. D. Sylvester, Interdependence in Judgments of Space, Time and Movement, *Acta Psychol.*, **11**:360–372 (1955).
123. B. Julesz, Binocular Depth Perception without Familiarity Cues, *Science,* **145**:356–362 (1964).
124. F. Attneave, Symmetry, Information and Memory for Patterns, *Am. J. Psychol.,* **68**:209–222 (1955).
125. B. F. Green, A. K. Wolf, and B. W. White, The Detection of Statistically Defined Patterns in a Matrix of Dots, *Am. J. Psychol.,* **62**:503–520 (1949).
126. L. A. Riggs, F. Ratliff, and U. T. Keesey, Appearance of Mach Bands with a Motionless Retinal Image, *J. Opt. Soc. Am.,* **51**:702–703 (1961).
127. A. L. Yarbus, A New Method of Studying the Activity of Various Parts of the Retina, *Biofizika,* **2**:165–167 (1957).
128. J. Krauskopf, Effect of Retinal Image Stabilization on the Appearance of Heterochromatic Targets, *J. Opt. Soc. Am.,* **53**:741–744 (1963).
129. D. M. Vowles, Maze Learning and Visual Discrimination in the Wood Ant (*Formica rufa*), *Brit. J. Psychol.,* **56**(1):15–31 (1965).
130. J. Z. Young, A Model of the Brain, Clarendon Press, Oxford, 1960.
131. N. S. Sutherland, Visual Discrimination of Orientation by Octopus, *Brit. J. Psychol.,* **48**:55–71 (1957).
132. N. S. Sutherland, The Visual System of Octopus, *Nature,* **186**:840–844 (1960).
133. F. W. Campbell, J. J. Kulikowski, and J. Levinson, The Effect of Orientation on the Visual Resolution of Gratings, *J. Physiol.,* **187**:427–436 (1966).
134. B. Hassenstein and W. Reichardt, Wie sehen Insekten Bewegungen? *Die Umschau,* **10**:302–305 (1959).
135. C. McCollough, Color Adaptation of Edge-detectors in the Human Visual System, *Science,* **149**:115–116 (1965).
136. L. Ronchi and G. Salvi, The Neural Organization of the Central Retina as Revealed by an Experiment on Simultaneous Contrast, *Pubbl. Inst. Nazl. Ottica,* **XX**(2):192–199 (1965).
137. B. Julesz, Some Neurophysiological Problems of Stereopsis, *Proc. Symp. Inform. Processing Sight Sensory Systems,* California Institute of Technology, Pasadena, Calif., 1965.
138. R. M. Pritchard and D. O. Hebb, Visual Perception Approached by the Method of Stabilized Images, *Can. J. Psychol.,* **14**:67–77 (1960).
139. C. R. Evans and D. J. Piggins, A Comparison of the Behavior of Geometrical Shapes when Viewed under Conditions of Steady Fixation and with Apparatus for Producing a Stabilized Retinal Image, *Brit. J. Phys.,* **20**(4):1–13 (1963).
140. B. Julesz, Some Recent Studies in Vision Relevant to Form Perception (1964), in Wathen-Dunn (ed.), "Symposium on Models for the Perception of Speech and Visual Form," pp. 136–154, MIT Press, Cambridge, Mass., 1967.
141. M. S. Mayzner, M. E. Tresselt, and M. S. Helfer, A Provisional Model of Visual Information Processing with Sequential Inputs, *Psychonomic Monographs,* suppl. 2, **7**(23):91–108 (1967).
142. M. F. Bassett and C. J. Warne, On the Lapse of Verbal Meaning with Repetition, *Am. J. Psychol.,* **30**:415–418 (1919).
143. E. Severence and M. F. Washburn, The Loss of Associative Power in Words after Long Fixation, *Am. J. Psychol.,* **18**:182–186 (1907).
144. W. E. Lambert and L. A. Jakobovits, Verbal Satiation and Changes in the Intensity of Meaning, *J. Exptl. Psychol.,* **60**:376–383 (1960).
145. L. G. Voronin and E. N. Sokolov, Cortical Mechanisms of the Orienting Reflex and Its Relation to the Conditioned Reflex, *Intern. J. EEG Clin. Neurophysiol.,* suppl. 13, pp. 335–346 (1960).

146. S. Sharpless and H. Jasper, Habituation of the Arousal Reaction, *Brain,* **79:**655–680 (1956).
147. L. A. Jakobovits and W. E. Lambert, Semantic Satiation among Bilinguals, *J. Exptl. Psychol.,* **62:**576–582 (1961).
148. D. M. MacKay, Interactive Processes in Visual Perception, in W. A. Rosenblith (ed.), "Sensory Communication," pp. 339–357, MIT Press, Cambridge, Mass., 1961; John Wiley & Sons, Inc., New York, 1961.
149. W. C. Hoffman, The Lie Algebra of Visual Perception, *J. Math. Psychol.,* **3**(1):65 (1966).
150. D. R. Brown and D. H. Owen, The Metrics of Visual Form: Methodological Dyspepsia, *Psychol. Bull.,* **68:**243–259 (1967).
151. R. Narsimhan, Labeling Schemata and Syntactic Descriptions of Pictures, *Inform. Control,* **7:**151–179 (1964).
152. J. Piaget, "The Psychology of Intelligence," Harcourt, Brace, New York, 1950.
153. R. Jakobson and M. Halle, "Fundamentals of Language," Mouton and Co., The Hague, 1956.
154. F. Attneave, Some Informational Aspects of Visual Perception, *Psychol. Rev.,* **61:**183–193 (1954).
155. I. Pollack and E. T. Klemmer, Visual Noise Filtering by the Human Operator, II: Linear Dot Patterns in Noise, Tech. Rept. 5415, Air Force Clinical Research Center, Bolling Air Force Base, Washington, 1954.
156. W. R. Garner, To Perceive Is to Know, *Am. Psychologist,* **21:**11–19 (1966).
157. R. L. Gregory, "Eye and Brain," Weidenfield and Nicholson, London, 1966.
158. R. N. Shepard, Circularity in Judgments of Relative Pitch, *J. Acoust. Soc. Am.,* **36:**2346–2353 (1964).
159. R. N. Shepard, The Analysis of Proximities: Multidimensional Scaling with an Unknown Distance Function, I and II, *Psychometrica,* **27:**125, 219 (1962).
160. J. B. Kruskal, Multidimensional Scaling by Optimizing Goodness of Fit to a Nonmetric Hypothesis, *Psychometrica,* **29:**1, 115 (1964).
161. R. N. Shepard, Attention and the Metric Structure of the Stimulus Space, *J. Math. Psychol.,* **1:**54–87 (1964).
162. G. Fairbanks and M. H. Goldstein, Word Intelligibility as a Function of Time Compression, *J. Acoust. Soc. Am.,* **29:**636–641 (1957).
163. N. Guttman and B. Julesz, Auditory Memory, *J. Acoust. Soc. Am.,* **35:**63 (1963).

CHAPTER NINE

Computing Displays and Programming Languages

K. C. KNOWLTON and E. E. ZAJAC

Communication, like other human enterprises, is being done these days by means of increasingly complex devices. We will here discuss several distinct modes of human communication and then explore some of the roles being played in them by our most advanced technical equipment—electronic digital computers. In particular, we will discuss communication processes which may surprise the uninitiated: processes in which the computer manipulates information and ultimately passes it on in the form of graphic and pictorial displays and movies.

Indeed, the easy production of computer pictures has been slow in coming to pass. In the early days of digital computing, computer results were put out as tables of numbers, usually by means of teletypewriters or punched-card tabulators. But pictures are often a more powerful way of representing results than are tables of numbers. And indeed, it was quickly realized that teletypewriters and tabulators could be used to make pictures: one had only to imitate the facsimile process of Wirephotos. Dark areas of the picture could be made by printing dense characters such as 4, intermediate shades by printing periods, and white areas by "printing" blanks. The careful selection of letters yielded several shades of dark and light. Figure 9.1, taken from a paper by E. N. Gilbert [1], was made by this process. It shows computed energy levels of radio waves arising in a mobile radio study. Likewise, this pictorial capability was used to produce line graphs of computer output; automatic graphing on typewriters and printers was commonplace in digital computing installations almost from the outset. An example is shown in Fig. 9.2.

However, digital computing installations are dominated by programmers, bent on getting their creations—programs—through the computer as quickly as possible. The horrible inconsistency in speeds in the above process was not generally appreciated; in fact, it is not gen-

Fig. 9.1. Level plot made on a line printer, showing energy densities of radio waves. Areas corresponding to 9 energy levels are indicated by different shades of gray, made by printing the characters: 0, ., 1, ,, 2, —, 3, /, 4.

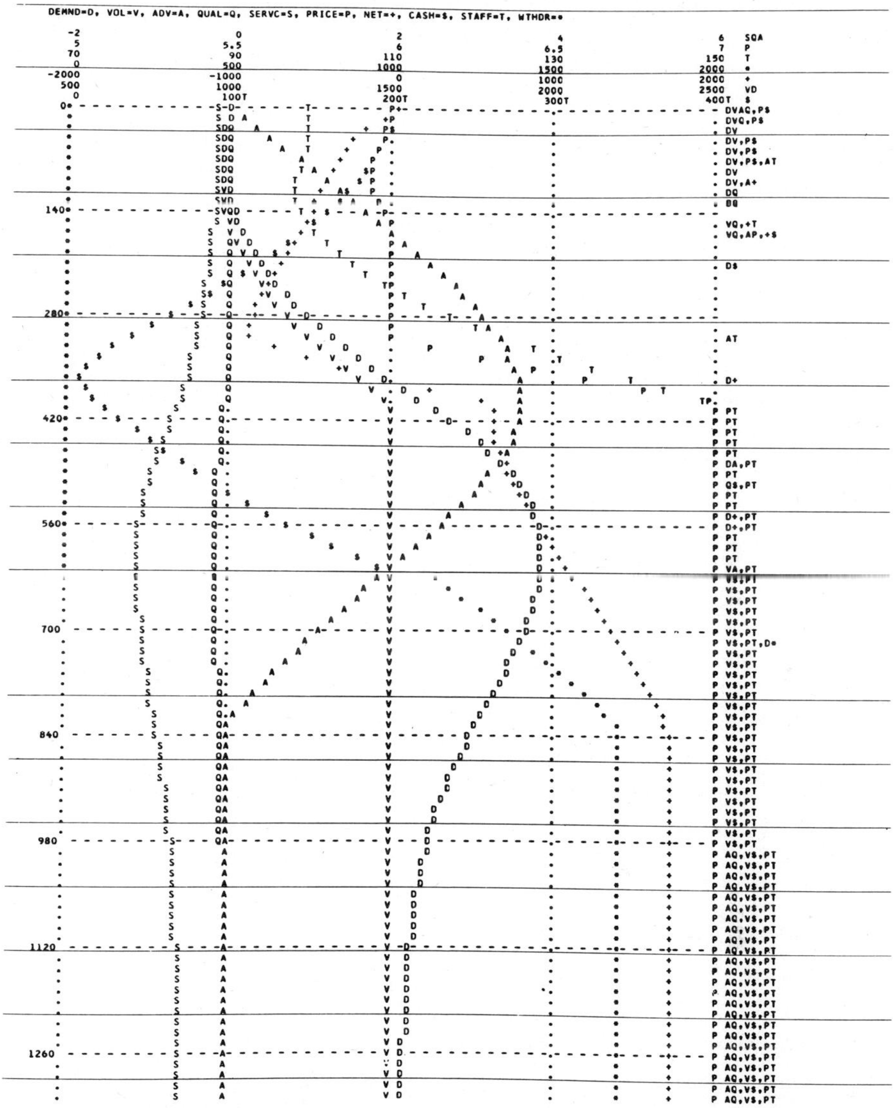

Fig. 9.2. Automatic graphing by line printer. The independent variable, time, is printed at the beginning of each line, so that the plot must be rotated counterclockwise by 90° after it is taken from the printer. Ten different curves are superimposed, indicated by labels on the first printed line. (*Produced by the Dynamo program of Alexander Pugh.*)

erally appreciated at the time of this writing. The process is an example of a machine-to-man link in a communication system, symbolized as follows:

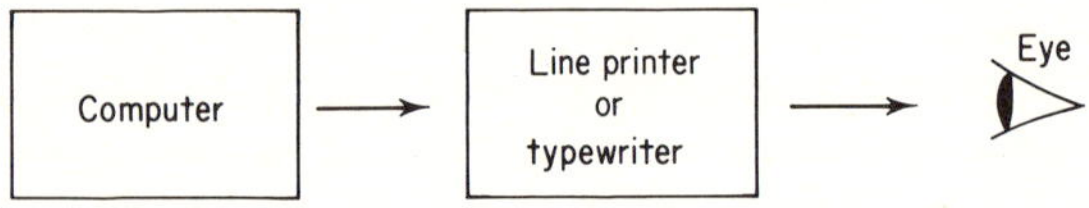

At one end, the digital computer typically puts out results at rates on the order of 100,000 to 1,000,000 bits per second. At the other end, the human eye is capable of accepting results at comparable rates. Interposed, however, is the typewriter or line printer, capable of converting computer results into pictures at rates on the order of only 100 to 1,000 bits per second. The bottleneck is comparable to a few telephone lines handling all present telephone communication between New York and Washington.

To remove this bottleneck, one obviously attacks the slow-working, mechanical typewriter or printer. What is clearly needed is a device which produces pictures at the electronic speeds of the digital computer. Such a device is a cathode-ray tube (CRT), similar to a television tube, which has been the standard picture-producing device in experimental science for several decades. The use of cathode-ray-tube output also goes back to the earliest days of digital computing. But again, in the early days the full potential of the machine-CRT-eye channel was not realized. It is not enough to provide a pictorial device with speeds comparable to a digital computer; one must also control the device with a logical power inherent in the digital computer. The mobilization of this power to produce high-level programming "languages" such as Fortran [2] and Algol [3] has revolutionized computing; likewise, only in the last few years, when picture-producing commands have been couched in languages like Fortran and when special-purpose pictorial languages have been developed, have we begun to realize the potential of pictorial computing.

Nowadays the computer draws and records pictures by sending appropriate signals to a device which contains a cathode-ray tube with a camera focused on it (often called a *microfilm recorder*). The basic commands which this machine understands are simple instructions such as those for advancing the film in the camera, displaying a spot of a certain brightness at specified coordinates of, typically, a 1,024-by-1,024 raster on the tube face, or drawing straight line segments from one such point to another.

In spite of the simplicity of its elementary operations, the machine can compose complicated pictures or series of pictures from a sufficiently large number of appropriately placed points and lines; it can draw and film these elements fast enough to make this not only a feasible but a desirable way to produce long series of such pictures. Current speeds for such devices lie in the range of 10,000 to 100,000 points, lines, or characters per second. This is fast enough to produce in a matter of seconds a television-quality image consisting of a fine mosaic of closely spaced spots, or fast enough to turn out simple line drawings at a rate of several frames per second.

We will here explore the use of this machine, and the computer that controls it, in several different modes of communication; we will then examine the physical machinery ("hardware"), and finally the logical machinery ("software," or programming languages and systems) which are crucial to the development of this new technology.

Modes of Communication

In order to see just where these machines and techniques fit into the larger picture, let us first examine, in more general terms, the principles of information transmission and processing in various modes of communication; for each such mode of communication we will cite an example of the roles that can be played by picture-producing computers.

The mode of communication which comes most readily to mind is that in which the message is transmitted directly from one man to another. This *person-to-person* mode we can picture like this:

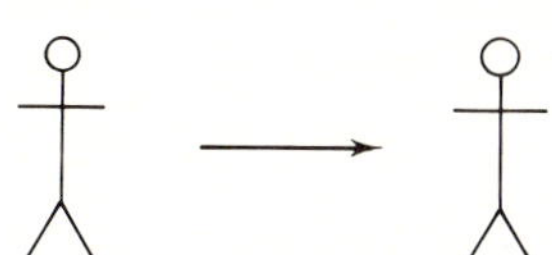

①

but a more complete representation of the process, of course, would recognize the role of intervening matter, devices, or processes, here represented by a box:

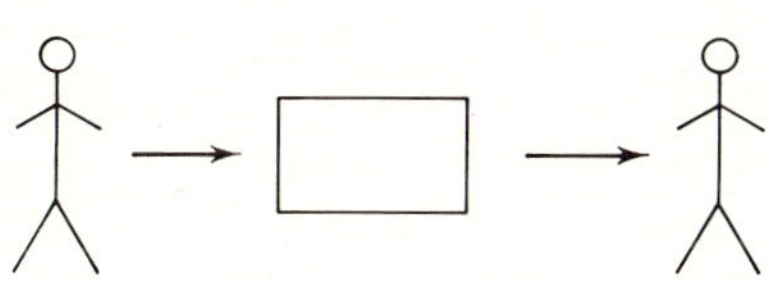

②

In the case of ordinary speech, the box represents the air which transmits the sound waves; in the case of television, it represents a great deal of mechanical, electrical, and electronic equipment.

The devices used for person-to-person communication assume a wide variety of forms, including such objects as microfilms, pencils, billboards, telephones, movie cameras and projectors, violins, printing presses, voting machines, and automobile turn signals. Such devices, individually or collectively, serve to record, code, amplify, analyze, transmit, synthesize, reconstitute, or otherwise process the input message or its derivatives. Sometimes this equipment is used to reproduce the input signal—as in the case of the telephone or tape recorder. In other instances it is used to process the input in order to yield a meaningful result of quite a different form, as in the case of a typewriter, which translates a sequence of thrusts of the fingertips into a visual display of alphabetic characters.

The computer and microfilm recorder have entered into man-to-man communication most notably in the production of animated movies for educational purposes—particularly movies in which the picture elements or their motions are inherently mathematical in form. Scenes from one such movie, done entirely by short line segments, are shown in Fig. 9.3. This film, entitled "Force, Mass, and Motion" [4] produced by F. W. Sinden of Bell Laboratories, describes the motion of two bodies acting under Newton's law, $f = ma$, for a number of different central force laws and a range of initial velocities. For example, the first scene depicts two bodies with different masses (indicated by different-sized circles) to which velocities, shown by arrows, are to be imparted and whose motion is to be governed by the inverse square law. The center of mass of the system is marked by the cross. The resultant motion of these bodies is the apparently complicated pair of paths traced out in the animated sequence, one frame of which is shown in Fig. 9.3*b*. The film then views the same motion from a frame of reference in which the center of mass is fixed, demonstrating that the motion is simpler than it first appeared, as exhibited by the motion being traced out in Fig. 9.3*c*.

Sinden's film contains many other scenes demonstrating motion under other central forces: those which vary as r^{-3}, r^{-1}, r^3, and r^{∞}. The last scene of Fig. 9.3, for example, shows two bodies tracing out their paths as determined by a force which varies as the cube of the separating distance. Arrows in the figure show instantaneous direction and magnitude of the force on each body.

This 10-minute film is an elegant and esthetically beautiful lesson in physics: its communicative effect cannot be matched by hours of hand-waving at a blackboard or with any physically realizable demonstration equipment (the world of the computer is in one sense the ideal physics laboratory, for here the laws of physics can be methodically abstracted, idealized, or revised to degrees which other teaching aids cannot possibly approximate). And, we should note, a film like this would probably not have been made by traditional manual animation,

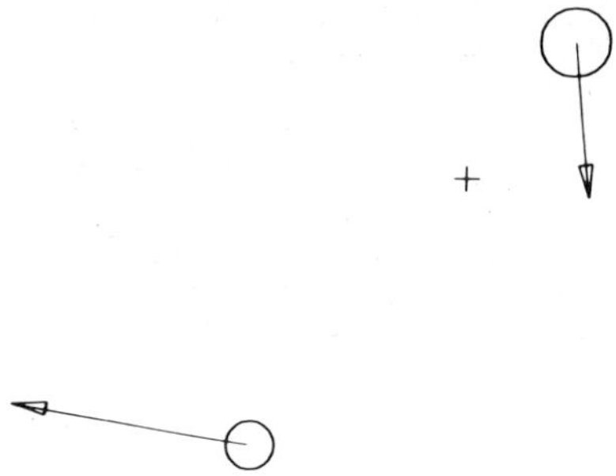

Fig. 9.3. (*a*)

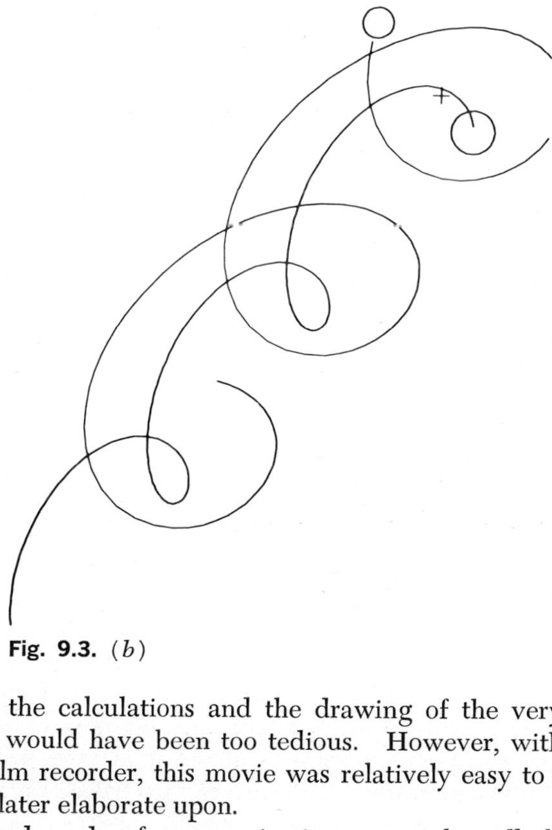

Fig. 9.3. (*b*)

for both the calculations and the drawing of the very precise pictures required would have been too tedious. However, with a computer and a microfilm recorder, this movie was relatively easy to make, for reasons we shall later elaborate upon.

A second mode of communication we might call the *man-to-himself* mode, to describe the case in which the sender and recipient of a message are the same person:

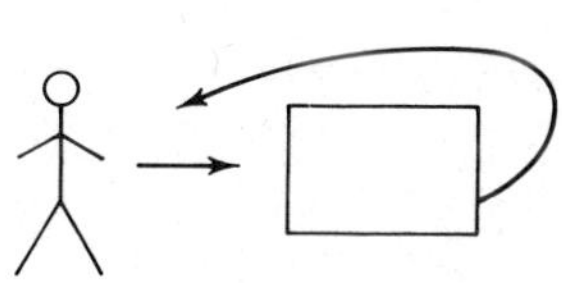

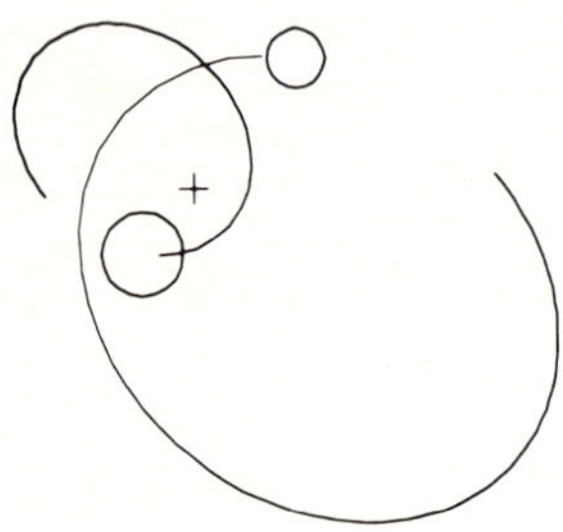

Fig. 9.3. (c)

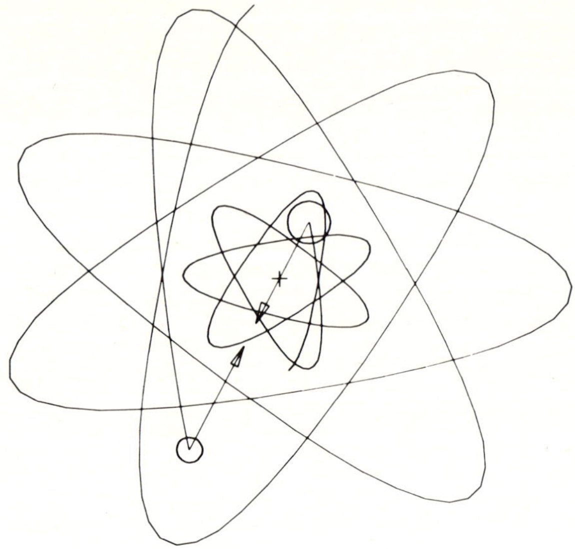

Fig. 9.3. (d)

Fig. 9.3. Scenes from computer-produced film "Force, Mass, and Motion." (a) Two bodies acting according to inverse square law, with arrows showing velocities to be imported to them at time $t = 0$. (b) Bodies tracing paths which result from initial conditions and inverse square (gravitational) force; cross indicates center of mass of the system. (c) Same motion as (b), but viewed in frame of reference moving with center of mass. (d) Two bodies acting under a force which varies as the cube of the separating distance; arrows show instantaneous direction and magnitude of the force on each.

Here the purpose of auxiliary equipment may be simply to store information, either from moment-to-moment as with an abacus, which records successive partial sums, or day-to-day and week-to-week as with a desk calendar or check stub. Or the purpose of the equipment may be to yield some desired function of its input—i.e., to render explicit something which is only implicit in the input—as in the case of the desk calculator. In either case, the man-to-himself communication task is one which is set up by a single person in order to increase his powers of thought and memory. Like the person-to-person mode, it is used in a variety of circumstances and it may involve a variety of devices, ranging from pencils to computers.

Computers are often used, in this reflexive communication link, to help a scientist or engineer to determine the logical or mathematical consequences of a situation which he hypothesizes. And sometimes it is particularly convenient to have these consequences presented as a movie. Such was the case in a study of satellite orientation undertaken by E. E. Zajac which resulted in a computer-produced movie, scenes of which appear in Fig. 9.4 [5, 6]. The problem was one of celestial mechanics: Given a certain mechanism for orientation and stabilization of a communications satellite with respect to the earth, and given certain initial conditions of insertion of the satellite into orbit, what is the satellite's resultant motion? The hypothetical satellite under investigation had a long axis, and it is represented by a domino-shaped

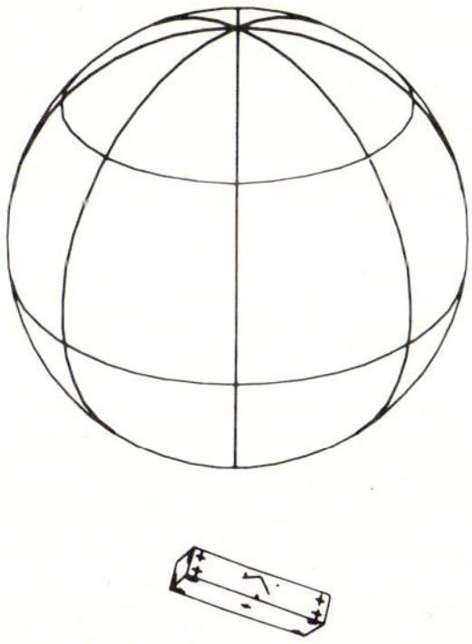

Fig. 9.4. (*a*)

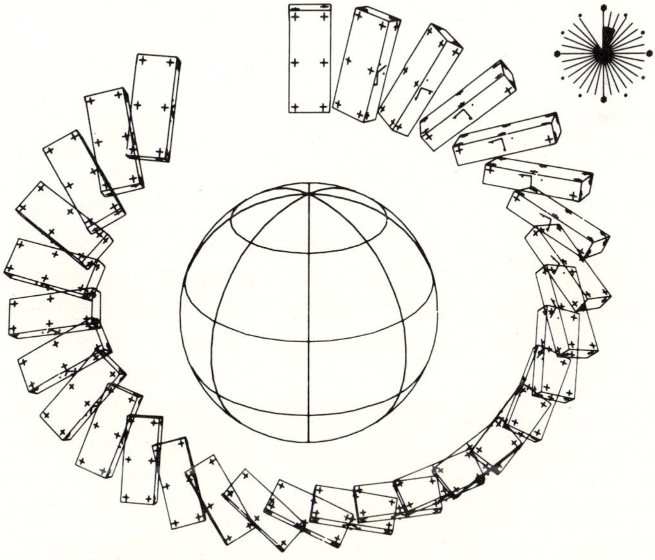

Fig. 9.4. (*b*)

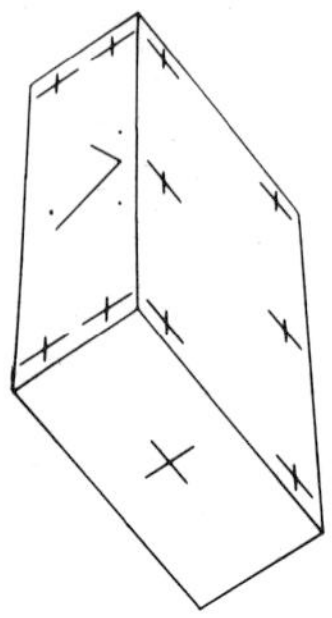

Fig. 9.4. (*c*)

Fig. 9.4. (*a*) Single frame from computer-produced film produced during Zajac's study of satellite orientation. Clock, also computer drawn, counts orbits. (*b*) A composite of several frames, showing the earth only once but with multiple exposures of satellite and clock. (*c*) Another view of the motion illustrated in the preceding scene, but from a frame of reference that moves with the satellite (lines on side show instantaneous orientation of gyros).

box in the scenes shown. Orientation of the satellite, with one face eventually pointing constantly towards the earth, is achieved by the gravity-gradient torque—that is, the torque resulting from the earth's gravity's pulling ever so slightly harder on the end of the satellite which is nearer to the earth. This results, in general, in an oscillatory motion; damping of this oscillation is accomplished by two gyros mounted within the satellite, with axes free to swing through a prescribed range, but with viscous damping.

The satellite's motion is described by complicated differential equations for which we have no solution in closed form. In such a situation, the applied mathematician usually resorts to numerical integration by computer, as Zajac did, to determine by iterative procedure the position, velocity, orientation, and angular momentum of the satellite and its gyros for successive moments of time. But the resulting tabulation of these quantities, if such a listing had actually been produced, would have been difficult to interpret even for the specialist, and of no use to the layman. Instead, the results of the computation were automatically put out as a series of perspective drawings showing the computed position of these objects as a function of time. The result is a movie which gives a much better feeling of the dynamics of the process than would the reams and reams of paper output.

Another result of a man-to-himself communication process appears

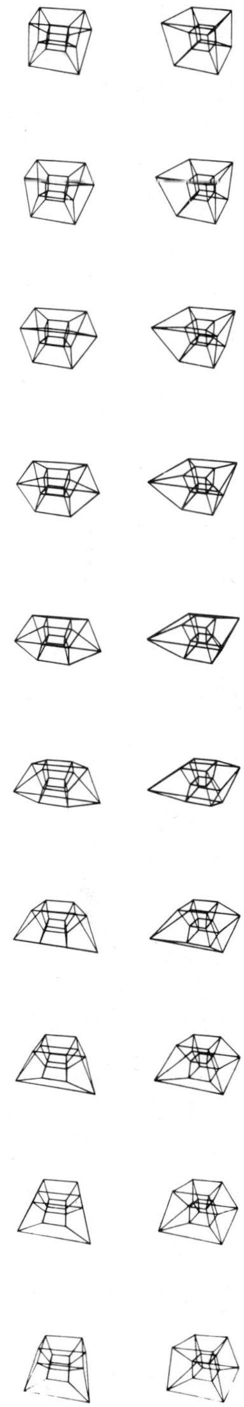

Fig. 9.5. Selected frames from a computer-generated three-dimensional movie showing the three-dimensional perspective projection of a four-dimensional hypercube. The hypercube is being viewed from the x_4 axis and is rotating in the x_1—x_3 plane. To view this figure in 3-D, place a sheet of paper on edge between one stereo pair. Postion your head so each eye sees only one image. The pictures should then seem to merge and appear three dimensional.

in Fig. 9.5—this sequence of stereoscopic views of a four-dimensional hypercube was produced by A. M. Noll [7]. Noll's intent here is to use the computer to generate three-dimensional projections of four-dimensional "hyperobjects"—which are generated and manipulated according to prescribed equations—in an attempt to gain insight into the meaning of these objects and their transformations. Figure 9.5 is actually a sequence of pairs of views from a movie; customarily these views are superimposed by a special projector and viewed by means of the familiar crossed-polaroid glasses. This method of display has been effective for other four-dimensional material, and similar processes have been useful for educational (i.e., person-to-person) films in situations where it is important to visualize things in three dimensions [8].

A third, and for our purposes, final mode of communication we will call the *environment-to-man* mode, which includes all communication paths set up to inform a man about his environment:

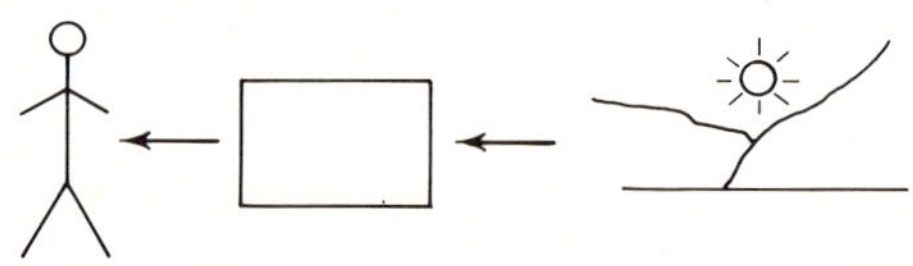

The variety of equipment involved is unspeakably vast, and even a small subcategory—say that of all cameras—proliferates into special cameras or attachments used for recording objects or events that are too slow (e.g., flower blooming), too fast (bullet), too large (hurricane), too small (bacterium), too remote (Mars), or too hostile (bomb test) for the unaided eye. This category of equipment includes almost everything used in scientific research and a great deal more.

Computers enter this communication arena most notably in data reduction, where they accept large quantities of "raw" measurements and process them, passing on only a few properties derived from the original data. Yet even this resulting information may be too much for anything but two- or three-dimensional visual display, where subsequent pattern recognition, it is hoped, will be done in the retina and brain of the investigator. Figure 9.6 is an example of one such computer-produced display. It depicts radiation above the earth's atmosphere as determined after a large amount of data processing from information telemetered back from the first Telstar satellite [9].

One might think of other modes of communication, such as a *man-to-environment* mode, but this we will rule out. Some machines are indeed found in this position, but they generally serve not to communicate information to the environment but rather to make physical assault upon it. The first part of this process could properly be called *man-to-machine* communication, the machine here being the intelligent recipient

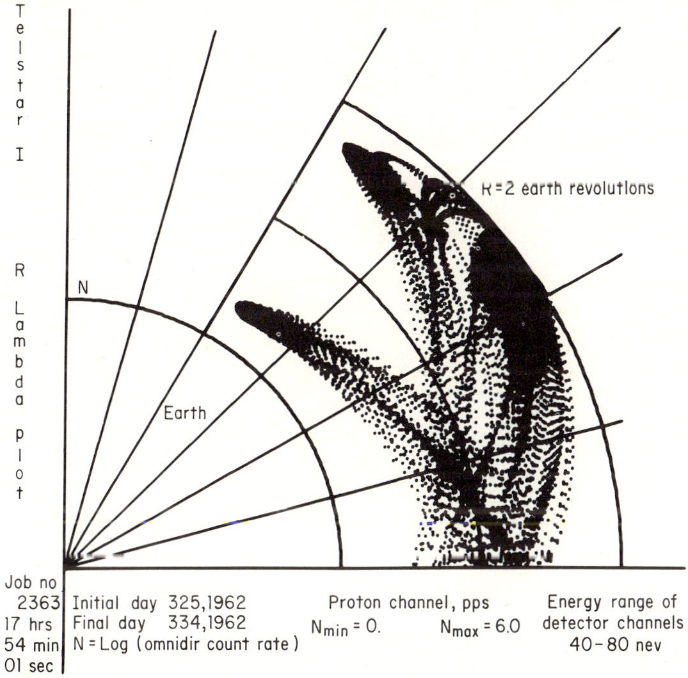

Fig. 9.6. Plot made automatically by the SC-4020 in the Telstar radiation experiment. Points indicate latitude and altitude at which high energy protons were found during Telstar's orbit. Points in the southern hemisphere have been folded up into the northern hemisphere, with the result that two main data "spines" emerge.

and understander of information. The action upon the environment, however, is overt rather than symbolic; hence it should not be thought of as communication of information.

Hardware for Computer-produced Pictures

Having reviewed several examples of the picture-making role played by computers in different modes of communication, let us now turn to the actual machinery which makes the pictures. A skeletal outline of the hardware used to produce these displays is shown in Fig. 9.7. The picture to be produced is specified by numbers computed in a digital computer. In many systems, these numbers are stored on magnetic tape or disks until the graphical computer is ready to process them; alternatively, the numbers are sometimes read directly into the graphical computer.

The numerical code generated by the digital computer and recognized by the graphical computer takes on many forms, depending on the par-

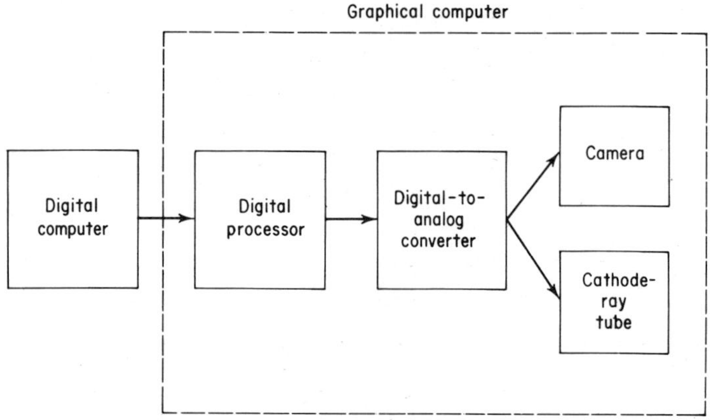

Fig. 9.7. Skeletal outline of hardware used to produce computer-made displays. The digital computer produces lists of numbers which define the picture. These numbers are then interpreted to command the graphical computer to produce voltages in a cathode-ray tube or to advance the film in the camera. The magnitudes of the voltages are obtained by converting numbers from digital to analog form.

ticular graphical computer. In one system, the Stromberg-Carlson 4020* graphical computer [10], the numerical coding is stored in 36-bit words. The SC-4020 recognizes a repertoire of 18 operation codes. An example is

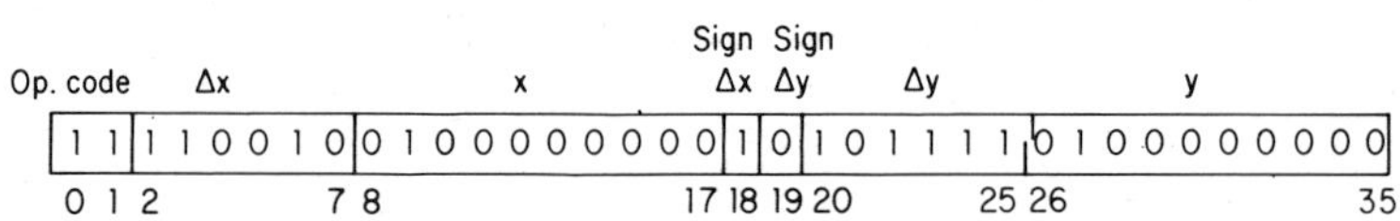

One bits in position 0 and 1 mean "this word signifies the drawing of a line segment, specified in positions 2 through 35." The effect of this instruction is to produce the line segment here shown:

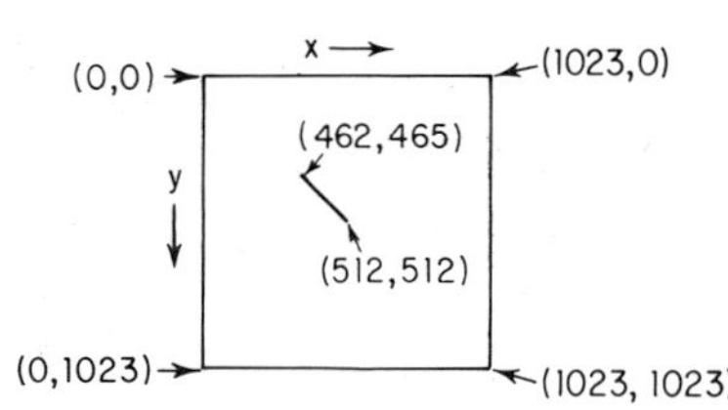

When a word is received by the SC-4020, its digital processor interprets the first two bits as a line-drawing command and sends the succes-

* Since the time of this writing, the name of the Stromberg-Carlson 4020 computer has been changed to the *DatagraphiX 4020*. The special cathode-ray tube employed in the 4020 is available under the registered trademark "Charactron®" from Stromberg DatagraphiX, Inc.

sive bit patterns to the digital-to-analog converter to be translated from their digital form to appropriate voltages to drive the electron beam in the cathode-ray tube.

The remaining 17 operations recognized by the SC-4020 from the leading bit pattern of a 36-bit word are:

Plot an alphabetic character
Expose heavy
Expose light
Stop typing
Type at a specified point
Type at current point
Generate x axis
Generate y axis
Select camera 1
Select camera 3
Select both cameras
Expand image
Reduce image
Advance film
Project the form slide
Carriage return
Reset

In each case, a Fortran or Algol instruction can be written which will translate commands specified in Fortran or Algol English and in numbers into the appropriate bit patterns for the SC-4020.

No standard set of operation codes has been adopted. Each graphical computer has its own, which differs in detail and philosophy from the illustrative set of the SC-4020 shown here.

In addition to the ability to generate a line segment, most cathode-ray-tube graphical computers are able to generate alphabetic and numeric characters. Two main processes are used, namely, the shaped-beam and the beam-writing methods. In the former, employed by the SC-4020, the electron beam is shaped by extrusion through a template or stencil containing a font of alphabetic and numeric characters. The arrangement is shown in Fig. 9.8. Selection plates in the cathode-ray tube (trademark Charactron by Stromberg-Carlson) send the beam through the appropriate character in the stencil; subsequent "reference" plates bring the beam back to the tube axis, and finally, the deflection yoke sends the shaped beam to the desired position on the face of the cathode-ray tube. In this way, any character out of the template's font can be positioned at any of the 1,024 by 1,024 grid points on the tube's face.

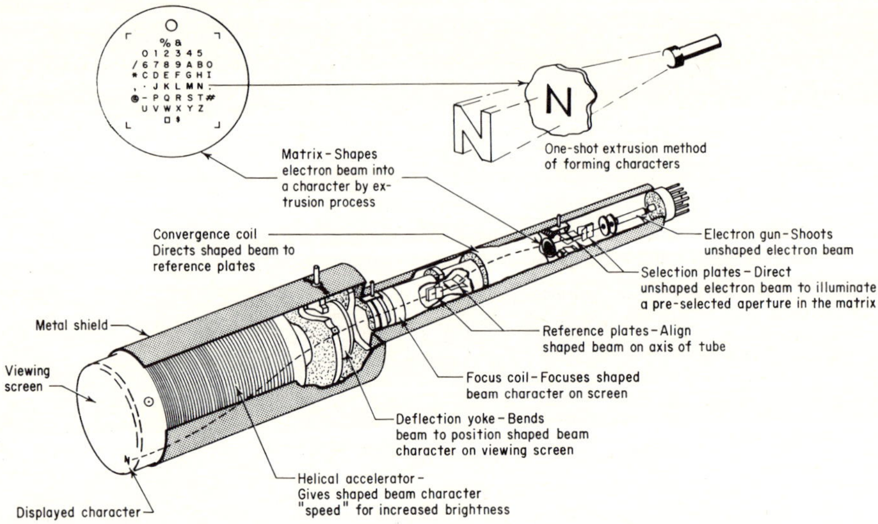

Fig. 9.8. Method of alphabetic character generator used by the SC-4020.

In the second main method, a cross section of the beam is not shaped; it remains circular in a constant diameter on the tube face. One variant uses *stroke generators.* This is a piece of hardware which deflects the beam in a sequence of line segments that trace out the character. In fact, this is a hardware embodiment of a sequence of line-generating commands. In another variant, the beam sweeps out a zig-zag pattern. As it sweeps, hardware alternately shuts the beam on and off so as to create the desired character.

Software for Computer-drawn Pictures

As stated earlier, it is not enough to have a high-speed picture-making device; one must also bring to bear the logical capability and speed of digital computing.

Let us assume, as before, that the face of the cathode-ray tube on which the computed pictures appear is ruled into a square grid of 1,024 × 1,024 points, numbered 0 to 1,023 from left to right horizontally and 0 to 1,023 from top to bottom vertically (0,0 is the upper left corner).

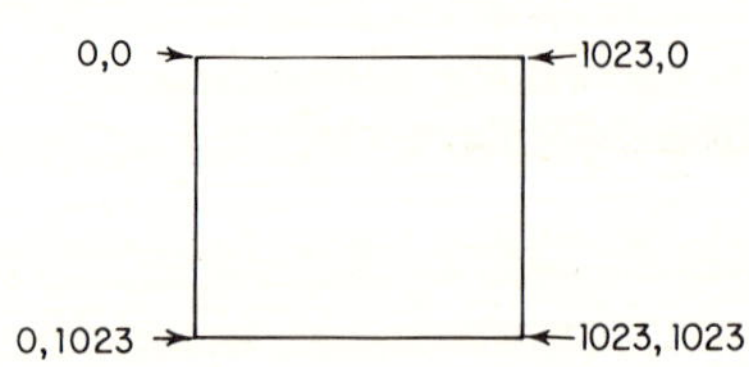

These assumptions are somewhat arbitrary; some microfilm recorders of higher resolution have 4,096 $\times$ 4,096 grid points; the numbering need not be from 0 to 1,023, since automatic scaling methods allow any values to be assigned to the corners of the plotting area, but we shall stick with these for simplicity of discussion.

Suppose then we wish to have appear a horizontal line stretching across the middle of the picture. In Fortran, the command to do this would be

CALL LINE (0,512,1023,512)

This Fortran instruction would cause transfer to a set of instructions which would "pack" bits into a word in computer storage into the form indicated in the previous section, and would cause this either to be read directly into the SC-4020 computer or would write the word on magnetic tape for future reading into the SC-4020. In either case, the control word would enter the digital processor of the SC-4020 (Fig. 9.7) and the point with tube face coordinates $x = 0$, $y = 512$ would be joined to the point with coordinates $x = 1023$, $y = 512$.

The above is a very simple example of a result produced by communication to the computer in something akin to ordinary English. The example chosen is very simple; the Fortran instruction converts in an obvious way to the computer output. However, Fortran and related languages are capable of much more, with sequences of English-like Fortran instructions that translate into complicated logical and arithmetic operations and results that are not apparent from a cursory reading of the Fortran text. Indeed, this capability is one of the triumphs of modern computing, and is one of the elements that gives computer-drawn pictures their power.

The possibility of coding a digital computer in instructions that look like ordinary language has evolved with the evolution of ever increasing computer sizes and speeds. In the first digital computers, the logical steps for executing a program were kept separate from the arithmetic operations. The logical steps were wired onto a "breadboard," which when connected to the arithmetic unit (resembling a desk calculator) would lead the arithmetic unit through the sequence of steps necessary to complete the desired calculation. Partial results which would be required at some subsequent stage of the computation were stored in temporary "storage registers."

With the original, slow digital computers using mechanical relays, this division of labor seemed natural. However, the advent of electronic digital machines quickly made it apparent that the time-consuming process of wiring up a new breadboard for each problem was a large stumbling block. The solution hit upon (usually credited to mathematician von Neumann) was to assign each logical operation a number, and then to design electronics into the computer which would recognize these numbers and execute the corresponding logical operations. The logical steps for a computation were thus implemented in "software" by a sequence of numbers rather than in "hardware" by a sequence of wires on a board.

Although programming by software instead of hardware was a giant step forward, the tedium of instructing the computer in the numbers of machine code was still considerable. Only after several years was it appreciated that the introduction of software coding had larger ramifications. The computer no longer processed numbers for doing arithmetic only. It was really processing "numerals," i.e., symbols which stood sometimes for numbers and sometimes for logical operations. The computer was better regarded as a symbol processor rather than a number processor. The numerals processed could symbolize not only numbers but logical operations and other entities as well. In particular, by assigning each letter of the alphabet a numerical code, the computer could process alphabetic information. It could, for example, translate English-like instructions such as CALL LINE into numerical instructions of machine code. Furthermore, the translation could be made differently depending on the application. For example, the same instruction could generate machine code for a cathode-ray-tube plotter or a different machine code for a mechanical plotter.

Fortran (standing for *For*mula *tran*slator) is one of the first "high-level" languages which does such translation. A Fortran program takes two passes through the computer to be completed. In the first pass, the alphabetic commands of Fortran are translated into machine-language instructions; in the second pass machine-language instructions are executed to produce final computer output (in some higher-level languages, and in some of the more elaborate versions of Fortran, several passes are executed, the result of each pass except the last being a program in a lower-level language).

By combining the enormous logical arithmetic power of computing, couched in English, with picture-producing hardware, we get a very powerful tool. We shall illustrate this capability in terms of the hardware described in the previous section. This is capable of generating only two rudimentary picture elements: straight-line segments and characters of a fixed size. However, let us see what results when Fortran is brought to bear on the rudimentary straight-line generation capability.

We consider the development of a Fortran program for a simple movie. The Fortran instruction defined earlier

```
CALL LINE (0,512,1023,512)
```

causes the beam in the cathode-ray tube to sweep a straight line from the point $x = 0$, $y = 512$ to the point $x = 1{,}023$, $y = 512$.

An alternative way to produce the same line is to write

```
Y = 512
CALL LINE (0,Y,1023,Y)
```

This seems like a step backward, since we have replaced a single instruction by two instructions. However, it shows an important fact: Fortran can deal directly in terms of symbols; the programmer is not doomed to programming in numbers. CALL LINE is now like an algebraic expression which depends on the variable Y. The actual value of Y can be calculated in any way we choose. For example

```
Y = SQRT (262144)
CALL LINE (0,Y,1023,Y)
```

SQRT (Square root function) is the Fortran command for taking the square root. Since the square root of 262,144 is 512, we get the same result as before. This command also illustrates Fortran's algebraic manipulation capability. For animation purposes, a useful way to specify Y for the CALL LINE instruction is by means of a *computer loop*. We first label the CALL LINE instruction with a reference number, say 17 (the reference number is arbitrary). Then we write

```
   DO TO 17 FOR Y = 1 to 100
17 CALL LINE (0,Y,1023,Y)
```

The DO instruction says to the computer "Do the following instruction up to and including the one labeled 17, letting Y take on successive values 1, 2, 3, 4, . . . , 100." In this case, the result is horizontal lines spaced one unit apart between $y = 1$ and $y = 100$.

To produce an animated film, we merely add a new instruction, CALL FRAME, transferring the label 17 at the same time:

```
   DO TO 17 FOR Y = 1 to 100
   CALL LINE (0,Y,1023,Y)
17 CALL FRAME
```

CALL FRAME causes the film to advance in the camera by one frame. The variable Y is now first given the value 1, then CALL LINE causes a horizontal line to be drawn from $x = 0$, $y = 1$ to $x = 1{,}023$, $y = 1$, and CALL FRAME brings in the next frame of film. The variable Y is next given the value 2, a horizontal line is drawn with Y = 2 on the new frame, and the film is advanced again. The process continues 100 times. The result is 100 horizontal lines spaced one unit apart, but now the lines each occur on a different frame of film. When the film strip is run through a projector, we see a vertical line which moves steadily downward.

The idea of a computer loop is a central concept of modern computing. Note that the computer loop differs from a film loop. In the computer loop, the same sequence of *instructions* is executed over and over again. The events that result in each pass through the loop are, however, based on differing data. Hence, each pass through the computer loop yields a *different event.* In the film loop, one sees the *same event* over and over again.

The symbolizing or naming power of programming illustrated by the use of the symbol Y extends further. To illustrate, assume that we are writing a number of programs for animated films and the need for a sequence showing the steady downward motion of a horizontal line arises frequently. We want to avoid writing the program for this animation time after time, short as it is. We give the program a name, say DOWNWARD, and affix two instructions:

```
   SUBROUTINE DOWNWARD
   DO TO 17 for Y = 1 to 100
   CALL LINE (0,Y,1023,Y)
17 CALL FRAME
   RETURN
```

This "subroutine" can now be stored either in computer memory or, if memory is at a premium, on punched cards, magnetic tape, or magnetic disks. When the user needs the downward-moving line in some subsequent program, he need only write

```
CALL DOWNWARD
```

This instruction sends program control to the subroutine DOWNWARD, causing the sequence of instructions for a downward-moving line to be executed. When these are executed, RETURN sends control back to the main program. The reader will note that CALL LINE and CALL FRAME are themselves calls to subroutines.

The ability to eliminate having to write the same sequence of instructions over and over again is a great convenience. But more important is the conceptual power of symbolization. One does a task once and for all, gives the task a name, DOWNWARD, and from then on thinks of the task in terms of this name.

Furthermore, a program which calls a subroutine can itself be made into a subroutine, which in turn can be incorporated into another subroutine, and so on. The result is a hierarchical structure like an onion; each layer encloses another layer which encloses another layer, etc.

Just as we use the ability for CALL LINE to accept information in symbolic form, so can we incorporate symbols into subroutines to increase their flexibility. For example, suppose we wish subroutine DOWNWARD to show a line moving downward at one-half the rate we originally programmed. We first make the action extend over 200 frames instead of 100 by changing the upper number in the DO instruction from 100 to 100 × 2:

```
DO TO 17 FOR Y = 1 TO 100 × 2
```

Also, we advance the line vertically one-half unit each frame instead of a full unit.

```
CALL LINE (0,Y/2,1023,Y/2)
```

The resulting subroutine for DOWNWARD is now:

```
   SUBROUTINE DOWNWARD
   DO TO 17 FOR Y = 1 to 100 × 2
   CALL LINE (0,Y/2,1023,Y/2)
17 CALL FRAME
   RETURN
```

But we see that we can easily make the line move one-*n*th as fast:

```
   SUBROUTINE DOWNWARD (N)
   DO TO 17 FOR Y = 1 to 100 × N
   CALL LINE (9,Y/N,1023,Y/N)
17 CALL FRAME
   RETURN
```

DOWNWARD, which now depends on the variable N, might appear in the main program as

```
N = 4
CALL DOWNWARD (N)
```

or, simply as

```
CALL DOWNWARD (4)
```

In either case, the resulting line would move downward ¼ as fast as orginally programmed. Subroutines, especially with a flexibility of variable dependence, allow the programmer to think in terms of dynamic visual symbols. Thus, for example, in programming an educational movie on Euclidean geometry, one would write a set of subroutines to show the striking of an arbitrary arc, the dropping of a perpendicular to a line, the bisection of an angle, and so on. These names of subroutines would then become the elements of a symbolic "language" by which the programmer would communicate with the computer in order to produce the sequences of his movie.

For a variety of tasks, especially where formula evaluation plays a heavy role, and where pictures can be composed of white lines on black background or vice versa, the visual symbols afforded by a Fortran-like language are sufficient. At other times, however, we may want to fill the entire picture area with various shades of gray. The picture would thus consist of a rectangular area of tens of thousands of picture elements, much like a television picture.

K. C. Knowlton has developed just such a system, called BEFLIX (for "Bell Flicks"), in which each picture consists of about 200 lines, with about 250 picture elements per line [11]. Thus, before putting out such a picture, the computer must first develop internally a complete and explicit array of 50,000 numbers from 0 to 7 (each representing one of eight shades of black, white, or gray). For example, suppose the programmer wants to represent a punched card by the three shades of picture elements shown in Fig. 9.9*a*. What he would actually be instructing the computer to construct is an array of numbers such as that shown in Fig. 9.9*b*, where 0 stands for a black picture element, 1 for dark gray, and 5 for white.

A BEFLIX system is designed specifically for constructing and manipulating pictures in just these terms, and for putting them out by sending appropriate commands to a film-exposing device. Figure 9.10 is an example of a picture produced by this process—it is a scene from an animated movie about the BEFLIX system [12]. The reader will note that the punched card of Fig. 9.9*a* appears as a part of Fig. 9.10.

In the operational BEFLIX system at Bell Laboratories, pictures are made by using the SC-4020 in its "typewriter" mode: a tiny character is typed for each picture element, with characters chosen for their overall brightness as viewed from a distance. Figure 9.10, for example, consists entirely of apostrophes in the dark gray region, degree signs in the light gray background area, and blanks which produced black areas and lines in this, a positive image.

The actual computation involved in constructing and manipulating a picture such as Fig. 9.10 involves the execution of sequences of instructions of the machine's basic repertoire. Such a sequence, expressed symbolically, might be

```
CLA  10321
ARS  9
ANA  =Ø7
SUB  =5
TZE  572
```

which means: "Clear the accumulator to zero and add into it the contents of register 10321, shift this number right nine bit positions, mask out

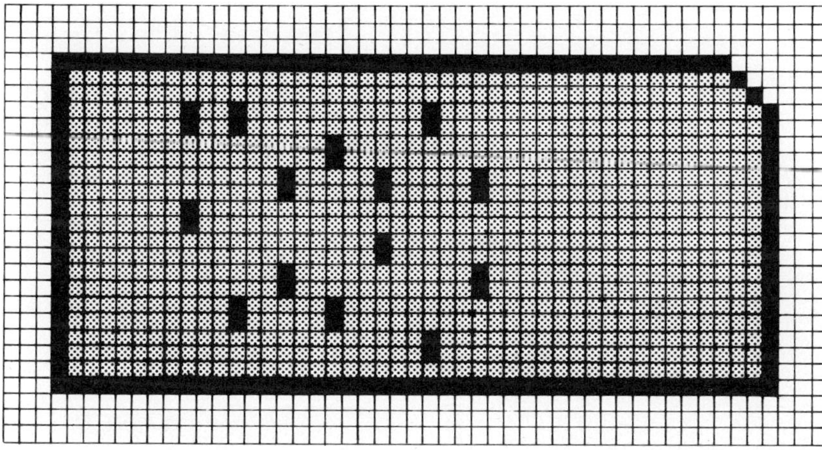

(a)

5	5	5	5	5	5	5	5	5	5	5	5	5	5	5	5	5	5	5	5	5	5	5	5	5	5	5	5	5	5	5	5	5	5	5	5	5	5	5	5	5	5	5	5	5	5	5	5	5	5	5
5	5	5	5	5	5	5	5	5	5	5	5	5	5	5	5	5	5	5	5	5	5	5	5	5	5	5	5	5	5	5	5	5	5	5	5	5	5	5	5	5	5	5	5	5	5	5	5	5	5	5
5	5	5	5	5	5	5	5	5	5	5	5	5	5	5	5	5	5	5	5	5	5	5	5	5	5	5	5	5	5	5	5	5	5	5	5	5	5	5	5	5	5	5	5	5	5	5	5	5	5	5
5	5	5	0	0	0	0	0	0	0	0	0	0	0	0	0	0	0	0	0	0	0	0	0	0	0	0	0	0	0	0	0	0	0	0	0	0	0	0	0	0	0	0	0	0	5	5	5	5	5	5
5	5	5	0	1	1	1	1	1	1	1	1	1	1	1	1	1	1	1	1	1	1	1	1	1	1	1	1	1	1	1	1	1	1	1	1	1	1	1	1	1	1	1	1	1	0	5	5	5	5	5
5	5	5	0	1	1	1	1	1	1	1	1	1	1	1	1	1	1	1	1	1	1	1	1	1	1	1	1	1	1	1	1	1	1	1	1	1	1	1	1	1	1	1	1	1	1	0	5	5	5	5
5	5	5	0	1	1	1	1	1	1	0	1	1	0	1	1	1	1	1	1	1	1	1	1	1	0	1	1	1	1	1	1	1	1	1	1	1	1	1	1	1	1	1	1	1	1	1	0	5	5	5
5	5	5	0	1	1	1	1	1	1	0	1	1	0	1	1	1	1	1	1	1	1	1	1	1	0	1	1	1	1	1	1	1	1	1	1	1	1	1	1	1	1	1	1	1	1	1	0	5	5	5
5	5	5	0	1	1	1	1	1	1	1	1	1	1	1	1	1	1	1	0	1	1	1	1	1	1	1	1	1	1	1	1	1	1	1	1	1	1	1	1	1	1	1	1	1	1	1	0	5	5	5
5	5	5	0	1	1	1	1	1	1	1	1	1	1	1	1	1	1	1	0	1	1	1	1	1	1	1	1	1	1	1	1	1	1	1	1	1	1	1	1	1	1	1	1	1	1	1	0	5	5	5
5	5	5	0	1	1	1	1	1	1	1	1	1	1	1	1	0	1	1	1	1	1	0	1	1	1	1	1	0	1	1	1	1	1	1	1	1	1	1	1	1	1	1	1	1	1	1	0	5	5	5
5	5	5	0	1	1	1	1	1	1	1	1	1	1	1	1	0	1	1	1	1	1	0	1	1	1	1	1	0	1	1	1	1	1	1	1	1	1	1	1	1	1	1	1	1	1	1	0	5	5	5
5	5	5	0	1	1	1	1	1	1	0	1	1	1	1	1	1	1	1	1	1	1	1	1	1	1	1	1	1	1	1	1	1	1	1	1	1	1	1	1	1	1	1	1	1	1	1	0	5	5	5
5	5	5	0	1	1	1	1	1	1	0	1	1	1	1	1	1	1	1	1	1	1	1	1	1	1	1	1	1	1	1	1	1	1	1	1	1	1	1	1	1	1	1	1	1	1	1	0	5	5	5
5	5	5	0	1	1	1	1	1	1	1	1	1	1	1	1	1	1	1	1	1	1	0	1	1	1	1	1	1	1	1	1	1	1	1	1	1	1	1	1	1	1	1	1	1	1	1	0	5	5	5
5	5	5	0	1	1	1	1	1	1	1	1	1	1	1	1	1	1	1	1	1	1	0	1	1	1	1	1	1	1	1	1	1	1	1	1	1	1	1	1	1	1	1	1	1	1	1	0	5	5	5
5	5	5	0	1	1	1	1	1	1	1	1	1	1	1	1	0	1	1	1	1	1	1	1	1	1	1	1	0	1	1	1	1	1	1	1	1	1	1	1	1	1	1	1	1	1	1	0	5	5	5
5	5	5	0	1	1	1	1	1	1	1	1	1	1	1	1	0	1	1	1	1	1	1	1	1	1	1	1	0	1	1	1	1	1	1	1	1	1	1	1	1	1	1	1	1	1	1	0	5	5	5
5	5	5	0	1	1	1	1	1	1	1	1	1	0	1	1	1	1	1	0	1	1	1	1	1	1	1	1	1	1	1	1	1	1	1	1	1	1	1	1	1	1	1	1	1	1	1	0	5	5	5
5	5	5	0	1	1	1	1	1	1	1	1	1	0	1	1	1	1	1	0	1	1	1	1	1	1	1	1	1	1	1	1	1	1	1	1	1	1	1	1	1	1	1	1	1	1	1	0	5	5	5
5	5	5	0	1	1	1	1	1	1	1	1	1	1	1	1	1	1	1	1	1	1	1	1	1	0	1	1	1	1	1	1	1	1	1	1	1	1	1	1	1	1	1	1	1	1	1	0	5	5	5
5	5	5	0	1	1	1	1	1	1	1	1	1	1	1	1	1	1	1	1	1	1	1	1	1	0	1	1	1	1	1	1	1	1	1	1	1	1	1	1	1	1	1	1	1	1	1	0	5	5	5
5	5	5	0	1	1	1	1	1	1	1	1	1	1	1	1	1	1	1	1	1	1	1	1	1	1	1	1	1	1	1	1	1	1	1	1	1	1	1	1	1	1	1	1	1	1	1	0	5	5	5
5	5	5	0	0	0	0	0	0	0	0	0	0	0	0	0	0	0	0	0	0	0	0	0	0	0	0	0	0	0	0	0	0	0	0	0	0	0	0	0	0	0	0	0	0	0	0	0	5	5	5
5	5	5	5	5	5	5	5	5	5	5	5	5	5	5	5	5	5	5	5	5	5	5	5	5	5	5	5	5	5	5	5	5	5	5	5	5	5	5	5	5	5	5	5	5	5	5	5	5	5	5
5	5	5	5	5	5	5	5	5	5	5	5	5	5	5	5	5	5	5	5	5	5	5	5	5	5	5	5	5	5	5	5	5	5	5	5	5	5	5	5	5	5	5	5	5	5	5	5	5	5	5
5	5	5	5	5	5	5	5	5	5	5	5	5	5	5	5	5	5	5	5	5	5	5	5	5	5	5	5	5	5	5	5	5	5	5	5	5	5	5	5	5	5	5	5	5	5	5	5	5	5	5

(b)

Fig. 9.9. (*a*) A pictorial representation of a punched card, in terms of an array of picture elements of different shades of gray. (*b*) Representation of the picture of (*a*) above within the computer, in terms of numbers representing different shades of gray. In the 7094 version of BEFLIX, twelve of these numbers are packed into a single machine register.

Fig. 9.10. Scene from "A Computer Technique for the Production of Animated Movies," a film about the BEFLIX system, and produced entirely by this system.

everything but the rightmost three bits, subtract five, and now if the result is zero, go to location 572 for the next instruction, otherwise continue with the very next instruction in this sequence, . . ." Obviously one could not tolerate the thought of building and changing pictures like that of Fig. 9.9*b* by programming in these terms, much less the thought of doing a large picture or a sequence of pictures for a movie. What is needed is a kit of tools—both in terms of more appropriate notation and in terms of pieces of program ("subroutines"), already written and checked out, which are generally useful. Fortran is one answer to this need for more powerful and better notation; in the present case, BEFLIX is the language which affords just the aids to picture building that we need.

The BEFLIX programmer imagines that within the computer there are large drawing boards laid out in squares which hold numbers from zero to seven as shown in Fig. 9.9*b*, but whose sizes are about 200 lines of 250 squares each. On these boards the programmer imagines a number of scanners or "bugs," each of which is sitting on a particular square at any time. A bug can read the number it is sitting on, can write a new number into this square, and can move right, left, up, or down any integral number of positions to a new square. There are 26 bugs in all, each named by a different letter of the alphabet.

The BEFLIX language may be divided into two distinct parts. The first (and historically older) part consists of those instructions for drawing and changing pictures by explicit manipulation of the bugs. An example of an instruction in the "bug language" is

```
IFANY (B,R,10)(B,A,C)(A,E,7)THEN(A,T,B)(A,U,2)(A,W,3)L5
```

which says "if any of the following is true: that bug B is right of $x = 10$, or that bug B is above (in a line higher than) bug C, or that bug A is sitting on a number equal to 7, then the following operations are to be performed: bug A is to move to the same square as bug B, bug A should then move up two squares, and bug A should write the number 3 on this square, and control should then go to the line of coding labeled L5; if none of the three elementary conditions is satisfied, no operations are performed and control goes to the next line of coding." Different numbers of elementary tests and operations may appear on a line, and the compound condition alternatively may be made to succeed *if all, if not all,* or *if none* of the elementary conditions are satisfied.

The other part of the movie language may be called the "movie language proper." It consists of more powerful instructions which in general compile into calls to subroutines written primarily in the bug language (these subroutines actually use an additional set of 26 bugs which the programmer need not know about). Instructions of the movie language proper fall logically into three categories: Instructions for controlling the output or temporary storage of pictures, instructions for performing drafting and typing operations, and instructions for modifying the contents of rectangular picture areas.

The facilities for drafting include the ability to draw straight lines, arcs, and arbitrary curves. These lines may be made to appear instantaneously in the movie, or they may be made to appear gradually as they are drawn. Lettering may be done by "typing" letters of several different sizes.

Operations on drawing boards or rectangular subareas include "painting" such an area by filling all of its squares with one particular digit. The contents of an area may also be shifted an integral number of positions up, down, right or left, or they may be "expanded" (by repeating rows or columns) or "squashed" (by deleting rows or columns) in any of the four directions, or one such area may be copied into another area. Certain local operations may be performed throughout an area such as adding incremental layers to regions defined by a certain number, or rounding sharp corners. There are operations which approximate the effect of a zoom lens by enlarging or reducing, by an integral factor, of the patterns of numbers within a rectangular area while the camera routine is putting out pictures of the intermediate states of the picture. There is also a facility for "dissolving" one picture onto another by sprinkling the new numbers onto the old ones, again while the output routine is putting out the intermediate states of the dissolve.

The drafting instructions and those for manipulating contents of rectangular areas in general require several parameters specifying just where and how the operation is to be performed. A sample of programming in the language is here given:

```
.
.
.
PAINT    A,B,WRITE,0
LINE     D,E,WRITE,2,3,15
TYPE     CAPT,C,5X7,1,3,WRITE,4
CAMERA
.
.
.
```

These four lines instruct the computer, first, to "paint" the rectangular area specified by bug A at the top right corner and bug B at the bottom left by writing a zero in each square. Then a "straight" line is to be drawn (as well as it can reasonably be done in terms of squares) from bug D to bug E by writing 2's in affected squares; the line is to be three squares wide, and it is to advance 15 squares per frame of movie output. The third line of code instructs the computer to type the text which has elsewhere been entered and labeled "CAPT," starting at bug C, in 5×7 font, with one square of horizontal spacing between letters and three vertically between lines, by writing 4's in affected squares. Finally, the "camera" subroutine is called to put out the frame containing the resulting picture.

As in Fortran programming, subroutines may be written once and may later be "called" any number of times by simply naming them; and subroutines may in turn be called into operation by other subroutines. Thus, the programmer has the ability to create a hierarchy of tools or facilities for drawing the objects or performing just the operations he needs for a particular area of work. When he has developed such a "library" of subroutines, he has in effect constructed a specialized and powerful language for drawing his type of pictures.

The BEFLIX system has been used to produce visual displays for psychophysical experiments and to generate artistic effects. It has been used to produce a set of expository films about a new programming language [13]. In general, it is useful for movies consisting of simple, but animated, schematic and geometric diagrams; films of this sort can be produced for less than $500 per minute of movie; they can be made quickly by one or two people, and can easily be revised: the marginal cost of redoing a scene of a movie is an order of magnitude less than by a conventional means, simply because the program needs only to be corrected and rerun.

Summary

In summary, we note that the computer is playing increasingly important and varied roles in communication processes, in particular with those processes which ideally deliver their outputs as visual displays for any of a number of reasons: because the material is inherently two- or three-dimensional, or because the sheer quantity of information is too great for other media, or because the next step in processing must be a difficult-to-specify pattern-recognition process, to be performed by the human eye and brain. In these areas, computers and their associated display equipment are becoming ever more useful because of their speed, accuracy, and economy, and because of their ability to handle mathematical situations and models easily. They are, for example, beginning to produce movies which heretofore would have been entirely beyond the realm of feasibility—such as films of three-dimensional vector fields, changing in time, as encountered in fluid dynamics and electrodynamics [14].

We note also that the use of computers in information transmission and processing affords another example of a familiar principle of communication in both biological and engineering systems: the tasks of computation and display, as elsewhere, consists of a more or less orderly collection of subtasks, and these subtasks in turn consist of still simpler but more basic processes. The entire situation is best thought of in terms of a hierarchy of messages and jobs.

REFERENCES

1. E. N. Gilbert, Energy Reception for Mobile Radio, *Bell System Tech. J.*, **44**:1779–1804 (October 1965).
2. E. I. Organick, "A Fortran Primer," Addison-Wesley, London, 1963.
3. E. W. Dijkstra, "Primer of ALGOL 60 Programming," Academic Press, New York, 1962.
4. F. W. Sinden, "Force, Mass, and Motion," 10-minute 16-mm black and white sound film; available on loan from Technical Information Libraries, Bell Laboratories, Murray Hill, New Jersey.
5. E. E. Zajac, "Two-gyro, Gravity Gradient Attitude Control System," 4-minute 16-mm black and white sound film; available on loan from Bell Laboratories (see Ref. 4).

6. E. E. Zajac, Computer-made Perspective Movies as a Scientific and Communication Tool, *Commun. ACM,* **7:**169–170 (March 1964).
7. A. Michael Noll, A Computer Technique for Displaying n-Dimensional-Hyperobjects, *Commun. ACM,* **10:**469–473 (August 1967).
8. A. Michael Noll, Computer-generated Three-dimensional Movies, *Computers Automation,* **14:**(11):20–23 (November 1965).
9. W. L. Brown, J. D. Gabbe, and W. Rosenzweig, Results of the Telstar Radiation Experiment, *Bell System Tech. J.,* **47:**1505–1559 (July 1963).
10. "Programmers' Reference Manual, SC-4020 High-speed Microfilm Recorder," Stromberg-Carlson Division of General Dynamics, San Diego, California.
11. K. C. Knowlton, A Computer Technique for Producing Animated Movies, *Am. Federation Inform. Processing Soc. Conf. Proc.,* **25:**67–87 (April 1964).
12. K. C. Knowlton, "A Computer Technique for the Production of Animated Movies," 17-minute 16-mm black and white silent film; available on loan from Bell Laboratories (see Ref. 4).
13. K. C. Knowlton, "L^6: Bell Laboratories Low-level Linked List Language," 16-minute film, and "L^6: Part II—An Example of L^6 Programming," 32-minute film. Both are 16-mm black and white films with sound; available on loan from Bell Laboratories (see Ref. 4).
14. "Movies from Computers—An Interim Report," 20-minute 16-mm sound film containing several examples of computer animation; available on loan from Educational Development Corp., 39 Chapel St., Newton, Mass. 02160.

CHAPTER TEN

*Speaker Identification by Speech Spectrograms: A Scientists' View of Its Reliability for Legal Purposes**

RICHARD H. BOLT

FRANKLIN S. COOPER

EDWARD E. DAVID, JR.

PETER B. DENES

JAMES M. PICKETT

KENNETH N. STEVENS

Preface

Can one reliably identify a person by examining the spectrographic patterns of his speech? This is a scientific problem of social importance because of the legal consequences of this question. The Technical Committee on Speech Communication of the Acoustical Society of America

* Reprinted from the Journal of the Acoustical Society of America, vol. 47, no. 2, part 2, February 1970.

has asked some of its members to review the matter from a scientific point of view. The topics they considered included the nature of speech information as it relates to speaker identification, a comparison of voice patterns and fingerprint patterns, experimental evidence on voice identification, and requirements for validation of such identification methods. Findings and conclusions are reported; supporting information is given in the appendixes.

Introduction

The sound spectrograph is an instrument that finds widespread use in current research on speech sounds. It portrays, in graphical form, the time variations of the short-term spectrum of the speech wave [1]. Examples of such speech spectrograms are shown in Fig. 10.1 for four instances of the word "science." In each spectrogram, the horizontal dimension is time, the vertical dimension represents frequency, and the darkness represents intensity on a compressed scale. This representation of the sound patterns of speech has proved to be extremely powerful in research on the phonetic aspects of speech because the spectrogram gives valuable information about speech articulation. In the examples of Fig. 10.1, the middle portions of the patterns show effects of the articulations corresponding to the vowels of "science." The initial and final portions of each spectrogram show sudden changes in the frequency pattern where consonants and vowels join.

When two persons speak the same word, their articulation is similar but not identical; therefore, spectrograms of these words will be similar but not identical. There are also similarities and differences even when the same speaker repeats the same word. These facts are apparent in the spectrograms of Fig. 10.1. The two spectrograms at the top were made by the same speaker on two different occasions; the two spectrograms at the bottom were made by two other speakers.

Speech scientists have found spectrograms very useful in studying how people pronounce different words. Can spectrograms also be applied to distinguishing one person from another? In several recent court hearings, evidence has been presented both for and against the use of speech spectrograms, or "voiceprints," for personal identification. Scientists in speech research have been concerned, for reasons of social importance and scientific credibility, about such use of speech spectrograms; the Technical Committee on Speech Communication of the Acoustical Society of America asked six members of the Society (the authors of this paper) to study and report on this issue.* In considering this problem, we asked questions such as the following: When two voice spectrograms look alike, do the similarities mean "same speaker"

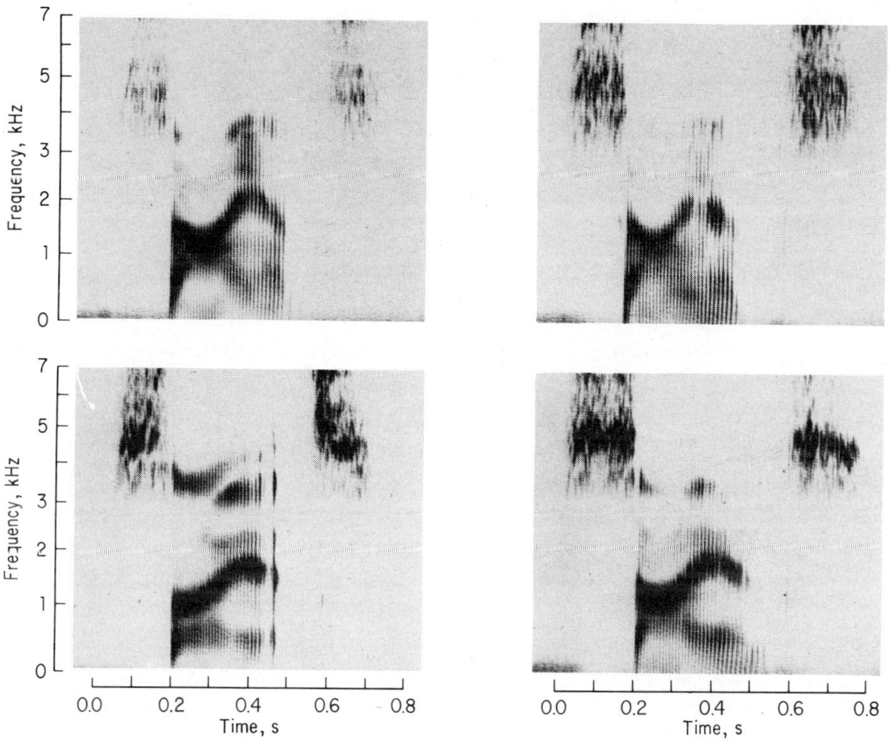

Fig. 10.1. Four spectrograms of the spoken word "science." The vertical scale represents frequency, the horizontal dimension is time, and darkness represents intensity on a compressed scale. Three of the spectrograms are from three different speakers and the remaining spectrogram is a repetition of the word by one of the speakers (see text). The spectrograms were made on a Voiceprint Laboratories sound spectrograph.

or merely "same word spoken"? Are the irrelevant similarities likely to mislead a lay jury in assessing conflicting testimony from opposing experts? How permanent are voice patterns? How distinctive are they for the individual? Can they be successfully disguised or faked?

Whatever the future may hold for voice printing as a method of identification, expert witnesses at the present time do not agree as to its reliability, and various courts of law have ruled both for and against the admission of such evidence [3]. These differences of opinion are, however, only the surface reflections of deep-lying difficulties, inherent in the nature of spoken language, that serve to make voice identification equivocal for the expert and confusing to the layman.

* The views given here are those of the authors as individuals. Additional background on this report can be found in Ref. 2.

It is against this background that we have undertaken to point up the difficulties inherent in voice identification, to review and assess the relevant scientific knowledge available today, and to examine the problem of scientific validation for the use of voiceprint identification as legal evidence.*

The Nature of Speech Information and Voice Identification

The aim of speech is communication. For this purpose, speakers of a given language use a common code and a common set of speech sounds. Thus, the same message produced by different speakers uses basically the same sequence of sounds; when a person speaks a word or phrase, he tries to produce sound patterns like those of other speakers of his dialect. In fact, however, only certain aspects of the sound are the same when two speakers produce the same word or when one speaker says the same word on different occasions.

There are several reasons why some aspects of the sound pattern of a word are different on different occasions. For different speakers, the vocal anatomy may be different. Regardless of the speaker, some aspects of the sounds are nonessential in the sense that they are not used to identify words, and speakers are free to produce them in various ways. Different speakers may develop characteristically different habits in using these nonessential features, or a single speaker may show considerable variation in their use from one utterance to another. Thus, the speech sounds carry several submessages, including information about the speaker's identity, his mood, and his manner of speaking, as well as the words he says. At present, we do not have a clear understanding of which sound features are likely to be invariant for a given speaker, and which are likely to show variation from one speaker to another [5, 6].

A further complication is that the sound features do not fall neatly into separate sets that refer to the various submessages carried in speech. All these submessages are merged into a complex sound stream; moreover, all of them can affect all the sound features, so that there is no simple, obvious relation between messages and features [7].

Yet recovering one of these submessages is the essence of speaker identification; the task is to tease out from the sound patterns those

* Technical details in support of these discussions are contained in Appendixes A to D. A detailed scientific review of voice identification has been prepared by M. Hecker [4].

features that correspond to the talker's vocal anatomy and his habits of forming speech sounds, since these might characterize him as a speaker. This is usually attempted by comparing different utterances of the same word or phrase, one from a known speaker, and interpreting the similarities and differences. There will be many similarities because the same words were used; there will also be differences that may be due either to a difference in speakers, or to the free variations of a single speaker.

The correct assignment of the differences, given all these complexities, is a difficult matter. Yet, we know that almost everyone can identify some voices just by listening to them. We know also, from controlled experiments, that identification by ear alone is not highly reliable [8–10].

A newer method of voice identification uses visual comparison of the graphic patterns resulting from a gross acoustic analysis using the sound spectrograph. Not all details of the acoustic patterns are presented in this graphic display; moreover, the display is designed to emphasize those features that characterize the words of the spoken message. Speech-sound spectrograms of this type are the primary material used forensically for voice identification. The identification is done, not by the spectrograph, but by means of visual comparison of the spectrograms and by subjective judgments about the identity of the speakers represented [11, 12].

Could a better instrument be developed? One possibility would be a device with a display emphasizing those sound features that are most dependent on the speaker. The patterns could then be judged with greater confidence by human experts. We do not yet know how to design such an instrument, primarily because of the inherent complexity of speech sounds. We are even farther from having a fully objective procedure by which the features that characterize an individual speaker could be extracted and evaluated automatically [13].

Voice Patterns and Fingerprint Patterns

How similar is voice identification by spectrogram to fingerprint identification? The differences between them seem to exceed the similarities, as the following comparative summary shows.

Fingerprints show directly the physical patterns of the fingers producing them and these patterns are readily discernible. Spectrographic patterns and the sound waves that they represent are not, however, related so simply and directly to vocal anatomy; moreover, the spectrogram is not the primary evidence, but only a graphic means for examining the sounds that a speaker makes.

In fingerprint identification, the gross types of ridge patterns, such as loops and whorls, are used for classification and indexing; these types are determined mainly by heredity and thus have only limited power in differentiating persons. The minute details of the ridges are then compared for final identification and all points of similarity strongly imply a match, while any point of dissimilarity strongly implies a mismatch. In comparing voice patterns, we are not able to interpret similarities and differences in such simple ways.

The fingerprint features that are ultimately used for identification are the most minute details of the skin ridge patterns such as bifurcations, terminations, and interruptions. These details are determined mainly by random processes in prenatal skin development. There are a sizable number of these minute anatomical features on each finger. There are an enormous number of possible combinations of these features, and it is known that their patterns remain unchanged throughout life [14, 15]. Comparable voice features for identification, if they exist, have not been established; moreover, changes with growth and environmental influences could be expected.

Whereas fingerprint patterns cannot easily be faked or disguised, a speaker can learn to alter his voice and imitate, with some success, the speech of other persons.

Variations found in fingerprint patterns do not consist of changes in patterns from one type to another, but rather in expansions (with growth), obliterations (of some features), smudges, or incompleteness. Spectrographic patterns are affected in a more fundamental way by the distortions of frequency, energy, and time that are commonly encountered in the transmission, recording, and analysis of sound. The very dimensions of the pattern are those that are changed by such sound distortions.

In view of basic differences between fingerprints and voice patterns, and the inherent complexity of spoken language, we doubt that the reliability of voice identification can ever match that of fingerprint identification.

Experimental Evidence on Voice Identification

Both objective and subjective methods have been used to try to identify voices. In objective methods, a piece of equipment makes all the decisions. Subjective methods may also involve equipment, such as a sound spectrograph, to display the acoustic information, but the final decision—the judgment—is made by a man.

Objective methods of voice identification have used automatic pattern matching, applied to voice patterns. In one study, average spectral patterns were obtained for each of 10 talkers and stored in a computer. To make identifications, a new pattern from each of the talkers was compared with each of the stored patterns to find the one most similar; identification errors were about 10 percent [16, 17].

Subjective experiments using speech spectrograms have been of two types: (1) sorting experiments, in which the observer sorts a set of spectrograms of a test word into individual talker categories, and (2) matching experiments, in which the observer identifies spectrograms of single talkers by matching them against spectrograms in a catalog of talkers, all speaking the same word or set of words.

In the sorting experiments, the observers knew how many talkers there were and how many examples were taken from each talker. In these experiments, test sets of 5 to 12 talkers were drawn at random from a pool of 123 male talkers selected to be homogeneous in regional accent [11, 17]. In a test, there were four examples of each test word from each talker. With 12 talkers, for example, 48 spectrograms were given to the observer and his task was to sort them into 12 categories corresponding to the individual talkers. Trained observers were used. In one such experiment [11], which used test sets of 5, 9, or 12 talkers, the average error rates, pooled over observers, ranged from 0.35 percent for 5 talkers in the set to 1 percent for 12 talkers in the set. In another sorting experiment [18], the observers were nine law-enforcement officers, of whom seven were fingerprint experts; all were first trained in voice identification from spectrograms; test sets of 12 talkers were used; the observers' error rates ranged from 0 to 3.48 percent, with a median of 0.42 percent.

The matching experiments reported to date have employed test sets of talkers ranging in size from 5 to 50. In one matching experiment [11], nine talkers were used in the catalog; the catalog contained two examples of a test word as spoken by each talker and the observer's task was to match a third example of the word spoken by one of the nine talkers; the average error rate was 1 percent; the range of error rates, over the 10 different test words employed, was 0 to 3 percent. In another matching experiment [18], with 50 talkers drawn from the pool of talkers mentioned above, the catalog of spectrograms consisted of two examples of each of five words spoken in context by each talker. Nine trained observers matched new sets of the same five words, each set spoken by a talker who was one of the 50 talkers in the catalog. The error rate for observers working individually ranged from 0 to 11.1 percent, with a median of 5.7 percent. The error rate for observers working together in pairs ranged from 3.2 to 14.3 percent, with a median of 7.7 percent.

In another matching experiment [19] using a set of five talkers and trained observers, the average error rate was 21.6 percent for words spoken in isolation. When the words were spoken in fluent context and matched against a catalog taken from context, the error of talker identification was 62.7 percent.

In still another matching experiment [20], the results obtained from listening only were compared with the results obtained solely by visual examination of spectrograms, using the same set of utterances for the two methods of identification. A set of eight talkers was used and a series of 14 identification tests was carried out. The performance of the observers improved over the series. The error rate for listening was always lower than for visual identification; at the best levels of performance, the average error rate was 6 percent for listening and 21 percent for visual identification. In further tests using new unknown talkers among the test samples, the observers were asked to judge whether a sample was spoken by any of the eight known talkers in the catalog. By listening, 6 to 8 percent of the unknown talkers were incorrectly called known; by visual examination of the spectrograms, 31 to 47 percent of the unknown talkers were called known. This result indicated that visual comparisons between spectrograms of talkers were less reliable than auditory comparisons.

The wide differences in error rate seen in these experiments reflect the strong dependence of voice identification judgments on specific conditions on the experimental test procedures, in particular, but also on the experience and training of the observers, on the speaking conditions under which the speech samples are collected, and on instrumentation.

How relevant are these experiments to voice identification as used in legal trials? The task of the expert witness usually consists of judging the identity of a speaker from two sets of spectrograms, one from a known speaker (the accused) and the other from a speech sample associated with the case but produced by an unidentified speaker. This is neither a sorting nor a matching task. It is not matching because there is only one entry in the catalog of known speakers and the unknown speaker may not even be in this catalog. It is not sorting, because the spectrograms are already sorted into two categories: known and unknown. Further, all matching and sorting experiments reported in the literature employed a closed set of known size; the unknown sample with which the expert witness is confronted is drawn from an indefinitely large set of unidentified speakers. *None of the experiments in the literature has employed a comparable task.*

In addition to the results of controlled experiments, there are essentially anecdotal accounts of experiences in applying the methods of spectrographic voice identification to law-enforcement problems. For example, we are informed that ". . . over 250 cases were processed for over 48 different law enforcement agencies in the United States and Europe which [is believed to be] a considerable body of practical proof, since no report of an error has occurred"; also, that a police officer has ". . . produced approximately 25 verified identifications where suspected persons admitted their guilt. In 37 cases the suspected persons were eliminated and released from any charges . . ." [21, 22]. The question of what interpretation or reliance to put on reports of this general kind is a difficult one, because (1) the relevant facts may not be publicly available in some types of investigations, or the facts may be fragmentary and disputed, as in courtroom proceedings; (2) actual cases usually involve other kinds of evidence, so that the contribution of voice identification to the resolution of the case cannot be determined; and (3) neither legal resolution of a case nor confession of guilt gives reliable information about the correctness of voice identifications that may have been made. Perhaps a careful analysis of experience with the investigative uses of spectrographic voice identification could lead to dependable estimates of the practical reliability of the method as applied to courtroom proceedings; however, other methods using controlled experiments could be far more direct and would gain credibility by full disclosure of data and procedures.

Situations in which one speaker attempts to mimic another have not been examined in depth, but speech scientists have noted cases in which spectrograms of different talkers are very similar [23] and in which an experienced mimic with special playback aids can produce speech sequences whose spectrographic patterns are capable of being confounded with those of another talker [24]. There have also been reports of instances in which the speech spectrograms of a mimic appeared quite different from those of the individual being mimicked [25].

Requirements for Validation of Voice-identification Methods

What kinds of evidence would convince scientists of the reliability of speaker identification based on voice patterns?

The usual basis for the scientific acceptance of any new procedure is an explicit description of experimental methods and of results of relevant tests. The description must be sufficient to allow the replication of experiments and results by other scientists. We have seen, in the preceding section, two doubts that arise when we apply this criterion to voice identification based on spectrograms. First, fully reliable identifications were not the usual result, even in small-scale sorting and matching experiments. Second, even when experimental methods were explicit, they differed in kind and complexity, as well as in scale, from the practical task of positively identifying a man solely on the basis of voice patterns.

Lacking explicit knowledge and procedures, can individuals nevertheless acquire such expertise in identification from voice patterns that their opinions could be accepted as reliable? This possibility may exist, for the human eye and brain are superb instruments. But it cannot be assumed without proof. Validation of this approach to voice identification becomes a matter of replicable experiments on the expert himself, considered as a voice-identifying machine.

Thus, voice identification might be accomplished either on the basis of explicit knowledge and procedure available to anyone, or on the basis of the unexplained expertise of individuals. In either case, validation requires experimental assessment of performance on relevant tasks.

Explicit procedures might be developed, based on specification of voice features useful for identification. Once the features were known, it would be important to learn how such features were distributed in the population. These distributions would permit an estimate of the size of the population of discriminable voices, and so give an indication of the reliability that would be theoretically attainable in specific situations [8].

What would we need to know about the performance of the expert whose procedures are not fully explicit? First, the experiments with experts should be statistically valid models of the practical task. The tests should include judgments of whether two speakers are identical when one spectrogram is available from each speaker, and when more than one spectrogram is available. It may also be appropriate to perform tests in which the unknown talker, whose identity is to be determined from a spectrogram, may be drawn from a set of known talkers or may not be a member of this set. Test formats should yield information about the probabilities of missed identification as well as false identification, and the trade-off between them; also, about the effects of size of population, the nature of the spoken context in both known and unknown samples, and the type of display of voice pattern and its sensitivity to noise, distortion, or deliberate attempts to disguise the unknown voice.*

It may be objected that this minimal set of tests is unreasonably

* Research projects on spectrographic voice identification, under sponsorship of the U.S. Department of Justice, are currently in progress at Michigan State University [18] and at Stanford Research Institute [4].

arduous. We do not believe that it is. As scientists, we could accept no less in checking the reliability of a "black box" supposed to perform speaker identification. This is how we must view the expert until he can provide an explicit and testable explanation of his methods.

Scientific Criteria and Legal Acceptance

Scientific and legal judgments differ in this basic respect: scientific acceptance is closely tied to technical evidence, whereas court determinations may rely heavily on the opinions of expert witnesses. When experts in recognized specialties differ in their opinions, the court may leave to a jury the assessment of conflicting opinions and of the relative expertise of witnesses. When new kinds of expert testimony are offered (e.g., speaker identification by spectrographic voice patterns), the court, before accepting such evidence, may first scrutinize the nature of the proffered expertise in relation to the consensus of informed scientific opinion. Today's consensus suggests that speaker identification by voice patterns is subject to error at a high, and as yet undetermined, rate.

Court determinations may also depend on the apparent validity of exhibits brought in evidence. Spectrographic evidence may often display features that are overwhelmingly influenced by the words spoken rather than by the speaker's identity. Judge and jury may therefore be misled in understanding the evidence and in assessing an expert's testimony.

Summary and Conclusions

1. Speech carries many simultaneous messages interwoven in a complex of words and phrases, moods, and individual voice characteristics. In their acoustic realization as speech, these messages are highly interdependent and thus difficult to disentangle. However, human observers can, to a limited extent, identify voices by ear or by visual examination of the acoustic patterns of speech.

2. The acoustic speech signal can be analyzed for frequency, energy, and time, and recorded graphically to produce a spectrogram. Neither the spectrogram nor any other known process can directly display an individual's voice traits, because of the intermixing of these traits with the features that characterize words and phrases. At present, a human observer must examine the patterns of spectrograms and decide subjectively about the identities of talkers.

3. Similarities and differences among spectrographic patterns are am-

biguous and may be misleading. Prominent similarities usually indicate that similar sounds were spoken, but do not necessarily imply that they were spoken by the same person; differences in pattern, when the words are the same, may reflect differences of speaker or only normal variations in the utterances of a single speaker.

4. Speech spectrograms, when used for voice identification, are not analogous to fingerprints, primarily because of fundamental differences in the sources of the patterns and consequent differences in their interpretation. For example, fingerprint patterns are a direct representation of anatomical traits. Vocal anatomy, on the contrary, is not represented in any direct way in voice spectrograms. In the interpretation of fingerprints, all points of similarity imply a match, although some more strongly than others; this simple relationship does not hold for the interpretation of voice patterns.

5. Experimental studies of voice identification using visual interpretation of spectrograms by human observers indicate false identification rates ranging from zero to as high as 63 percent, depending on the type of task set for the observer, the observer's training, and other factors. Reliable machine methods for voice identification have not yet been established.

6. Experience in applying spectrographic voice identification in law enforcement has led proponents of the method to express confidence in its reliability. The basis for this confidence is not, however, accessible to objective assessment.

7. Experimental studies to assess the reliability of voice identification under practical conditions, whether by experts or by explicit procedures, have not yet been made, but the requirements for such studies have been outlined.

We find, in brief, that spectrographic voice identification has inherent difficulties and uncertainties. Anecdotal evidence given in support of the method is not scientifically convincing. The controlled experiments that have been reported give conflicting results. Furthermore, the experiments reported thus far do not provide a direct test of the practical task of determining whether two spoken passages were uttered by the same speaker or by two different speakers, one of whom may be a person unknown.

We conclude that the available results are inadequate to establish the reliability of voice identification by spectrograms. We believe this conclusion is shared by most scientists who are knowledgeable about speech; hence, many of them are deeply concerned about the use of spectrographic evidence in the courts. Procedures exist, as we have suggested, by which the reliability of voice identification methods can be evaluated. We believe that such validation is urgently required.

APPENDIX A THE NATURE OF SPEECH INFORMATION AND VOICE IDENTIFICATION

The root of the voice identification problem lies in the nature of speech itself. This may not be immediately apparent, because speech is so familiar and so seemingly simple, but intensive research, especially over the past 20 years, has shown it to be a very complex process that is only partially understood even now. We do know, however, one important way in which this complexity affects the problem of voice identification: speech carries many different messages simultaneously, about the speaker as well as about the words spoken, and it does this by blending them into a single acoustic stream. Thus the speaker combines and encodes these messages for acoustic transmission and the listener must decode them. But now the component messages are no longer distinct, nor are message elements represented in any simple, direct way by acoustic elements of the speech.

The encoding operation, at least for the primary message of words and sentences, is a straightforward consequence of the articulatory process. As an example, in saying the word "tag," the vocal tract is first closed momentarily by bringing the tip of the tongue up to the dental ridge; then the tract is open wide by depressing the tongue tip rapidly while lowering the tongue body and jaw and again closed by lifting the back of the tongue. At every moment of this smoothly flowing gesture, the vocal cavities can serve as resonators to reinforce selectively certain frequency regions (the formants) of whatever sound is produced at the vocal cords or by turbulent air flow at narrow constrictions. The resulting acoustic stream has an overall spectral pattern that is distinctive for the word "tag," but it does not have distinctive parts for the component gestures of "t" or "a" or "g." Each of the component gestures affects most of the tract for much of the time and generates a correspondingly encoded acoustic signal. A listener can, to be sure, hear "tag," and can identify the component speech sounds, but the perceptual processes by which he decodes the acoustic signal are far more involved than introspection would suggest. Indeed, much remains obscure about the perception of all the messages carried in speech.

What are these messages, and how do they relate to voice identification? There is, of course, the primary message comprising the words and sentences that were said. But *how* were they said (in what manner and mood and with what emphasis), by what class of speaker (man or woman, of what dialect and occupational group), in what assumed interpersonal relationship to one or many listeners, and even in what state of the speaker's health? These are some of the other messages carried by the speech and encoded into it. In addition, there is information about who is speaking. This is, for voice identification, the one message that must be teased apart from all the others.

By ear, identification seems an easy task, at least for the speech of friends and regular acquaintances. But wrong identifications are not uncommon, and there is no way to scrutinize directly the basis on which auditory identifications are made. An indirect method, employing the conversion of speech sounds into graphic patterns for recognition by eye, would seem to be an attractive alternative. Such a procedure, using sound spectrograms (voiceprints), was described by Kersta [11] in 1962 and has been used by him and others since that time. There was earlier work dating back to the 1940s, in conjunction with military communications, but few records and no publications resulted.

The proponents of voiceprint identification have advanced a two-part theoretical basis for their methods: (1) people differ anatomically, e.g., in the size and shape of their oral and nasal cavities, in the structure of the larynx, etc., and (2) people have different but stable habit patterns in the ways they use this vocal apparatus in speaking. All of these affect their speech spectrograms. Thus it may be supposed that the combination of so many factors would uniquely characterize a particular speaker and set him apart from all others. The sound spectrogram, or voiceprint, is then used as an objective display in which to seek for enough points of similarity between the patterns of two spectrograms (one from a known speaker) to conclude that the known and unknown (but suspected) speakers are (or are not) the same person.

Clearly, these points of similarity should reflect only, or mainly, those things that characterize the speaker, i.e., his anatomy and his individualistic speech habits. Otherwise, the information about the identity of the speaker is contaminated by the other messages in his speech. This is a major difficulty, for as we have seen, it is inherent in the nature of speech that the messages are acoustically interdependent, and in fact the spectrographic patterns do show the mixed influences of quite different kinds of information.

An example of these mixed influences is provided by the vowels, which are among the simplest of speech sounds. A steady "ah," made with the vocal tract in a relaxed open-mouth position, has peaks, or formants, in the spectrogram that are determined mainly by the length and shape of the pharynx and mouth, and so reflect directly these anatomical and physiological dimensions of the speaker. But other vowels are characterized by different formants, which are produced by changing the positions and shape of jaw, tongue, and lips. Some effects of the speaker's body dimensions will remain, but these effects are changed in unobvious ways by how he moves his articulators to approximate the vowel formants that are typical of the dialect he speaks. Thus, formant frequencies are affected by at least three factors: the speaker's dialect, his tactics and precision in matching its norms, and the set of bodily dimensions that set him apart in some degree from other speakers.

Actually, the situation even for vowels is more complex. Vowels rarely occur as steady sounds; usually the formants are changing continuously. Often vowel formants do not reach their "target" frequencies (corresponding to the steady state of the vowel) at any point in a spoken syllable. Always they are much affected by the particular consonants that precede and follow them. Speech is, in short, a highly dynamic set of gestures that so contorts the vocal tract as to make difficult and uncertain any precise inferences about its "normal" dimensions.

The gestures of speech are, however, highly repetitive, which should lead to stable habit patterns characteristic of the individual. But here, also, there is interaction between personal traits and the need to communicate. The latter imperative implies an agreed set of speech sounds that each speaker of a dialect must use if he is to be understood. But not every sound feature is so tightly specified; some may be varied at will without violating the phonetic rules, thus permitting each speaker some freedom to be individualistic in his speech gestures. Nevertheless, the fact that he and every other speaker of the same dialect must conform to its sound patterns implies that there will be more similarities than individual differences among their speech patterns. Clearly, such points of similarity, as they are reflected in spectrograms, must be carefully avoided in attempting to establish speaker identity. But differences in the spectrographic patterns can also be misleading. They may indicate that the sound came from different speakers, or only that a single speaker was free to vary this sound feature and had done so. Thus, it would appear that neither points of similarity nor points of difference between two spectrograms will, in general, give unambiguous evidence as to whether the speech they represent came from the same speaker or from different speakers.

Are there, nevertheless, some points of similarity or difference that are not equivocal? Some that could serve as reliable "markers" of individual voices? As a technique for speaker identification, voiceprinting appears to be dependent on the existence of such similarities in spectrograms and on human ability to recognize them by eye.

In assessing the method, it will be important to note what functions are performed by the spectrograph and what by the eye, and to weigh their respective roles in arriving at a subjective judgment about the speaker. Let us start with the instrument, what it does, and what it can tell the eye about speech.

The principles underlying the operation of the sound spectrograph were well known long before they were adequately implemented; indeed, a crude hand-drawn spectrogram, based on months of laborious analysis, had been published in the early thirties [26]. The announcement made by Bell Laboratories [27] of an easy-to-use instrument that could make high-quality spectrograms, plus a brilliant exposition by Martin Joos [28] of their relevance to acoustic phonetics, excited much interest and motivated a number of efforts to interpret spectrograms, to teach people to "read" them, and to devise automatic methods of speech recognition. It is a measure of the inherent difficulty, as well as the challenge, of these problems that the efforts to solve them have continued to the present time.

Although various types of sound spectrograph have been built for special purposes, the original instrument—and most of those now in common use with speech—are similar in principle and make very similar spectrograms. They analyze a recording of speech that is about 2 s in duration by replaying it repeatedly through a band-pass filter that has its effective center frequency swept slowly through the audio frequency range, typically about 0 to 8 kHz. The short-time-average amplitude of the filter output is recorded along the horizontal (time) axis of a sheet of electrosensitive paper, in step with the speech sample. Recordings of successive analyses are displaced upward along the vertical (frequency) axis in proportion to incremental increases in the center frequency of the filter. Thus, the spectrogram is generated as a raster of closely spaced horizontal lines. When average amplitude is recorded as degree of blackening, the spectrogram constitutes a "picture" of the spoken words (reading from left to right), with the dominant frequency components shown as the darker areas.

Originally, two types of spectrogram could be recorded, using either a wide-band or a narrow-band filter for the analysis. A third type, known as a contour spectrogram, was developed later and can be made on most present-day spectrographs. One might wonder, since all three types of spectrogram contain essentially the same information, what reasons there may be for this variety. Actually, the justification for three different displays lies partly in the nature of speech and partly in the characteristics of visual pattern perception. The relationship between these factors will emerge from descriptions of the different types of spectrograms.

Contour spectrograms capitalize on the preference of the eyes for closed figures with sharp boundaries, as do conventional contour maps, which they resemble. In a contour spectrogram, it is the transition from one amplitude level to another that is recorded as a dark line. The line will then enclose an area on the spectrogram for which all amplitudes lie above (or below) this particular transition amplitude. The areas between adjacent contour lines is shaded to give an approximate indication of absolute levels. Typically, successive contour lines (and shadings) change by 6-dB steps. The visual patterns of contour spectrograms are far more striking than those of narrow-band or wide-band spectrograms, and quantitative estimates of spectrum level can be made directly by eye with greater ease and accuracy than for the other two types. The visual patterns change substantially, though, with changes in amplitude distributions small enough that the ear would scarcely notice them; thus, two utterances that sound very alike may look quite different. It is not surprising, then, that contour spectrograms have gained little favor in speech research, despite their striking appearance and quantitative advantages. In the simplest terms, they emphasize to the eye a dimension of speech to which the ear is largely inattentive.*

In generating narrow-band spectrograms, the effective width of the analyzing filter is about 45 to 50 Hz, and so resolves the individual harmonics of all but the deepest male voices. Consequently, the spectrograms consist of many equally spaced horizontal lines that may sweep upward and diverge, or turn downward and converge, as voice pitch rises or falls in a voiced passage. Those harmonics that are close in frequency to the vocal cavity

* The ear is even less attentive to the relative phases of the component frequencies of speech. Since relative phases are ignored in spectrograms but strongly affect the wave shapes of oscillograms, it may be that spectrograms owe a substantial part of their superiority as visual patterns to the fact that they omit phase information.

resonances are selectively reinforced and so appear as darker regions on the general background of (more or less) horizontal bands. The temporal resolution of the impulsive sounds of speech is smeared somewhat, though not excessively. The primary effect of the narrow-band filter is, however, to emphasize voice pitch and, accordingly, to deemphasize other features of the utterance.

Wide-band spectrograms, for which the analyzing filter has a bandwidth of about 300 Hz, do not resolve the voice harmonics (except for very high-pitched voices), but merge all of the harmonics within a formant region into one solid "bar" that will tilt up or down as the shape of the vocal tract is changed. The emphasis, for the eye, has been shifted to the changing shapes of the vocal tract, whereas voice-pitch information has been minimized though not removed, since it can still be seen in the spacing of the vertical striations during voiced sounds. The overall patterns for wide-band spectrograms look simpler to the eye than do the corresponding patterns for narrow-band spectrograms, although they contain approximately the same amount of information.

The advantage of wide-band spectrograms lies only partly in their apparent simplicity; another and more important factor is that they emphasize the information that characterizes the primary message, i.e., the words or phrases that the speaker articulates. Indeed, the primary objective in developing the spectrograph was to find a way of recording speech that would emphasize the similarities and differences among words. It follows that other differences, and in particular the differences between speakers, have been subordinated to this primary objective. Clearly, we need—but do not know how to build—an instrument that would give good graphic patterns that emphasize the distinctive characteristics of speakers. It may be that, when we have learned much more about the sound features that characterize individual speakers, it will be possible to design an instrument that can be a powerful aid to the eye in voice identification, or even one that can operate automatically in a completely objective manner.

BIBLIOGRAPHY

Denes, P. B., and E. N. Pinson "The Speech Chain," Bell Laboratories, 1963; obtainable through Bell System educational representatives.

Fant, G., "Acoustic Theory of Speech Production," Mouton and Co., The Hague, 1960.

Flanagan J. L., "Speech Analysis Synthesis and Perception," 2d edition, Springer-Verlag, 1972.

Liberman, A. M., F. S. Cooper, D. P. Shankweiler, and M. Studdert-Kennedy, Perception of the Speech Code, *Psychol. Rev.*, **74:**431–461 (1967).

Liberman, A. M., F. S. Cooper, D. P. Shankweiler, and M. Studdert-Kennedy, Why Are Speech Spectrograms Hard to Read? *Am. Ann. Deaf*, **113:**127–133 (1968).

Potter, R. K., G. A. Kopp, and H. Green Kopp, "Visible Speech," Dover Publications, New York, 1966.

Stevens, K. N., and A. S. House, An Acoustical Theory of Vowel Production and Some of Its Implications, *J. Speech Hearing Res.*, **4:**303–320 (1961).

APPENDIX B
VOICE PATTERNS AND FINGERPRINT PATTERNS

The term *voiceprint* implies an analogy with fingerprints. In this appendix we compare voice identification and fingerprint identification in their details, to see just how far they may be analogous. First, we review briefly the history and procedures of fingerprint identification [14, 15].

The first classification of fingerprint patterns, i.e., the ridge patterns on the underside of the finger tips, was made by J. Purkinje in 1823. He was concerned with these patterns only as part of the tactile sensory system and did not mention them as a basis for personal identification. In 1880, H. Faulds, a British medical missionary in Japan, first reported on the use of fingerprints as a device for identification in two criminal cases. From 1886 to 1888, Faulds attempted to interest Scotland Yard, but he was unsuccessful, probably owing to the lack of a workable classification scheme for files. Upon Fauld's publication, W. Herschel, an administrator in India, published an account of his 20-year use of fingerprints against impersonation and repudiation of signatures, and in registering prisoners. In this paper, Herschel also observed the permanence of fingerprint patterns, basing his conclusion on repeated prints of the same persons over intervals as long as 30 years. His use of fingerprints began in 1858 and official use in a few Indian government departments began in 1877.

Francis Galton, the great British geneticist and anthropologist, carried out the first extensive scientific study of fingerprints as compared with other methods of personal identification. His work began in 1888 and culminated in 1894 with the adoption of fingerprint classification as a main filing method used by the British government and as the ultimate proof of a person's identity. About 1901, fingerprint classification was adopted as the basis of the filing method. Subsequent developments in classification systems stemmed from those adopted in India by E. Henry (published in 1900) and in Argentina by Vucetich (beginning in 1891). Henry, during his early work, consulted Galton extensively.

Galton's studies on identification by fingerprints covered the following problems: (1) print persistence with growth, (2) probability of false identification, (3) indexing methods, (4) practical uses, and (5) comparison with other methods.

The work on *persistence* used Herschel's material, which was taken from 15 persons over age ranges beginning at various stages in life from infancy onward. The longest period studied was 30 years, the shortest 12 years. Repeated prints from about 25 different fingers were available. Certain general features of a print were found to change somewhat with age; for example, the sizes and distances increased with growth and the print texture or grain might change because of calluses or old age. However, the pattern type and the minute details remained remarkably constant. The details noted were the points of appearance or disappearance of a ridge, the occurrences of islands and enclosures, and the number of ridges involved in typical parts of the patterns, such as the whorls, loops, and deltas. The exact imprinted textures of these details would vary somewhat with changes in skin condition and with print-inking conditions. However, the details, when compared with age, were always identifiable by their unchanging pattern, ridge count, and positions relative to each other. Six hundred ninety-nine out of seven hundred such details, when compared with the same print at the later age, remained unchanged as to type of feature, ridge count, and relative location. The one point changed from a divided ridge to a single ridge.

In this study of the *probability of false identification,* Galton first classified the thumb prints of 1,000 different persons into 100 classes based on general pattern types, attempting to make the 100 classes appear equally different from each other. However, two-thirds of the prints fell into only 12 classes; thus, there was the chance of about one in 18 that two patterns of the same class would be from different persons. This error rate (about 5.6 percent) was not acceptable in relation to the low rates to be had by considering the minute details of each print, which, conservatively estimated, numbered about 30 per print. Galton noted that a disagreement in general pattern type for the same finger would be conclusive evidence that the two prints were from different persons.

To estimate the probability of false identification based on the minute details, Galton first estimated the size of a square (in terms of ridge intervals) within which the detailed ridge pattern was 50 percent predictable if only ridge patterns outside the square are known; i.e., he then estimated that there was an equal chance of being right or wrong as to the pattern within the square. Conservatively estimated, there were 24 such independent squares in a single print, and thus the probability that two different prints would correspond exactly within the independent squares was estimated as 1 in 2^{24}. When Galton included the chances of guessing the number and course of the ridges outside each independent square, the chance of false identity was estimated as 1 in 2^{36} or about 1 in 64,000,000,000. For two fingerprints, this estimate is squared, for three cubed, etc. The chance of three fingerprints of two persons being identical in their minute details was estimated as 1 in $64^3 \times 10^{27}$.

Usually, there were about 35 details in a print. Not all might agree in two different prints of the same finger. If, for example, there are 35 points

TABLE 10.1 Decision Matrix Showing Possible Correspondences of Fingerprint Patterns to Subjects to Be Identified

Type of prints	*S* (Same person) Correct identification	*D* (Different persons) False identification
S (Same prints, one finger)	$P_{SS} = 1 \frac{1}{64 \times 10^9}$	$P_{SD} = \frac{1}{64 \times 10^9}$
D (Different prints)	Incorrect rejection	Correct rejection

of comparison and all but four agree, the chances are estimated as 1 in 2^{29} that they are prints from different fingers.

In terms of modern theory a possible decision matrix would be as shown in Table 10.1, where P_{SS} is the probability of the same print corresponding to the same person (i.e., the hit rate) and P_{SD} is the probability of the same print corresponding to different persons (i.e., the false-alarm rate). Galton's probability calculations are used in the "same prints" row. The probabilities in the "different prints" row would reflect the fact that it is very easy to detect different prints by general pattern type, and thus the chances would be very small for an incorrect rejection or miss and correspondingly very high for a correct rejection.

Galton worked with 3,000 prints to develop index methods for establishing files. This was important for his demonstrations and tests in his campaign for official adoption. His index system was the one initially used in 1894.

Another important aspect of Galton's work was a study of the relative power of fingerprint identification and the then-current identification method of Bertillon, which employed a standard set of body measurements. The theoretical error rate of the basic body set was about 1 in 1,000,000; but Galton sought to see if, as with his general types of fingerprint patterns, there was significant correlation between classes of the measures. He made the set of body measurements on 500 persons and then distributed the measures into 243 Bertillon classes; two or three additional measures were then necessary to resolve the 24 cases falling in the largest class. He concluded that about 2,000 persons could thus be distinguished. As an example of a Bertillon-indexed register of persons, a total of 20,000 persons were assumed, and then Galton pointed out that, with fingerprints added, this register could be expanded to 10,000,000 assuming that only 500 persons could be perfectly distinguished by fingerprints alone.

Thus Galton modestly looked on fingerprints as a powerful supplement to current identification classes of body measurements. But only seven years elapsed before fingerprint classification in England officially superseded classification by body characteristics.

We note that, in contrast to the current practice of voice identification, the use of fingerprint identification in the 1890s rested on a rather large body of experience, on scientific studies of pattern permanence over time and of the statistical distribution of the pattern features, and on the development of a classification system.

The current American classification system for registering complete sets of fingerprints is virtually the same as the original one of Henry. The primary classes are based on the overall pattern types, such as whorls, arches, and loops, rather than on the minute details such as enclosures, ridge counts, islands, deltas, terminations, origins, and bifurcations. Each set is first classed according to the pattern, over the 10 fingers, of the presence or absence of a whorl in each print. There are thus 2^{10} (i.e., 1,024) such classes; they are called primary classes. As Galton found, some of these classes contain many more cases than others; for example, the class *no whorls* contains about 25 percent of all the cases. Thus the primary classes must be subdivided into secondary classes based on patterns, over the 10 prints, of occurrences and types of arches and loops. Further subordinate divisions are made by ridge counts of loops and whorls.

Anatomical studies of the ridge patterns have established that the general pattern types, such as loops and whorls, are due to hereditary factors. However, the minute details such as the bifurcations, terminations, and interruptions of ridges, are the final bases for fingerprint identification. These minutiae are determined mainly by random processes in the prenatal development of the skin.

The randomness of the minutiae and their number per print form a statistical basis for individual identification that is virtually unequivocal. Cummins and Midlo [14, p. 151] estimated that the chance that prints from two different fingers will match in all details is about 1 in 3×10^{42}. This probability is based on the number of the combinations of 25 binary events falling in

TABLE 10.2 Comparison of Fingerprints and Voiceprints

This comparison shows that fingerprint identification is basically different from voice-pattern identification in several essential and critical aspects; further, it indicates that voice identification is inherently more complex and more susceptible to error than fingerprint identification.

Finger-ridge patterns	Voice patterns
1. Patterns are inherent in anatomy, not changeable in kind, i.e., they cannot be changed from one pattern to another. Parts of pattern, large or small, can only be obliterated.	1. Patterns are only partially dependent on anatomy and are changed by the articulatory movements needed to realize the language code.
2. Details of patterns are: *a.* Permanent *b.* Not affected by growth (aging merely changes the size or the print grain) *c.* Not affected by habits (calluses merely change the print grain)	2. Details of patterns are: *a.* Just as variable as the overall patterns *b.* Affected by growth *c.* Affected by habits (learning new dialects and voice qualities)
3. Pattern similarity depends entirely on underlying anatomical structure.	3. Pattern similarity depends primarily on acquired movement patterns used to produce language code and only partially on anatomical structure.
4. Patterns result from a direct transfer from the skin of the finger to the surface touched by it.	4. Patterns result from an analysis of voice sounds which, in turn, are related only indirectly to the vocal anatomy of the speaker. Moreover, the transmission channel from speaker to spectrograph is vulnerable to acoustical and electrical distortions.

all the possible patterns at 25 locations in the print [1 in $(\frac{1}{2} \times 25)^{25}$].

The matching of a single chance print depends much more on the pattern of minute features than on the overall pattern. Classification of single prints, where such files are kept, generally starts with a police category related to the crime at which the print was collected.

Partial prints are sometimes the only print samples available for a fingerprint identification. In these cases, the fingerprint expert first attempts to decide which finger of which hand each print belongs to. Then the partial prints are compared with filed prints. As far as we could determine, there are no published experimental studies of the statistical success of identification by partial fingerprints. Experts agree that perfect correspondence of 12 points of comparison, and no discordances, proves that two prints originate from the same finger [14, pp. 152–155, 182–183].

Using the foregoing information, we have compared fingerprint identification and voice-spectrogram identification as to their basic pattern sources. We have arranged the essential points of our comparison in Table 10.2.

APPENDIX C
EXPERIMENTAL EVIDENCE ON VOICE IDENTIFICATION

Identification by Subjective Examination of Spectrograms

Several experimenters have investigated the ability of observers to identify talkers by visual examination of voice spectrograms. In most of these experiments, a limited group of talkers was used. Spectrograms were available of each of the talkers uttering a fixed set of words or phrases several times. The exact nature of the observers' tasks differed considerably among the various experiments.

The first experiments were reported by Kersta [11, 25, 29–31]. His observers were female high-school students who worked in pairs in the final test experiments. They were given about one week of training in the interpretation of voice spectrograms. In some of the experiments reported, their task consisted of sorting an array of spectrograms into individual talker categories; they knew the number of different talkers and the number of examples from each talker. The experiments involved 5, 9, and 12 talkers who were drawn at random from a pool of 123 male talkers. In a typical experiment (say with 12 talkers), spectrograms were made of four utterances of a one-syllable word, such as "you," spoken in isolation by each talker. The observers were given the 48 spectrograms and were asked to sort them into 12 piles corresponding to the 12 different talkers. No further details of the training and test procedures, nor of the instructions to the observers, are reported. Error scores of individual observers range from zero to 2 percent; average error rates, pooled over all observers, ranged from 0.35 percent for five talkers in the set to 1 percent for 12 talkers in the set. In another task, the observers had to identify a talker by matching his spectrograms against those in a catalog of a set of talkers; the size of the set ranged from 9 to 15 talkers; the test words were spoken in context; the average error score was 1 percent.

Experiments with a matching procedure were carried out by Stevens et al. [20]. For the most part, these experiments employed a closed set of eight talkers. The observers were college students with no previous training in reading spectrograms. In a number of experimental sessions, observers working individually were given a set of eight "standard" spectrograms, representing a given utterance spoken by each of the eight talkers. They were then presented "unknown" spectrograms, one at a time, each representing the same utterance by one of the talkers, and were asked to make an identification of the talker. Some learning and consequent improvement of error scores occurred in the first few sessions, and then the scores reached a relatively uniform level. Error scores ranged from 18 to 50 percent, depending upon the utterance; error scores were generally higher for brief monosyllabic utterances than for utterances with more syllables.

A procedure similar to that of Stevens et al. was followed in an experiment by Young and Campbell [19]. Their observers, however, had some training in spectrogram interpretation for purposes of matching talkers; also, the experiment was designed to compare identification using words spoken in context *versus* identification using words spoken in isolation. The observers examined spectrograms of two different words (*it* and *you*) spoken by five talkers. The catalog for matching consisted of all five talkers. The observers were first trained and tested with spectrograms of the isolated words; then they were tested on the words taken from context. With the words spoken in isolation, the average error score was 21.6 percent. With the words spoken in context, the average error score was 62.7 percent. Young and Campbell point out that words spoken in context have shorter durations and different acoustic patterns than words spoken in isolation and that these differences may have been responsible for the large difference in identification.

An experiment similar to that of Young and Campbell just described was carried out by R. Bruce [32]. He used six talkers, and his "standard" spectrograms consisted of 10 key words ("the," "to," "and," "me," "on," "is," "you," "I," "it," and "a") spoken in isolation. He had one test utterance, which was a long sentence containing all of these words, and again the task of the observer was to determine the speaker of the test utterance, using all 10 spectrograms of key words as standards. The error rate for this task was about 50 percent.

Other evidence with regard to identification of speakers from spectrograms has been reported by Ladefoged and Vanderslice [23]. Although these investigators did not carry out formal experiments, they provide examples to show that spectrograms of the same speaker producing the same utterance twice can appear to be quite different, whereas two different speakers can produce very similar spectrograms. Other investigators have reported informally on situations in which one speaker attempts to mimic another; in one of these situations, an experienced mimic with special aids produced speech sequences whose spectrographic patterns appeared capable of being confounded with those of the talker being mimicked; in another case, the spectrograms of a famous mimic appeared to be different from those of the speaker being mimicked [24, 25, 29–31].

Tosi [18] recently reported confirmation of the average error rate, about 1 percent, in the spectrogram sorting task originally used by Kersta. Further, in a matching task, Tosi used two utterances of each of five test words arranged in a catalog of 50 different talkers selected from a larger set of 123 talkers. The spectrograms were the same as those used for the work reported by Kersta [25, 29–31]. Seven of Tosi's observers were police fingerprint technicians. Several days of training preceded the experimental tests. The error rate for observers working individually ranged from zero to 11.1 percent, with a median of 5.7 percent. The error rate for observers working together in pairs ranged from 3.2 to 14.3 percent, with a medium of 7.7 percent.

None of the experiments reported to date has employed an observer's task that simulates the task commonly encountered by the expert in voiceprint identification, namely, the task of deciding the identity of a speaker of a known key utterance and the same utterance spoken by an unknown speaker. However, Stevens et al. [20] carried out some tests where the observers were asked to judge whether a sample was produced by any of the eight known talkers in a catalog. New "unknown" talkers among the test samples were incorrectly called "known" 6 to 8 percent of the time by listening and 31 to 47 percent of the time by visual examination of the corresponding spectrograms.

Identification by Listening

A number of experiments have examined how well a listener can identify a talker from the sound of his voice. In most of these experiments, the task of the listener was to identify a talker from an ensemble of several (typically 5 to 10) talkers that were known to him or whose voices were available to him on recordings. Error scores in such experiments are in the range of 5 to 19 percent, depending on the conditons of the experiment [20, 33, 34]. Stevens et al. [20] found that listening gave better talker identification than the examination of spectrograms of the same utterances. The observers also reported higher confidence in listening than in their visual identifications.

There is an appreciable decrease in error scores for a two- or three-syllable sample of speech compared with a one-syllable sample [10, 20]. Recognition scores are fairly steep functions of the duration of the speech sample for durations up to 1.2 s, but the increase in score above 1.2 s is rather small [33]. Several investigators have shown that fairly high aural recognition scores are obtained when the task is to identify two sequential speech samples as being spoken by the same talker or by different talkers. Correct identification was 93 percent in such tests using one-syllable words [35]. With five-syllable speech samples, Clarke et al. [8] found about 89 percent correct same-different decisions for two samples, about 85 percent correct for matching an unknown sample to one of two different samples, and about 60 percent correct matching to four samples.

It has been observed that some parts of the speech frequency range are more important than others in their contributions of cues for speaker recognition. For example, when speech is processed by octave-band filters, the best recognition scores are obtained with the filter 1,200 to 2,400 Hz. Low-pass filtering at 3,000 Hz or high-pass filtering at 500 Hz caused little deterioration relative to wide-band speech. Noise affects the ability of a listener to recognize a talker's voice, but there are conflicting data on how much noise gives a substantial decrease in score. For white noise, the decrease in performance seems to occur for signal-to-noise ratios in the range −4 to +8 dB [8, 36].

Identification by Objective Methods

There have been a number of experiments on the design and evaluation of methods for objective voice identification using completely automatic procedures [13, 10, 17, 25, 29–31, 37–39]. Typically these studies have employed sets of about 10 talkers and a process of spectrum analysis to produce the voice patterns. The patterns were fed to a computer where they were processed statistically to yield a reference pattern for each talker. A new utterance from one of the talkers is then analyzed and fed to the computer for comparison with each reference pattern. A measure of the similarity of the new pattern to each reference pattern is then computed and the reference talker yielding the highest similarity is chosen as the identity of the talker of the new utterance. Error rates in these experiments were about 10 percent.

APPENDIX D
REQUIREMENTS FOR VALIDATION OF VOICE-IDENTIFICATION METHODS

Any identification method that is highly reliable will depend ultimately on the use of a sufficient number of independent identifying features that are stable for the individual and have a wide variation in the population. Voice features having these characteristics may eventually be found, but we can expect that considerable research will be necessary because of the complexity of speech.

Several investigators have studied identification features of voice that may be useful [8, 9, 13]. The statistical methods they [8, 13, 16] describe seem to be promising approaches to identification from a population of talkers. Research on individual voice features is still in its early stages, and there is no large body of data and experience on which to base a system of features for identification.

An alternative to using a well-defined set of identification features is to train a human observer to perform voice identification, using whatever procedures seem to yield the best results. Experimental tests of such observers, as summarized in Appendix C, have not been extensive, and some have not employed appropriate statistical designs. All the reported tests have used sorting or matching tasks and closed (usually small) sets of speakers and subjects. None of the tests has covered identification tasks that resemble real-life situations.

Validation of any method of identification poses important problems in statistical decision making. Some of the important questions are these: What is the probability that the same person will be judged as different (missed identification) and the probability that different persons will be called the same (false identification)? How do these errors trade off against each other, and what is the influence of population size? It is instructive to formulate these questions in terms of statistical decision theory.

An appropriate model assumes that each observation of a talker's voice defines a point in a multidimensional space. Successive utterances of the talker define a distribution of points in that space. Comparable utterances by other people define other distributions. The reliability of identification is tied up with the degree of overlap between the distributions. The dimensions of the multidimensional space concern properties of speech used in the identification scheme. The dimensions may be either subjective (pitch or loudness, for example) or objective (fundamental voice frequency or sound intensity, for example), depending upon whether the identification judgment is made entirely subjectively by a human observer or is based upon physical measurements taken from a spectrogram or some other physical analysis. This decision model can form the basis for validation of a voice-identification scheme.

The problem of determining the probability that two samples are drawn from the same distribution, i.e., that they came from the same speaker, is well known in statistical theory. There are well-documented decision techniques for deciding (with stated probabilities of error) whether two observations come from the same or different multidimensional distributions. However, the application of these techniques depends upon knowledge of the distributions involved as well as on the dimensions in which they are defined. These dimensions are closely tied to the "features" in a pattern which distinguish it from patterns drawn from other distributions. In the case of speech spectrograms, we know neither the dimensions nor their distributions. Thus current experiments run the risk of producing atypical results because of selection of test materials and subjects.

The applicable distributions and dimensions depend not only on the "natural" voice characteristics of the statistical population, but also on the instrumentation used to display the voice, on factors in the recording environment, on the context in which key words, phrases, or sounds are spoken, and on attempts to disguise the voice. Also, the experimental paradigm of a voice-identification test must be such that the data collected can be readily interpreted in terms of the statistical model discussed above.

With these considerations in mind, specific investigations can be proposed to determine the validity of personal identification using speech spectrograms. We assume that the relevant task is to decide from samples of two utterances if these were spoken by the same or different talkers. The various types of investigations fall into four classes: (1) those concerned with understanding and characterizing the normal subjective process of comparing speech spectrograms for identification; (2) experiments comparing the subjective findings with comparable results from other, more "objective" methods of talker identification; (3) studies to assess the performance of experts in voice identification by means of speech spectrograms; and (4) studies to define statistical procedures for validation of a specific identification.

Understanding and Characterizing the Process of Subjective Identification Using Speech Spectrograms

One way to achieve quantitative results from the subjective process is the following. The observers are given all the possible talker pairs of test spectrograms, one pair at a time. Pairs of separate utterances of the test words by the same talker are included, but the observer is not told how many talkers there are. For each pair, the observer's task is to judge whether they are from the same talker or from different talkers. A matrix is then constructed to show the percentages of "same" judgments for all the voice pairs. The confusion rates can then be used as input measures of similarity to multidimensional scaling, cluster analysis, and other similar techniques. These provide metric representations that, as quantitative descriptions of the subjective process of identification, *may* lead to some insight into physical dimensions underlying the process. For further analyses, one could also calculate various summary statistics (e.g., interpoint distances, measures of "tightness" of clusters, etc.) and derive statistical properties, such as their distributions. Further experiments could vary the number of talkers and thereby study the behavior of the patterns in the confusion matrices, their summary statistics and statistical distributions, and their correlations with physical dimensions. This would clarify the dependence of these statistical measures on the number of talkers and help to evaluate their stability.

Comparisons with Objective Methods of Talker Identification

One could compare the confusion matrices and the values and distributions of the summary statistics, as obtained in the subjective experiments, with the corresponding entities obtained in more directly quantifiable and objectively describable processes of talker identification applied to an acoustic analysis of the same set of utterances. Such comparisons would help to detect the existence and nature of differences between the subjective process and these more objective procedures. Also, the objective procedures may be employed to guide the selection of the acoustical samples for further subjective experiments.

Assessment of Expertise

To compare performance in the task of voice identification of "experts" with that of "average" persons, the experiments described above (which would ordinarily use "average" persons as subjects) could be repeated with a group of "experts." The resultant data summaries could then be compared with the data from "average" subjects to determine if, for example, (1) the confusion matrix for experts is more nearly "diagonal" in structure (i.e., sparse almost everywhere except for the same-speaker pairs) than the matrix for "average" subjects; (2) the clustering is "tighter" for the experts; etc.

Validation of a Specific Identification

For "validating" an identification based on a single pair of speech spectrograms, one possibility is to obtain direct measures of the physical dimensions (uncovered by the approach described above) for the pair of spectrograms in question. One can, in such a case, calculate a statistic to measure the closeness of the pair (e.g., the "intervoice" distance in multidimensional space) and see where its value falls in the reference distribution for these physical dimensions.

Investigations of the four types suggested are minimal for judging the validity of voice identification using speech spectrograms. In practice, it seems likely (and desirable) that acceptance of any scheme for general use would be based upon both an analysis of laboratory data *and* usage tests under realistic conditions undertaken to confirm the results from the experiments.

Apart from the statistical model suggested above, one might well ask whether it is possible to validate entirely through actual use. The question in this form is difficult to answer in more than a "common sense" fashion. From this viewpoint, it would seem that validation would require experience with some substantial fraction, say 1 to 10 percent, of the population of the community in question (the United States, for example). Experience might be limited to a smaller fraction of the population, but there would be the nagging doubt that troublesome cases might show up until a larger number of cases had been examined. This doubt could not be removed by any sampling procedure since the relevant voice characteristics are unknown. Granted that a long string of successes under these conditions might eventually convince many people, the point at which the case was "proved" would remain very much a value judgment based on inference, and could not be said to be established in a scientific sense.

REFERENCES

1. W. Koenig, H. K. Dunn, and L. Y. Lacey, The Sound Spectrograph, *J. Acoust. Soc. Am.,* **18:**19 (1946).
2. J. M. Pickett, Speech Communication, *J. Acoust. Soc. Am.,* **46:**867–868 (1969).
3. *State v. Cary,* 49 N.J. 343 (1967), 99 N.J. Super. 323 (L. D 1968), N.J. Supreme Court, Docket C-207; *People v. King,* Calif. App. 2nd Dist., 2nd Crim. 13588; *United States v. Wright,* 17 U.S.C.M.A. 183 (1967).
4. M. Heckes, "Methods for Measuring Speaker Recognition," Stanford Research Institute, Menlo Park, Calif., April 1969.
5. G. Fant, "Acoustic Theory of Speech Production," Mouton and Co., The Hague, 1960.
6. K. N. Stevens and A. S. House, An Acoustical Theory of Vowel Production and Some of Its Implications, *J. Speech Hearing Res.,* **4:**303 (1961).
7. A. M. Liberman, F. S. Cooper, D. P. Shankweiler, and M. Studdert-Kennedy, Why Are Speech Spectrograms Hard to Read?, *Am. Ann. Deaf,* **113:**127 (1968); Perception of the Speech Code, *Psych. Rev.,* **74:**431–461 (1967).
8. F. R. Clarke, R. W. Becker, and J. C. Nixon, Characteristics That Determine Speaker Recognition, Rept. ESD-TR-66-636, Decision Sciences Laboratory, Hanscom Field, Bedford, Mass., December 1966 (report under contract to Stanford Research Institute, Menlo Park, Calif.).
9. W. D. Voiers, Perceptual Bases of Speaker Identity, *J. Acoust. Soc. Am.,* **36:**1065–1073 (1964).
10. C. E. Williams, The Effects of Selected Factors on the Aural Identification of Speakers, sec. 111 in "Methods for Psychoacoustic Evaluation of Speech Communication Systems," Rept. ESD-tdr-65-153, Electronic Systems Division, Air Force Systems Command, Hanscom Field, Mass., 1964.
11. L. G. Kersta, *Nature,* **196:**1253–1257 (1962).
12. H. Mennen, H. Tillman, and G. Ungeheuer, "Entwicklung eines Systems von Beschreibungsmerkmalen für Kontursonagramme zum Zwecke der Sprecheridentifikation," T-888-L-203, Institut für Phonetik und Kommunikationsforschung, Universität Bonn, November 1968.
13. S. Pruzansky, Pattern-matching Procedure for Automatic Talker Recognition, *J. Acoust. Soc. Am.,* **35:**354–358 (1963).
14. H. Cummins and C. Midlo, "Fingerprints, Palms and Soles: An Introduction to Dermatoglyphics," Dover Publications, New York, 1961.
15. Francis Galton, "Finger Prints," Macmillan and Company, Ltd., London, 1892; facsimile reprint, Da Capo Press, New York, 1965, with historical introduction by H. Cummins.
16. S. Pruzansky and M. V. Mathews, Talker-recognition Procedure Based on Analysis of Variance, *J. Acoust. Soc. Am.,* **36:**2041–2047 (1964).
17. L. G. Kersta, Paper B7, Preprints of 1967 Conf. on Speech Communication and Processing, pp. 100–103, Air Force Cambridge Research Laboratory, Bedford, Mass., November 1967.
18. O. Tosi, Speaker Identification through Acoustic Spectrography, paper presented at XIV Intern. Congr. Logopedics and Phoniatrics, Paris, September 1968.
19. M. A. Young and R. A. Campbell, Effects of Context on Talker Identification, *J. Acoust. Soc. Am.,* **42:**1250–1254 (1967).
20. K. N. Stevens, C. E. Williams, J. P. Carbonell, and B. Woods, Speaker Authentication and Identification: A Comparison of Spectrographic and Auditory Presentations of Speech Material, *J. Acoust. Soc. Am.,* **44:**1596–1607 (1968).

21. L. G. Kersta, private communication, 1969.
22. O. Tosi, private communication, 1969.
23. P. Ladefoged and R. Vanderslice, The "Voiceprint" Mystique, Working Papers in Phonetics, Department Linguistics, UCLA, pp. 126–142, November 1967.
24. A. Fourcin and A. W. F. Huggins, private communication, 1969.
25. L. G. Kersta, Voiceprint-identification Infallibility, *J. Acoust. Soc. Am.,* **34:**1978 (1962). (Abstract)
26. J. C. Steinberg, *J. Acoust. Soc. Am.,* **6:**16–24 (1934).
27. R. K. Potter et al., *J. Acoust. Soc. Am.,* **18:**1–89 (1946). (A series of six articles)
28. M. Joos, Acoustic Phonetics, *Language Monographs,* No. 23 (1948).
29. L. G. Kersta, Voiceprint Identification, *J. Acoust. Soc. Am.,* **34:**725 (1962). (Abstract)
30. L. G. Kersta, Voiceprint Classification, *J. Acoust. Soc. Am.,* **37:**1217 (1965). (Abstract)
31. L. G. Kersta, Voiceprint Classification for an Extended Population, *J. Acoust. Soc. Am.,* **39:**1239 (1966). (Abstract)
32. R. Bruce, unpublished study, MIT, 1966.
33. I. Pollack, J. M. Pickett, and W. H. Sumby, On the Identification of Speakers by Voice, *J. Acoust. Soc. Am.,* **26:**403–406 (1954).
34. P. D. Bricker and S. Pruzansky, Effects of Stimulus Content and Duration on Talker Identification, *J. Acoust. Soc. Am.,* **40:**1441–1449 (1966).
35. J. A. Williamson, An Investigation of Several Factors Which Affect the Ability to Identify Voices as Same or Different, unpublished dissertation, University of Edinburgh, 1961.
36. R. W. Peters, Studies in Extra-messages: Listener Identification of Speakers' Voices under Conditions of Certain Restrictions Imposed on the Voice Signal, Project Rept. NM 001-064.01.03, U.S. Naval School of Aviation Medicine, Pensacola, Fla., October 1954.
37. W. A. Hargreaves and J. A. Starkweather, Recognition of Speaker Identity, *Language and Speech,* **6:**63–67 (1963).
38. K. P. Li, J. E. Dammann, and W. D. Chapman, Experimental Studies in Speaker Verification Using an Adaptive System, *J. Acout. Soc. Am.,* **40:**966–978 (1966).
39. S. K. Das, A Method of Decision Making in Pattern Recognition, *IEEE Trans. Computers,* **C-18:**329–333 (1969).

CHAPTER ELEVEN

Automatic Speech Recognition: A Critical Survey and Discussion of the Literature

S. R. HYDE

Introduction

This chapter* covers the literature now available on the subject of automatic speech recognition and presents some specific conclusions which were drawn as a result of this study. The literature refers to about 30 quite separate studies. It shows that there is much overlap in the work and a similarity in the degree of achievement.

In the literature available in 1970 it is possible to identify about 60 different studies. A few of these are claiming recognition scores of about 98 percent for about 30 isolated words spoken by about 30 speakers. In general these figures represent improved performance using earlier techniques and not the implementation of fundamentally new ideas on the subject. There are still no devices which can perform even moderately well on normal (conversational) speech in normal (noisy) environments by a normal range of talkers. Although this chap-

* Originally written as a British Post Office research report in 1968.

ter itself may not therefore adequately represent the current position, the conclusions are still valid.

The chapter is divided into three major parts. In the first part we give a summary of the nature of the speech process and outline some of the lines of general speech research which have influenced speech recognition studies. If further reading is required Flanagan's book [1] provides a good coverage of the field of speech research and contains many valuable references.

In the second part we examine the automatic speech recognition literature. If a more comprehensive description of the earlier studies is required the reader is referred to the literature reviews of Lindgren [2] and Marill [3], to secs. 11.2, 11.4, and 12.2 of Saposhkov [4], and to sec. 5.5 of Flanagan [1].

In the third part we present certain conclusions drawn from the study regarding the important conditions to be met in a general-purpose recognition device. These conclusions cover several aspects of the recognition problem and each conclusion is briefly discussed as it is introduced.

The Nature of Speech

Speech is a form of communication between human beings which involves the generation and reception of a complex acoustic signal. The process by which thoughts in the mind of the talker are communicated, and so form reciprocal thoughts in the mind of the listener, may be thought of as a coding operation which takes place over a hierarchy of processing levels. At the highest level we have the thoughts, or possibly the fundamental concepts which give rise to these thoughts. The thoughts are encoded on a lower level, which we shall refer to as the *linguistic level,* in the form of words. The words are encoded on successively lower levels, involving neural processing and articulatory movements, until the lowest level is reached with the acoustic signal.

At each level redundancy is used to overcome the inherent ambiguities at that level. One form of redundancy is seen in the multiplicity of perceptual "cues" used to distinguish between different speech elements. Thus the sound /s/ is distinguished from other speech sounds by the presence of fricative noise, by the initial rate of rise in energy, by the concentration of energy in certain regions of the frequency spectrum, by its relative intensity, etc. Another form of redundancy involves feedback between levels. Thus an error made in identifying a speech sound from its acoustic pattern may be corrected by reference to rules governing the production of such sounds (physical, linguistic, etc.), knowledge about the vocal characteristics of the talker, and even whether the total message "makes sense."

Naturally, the redundancy added at each processing level results in an increase in the channel capacity necessary to transmit the information. The acoustic waveform covers a frequency range of about 10 kHz, although almost no intelligibility is lost if the range is limited to the region 200 Hz to 4 kHz. It has been estimated that, if the basic message could be extracted from the speech signal (by automatic recognition) and transmitted in the form of phonemic elements (see reference to the phoneme later), a saving of the order of 1,000:1 would be possible in the required channel capacity compared with that needed to transmit the acoustic waveform.

The acoustic signal is the result of the interaction of two separate functions of the human vocal system. We shall refer to these functions as the *spectral-envelope function* and the *excitation function.* To a first order these functions are independent of each other.

The spectral envelope function is due to multiple acoustic resonance in the vocal tract. It is varied by means of the articulators: the tongue, lips, jaw, and velum. An adequate description of the envelope function is possible in terms of the frequency positions and relative amplitudes of the first three or four spectral peaks. These peaks are termed *formants* in voiced sounds, and it is convenient to consider them as separate measurable entities. Much of the message information in speech is conveyed by the envelope function and, in theory, it should be possible to extract this information if formant measures and the variation in overall energy level are known.

The excitation function, on whose spectrum the pattern of the vocal-tract resonances is impressed, is produced by two basically different processes.

One of these processes is due to the action of the vibrating vocal cords, which give a pulse-like air-flow waveform whose spectrum is very rich in harmonic components. The spectrum is seen as a series of harmonically related spectral lines, of which the first 50 to 100 have significant energy. The sensation of vocal pitch depends on the frequency with which the individual pulses occur.

The second excitation process is due to air turbulence generated by forcing a strong current of air through a narrow constriction in the vocal tract, for example between the tongue and the alveolar ridge. The hissing sound produced is random in nature and is referred to as *fricative noise.* The spectrum is continuous and covers a wide frequency range, but is modified by the vocal-tract resonances, particularly those associated with that part of the tract in front of the point of generation.

Although an electrical analog of the speech waveform may be viewed by means of an oscilloscope, a much more informative display is obtained from a running description of the short-time energy spectrum. This can be obtained by means of the sound spectrograph [1, p. 126], which analyzes a recorded section of speech and displays the result as a three-dimensional graph called a *spectrogram.* In this the two spatial dimensions represent frequency (vertical displacement) and time (horizontal displacement), and intensity is represented by the intensity (blackness) of the trace.

Spoken words are perceived as consisting of successions of elemental sound units. These perceptual units are referred to by the phonetician as *phonemes.* They function in the spoken language much as do letters in the written language. The various sounds which are perceived by the listener as being appropriate to the same phoneme are seen to result in spectrogram patterns with certain common characteristics. In fact, with suitable training it is often possible to "read" the spectrogram and repeat what was said. However, the patterns associated with a particular phoneme vary considerably with the talker, speed of utterance, presence of nearby phonemes, etc.; and quite different sounds, for example due to dialectal differences, may be correctly described by the listener as being due to the same phoneme.

Since the set of phonemes in a given language is quite small (there are about 40 different phonemes in English) compared with the set of all possible words, it is the phoneme which is often chosen as the unit of recognition in automatic speech recognition. Such a choice may be adequate for the case of a single cooperative talker and a small vocabulary of isolated words but is insufficient for the recognition of normal conversational speech.

Outline of General Speech Research

Speech research in general owes much to earlier workers in experimental phonetics such as Jones [5]. This work was able to quantify the relation between perceived phonemic quality and the occurrence of articulatory events related to tongue position and movement, lip shape, etc. It also revealed the independent nature of the sound-source and vocal-tract functions.

The fact that recognizable vowel sounds could be generated by combinations of acoustic resonators was known to Helmholtz and Rayleigh [6, p. 477], but the true nature of the dependence of the spectrum on the vocal-tract-area function was to await the development of cineradiographic techniques (e.g., the study by Russell, Ref. 7) and experiments with electrical vocal-tract analogs by Dunn [8] and Fant [9].

The mechanism of the operation of the human larynx (vocal cords, supporting cartilages, and operating muscles) was established by the work on cadaver larynxes by Van den Berg [10, 11], and the relation between intonation, intensity, etc., and prosodic information (grammatical stress, talker's emotional state and sex, etc.) has been investigated by workers such as Lieberman [12].

Important relationships between articulatory events and neural motor-function control have been revealed by electromyographic studies (e.g., Ref. 13). These suggest that, at the neural level, the physical correlates of phonemic elements are less dependent on phonemic environment than at the acoustic level.

An idea of the tolerance of the ear to certain forms of severe waveform distortion can be obtained from the paper by Licklider and Pollack [14]. They found that even limiting the waveform to two amplitude levels (infinite clipping), so preserving only information about the times at which the signal crosses the zero axis ("zero crossings"), still permits a high degree of intelligibility.

A great deal of useful research has been concerned with relations between the perceptual and acoustic aspects of speech communication. A comprehensive study of speech sounds analyzed by an early Bell Laboratories spectrograph led to the book by Potter, Kopp, and Kopp [15]. After twenty years this book is still considered to comprise a most valuable collection of data.

A considerable body of data concerning the acoustic correlates of phonemic quality (e.g., the acoustic patterns of vowels, semivowels, etc.) has resulted from the work directed by Peterson at the Communication Sciences Laboratory, University of Michigan, in which Lehiste has been most prominent (e.g., Refs. 16 and 17).

In a classic study, Peterson and Barney [18] obtained the perceptual responses of a large number of listeners to vowel sounds in speech by a large number of talkers, and plotted these as a function of the measured frequencies of the first two formants (F1 and F2). This showed a high degree of overlap between the different vowel judgments. For instance, the formant measurements for a particular vowel sound by one talker might be identical with those for a different vowel sound by another talker. This is particularly so when the range of speakers is not restricted in sex or age.

Clearly, specifying the first two formant frequencies alone does not provide sufficient information to uniquely identify a given vowel sound. It might be suggested that additional measures are required, perhaps related to higher formants. It is more likely that the judgment is related to perceived talker characteristics, so that the listener must become familiar with the talker's voice before reliable judgments can be made.

This notion is supported by an experiment reported by Ladefoged and Broadbent [19]. Using synthetic speech they generated utterances which sounded like the words "bit," "bet," and "bat." These utterances differed only in the formant frequencies used for the vowel sounds. In fact, F2 was the same in each case but F1 was higher for "a" than for "e" and higher for "e" than for "i." Each word was introduced by a short sentence, also in synthetic speech, and a panel of listeners was asked to decide which of the three words had been presented.

It was found that the listener's responses to the vowel sound could be controlled by varying the average value of F1 used in the introductory sentence. Thus, if a higher than average F1 was used throughout the preamble, a word which was earlier judged to be "bet" was now judged by the same panel to be "bit."

The great advantage in using synthetic speech for this type of experiment is in the precise way in which selected parameters may be varied while keeping others fixed. This is an advantage in many branches of speech research where the subject of study must be related to perceptual standards, as in automatic recognition. The value of synthetic speech in speech research was recognized and exploited in work performed at Haskins Laboratories on the isolation of the more important "cues" by which speech sounds are identified. A summary of the work performed in the early and middle 1950s is given by Delattre [20].

We conclude this introduction with a brief look at a group of papers of particular relevance to work on automatic recognition. These are concerned with theories on the way in which the human listener perceives speech when presented with the acoustic speech signal.

One such theory, known as *analysis by synthesis,* was proposed by Halle and Stevens of MIT [21, 22]. This postulates that in order to relate the speech signal to permissible strings of speech elements, the listener generates an internal speech signal under the known generative rules and matches these signals to signals derived from the incoming speech. A similar theory, called the *motor theory of speech perception,* has been suggested by Liberman of Haskins Laboratories [23]. This also suggests that the listener makes use of the mechanism for generating speech in order to turn the continuous acoustic signal into the discrete units in which speech is perceived.

The main difference between these two theories seems to be in the purpose for which the ideas are introduced. The MIT model is proposed in an explicit form, without regard for the detailed accuracy of the proposal, in order to stimulate research into specific attempts at speech recognition. The Haskins theory is used as a starting point from which research can proceed into the perceptual effects themselves.

Fant has criticized the details of these suggested active perceptual systems and has suggested a further model of the operations involved [24].

Fant is also co-author of a theory of speech production which has been fruitful in stimulating work on automatic recognition. This is the *distinctive-features* theory [25], which views the various phonemes of speech in terms of a smaller set of binary oppositions related to the manner of production. These oppositions are referred to by such terms as vocalic/nonvocalic, nasal/oral, tense/lax, etc. Some of these quantities can be directly related to measurable acoustic phenomena, such as the overall energy level and the presence of concentrations of energy in certain regions of the frequency domain; but the acoustic correlates of others have proved very elusive, and Fant himself has, more recently, been critical of some of the quantities chosen for the original set [24].

Survey of the Literature on Automatic Speech Recognition

The aim of this survey is not to give a detailed explanation of each system or to criticize the methods used, but to reveal the main theme on which each approach is based and to give an idea of the degree of success attained. This latter quantity, where given, usually takes the form of a percent-correct recognition score as reported by the experimenter. This measure should be used with great caution when comparing different systems, as it depends so much on the input material chosen and on the criteria used to determine it.

Earlier Studies

The first truly successful recognizer was reported in 1952 by Davis, Biddulph, and Balashek of Bell Laboratories [26]. This device could recognize the ten digits, spoken over the telephone by a single talker, with an accuracy approaching 100 percent. On the speech of a different talker, however, the accuracy could be as low as 50 percent. The talker was expected to speak clearly and to pause between digits. The recognition method used was to assign the spoken word to the most probable digit category on the basis of approximate F1/F2 measurements during vowel sounds.

The choice of the spoken digits as recognition material is a natural one due to the modest size of the vocabulary and its application in machine control, automatic dialing, etc. It does, however, contain word pairs which are easily confused even by humans, such as "five" and "nine."

In the following years the 1952 machine was considerably refined so that the device reported in 1958 [27] gave virtually perfect recognition for a single talker and could be used by other talkers if they learned to modify their voices, but it was not possible to significantly enlarge the vocabulary or increase the number of users without a considerable retraining period.

In 1956 Wiren and Stubbs [28] at Northeastern University produced a device which partially implemented the distinctive-feature binary oppositions. Phoneme classification was based on voiced/unvoiced, turbulent/nonturbulent, stop/fricative, and acute/grave determinations. This gave 94 percent correct recognition of the vowels in short words by 21 talkers. Also in 1956, Olson and Belar of RCA [29] reported a machine with a vocabulary of ten monosyllabic words with which a syllable recognition accuracy of 98 percent could be obtained in complete sentences by a single talker. "Careful" pronunciation was required with a pause between each syllable. Eight frequency bands and five time intervals per syllable were used to define an eight-cell by five-cell matrix. In each cell a "1" or a "0" was stored depending on whether the signal energy appropriate to that cell was above or below a threshold level. The decoded matrix pattern was used to operate a typewriter key and so a typed transcript of the sentence was obtained.

A later version of the Olson and Belar syllable recognizer was reported in 1961 [30]. Again this made use of eight frequency bands and five time samples, but these time samples were only taken when a significant change occurred in the spectral power distribution. The machine's vocabulary was increased from 10 to 100 syllables, but no recognition performance figures were given.

Following suggestions by Fry, Denes produced a speech recognizer at University College, London, in 1959 [31]. This consisted of a spectrum analyzer, a spectral pattern-matching system, and stored probabilistic information concerning the probability of any phoneme recognized by the machine following another in spoken English. The phoneme-recognition set comprised four vowels and nine consonants. The overall performance was not particularly good, but use of the linguistic data (phoneme pair probabilities) improved the word recognition accuracy from 24 to 44 percent.

We conclude this look at the earlier literature with the pioneering study by Forgie and Forgie at Lincoln Laboratories, reported in 1959 [32]. This used a 35-channel filter bank whose outputs were envelope-detected, sampled, and fed to a computer. The computer program made use mainly of the frequency positions of F1 and F2 and of fundamental voice-frequency measurements. It could recognize ten English vowels in isolated words of the form /b/-vowel-/t. For 21 male and female talkers, with no adjustment for the talker, the vowel recognition accuracy was 93 percent.

This work demonstrated the value of the digital computer in recognition studies; and the combination of computer and vocoder-type hardware analyzer was to appear in many future investigations, as we shall see in the following section.

Reports Since 1960

The availability of powerful, high-speed computers in recent years has brought about a significant change in research in this field.

One common use for a computer has been in place of the hardware concerned with classifying the utterance on the basis of output signals from a hardware spectrum analyzer. The spectrum analyzer is typically of the vocoder type, having a bank of filters followed by rectifying and smoothing circuits. Spectral analysis of speech in this manner is well established, and many such analyzers exist in speech-research centers. The computer time involved in simulating a conventional vocoder-type analyzer is therefore hardly justified. However, the recognition strategy, which determines the processing necessary in the later stages, is often subject to considerable modification as the study progresses. The flexibility which the computer offers is therefore very valuable in these stages.

Where the spectral analysis section is also subject to investigation there are considerable advantages in simulating the whole system by computer. However, where real-time operation is required, or where large amounts of speech material are to be processed, it has been common to fix the design during an initial period of complete simulation and then to build hardware units for those sections requiring long computer time. Now even this restriction has been greatly relaxed with the development of the "fast Fourier transform" algorithm of Cooley and Tukey [33]. Thus in many present-day laboratory investigations valuable research can be conducted with no further equipment than a tape recorder, an analog-to-digital converter, and a general-purpose computer.

The most interesting use to which computers have been put in some recently reported investigations has been in on-line computer studies using man-machine communication peripherals such as the light pen and RAND tablet. These highly flexible systems allow for rapid manipulation of the speech signal in intensive experimental sessions, which permit progress at a speed undreamed of in the special hardware days.

Hardware Studies

We begin this section with a look at three hardware devices reported from Japan in the early 1960s. A number of practical recognizers were demonstrated in that country at about this time and rather high recognition scores were claimed, although it has been suggested that this is partly due to the phonetic simplicity of the Japanese language.

A study of vowel recognition by Suzuki and Nakata of the Radio Research Laboratory, Tokyo, was reported in 1961 [34]. A 26-channel spectrum analyzer and separate wideband, formant-related channels were used. The channel outputs were separately grouped and connected to individual vowel-decision circuits. The speech was segmented into voiced and unvoiced segments, and envelope-intensity and fundamental voice-frequency measurements were also used. To reduce the errors due to formant movement during vowel sounds, separate recognition decisions were made at intervals throughout voiced segments. The final classification was then made by observing the phoneme most frequently recognized. If one phoneme was not clearly in the majority, the two most frequent were indicated.

Sakai and Doshita of Kyoto University reported a more comprehensive recognizer in 1962 [35]. This used separate circuits for segmenting the speech into vowels and consonants and for classifying the segmented phonemes. Zero-crossing analysis was combined with measurements of the variations of energy in various frequency regions. The segmentation operation made use of measures of the "stability" of, and the "distance" between, the digital patterns generated. Details of the recognition experiments were not given but it was claimed that 90 percent correct recognition was obtained on vowels and 70 percent on consonants, although it was pointed out that some phonemes were not allowed as input.

A device for recognizing Japanese digits spoken in isolation was reported by Nagata et al. of the Nippon Electric Co. in 1963 [36]. Recognition decisions were based on the number of voiced intervals in each utterance, the presence of an unvoiced consonant, and formant frequencies and frequency slopes at three time points in each voiced interval. Eight such features were detected, and the state of each was indicated by energizing one of a number of output lines. There were 56 lines in all, of which eight were energized at the end of each utterance. The output lines were connected to the columns of a resistor matrix. The rows of the matrix represented the 10 digits. The resistors were chosen such that the row appropriate to a particular digit had the highest voltage when the sequence of detected features made that digit the most likely. An indication of the fundamental voice frequency was derived and used to change the decision matrix for female talkers.

The matrix resistors were adjusted to suit a single male talker based on an analysis of 500 utterances of the digits. One thousand utterances by the same talker resulted in an error rate of 0.3 percent. The matrix was then adjusted on the basis of 600 utterances by 20 male talkers. One thousand utterances by the same talkers then gave a 2.1 percent error rate. After further adjustments, 500 utterances by 10 female talkers gave a 7 percent error rate.

A hardware study of massive proportions has been the subject of periodic reports by Martin et al. of RCA [37]. This system makes use of analog threshold logic (ATL) elements which are based on a model of the biological neuron. The ATL element is a transistor circuit having excitory and inhibitory inputs which provides an output only when the linear sum of input currents (inhibitory inputs are subtracted) exceeds a preset threshold. This output is then proportional to the sum of the inputs until saturation is reached. When reported in 1964 the system contained well over 500 of these circuits. The recognizer employed a 19-channel spectrum analyzer (which could handle a 60-dB dynamic range), ATL elements, AND gates, and monostable multivibrators. Various features of the speech signal were used for the recognition of individual phoneme patterns, such as steady-state and transitory spectral-energy patterns and intensity ratios. An interesting feature of the system was that no formant peaks or troughs were measured; it was found that a more invariant measurement was obtained from the "spectral regions of increasing and decreasing energy," i.e., the formant skirt slopes. The channel filters had Q factors ranging between 1 and 2.

In an article by Falter in 1965 [38] the machine's performance on CVC utterances by six male talkers was given. Recognition accuracies ranging from 82 to 99 percent were obtained for 22 different phonemes including vowels, stops, and vowel-like consonants. Work in hand at that time was expected to lead to improved performance on these phonemes and others not discussed, and it was claimed that the principle of operation could permit the recognition of connected speech. A great advantage of the approach adopted in this study is that it is possible to distinguish between patterns which differ only slightly in their physical characteristics. These differences can be detected and given greater weight then they would have in an overall view of the patterns.

A study made at the University of Illinois was described by Gazdag in 1966 [39]. In fact the recognition process was not completely implemented, so requiring human effort in the final stages, and the system was not fully tested at the time of reporting, but the report was mainly concerned with a mathematical investigation of the fundamental ideas involved. A 12-channel spectrum analyzer was used (highest frequency 3 kHz), and the measurement space defined by its outputs was partitioned by six hyperplanes, implemented by summing amplifiers and trigger circuits, each trigger circuit changing state as its amplifier's output passed through zero. The output pattern was thus in the form of six binary quantities whose time variation was characteristic of the spoken word. The outputs were recorded on a multichannel pen recorder and transcribed by human operators in sequences of six-digit binary numbers.

The machine was tested on 10 digits spoken by four talkers. Detailed results were not given but the performance was described as "promising." It was also claimed that the system was invariant to time variations but no proof of this was given.

A system for recognizing Italian numerals was described in 1967 by Gilli and Meo [40]. This used a 17-channel spectrum analyzer followed by threshold detectors which reduced the range of outputs from each channel to binary statements. These signals were sampled and connected to separate circuits for the recognition of each digit. The decisions were mainly based on the sequential occurrence of vowel and consonant patterns and patterns due to certain transitions.

For the 10 numerals spoken by 10 talkers, which were used to provide data on which the machine was designed, no errors occurred. For new utterances by the same talkers, correct recognition was obtained for 90 percent of the utterances. The authors claimed that the results proved that the crude patterns obtained were sufficient for recognition of the digits by a simple machine and that a redesign could have eliminated most of the errors.

Bezdel [41] of Standard Telecommunication Laboratories (STL) has described a system for discriminating sound class on the basis of zero-crossing analysis. This depends on the rate, and the differential rate, at which zero-crossing frequencies fall in previously defined bands. Some of the classes separated include long and short voiced and unvoiced sounds, two vowel classes, two fricative classes, and long and short periods of silence. It was claimed that an advantage of the system is that separate segmentation is not necessary, as this is inherent in the processing involved.

A word recognizer reported by Ross of RCA [42] was an extension of work by Olson and Belar. It used a four-channel spectrum analyzer and a digital disk storage system. A 20-bit binary pattern was generated for each word by sampling five two-state signals derived from the four frequency channels. Four of these signals were obtained by calculating the ratio of the mean energy level in each frequency channel to the mean energy in the overall signal. The fifth signal resulted from a comparison of the energy in the highest frequency channel with that in the two lowest. Each of these signals was compared with a threshold level to produce five binary outputs. The resulting patterns were classified by means of a "nearest neighbor" comparison with patterns stored in the machine. The permissible "distance" between patterns giving the same output response was under the control of the experimenter. The training procedure was to present a number of utterances representing a single word in sequence. If the incoming pattern was not sufficiently close to any of the patterns already stored, the new pattern was added to the stored patterns. Thus a set of different patterns were retained for each word in the machine's vocabulary.

After training, a new input pattern was given the same label as that of the nearest stored pattern if it was within the specified distance of one of these. Otherwise it was rejected. The machine was tested on spoken digits. When the permitted distance was set to one bit (i.e., two patterns were considered the same if they differed by only one bit out of the 20 pattern bits) 86 stored patterns were required to correctly identify the members of the training set. For ten new samples of each spoken digit, 56 gave the correct response, 8 gave incorrect responses, and 36 gave no response. When the permitted distance was zero (requiring an exact match), with 218 patterns stored, 46 out of 100 new digits gave the correct response, 2 gave incorrect responses, and 52 gave no response.

Computer Studies

Denes and Mathews [43] in 1960 reported a system for recognizing the 10 digits from complete word patterns. This used a 17-channel spectrum analyzer, the outputs of which were sampled and recorded on magnetic tape. This signal then formed the input to a computer. Time-frequency patterns for a number of utterances of each word were averaged and stored as reference patterns. Patterns from unknown utterances to be classified were compared, by a cross-correlation process, with each stored pattern in turn. The classification of the reference pattern giving the best match was chosen as that of the unknown utterance. A comparison was made of the results with and without time normalization of the patterns.

One female and six male talkers were used and the only restriction imposed on their pronunciation of the digits was that they should pause between each. The error rate averaged over all talkers was 6 percent with time normalization and 12 percent without. The authors concluded that forming the reference patterns by averaging over several talkers and the use of time normalization were both valuable techniques. They also suggested that, in time normalization, the consonant and vowel parts of the pattern should be treated separately rather than the whole pattern being simply stretched or compressed.

Another digit recognizer was briefly described in an abstract published in 1960 by Sebestyen of Litton Industries [44]. This combined an 18-channel vocoder analyzer and computer. The computer implemented linear transformations of the analyzer output signals to obtain maximal clustering of the data in the 361-dimensional space formed by time-sampling the channel outputs. Time normalization was used, and the normalization factor was included as one of the space dimensions.

Four hundred utterances of the 10 numerals by 10 talkers were used. It was claimed that, if at least seven examples of each numeral were used to optimize the clustering transformations, no recognition errors were made even when the talkers used in testing the recognizer were different from those used in training it.

The phoneme-recognition study by Meeker et al. of RCA [45] also used an 18-channel vocoder-type analyzer and a computer. Boundaries between phoneme-like segments were detected from changes in the channel energy levels. Long voiced segments in CVC words were considered to be vowels. For these the frequencies of the first two formants were determined at the center of the segment. The vowels were classified by comparison with the published data of Peterson and Barney [18]. Three types of consonant segment were recognized: stop, fricative, and nasal/liquid.

A total of 7,200 vowel sounds from words spoken by 10 male talkers were classified with an accuracy of about 40 percent. After an analysis of the results it was concluded that if the decision rules had been based on the speech of each talker separately, and if use had been made of vowel duration, the vowel recognition score would have been 97 percent. Ten consonants in 6,000 words were recognized with an accuracy of 60 percent.

A word-recognition system was reported in 1966 by Gold of MIT [46]. This used a 16-channel spectrum analyzer (maximum frequency 3 kHz), a pitch extractor, and a voicing detector. The computer program segmented the words into approximate phonemic units on the basis of voicing, magnitude, and spectral information. A further 15 spectral, durational, and intensity measurements were then made on a group of five segments centered on one segment which was defined as stressed. A scoring method based on the similarity with previous measurements on known words was used to classify the word. For 50 isolated words by 10 talkers, 86 percent were correctly identified and 96 percent received either the highest or the second-highest score.

An example of a system produced entirely by computer simulation is that of Sholtz and Bakis of IBM [47]. In this the spectral analyzer was assumed to have 40 filters, and the power output of each channel was obtained by convolving the time-sampled input signal with the impulse response of the appropriate filter. The input was in the form of isolated words. These were segmented into consonants and vowels (including vowel-like consonants) and compared with a library of stored word patterns. If a suitable match was obtained, the appropriate word was considered to be recognized; otherwise the utterance was rejected.

Eleven vowel and three consonant categories were used. Segment classification was on the basis of the following measurements:

1. Silence (power level 20 dB below average).
2. Total power slope (approximation to the time derivative of the total power).
3. A number of measurements obtained from the ratio of power contained in various bands; for example, the vowel/consonant decision was based on the ratio of the power in the band 0–800 Hz to that in the band 7–8 kHz. If greater than a given threshold value, vowel; otherwise consonant.

For each vowel applied to the classification process a set of 24 numbers was obtained relating to its power spectrum and time variation. The numbers were considered to specify a point in 24-dimensional space. This space was divided into 11 regions (ten vowel classes and one reject class) by hyperplanes implementing a Bayes decision, assuming equal a priori probabilities. The three consonant categories were stop (based on a rapid increase in power level following silence) and two types of fricative. In some cases a segment which did not fit into any of these three categories was rejected.

Utterances by 10 talkers were used to develop the recognition procedure. The system was then applied to words spoken by 40 new talkers in order to optimize the dictionary categories. If one word caused a particular sequence of phoneme categories, that word was assigned as the dictionary meaning of that sequence. If several words gave the same sequence, the most frequently occurring word was assigned as the dictionary meaning. When the recognition procedure was applied to the whole set of utterances (total of 493 words by 25 male and 25 female talkers), 97 percent of the words gave the correct response. It was claimed that the results were independent of the sex of the talker and that the process was more tolerant of intertalker differences than previously reported systems.

A word recognizer using a low-data-rate spectral-matching process has been developed by Shearme and Leach of J.S.R.U. [48]. The output of a 20-channel vocoder analyzer is sampled and fed to a computer. Each time sample is considered to define a point in 20-dimensional space. The variation of this point traces out a path in the space which is characteristic of the word and of the talker. Twenty different "prototype spectra" are chosen which represent certain fixed points in the space. The path taken by the signal during an utterance is specified by noting the nearest prototype point at each sampling instant. The result is a series of numbers in the range 1 to 20. It is this sequence which forms the pattern to be recognized in the matching process. Separate number sequences due to the utterance of words of known classification are first stored in the computer as "template" patterns. Unknown-word patterns are then compared with each prototype pattern and the classification of that giving the highest score is chosen.

For 32 isolated words by 10 talkers and using nine template patterns for each vocabulary word, an accuracy of 90 percent correct identification was obtained. No example of the input word by the talker under test was included in the set of prototype patterns. The scoring method provides two confidence measures, one relating to the probability of correct recognition and the other the probability that the word giving the highest score was, in fact, outside the vocabulary of the machine. One advantage of this type of system is the ease with which the template patterns may be changed to suit a different talker, dialect, or language. Another is the fact that the unit of recognition can be easily extended to a longer utterance than the word.

Purton [49] has produced a system which makes use of an autocorrelation technique. The signal is first split into two bands approximating the ranges of F1 and F2. The two waveforms are then infinitely clipped to produce zero-crossing signals. These signals are separately autocorrelated and time-sampled to produce a 36×30 matrix for each utterance. This pattern is compared with master patterns and the best match determined by a scoring method. The master patterns are formed from several utterances of known classification by one or by several talkers.

In single-talker experiments using a machine vocabulary of 10 words, 696 utterances gave individual accuracies ranging from 78 to 99 percent. The average accuracy was 89 percent. By using an "updating" procedure, where incoming patterns giving high scores are used to improve the master patterns, an average accuracy of 93 percent was obtained with 385 utterances by six talkers. As with the previous system, this system has the advantage that the stored patterns can be easily changed to suit the machine's use. Admitted disadvantages are the large storage requirements and the long processing time (about 3 s per utterance). It was claimed that these can be improved without loss of performance.

Lavington and Rosenthal [50] have been working on the recognition of verbal commands at Manchester University (Department of Computer Science). Their recognition system makes use of simple measurements of zero-crossing intervals, turn-arounds (points of zero time derivative), and amplitude-envelope information.

A total of 70 words from a vocabulary of 16 CVC monosyllables by 19 talkers with various accents were recognized with only one misclassification error and three "minor" errors. In each word the first consonant was /s/, /f/, /t/, or /n/, the final consonant was /s/ or /n/, and the vowel was /i/ or "or" (it is not clear whether this was /ɔ/ or /ɔr/, but in view of the range of dialects it is probable that both were included). The program was enlarged to accept all the initial consonants occurring in the 10 digits. There were 101 examples of these consonants pronounced by the same talkers and recognized without error, provided that no distinction was made between /θ/ and /f/.

Distinctive Features

In 1961 Hughes of MIT published a report on a limited recognition system based on a distinctive-features approach to phoneme classification [51]. The aim of the study was limited, being concerned with demonstrating that the distinctive-features approach was a valid one in speech recognition. The input to a computer program was in the form of purely spectral information from a 35-channel spectrum analyzer. Five acoustic features were detected: the frequencies of the first two formants, the presence of fricative noise, the approximate shape of the fricative spectrum, the occurrence of discontinuous changes in energy level and in formant frequencies, and the presence of silence. Six vowel and five consonant phoneme classifications were used, and no attempt was made to distinguish between consonants with similar spectral characteristics or between liquids, nasals, and glides.

For seven talkers pronouncing one- or two-syllable isolated words it was found that fairly good results were obtained for words containing a single stressed vowel but otherwise the results were poor.

Hughes was concerned with another distinctive-features scheme published in 1965 [52]. Again the input to the computer was in the form of spectral samples. Although the acoustic correlates of vowels and consonants were tested, detailed results were given only for vowels. A single-speaker approach was adopted and the results of machine recognition were compared with the performance of a panel of listeners as well as with the intentions of the talker.

In this study the vowel decisions were associated with measurements on the F1-F2 plane. The acute/grave, diffuse/compact, and flat/plain oppositions were implemented by means of linear decision boundaries (straight lines); the tense/lax decision was based on the relative distance from the neutral vowel and on the time duration. Consonant classification was based on the frequency of energy concentration and intensity for fricatives and various spectral and temporal measurements for stops and affricates. The decisions based on these measurements were given empirically derived weights in the classification process. The use of simple linguistic constraints concerned with vowel duration was also found to be useful in resolving some ambiguities. It was pointed out by the authors that it is necessary to distinguish between formant variations due to diphthong shifts and those due to the influence of adjacent phonemes.

The test material consisted of two-syllable nonsense utterances, a number of monosyllabic English words, and two English sentences. The overall vowel phoneme recognition accuracy was 92 percent, although it was believed that this could have been improved by a simple decision-boundary shift. The machine performance was similar to that of the human judges on excised vowels, and in some cases machine and listeners agreed on classifications that were different from those intended.

Adaptive (Learning) Recognizers

A report by Talbert et al. [53] demonstrates the application of "Adaline" networks (adaptive-threshold elements) to a speech-recognition task. For a description of the Adaline network, various adaptive systems using these networks and a discussion of important training theorems, see the book by Nilsson [54]. The reported system could recognize a small number of words by means of an eight-channel spectrum analyzer, four-level amplitude quantization and 10 time samples per word to generate a 240-spot binary pattern. This pattern was connected to a combination of Adaline networks simulated by computer. In a training operation several examples of each spoken word were presented to the system, which assigned a separate output signal to each word group. The training set was presented sequentially until each utterance was correctly categorized. New utterances were then presented for the system to identify.

It was found that, for the chosen set of "phonetically balanced" words, when the same talker was used for training and testing, 100 test utterances were recognized without error. For the 10 digits by a single talker, a 2 percent error rate was obtained. It was also found that when recognizing the utterances by five different talkers, better results were obtained if only one talker was used for training than when all five talkers were used to speak the training set. In an experiment in which new words were progressively added to the system's vocabulary, low error rates were obtained up to a vocabulary size of 16 words, but above this the error rate increased rapidly. This gave a measure of the "capacity" of the device.

A more detailed study of the application of adaptive-threshold elements to speech recognition was reported in 1965 by Dammann of IBM [55]. This phoneme-recognition system used a 15-channel spectrum analyzer and 13-level amplitude quantization, and the output, sampled every 10 ms, was fed to 10 adaptive threshold elements simulated by computer. Various phoneme categories were tried, but the best results were obtained with 20 classes, making no distinction between different stop consonants, between certain fricatives, or between a number of voiced continuants.

After training the system on the speech of a single talker, requiring 100 repetitions of the training set, 278 new isolated words by the same talker gave a phoneme-class recognition accuracy of 91.7 percent. For 343 words by a second talker the accuracy was 80 percent.

The adaptive word-recognition system of King and Tunis reported in 1966 [56] was rather more successful. This used a 15-channel spectrum analyzer and a computer. The computer program made use of a "peak picking" routine to find the frequency positions of the formants and based the recognition on a frequency-time matrix whose entries were 1 (peak) or 0 (no peak). The computer then implemented various transformations on this pattern in a series of experiments and classified the word by means of adaptive linear decision functions which had been trained on previous input data.

Two different vocabularies of 15 words each were recorded a number of times by a range of talkers. The recordings were used in various ways to test the system; for instance, the performance was observed when the same talker was used for the training and testing material, when different talkers were used, and when the material was formed from the combined utterances of several talkers. Different vocabulary sizes were also tried. The best result, obtained by using the same talker for training and recognition, gave only a 0.2 percent error rate. The worst result in the single-talker experiments (which was using a female talker) gave a 2.5 percent error rate. The training set consisted of 15 words repeated 35 to 50 times each. The recognition set consisted of different utterances of the same words repeated 90 to 115 times each. The worst result was obtained when the system was trained by one talker and then tried to recognize utterances by another talker. In that case the error rate was 46 percent, but when examples of both talkers were included in the training set, the error rate was 0.8 percent.

The above experiments made use of all the information contained in the matrix resulting from the utterance of each word. In a further set of experiments this matrix was transformed in various ways before the classification operation. In the first transformation a layer of feature detectors was used to detect the presence of steady formant patterns and of formant glides; in the second transformation detectors were applied to each column to detect particular sounds, e.g., particular formant distributions; in the third transformation the number of columns was reduced to three, so permitting only three time regions per word: early, middle, and late. None of these transformations resulted in better performance than was obtained without them, but the second and third transformations in series gave comparable results (0.6 to 1.9 percent errors) with significantly less information.

A word recognizer described by Fraipont in 1966 [57] divided the frequency range 300 Hz–3 kHz into ten channels, each of which was envelope-detected. Two more signals were formed from the energy above 3 kHz and the overall spectrum. These 12 signals were sampled for ½ second after the onset of a word, and the resulting 192 samples were punched on to paper tape which was subsequently fed into a computer. Word recognition was by means of linear decision hyperplanes which were adjusted to give optimum performance during a training session. The machine vocabulary comprised the 10 digits and five other words.

The training data were formed by 26 talkers each speaking the vocabulary words once. After training the machine for four hours the training set gave a correct-recognition score of 99 percent. Ten new talkers then spoke each of the words twice. This set resulted in 87 percent correct recognition, 6 percent errors, and 7 percent rejected.

Unusual Forms of Analysis

The successful transmission of speech over vocoder systems suggests that the smallest set of data containing sufficient information to specify the acoustic signal comprises eight measurements: the frequencies and amplitudes of the first three formants, the pitch of the voice in voiced sounds, and a binary indication concerning whether the sound is voiced or unvoiced. Of course, to these eight measurements must be added the human ability to resolve ambiguities by the use of linguistic and other constraints.

A recognition system proposed and tested by Teacher and Piotrowski [58] makes use of the single-equivalent-formant theory (SEF) devised by L. Focht of Philco Corporation. This theory is based on the experimentally established fact that a single resonance operating on a typical larynx-tone signal can elicit a sensation of vowel quality in the listener. It is argued that, if it were possible to obtain an estimate of the necessary resonance frequency from the acoustic waveform of natural speech, then the number of measurements required to classify these sounds would be reduced to four, i.e., only half that for a vocoder, with a consequent reduction in processing complexity. It has been shown that the SEF is closely related to the "dominant" formant in voiced sounds; this is usually defined as the formant having the highest amplitude when the speech signal is passed through a weighting network having a spectral "tilt" of +9 dB/oct.

In preliminary experiments with a simple word recognizer based on the SEF principle it was found that a small vocabulary of randomly chosen words could be recognized with an accuracy of 98 percent; however, it was expected that some confusion would occur between phonetically similar words with the system as it was at that time (1965).

In 1967 a complete, portable digit recognizer based on this earlier work was exhibited [59]. It contained a "pitch extractor" to give an indication of the beginning of each glottal cycle. The spectrum was modified by 9 dB/oct preemphasis. The SEF parameters were estimated from the period between the onset of the glottal cycle and the first zero crossing, and the maximum amplitude reached during this period. Logic circuits detected the occurrence of sequences of sound segments and identified the digit spoken.

The design was based on utterances by 10 male talkers. Further digits spoken by these talkers gave 90 percent correct recognition. When the system was tested on 34 new talkers, 25 percent of these were found to give good results.

A word-recognition system was reported by Weiss of the Federal Scientific Corporation (FSC) in 1966 [60]. This reduces the amount of data to be processed by sampling the spectrum at only three time positions in each phoneme pattern: at the initial and final boundaries and at the point of maximum power. The spectrum analyzer used was a commercial device manufactured by FSC called the Simoramic analyzer. This uses delay line feedback in a correlation technique simulating a continum of filters of uniform bandwidth. The spectral resolution depends on the number of recirculations, and the amplitude-frequency information (spectral cross section) is translated into a short, repetitive, amplitude-time signal, where frequency is measured along the time axis for each "sweep." This signal was sampled at the equivalent of 30-Hz intervals in frequency and stored for computer analysis. The computer program determined the frequencies of F1, F2, and F3 at each of the three "critical instants" for each vowel, and in the most successful experiment, use was made of a simple fricative/vowel phoneme classification and of a voiced/unvoiced indication.

For 30 isolated words (including 16 minimal phoneme pairs) each spoken twice by 19 talkers, using the first set of utterances to "train" the system and the second set as input material in the recognition experiment, 92.4 percent correct word recognition was obtained when basing the measurements on the single vowel segment in each word. It was also found that ignoring the data obtained at the point of maximum power, i.e., the point at which the vowel pattern was least influenced by adjacent phonemes, a drop of only 3 percent was found in the recognition performance. In the experiment no more than 15 data values per word were used. The recognition strategy assumed a normal distribution for the measured data about mean values, and a likelihood classification procedure was employed which minimized the expected probability of error.

A vowel-recognition system described by Cannon of the Aerospace

Medical Research Laboratory [61] performs the spectral analysis by means of an "analog ear." This simulates the operation of the cochlea by means of a 24-section low-Q ladder network, where the cutoff frequencies of the sections decrease logarithmically with distance from the input end. Outputs were taken at four points equally spaced over the region of maximum activity. The outputs were sampled at a high rate in 4-ms bursts synchronized with the onset of each glottal cycle. Analysis was performed by a computer by means of correlation operations. The 4-ms samples were first autocorrelated. The autocorrelation functions obtained were then cross-correlated with each of a set of seven stored prototype patterns of similar form. This produced a set of 28 cross-correlation coefficients (four signals per sound and seven prototype patterns). The coefficients obtained were considered to specify a point in 28-dimensional space. This space was partitioned into vowel regions by a simple linear adaptive network, giving seven vowel-recognition classes.

After using 250 utterances by 10 talkers in the training operation, 71 sounds by five talkers were classified with an accuracy of 97 percent. The utterances were apparently isolated vowels, and the talkers had various regional accents. The prototype patterns were obtained by averaging the autocorrelation coefficients over several utterances by each talker and then over all talkers so that only information common to all talkers was retained.

A report by Reddy on work for a Ph.D. thesis conducted at Stanford University [62] is of particular interest not for the success achieved but for the way in which the computer installation was employed. The recognition strategy involved ad hoc measurements on the speech waveform which were developed during on-line computer sessions. The microphone signal was input directly to the computer's disk store via an analog-to-digital converter. The stored waveform (up to 2 s long) was presented on a cathode-ray tube, and the signal could be monitored repeatedly by loudspeaker. A light pen was used to select portions of the displayed waveform for analysis, and, if required, segments of stored speech could be selected and joined together and then heard on the loudspeaker.

In many speech-analysis systems spectral analysis accounts for a significant amount of the computer time involved. In Reddy's work spectral analysis had a relatively minor role and formed one of the final stages of analysis before classification. A 2-s utterance was first divided into sustained and transitional segments on the basis of intensity and zero-crossing measurements; for each voiced segment a typical pitch period was then identified near the center of the segment, and a Fourier expansion of this period gave the amplitudes of the first 100 harmonics of the fundamental frequency. Approximate spectral energy distributions for unvoiced segments were obtained by the Fourier expansion of a 10-ms sample near the center. These computer routines resulted in a list of 21 parameter values related to duration, intensity, and frequency measurements. The segments were then classified, on the basis of these values, as vowel-like, fricative-like, etc., and tests were made to reject those segments which were due to transitions between speech elements. The remaining segments were then associated with English phonemes.

For a single talker pronouncing 1- to 2-s connected utterances, both nonsense and meaningful, 81 percent of 287 phoneme patterns were correctly recognized. For the reported study the time necessary to analyze each utterance was about 40 times real time. It was claimed that this is significantly less than that for many other comparable studies. It was also claimed that some of the measurements found useful could not have been easily derived from the output of a filter bank.

General Comments on the Literature

Many of the reported systems have been designed to recognize short isolated utterances, and some of these are seen to provide rather good recognition scores. While several of the better systems could probably be expanded to permit the recognition of larger vocabularies or to accept a wider range of talkers, it is most unlikely that any of them could be modified to cope with normal connected speech. In general they perform the recognition by means of ad hoc rules based on knowledge of the acoustic waveform alone, whereas human recognition requires instinctive and acquired knowledge from a number of sources.

Those systems which use adaptive techniques work rather well within the limitations of their input material, but again these are ad hoc schemes which could not cope with the highly ambiguous acoustic patterns found in normal speech.

Although in theory a successful phoneme-pattern recognizer would have wider application than a word recognizer with similar limitations on the size of the recognition set, most of the phoneme recognizers covered by this survey, like the word recognizers, depend too much on the measurable acoustic patterns. The feature-abstraction scheme by Martin et al. [37] looks more promising than many others, but this still seems to require a separable pattern for each phoneme, and this is just not found in normal connected speech. The arguments in favor of using feature recognition and against the existence of a unique phoneme–acoustic-correlate relationship are developed in the next section.

The reported distinctive-feature schemes, though based on a theory of human perception, do not exhibit a marked degree of talker invariability or processing simplicity.

Some of the reported investigations have achieved results which appear contradictory; thus, Denes and Mathews [43] and King and Tunis [56] found it better to form the stored patterns used in the recognition process from utterances by several different talkers; whereas Talbert et al. [53] and Shearme and Leach [48] found it better to store and use the patterns due to different talkers separately. These effects obviously depend on the type of pattern stored, the way in which different patterns are combined, and the degree of variability between similar utterances by the different talkers used in each study.

The processes by which the large amount of data contained in the acoustic waveform can be reduced, while retaining sufficient data on which to base the recognition procedure, are of considerable interest. Some designers have taken conventional vocoder analysis techniques and simply reduced the number of measurements in the frequency, time, and amplitude directions. Others have based their data reduction on the results of earlier studies. Weiss [60] found that the most valuable data were preserved if he took spectral samples near the junctions between phonemic elements; Reddy [62] segmented the speech into phoneme-sized elements on the basis of simple measurements and then performed a detailed spectral analysis on a single glottal period near the center of each; Gold [46] gave greatest attention to stressed segments; and Shearme and Leach [48] divided their measurement space up into cells which were most closely spaced in the more populated regions.

It must be accepted that an arbitrary reduction in the data preserved for recognition will be reflected in the restrictions necessary on the input material and in the reliability of the recognition results. For a high-performance recognizer requiring minimal restrictions on the input speech it is unlikely that a significant degree of data reduction will be possible; in fact it will be necessary to add a certain amount of a priori information before the recognition process can be completed.

In summary, the reported studies suggest that the aims of reliable machine control, requiring the recognition of a small vocabulary of isolated utterances by a limited range of cooperative talkers, could be achieved in the near future; but the recognition of less restricted connected speech requires knowledge of the speech process which is not yet available.

It is unlikely that a recognition system which could match the full range of human ability will ever be economically feasible, but it is quite possible that future recognizers will be able to perform valuable recognition on input speech having no severe restrictions. The next step toward this aim will probably be a device which can accept normal connected speech as input and will scan this for the occurrence of any of a small number of preselected words or phrases. This would have the advantage that the available storage and computing effort would be concentrated on the detection of these few utterances, and the system could provide a valuable test bed for the development of more advanced recognition strategies.

The following section of this report, based on a wider study than that covered by this recognition-literature review, is concerned with some of the requirements which it is believed must be met to make possible a recognizer of this type.

Discussion

In this section we discuss certain conclusions reached by the writer as a result of the literature study. These conclusions are concerned with the important conditions which it is believed must be met if a general speech-recognition device is to have a reasonable chance of success. They are of three main types: (1) those which have already been explicitly stated in the literature and are now generally accepted by workers in this field, (2) those which are clearly implied by certain reported experiments but which have not been explicitly stated or which are apparently not widely known, and (3) personal opinions formed by the writer from his study of the literature on general speech research. The class into which a particular conclusion falls is not generally indicated but references to supporting works are given in a few cases.

1. *The mechanical recognition operation must be closely related to the way in which a human recognizes speech.* It is unlikely that there exist in the speech waveform invariant features which can be used for general speech recognition that are not already exploited by the human listener. The human-speech communication process is remarkably resistant to very severe corrupting influences. There is evidence that the listener can make use of information from a great many sources, employing both instinctive and acquired knowledge, and different forms of information in the speech wave itself. It is most unlikely that, in developing the speech facility, the evolutionary process has omitted valuable information which can be derived by mechanical processing.

2. *The most efficient way to isolate important perceptual features in speech is by the use of speech synthesis and human judgment.* Of course, the analysis of natural utterances must form the first step in detecting the important features for recognition; but in determining the

relative weight to be given to the observed features, speech-synthesis techniques provide essential stability and precision which can be obtained by no other method.

3. *Feature extraction is better than pattern matching in recognition at the acoustic level.* It is possible to separate many of the reported recognition systems into two groups related to the fundamental nature of the recognition process employed. We shall refer to these two processes as the pattern-matching process and the feature-extraction process These processes have inherent advantages and limitations which should be considered before a particular method is selected; of course, some systems make use of both processes, but even then one process may be dominant and so have a general influence on the utility of the machine.

The pattern-matching process usually compares the patterns produced by the incoming speech with patterns stored in the machine, and then decides on the classification by detecting the stored pattern which gives the best match. The patterns are usually produced by a particular transformation of the speech wave, for instance by means of spectral or correlation analysis. The stored patterns are chosen to be typical of the utterances within the vocabulary of the machine.

The feature-extraction process generally employs a number of specialized circuits or processing routines designed to detect the presence of various features known to be characteristic of the speech sound elements. These features might be related to the simultaneous presence of formants in defined regions of the frequency domain, to the rate of change of formant frequency, to the overall energy level, to the presence of voicing, etc. Recognition of an utterance is then based on the sequential occurrence of certain features, and the output may be in the form of a simple indication that a particular sound element has been detected.

The advantages of the pattern-recognition system include the ease with which the stored patterns may be changed to suit changes in language, talker, or the size of the unit of recognition, the comparative simplicity of the overall system, and the ease with which the system can be made self-adaptive. The main disadvantage is that, since the matching process must cover the whole range in which a pattern can occur (e.g., the whole range of important speech frequencies), it is difficult to discriminate against prominent but irrelevant data. The advantages and disadvantages of the feature-extraction system are largely the reverse of these. It is frequently more complicated, requires a period of intensive study to cope with changes of language, etc., and is difficult to make self-adaptive; however, as each section is designed for the optimum detection of a particular feature, it is easier to specifically exclude irrelevant data and to distinguish between very similar though distinctly different sounds.

It is most likely that a combination of these two systems should be used for optimum results, that is, feature extraction should form the basis of recognition at the lowest level, the level of sound elements, but that patterns formed by sequences of sound elements should be recognized by a pattern-matching process.

4. *The question of whether to base the recognition on phonemes or syllables has yet to be resolved.* There is some evidence to support the view that the syllable is the basic unit of speech articulation (see, for example, Kozhevnikov and Chistovich, Ref. 63). It is not clear, however, that it is also the basis of perception. The significance of rhythm and other aspects of syllabic stress show that the syllable has an important function in speech perception, but the ease and consistency with which the phonetician can describe an utterance in terms of phonemic units argues for a subsyllabic unit of perception. This fact and the implicit signal-processing economy have convinced many workers that phoneme-level recognition is a sensible approach to mechanical processing.

The view expressed by Kozhevnikov and Chistovich is that making recognition decisions in terms of phoneme units is probably valid as long as the decisions are taken with regard to information distributed over the whole syllable. Although this view was reached on the basis of experimental evidence, the question has not been finally resolved and some work remains to be done on the subject.

5. *The speech signal cannot be directly segmented into phoneme units.* The term *phoneme* is often used in the literature in a way which might confuse the reader. Thus the use of a "phoneme recognizer" suggests that speech is composed of phonemes and that these phonemes can be physically isolated and identified. In fact, the term phoneme refers to a conceptual grouping of speech sounds and allows the listener to describe a speech utterance in terms of an alphabet of phonemic symbols. The phoneme is the smallest meaningful sound unit of speech which the listener can perceive. The acoustic correlates of a given phoneme depend on the language, the dialect, and the individual talker. There is no one-to-one relationship between sound elements measurable in the speech waveform and the listener's description in terms of a sequence of phonemes. The term "phoneme unit" might reasonably apply to a speech sound having phonemic proportions, but the notion that the speech wave can be segmented into units which can be equated one-for-one with the phonemic description is wrong.

It is true that speech sounds made in isolation can be related to phonemic elements and that modified forms of these sounds can often be detected in connected speech, but it is equally true that quite different sound elements may be correctly given the same phoneme label, that a signal which seems, acoustically, to be a single sound may be described by a sequence of phonemes, and that a phoneme can even be ascribed to an element whose acoustic correlate may be totally absent. Thus, in the Cockney pronunciation of the word "bottle," the /t/ may be replaced by a glottal stop and the /l/ by a sound related to /w/; whereas the standard English pronunciation results in a laterally released /t/ followed by /l/. If there is no intention to distinguish between the two dialects it is quite legitimate to transcribe both as /bɒtl/.

It is evident that a recognizer designed to recognize phoneme units without reference to knowledge about the talker or to linguistic information would have only limited application in the recognition of normal conversational speech. In the case of a small vocabulary of words and a few talkers such a system might be quite adequate. The argument against trying to use phoneme recognition alone in speech recognition was clearly put by Denes in 1963 [64].

6. *Crudely quantized measurements of spectral and temporal quantities are inadequate.* Quite small changes in formant frequencies can result in significant changes in the perceived speech sound. Certain brief sounds may persist for very short periods only. Many of the reported recognition schemes employ measurement processes whose resolutions in time and frequency are quite inadequate to preserve such information. The precision required in the measurement of normal speech has never been properly determined.

Formant frequency measurement by zero-crossing analysis has been popular for some years due to the simplicity of the method, but this technique can lead to serious error unless the formant being measured is much larger than other spectral peaks. This was demonstrated in the paper published by E. Peterson in 1951 [65].

7. *A simple single measurement of the spectrum cross section in high-pitched voiced sounds may not be sufficient to accurately determine the formant frequencies.* When the fundamental frequency of larynx vibration is higher than the formant bandwidths (of the order of 150 Hz), as it often is in female and child speech, it is quite possible that a particular formant does not occur sufficiently close to a voice harmonic to be adequately specified by a simple spectrum measurement. It might be necessary to track a formant as it crosses the various harmonics prior to the point of measurement, to measure nearby voice harmonics and decide on the position of the peak by interpolation, or to employ a form of "pitch synchronous" analysis to examine the waveform at particular points in the glottal cycle.

8. *The human listener can recognize extremely brief sounds.* It is probable that the excitation of the vocal-tract resonances by a single glottal pulse is sufficient for the human listener to identify a given vowel sound. It also appears that the listener can make use of extremely rapid formant shifts involving large formant-frequency changes between successive glottal pulses (which are typically spaced about 10 ms apart). Narrowband spectrum analyzers and spectrum-sampling rates of the order of 100 s^{-1} are probably inadequate to preserve this information. Martin et al. [37] restricted channel-filter Q factors to less than two for this reason, and Reddy [62] claimed that his system made use of data which could not be easily obtained from the output of a normal spectrum analyzer. The ability to converse intelligibly over vocoder systems shows that conventional hardware spectrum analyzers preserve sufficient information for such purposes, but some loss in intelligibility must be admitted, and a moderate amount of degradation can be compensated for by the use of grammatical context. In demonstrating speech recognition techniques it might be necessary to supplement conventional channel-type spectrum analyzers with special circuits or computer routines operating on the unprocessed input signal in order to preserve very brief features.

9. *Time normalization, by simply stretching or compressing one pattern to compare with another, is of very limited value.* Except where the necessary changes are very slight, this type of time normalization is of little value even when the patterns due to different types of speech sound are treated separately. The reason is apparent if spectrograms are examined of different utterances of a sound like /bɪb/. Considering F2 alone, in the vowel /ɪ/ spoken in isolation it normally takes a high position, near 2 kHz typically; at the point of release of the initial stop and the point of closure of the final stop it takes a low position, typically below 500 Hz. The variation of F2 throughout the sound depends on the speed at which the lips open and close. If the sound is long the central part may show F2 in its normal /ɪ/ position for a considerable time. If the sound is very short, F2 may rise and fall very rapidly without actually attaining its "target" position in the vowel. To stretch this short vowel pattern consisting entirely of formant transition and compare it with the longer example, where the transition regions occupy a very small fraction of the time, would result in a high error measurement. If, however, a measure of the formant's time derivative were available, it might be possible to predict its target position and so to estimate which vowel was intended. This is equivalent to taking account of articulator inertia and thus is related to analysis-by-synthesis. The fact that the listener does take account of phonemic environment in identifying a vowel sound has been demonstrated by Lindblom and

Studdert-Kennedy [66]. This work shows that the intended vowel is actually heard even though the formants do not reach their target positions.

10. *Some consonant judgments are discrete while vowel quality judgments are continuous.* The human recognition of continuous vowels and consonants on one hand and rapid vowel transients and stops on the other seem to be based on different processing mechanisms. Thus varying vowel formant frequencies and amplitudes continuously causes a continuous change in perceived vowel quality, whereas a continuous change in formant frequency and amplitude transitions causes discrete jumps in consonant perception. For instance, if the vowel /æ/ is synthesized with an initial transition in F2 which begins at some given point in frequency and this starting frequency is gradually varied from a low frequency to a high frequency, at first the syllable /bæ/ is heard; at some starting frequency near 1.0 kHz the sound suddenly changes to /dæ/; at a little higher frequency the sound becomes /gæ/, and this persists for all higher frequencies. This effect was demonstrated by work at Haskins Laboratories [20] in early experiments with synthetic speech.

It is known that in visual perception some parts of the human recognition mechanism specialize in the detection of particular visual features, say curves having a particular curvature lying at a particular angle in the field of vision. It seems reasonable to suggest that some parts of the hearing mechanism are similarly specialized, say to detect positive or negative transitions in spectral peaks having time derivatives lying within specific values.

11. *Nondistinctive articulatory states (e.g., nasalization) can cause severe modification of spectral patterns without changing listener phoneme judgments.* This is one of the arguments against the use of simple spectral pattern matching for phoneme-level identification. Nasalization of a vowel sound introduces additional resonances and causes a shift in vowel formant frequencies, among other effects. If nasalization is nondistinctive, as it is in English, its presence or absence may have no effect on listener judgments. A matching process which compares the whole of the frequency range in a nasalized and a nonnasalized vowel will result in a large error measurement. In a feature-extraction process it should be possible to allow for the effects of such nondistinctive properties in the feature-detection operation.

12. *The mechanical recognizer must be able to cope with distortions due to the talker's acoustic environment.* The human listener is able to perform well in conditions of intense background noise, reverberation, and the addition of other sounds, such as speech due to other talkers.

Speech transmission can also lead to severe waveform distortion without greatly affecting the intelligibility of the signal to human ears. A mechanical recognizer must have the same ability if it is to match the performance of the human listener. This requires knowledge of how the human listener can perform in such conditions; this knowledge is very limited at present.

13. *Recognition of speech sounds at the acoustic level requires talker normalization.* A child learns to speak by imitation of more fluent talkers. The degree to which one person can imitate the speech sounds of another is limited by physical characteristics, in particular by the length of the vocal tract. The various vowel sounds are produced by controlling the shape of the vocal tract by means of the articulatory organs (tongue, lips, jaw, and velum). The range over which these vary in speech is a large proportion of the maximum possible variation; that is, the permissible "generation space" is almost completely occupied. This implies that when listening to the speech of different talkers, the human listener either detects meaningful features of the speech that do not depend on talker characteristics (invariant features) or else is able to judge the speech sounds of a particular talker in relation to that talker's own characteristics. Many of the recognition systems reported to date imply an acceptance of the first (feature invariance) condition, and this imposes severe limitations where more than one talker is involved. There is some evidence that talker normalization is invoked in the human listener, and Fant has discussed certain aspects of such a process, including the probability of nonlinear scaling in the normalizing process [67]. In an experiment by Gerstman [68] use was made of the Peterson and Barney [18] data discussed earlier. The original data showed considerable overlap in the F1/F2 plots of judged vowel quality when the talkers included men, women, and children, whereas the vowel sounds by a single talker led to little or no overlap. Gerstman normalized each talker's vowel formant measurements by determining the highest and lowest frequencies of F1 and F2 for the set of vowels by each, setting these measurements to 999 and 0, respectively, and then determining intermediate values by interpolation. This is approximately equivalent to expanding or compressing the frequency scales to give coincidence for the formants in /i/, /a/ and /u/. Replotting this talker-normalized data resulted in unique vowel-cluster boundaries for all but 34 of the 1,368 vowels tested. Each of those which were misclassified also resulted in nonunanimous classification by the panel of judges in the original experiment.

Such talker normalization cannot correct for vowel patterns which differ because of dialect or accent differences, as these are often due to the substitution of one vowel phoneme for another or to a consistent shift in vowel quality. Differences due to these causes must be recognized as a characteristic of the individual talker.

Since certain vowel formants are related to (often continuous with) characteristic resonances in the consonants, talker normalization should aid the identification of consonants as with vowels.

14. *The single-talker approach is of limited value in the development of a general speech-recognition device.* Some workers have developed recognition procedures based on the analysis of the speech of a single talker with a view to expanding the procedures, when proved successful, to cope with a larger range of talkers.

A recognition strategy which is based on features observed in a particular set of utterances by a single talker is open to criticism on several counts. One is that the chosen features may not be invariant when considering a wider range of utterances even by the same talker. Another is that the features may be appropriate to that talker alone and their use in the recognition operations may actually reduce the ability of the machine to recognize speech by other talkers. A third point is that modifying a sophisticated recognition strategy which makes use of such talker-specific data may be more difficult than developing the strategy from the start.

However, the possibility should not be overlooked that such limited-value data may be learned and utilized by the human listener.

15. *The use of language by a talker and the precision with which he articulates his speech depend on his assessment of the listener's ability to comprehend.* In an informal conversational environment, e.g., when chatting with a friend, the talker will generally be less careful about the way his speech is articulated, will be less formal or precise in his use of the language, and may even use a special vocabulary. This latter consideration also particularly applies where talker and listener have a specialized interest, say in a technical subject.

16. *The identification of sounds at the acoustic level requires knowledge of prosodic features.* The prosodic features are features of the speech sound which convey information other than phonemic information. They tell the listener something about the talker (sex, age, etc.), his emotional state, his attitude towards the listener and towards the subject of conversation, and so on. They also perform certain linguistic functions; thus in English the pitch pattern of a sentence may distinguish between a question and a statement, and in Chinese the "tone" of a word distinguishes it from other words in the vocabulary with otherwise similar pronunciation. The prosodic features are related to the range and the use of pitch variation, intensity, and rhythm, knowledge of which is essential in determining the stress pattern. The precision with

which a sound is articulated depends very much on its relation to the stressed syllables. It is possible that some very familiar utterances can be recognized almost entirely by analysis of the stressed sounds and knowledge of the context in which the utterances are spoken.

17. *The general-purpose recognizer must be able to take account of linguistic information.* The range of words which can appear at a particular point in a sentence is greatly restricted by the operation of the linguistic rules (grammatical, semantic, lexical, etc.) under which sentences are generated. This allows for error correction or the removal of ambiguity at the word or phrase level. Human listeners certainly make use of such constraints, and for similar performance the mechanical recognizer must do the same.

18. *Probabilistic information must be used with caution.* By probabilistic information we mean the probability that, for instance, one speech sound or word may follow another speech sound or word. The rejection of an unlikely candidate in a recognition process in favor of a similar, more likely one may improve the overall recognition scores but at the expense of message "quality." In one sense at least, an unlikely word conveys more information than one which is more likely. This danger has been pointed out by Flanagan [1, p. 162].

19. *The set of features to be detected in the recognition of a phoneme pattern may be very large.* Analysis of the acoustic correlates of phonemic quality has shown that data on a large number of features is necessary to distinguish between similar phoneme patterns. For instance, to distinguish /s/ from other patterns it may be necessary to observe the intensity and duration of the sound, the spectral transitions introduced by its juxtaposition with other sounds, its initial rate of rise of intensity, its position in relation to other sounds in a given utterance, the absence of features known to be characteristic of other classes of sound (e.g., a stop gap or voicing), etc. If less than the complete set of these features is utilized, the overlap with the feature sets of other sounds may cause ambiguity. The complete set may include features which it is difficult or undesirable to include on an automated basis, such as the meaning of the whole utterance in relation to some personal knowledge held by the listener; the point here is that distortions, such as phonemic substitution, leading to ambiguity which the listener can easily overcome by use of context, will often not be suppressed by the talker.

20. *Learning systems have a place in automatic speech recognition but cannot be valuably exploited until the basic principles of recognition have been determined.* Although in theory a learning system taking account of every possible measurable quantity can be trained to recognize human speech, it is at present much more efficient to employ human

ingenuity to isolate the factors on which human recognition is based. When these factors have been established and demonstrated, learning techniques will be of value in adapting the recognizer to suit different talkers, accents, vocabularies, etc., but simply connecting a spectrum analyzer to a learning net and training it to cope with speech patterns is unlikely to aid the development of a general speech recognizer in the foreseeable future.

21. *It should be possible to limit the size of the storage requirements by choosing the vocabulary to suit the topic of conversation.* The use of simple phoneme recognition in reported recognition systems has often been dictated by the available data storage capacity. Extending the unit of recognition to the word or phrase level will greatly increase the quick-access storage requirements. It should be possible to relate the choice of less frequently used (and therefore more numerous) vocabulary items to the assumed topic of conversation, based on human judgment or partial recognition of earlier parts of the conversation.

22. *General theories on speech perception are not sufficiently developed or proven to make their use in studies of mechanical recognition an obvious choice at this time.* Although the distinctive-features theory has been partially implemented for recognition purposes, the acoustic correlates of the full set of features have not yet been isolated, and there is little evidence that the features employed in recognition attempts to date provide a high degree of talker invariance or can be applied to a very wide range of utterances; the analysis-by-synthesis methods reported are somewhat slow and cumbersome and, except for some general considerations, the motor theory does not yet lend itself to a practical realization.

General Conclusion

The main finding which these conclusions illustrate is that significant advances in speech recognition are likely to come not from researches into signal analysis, adaptive pattern matching, or computer implementation (although these fields have valuable techniques to offer the speech researcher), but from studies of speech perception and generation, phonetics, linguistics, and psychology. We need a much greater understanding of the whole speech process before an automatic recognizer can be built whose performance will approach human ability. Much of this work must follow where others have led and a great deal of valuable information is available in the literature on general speech research. A study of writings on automatic recognition alone is not sufficient. An extensive list of publications dealing with automatic speech recognition is given in the bibliography following the references.

REFERENCES

1. J. L. Flanagan, "Speech Analysis Synthesis and Perception," Springer-Verlag, Berlin, 1965.
2. N. Lindgren, Machine Recognition of Human Language, *IEEE Spectrum,* **2:**(3 and 4) (1965).
3. T. Marill, Automatic Recognition of Speech, *IRE Trans. Human Factors Electron.,* **HFE-2**(1):34–38 (1961).
4. M. A. Saposhkov, The Speech Signal in Cybernetics and Communications, translation by *Joint Publications Res. Serv.,* 28117 (1965).
5. D. Jones, "An Outline of English Phonetics," 9th ed., Heffer and Sons, London, 1960; first published in 1918.
6. J. W. Strutt (Lord Rayleigh), "The Theory of Sound," vol. II, Dover Publications, New York, 1945 (first published in 1878).
7. G. O. Russell, "The Vowel," Ohio State University Press, 1928; summary in *J. Acoust. Soc. Am.,* **I**(1) (1929).
8. H. K. Dunn, Calculation of Vowel Resonances and an Electrical Vocal Tract, *J. Acoust. Soc. Am.,* **22:**740–753 (1950).
9. G. Fant, "Acoustic Theory of Speech Production, Mouton and Co., The Hague, 1960.
10. J. van den Berg, Myoelastic-Aerodynamic Theory of Voice Production, *J. Speech Hearing Res.,* **1:**227–244 (1958).
11. J. van den Berg, "Voice Production: The Vibrating Larynx," instructional film, University of Gronigan, 1960.
12. P. Lieberman, Intonation, Perception and Language, *Res. Monograph* No. 38, MIT Press, Cambridge, Mass., 1967.
13. P. F. MacNeilage and G. N. Sholes, An Electromyographic Study of the Tongue During Vowel Production, *J. Speech Hearing Res.,* **7**(3):209–232 (1964).
14. J. C. R. Licklider and I. Pollack, Effects of Differentiation, Integration and Infinite Peak Clipping upon the Intelligibility of Speech, *J. Acoust. Soc. Am.,* **20:**42–51 (1948).
15. R. K. Potter, G. A. Kopp, and H. C. Green, "Visible Speech," Van Nostrand, New York, 1947.
16. I. Lehiste and G. E. Peterson, Studies of Syllable Nuclei 2, Rept. No. 4, University of Michigan, 1960.
17. I. Lehiste, Acoustical Characteristics of Selected English Consonants, Rept. No. 9, University of Michigan, 1962.
18. G. E. Peterson and H. L. Barney, Control Methods Used in a Study of the Vowels, *J. Acoust. Soc. Am.,* **24**(2):175–184 (1952).
19. P. Ladefoged and D. E. Broadbent, Information Conveyed by Vowels, *J. Acoust. Soc. Am.,* **29:**98–104 (1957).
20. P. Delattre, Acoustic Cues in Speech, First Report, Haskins Lab., N.Y.: first appeared in French in *Phonetica,* **2:**108–118, 226–251 (1958).
21. M. Halle and K. N. Stevens, Analysis by Synthesis, in W. Wathen-Dunn and L. E. Woods (eds.), *Proc. Seminar Speech Compression Processing,* vol. 2, Paper D7, December 1959.
22. M. Halle and K. N. Stevens, Speech Recognition: A Model and a Program for Research, *IRE Trans. Inform. Theory,* **IT-8**(2):155–159 (1962).
23. A. M. Liberman, F. S. Cooper, K. S. Harris, and P. F. MacNeilage, A Motor Theory of Speech Perception, *Proc. Speech Commun. Seminar,* Stockholm, 1962.
24. C. G. M. Fant, Auditory Patterns in Speech, in W. Wathen-Dunn (ed.),

Proc. Symp. Models Perception Speech Visual Form AFCRL, 1964, MIT Press, Cambridge, Mass., 1967.

25. R. Jakobson, C. G. M. Fant, and M. Halle, Preliminaries to Speech Analysis, *Tech. Rept.* No. 13, Acoustics Laboratory, MIT, 1952, reprinted 1963.
26. K. H. Davis, R. Biddulph, and S. Balashek, Automatic Recognition of Spoken Digits, *J. Acoust. Soc. Am.,* **24**(6):637–642 (1952).
27. H. Dudley and S. Balashek, Automatic Recognition of Phonetic Patterns in Speech, *J. Acoust. Soc. Am.,* **30**(8):721–733 (1958).
28. J. Wiren and H. L. Stubbs, Electronic Binary Selection System for Phoneme Classification, *J. Acoust. Soc. Am.,* **28:**1082–1091 (1956).
29. H. F. Olson and H. Belar, Phonetic Typewriter, *J. Acoust. Soc. Am.,* **28**(6):1072–1081 (1956).
30. H. F. Olson and H. Belar, Phonetic Typewriter III, *J. Acoust. Soc. Am.,* **33**(11):1610–1615 (1961).
31. D. B. Fry, Theoretical Aspects of Mechanical Speech Recognition; also P. Denes, The Design and Operation of the Mechanical Speech Recognizer at University College London; both in *J. Brit. Inst. Radio Engr.,* **19:**211–229 (1959).
32. J. W. Forgie and C. D. Forgie, Results Obtained from a Vowel Recognition Computer Program, *J. Acoust. Soc. Am.,* **31**(11):1480–1489 (1959).
33. J. W. Cooley and J. W. Tukey, An Algorithm for the Machine Calculation of Complex Fourier Series, *Math. Computers,* **19:**297–301 (1965).
34. J. Suzuki and K. Nakata, Recognition of Japanese Vowels—Preliminary to the Recognition of Speech, *J. Radio Res. Lab. Tokyo,* **8**(37):193–212 (1961).
35. T. Sakai and S. Doshita, The Phonetic Typewriter, Information Processing 1962, *Proc. IFIP Congr.,* Munich, August–September 1962.
36. K. Nagata, Y. Kato, and S. Chiba, Spoken Digit Recognizer for Japanese Language, *NEC Res. Develop.,* No. 6, 1963.
37. T. B. Martin, A. L. Nelson, and H. J. Zadell, Speech Recognition by Feature Abstraction Techniques, *Tech. Rept.* AL-TDR-64-176, Air Force Avionics Laboratory, 1964 (AD 604526).
38. J. W. Falter, Feature Abstraction: An Approach to Speech Recognition, *Proc. IEEE Nat. Aerospace Electron. Conf.,* pp. 192–198, 1965.
39. J. Gazdag, A Method of Decoding Speech, *Tech. Rept.* No. 9, AFOSR-66-2385, University of Illinois, June 1966 (AD 641132).
40. L. Gilli and A. R. Meo, Sequential System for Recognizing Spoken Digits in Real Time, *Acustica,* **19**(1):38–48 (1967/68).
41. W. Bezdel, Discriminators of Sound Classes for Speech Recognition Purposes, *AFCRL Conf. Reprints,* Section B8, pp. 104–108, Conf. on Speech Communication and Processing, 1967.
42. P. W. Ross, A Limited-vocabulary Adaptive Speech-recognition System, *J. Audio Eng. Soc.,* **15**(4):414–419 (1967).
43. P. Denes and M. V. Mathews, Spoken Digit Recognition Using Time-Frequency Pattern Matching, *J. Acoust. Soc. Am.,* **32**(11):1450–1455 (1960).
44. G. Sebestyn, Automatic Recognition of Spoken Numerals, *J. Acoust. Soc. Am.,* **32**(11):1516 (1960). (Abstract)
45. W. F. Meeker, A. L. Nelson, and P. B. Scott, Voice to Teletype Code Convertor Research Program, Part II: Experimental Verification of a Method to Recognize Phonetic Sounds, *Tech. Rept.* No. ASD-TR 61-666, Wright-Patterson A.F., Ohio, 1962 (AD 288099).
46. B. Gold, Word-recognition Computer Program, Rept. No. 452, Research Laboratory of Electronics, MIT, June 1966.

47. P. N. Sholtz and R. Bakis, Spoken Digit Recognition Using Vowel-Consonant Segmentation, *J. Acoust. Soc. Am.*, **34**(1):1–5 (1962).
48. J. N. Shearme and P. F. Leach, Some Experiments with a Simple Word Recognition System, *IEEE Trans. Audio Electroacoust.*, **AU-16:**256–261 (1968).
49. R. F. Purton, Speech Recognition Using Autocorrelation Analysis, *IEEE Trans. Audio Electroacoust.*, **AU-16**(2):235–239 (1968).
50. S. H. Lavington and L. E. Rosenthal, Some Facilities for Speech Processing by Computer, *Computer J. Brit. Computer Soc.*, **9**(4):330–339 (1967).
51. G. W. Hughes, The Recognition of Speech by Machine, *Tech. Rept.* No. 395, MIT Research Laboratory of Electronics, 1961.
52. G. W. Hughes and J. F. Hemdal, Speech Analysis, Report AFCRL-65-681, Purdue University, 1965 (P 137552).
53. L. R. Talbert, G. F. Groner, J. S. Koford, R. J. Brown, P. R. Low, and C. H. Mays, A Real-time Adaptive Speech Recognition System, *Tech. Rept.* No. 6760-1 (ASD-TDR-63-660) (P 133441), prepared by Stanford Electronics Laboratory.
54. N. J. Nilsson, "Learning Machines," McGraw-Hill, New York, 1965.
55. J. A. Dammann, Application of Adaptive Threshold Elements to the Recognition of Acoustic-phonetic States, *J. Acoust. Soc. Am.*, **38**(2):213–223 (1965).
56. J. H. King and C. J. Tunis, Some Experiments in Spoken Word Recognition, *IBM J. Res. Develop.*, **10**(1):65–79 (1966).
57. D. Fraipont, Voice Actuated Address Mechanism. Report No. 3, Electronics Associates, Inc., 1966 (AD 633711).
58. C. F. Teacher and C. F. Piotrowski, Voice Sound Recognition, *Tech. Rept.* No. RADC-TR-65-184, Rome Air Development Center, July 1965 (AD 619964).
59. C. F. Teacher, H. G. Kellett, and L. R. Focht, Experimental, Limited Vocabulary, Speech Recognizer, *IEEE Trans. Audio Electroacoust.*, **AU-15**(3):127–130 (September 1967).
60. M. Weiss, A Study of Critical Instant Sampling of Speech Parameters for Automatic Recognition of Spoken Words, Rept. No. RADC-TR-65-371, Rome Air Development Center, July 1966 (AD 638380).
61. M. W. Cannon, A Method of Analysis and Recognition for Voiced Vowels, *IEEE Trans. Audio Electroacoust.*, **AU-16**(2):154–158 (1968).
62. D. R. Reddy, An Approach to Computer Speech Recognition by Direct Analysis of the Speech Wave, *Tech. Rept.* No. CS49, Computer Science Dept., Stanford University, September 1966; paper based on this report presented in *J. Acoust. Soc. Am.*, **42**(2):329–347 (August 1967) Computer Recognition of Connected Speech.
63. V. A. Kozhevnikov and L. A. Chistovich, Speech: Articulation and Perception. Translation by *Joint Publications Res. Serv.*, 30543 (1965).
64. P. Denes, On the Statistics of Spoken English, *J. Acoust. Soc. Am.*, **35**(6):892–904 (1963).
65. E. Peterson, Frequency Detection and Speech Formants, *J. Acoust. Soc. Am.*, **23**(6):668–674 (1951).
66. B. E. F. Lindblom and M. Studdert-Kennedy, On the Role of Formant Transitions in Vowel Recognition, *J. Acoust. Soc. Am.*, **42**(4):830–843 (1967).
67. G. Fant, A Note on Vocal Tract Size Factors and Non-uniform F-pattern Scalings, *Speech Transmission Lab. Quart. Progr. Status Rept. Roy. Inst. Technol. Stockholm,* No. 4/1966, pp. 22–30, January 1967.
68. L. J. Gerstman, Classification of Self-normalized Vowels, *IEEE Trans. Audio Electroacoust.*, **AU-16**(1):78–80 (1968).

BIBLIOGRAPHY

Baumann, R. H., J. C. R. Licklider, and B. Howland, An Electronic Word Recognizer, *J. Acoust. Soc. Am.*, **26**(1):137–138 (January 1954).

Bezdel, W., and J. S. Bridle, Speech Recognition Using Zero-crossing Measurements and Sequence Information, *Proc. IEE*, **116**(4):617–623 (April 1969).

Bezdel, W., and H. J. Chandler, Results of an Analysis and Recognition of Vowels by Computer Using Zero-crossing Data, *Proc. IEE*, **112**(11):2060–2066 (November 1965).

Bobrow, D. G., and D. H. Klatt, A Limited Speech Recognition System, Rept. No. 1667, Bolt, Beranek and Newman, Inc., May 1968.

Bobrow, D. G., and D. H. Klatt, Studies in Word Recognition by Computer, *J. Acoust. Soc. Am.*, **44**(1):385 (July 1968). (Abstract)

Chiba, S., Spoken Word Recognition by Multiple Linear Separation, *Rept. 6th Intern. Congr. Acoustics*, Tokyo, August 1968, Paper B-4-4, pp. B123–B126.

Chiba, S., and H. Sakoe, Calculation of Classification Functions Using a Large Number of Spoken Word Samples, *J. Acoust. Soc. Am.*, **47**(1, pt. 1):83 (January 1970). (Abstract)

Clapper, G. L., Machine Looks, Listens, Learns, *Electronics*, **40**(22):91–102 (October 30, 1967).

Clapper, G. L., Word Recognition System, *IBM Tech. Disclosure Bull.*, **11**(6):603–605 (November 1968).

Comer, D. J., The Use of Waveform Asymmetry to Identify Voiced Sounds, *IEEE Trans. Audio Electroacoust.*, **AU-16**(4): 500–506 (December 1968).

Denes, P., The Design and Operation of the Mechanical Speech Recognizer at University College London, *J. Brit. IRE*, **19**(4):219–229 (April 1959).

Denes, P. B., and T. G. von Keller, Articulatory Segmentation for Automatic Recognition of Speech, *Rept. 6th Intern. Congr. Acoust.*, Tokyo, August 1968, Paper B-4-9, pp. B143–B146.

Derkach, M., Heuristic Models for Automatic Recognition of Spoken Words, *Speech Transmission Lab. Quart. Progr. Status Rept. Roy. Inst. Technol. Stockholm*, No. 1/1970, April 15, 1970.

Dersch, W. C., Shoe-box, A Voice Responsive Machine, *Datamation*, **8**(6):47–50 (June 1962).

Ewing, G. D., and J. F. Taylor, Computer Recognition of Speech Using Zero-crossing Information, *IEEE Trans. Audio Electroacoust.*, **AU-17**(1):37–40 (March 1969).

Falter, J. W., and K. W. Otten, Cybernetics and Speech Communications: A Survey of Russian Literature, *IEEE Trans. Audio Electroacoust.*, **AU-15**(1):27–36 (1967).

Fant, G., The Nature of Distinctive Features, *Speech Transmission Lab. Quart. Progr. Status Rept. Roy. Inst. Technol. Stockholm*, No. 4/1966, pp. 1–14, January 1967.

Forgie, J. W., C. D. Forgie, and E. P. Dickey, A Recognition Program for English Fricative Consonants, *J. Acoust. Soc. Am.*, **33**(11):1676–1677 (November 1961). (Abstract)

Foulkes, J. D., Computer Identification of Vowel Types, *J. Acoust. Soc. Am.*, **33**(1):7–11 (January 1961).

Fujisaki, H., and N. Nakamura, Normalization and Recognition of Vowels, Research on Information Processing, *Ann. Rept. Eng. Res. Inst. Univ. Tokyo*, **28:**61–66 (1969).

Fukumura, T., and K. Adachi, Phoneme Recognition of Japanese Vowels Based Upon the Order Relations of Their Frequency-band Components, *Electron. Commun. Japan*, **47**(10):67–79 (October 1964).

Hemdal, J. F., and G. W. Hughes, A Feature Based Computer Recognition Program for the Modeling of Vowel Perception, in W. Wathen-Dunn (ed.), "Models for the Perception of Speech and Visual Form," pp. 440–453, MIT Press, Cambridge, Mass., 1967.

Hill, D. R., Automatic Speech Recognition—A Problem for Machine Intelligence, *Machine Intelligence,* **I**:199–226, Oliver and Boyd (October 1966).

Hill, D. R., An Esoteric Approach to Some Problems in Automatic Speech Recognition, *Intern. J. Man-Machine Studies,* **1**(1):101–121 (January 1969).

Hillix, W. A., M. N. Fry, and R. L. Hershman, Computer Recognition of Spoken Digits Based on Six Nonacoustic Measures, *J. Acoust. Soc. Am.,* **38**(5):790–796 (November 1965).

Hiramatsu, K., and K. Kotoh, A Spoken Digit Recognition System Using Error Correcting Procedure, *Rept. 6th Intern. Congr. Acoust.,* Tokyo, August 1968, Paper B-4-3, pp. B119–B122.

Hogan, D. L., Automatic Recognition of a Limited Set of Syllables, MIT *Quart. Progr. Rept. Res. Lab. Electron.,* No. 62, pp. 202–203 July 1961.

Hollabaugh, J. D., Methods for Phonemic Recognition in Speech Processing, MSC thesis, US Naval Postgraduate School, 1963 (AD 481756).

Holmgren, G. L., Speaker Recognition, Speech Characteristics, Speech Evaluation, and Modification of Speech Signal—A Selected Bibliography, *IEEE Trans. Audio Electroacoust.,* **AU-14**(1):32–39 (1966).

Inoue, S., and A. Kurematsu, Speech Recognition with Time-normalized Frequency Pattern, *Rept. 6th Intern. Congr. Acoust.,* Tokyo, August 1968, Paper B-4-5.

Keller, T. G. von, Automatic Recognition of Spoken Words, *J. Acoust. Soc. Am.,* **44**(1):385 (July 1968). (Abstract)

Ye Kirillov, N., and L. V. Fatkin, Experiments in the Recognition of Speech Sounds by Automatic Machines, Foreign Developments in Machine Translation and Information Processing, No. 107, *Joint Publ. Res. Serv.,* 15754 (October 1962).

Lecours, M., and J. J. Sparkes, Adaptive Spectral Analysis for Speech-sound Recognition, *IEEE Trans. Audio Electroacoust.,* **AU-16**(4):523–525 (December 1968).

Makhoul, J. I., Speaker-Machine Interaction in a Limited Speech Recognition System, *J. Acoust. Soc. Am.,* **47**(1, pt. 1):84 (January 1970). (Abstract)

Mendress, M., An Approach to the Computer Recognition of Single-syllable English Words, *J. Acoust. Soc. Am.,* **47**(1, pt. 1):83–84 (January 1970). (Abstract)

Miller, J. C., P. W. Ross, and C. M. Wine, An Adaptive Speech Recognition System Operating in a Remote Time-shared Computer Environment, *IEEE Trans. Audio Electroacoust.,* **AU-18**(1):26–32 (March 1970).

Nelson, A. L., M. B. Herscher, T. B. Martin, H. J. Zadell, and J. W. Falter, Acoustic Recognition by Analog Feature Abstraction Techniques, in W. Wathen-Dunn (ed.), "Models for the Perception of Speech and Visual Form," pp. 428–440, MIT Press, 1964.

Newell, A. F., and C. D. Nabavi, VOTEM: The Voice Operated Typewriter Employing Morse Code, *J. Sci. Instr.,* Series 2, **2**:655–657 (1969).

Ohlendorf, R. C., and C. L. Coates, Recognition of Spoken Digits Utilizing Sequential Patterns, *Tech. Rept.* No. 57, Electronics Research Center, University of Texas, November 1968 (AD 685128).

Olson, H. F., H. Belar, and E. S. Rogers, Speech Processing Techniques and Applications, *IEEE Trans. Audio Electroacoust.,* **AU-15**(3):120–126 (September 1967).

Paul, J. E., Jr., A Limited-vocabulary, Multi-speaker Automatic Isolated Word Recognition System, North Carolina State University, September 1969 (AD 696206).

Petrick, S. R., and H. M. Willet, Digital Automatic Word Recognition Procedure, *J. Acoust. Soc. Am.,* **32**(11):1517 (November 1960). (Abstract)

Robinson, E. F. V., Voice Control of Computers, *Bull. Radio Elec. Eng. Div. Nat. Res. Council Canada,* **18**(4):13 (October–December 1968).

Rogers, E. S., and E. G. May, Performance of a 200-syllable Communication System, *J. Acoust. Soc. Am.,* **41**(6):1594–1595 (June 1967). (Abstract)

Rogers, E. S., W. H. Jamison, and P. W. Ross, Syllable Coder Communication System, *Final Rept.,* Defense Communication Agency, Washington, May 1967 (AD 658530).

Sakai, T., and S. Doshita, The Automatic Speech Recognition System for Conversational Sound, *IEEE Trans. Electron. Computers,* **EC-12**(5):835–846 (December 1963).

Scarr, R. W. A., Word Recognition Machine, *Proc. IEE,* **117**(1):203–212 (January 1970).

Smith, C. P., A Phoneme Detector, *J. Acoust. Soc. Am.,* **23**(4):446–451 (July 1951).

Smith, J. E. K., and L. Klem, Vowel Recognition Using a Multiple Discriminant Function, *J. Acoust. Soc. Am.,* **33**(3):358 (March 1961). (Letter)

Trunin-Donskii, V. N., A. S. Firer, and G. I. Tsemel, Recognition of Spoken Word Ensembles with the Aid of a Digital Computer, Foreign Technology Division, Wright-Patterson, AFB, Ohio, February 1969 (AD 687227); *Computer Abstr.,* **13**(11): Abstr. No. 3100 (November 1969).

Tsemel, G., and V. Trunin, Words of Command, *Computer Weekly,* February 20, 1969.

Velichko, V. M., and N. G. Zagoruyko, Automatic Recognition of 200 Words, *Intern. J. Man-Machine Studies,* **2**(3):222–234 (July 1970).

Vicens, P., Aspects of Speech Recognition by Computer, Dept. of Computer Science, Stanford University, Calif., April 1969 (AD 687720); *Computer Abstr.,* **13**(11):Abstr. No. 3098 (November 1969).

Washizawa, S., M. Okamoto, T. Shiga, and S. Inomata, A Spoken Digit Recognition Scheme and Its Computer Simulation, *Rept. 6th Intern. Congr. Acoust.,* Tokyo, August 1968, Paper B-4-7, pp. B135–B138.

Zaytsev, V. H., Information and Interpolation Systems Recognition of a Limited Set of Words, *Sov. Autom. Control (IEEE),* **13**(2):28–33 (March–April 1968).

Index